THE SCIENCE OF LEARNING

THE SCIENCE
OF LEARNING

Joseph J. Pear

Department of Psychology
University of Manitoba

USA	Publishing Office:	PSYCHOLOGY PRESS
		A member of the Taylor & Francis Group
		325 Chestnut Street
		Philadelphia, PA 19106
		Tel: (215) 625-8900
		Fax: (215) 625-2940
	Distribution Center:	PSYCHOLOGY PRESS
		A member of the Taylor & Francis Group
		7625 Empire Drive
		Florence, KY 41042
		Tel: 1-800-624-7064
		Fax: 1-800-248-4724
UK		PSYCHOLOGY PRESS
		A member of the Taylor & Francis Group
		27 Church Road
		Hove
		E. Sussex, BN3 2FA
		Tel: +44 (0) 1273 207411
		Fax: +44 (0) 1273 205612

THE SCIENCE OF LEARNING

1 2 3 4 5 6 7 8 9 0

Printed by Edwards Brothers, Ann Arbor, MI, 2001.
Cover design by Marja Walker.

A CIP catalog record for this book is available from the British Library.
   The paper in this publication meets the requirements of the ANSI Standard Z39.48-1984 (Permanence of Paper).

Library of Congress Cataloging-in-Publication Data
Pear, Joseph, 1938–
    The science of learning / Joseph J. Pear
       p. cm.
    Includes bibliographic references and index.
       ISBN 1-84169-036-8 (case : alk. paper) — ISBN 1-84169-037-6 (pbk : alk. paper)
       1. Learning, Psychology of. I. Title.
BF318 .P43 2001
153. 1'5—dc21

                                                                      00-045893

ISBN 1-84169-036-8 (case)
ISBN 1-84169-037-6 (paper)

To Fran

Contents

Appendices

References

Author Index

Subject Index

Preface

For over a century the science of learning has been growing at an ever-increasing pace to where it now comprises an extensive systematic body of knowledge. This book is designed to provide an introduction to and an overview of that body of knowledge.

This book is intended primarily for students in introductory undergraduate courses in the science of learning. It was also written with the following readers in mind: specialists in the science of learning wishing to read a systematic overview of the state of knowledge in their field; advanced undergraduate and graduate students in courses on the science of learning; and scientists and practitioners in various fields (biology, education, clinical psychology) who wish to acquaint themselves with the fundamental knowledge in this science.

The solid body of basic concepts and facts that have developed as the science of learning has matured demands a comprehensive, systematic introduction. In fact, as we move into the information age it is hard to think of anything more important than making the fundamental knowledge gleaned through the science of learning readily accessible to students and professionals in a wide variety of fields. Emphasizing well-established factually based concepts rather than theory, this book provides such an introduction. Because its focus is on what is known rather than what is speculated, this book differs from other texts on learning by not dwelling on which learning theories are in vogue and which are not. The focus is squarely on the science and the body of knowledge it has generated.

This is not to say that theories are unimportant. When excessively speculative, however, theories can obscure more than they illuminate—especially in an introduction to a field. In addition, I believe that individuals who are well grounded in the basic factual concepts of learning are in a better position to appreciate and evaluate theories of learning than are individuals who have little knowledge of the factual basis of the science. Similar points apply with regard to many historical, methodological, and philosophical issues that, though undeniably important, receive less attention in this book than in most books on learning.

The comprehensive review of the research in this book is illuminated by practical applications. Although not the focus, practical applications receive frequent mention as illustrations of the knowledge with which this book deals. Reference to the widespread application of learning concepts also serves to drive home the power of the science, for an effective technology implies the existence of a well-developed science on which it is based.

Completion of this book was facilitated by a grant from the Social Sciences and Humanities Research Council of Canada.

Although learning is usually considered to be part of psychology, the present approach is based more on that of the typical natural science textbook than that of the typical psychology textbook. The typical biology, chemistry, or physics textbook, for example, devotes little space to the relative merits and demerits of unconfirmed theories. Instead, the typical natural science textbook concentrates almost exclusively on expounding in a highly systematic manner the basic knowledge in its field. Perhaps because so little systematic knowledge exists in most areas of psychology, most psychology textbooks are replete with theories pointing the way to what we have yet to learn. The field of learning is an exception to this lack of systematic knowledge, however, which is why I call it the "science of learning."

The plan of this book is from the general to the specific. Part I gives an overview of basic terms and concepts. Part II deals in more detail with respondent and operant conditioning, using the concept of contingency as the unifying theme. The first chapter of this two-chapter part presents a classification of the various effects of stimulus-stimulus contingencies, while the second chapter describes the effects on response rate of the response-reinforcer contingencies in simple schedules of reinforcement. Part III delves into the ramifications of complicating the contingencies discussed in the previous part; for example, by adding discriminative stimuli to produce successive and simultaneous discriminations, by adding further antecedent stimuli to produce conditional discriminations, by sequencing stimuli and responses to produce complex chains of behavior, and by operating several contingencies simultaneously to produce concurrent performances. Part III also treats in some detail how these complex contingencies generate complex behavior such as concept formation, language, and choice. Part IV covers material that is often placed in the areas of motivation or emotion. The focus of this part is on the effects of deprivation and aversive stimulation, and how aversive segments of reinforcement schedules can instigate the release of phylogenetic behavior patterns. Finally, Part V deals with how the principles described in the previous parts apply to animals in their habitats and to humans in social settings. This part highlights some of the broader implications of the material in the book.

Although this book focuses on well established, factually based concepts rather than on speculative theories, it includes appendices on current mathematical theories of learning. This is a reflection of the fact that there have been important—and indeed remarkable—advances in certain mathematical theories of learning in recent years. These advances have been so great that, in many respects, these theories are in remarkably close accordance with the factual knowledge of the science. In fact, they are so much in accordance with that knowledge that they serve to compress the most fundamental concepts in the field. Studying these theories and their relationships to each other can thus provide, to the mathematically inclined, an excellent review of that knowledge as well as a deeper understanding of it. Since many readers will not be mathematically inclined, however, it seemed appropriate to put this material in appendices rather than to integrate it with the main body of the text. References to specific appendices are made at relevant points in the text.

In writing this book, I have benefited immensely from the feedback of many people: friends, colleagues, and countless students in my undergraduate and graduate learning courses. I wish to specifically acknowledge my deep appreciation to: Mark V. Abrahams, Anna E. Bergen, Wayne S. Chan, Thomas S. Critchfield, Darlene E. Crone-Todd, Frances M. Falzarano, Bruce E. Hesse, M. Jackson Marr, Frances K. McSweeney, Jack Michael, James B. Nickels, David W. Schaal, Francisco J. Silva, Robert W. Tait, and Ben A. Williams. Although the above mentioned deserve much credit for the merits of this book, the author as usual bears sole responsibility for its faults.

PART *I*

BASIC TERMS
AND CONCEPTS

*E*very science has a set of basic terms and concepts that are used in all discourse concerning the principles and phenomena of that science. The science of learning is no exception. As with other sciences, its basic terms and concepts form the building blocks of the science. Moreover, as with other sciences, proper terminology is crucial to understanding the phenomena covered by the science.

1

Introduction

*T*he word *science* has a number of definitions. One definition—the one emphasized in this book—is *a growing systematic body of factual knowledge derived through observation and experimentation showing the operation of general scientific laws.* A *scientific law* is a *statement of a relation that is invariable under the same conditions.* There are many definitions of learning. However, the term *learning* generally refers to the effect on behavior of certain types of interactions between the individual and the environment, which includes all sources of stimulation impinging on the individual's sense receptors within a given period. Thus, this book is concerned with scientific laws that describe how specific types of interactions with the environment affect behavior.

Obviously, some laws are more general than others; that is, some laws apply to more types of situations than others. One goal of science is to develop laws that are as general as possible. Another is to organize the laws of a science into theories, which are then used to make predictions; in fact, the supreme test of any theory is its ability to accurately predict new observations.

The first part of this chapter provides an overview of the theoretical position of this book with references to various theoretical approaches that have been taken by scientists who study learning. The chapter then discusses the theory of evolution, which is a powerful organizing theory that has unified all of the life sciences. Finally, the chapter presents a more detailed definition of learning than that given above and considers how learning evolved.

THEORETICAL APPROACHES TO LEARNING

The science of learning is relatively young and many of its more general theories are highly speculative. While there is an extensive literature on these theories, this book makes little direct reference to that literature because its purpose is to cover what is known about learning rather than speculations about it. The history of science repeatedly shows that what was believed or theorized at one point in time often turned out to be false later on. What is presented in this book, however, is well documented and appears likely to survive the test of time.

While there are many theories of learning, we may classify them according to five major categories: folk, physiological, behavioral, cognitive, and mathematical. The following summarizes the approach of this book with regard to each of these categories.

Folk Theories

A folk theory is an organized set of concepts that many members of a culture share about a particular domain of phenomena and is used to explain, manipulate, and predict those phenomena (Churchland, 1991). Because of the great importance of phenomena in the area of learning to human individual and group survival, folk theories of learning abound in every culture. The folk theories of learning in our culture contain a number of terms that seem to refer to things going on inside of an individual. We may group these terms under the headings of "cognition," "motivation," and "emotion." Under cognition we may list such folk terms as "thought," "belief," and "expectation;" under motivation we may list terms like "hunger," "thirst," "needs," and "desires;" and, under emotion we may list terms like "fear," "anger," "joy," and "love." The above terms are sometimes called "mentalistic terms" because they seem to refer to an entity called "the mind" which folk theory holds to cause behavior (e.g., as when someone asks what got into a person's mind to cause him or her to do something).

When scientists start developing theories in a totally new area they often borrow liberally from folk theories. This has been true of many learning scientists. Thus many learning theories postulate inner processes that have names derived from folk theories of learning. A major argument for this approach is that even though they may not have used strict scientific methods, those who gave us our folk theories were keen observers of behavior and had been observing and dealing with it thousands of years before we were born. It is therefore likely that they were correct about many things. While there is validity to this argument, we should also recognize that they were wrong about many things because they did not have the scientific methodology that is available to us today. (If they were not often wrong science would be unnecessary; folk wisdom would suffice.) Moreover, the language of folk theories is often imprecise and misleading, and often makes distinctions that turn out not to be scientifically important while failing to make distinctions that do turn out to be scientifically important. Folk theories and the terminology of folk theories therefore are not ideally suited to describe learning scientifically.

Physiological Theories

Although the folk terms exemplified above appear to refer to inner things, they are not physiological terms and they do not refer to anything that physiologists directly observe as part of their subject matter. Physiologists studying the nervous system, for example, observe such things as brain tissue, nerves, and the interactions among nerves and other parts of the body. They do not, as physiologists, directly observe such things as thought, hunger, or fear.

The laws of learning result directly from the combined action of all the organ systems of the body. These include the nervous, endocrine, circulatory, respiratory, digestive, reproductive, excretory, skeletal, and muscular systems, as well as the skin and its derivatives. The nervous system is clearly crucial to learning; in vertebrates, at least, the brain is the part of the nervous system that is most important for learning. Little is currently known, however, about how the brain is involved in learning.

There are a number of theories relating learning to the brain, including computer models of brain processes (e.g., neural nets), and the interested reader is encouraged to consult the literature on those theories (e.g., Donahoe & Palmer, 1994; Donahoe, Palmer, & Burgos, 1997). At present these theories are all highly speculative, however, and it does not serve our purpose to describe them here. Fortunately, it is not necessary to know how neurological and other physiological processes result in learning in order to describe functional relationships between learning and the environment. Learning is clearly a function of physiological processes, but physiological processes are a function of the environment. A function of a function is also a function; therefore, learning is a function of the environment. Since laws are functional relationships, it is possible to discover and formulate laws of learning without reference to physiological processes. As more information about how learning is related to physiology becomes available, it will of course be important to integrate this information into a unified theory of learning. In this book, however, little attention will be given to physiological theories of learning because of their current speculative nature.

Behavioral Theories

Behavioral theories attempt to relate units of behavior, called *responses*, to units of the environment, called stimuli (plural of stimulus). Although they focus on externally observable stimuli and responses, behavioral theories usually acknowledge that some stimuli and responses are not directly observable to anyone other than the individual experiencing or engaging in them. Stimuli and responses that are not externally observable are said to be private or covert. While maintaining that we may infer private stimuli and responses from overt (i.e., directly observable) behavior, behavioral theories are generally strict about when and how such inferences are scientifically permissible.

As previously mentioned, although many folk terms related to learning appear to refer to inner things, they do not refer to anything that physiologists directly observe as part of their subject matter. Behavioral theories tend to regard these folk terms in either of two ways. One of these is simply to dismiss them as so vague as to be essentially meaningless. The other (and the approach favored in this book) is to regard them not as referring to something entirely inside the individual (as folk theory seems to suggest) but rather to behavior (both covert and overt). Consider, for example, the folk term "expectancy." When a dog salivates in response to a bell that has rung just before the dog received food, it is sometimes said that this is because the bell causes the animal to "expect" or "anticipate" food. But how do we observe that the dog expects or anticipates food? We do this only by observing that the dog salivates in response to the bell and perhaps engages in certain other behavior that animals characteristically exhibit when presented with a stimulus that has been paired with food. The "expectation of food" or "anticipation of food" is therefore simply a label for these responses that we might therefore call "anticipatory behavior," and is not an internal state or process.

Similarly, to say that an animal is "hungry" simply means that it shows a strong tendency to eat—typically as a result of having been without food for a period of time—and to engage in other behavior that has been reinforced with food. Thus, the term "hunger" also refers to behavior and not to an internal state or process.

Finally, to take an example from the third category of folk theory (emotion), to say that an animal is "fearful" is simply to say that the animal shows a strong tendency to cower or to flee in certain situations. Once again, the term does not refer directly to an inner state or physiological process.

Given the above, why do we tend to have such strong feelings that folk terms refer to internal states or processes? There are several reasons, but probably the most important is that we are observers of our own environments and behavior as well as those of others. A small part of the environment and behavior of each of us is contained within our own skins. Each of us is closer to that part of our own environment and behavior than anyone else is; in fact, it is private in that it is accessible only to ourselves. Private events—both private stimuli and private responses—occur within that environment (Skinner, 1974). My toothache, for example, is a private stimulus in that only I can directly observe—that is, respond to—it. Similarly, I can observe my own anticipatory responses—for example, increased heart rate prior to some aversive event—which others cannot, unless they use special instruments. I can observe internal stimuli that are often correlated with what I identify in myself as "hunger," such as stimuli produced by my stomach contractions and decreased blood sugar level. Likewise, I can observe private responses involved in fear behavior, and even use them as a cue to hide or disguise the overt fear behavior. Furthermore, I believe that you and others can also do these things, although of course I have no direct knowledge of this. Probably because we are closer to them, private stimuli and responses are often more salient to us than the corresponding public behavior is (although there are exceptions to this, as when a person who sincerely claims not to be hungry proceeds to eat a huge meal). This makes it easy for us to attach more importance to such private events than they actually merit.

There is one folk term, however, that many behavioral theorists would accept as referring more to covert than to overt behavior; namely, the term "thinking." Verbal behavior can occur both overtly and covertly, and when it occurs covertly we often call it "thinking." Except when "thinking out loud," a person who is said to be thinking is typically characterized by a lack of overt activity. When talking covertly, only the speaker can "hear" or otherwise respond in some way to the verbal behavior he or she is emitting. The behavior is said to occur subvocally or below the vocal level. Although all of us no doubt experience subvocal behavior, its exact locus has not been well studied and is largely unknown. Although electrical activity normally occurs in the muscles of the tongue and upper lip when a person is instructed to think of words silently (Jacobson, 1932), subvocal speech does not necessarily occur only when there is muscular movement in the vocal apparatus. It can occur even when all skeletal muscles (including those of the vocal apparatus) are paralyzed (Smith, Brown, Toman, & Goodman, 1947).

Another type of thinking appears to involve covert sensing, such as covert visualization. Essentially, this means having a sensation of something that is not actually there. Covert seeing is often referred to as visualizing, imagining, or having a mental image. If strong enough, a covert visual image might be a visual hallucination. Other types of covert sensing, such as covert hearing, feeling (in the sense of touching or being touched), tasting, and smelling also occur. In most behavioral theories (at least those that talk about visual images and other types of covert sensing), sensing is not a passive process but, rather, a response made to the stimulus that is sensed.

We should not take the fact that sensing can occur in the absence of what is sensed to mean, however, that covert sensory responses occur in some other-worldly region called "the mind" (even though the term "mental image" stems from the philosophy that they do). Research indicates that mental images occupy the same or nearly the same locus in the nervous system as sensory responses to actual objects; that is, the neural pathways in the brain that become active when a person has a mental image of a stimulus overlap with those that become active when the actual stimulus occurs (Farah, 1988).

According to behavioral theory, it can be quite misleading to attribute behavior to hypothetical inner causes. For example, if hunger is simply a tendency to eat, it is clearly invalid to say that hunger causes eating. There is a sense, however, in which thinking may be said to cause behavior. This would occur when it is part of a behavioral chain. Suppose, for example, that you are asked to solve an addition problem without using pencil and paper or talking out loud. In order to solve the problem you might have to either covertly verbalize the steps (e.g., "eight plus nine is seventeen, carry the one") or visualize them, or do both. These covert responses might be called "thinking," and thus we might say that thinking or a thought process produced the answer. Technically, however, it would be more accurate to say that a behavioral chain that was partly covert or private produced the answer. Later in this book we discuss the properties of behavioral chains. The point emphasized here, however, is that behavioral theories postulate that there is little or no fundamental difference between private and public behavior; thus, facts pertaining to the latter should also apply (with certain qualifications) to the former. This provides one justification for the focus on overt behavior, to the almost complete exclusion of interest in private behavior, by many behavioral theorists.

In this book we use the language of behavioral theory because it is specifically designed to deal with the facts of learning. We do not rule folk theory entirely out of bounds, however, because of the valuable insights it can give us into learning. In addition, because folk language is the language of common, everyday speech, it is often useful to translate between behavioral and folk terminology (Pear, 1983).

Cognitive Theories

Cognitive theories look at the individual as an information processing system analogous to a modern computer. In some respects, cognitive theories are more similar to folk theories than behavioral theories are because computer programs are internal to a computer in the same way that folk theories hold that expectancies, beliefs, and other mentalistic constructs are internal to an individual. In fact, folk terms are often indistinguishable from the terms in cognitive theories. Thus, for example, the word "belief" may be used in a cognitive theory in essentially the same way that it is used in folk theories.

No one can say with certainty whether cognitive or behavioral theories (or either) will ultimately turn out to be more fruitful in advancing the science of learning. By deliberate design, however, cognitive theories are more speculative than behavioral theories are. Although it may seem less natural, more cumbersome, and more difficult to learn than the language of cognitive and folk theories (O'Donohue, Callaghan, & Ruckstuhl, 1998), behavioral terminology is much more precise in dealing with the basic facts of learning. Indeed, it is the terminology of choice when dealing strictly with the facts of learning even for those who subscribe most strongly to cognitive learning theories. Because our purpose is to present a factual account of the science of learning, we consistently use behavioral terminology in this book. (We return to the issue of cognitive versus behavioral terminology in Chapter 10.)

Mathematical Theories

Mathematics is the language designed to describe functional relations concisely and with the highest degree of precision and generality, and is therefore ideal for describing the laws of learning. Mathematical theories not only have the advantage of precision and conciseness; they also do *not* require pictures of the functional relations that they describe (Marr, 1993, 1999). Physicists, for example, do not require a picture of an electron in order to describe it mathematically. This is important because, although they can sometimes be helpful, pictures are often misleading.

The science of learning, particularly the study of animal learning, has advanced to the stage at which remarkably accurate mathematical formulations of some of the most basic principles and procedures appear possible (see Church, 1997). Perhaps future science of learning texts will resemble books in physics with regard to the amount of mathematics they contain. At present, even the best mathematical learning theories are speculative and incomplete, and are touched on only briefly in the main body of this book. Appendices A to E, however, detail several of the more powerful of the mathematical learning theories developed thus far to describe some of the most basic findings in the science of learning. Studying the material in the appendices should be helpful in summarizing and clarifying some of the central concepts in this book. Reference to a specific appendix is made when material relevant to that appendix is discussed.

THE THEORY OF EVOLUTION

Although evolution is called a "theory," and like all theories was once speculative, the weight of evidence has given it the status of a fact. Along with many other attributes that animals possess, the capacity to learn evolved as a way to adapt to the environment. We therefore give a brief overview of what is known about evolution in general, and the evolution of learning in particular. In order to appreciate the current state of knowledge about evolution, it is important to clearly separate the fact that evolution occurred from the manner or mechanism of its occurrence. We consider each of these in turn.

The Evolution of Species

We illustrate the fact of evolution with a brief outline of the evolutionary history of humans. Although uncertainty exists over the exact manner in which evolution operated (Campbell, 1996, pp. 477–479), evidence is strong that it occurred. Buried in the ground or embedded in rock are the fossilized remains and traces of plants and animals, many of which belonged to species that no longer exist. These fossils occur in a definite sequence in the layers of rock that are stacked on top of each other throughout the world. The few exceptions to this sequence are due to geological disturbances after the layers of rock were formed.

Since the lower layers of rock formed before the upper layers, we must conclude that the layer in which a fossil occurs is a strong indicator of the period in which the organism that produced it lived. In addition, various methods of dating fossils give approximate times at which the organisms that produced them lived. Examination of fossils all over the world reveals an orderly progression in which many life forms gradually acquired more sophisticated or elaborate characteristics. Other types of evidence, such as that from embryology and comparative anatomy, complement the fossil record by pointing to the common origins of various anatomical structures across species. Perhaps the most compelling evidence, however, comes from studies of the genetic material, or DNA, of different species. Among other things, these studies provide a way of estimating the periods at which different species evolved that generally agrees well with dates given by the fossil record.

The evidence shows that evolution operated over an incredibly long span of time (see Fig 1.1). Found in ancient sedimentary rock, the earliest known fossils are those of primitive bacteria dating back to 3.5 billion years ago (Campbell, 1996, pp. 458, 487; Schopf, 1993). Thus, life may have first appeared as many as 4 billion years ago—which was about 500 million years after the formation of the planet. Multicellular algae may have evolved by 1.9 billion years ago (Knoll, 1994), but multicellular animals did not appear until about 600 million years ago (Gould, 1994). The first sizeable multicellular animals had evolved by about 575 million years ago (Kerr, 1993). Then, in what is known as the Cambrian explosion, a vast diversification of animals took place over a 5-million-year period between about 530 and 525 million years ago. Virtually all the basic animal body designs—including many that for unknown reasons became extinct—arose during that relatively brief evolutionary period (Gould, 1994).

About 460 million years ago plants, having originated from green algae, began to colonize land (Campbell, 1996, p. 458). Around the same time, creatures similar to modern centipedes and millipedes had begun to walk on land (Johnson, Briggs, Suthren, Wright, & Tunnicliff, 1994). More time had to pass, however, before one of our ancestors crawled out of the ocean.

The earliest known vertebrates were small fish-like creatures called ostracoderms. Although these animals, which have been dated back to 460 million years ago, became extinct about 450 million years ago, they gave rise to most existing vertebrate species including humans (Forey & Janvier, 1994). By 400 million years ago vertebrates were well established

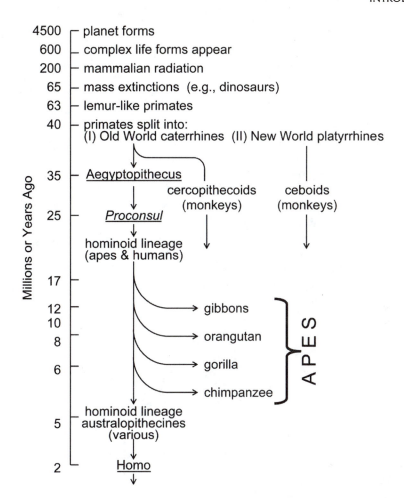

FIGURE 1.1. Approximate numbers of millions of years ago at which various species related to humans first appeared. Note that the apes have no common ancestor that is not also an ancestor of humans; thus, the ape-human distinction is arbitrary from an evolutionary point of view. (From Bradshaw & Rogers, 1993)

throughout the earth's oceans (Campbell, 1996, pp. 458, 634). Fishes predominated from 400 to 350 million years ago. The oldest amphibian fossils are 365 million years old; the oldest reptilian fossils are 300 million years old. Dinosaurs and flying reptiles evolved 200 million years ago, and birds around 208 to 144 million years ago. Although the first mammals may have appeared 220 million years ago, they did not begin to predominate until after a catastrophic collision of an asteroid with the earth led to a mass extinction of their large reptilian competitors about 65 million years ago (Gould, 1994, p. 90). From one successful order of tree-living mammals, the *Primates*, arose the suborder *Anthropoidea*—that today includes monkeys, apes, and humans—at least 45 million years ago (Beard, Tong, Dawson, Wang, & Huang, 1996).

Contrary to some popular beliefs, humans did not evolve from monkeys or apes. As illustrated in Figure 1.1, a sequence of divergences from common ancestors of apes and humans occurred over millions of years. DNA evidence shows the ape and human lines finally completely diverged (with the last of these divergences being between chimpanzees and human) between about 8 and 5 million years ago (Horai, Hyasaka, Kondo, Tsugane, & Takahata, 1995; Ruvolo, Disotell, Allard, Brown, & Honeycutt, 1991). From the fossil record, the first hominid appeared at least 4.4 million years ago, and existed with little change for over 3 million years.

The earliest hominid to be classified in the genus *Homo* appeared about 2.2 million years ago (see Fig. 1.2). While earlier hominids (i.e., those in the genus *Austrolopithecus*) had brains no larger than that of a chimpanzee, this hominid (*Homo rudolfensis*) had a larger brain. It gave rise to another hominid (*Homo habilis*) that made stone tools (Hill, Ward, Deino, Curtix, & Drake, 1992). Later arising hominids (*Homo ergaster* and *Homo erectus*, originally thought to be one species) spread out from Africa and populated Europe and Asia (Swisher, Curtis, Jacob, Getty, & Widiasmoro, 1994). One of these hominids may have been ancestor separately both to the Neanderthals (*Homo neanderthalensis* or *Homo sapiens neanderthalensis*) who existed from the period of about 230,000 to 35,000 years ago, and to us. The first anatomically modern humans (*Homo sapiens* or *Homo sapiens sapiens*) seem to have originated in Africa perhaps as many as 200,000 years ago (Gibbons, 1995; Horai et al., 1995; Lieberman, 1995; Relethford, 1995; Stoneking, 1993; Stringer & McKie, 1996).

Although there is an understandable tendency for us to think of evolution as a straight-line progression to us, the evidence shows that this is not the case. One reason it may appear

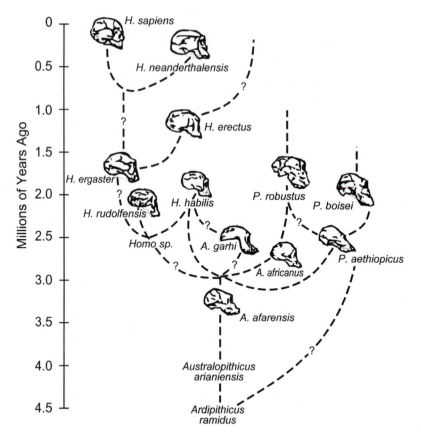

FIGURE 1.2. Although undoubtedly incomplete, the current picture of the human family tree indicates that it is more a bush than a tree. As is typical for other surviving species, the evolutionary path to *Homo sapiens* resembles trial-and-error rather than a straight-line progression. (From Hublin, 1999)

that way is that all the branches of the hominid tree except ours died out. In fact, as indicated in Figure 1.2, the hominid "tree" is more accurately thought of as a dense bush of which we have only partial knowledge (Rightmire, 1995). Many different human forms appeared and some coexisted, but only one exists today. It is unusual for all the species but one in any given genus—let alone in a biological family—to become extinct, but that is what has happened in the case of the hominids. At present we have no clear explanation for the extinction of all the hominid species except ours.

Thus, all species are related and some are more closely related than others are, depending on how long ago their ancestors diverged. DNA studies show how closely related different species are on the basis of similarities in the sequences in their genetic codes. For example, DNA studies show that chimpanzees and humans are more closely related to each other than they are to any other species: there is less than 2% difference between the genetic codes of humans and chimpanzees (Caccone & Powell, 1989; Goodman et al., 1990; Sibley, Comstock, & Ahlquist, 1990). Although differing by only about 1.9% from that of humans, chimpanzee DNA differs 4.0% from that of gorillas, 8.2% from that of orangutans, and 16.8% from that of baboons (Kim & Takenaka, 1996). For the purpose of comparison, the difference between chimpanzee and human DNA is small relative to that between many species that are so closely related as to be indistinguishable to a casual observer (Sibley, Ahlquist, & Monroe, 1988).

The Mechanism of Evolution: Natural Selection

The fossil record and DNA evidence tell us that evolution occurred and the approximate dates at which various species appeared, but not how evolution occurred. Traces of evolution are present, but the process itself left no trace. Although presumably it is still occurring, its rate of occurrence is so slow as to be virtually invisible.

The following three statements taken together describe the general mechanism by which evolution probably operated (Gould, 1977, p. 11):

- The characteristics of organisms differ, and these differences are at least partly inherited.
- More organisms are produced than can possibly survive.
- Those organisms whose characteristics are more favorably adapted to their environments are more likely to survive and produce offspring than will those organisms whose characteristics are less favorably adapted to their environments. Therefore, the characteristics of the former organisms are more likely to be passed on from generation to generation than will the characteristics of the latter organisms.

For example, swiftness is a characteristic that is particularly advantageous to animals such as antelopes and gazelles that graze on flat grasslands. These animals must escape their predators by running, since there is no place for them to climb or hide in their feeding areas. Those that are too slow would likely not live long enough to produce offspring. Because of this, members of these species have become increasingly swifter. This process is called *natural selection*. Characteristics that promote the survival of a species are said to have *survival value*, and the tendency for such a characteristic to be naturally selected is called a *selection pressure* for that characteristic.

Note that natural selection may operate on both physical and behavioral characteristics. It operated on physical characteristics of the animals in the above example because swiftness requires a sleek, lean body equipped with quick-acting muscles. It also operated on behavioral characteristics of these animals in that the muscles move the legs in a certain manner. Both physical and behavioral characteristics can be inherited. (Technically speaking, of course, behavioral characteristics are physical in the sense that they are the result of various physical aspects of the nervous system.)

It should be noted that although natural selection is the most important mechanism driving evolution, it is not the only one. Fortuitous events have also played a major role (Gould, 1994).

A DEFINITION OF LEARNING

As indicated at the beginning of this chapter, learning has to do with the manner in which an individual's behavior is related to the environment. In this book we define *behavior* as

> any neurological activity that is typically (but not necessarily) measured or observed as motor—that is, muscular or glandular—activity.

Note that with this definition behavior need not always be overt because neurological activity can occur with little or no direct muscular or glandular effects. Thus, this definition includes covert or private behavior, as discussed earlier in this chapter.

Learning can then be defined as

> a dependency of current behavior on the environment as a function of a prior interaction between sensory-motor activity and the environment.

For example, suppose that a bear characteristically goes to a particular stream to feed. If the bear stops going to that stream as a result of experiencing that it no longer contains fish, then we would say that learning has occurred: the bear has learned in its current environment to go elsewhere for food.

Note that according to the above definition, learning is an ongoing process that occurs continuously regardless of whether the environment changes. When an individual's current behavior changes following a change in the environment, we might say that the individual has "learned that" the environment has changed. When an individual's current behavior remains the same following no change in the environment, we might say that the individual has "learned that" the environment has not changed. In either case, what the individual has learned is always to be measured by the effect that the individual's prior interaction with the environment has had on the individual's current behavior.

Also note that learning is not necessarily a process that one can verbalize. Clearly, animals and nonverbal humans cannot verbalize what they have learned. Moreover, although people have developed special methods and techniques for enhancing their own learning and that of others, learning does not necessarily involve any conscious effort or intention to learn.

THE EVOLUTION OF LEARNING

Learning is the result of the same evolutionary processes that produced species and behavior. Through a progression of innumerable small physical changes, selection pressures operating over millions of years produced the immense variety of species that inhabit our planet. Evolution is incremental in that it generally proceeds in small steps. The incremental nature of evolution follows from the fact that a large change in the environment may drive a species into extinction, whereas gradual changes permit the accumulation of small adaptations that promote survival. This may be summarized in the following rule referred to in this book as the principle of small increments:

> Given two environmental states, A and B, the effect of B relative to that of A will be less drastic if there is a transition in small increments from A to B (i.e., if the transition from A to B is gradual rather than sudden).

Environmental conditions can change so rapidly that behavior that once promoted survival may quickly cease to do so, and behavior that once lacked survival value may suddenly acquire it. Suppose for a particular species natural selection had favored the behavior of going to a particular location for food because members of that species that had gone to that location had found food and survived, while those that had gone elsewhere did not find food and died. Now suppose that food was no longer to be found at the original location but at another instead. Since it might take thousands or tens of thousands of years for natural selection to produce the appropriate change in behavior corresponding to this change in the environment, clearly the species in this example would become extinct before it adapted to the new location of food. Indeed, since the environment is highly variable, the location of the food source would probably have changed many times before the species adapted even to a single change. Natural selection is not a very efficient process in a rapidly changing environment.

There is therefore a selection pressure against behavior depending too heavily on natural selection. This has resulted in the evolution of a set of processes that are more efficient than natural selection in a rapidly changing envionment. These are the learning processes, which make it possible for the behavior of a single individual to be changed in ways that promote its survival and tendency to reproduce as a function of changes in its environment. Interestingly, in addition to its role in evolution, the principle of small increments applies (though on a much smaller time scale) to many aspects of learning.

From the foregoing, we may say that there are two broad sets of variables that determine an individual's behavior:

- *phylogeny*, which refers to the evolutionary history of the individual (i.e., the selection pressures operating on its ancestors); and
- *ontogeny*, which is the history of the individual's interactions with its environment.

Phylogenetic characteristics are often referred to as genetic, hereditary, or innate, while ontogenetic characteristics are typically called acquired or learned.

It is important to keep in mind, however, that virtually all behavior consists of both types of characteristics. Phylogeny and ontogeny interact, and no behavior can be attributed simply to one or the other. For example, writing might be thought to be a purely learned behavior because of the obvious importance of ontogeny in developing it. However, it also has a phylogenetic component in that it involves opposing the thumb and fingers in a uniquely human manner, which we have inherited from our early tool-using ancestors.

It is also important to understand that there are ontogenetic factors that we would not classify as learning. For example, although having exactly the same DNA, identical twins differ slightly in their physical characteristics simply because of different mechanical and chemical effects that operated on their fetal development due to their different positions in the uterus. We would not consider effects such as these to be learning, any more than we would consider other purely physical effects to be.

SUMMARY AND CONCLUSIONS

This chapter began by considering five approaches to theory: folk, physiological, behavioral, cognitive, and mathematical. All five have their merits. This book, however, uses the language of behavioral theory because its terminology is most suited to our purpose—namely, to precisely describe the scientific knowledge that exists in the field of learning. The appendices introduce some mathematical theories that seem to have a high potential for eventually describing learning in a compact and precise manner.

In taking a scientific approach to learning, it is important to use clear and precise terminology. Many words and common expressions in English, while fine for nonscientific speech, lack the necessary precision. The terms used in this book refer to events and entities that can be observed, with high agreement, by everyone. No one has ever seen a belief, an expectation, or an intention, for example, and so we avoid terms such as these in this book. People do observe physical objects and events, and so we use a language that is suited to talking about these. People also observe private events, such as images and covert speech, and so we do not avoid reference to these things when relevant. We must exercise considerable scientific caution when speaking about private events, however, because (by definition) only one person can observe any particular private event. Evidence that a particular private event has occurred, therefore, is always indirect except for the individual who experienced it.

Learning evolved because survival and reproduction depends on the adjustment of behavior to a changing environment. As is the case with evolution, learning often follows a principle of small increments in that it tends to be most efficient when changes in the environment are small rather than large.

2

Nonassociative Learning

*T*here are two broad categories of learning: nonassociative and associative. In this chapter we deal with nonassociative learning. In nonassociative learning, behavior is modified simply by the occurrence of a stimulus without that stimulus having to be paired (i.e., associated) with any other stimulus. We consider several types of nonassociative learning.

SENSITIZATION AND HABITUATION: TWO OPPOSING PROCESSES

The presentation of certain stimuli may have either of two opposite effects on the future power of that stimulus (or some other stimulus) to elicit a particular response. Generally, these effects last only for a fairly short time. These effects are sensitization and habituation.

Sensitization

Sensitization is an increase in the eliciting effect of a stimulus as a result of prior presentations of either that stimulus or some other stimulus. For example, a buzzer sound presented to a rat will elicit increased activity; however, the buzzer sound will tend to elicit a greater increase in activity if the rat had recently received an electric shock (Harris, 1943). In this case we say that the shock *sensitizes* the animal to the buzzer. A familiar human example is a creaking floorboard eliciting an uncharacteristically large startle response in someone who has just watched a TV horror movie. In this case the large startle response to the creaking sound occurs because of the sensitizing effect of stimuli in the movie.

   In the above examples, the first stimulus presented (e.g., the electric shock or some frightening event in the horror movie) was different from the second stimulus (e.g., the buzzer or the creaking sound). A stimulus can also sensitize responses to itself. For example, if several electric shocks are presented to a rat, the later shocks will tend to elicit more squealing than will the earlier shocks (e.g., Badia, Suter, & Lewis, 1966). Similarly, a low-intensity electric shock presented a short time after a more intense shock will elicit a greater reaction than it would have if it had been preceded by a shock of the same intensity.

Habituation

Acting in direct opposition to sensitization is the process of habituation, which is a decrease in the eliciting effect of a stimulus as a result of repeated presentations of that stimulus. For example, a tone sounded within hearing range of a dog will probably cause the dog's ears to raise. With repeated presentations of the tone, however, the ear-raising response will diminish.

Discrete responses (such as the dog pricking up its ears in the preceding example) or more diffuse (e.g., emotional) behavior may occur to specific stimuli (such as the tone in the preceding example) or to all stimuli in a particular situation. The following general rules apply to habituation:

- If a stimulus to which a response has habituated is withheld for a period of time, an increased response will occur when the stimulus next occurs. (In Chapters 3 and 4 we see that this is similar to a phenomenon called spontaneous recovery in associative learning.)
- If a response goes through the habituation process a number of times, the amount of this recovery steadily decreases (which is also what occurs with spontaneous recovery in associative learning). Eventually the response does not occur at all, even when the stimulus that previously elicited it occurs after a long delay. This is called long-term habituation. It is distinguished from short-term habituation which typically occurs within, rather than across sessions.

Habituation proceeds more rapidly for stimuli that occur at a high rate than for stimuli that occur at a low rate. It also proceeds more rapidly for weak than for strong stimuli. In fact, if a stimulus is very strong habituation may not occur at all (Thompson & Spencer, 1966, p. 19). If the intensity of a stimulus gradually increases over trials to a given level, however, the response to that stimulus will be less than it would have been had the stimulus occurred at that intensity throughout the habituation process (Groves & Thompson, 1970, pp. 426–427). In other words, habituation develops more rapidly to a stimulus that gradually increases in intensity to a given level than to one that starts at that given intensity. Note that this is an instance of the principle of small increments mentioned in the previous chapter. Recall that this principle states that changing from situation A—in this case, a small intensity of stimulus—to situation B—in this case, a large intensity of stimulus—by small increments has a less drastic effect—in this case, a weaker response—than would have resulted from presenting B directly (i.e., in one large step).

Although, as stated above, habituation develops more rapidly to weak than to strong stimuli, a strong stimulus will elicit a stronger response if habituation had occurred to a weak stimulus than if it had occurred to a strong stimulus. Likewise, a weak stimulus will elicit a weaker response if habituation had occurred to a strong stimulus than if it had occurred to a weak stimulus. (Groves & Thompson, 1970, p. 425). In subsequent chapters we see other examples of elevated responding in situations that replace or alternate with those in which lower responding tends to occur, and attenuated responding in situations that replace or alternate with those in which higher responding tends to occur. Such effects are called contrast effects.

Habituation and sensitization act in opposition to each other when a stimulus occurs repeatedly (Groves & Thompson, 1970). If a strong stimulus occurs repeatedly at a low rate, we will see sensitization first (i.e., there will be an increase in the intensity, magnitude, or amount of the response) followed by a gradual decrease in the response with repeated presentations of the stimulus. If the stimulus is not so strong or occurs at a higher rate, we will see less sensitization during the early presentations of the stimulus. If a weak stimulus occurs at a high rate, only a decrease in the response will occur over stimulus presentations; that is, we will observe only habituation.

If a response has decreased to a low level over repeated presentations of a stimulus and a somewhat different stimulus occurs—for example, the same stimulus at a different intensity or a similar stimulus—the response will increase and then further decrease with repeated presentations of the habituation stimulus. It was once thought that this process was a reversal of the habituation process, and accordingly it was given the name *dishabituation*. It now appears, however, that it may be due to the superimposition of the sensitization process on the habituation process. To put this a bit more precisely, it may be that while habituation results from a single decremental process, both sensitization and dishabituation result from a single (that is, the same) facilitative process. The primary evidence for this is that an habituated response that has increased following the occurrence of a different stimulus quickly decreases to the level of habituation it would have reached if only repeated presentations of the habituation stimulus had occurred (Groves & Thompson, 1970, pp. 422–424).

Habituation of discrete responses to specific stimuli.   Examples of habituation of discrete responses to specific stimuli include the startle response in rats (Davis & Wagner, 1969) and humans (Gogan, 1970; Ornitz & Guthrie, 1989) to sudden sounds, visual fixation by human infants on complex (e.g., checkerboard) visual patterns (Kaplan & Werner, 1986; Peterzell, 1993), biting by restrained squirrel monkeys on a rubber tube following electric shocks to their tails (Hutchinson, Renfrew, & Young, 1971), flight by male white-crowned sparrows toward a song of their species played on a speaker in their territories (Petrinovich & Peeke, 1973), and approach and aggressive displays by male Siamese fighting fish (Bronstein, 1994) and threespine sticklebacks (Peeke & Dark, 1990) toward another male of their species introduced behind glass into their territories.

Habituation of emotional behavior.   Emotional behavior to stimuli for phylogenetic reasons, such as a fear response to stimuli that occurs because of its survival value, may produce habituation. An example is fear of cat odor by rats. Figure 2.1 shows an apparatus for studying the habituation of a rat's fear of cat odor. It is interesting that a fear that has such a strong genetic basis can be affected by learning.

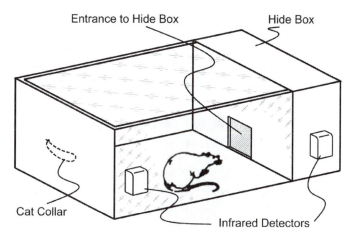

FIGURE 2.1. A worn cat collar placed in the position shown in the figure initially causes the rat to go into the hide box. Over trials the tendency for the cat collar to elicit hiding gradually decreases; i.e., the rat approaches the hide box less and less rapidly and spends less and less time in it. (From Dielenberg & McGregor, 1999)

Habituation to novel environments.   An animal that finds itself in a novel environment may react in several different ways. For example, it may tend to *freeze*—i.e., tense up and remain motionless—during the first few sessions in which it is put into an unfamiliar environment. Over sessions, however, the animal freezes less and less each time it is put into the same (no longer novel) environment. We sometimes use the term adaptation to refer to this type of habituation. When the animal no longer freezes when placed in the formerly novel environment, we say the animal has adapted to it.

Rather than freezing, or after freezing has habituated, animals may move about to a considerable extent in the new environment while bringing their sense receptors into contact with parts of the environment. Rats, for example, will rear and sniff the air while moving their heads from side-to-side or will stick their snouts into small openings and sniff (Bronstein, Neiman, Wolkoff, & Levine, 1974; Feigley, Parsons, Hamilton, & Spear, 1972). This activity, which is called exploratory behavior, also habituates as the animal gains experience with the environment. Eventually, the animal will remain fairly still and relaxed in the environment as long as it remains free of sudden stimuli.

EXPOSURE-BASED LEARNING

The types of nonassociative learning we have considered so far apply to a wide variety of stimuli and responses. We now look at three types of nonassociative learning that apply to very specific types of stimuli (i.e., odors, visually moving objects, and vocal sounds). We will call these types of learning exposure-based learning. Two of these types of learning may be limited to young animals; the third type (birdsong learning) occurs exclusively in the young of some species, but in the adults as well as the young of others.

Exposure-Based Odor Learning

Mere exposure can cause some odors to have specific effects on the behavior of some animals. For example, giving an infant rat a short (e.g., a few minutes) exposure to a neutral odor results in the animal subsequently learning to go to a location scented with that odor rather than another location scented with an odor that is unfamiliar to the animal (Alberts, 1984; Caza & Spear, 1984; Leon, Galef, & Behse, 1977). Moreover, an approximately 2-week-old rat exposed to a particular odor will subsequently huddle with soft, infant-rat-size objects that have been scented with that odor in preference to objects scented with an unfamiliar odor (Brunjes & Alberts, 1979). The evolutionary significance of this learning appears to be in keeping the young animal in the vicinity of its siblings and its mother, thereby facilitating thermoregulation, feeding, and protection.

Exposure to distinctive odors in streams and rivers as salmon fry migrate to the sea causes those salmon to swim toward higher concentrations of those odors when they become adults. This is the mechanism responsible for the migration of salmon back to their stream of origin as the time for them to spawn approaches (Hasler, Schulz, & Horrall, 1978).

Exposure-based odor learning is sometimes called olfactory imprinting, because of its similarity to (standard) imprinting—which is discussed next.

Imprinting

Studied mainly in precocial birds (i.e., birds that can walk immediately after hatching), although it may also occur in other animals, imprinting encompasses two categories of learning that depend on early exposure to a stimulus: filial (or parental) and sexual.

Filial imprinting is a process whereby exposing an individual to a moving visual stimulus creates a tendency in that individual to approach and follow that stimulus. For example, if a duckling has been exposed a few hours after hatching to a foster mother of another species (e.g., a goose), rather than its own mother, it will tend to follow the foster mother and avoid its own mother (e.g., Lorenz, 1935/1970, 1937/1970).

Sexual imprinting is a process whereby individuals tend, upon reaching sexual maturity, to court or exhibit other sexual behavior toward an object resembling one to which they had been filially imprinted. For example, male ducklings that have been raised with a foster mother of another species may upon reaching maturity court and attempt to mate with members of the foster mother's species rather than their own (e.g., Schutz, 1965, 1971).

Figure 2.2 shows an apparatus used to study imprinting. In the figure, a newly hatched duckling is being imprinted to a decoy of a male mallard duckling. The decoy is suspended from an elevated rotating arm that moves the decoy in a circular manner behind a transparent plastic (Plexiglas) wall. The decoy contains speakers over which sounds can be played through a tape recorder. The number of rotations the duckling makes relative to the decoy provides an index of the strength of imprinting. This apparatus is useful for studying the amount of imprinting that occurs on objects displaying different types of visual and auditory stimuli.

Ducklings will imprint on a wide variety of objects, including a flashing light, a dangling ball, and a stuffed hen (Shettleworth, 1994, p. 188). Imprinting does not occur instantaneously with one exposure to an object, as was once thought, but rather develops gradually with continued exposures (ten Cate, 1989). It should be noted that imprinting is generally much stronger in the laboratory than in nature, because young precocial birds tend to be more attracted to their broodmates than to their mother (Darczewska & Shapiro, 1997; Lorenz, 1935/1970, p. 235).

It was once thought that imprinting could occur only during a brief critical period. It now appears, however, that there is no abrupt demarcation between when imprinting can and cannot occur; instead, there appears to be a gradual increase and then a gradual decrease in the individual's sensitivity early in life. Thus, the term "sensitive period" (Bateson, 1979) has tended to replace "critical period" in the terminology of imprinting. It was also once believed that the

Figure 2.2. A duckling is being imprinted on a decoy attached to a rotating arm. In front of the apparatus is a console for controlling such variables as the speed of the rotating arm, intermittent movements of the decoy, the temperature of a heating element in the decoy, and the presentations of sounds through speakers in the decoy. The console also contains counters for displaying number of rotations of the decoy and the duckling. (From Hess, 1959)

critical or sensitive periods for filial and sexual imprinting were identical, and that the two types of imprinting occurred at the same time. Evidence now indicates that this is not the case (Bateson, 1979; Bolhuis, 1991; Bolhuis, deVos, & Kruijt, 1990; Videl, 1980).

Birdsong Learning

Simply as a result of being exposed to a song at a particular time, a bird may sing a similar song at a later time. Most of our knowledge about song learning comes from studies of the white-crowned sparrow of North America (*Zonotrichia* leucophrys)—a species with a well-defined song. Extrapolating largely, but not exclusively, from the research done on this species, we may list the following basic facts about song learning.

- Some species tend to learn any birdsong they are exposed to a sufficient number of times (Baptista & Petrinovich, 1986), although there appears to be a tendency to learn songs of one's own species more readily (as indicated by the number of repetitions required of the song in order for it to be learned) than those of other species (Petrinovich, 1988, p. 257).
- Some species learn songs simply from hearing them played on tape (Marler, 1970).
- For some species there is a sensitive period in development (perhaps similar to the sensitive period for imprinting) during which they learn songs more readily than at other times (Marler, 1970). This sensitive period is particularly evident when the song is played on tape rather than when it is sung live (Baptista & Petrinovich, 1986).
- A considerable time (e.g., many months) can elapse between a bird hearing a song and singing that song for the first time (Marler & Peters, 1981).
- Some species continue learning new songs or modifications of old songs even as adults (Petrinovich & Baptista, 1987). In some cases this may be true only to a limited extent, and perhaps only for the males (Baptista & Morton, 1982; Petrinovich & Baptista, 1984). Other species (e.g., canaries) readily learn new songs throughout their lives; indeed, some species (e.g., parrots, mynahs) learn vocalizations, such as those mimicking human speech, that are quite different from what is typically thought of as birdsongs.
- There is a phylogenetic (or innate) tendency for birds to sing regardless of their exposure to songs. Birds that have been prevented from hearing songs, either through isolation or from being made deaf, develop songs. A bird that has never heard birdsongs, however, develops an abnormal song (Marler, 1970). For some species a normal song will develop if the bird is later exposed to a normal song (Eales, 1985), but for other species the abnormal song persists (Petrinovich & Baptista, 1987).

Although we have classified birdsong learning as nonassociative, there is evidence that associative learning may also be involved. We take up the associative aspects of birdsong learning in the next chapter (pp. 48–49).

From an evolutionary point of view, singing by birds serves several functions. It delineates the territories of different members of a species, it attracts sexual partners, and it enables members of a flock to locate other members and mates within the flock, even when separated by great distances (Bertram, 1970; Thorpe & North, 1965). The tendency to learn the songs of other members of one's flock and of one's mate therefore would appear to be important to a bird's survival and reproduction.

It should be noted that birds are not the only animals that learn distinctive vocalizations as a result of being exposed to them. Although exposure-based vocal learning appears not to be common in mammals (Janik & Slater, 1997), at least one species of bat (Boughman, 1998; Boughman & Wilkinson, 1998) and at least two species of marine mammals (Ford, 1989, 1991; Ford & Fisher, 1983; Guinee, Chu, & Dorsey, 1983; Payne & Guinee,1983; Strager, 1995) learn calls or songs distinctive of their social groups. This appears to have at least one of the same evolutionary functions for these animals as songs do for birds—namely, to help keep members of a social group together. It is interesting that the mammals (bats, dolphins, and whales) that learn their groups' social vocalizations are the ones that navigate and detect prey through echolocation. This appears to be an example of the same physiological apparatus serving two evolutionary functions.

NERVOUS SYSTEM REQUIRED FOR NONASSOCIATIVE LEARNING

Most of our knowledge of learning comes from studies of vertebrates (i.e., fish, amphibians, reptiles, birds, and mammals) whose nervous systems are relatively complex and have a relatively large brain. There is evidence, however, that a large, vertebrate brain is not necessary for at least some categories of learning. Much of this evidence comes from studies of invertebrates, most of which have simple nervous systems and nothing that could be classified as a "brain" of the type found in vertebrates. In this section we look at some of this evidence with regard to nonassociative learning.

Sensitization and Habituation

Sensitization and habituation can occur in vertebrates without the participation of the brain. For example, these two processes can be observed in the flexion response elicited by electric shock to the leg of a cat whose spinal cord has been severed just below the brain (Groves, Lee, & Thompson, 1969; Thompson & Spencer, 1966).

Habituation occurs as far down on the phylogenetic scale as one-celled animals—the protozoans. The contraction responses of these animals to vibratory or photic (i.e., light) stimulation repeated within a short time span decreases gradually (Corning & Von Burg, 1973; Wood, 1973). Similarly, habituation of contraction elicited by vibration occurs in hydras, which are simple multicellular animals with diffuse nervous systems (Rushforth, 1973; Rushforth et al., 1963). The sea anemone, a member of the same phylum (*Coelenterata*) as the hydra, shows habituation of contraction elicited by a stream of fresh water directed at it (Logan, 1975). Interestingly, diminished responding may persist for up to four days (Logan & Beck, 1978). The planarian, which is a member of the phylum (*Platyhelminth*) containing animals (flat worms) with the most primitive bilateral symmetry in the animal kingdom, shows habituation of contraction in response to being touched with a 100-micron wire (Westerman, 1963) or a drop of water from an eyedropper on its anterior region (Owren & Scheuneman, 1993).

In the sea slug *Aplysia*, which is a mollusk (or, actually, a family of mollusks) that has a very primitive centralized nervous system, lightly touching the siphon (an organ for taking in and expelling water) elicits withdrawal of that organ and the gill (Leonard, Edstrom, & Lukowiak, 1989). (See Fig. 2.3.) This response is decreased by repeated presentation of the stimulus, and the response may take at least three weeks to recover its original level (Carew et al., 1979). Sugar applied to the tarsus (bottom part of the foot) of some insects, such as fruit flies (*Drosophila*), elicits extension of the proboscis. Repeated application of sugar to the tarsus over a short time span causes the response to decrease, with the speed at which this habituation occurs being lower for older flies (Fois, Medioni, & leBourg, 1991).

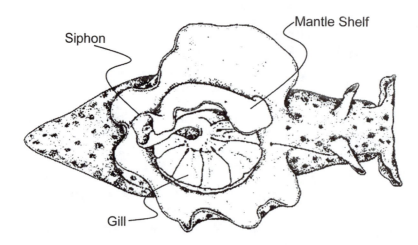

FIGURE 2.3. The gill of this invertebrate (sea slug, Aplysia) withdraws when either the siphon or the mantle shelf is stimulated. This response undergoes habituation. (From Kandel, 1979)

Sensitization and dishabituation of a planarian's contraction response to touch can be produced by drawing the planarian in and out of an eyedropper several times (Owren & Scheuneman, 1993). The results support the view, mentioned earlier, that sensitization and dishabituation are produced by the same facilitative process. Dishabituation occurs in at least one coelenterate: touch with a glass rod will reinstate a sea anemone's habituated contraction to a stream of fresh water directed at it (Logan & Beck, 1978). Presentation of brief electric shock sensitizes a sea slug's siphon-and-gill-withdrawal response to touch, and the enhanced responding to touch lasts at least three weeks (Pinsker, Hening, Carew, & Kandel, 1973). Strong tail shock to a slug produces a sensitization that does not start until 30 to 50 minutes after the shock, and hence is called delayed-onset sensitization (DOS). Although slugs show dishabituation by about 50 days after metamorphosis, they do not show DOS until at least 30 days later (Wright, McCance, Lu, & Carew, 1992). This suggests that, at least for slugs, dishabituation and sensitization may be different processes. Other evidence supporting this conclusion is that the onset of dishabituation is not delayed to the same extent and dishabituation is produced by a less intense stimulus (Marcus, Nolen, Rankin, & Carew, 1988).

Exposure-Based Learning

Some apparent examples of olfactory imprinting in insects are as follows:

When a female parasitic wasp is ready to deposit her ova, she is likely to select the species of host larva on which she herself was reared (Taylor, 1974; Thorpe & Jones, 1937). Social wasps, which are raised with their own kind, discriminate nest mates from others as a result of only one to two hours exposure to the natal nest and nest mates at emergence (Pfennig et al., 1983). This learning seems to be based on exposure to the odor of the nest mates or nest, or both, soon after emergence.

The acceptance or rejection by guard bees of bees entering a nest is based on whether the entering bees' odor resembles that of the nest mates of the guard bees (Buckle & Greenberg, 1981). This discrimination seems to result from exposure of guard bees when young to the odor of their nest mates. Another apparent example of olfactory imprinting in bees pertains to the way in which these insects locate food. Worker bees foraging for food fly toward a food source communicated to them at the hive through a "dance" performed by a bee that had just returned from that site (von Frisch, 1967). The dance, however, appears to be sufficient only to get the worker bee in the vicinity of the food source. The odor that the communicator bee brings back to the hive from the food source appears to get the worker to the rest of the way to the site (Wenner & Johnson, 1967; Wenner, Wells, & Johnson, 1969).

SUMMARY AND CONCLUSIONS

Nonassociative learning involves the modification of behavior as a result of the occurrence or repeated occurrence of a single stimulus. The types of nonassociative learning include sensitization, which is the increased tendency of a given stimulus to elicit a response as a result of that stimulus being preceded by itself or a different stimulus within a short time period; habituation, which is the opposite of sensitization (i.e., the decreased tendency of a given stimulus to elicit a given response as a result of the repeated occurrence of that stimulus within a short time period); and exposure-based learning, which is the development of new responses to specific stimuli (i.e., odors, visually moving objects, and vocal sounds) simply as a result of exposure to those stimuli.

The types of nervous systems required for nonassociative learning appear not to be very complex. Nonassociative learning occurs in simple multicellular animals, mollusks, insects, and other invertebrates, and the isolated spinal cords of vertebrates as well as intact vertebrates.

3

Associative Learning

A ssociative learning results from the *pairing* or *association* of two events close together in time. The two events may be either two stimuli or a response followed by a stimulus. The former we call stimulus-stimulus learning, while the latter we call response-stimulus learning. Two more common names for these types of associative learning are respondent conditioning and operant conditioning, respectively.

RESPONDENT BEHAVIOR

Some stimuli elicit particular responses in an individual due to the individual's evolutionary history. For example, meat placed in the mouth of a dog that has been deprived of food is a stimulus that elicits salivation, because this facilitates digestion of food and thus promoted the survival of the dog's ancestors. Stimuli that do not elicit particular responses come to do so by being paired with other stimuli that elicit those responses. Conditioned respondent behavior is behavior that is acquired in this way; that is, behavior that is learned through a process called respondent conditioning. Respondent conditioning appears to have evolved because it prepares an animal to respond to impending events.

Respondent Conditioning

A stimulus-response relationship that depends on phylogeny rather than ontogeny is called an unconditioned reflex. The stimulus member (e.g., meat) of the unconditioned reflex is called the unconditioned stimulus, and the response member (e.g., salivation) is called the unconditioned response.

Consider a stimulus, such as the sound of a bell, which does not elicit the unconditioned response in the above example. Such a stimulus is called a neutral stimulus with respect to that particular response (although it may be an unconditioned stimulus with respect to some other response, such as ear raising or orienting toward the bell). Suppose, however, that this neutral stimulus occurs just prior to presenting an unconditioned stimulus (e.g., a piece of meat) on a number of occasions. The result of pairing these two stimuli is that the neutral stimulus will elicit a response similar to (but not identical to) the response elicited by the unconditioned stimulus. That is, if the sound of a bell is repeatedly paired with the presentation of meat to a dog, eventually the sound of the bell by itself (i.e., without the meat) will elicit salivation. A stimulus-response relationship of this type is called a conditioned reflex. The stimulus member (the sound of the bell) of the conditioned reflex is called the conditioned stimulus, and the response member (salivation) is called the conditioned response. The above process of establishing a conditioned reflex is called respondent conditioning. (It also is known as Pavlovian conditioning, after the Russian physiologist I. P. Pavlov who studied it extensively, and as classical conditioning because it was the first process to be labeled "conditioning.") Because respondent conditioning is the association between a conditioned stimulus and an unconditioned stimulus, it is classified as stimulus-stimulus associative learning.

The process of respondent conditioning can be diagramed as follows (US = unconditioned stimulus; UR = unconditioned response; CS = conditioned stimulus; CR = conditioned response):

Given that US → UR, then:
(CS, US), (CS, US), . . . , (CS, US) ⇒ CS → CR.

We may use the above diagram to represent the conditioning of salivation in a dog to the sound of a bell as follows:

Given that meat → salivation, then:
(bell, meat), (bell, meat), . . . , (bell, meat) ⇒ bell → salivation.

Figure 3.1 illustrates an early respondent (Pavlovian) conditioning experiment with a dog.

Respondent Extinction

In respondent extinction a stimulus that previously reliably preceded an impending event no longer does so, and the conditioned response eventually ceases to occur.

For example, suppose that a dog has been conditioned to salivate to the sound of a bell as described above. If the bell is now repeatedly rung without being followed by the presentation of food, the salivary response will gradually decrease until eventually the bell elicits no salivation at all. When this happens we say that the conditioned response has been extinguished. Since unnecessarily producing saliva is wasteful of body fluid and energy, we can see that the process of respondent extinction, like that of respondent conditioning, has survival value. It should be understood, of course, that the survival value of these processes is by no means limited to the salivary response, which is used here as merely one of many possible examples. In later chapters other examples of these processes will be discussed.

Using the same notation as above, we may represent respondent extinction as:

(CS, ~US), (CS, ~US), . . . , (CS, ~US) ⇒ CS → ~CR,

indicating that after repeated presentations of the conditioned stimulus without the unconditioned stimulus (the symbol "~" means "no" or "not" here) the conditioned stimulus eventually no longer elicits the unconditioned response.

If a conditioned stimulus has not occurred for a relatively long period of time after the conditioned response has been extinguished, presenting the conditioned stimulus may elicit a stronger response than had occurred on the previous presentation of the conditioned stimulus. In other words, a conditioned stimulus may recover some of the eliciting strength it lost during extinction if a relatively long period of time passes in which the conditioned stimulus does not occur. This phenomenon is called spontaneous recovery. The phenomenon is not

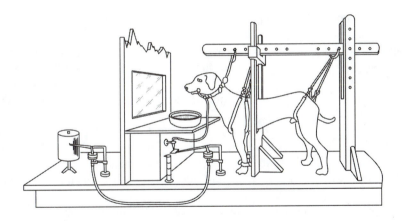

FIGURE 3.1. A sound that consistently precedes food eventually elicits a recording pen on a rotating drum and accumulates in a calibrated glass tube. (From Yerkes, & Morgulis, 1909)

permanent; subsequent occurrences of the conditioned stimulus without the unconditioned stimulus will result in further decreases in the conditioned response.

Respondent Stimulus Generalization

When a given stimulus has become a conditioned stimulus, stimuli that are similar to that stimulus will also tend to elicit the conditioned response. This principle is called respondent stimulus generalization. For example, if the sound of a given bell is a conditioned stimulus for salivation by a particular dog, the sounds of other bells will also elicit salivation in that dog—even if those other bells are of higher or lower frequencies than the conditioned stimulus. The more different these other stimuli are from the conditioned stimulus, the weaker their conditioned response will be.

Stimulus generalization occurs with respondent extinction as well as with respondent conditioning. A conditioned response will be more weakly elicited by any stimulus (not necessarily the conditioned stimulus) if a similar stimulus has repeatedly occurred without being paired with the unconditioned stimulus.

With regard to respondent conditioning, stimulus generalization is defined as the tendency for a conditioned response to occur to a stimulus other than the stimulus to which it was conditioned. A corresponding definition holds for stimulus generalization of respondent extinction.

It is not difficult to see the evolutionary reason for respondent stimulus generalization. Stimuli that are important to the organism vary. For example, not all food items look or smell exactly alike. An animal that has a conditioned salivation response only to food items that looked exactly like the ones it has already eaten would never salivate in advance of having food in its mouth.

Respondent Stimulus Discrimination

Although responses tend to occur to stimuli other than those to which they have been conditioned, this tendency is less than that to stimuli to which they have been conditioned. Thus, opposite to respondent stimulus generalization there is a process, called respondent stimulus discrimination, which is defined as the tendency for a conditioned response *not* to occur to a stimulus other than the stimulus to which it was conditioned.

Respondent stimulus discrimination may be enhanced by alternating the conditioned stimulus with another stimulus, while following the conditioned stimulus with the unconditioned stimulus but not following the other stimulus with the unconditioned stimulus. For example, using a dog as the experimental subject, we might alternately follow the sound of a high-pitched bell with meat and the sound of a low-pitched bell with nothing. The result would be that the dog would salivate copiously to the high-pitched bell and salivate very little or not at all to the low-pitched bell. In this experiment, the high-pitched bell is called a positive conditioned stimulus (abbreviated CS+, which is pronounced "see-ess plus") and the low-pitched bell is a negative conditioned stimulus (abbreviated CS–, which is pronounced "see-ess minus").

We may diagram the development of a respondent stimulus discrimination as follows:

Given two arbitrary stimuli, abbreviated CS+ and CS–, and an unconditioned stimulus (US), then:
(CS+, US), (CS–,~US), . . . , (CS+, US), (CS-,~US) $\Rightarrow$ CS+ $\rightarrow$ CR, CS– $\rightarrow$ ~CR.

It is not difficult to see the evolutionary reason for respondent stimulus discrimination. Stimuli that are important to an animal may be similar to ones that are unimportant or important in the opposite way. For example, inedible substances may resemble food items, but it would be wasteful of its resources for an animal to salivate to inedible material. Thus, we see that respondent stimulus generalization and respondent discrimination are important. The former helps ensure that an animal will respond effectively to stimuli it has not yet encountered, the latter that an animal does not respond ineffectively to stimuli that are unimportant to it.

Higher-Order Conditioning

It is not necessary for stimuli to be directly paired with an unconditioned stimulus in order to elicit a conditioned response based on that unconditioned stimulus. For example, once a stimulus has been established as a conditioned stimulus for a particular response it can then be an unconditioned stimulus for establishing a new conditioned stimulus for that response. This is called higher-order conditioning. For example, a bell that elicits salivation due to having been paired with food can be used as an unconditioned stimulus for conditioning salivation to a light. This would be done by repeatedly presenting the light followed immediately by the bell (but not the food) until eventually the light elicited salivation (Shapiro, Sadler, & Mugg, 1971). Using this example, higher-order conditioning can be diagramed according to the following two-step procedure:

1. Given that meat $\rightarrow$ salivation, then:
   (bell, meat), (bell, meat), . . . , (bell, meat) $\Rightarrow$ bell $\rightarrow$ salivation.
2. Given that bell $\rightarrow$ salivation, then:
   (light, bell), (light, bell), . . . , (light, bell) $\Rightarrow$ light $\rightarrow$ salivation.

Higher-order conditioning is not a powerful process, however, for at least two reasons: (1) experimentally demonstrating it requires presenting the original conditioned stimulus without following it by the original unconditioned stimulus, which is also the procedure for extinction (p. 26); (2) experimentally demonstrating it requires pairing the new conditioned stimulus with the original conditioned stimulus on trials on which the original unconditioned stimulus does not occur, which causes the new conditioned stimulus to inhibit (i.e., prevent) the occurrence of the response to the original conditioned stimulus. In other words, the conditioned response does not occur to the combined stimuli because the unconditioned stimulus does not follow the stimuli presented in combination. This is called conditioned inhibition; we discuss this concept in more detail in Chapter 4.

Sensory Preconditioning

We have seen that through higher-order conditioning a stimulus that has not been directly paired with an unconditioned stimulus can elicit a conditioned response based on that unconditioned stimulus. There is another way that this sort of indirect conditioning can happen. Suppose that two neutral stimuli (i.e., two stimuli that do not elicit any obvious strong response) are paired and then one of these neutral stimuli becomes a conditioned stimulus for a particular response. The result of this procedure, which is called sensory preconditioning, is that the other stimulus will then also elicit that response (we might say that it has been preconditioned). Suppose, for example, that a light is presented to a dog just before a bell sounds, and that this procedure is repeated a number of times. Next, suppose that the bell sounds just before a shock to the leg, which elicits a strong leg-flexion response. After several such pairings, the bell alone will elicit the flexion response, simply as a result of respondent conditioning. In addition, however, the light also will tend to elicit the flexion response as a result of having been previously paired with the bell (Brogden, 1939).

We may see sensory preconditioning as a form of respondent conditioning if we assume that any stimulus elicits covert responses that then act as stimuli that can become conditioned stimuli. For example, following our discussion of covert or private stimuli and responses in Chapter 1, we assume that presenting the sound of a bell to a dog elicits a covert response which in turn produces a covert stimulus we might call "hearing the bell." If a light occurs just prior to the bell a number of times, then by the principle of respondent conditioning the light should begin to elicit "hearing the bell." (A less formal way of putting this is to say that the light "reminds" the dog of the bell.) Now suppose that the bell has been paired with a shock to the dog's leg. Since the shock elicits the leg flexion response, the bell will also elicit this response through respondent conditioning. It is not difficult to see why a light that had been previously paired with the bell would also elicit the flexion response. The light would elicit the response "hearing the bell" (or a similar response) and it would be this response which, acting now as a stimulus, would (because of its similarity to the original conditioned stimulus) directly elicit the flexion response. This can be diagramed according to the following three-step procedure:

1. Given that bell → hearing bell, then:
   (light, bell), (light, bell), . . . , (light, bell) ⇒ light → hearing bell.
2. Given that shock → flexion, then:
   (bell, shock), (bell, shock), . . . , (bell, shock) ⇒ bell → flexion.
3. Given that light → hearing bell (the result of Step 1) and bell → flexion (the result of Step 2), then:
   light → hearing bell → flexion.

Thus, sensory preconditioning can be considered to be a special case of respondent conditioning on the basis of the following two assumptions:

- external stimuli elicit covert or private "sensory" responses (e.g., "hearing the bell");
- these "sensory" responses can act as stimuli which can be conditioned to elicit other responses (e.g., flexion in the above example).

Sensory responses (or "mental images" as they are often called) are discussed further in later chapters).

Distinguishing Neutral From Unconditioned Stimuli

As mentioned, any neutral stimulus can become a conditioned stimulus for any response that can be elicited by an unconditioned stimulus. It is important to be very clear on what we mean when we use the term "neutral stimulus." A stimulus that is neutral for one response (and hence a potential conditioned stimulus for that response) may be an unconditioned stimulus (and hence not neutral) for another response (Gormezano & Tait, 1976). For example, a mild electric shock near the orbit of a rabbit's eye will elicit a blink and is therefore an unconditioned stimulus for the blink response. Water injected through a tube into a rabbit's mouth elicits jaw movements and is therefore an unconditioned stimulus for jaw movements. An electric shock near the orbit of a rabbit's eye will not elicit jaw movements and water injected into a rabbit's mouth will not elicit a blink; therefore, each of these stimuli is neutral with respect to the response elicited by the other. Accordingly, if we pair shock near the orbit of a rabbit's eye with water in the animal's mouth, the shock will (after a number of such pairings) elicit jaw movements. Similarly, if we pair water in the mouth with shock near the orbit of the eye, the water will (after a number of such pairings) elicit the blink response (Tait, 1974). (Note that in each case, the stimulus that becomes the conditioned stimulus is the one that occurs prior to the other stimulus in the pairing procedure; we discuss the importance of order of stimulus-stimulus pairings in respondent conditioning in Chapter 4.)

It is also possible to use the unconditioned stimulus of one response as the conditioned stimulus for another in higher-order conditioning and in sensory preconditioning. First consider higher-order conditioning. To continue using the rabbit example, we might first pair water in the mouth (which elicits jaw movements) with shock near the orbit of the eye (which elicits the blink response), and then pair a tone with water in the mouth. The result is that the tone will come to elicit both jaw movements, due to simple conditioning, and the blink response due to higher-order conditioning.

Now consider sensory preconditioning, again using a rabbit example. This time we first pair the tone with water in the mouth, which will result in the tone eliciting jaw movements through simple conditioning. Next we pair water in the mouth with shock near the orbit of the eye. The result is exactly the same as in the preceding example; that is, the tone will elicit both jaw movements and the blink response (Tait, Quesnel, & Ten Have, 1986).

We can see from the above that although the procedures of simple respondent conditioning, higher-order conditioning, and sensory preconditioning differ, the basic processes operating are the same. In addition, we see that the terms "neutral stimulus," "unconditioned stimulus," and "conditioned stimulus" are relative. The essential fact about respondent conditioning is that it is the result of pairing two stimuli, regardless of the terms by which we designate those stimuli.

OPERANT BEHAVIOR

Respondent conditioning is one of the two major types of associative learning. The other major type is called operant conditioning (also known as instrumental conditioning). In respondent conditioning, as we saw above, a response similar to one that occurs to one stimulus is made to occur to another stimulus by presenting the two stimuli close together in time (i.e., pairing or associating them). In operant conditioning a response that occurs with some minimum frequency is made to occur more frequently by following it with a particular type of stimulus event (which could be either the presentation or the removal of stimulus) called reinforcement. That is, unlike respondent conditioning, operant conditioning involves associating a response with a stimulus event rather than a stimulus with a stimulus (and is therefore classified as response-stimulus associative learning). Behavior that has been learned through operant conditioning is called operant behavior. While respondent conditioning is important in preparing an animal to respond (often internally) to impending events, operant conditioning is the major way in which an animal learns to interact with its surroundings.

Positive Reinforcement

There are two types of reinforcement that condition new operant behavior: positive and negative. Positive reinforcement is the presentation of a stimulus (called a positive reinforcer) immediately following a response. A positive reinforcer is defined as any stimulus whose presentation immediately following a response increases the probability (i.e., the frequency or rate of occurrence) of that response.

A standard experimental apparatus for studying operant conditioning in a small mammal (e.g., a rat) is an enclosure containing a food tray and a protruding lever. This enclosure, which is often called a Skinner box after its inventor (B. F. Skinner), is more descriptively referred to as an operant conditioning chamber. The lever inside the operant conditioning chamber is electrically connected to a feeder mechanism that delivers a small pellet of food into the tray when the lever is pressed. A test animal, such as a laboratory rat, that has been deprived of food is placed in the chamber. Even though the animal has had no prior exposure to this situation, except for some experience eating from the food tray, it will eventually begin performing a response that its distant ancestors never performed—it will begin pressing the lever at a fairly high rate. In this example the food pellet is a positive reinforcer because its presentation immediately following the response of lever pressing increased the probability of that response.

Positive reinforcement can be diagramed as follows (R = response):

Given that S (a stimulus) is a positive reinforcer, then:
(R, S), (R, S), . . . , (R, S) $\Rightarrow \uparrow$R (increased probability of R).

Thus the diagram illustrates that repeated instances of positive reinforcement of a response produces an increased probability or rate of occurrence of that response. (The up arrow indicates increased probability.) An example of the operant conditioning of a lever press with food as the positive reinforcer can be diagramed as follows:

Given that food is a positive reinforcer, then:
(lever press, food), (lever press, food), . . . , (lever press, food) $\Rightarrow \uparrow$ lever press

Figure 3.2 shows some examples of experimental apparatuses for the study of operant conditioning. Pigeons pecking response keys—which are small plastic disks that can be transilluminated (i.e., illuminated from behind) with differed colored lights—for food are very commonly studied in operant conditioning experiments (as illustrated in the top left panel of the figure). Other species and reinforcers are also studied, however.

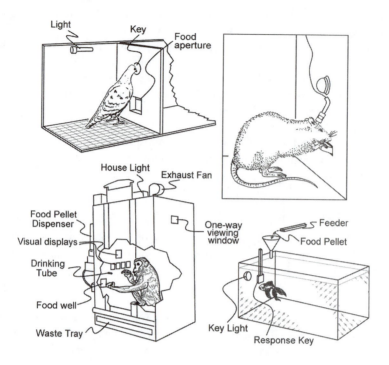

Figure 3.2. Examples of operant conditioning apparatuses. Top left: Apparatus for reinforcing a pigeon's key pecking with food (from Verhave, 1966); top right: Apparatus for reinforcing a rat's lever pressing with electric stimulation to a reinforcing brain region (from Routtenberg, 1978); bottom left: Apparatus for reinforcing a chimpanzee's lever pressing with food (from Rohles, 1961); bottom right: Apparatus for reinforcing a fish's key pushing with food (from Talton et al., 1999).

Any positive reinforcer generally produces a specific behavioral interaction with it; for example, food evokes eating the food, a sex partner evokes copulation. The behavioral interaction that typically occurs with a positive reinforcer is called *consummatory behavior*, and there is generally a direct relationship between the strength or effectiveness of the reinforcer and the amount or intensity of the consummatory behavior it evokes. Note that "consummatory" in the sense we use it here does not necessary imply "destroying" or "using up" the reinforcer.

The strength of a positive reinforcer, or in other words an individual's motivation for it, usually depends on a prior event or occurrence called an establishing operation (Michael, 1982, 1993). For example, engaging in sustained physical activity (i.e., "working up an appetite") is an establishing operation for food reinforcement because it increases the effectiveness of food as a reinforcer. Becoming overheated or eating salty food are establishing operations for water reinforcement because they increase the effectiveness of water as a reinforcer.

One of the most effective establishing operations, and the one most commonly used in basic laboratory research with animals, is deprivation. This involves withholding a reinforcer from an individual for some period of time prior to a session in which that reinforcer is used. Typically, when food deprivation is used to establish food as a reinforcer, the animal is maintained at some reduced percentage (e.g., 80%) of its body weight through food deprivation during the period in which an experiment is carried out.

The opposite of deprivation (i.e., a term meaning "no deprivation") is satiation. If an individual has not been deprived of a particular reinforcer for any length of time, that individual is said to be satiated on that reinforcer.

Negative Reinforcement

Negative reinforcement is the removal, or termination, of a stimulus called a negative reinforcer immediately following a response. A negative reinforcer is defined as any stimulus whose removal immediately following a response increases the probability of that response. Suppose, for example, that an operant conditioning chamber is equipped with, instead of a feeder, a device for delivering electric shock to the feet of a test animal. If during the occurrence of shock each lever press terminates (i.e., turns off) the shock for a brief period, the animal will eventually press the lever as soon as the shock begins. In this example shock is a negative reinforcer because its termination immediately following the response of lever pressing increased the probability of that response (i.e., lever pressing).

We may diagram negative reinforcement as follows:

Given that S is a negative reinforcer, then:
$$(R, -S), (R, -S), \ldots, (R, -S) \Rightarrow \uparrow R$$

where (R, –S) represents one pairing of the response with the removal of S. Thus the diagram illustrates that repeated instances of negative reinforcement of a response produces an increased probability or rate of occurrence of that response.

Note that a negative reinforcer differs from a positive reinforcer in the following ways:

- there is no consummatory response for a negative reinforcer (because the individual tends to respond in such a way as to remove it, rather than interact with it)
- a sufficient establishing operation for a negative reinforcer is the negative reinforcer itself (because simply presenting the negative reinforcer ensures that its removal will increase the probability of a preceding response)

Later we shall see that stimuli paired with a negative reinforcer can also be establishing operations for that negative reinforcer. Negative reinforcement is often referred to as escape conditioning because it results in an individual escaping from a particular stimulus (given that, from a relativistic point of view, engaging in an action that removes a particular stimulus is functionally equivalent to removing oneself from that stimulus—which is the usual meaning of escape in common, everyday speech).

In addition to learning to remove, or terminate, negative reinforcers, individuals also learn to avoid them, that is, to prevent or postpone them. This is called avoidance conditioning. In one standard avoidance-conditioning procedure, for example, a neutral stimulus such as a light is followed within a short interval by a shock. If the individual emits some specific response (e.g., lever press) before the shock is scheduled to occur, however, its occurrence is canceled. We may diagram avoidance conditioning as follows:

Given that S is a negative reinforcer, then:
$$(\sim R, S), (\sim R, S), \ldots, (\sim R, S) \Rightarrow \uparrow R$$

where ~R represents the nonoccurrence of the response, R, and (~R, S) represents one pairing of the nonoccurrence of the response with the stimulus. Thus the diagram illustrates that repeated instances of a negative reinforcer in the absence of a particular response increases the probability or rate of occurrence of that response.

In Chapter 13 we discuss processes by which behavior is reinforced by the prevention or postponement of negative reinforcers.

Operant Extinction

In operant extinction reinforcement is omitted after the response has been operantly conditioned. The typical result is that the frequency of occurrence (or rate) of the response decreases back to the level it was at prior to conditioning. When this happens, we say that the response has been effectively extinguished. (Sometimes the word "effectively" is omitted; however, it is an important qualifier because it helps avoid confusing the procedure of extinction with its effect.) In the case of positive reinforcement, extinction involves no longer delivering the reinforcer after responding occurs; for example, no longer delivering food pellets following lever presses, if lever pressing had originally been reinforced by food pellets. In the case of negative reinforcement, extinction involves no longer terminating the reinforcer after responding occurs; for example, no longer terminating shock following lever presses, if lever pressing had originally been reinforced by shock termination. Given a response, R, that has been reinforced with a positive reinforcer, S, we may diagram operant extinction as follows:

$$(R, \sim S), (R, \sim S), \ldots, (R, \sim S) \Rightarrow \downarrow R \text{ (decreased probability of R)}.$$

Spontaneous recovery occurs in operant extinction in an analogous manner to its occurrence in respondent extinction. That is, if a relatively long period of time passes in which an operant response has no opportunity to occur after the response has decreased due to extinction, the response may occur at an increased rate on the next opportunity for it to occur. As with respondent spontaneous recovery, operant spontaneous recovery is a short-lived phenomenon. Subsequent extinction causes responding due to decrease.

Other effects of operant extinction include extinction bursts, which are increases in responding above the level that occurred during reinforcement of the response just prior to extinction (Skinner, 1933), aggression toward nearby animate or inanimate objects (Azrin, Hutchinson, & Hake, 1966; Flory, Smith, & Ellis, 1977), and distress calling (Hoffman, 1996). Collectively these effects are called emotional effects. Although common, emotional effects do not always occur during extinction (Lerman & Iwata, 1995; Lerman, Iwata, & Wallace, 1999); when they do occur, they are temporary and decrease as extinction progresses.

Negative Reinforcement Compared With Punishment and Extinction

Negative reinforcement should not be confused with a process called punishment, which technically is defined as the presentation of a stimulus, called a punisher, following a response. A punisher is defined as any stimulus whose presentation immediately following a response decreases the probability of that response. For example, suppose that a rat's lever pressing is being positively reinforced with food and is therefore occurring at a high rate. If a brief shock then occurs immediately following each lever press, the rate of lever pressing will decrease and we would say that the response has been punished. Punishment may be diagramed as follows:

Given that S is a punisher, then:
(R, S), (R, S), . . . , (R, S) $\Rightarrow$ $\downarrow$R.

Note that although the same stimulus can be both a negative reinforcer and a punisher, the processes of negative reinforcement and punishment have quite different results. In the former case the rate of a response is increased; in the latter case it is decreased. Just as punishment should not be confused with negative reinforcement, however, it also should not be confused with extinction even though both processes have a similar result. In extinction, no stimulus follows the response; in punishment a punisher follows the response. Moreover, in the above example of punishment, the lever pressing response continued to be reinforced. Clearly this does not satisfy the definition of extinction, which specifies that the response no longer be reinforced. (Compare the preceding diagrams of negative reinforcement and extinction with the above diagram of punishment.)

It is often useful to have a single term to refer to either a negative reinforcer or a punisher; the term aversive stimulus serves this purpose. Similarly, the expression aversive control refers to the control of behavior by either negative reinforcement or punishment.

Operant Stimulus Generalization and Discrimination

If a particular stimulus is present when a particular response is reinforced, the response will be more likely to occur in its presence than in its absence. This is called operant stimulus generalization, and it is exactly analogous to respondent stimulus generalization (discussed earlier in this chapter). Moreover, there is a process of operant stimulus discrimination that is exactly analogous to the process of respondent stimulus discrimination (also discussed earlier in this chapter). An operant stimulus discrimination develops (or is enhanced) when a particular response is reinforced in the presence of a particular stimulus and extinguished in its absence. For example, suppose that lever presses are sometimes reinforced with food and sometimes not. If a specific tone is present whenever a lever press is followed by food and a different tone is present whenever a lever press is not followed by food, eventually the animal will respond only when the first tone is present. We say that that tone has acquired stimulus control over the response of lever pressing, and we call that tone a discriminative stimulus for responding. Commonly we use the symbol S^D (pronounced "ess-dee") to represent a discriminative stimulus for responding. Likewise, we would say that the second tone has acquired control over not responding, and we call that tone a discriminative stimulus for not responding. Commonly we use the symbol S^Δ (pronounced "ess-delta") to represent a discriminative stimulus for not responding ("Δ" being the Greek letter delta, corresponding to the Roman letter "D"). Note that an S^D in operant conditioning is analogous to a CS+ in respondent conditioning, and an S^Δ in operant conditioning is analogous to a CS– in respondent conditioning.

The reasons that operant stimulus generalization and discrimination evolved are similar to those for respondent stimulus generalization and discrimination. Objects that have similar properties vary, so that an animal would likely not survive if it emitted responses only in the presence of stimuli exactly like stimuli that was present when the responses were previously reinforced. For example, a tiger would not learn to chase different prey of the same species. Conversely, animals that responded indiscriminately to stimuli that resembled each other would waste energy and time. For example, a tiger that failed to learn *not* to chase prey that were too swift for it to catch would waste energy in fruitless chases and waste time that would be more effectively used chasing easier prey.

We may diagram the development of an operant stimulus discrimination as follows:

Given two arbitrary stimuli, S^D and S^Δ, and a positive reinforcer, abbreviated S^r, then:
$(S^D, R, S^r), (S^\Delta, R, \sim S^r), \ldots, (S^D, R, S^r), (S^\Delta R, \sim S^r) \Rightarrow S^D \to R, S^\Delta \to \sim R.$

Note the similarity between a discriminative stimulus for responding (in operant conditioning) and a conditioned stimulus (in respondent conditioning). Both an operant discriminative stimulus and a conditioned stimulus occur prior to the response that they may be said to "cause," "produce," or "control." Moreover, as with a conditioned stimulus, stimuli similar to a discriminative stimulus tend to produce the same response that the discriminative stimulus produces. The more similar a given stimulus is to the discriminative stimulus, the more similar its response-producing effect will be to that of the discriminative stimulus. Thus, stimulus generalization occurs with operant conditioning as it does with respondent conditioning.

Conditioned Reinforcement

Some stimuli, such as food and water, are reinforcers due to phylogeny (i.e., the evolutionary history of the species). These stimuli are called primary reinforcers. Other stimuli can become reinforcers due to events that occur in the history of an individual. Typically, these reinforcers have been paired with existing reinforcers. For example, if a tone regularly precedes food, the tone will become a reinforcer—that is, it can be used to operantly condition an arbitrary response such as a lever press. A conditioned reinforcer is a stimulus that has become a reinforcer by being paired with a reinforcer. Conditioned reinforcement expands the range of stimuli that can become reinforcers. The evolutionary significance of conditioned reinforcement is that responding to produce a stimulus that has occurred in close temporal association with a primary reinforcer is likely to bring the animal closer to the primary reinforcer. Natural selection would favor this because primary reinforcers usually benefit the animal or its reproductivity.

The development of a conditioned reinforcer can be diagramed as follows:

Given that S_1 is an arbitrary stimulus and S^r is a reinforcer, then:
$(S_1, S^r), (S_1, S^r), \ldots, (S_1, S^r) \Rightarrow S^r_1.$

The diagram depicts the fact that through repeated pairings of S_1 with S^r, S_1 becomes a conditioned reinforcer.

Conditioned reinforcers enable the development of stimulus-response sequences called behavioral chains. Consider, for example, a behavioral chain consisting of (1) a lever press response, followed by (2) the "click" sound of a feeder depositing food in a trough response, followed by (3) running to the food trough response, followed by (4) food stimulus, followed by (5) eating the food response. Note that in this behavioral chain, the lever press is not reinforced directly by the food. Rather, the lever press is reinforced directly by the "click" sound of the feeder, which is a conditioned reinforcer because it has been paired with food. The food maintains the chain by directly reinforcing running to the food trough following the "click" sound (which is therefore an S^D for running to the food trough) so that the "click" sound becomes and remains a conditioned reinforcer. Much longer behavioral chains can also be formed through conditioned reinforcement in this same general manner, as will be discussed in Chapter 11. A two-link behavioral chain may be diagramed as follows:

$$S^D_1 \to R_1 \to S^{r,D}_2 \to R_2 \to S^r_3$$

where R_1 and R_2, are two different responses, and S^D_1 is a discriminative stimulus for R_1, $S^{r.D}_2$ is both a conditioned reinforcer for R_1 and a discriminative stimulus for R_2, and S^r_3 is the primary reinforcer that maintains the chain in strength.

One type of conditioned reinforcer that is common in practical applications of the science of learning—for example, behavior modification and behavior therapy procedures—is a reinforcement token, which is an object or other stimulus that can be saved and accumulated with other tokens and then exchanged for other reinforcers. For example, children in a classroom might receive points, plastic chips, certificates, stickers, and so forth for correct answers in a workbook. Periodically, during a "store time," the children exchange their tokens for desired items such as candy, toys, and books. Air-mile points, which can be accumulated and exchanged for airline tickets, are tokens that many businesses have found to be highly effective reinforcers of purchasing merchandise ("Air miles plan," 1996).

The reinforcers for which tokens can be exchanged, called backup reinforcers, maintain the tokens as conditioned reinforcers so that they can continue to be used to strengthen behavior. A setting, such as a classroom, in which tokens are used with a group of individuals to strengthen and maintain specific behavior, is called a token economy (Ayllon & Azrin, 1968; Kazdin, 1977).

It should be noted that the process of conditioned reinforcement can make an aversive stimulus become less aversive as well as make a neutral stimulus reinforcing. For example, if shock has been followed by water reinforcement to a water-deprived animal, shock will be less punishing than if it had not been followed by water (Scavio, 1974, 1975). It appears that pairing a punisher with a positive reinforcer subtracts (or adds negatively) to the aversiveness of the punisher.

Analogous to the extinction of a respondently conditioned response, a conditioned reinforcer is weakened if it occurs repeatedly without being followed by a primary reinforcer.

Conditioned Punishment

Analogous to conditioned reinforcers are stimuli called conditioned punishers. That is, just as some stimuli are reinforcers due to phylogeny, there are other stimuli that are punishers due to phylogeny. These stimuli are called primary punishers. Other stimuli can become punishers by being paired with stimuli that are already punishers. For example, if a tone regularly precedes an electric shock, the tone will become a conditioned punisher. Conditioned punishment expands the range of stimuli that can become punishers. The evolutionary significance of conditioned punishment is that ceasing to produce a stimulus that has occurred in close temporal association with a primary punisher is likely to take the animal farther from the primary punisher, which likely is something that is harmful to the animal.

Although a period in which reinforcement does not occur (e.g., when a response is undergoing extinction) is not a stimulus, and is therefore by definition not a punisher, stimuli that have been paired with such periods are conditioned punishers. The term "timeout" is commonly used to describe the occurrence of a stimulus that has been paired with the absence of reinforcement. Although, as mentioned above, extinction is not to be confused with punishment, timeout does satisfy the definition of punishment if—as is often the case—the occurrence of a timeout stimulus (or S^Δ) results in a decrease in a response that it follows. A familiar example of timeout is a teacher seating a child far from the other pupils for a period of time following instances of disruptive behavior by the child. This constitutes a timeout stimulus for the child since it is coupled with the absence of social reinforcement. The likely result is that future instances of disruptive behavior will be suppressed when the child is once again in close proximity to the other pupils.

Operant Response Classes

It is inaccurate to view any operant response as simply a single fixed movement or even a single fixed series of movements. Consider, for example, an operant response such as a rat's lever press. There are many different ways in which the rat can press the lever—with its left paw, its right paw, both front paws together, its snout, and so on. Each of these lever presses consists of different movements, but they are all considered lever presses. We call all responses that have a given effect on the environment, and vary together as a function of reinforcement (i.e., their probability increases together when one of them is reinforced), an operant response class (also called simply a response class or an operant). For convenience, however, we use "response" or "operant response" to refer to an operant response class, unless otherwise indicated.

As an operant response class is repeated, the members that occur tend to narrow down to the more efficient ones. This is because more efficient reponses (by definition) result in more immediate reinforcement. The tendency of a response to become more efficient with repetition is called the law of practice (Snoddy, 1926).

Generally, when an operant response class is well conditioned, just a few members of the class occur. If those members that typically occur are prevented from doing so, however, then other members will occur. For example, a right-handed person whose right hand has been injured may pick up objects with his or her left hand because picking up objects with the left hand belongs to the same response class as picking up objects with the right hand.

Operant response classes do not have to be responses with a single mechanical effect on the environment such as lever presses. For example, as we shall see in Chapter 5, with special training imitation can become an operant response class in a few species (e.g., higher primates such as chimpanzees and humans).

DIFFERENCES BETWEEN RESPONDENT AND OPERANT BEHAVIOR

Despite the fact that there are many similarities between respondent and operant behavior, it is important to keep their differences firmly in mind. The defining difference is that the latter is affected by its consequences whereas the former is not—that is, it is neither increased nor decreased in frequency or probability of occurrence by what follows it. Ramifications of this fact are discussed below.

Distinguishing Respondent From Operant Conditioning

It is often difficult to be certain that respondent conditioning rather than operant conditioning is responsible for a given instance of conditioning. Consider, for example, the following sequence:

bell → food → salivation

As we have seen, repeating this sequence eventually results in:

bell → salivation → food → salivation

The salivation that occurs right after the bell in this new sequence is a conditioned response, and we have said that it is a respondently conditioned response; that is, we have said that it is the result of pairing the bell with food. There is, however, another logical possibility.

Perhaps the first occurrence of salivation right after the bell was due simply to the general feeding situation that the animal was in, and the food that followed this first occurrence of salivation right after the bell reinforced it. This would result in future occurrences of salivation right after the bell, which the subsequent occurrences of food would also reinforce and thereby further strengthen the conditioned response. In this scenario the conditioned response would be operant, not respondent, and the bell would be a discriminative stimulus instead of a conditioned stimulus. A similar interpretation is possible whenever the unconditioned stimulus in a respondent conditioning procedure is a positive reinforcer. The question thus arises: how can we rule out the possibility that what has taken place in such cases is operant rather than respondent conditioning?

There are a number of indirect indicators that a given conditioned response to a stimulus that has been paired with an unconditioned stimulus is respondent rather than operant. One indicator, for example, is that the conditioned response resembles the response to the unconditioned stimulus; another is that it rapidly comes under the control of the stimulus paired with the unconditioned stimulus; yet another is that simply reinforcing the response does not readily increase its probability of occurrence. There is, however, only one known definitive way to show that a given conditioned response is the result of respondent rather than operant conditioning. This is to omit the unconditioned stimulus every time the conditioned response occurs; that is, to have the conditioned response prevent the unconditioned stimulus.

This procedure, which is called omission training (because the unconditioned stimulus is omitted when the conditioned response occurs), may be diagramed in two different ways depending on whether conditioning occurs or not. If respondent conditioning occurs, the procedure may be diagramed as follows:

$$(CS, \sim CR, US), (CS, CR, \sim US), \ldots, (CS, \sim CR, US), (CS, CR, \sim US) \Rightarrow CS \rightarrow CR$$

The above diagram indicates that the unconditioned stimulus follows the conditioned stimulus only if the conditioned response does not occur. Basically, respondent conditioning and extinction will alternate with this procedure. Thus, respondent conditioning will occur because the unconditioned stimulus will sometimes follow the conditioned stimulus.

If no conditioning occurs, however, the following diagram probably applies:

$$(S^D, \sim R, S^r), (S^D, R, \sim S^r), \ldots, (S^D, \sim R, S^r), (S^D, R, \sim S^r) \Rightarrow S^D \rightarrow \sim R$$

The above diagram indicates that the antecedent stimulus (i.e., the stimulus that occurs prior to the response) is not a conditioned stimulus, but instead is a discriminative stimulus for not responding because responding is never reinforced following the stimulus; and, in fact, reinforcement occurs when responding does not occur (which makes the stimulus an even stronger discriminative stimulus for not responding). Thus, no operant conditioning of the response will occur with this procedure. Any conditioning that occurs with an omission procedure must, therefore, be respondent conditioning as illustrated by the first diagram above.

Using the example of conditioning salivation to a bell, another way to diagram omission training is as follows:

- *bell → food → salivation*
- *bell → salivation → no food*

Note that with this procedure, salivation to the bell cannot be reinforced. Therefore, the reliable occurrence of salivation to the bell must be due solely to the pairing of the bell with food, and hence salivation to the bell is not an operant response.

Because it involves extinction on some trials, omission training generally is used only when it is important to establish conclusively that the conditioning of a given response is respondent and not operant. Another point to note about omission training is that the procedure is identical to avoidance conditioning, except that it is used with a positive rather than a negative reinforcer (see pp. 33–34). We would not use omission training to prove respondent conditioning if the unconditioned stimulus was aversive. In fact, we would do just the opposite; that is, we would ensure that the conditioned response did not prevent the occurrence of the unconditioned stimulus.

Before concluding this discussion of the distinction between respondent and operant conditioning, it is important to note that pure instances of either are rare. Most learned behavior consists of both. This is analogous to the rarity of elemental hydrogen and oxygen, but the abundance of H_2O.

Terminological Distinctions

In the science of learning, as in any science, the rules and conventions for talking about the subject matter are crucial. Nowhere are terminological distinctions more important than when differentiating between respondent and operant conditioning. The following highlights these distinctions.

Elicited versus emitted responses.   Because a discriminative stimulus for responding controls operant behavior in a somewhat different manner from that in which a conditioned stimulus controls respondent behavior, it is important to talk about these two types of control in somewhat different ways. We say that a conditioned stimulus *elicits* its response but that a discriminative stimulus *evokes* its response. It is technically incorrect to speak of an operant response as elicited. Instead, we say that an individual emits operant responses. Analogizing from another science, physics, a conditioned or unconditioned stimulus eliciting a conditioned or unconditioned response is like one object hitting another and thereby causing it to move. In contrast, a discriminative stimulus evoking responses is like an electrical current causing the filament in a light bulb to emit photons.

Note that for respondent behavior there is a one-to-one correspondence between an eliciting stimulus and its resulting response, whereas one presentation of a discriminative stimulus may cause many operant responses to be emitted. Therefore, we sometimes say that, as opposed to eliciting a response, a discriminative stimulus for responding sets the occasion for responding.

Contingencies in respondent and operant conditioning.   Thus far we have talked about conditioning as resulting from the pairing of two events; that is, two stimuli or a response and a stimulus event (called reinforcement). The term "pairing," however, is somewhat imprecise; rather than talking about pairing of events, it is more accurate to talk about contingencies between events. A contingency exists between two events if the prior occurrence of one event increases the probability of the subsequent occurrence of the other event.

Contingencies in Respondent Conditioning. In respondent conditioning the unconditioned stimulus is contingent on the conditioned stimulus. Technically, this means that the probability that the unconditioned stimulus will occur is greater given the occurrence of the conditioned stimulus than it is at other times. This contingency can be expressed symbolically as follows:

$p(\mathrm{US}|\mathrm{CS}) > p(\mathrm{US}|{\sim}\mathrm{CS}),$ \qquad (Inequality 1)

where $p(\mathrm{US}|\mathrm{CS})$ is the probability of the unconditioned stimulus given the occurrence of the conditioned stimulus, and $p(\mathrm{US}|{\sim}\mathrm{CS})$ is the probability of the unconditioned stimulus given that the conditioned stimulus has not occurred. Note that Inequality 1 holds in most of the examples of respondent conditioning that we have discussed. Specifically, in most of the examples discussed above, $p(\mathrm{US}|\mathrm{CS})$ was equal to 1.00 and $p(\mathrm{US}|{\sim}\mathrm{CS})$ was equal to 0; that is, the unconditioned stimulus followed every occurrence of the conditioned stimulus and never occurred when the conditioned stimulus did not occur. Therefore, we can say that in the examples discussed, the unconditioned stimulus was contingent on the conditioned stimulus.

In the case of respondent extinction, however, Inequality 1 does not hold. Instead,

$p(\mathrm{US}|\mathrm{CS}) = p(\mathrm{US}|{\sim}\mathrm{CS}) = 0,$

and we say that the unconditioned stimulus is not contingent on, or is independent of the conditioned stimulus. It follows from Inequality 1 that to eliminate the contingency between the conditioned stimulus and the unconditioned stimulus, $p(\mathrm{US}|\mathrm{CS})$ and $p(\mathrm{US}|{\sim}\mathrm{CS})$ need not be equal to zero. That is, no contingency exists between the two stimuli if the probability of the unconditioned stimulus occurring on a trial in which the conditioned stimulus occurs is equal to the probability of the unconditioned stimulus occurring on a trial in which the conditioned stimulus does not occur. Note that if those probabilities are equal but greater than zero, some chance pairings of the conditioned stimulus with the unconditioned stimulus necessarily will occur. Nevertheless, this will not result in conditioning (Ayres & Quinsey, 1970; Bull & Overmier, 1968; Davis & McIntyre, 1969; Rescorla, 1968). Hence, strictly speaking, we should not say that respondent conditioning depends simply on the pairing of two stimuli. Instead, to be technically correct, we should say that respondent conditioning depends on the existence of a contingency between two stimuli. (See Appendix A for a mathematical treatment of the concept of contingency, as described above.)

Note that although $p(\mathrm{US}|\mathrm{CS})$ is less than 1.00 during omission training, discussed on pages 39–40, Inequality (1) still holds because $p(\mathrm{US}|{\sim}\,\mathrm{CS})$ is equal to 0 and the omission procedure ensures that $p(\mathrm{US}|\mathrm{CS})$ must always be greater than zero. Therefore, during omission training the unconditioned stimulus is contingent on the conditioned stimulus.

Contingencies in Operant Conditioning. In operant conditioning a stimulus (namely, a reinforcer) is contingent on a response rather than another stimulus as is the case in respondent conditioning. This contingency implies that the probability that the reinforcer will occur (or be removed in the case of negative reinforcement) is greater given the emission of the operant response than at other times. We can express a contingency in operant conditioning symbolically as follows:

$p(\mathrm{S^r}|\mathrm{R}) > p(\mathrm{S^r}|{\sim}\mathrm{R}),$ \quad (Inequality 2)

where $p(\mathrm{S^r}|\mathrm{R})$ is the probability of reinforcement given the occurrence of the response, and $p(\mathrm{S^r}|{\sim}\mathrm{R})$ is the probability of reinforcement given that the response has not occurred. Note that Inequality 2 holds in all of the examples of operant conditioning that we have discussed. Specifically, in those examples $p(\mathrm{S^r}|\mathrm{R})$ was equal to 1.00 and $p(\mathrm{S^r}|{\sim}\mathrm{R})$ was equal to 0; that is, reinforcement followed every occurrence of the operant response and never occurred when the response did not occur. Therefore, we can say that in the examples discussed, reinforcement was contingent on the response.

In the case of operant extinction, however, Inequality 2 does not hold. Instead,

$$p(S^r|R) = p(S^r|{\sim}R) = 0,$$

and we say that reinforcement is not contingent on, or in other words is independent of, the response. It follows from Inequality 2 that to eliminate the contingency between the response and the reinforcer, it is not necessary that $p(S^r|R)$ and $p(S^r|{\sim}R)$ both be equal to zero. All that is necessary is that they both be equal to each other. That is, no contingency exists between the response and the reinforcer if the probability of the reinforcer occurring when the response occurs is equal to the probability of the reinforcer occurring when the response does not occur. Note that if those probabilities are equal but greater than zero, some chance pairings of the operant response with reinforcement necessarily will occur. It turns out that, while chance pairings of the conditioned and unconditioned stimuli when there is no contingency between the conditioned and unconditioned stimuli do not result in respondent conditioning, chance pairings of a response with reinforcement may produce operant conditioning.

The effect on operant behavior of presenting reinforcement noncontingently on (i.e., independent of) responding is rather complex. In a classic experiment (Skinner, 1948a), eight pigeons placed individually in an experimental chamber received food periodically for a few seconds regardless of their behavior. The interval between food presentations was initially 15 seconds, but was later increased to as much as two minutes in some cases. After exposure to the response-independent periodic reinforcement for some time, six of the eight birds developed repetitive responses. One bird repeatedly made counterclockwise turns about the chamber; another repeatedly thrust its head into one of the upper corners of the chamber; a third developed a "tossing" of the head response; two birds developed a pendulum motion of the head and body; another made incomplete pecking or brushing movements toward the floor. These responses appeared to be the result of an "accidental reinforcement" or, more technically, an adventitious reinforcement process. Apparently, food presentations reinforced whatever each pigeon was doing when the food appeared, so that that response had an increased probability of occurring when the next food presentation occurred. This would strengthen the response still further, and subsequent reinforcement of the response would therefore become even more probable.

Operant responses conditioned in this adventitious manner are called superstitious behavior. Similar behavior in humans may include rituals for bringing about desired consequences—for example, blowing on dice for luck. A few accidental connections between the ritual and the favorable consequence suffice to set up and maintain the behavior. (Cultural variables, as discussed in Chapter 17, also play an important role in the development and maintenance of many human superstitions.) Although there is considerable evidence that superstitious behavior is a real phenomenon (e.g., Neuringer, 1970), its interpretation is complicated by the fact that response-independent reinforcement can also generate behavior that is not operant (as will be discussed in Chapter 15).

Besides operant contingencies for responding, there are also operant contingencies for not responding. Such a contingency exists if

$$p(S^r|{\sim}R) > p(S^r|R) \quad \text{(Inequality 3)}$$

The typical result of this contingency is that operant responding decreases to zero. Note that omission training, described previously, involves an operant contingency for not responding.

The Three-Term Contingency. So far we have talked about contingencies between just two events. We have seen, however, that operant responses come under the control of stimuli in the presence of which they have been reinforced. We describe this as a contingency that contains three terms: an antecedent stimulus, a response, and reinforcement. We can express this three-term contingency symbolically as follows:

$$p(S^r|S^D \text{ and } R) > p(S^r|{\sim}S^D \text{ or } {\sim}R), \qquad \text{(Inequality 4)}$$

where $p(S^r|S^D \text{ and } R)$ is the probability of the reinforcer given the occurrence of the discriminative stimulus for responding *and* the response, and $p(S^r|{\sim}S^D \text{ or } {\sim}R)$ is the probability of reinforcement given that either the discriminative stimulus for responding *or* the response has not occurred. Note that $p(S^r|{\sim}S^D \text{ or } {\sim}R)$ may also be written $p(S^r|S^) \text{ or } {\sim}R)$. Typically, $p(S^r|S^\Delta \text{ or } {\sim}R)$ is equal to zero and $p(S^r|S^D \text{ and } R)$ is greater than zero.

Voluntary versus involuntary behavior.   Subjectively speaking, respondent behavior usually feels involuntary (when one is aware of it at all). This may be related to the fact that respondent behavior generally involves smooth muscles and glands, which have relatively few sensory feedback receptors. Operant behavior often (but not always) has a voluntary feel to it. Interestingly, and contrary to intuition, this voluntary feeling cannot be the cause of the behavior because it occurs after the commencement of the neurological activity leading up to the behavior (Deeke, Grötzinger, & Kornhuber, 1976; Libet, 1985; Libet, Curtis, Wright, & Pearl, 1983).

RESPONDENT AND OPERANT ATTENDING RESPONSES

Thus far in our discussion of how stimuli come to control behavior, we have glossed over an important precondition. In order for a stimulus to control behavior, it must come into contact with a sense receptor. In order for a visual stimulus to have an effect on behavior, for example, the eyes must be directed toward the stimulus. More generally, we say that the individual must be attending, or paying attention to, the stimulus. An individual who is attending to something is engaging in behavior consisting of attending responses. In order for a stimulus to control behavior—either as a conditioned stimulus or a discriminative stimulus—certain attending responses must occur.

There are both respondent and operant attending responses. Respondent attending responses are elicited by particular stimuli. A loud noise or a sudden movement, for example, causes the head to turn in the direction of noise or movement, and the ears may tend to rise. Another name for a respondent attending response is orienting reflex.

Like other operant responses, operant attending responses are learned through reinforcement. Consider, for example, a child who has been asked to watch for an expected visitor. Although looking out the window as instructed, the child may not see the approaching guest. Instead, although the child's eyes may be pointed in the general direction of the guest, whose image may even stimulate the child's retinas, the child's attention may be focused on something else—perhaps two squirrels playing—and so the parent receives no warning before the doorbell rings. This might result in a harsh word from the parent. If, however, the child had attended to the relevant stimulus—that is, the approaching guest—the likely result would have been praise, which would have tended to positively reinforce the child's attentive behavior.

As we know from personal experience, it is possible to seem to be looking at something but not see it. Clearly, some attending responses are covert, because we cannot always tell whether someone is responding to a visual stimulus just from observing the position of his or her eyes. It is even more difficult to tell what someone is listening to than it is to tell what that person is seeing on the basis of overt behavior. Some attending responses for auditory stimuli therefore must also be covert. Whether these are the same as the attending responses for visual stimuli is not known, because we do not know specifically what these attending responses are. Similarly, we do not know whether there are attending responses specific to other sensory modalities. Regardless, it is clear that while attending responses are frequently difficult to observe in other individuals, they are more accessible to self-observation—that is, I usually know when I am attending to a particular stimulus even when others observing me do not.

EVOLUTIONARY BASES OF RESPONDENT AND OPERANT CONDITIONING

Respondent conditioning evolved because the long-term survival of individuals and their progeny depends on the speed at which they respond to biologically significant stimuli. An individual who begins responding to a biologically significant stimulus before it occurs, rather than after it occurs, has an increased chance of surviving and producing viable offspring. For example, an animal that begins salivating before food enters its mouth digests the food and derives nourishment from it more quickly than an animal that ingests food with a dry mouth. An animal that increases its breathing and heart rate in preparation to fight an opponent or flee from a predator before the opponent or predator attacks is more likely than an unprepared animal to fight off the opponent or escape the predator. A mother who begins lactating before her baby starts to suck her nipple will nourish the baby more quickly than a mother who lactates only after the baby starts sucking the nipple. In each of these examples, the individual responds to a biologically significant stimulus (e.g., food in the mouth, being attacked, suction on the nipple) *before* it occurs by responding to a stimulus (e.g., the sight or sound of an edible object, an opponent or predator, a crying baby) that reliably precedes it.

The reason for the evolution of operant conditioning is also not hard to understand. Animals whose behavior was positively reinforced by food, water, sexual contact, and other stimuli that promoted their survival and reproduction, and whose behavior was negatively reinforced and punished by harmful stimuli, produced more offspring than did animals that were not affected in these ways by such stimuli.

The reason for the evolution of respondent and operant extinction is also clear. Animals that ceased to respond to a conditioned stimulus when the unconditioned stimulus no longer followed it, and that ceased to emit previously reinforced responses when reinforcement no longer followed them, conserved energy that otherwise would be wasted. Similarly, it is not difficult to infer evolutionary reasons for most of the other associative learning principles and phenomena discussed in this book.

Despite the clear evolutionary reasons for respondent and operant conditioning, one cannot use survival value to predict with perfect accuracy which stimuli will be unconditioned stimuli, primary reinforcers, and primary punishers for any given species. Sugar and fat, for example, are strong positive reinforcers, yet too much sugar causes tooth decay and overconsumption of fat causes many health problems. The reason that these stimuli are such powerful reinforcers is that in the environment in which our species originally evolved they were not as readily available as they are today, and survival depended on obtaining as much of them as possible. The presence of sugar in a fruit or vegetable indicates that it is ripe and nutritious, while fat is a source of highly concentrated energy in addition to being an essential nutrient. Although foods that contain lots of sugar and fat are harmful when consumed regularly over many years, such foods have become widely available only in the past century and there has not been enough time for natural selection to produce the appropriate adaptation to this recent change in our environment.

Because we have incomplete knowledge of environments in the distant past, the only way to determine which stimuli are unconditioned stimuli, primary reinforcers, and primary punishers for a given species is empirically; that is, by performing an experiment in which the definitions of unconditioned stimulus, primary reinforcement, and primary punishment are strictly applied. Thus, a given stimulus is an unconditioned stimulus if and only if without prior pairing with other stimuli it consistently elicits a specific response. A given stimulus is a positive reinforcer if and only if the rate of a response that it follows increases. A given stimulus is a negative reinforcer if and only if the rate of a response that its removal follows increases. A given stimulus is a punisher if and only if the rate of a response that it follows decreases. Stimuli are primary reinforcers or punishers if and only if they have not become reinforcers or punishers through learning (e.g., by being paired with other reinforcers or punishers). We may try to guess whether a given stimulus will fit one of these definitions, but such guesses are never scientifically valid substitutes for empirical tests.

A NOTE ABOUT ASSOCIATIVE TERMINOLOGY

In using the term "associative learning" we are assuming no particular theoretical position about what is going on within an individual when associative learning occurs. The term "associative learning" in this book refers simply to learning that occurs due to a contingency between two events—either two stimuli or a response and a stimulus. Clearly, in order for learning to occur, there must be certain changes within the individual. What these change are, however, is a matter that is beyond the scope of this book.

Thus, in a respondent conditioning experiment involving the pairing of a bell with food, we would not say that the animal "associates" the bell with food. Likewise, in an operant conditioning experiment involving reinforcing lever pressing with food, we would not say that the animal "associates" lever pressing with food. This is not to question the fact that humans do make associations as memory aids. For example, when parking my car, I often covertly pair some easy-to-spot landmark with the location of my car. This is a self-conditioning process that I have learned to do so that the landmark will elicit responses that will help me find my car. Although I do not know when I learned to engage in this memory-aiding behavior, I am quite sure that it was made possible through teaching (including language training) provided by my culture. This sort of teaching does not apply to animals that have not received language training; therefore, it is highly unlikely that they make associations in this sense. In later chapters we delve further into issues involving language training and how it facilitates other learning and memory.

RELATIONSHIPS BETWEEN ASSOCIATIVE AND NONASSOCIATIVE LEARNING

In the previous chapter we covered the various types of nonassociative learning: sensitization, habituation, dishabituation, and exposure-based learning (including odor-based learning, imprinting, and birdsong learning). Although we have distinguished between nonassociative learning and associative learning (i.e., respondent and operant conditioning), we should note that there are a number of similarities and interactions between these two broad categories of learning.

Sensitization and Habituation

Recall that sensitization is the process by which a response to a stimulus becomes more probable simply as a result of the prior occurrence of that or some other stimulus; and that habituation is the process by which a response to a stimulus becomes less probable as a result of the prior occurrence of that stimulus. Sensitization and habituation are similar to respondent conditioning and extinction, respectively. In addition, to complicate matters, they interact with them in various ways.

Similarities with conditioning and extinction. Sensitization is similar to respondent conditioning and conditioning an operant response to an S^D: In all three cases, a response that did not previously occur to a particular stimulus (or did not occur so strongly) now occurs to it (or more strongly than it did before). In fact, in respondent conditioning experiments, sensitization can be mistaken for respondent conditioning because responding to the conditioned stimulus may be due to the sensitizing effect of either the unconditioned stimulus or the conditioned stimulus rather than to the pairing of the two stimuli. For this reason sensitization is sometimes called pseudoconditioning. [1]

Habituation is similar to respondent extinction and the extinction of an operant response to an S^D (Thompson & Spencer, 1966). In all three cases, a response to a stimulus decreases as a result of repeated presentations of, or continuous exposure to, a stimulus. The difference is that in the latter two cases it is the conditioned stimulus or S^D that occurs repeatedly or continuously without the occurrence of an unconditioned stimulus or reinforcement.

In habituation (as discussed in Chapter 2), if a stimulus to which a response has habituated is withheld for a period of time an increased response will occur when the stimulus next occurs. This is similar to spontaneous recovery after respondent or operant extinction. Moreover, if a response goes through the habituation process a number of times, the amount of this recovery steadily decreases—which is also what occurs with spontaneous recovery when a conditioned response goes through the extinction process on separate occasions a number of times (with no intervening re-conditioning).

Habituation is also similar to respondent extinction in that it shows stimulus generalization. When a response to one stimulus has been reduced by habituation, responses to similar stimuli will also show decreases.

Finally, a process similar to dishabituation may occur with both respondent and operant extinction (see p. 17): If a novel or strong stimulus occurs during extinction, the response may temporarily recover to some extent (Bottjer, 1982; Brimer, 1970, 1972; Hearst et al., 1974; Pavlov, 1927; Razran, 1939; Switzer, 1933).

Interactions with respondent and operant conditioning. Although distinct from respondent and operant conditioning, habituation can affect—that is, interact with—them in several ways, as detailed below.

Habituation of Attention. As we have already seen, in order for a particular stimulus to become a conditioned stimulus or a discriminative stimulus—that is, in order for respondent or operant conditioning to occur to a particular stimulus—that stimulus often must first elicit an attending response. In less technical language, we might say that a particular stimulus

---

[1]Experiments on respondent conditioning usually control for pseudoconditioning by comparing responding to the conditioned stimulus after the conditioned and unconditioned stimuli have been presented unpaired with responding to the conditioned stimulus after these two stimuli have been paired.

cannot become a conditioned or discriminative stimulus for an individual if the individual does not "attend to" or "pay attention to" that stimulus. We have already distinguished between respondent attending responses and operant attending. A dog pricking up its ears and turning its head toward a ringing bell is an example of a respondent attending response or orienting reflex. Undoubtedly, there are other orienting reflexes that are covert.

Orienting reflexes elicited by specific stimuli can habituate, just as other responses can. This process accounts (at least in part) for a phenomenon called latent inhibition, whereby presenting the conditioned stimulus a number of times by itself prior to respondent conditioning retards the development of the conditioned response to that stimulus (Lubow, 1973, 1989; Lubow & Moore, 1959).

For example, conditioning a salivary response to a bell will take longer if the bell sounds alone a number of times before being paired with food. One explanation for this is that presenting the bell alone habituates the attending responses that the bell elicits (Lubow, 1989). When the bell is finally paired with food, the individual's attending to the bell has habituated; a stimulus can become a conditioned or discriminative stimulus only to the extent that it elicits an attending response. An alternative description of latent inhibition is to say that novel stimuli condition more readily than familiar stimuli do.

The above discussion applies only to respondent attending responses. Operant attending responses to a particular stimulus will also decrease if the stimulus occurs repeatedly and the attending response is not reinforced. This, however, is operant extinction, not habituation.

Habituation to novel environments. In Chapter 2, we spoke of two types of habituation that occur in novel environments (a) habituation of freezing, and (b) habituation of exploratory behavior. Since freezing interferes with operant conditioning, habituation must occur before operant conditioning can occur. Exploratory behavior, in contrast, facilitates operant conditioning because it increases the probability that an animal will emit a response that will be reinforced (which is probably the evolutionary significance of exploratory behavior). The habituation of exploratory behavior can therefore retard operant conditioning. An interesting feature of exploratory behavior is that it tends to counteract its habituation because it brings the individual into contact with novel stimuli (Welker, 1961).

Motivation. It appears that individuals first sensitize and then habituate to a reinforcer when it is presented repeatedly during operant conditioning (McSweeney & Swindell, 1999). That is, with repeated presentations over a short period, the strength of a reinforcer—that is, its ability to condition and maintain behavior—first increases and then decreases. An example of the increase that everyone is familiar with is an appetizer increasing the reinforcing effectiveness of the subsequent main course. Habituation to a reinforcer, however, is only partly responsible for satiation. Other factors (e.g., stomach distension, blood glucose levels) are also involved (Bizo, Bogdanov, & Killeen, 1998).

An associative effect on habituation: the "surprise" effect. As we have seen, the repeated presentation of a stimulus eventually (often after first producing sensitization) produces habituation. Because the unconditioned stimulus is repeated over trials during respondent conditioning, we would expect the unconditioned response to habituate. That is, we would expect the unconditioned response to gradually become weaker and weaker, even while the conditioned response is becoming stronger. Suppose, however, that at some point in this process we present the unconditioned stimulus without preceding it with the conditioned stimulus. This produces what we might call a "surprise" effect: the unconditioned response intensifies, that is, habituation decreases, as a result of the omission of the conditioned stimulus. For example, if a tone (conditioned stimulus) repeatedly precedes a light (unconditioned stimulus), rats will orient (unconditioned response) more readily to the light when the tone does not precede it than they will when the tone does precede it (Honey & Good, 2000; Honey, Good, & Manser, 1998). Similarly, in an experiment in which a tone repeatedly precedes an electric shock, the unconditioned response to the shock will be greater on trials in which the shock occurs without being preceded by the tone (Donegan, 1981). This surprise effect indicates that habituation itself may be conditioned or come under stimulus control.

Exposure-Based Learning

In Chapter 2, we saw that mere exposure to certain stimuli early in the life of an animal can cause those stimuli to elicit behavior that they did not previously (and would not otherwise) elicit.

In addition, exposure-based learning affects the reinforcing power of stimuli. For example, an object on which an animal has been imprinted is an exposure-produced reinforcer. This is indicated by the fact that ducklings will learn to peck a response key when key pecks enable the duckling to view a stimulus it has been exposed to within 24 hours after hatching (Hoffman & Kozma, 1967; Hoffman, Searle, Toffey, & Kozma, 1966; Peterson, 1960). An apparatus for studying the reinforcing effect of an imprinted stimulus in shown in Figure 3.3, and some data showing that an imprinted stimulus is a reinforcer is seen in Figure 3.4.

Similarly, it appears that early exposure of birds to certain songs makes those songs into

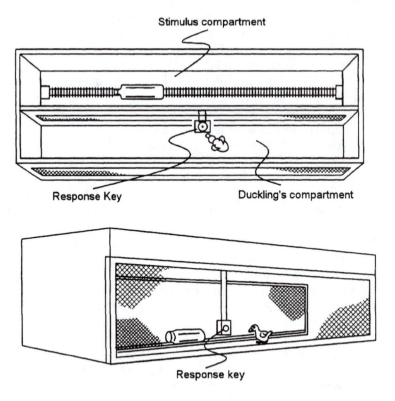

FIGURE 3.3. Apparatus for studying an imprinted stimulus as a reinforcer. Key pecks are reinforced by the light in the stimulus compartment turning on, providing the duckling with a view of a moving stimulus (a milk bottle on a toy train) that the duckling has been imprinted on. (From Hoffman, 1996)

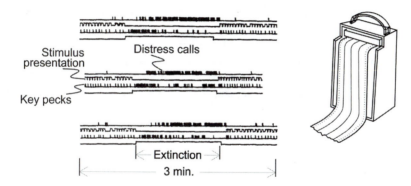

Stimulus presentation

Distress calls

Key pecks

Extinction

3 min.

FIGURE 3.4. An event recorder and some sample data from an imprinting study. As paper, moving at a constant speed, rolls out of the event recorder shown in the right part of the figure, pens in the recorder mark the occurrence of various events. All the sample event records in the left part of the figure are from the same duckling. The duckling's distress calls are recorded by the top pen, reinforcements (stimulus presentations) by the pen next to that pen, key pecks by the next pen, and periods of extinction (no reinforcement) by the bottom pen. Note that during periods of extinction, key pecking decreased. In addition, distress calling increased, illustrating an emotional effect of extinction. (From Hoffman, 1996)

reinforcers for those birds, so that producing them is reinforcing (Petrinovich, 1988, p. 257). Genetics, as well as reinforcement, play an important role in birdsong learning. For the white-crowned sparrow discussed in the previous chapter, for example, songs that have at least some characteristics of the bird's species tend to be reinforcing to that bird even if the bird has never heard the song of its own species. This is shown by the fact that birds that have been deafened early in life and thus cannot hear their own singing, develop songs that are more abnormal than those developed by birds with normal hearing that, through isolation, have never been exposed to songs (Konishi, 1965).

Although it is distinct from exposure-based learning, operant conditioning may affect it. A striking demonstration of the role that operant conditioning plays in singing specific songs is shown by the fact that songs may be reinforced or punished by the reactions of other individuals toward them. For example, certain song characteristics may be reduced through punishment if the song elicits aggression directed at the singer (Marler & Nelson, 1993; West & King, 1988).

Summary of Relationships Between Associative and Nonassociative Learning

In one sense associative and nonassociative learning are quite different. The former is based on an association between a stimulus and another stimulus or between a response and a stimulus, whereas the latter is based on the repeated occurrence of a stimulus. Nevertheless, there are some similarities.

The repeated occurrence of a stimulus can produce conditioning-like effects (sensitization). In addition, it can produce extinction-like effects (habituation). Moreover, the repeated occurrence of a stimulus can make that stimulus into a positive reinforcer (e.g., olfactory, filial, and sexual imprinting, and song learning). Once a stimulus becomes a positive reinforcer, it can then enter into associative learning in developing and maintaining new responses by following those responses and in developing conditioned reinforcers by being paired with neutral stimuli.

NERVOUS SYSTEM REQUIRED FOR ASSOCIATIVE LEARNING

Unlike the case with sensitization and habituation (discussed in the previous chapter), there is no convincing evidence for either respondent or operant conditioning in the isolated spinal cords of vertebrates or in organisms less complex than planarians. There is considerable evidence, however, for these processes in planarians (Corning & Kelly, 1973) and more complex invertebrates.

Respondent Conditioning

Some examples of respondent conditioning in invertebrates are as follows. Pairing light as a conditioned stimulus (even though it elicits a small degree of contraction) with electric shock as an unconditioned stimulus for contraction in planarians will result in light eliciting stronger contraction than is the case when light has not been paired with shock (Jacobson, Horowitz, & Fried, 1967). (However, there are results that contradict this conclusion; e.g., Brown, 1967).

Pairing a moderate increase or decrease in seawater concentration, as a conditioned stimulus, with electric shock to a sea hare, a sea slug, or member of the genus *Aplysia*, causes the animal's respiratory pump rate to increase in response to the conditioned stimulus (Levy, Welle, & Susswein, 1994). It is also possible to condition respondent stimulus discrimination and higher-order conditioning in the sea slug (Hawkins, Greene, & Kandel, 1998).

Pairing touch, as a conditioned stimulus, with electric shock as an unconditioned stimulus for contraction in leeches will result in touch eliciting contraction (Sahley, Boulis, & Schurman, 1994). Exposing the animal to the conditioned stimulus a number of times before conditioning retards the development of the conditioned response; thus, these animals manifest latent inhibition. Pairing mild vibration, as a conditioned stimulus, with either light or electric shock as an unconditioned stimulus for withdrawal in earthworms, will result in vibration coming to elicit withdrawal (Ratner & Miller, 1959). A solution of squid extract will normally elicit feeding movements in a sea slug. Pairing the presentation of this solution to a slug with electric shock will result in the solution eliciting rapid contraction of the body and head followed by movement away from the solution (Mpitsos & Collins, 1975). Similarly, pairing a novel food with carbon dioxide, which is toxic and aversive to a slug, will result in the novel food becoming aversive to the slug (Gelperin, 1975). Sugar applied to chemoreceptive hairs on the legs of a blowfly, an insect, is an unconditioned stimulus for proboscis extension. Repeatedly presenting either salt water or distilled water, as a conditioned stimulus, followed by sugar to a blowfly's legs will result in the conditioned stimulus eliciting proboscis extension (Nelson, 1971). Similarly, presenting a distinctive odor (e.g., jasmine, peppermint, or geraniol) followed by sugar to a harnessed honeybee will condition proboscis extension to the odor (Batson, Hoban, & Bitterman, 1992).

Operant Conditioning

With regard to operant conditioning in invertebrates, planarians learn to follow a specific swimming route if this has led to food (P. Wells, 1967). Planarians also learn escape responses, such swimming through a photocell beam whose interruption causes an intense (and presumably aversive) overhead light to turn off (Crawford & Skeen, 1967; Lee, 1963). Similarly, a sea slug uncovered in shallow water will move through a photocell beam whose interruption causes the water level to rise (Lee, 1969). Cephalopods (squid, octopuses, and cuttlefish) are mollusks with well developed brains, eyes, and appendages. Despite membership in a phylum that includes oysters, clams, and snails, cephalopods (especially octopuses) perform comparably to higher vertebrates on complex operant conditioning tasks (Dilly, 1963; Fiorito, von Planta, & Scotto, 1990; Messenger & Sanders, 1972; M. Wells, 1964, 1967, 1978; Wells & Young, 1970 a,b), such as those discussed later in this book.

Numerous experiments demonstrate that insects exhibit simple and, in some cases, quite complex operant conditioning. Locusts learn to go into a chamber marked with either yellow or blue cellophane when this response is reinforced with water (Raubenheimer & Blackshaw, 1994). Crickets learn to go to one side of a Y-shaped maze when this response leads to water (Jaffe et al., 1990). Cockroaches shocked on one side of a box learn to remain on the other side, even when the side the shock occurs on is dark and the other side is lighted (Alloway, 1973). Cockroaches also learn to flex a leg when this response prevents shock (Pritchatt, 1968) or turns off a light (Harris, 1943).

Foraging ants learn to traverse rather complex mazes from their nest to food and from food to their nest (Schneirla, 1943, 1946). Ants also learn a maze when opportunity to care for offspring is the reinforcer (Dashevskii, Karás, & Vdalova, 1990). Moreover, they learn to go to specific sites at different times when reinforcement has been at those sites at those times on previous days (Schatz, Beugnon, & Lachaud, 1994), and they alter their behavior appropriately when the site of a reinforcer changes (Dashevskii et al., 1990).

A female parasitic wasp will learn to insert her ovipositor through a silk cloth in the presence of the odor of larvae hidden under the cloth when this response had led to the depositing of her ova into larvae under silk cloths (Taylor, 1974). A female parasitic wasp will also learn to go toward an odor that has been paired with food when she has been deprived of food, and to go toward an odor that has been paired with a host when she has been well fed (Lewis & Takasu, 1990).

Honeybees show operant conditioning by entering a Plexiglas tube when this response is reinforced with a sugar solution and extinction when the response is no longer reinforced, and also show many of the reinforcement-schedule-effects that are discussed in the next chapter and elsewhere in this book (Grossman, 1973). Foraging honeybees learn to land on targets (sometimes characterized as artificial flowers) having distinctive colors or scents (Couvillon & Bitterman, 1980; Menzel, Erber, & Mashur, 1974) or located near specific landmarks (Huber, Couvillon, & Bitterman, 1994) when they have found sugar water on targets with similar distinguishing characteristics, and show extinction just as (as far as we can tell) vertebrates do when reinforcement is no longer available. Moreover, bees learn to go to a particular location at a particular time when food has been at that location at that time on previous days (Koltermann, 1974). Bumble bees obtain nectar from complex flowers more and more rapidly as a result of the reinforcement that occurs when they find the nectar (Laverty, 1994). As might be expected, then, a bee's foraging skills improve considerably over her lifetime; by the end of her first week of foraging, which is half her expected lifetime, the typical honeybee's forage uptake has doubled (Dukas & Visscher, 1994).

Bees are also responsive to punishment. If in the presence of an arbitrary stimulus such as an odor, airstream, or vibration, proboscis extension by honeybees in response to sugar is followed by electric shock, this response will be suppressed in the presence of the arbitrary stimulus—although it will still occur in the presence of a stimulus that was not coupled with the punishment of proboscis extension (Abramson & Bitterman, 1986; Smith, Abramson, & Tobin, 1991). Similarly, bees that have been intercepted by a spider web and escaped avoid webs with similar decorations, although this learning occurs more readily for some types of webs than for others (Huber et al., 1994).

Generality of the Learning Processes

The learning processes discussed in this book have extremely widespread generality throughout the animal kingdom. It is particularly remarkable that the basic learning phenomena described in this book apply to so many invertebrate species, given that the structure of their nervous systems, beyond the simple neuron (or nerve cell), synapse (i.e., the connections between neurons), and (in the case of arthropods) nerve cord evolved along different lines from those of the vertebrates. (Although at opposite locations in their respective bodies, the nerve cords of arthropods and vertebrates nevertheless may have arisen from a common ancestor (Arendt & Nübler-Jung, 1994). That is to say, the vertebrates split off from the invertebrates before any of the latter had developed much of anything resembling a brain. This raises the interesting evolutionary question of whether the same learning processes evolved independently in invertebrates and vertebrates or whether these processes were already present in vertebrates when the vertebrate-invertebrate split occurred.

SUMMARY AND CONCLUSIONS

There are two basic types of associative learning: respondent conditioning, which is the development of new stimulus-response (conditioned stimulus → conditioned response) relations as a result of stimulus-stimulus (conditioned stimulus – unconditioned stimulus) pairings; and, operant conditioning, which is the increased probability of a given response as a result of that response being followed by an event called reinforcement (which may be either the presentation of a stimulus called a positive reinforcer or the removal of a stimulus called a negative reinforcer) or the decreased probability of a response as a result of that response being followed by an event called punishment. Although developed by stimuli that follow it, an operant response may come under the control of a stimulus, called a discriminative stimulus, which precedes it.

If a conditioned stimulus is no longer followed by an unconditioned stimulus, or if an operantly conditioned response is no longer followed by reinforcement, the probability of occurrence of the conditioned response decreases. This is called extinction.

Stimulus generalization is the process whereby a respondently conditioned response occurs to a stimulus other than one to which it was originally conditioned, or an operant response occurs under the control of a stimulus other than one in whose presence it was originally reinforced. *Stimulus discrimination* is the tendency for responses to occur with a lower probability or less intensity to stimuli other than those to which they were originally conditioned (respondent conditioning) or in the presence of which they were originally reinforced (operant conditioning). A respondent conditioned discrimination is enhanced by alternating a positive conditioned stimulus (CS+), which is followed by the unconditioned stimulus, with a negative conditioned stimulus (CS−), which is not. An operant stimulus discrimination is enhanced by alternating a discriminative stimulus for responding (S^D), in the presence of which responding is reinforced, with a discriminative stimulus for not responding (S^Δ), in the presence of which responding is not reinforced.

If an operant response is followed by a stimulus called a punisher, the probability of occurrence of that response will decrease. This process is called punishment. Negative reinforcers and punishers are called aversive stimuli. It is very important to clearly distinguish between the concepts of punishment, negative reinforcement, and extinction.

A stimulus that has been paired with a reinforcer is a conditioned reinforcer; a stimulus that has been paired with a punisher is a conditioned punisher. Analogous to the extinction of a respondently conditioned response, a conditioned reinforcer or punisher is extinguished by occurring repeatedly without being followed by primary reinforcement or punishment, respectively.

It is inaccurate to view any operant response as simply a single fixed movement or even a single fixed series of movements. All responses that have a given effect on the environment, and vary together as a function of reinforcement (i.e., their probability increases together when one of them is reinforced), are an *operant response class*.

Omission training, which involves omitting the unconditioned stimulus every time the conditioned response occurs, is the only known definitive way to show that a given conditioned response is the result of respondent rather than operant conditioning.

There is a one-to-one relationship between a respondent response and the stimulus that elicits it, whereas generally the discriminative stimulus controlling an operant response is simply present when the response occurs. Thus, we do not say that a discriminative stimulus for responding elicits the response that it controls, but rather that the discriminative stimulus evokes it or that the individual emits the response in the presence of the discriminative stimulus.

It is more accurate to talk about respondent and operant conditioning resulting from a contingency between two events rather than the pairing of two events (two stimuli in the former case, a response and a stimulus in the latter case). A contingency between two events exists when one event is more probable given the occurrence of the other event. In respondent conditioning, the unconditioned stimulus is contingent on the conditioned stimulus; in operant conditioning, reinforcement is contingent on responding. If a neutral stimulus and an unconditioned stimulus are presented randomly, so that the latter is not contingent on the former, no conditioning will occur. However, if reinforcement occurs randomly, chance coinciding of an operant response with reinforcement may condition the response. This may result in further coinciding of the response with reinforcement, resulting in maintenance of responding at a high level. We call this process adventitious reinforcement, and the conditioned responding that it produces we call superstitious behavior.

A three-term contingency is a contingency between a response and two other events: an antecedent stimulus and reinforcement. The result is stimulus control over responding.

There are both respondent and operant attending responses. The former are elicited by particular stimuli. Another name for respondent attending response is orienting reflex. Operant attending responses are learned through reinforcement. Attending responses appear to be necessary in order for stimuli to become conditioned or discriminative stimuli for other responses.

Respondent conditioning evolved because the long-term survival of individuals and their progeny depends on the speed at which they respond to biologically significant stimuli. An individual who begins responding to a biologically significant stimulus before it occurs, rather than after it occurs, has an increased chance of surviving and producing viable offspring. Operant conditioning evolved because animals whose behavior was positively reinforced by food, water, sexual contact, and other stimuli that promoted their survival and reproduction, and whose behavior was negatively reinforced and punished by harmful stimuli, produced more offspring than did animals who were not affected in these ways by such stimuli.

In using the term "associative learning" we are assuming no particular theoretical position about what is going on within an individual when associative learning occurs. The term associative learning in this book refers simply to learning that occurs due to a contingency between two events—either two stimuli or a stimulus and a response. Nonassociative learning, therefore, is simply learning that does not involve a contingency between two events (or any sort of pairing, adventitious or otherwise). There are a number of similarities and interactions between nonassociative and associative learning. For example, sensitization is similar to conditioning, and habituation is similar to extinction. Habituation of attention and of exploratory behavior can retard conditioning, and habituation of freezing can facilitate conditioning. Exposure-based learning can create new reinforcers.

The learning processes discussed in this book have extremely widespread generality throughout the animal kingdom, including the invertebrates. This has potentially important implications regarding the type of nervous systems necessary for the learning principles discussed in this book.

4

Basic Respondent and Operant Processes

While the previous chapter focused primarily on basic *concepts* of associative learning, this chapter is concerned more with the *processes* involved in associative learning. That is, in this chapter we focus on how respondent and operant conditioning develop and manifest themselves over time and how the temporal sequencing of various events affect them. All complex learning, from learning to fear a particular stimulus to how to solve a complex problem, or from learning to joyfully anticipate happy events to skillfully meeting physical challenges, involves respondent and operant conditioning. In order to understand complex learning, therefore, we need to understand the processes involved in respondent and operant conditioning.

ACQUISITION AND EXTINCTION

In both respondent and operant conditioning a person or animal acquires behavior that the individual did not previously possess. Two general names for this are conditioning and acquisition. (See Appendix A for a mathematical treatment of acquisition and extinction in both respondent and operant conditioning.) After acquisition of a conditioned response, continued pairing of the conditioned and unconditioned stimuli (in the case of respondent conditioning) or continued reinforcement of the conditioned response (in the case of operant conditioning) will cause the conditioned response to keep occurring. This is called behavioral maintenance. If after the conditioned response has been acquired, however, the unconditioned stimulus or the reinforcer ceases to occur while the conditioned stimulus or conditioned operant response continues to occur, the conditioned response will decrease to the level it was at prior to conditioning (typically, zero). This, as we have seen, is extinction. We now look at some of the major factors affecting the acquisition and extinction of both respondent and operant behavior.

Acquisition: Respondent Conditioning

In respondent conditioning two stimuli are paired (i.e., associated in time) resulting in the creation of a new reflex, or new stimulus-response connection or relationship. A stimulus that did not previously elicit a response becomes a conditioned stimulus for that response, which is now the conditioned response for that stimulus.

There are a number of ways to pair stimuli, but they are not all equally effective in conditioning a response to a stimulus. Probably the most obvious way to pair two stimuli is to present them at exactly the same time. For example, in an experiment on conditioned salivation, we might present a tone to a dog at the exact instant that meat powder is injected into the dog's mouth and continue the tone until the animal swallows the food. This procedure does not, however, appear to be very effective. Possibly the unconditioned stimulus in this procedure interferes with the animal's attention to the conditioned stimulus; that is, the response elicited by the unconditioned stimulus interferes with the attending responses elicited by the stimulus that is being paired with the unconditioned stimulus, and this prevents that unconditioned stimulus from becoming a conditioned stimulus. (We shall discuss similar interference later in this chapter.)

Delay versus trace conditioning.   Conditioning is most effective when the onset (i.e., the beginning) of the conditioned stimulus precedes the onset of the unconditioned stimulus. There are two general versions of this procedure. In one version the conditioned stimulus continues up to and during the onset of the unconditioned stimulus. For example, in the respondent conditioning of a tone-salivation reflex in a dog, the tone might turn on five seconds before meat powder is presented and remains on until and during the presentation of the meat powder. This procedure is called delay conditioning because there is a delay between the onset of the conditioned stimulus and the onset of the unconditioned stimulus.

In the other version of the procedure in which the onset of the conditioned stimulus precedes the onset of the unconditioned stimulus, the conditioned stimulus terminates prior to the onset of the unconditioned stimulus. For example, the tone might come on five seconds before the presentation of the meat powder and off two seconds before the presentation of the meat powder. This procedure is called trace conditioning because when the conditioned stimulus turns off its sensory effect on the nervous system persists for a brief period as an after-effect called a "stimulus trace." This stimulus trace is assumed to overlap with the onset of the unconditioned stimulus and thus account for the conditioning that occurs during trace conditioning.

Delay conditioning appears to be consistently more effective than trace conditioning (when, of course, the interval between the onset of the conditioned stimulus and the onset of the unconditioned stimulus is the same in the two procedures). It was once thought that the reason for this was a weakening of the stimulus trace during the interval between the termination of the conditioned stimulus and the onset of the unconditioned stimulus. A more likely possibility, however, is that the conditioned stimulus in trace conditioning tends to inhibit—that is, suppress or prevent—the conditioned response due to the fact that the stimulus immediately precedes a period in which the unconditioned stimulus does not occur. This explanation is supported by a finding that has been made on the conditioned blink of rabbits. If, for example, a rabbit receives trials in which a tone lasting 0.6 seconds is followed 10 seconds later by a shock near the orbit of the eye, conditioning of the blink to the tone generally will not occur. This, despite the fact, that the blink is the response that is elicited by the shock. Suppose that the same rabbit is now given trials in which a visual stimulus, such as a dimming of the light in the experimental chamber, occurs for 10.6 seconds followed immediately by the electric shock. In this case conditioning is much more likely to occur, since it involves delay conditioning whereas the previous procedure used trace conditioning. Now suppose that a test is given in which the tone occurs at the same time as the visual stimulus. The result is that the conditioned blink response will be less likely to occur than it will when the visual stimulus occurs alone (Hinson & Siegel, 1980). Thus it appears that a conditioned stimulus in trace conditioning can inhibit the conditioned response. It should be noted, however, that although even short (e.g., 10 seconds) trace-conditioning intervals are generally ineffective in conditioning blink responses in rabbits, much longer trace-conditioning intervals can result in conditioning other responses in other animals (e.g., conditioned salivation in the dog).

We will discuss the concept of inhibition in more detail when we talk about stimulus discrimination later in this chapter.

Backward conditioning. The least effective type of conditioning is called backward conditioning. As its name suggests, this procedure consists in presenting the two stimuli in the reverse of their proven effective order, variations of which (trace and delay) are collectively called forward conditioning. Thus, in backward conditioning the unconditioned stimulus occurs prior to the conditioned stimulus. The reason for the ineffectiveness of backward conditioning appears to be similar to the reason for the decreased effectiveness of trace conditioning relative to delay conditioning. That is, in backward conditioning the conditioned stimulus tends to be inhibitory because it immediately precedes a period in which the unconditioned stimulus does not occur. The evidence for this is similar to the evidence that the conditioned stimulus in trace conditioning can be inhibitory. A stimulus paired backward with an unconditioned stimulus will suppress responding to a conditioned stimulus that it is presented in combination with; and, in addition, will take longer to establish as a conditioned stimulus in a forward conditioning procedure than will a stimulus that has never been paired (forward or backward) with the unconditioned stimulus (Hall, 1984; Plotkin & Oakley, 1975; Siegel & Domjan, 1971, 1974).

It should be noted, however, that there are certain conditions under which backward conditioning is effective (Ayres, Albert, & Bombace, 1987; Burkhardt, 1980; Heth, 1976; Mahoney & Ayres, 1976; Shurtleff & Ayres, 1981; Singh, 1959; Tait & Saladin, 1986; Williams, Dyck, & Tait, 1986). These will be discussed in Chapter 6.

Simultaneous conditioning. To summarize, there are three effective ways to pair conditioned and unconditioned stimuli. In order of effectiveness they are delay conditioning, trace conditioning, and backward conditioning. Delay conditioning is especially effective if the interval between the onset of the conditioned stimulus and the onset of the unconditioned stimulus is quite short; in such cases it is often called simultaneous conditioning. This should not be confused with the case in which the conditioned and unconditioned stimuli overlap completely, however, and which we have already said appears to be ineffective—at least in vertebrates. There is evidence that simultaneous conditioning may be almost as effective as forward conditioning in establishing a conditioned proboscis-extension response in honeybees (Batson et al., 1992; Hoban, Couvillan, & Bitterman, 1996).

Temporal conditioning. Respondent conditioning also can occur simply on the basis of time in the absence of an explicit conditioned stimulus. For example, a hungry (i.e., food-deprived) dog that is given a bite of food every 30 minutes will eventually salivate profusely near the end of each 30-minute interval. This type of conditioning is called temporal conditioning.

Probably the conditioned stimuli for temporal conditioning are stimuli (e.g., those produced by the body in digesting food) that appear fairly regularly in time following the previous presentation of the unconditioned stimulus.

Acquisition: Operant Conditioning

Operant behavior has a peculiar relationship to the environment. Unlike respondent behavior, it does not appear to be elicited by specific, identifiable stimuli. For that reason it is said to be emitted rather than elicited, analogous to the way in which a light bulb is said to emit light. Although the effects of the environment on operant behavior are rather subtle, operant behavior generally has quite definite effects on the environment. It operates on the environment to change it in some manner, which is why it is called operant behavior. (Another name for operant conditioning is instrumental conditioning.)

As a result of a response being reinforced in the presence of a given stimulus, that stimulus acquires control over the response. The control that develops is similar to the control that a conditioned stimulus acquires over its conditioned response in respondent conditioning: The response tends to occur in the presence of the stimulus and not in its absence. Many of the statements that this text makes about an operant controlling stimulus also apply to a conditioned stimulus, and vice versa. Therefore, we shall use the term "controlling stimulus" to refer to a conditioned stimulus as well as an operant controlling stimulus, and the term "stimulus control" to refer to control by a conditioned stimulus as well as an operant controlling stimulus. We use the term "discriminative stimulus" to refer to an operant controlling stimulus.

Discrete-trial versus free-operant conditioning. There are two major types of operant conditioning procedures. In a discrete-trials conditioning procedure, a distinct stimulus occurs for a brief period during which a response can occur only once. Each presentation of the stimulus is called a trial. An example of discrete-trials conditioning would be training carried out in a T-maze, such as shown in the left side of Figure 4.1. An even simpler example is training in an apparatus called a runway, shown in the right side of Figure 4.1. Each trial

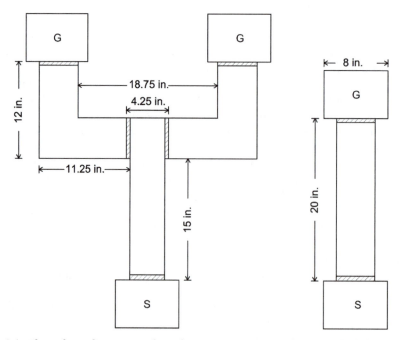

FIGURE 4.1. Floor plans of two types of simple mazes. A T-maze is shown on the left; a runway on the right. "S" and "G" indicate start and goal boxes, respectively. (From Saltzman, 1950)

begins when the experimenter raises a partition in the start box, thus allowing the animal to move down the main alley of the T-maze or the runway. Typically, a reinforcer is present in one of the distinctive goal boxes of the T-maze or in the single goal box of the runway. Conditioning is measured by the animal's running speed and, in the case of the T-maze, by the percentage of trials on which the animal enters the goal box containing the reinforcer.

In free-operant conditioning, the response may occur repeatedly without restriction. Studies on free-operant conditioning typically use an operant conditioning chamber containing a device called an operandum that records instances of the operant response. As the term suggests, an operandum (sometimes also called a manipulandum) is usually designed to be operated by a characteristic behavior of the species under study (Skinner, 1980). With rats, for example, the operandum is usually a lever because rats have a tendency to manipulate movable objects in their environments. With pigeons, on the other hand, the operandum is typically a round plastic disc, called a key, that the bird can peck. Because operant behavior operates on the environment, it can be recorded by an electrical switch that is operated by movement of the operandum. The switch can then be wired to devices that automatically reinforce the behavior and record it. For some examples of operant conditioning chambers see Chapter 3 (Figure 3.2, p. 32).

A useful devices for recording free-operant behavior is a cumulative recorder. As its name implies, this device records the cumulative number of responses that have occurred over a given period of time. The device is more useful for the information it provides about rate of responding, however, than for the information it gives as to total number of responses. The manner in which it records operant behavior is illustrated in Figure 4.2. In many laboratories,

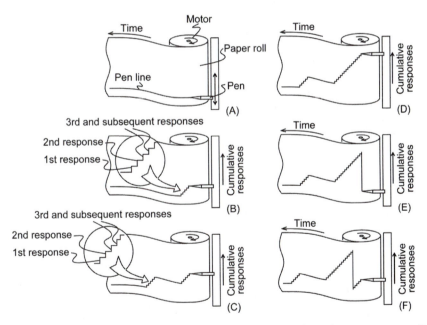

FIGURE 4.2. The parts of the figure are as follows: (A) The point of an ink pen rests on a roll of paper being turned by an electric motor. The paper unrolls at a constant speed so that the horizontal length of the line drawn by the pen corresponds directly to the amount of time that has passed. (B) Every time the individual responds the pen moves up one "notch" or unit. The units are very small, as illustrated in the lower portion of B where the first five responses are shown magnified. (C) The first five responses are followed by a fairly long period in which no responses occur. Then, after this pause in responding, more responses occur rather close together. (D) The pen has reached the top of the paper. (E) In order to continue recording, the pen quickly resets to the bottom of the paper. (F) The pen continues graphing responses cumulatively over time.

computer graphing programs have replaced cumulative recorders in producing cumulative records of data.

Some representative cumulative records of the acquisition of free-operant behavior are shown in Figure 4.3. Each curve was made by a food-deprived rat that had previous experience eating from the food tray in the chamber immediately upon hearing the sound of the feeder. Thus, the sound of the feeder was a conditioned reinforcer for these rats. Prior to the start of the sessions in which the records shown in the figure were made, however, the rats had never received reinforcement for lever pressing. Conditioning was carried out simply by arranging for the lever to operate the feeder and placing the rat in the chamber.

The record in the top panel of Figure 4.3 was produced by a rat that required four lever presses to acquire the lever-press operant response. The first lever press occurred five minutes after the rat was released into the chamber, but the resulting reinforcement had no ob-

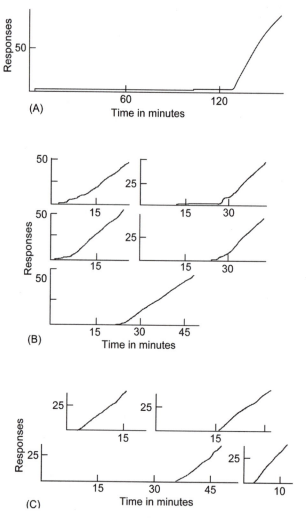

FIGURE 4.3. Cumulative records of the operant conditioning of 10 rats. (A) conditioning did not occur until the fourth reinforcement. (B) conditioning occurred with the first or second reinforcement, although the rate was not immediately at maximum. (C) the first reinforcement produced an immediate change to the maximum response rate. (From Skinner, 1938)

servable effect on the behavior. The second response occurred 51.5 minutes later, but again there was no observable effect on the behavior. The third response occurred 47.5 minutes later and the fourth 25 minutes' after that. Immediately after the fourth response the rate of responding suddenly increased and accelerated to a maximum. After being maintained at an essentially constant rate for a period of time, responding then began to slow down due to satiation of the animal on the food reinforcer. This can be seen in the negative acceleration (or deceleration) in the last part of the record.

The records in the middle panel show cases of more rapid conditioning. In these cases conditioning occurred with the first or second reinforcement, although the rate of responding did not immediately reach its maximum level. The records in the bottom panel show even more rapid conditioning. In each of these cases response rate increased to its maximum level immediately after the first reinforcement.

Response shaping.   Probably the most impressive aspect of the records in Figure 4.3 is the rapidity with which operant conditioning can occur. In order for operant conditioning to occur, however, the response must occur at some minimum rate so that it can be reinforced. The rate at which an operant response occurs prior to conditioning is called the operant level of that response. Sometimes the operant level of a response is so low that it would take an extremely long time for it to be conditioned. The speed of conditioning the response can, however, be greatly increased by a procedure known as the method of successive approximations or, more simply, response shaping.

Response shaping involves gradually developing a particular response by successively reinforcing responses that more and more closely resemble that response. Thus, response shaping is an example of the principle of small increments mentioned in Chapter 1. In shaping lever pressing in a rat, for example, one might use a hand switch connected to the feeder. The rat would have been previously trained to eat from the food tray as soon as the feeder operates. When the rat makes a movement in the direction of the lever, one would operate the hand switch to reinforce that movement. One would continue to administer reinforcement whenever that particular movement occurs until a closer movement occurs, at which point the closer movement would be reinforced. One would then continue to reinforce that movement until an even closer movement occurs.

Eventually the rat will touch the lever, and one would reinforce that response until a slight depression of the lever occurs. Then these slight depressions would be reinforced. Finally the rat will press the lever with sufficient force to activate the switch that operates the feeder. At that point the behavior will most likely have been conditioned and no additional hand-delivered reinforcements should be given.

Extinction and Spontaneous Recovery

Respondent extinction consists of repeatedly presenting the conditioned stimulus without presenting the unconditioned stimulus. Operant extinction consists of permitting the response to occur without reinforcing it. In both cases the conditioned behavior gradually weakens. In the case of respondent extinction the time between the conditioned stimulus and the conditioned response becomes increasingly longer and the magnitude of the conditioned response becomes smaller and smaller (e.g., fewer drops of saliva are secreted). In the case of operant extinction the rate of responding gradually decreases. It does not do so, however, in a smooth manner.

Figure 4.4 (solid lines) shows four typical cumulative records of operant extinction. The records were generated by four rats that had been conditioned with about 100 responses

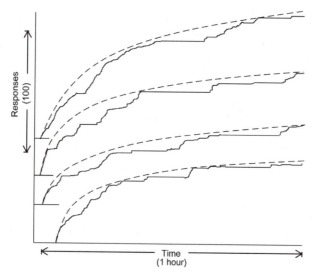

FIGURE 4.4. Four typical operant extinction curves. These extinction curves were made after continuous reinforcement (every response reinforced) of lever pressing in rats. Note the negative acceleration indicated by the dashed lines. (From Skinner, 1938)

reinforced on the day prior to extinction. During extinction the rats were in the same state of food deprivation as during conditioning. Note that each of the four rats responded at a high rate for a short time at the beginning of the session. (This could be extinction bursting as described in Chapter 3, although comparison with the session immediately prior to extinction would be necessary to determine this.) The rate then decreased, sometimes to zero, and then increased again. Periods of high and low rates alternated throughout the extinction session, with the low rate periods becoming longer and longer. The dashed lines in the figure indicate that the obtained extinction records may be viewed as consisting of deviations from smoothly decelerating curves. The deviations from a smooth curve take the form of depressions in the curve followed by "compensatory" increases in rate—that is, increases that compensate for the deviations from the curve (Skinner, 1938, p. 74). Eventually, if extinction is carried out long enough, the behavior returns to its operant level (i.e., its level prior to conditioning).

If an animal is removed for a period of time from an extinction situation and then placed back into it, responding will increase above the level it was at when the animal was removed. This phenomenon, which we discussed in Chapter 3 in connection with habituation and sensitization, is called spontaneous recovery, and it occurs with both respondent and operant behavior. Extinction may then be carried out again, and will generally proceed more rapidly than it did during the previous extinction period.

Figure 4.5 shows a cumulative record of the spontaneous recovery of a rat's lever pressing behavior. The portion of the curve to the left of the center line is from the first extinction session. The portion to the right is from the second extinction session, which was conducted 48 hours later. The rat was at the same level of food deprivation during both sessions. In spite of the fact that there was no reinforcement of the response between the two sessions, on the second day of extinction the rate of responding began at a value many times that of the final value on the first day.

The spontaneous recovery that occurs in operant extinction was thought to be a special case of stimulus control (Reid, 1957; Skinner, 1950). Recall from Chapter 3 that a stimulus that is present when a response is reinforced will tend to acquire control over that response. In seeing how stimulus control can explain spontaneous recovery, note that the beginning of a session contains stimuli (e.g., the stimuli involved in having just been placed in the chamber) that are quite distinct from stimuli that occur during the remainder of the session. The distinctive stimuli at the beginning of a session are present for only a short time, and thus there is not enough time for the response to fully extinguish in their presence during a single extinction session. Hence, according to this explanation, spontaneous recovery is due to the reintroduction of stimuli at the beginning of the session that still control the response because it has not been fully extinguished in their presence.

The evidence does not, however support the above explanation. For example, similar response patterns (i.e., increasing response rate early in a session followed by decreasing response rate as the session progresses) occur within sessions when responding is not undergoing extinction (McSweeney, 1992; McSweeney & Swindell, 1999). Moreover, stimuli paired with the beginnings of sessions do not produce spontaneous recovery when presented immediately after extinction (Burdick & James, 1970; Ellson, 1939; Lewis, 1956; Robbins, 1990; Thomas & Sherman, 1986). Thus some process other than (or in addition to) stimulus control appears responsible for spontaneous recovery. This other process may be the same one that produces spontaneous recovery in habituation (Chaper 2). (As we saw in Chapter 3, there are striking similarities between habituation and extinction, suggesting that some of the same processes may be involved in both.) That is, the decrease in responding during extinction and subsequent spontaneous recovery may be at least partly due to habituation (or processes involved in habituation) to stimuli present in the situation followed by spontaneous recovery from habituation (Humphrey, 1930; McSweeney et al, 1996; Thompson & Spencer, 1956; Windsor, 1930).

In addition, taking an animal out of an experimental situation and putting it back into it is not necessary for spontaneous recovery to occur. It may occur after responding has remained at zero for a time within a long extinction session. If a session lasts for several 24-hour periods and (in what is called a circadian rhythm) responding for the reinforcer tends to occur at about the same time each day, spontaneous recovery may tend to occur at that time (Iversen, 1998).

PARTIAL REINFORCEMENT

Up to now we have spoken of conditioning and maintaining a response by pairing the unconditioned stimulus with each occurrence of the conditioned stimulus in the case of respondent conditioning, and by reinforcing every emission of the response in the case of operant condi-

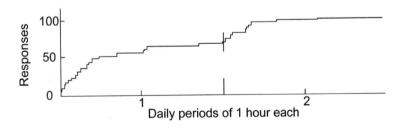

FIGURE 4.5. Spontaneous recovery from operant extinction. The first curve (right) is the bottom extinction curve in Figure 4.4. The second (left) was produced by the same rat 47 hours later with no intervening conditioning. Note the increased response rate at the beginning of the second session relative to the response rate at the end of the first session. (From Skinner, 1938)

tioning. The procedure is called continuous reinforcement in the case of respondent conditioning as well as in the case of operant conditioning. It is to be contrasted with partial reinforcement, which is pairing the unconditioned stimulus with fewer than 100% of the presentations of the conditioned stimulus or reinforcing fewer than 100% of the occurrences of the conditioned response in the cases of respondent and operant conditioning, respectively. In partial reinforcement, presentations of the conditioned stimulus paired with the unconditioned stimulus are interspersed among presentations of the conditioned stimulus that are not paired with the unconditioned stimulus (in the case of respondent conditioning), and reinforced instances of the response are interspersed among unreinforced instances of the response (in the case of operant conditioning).

Effect of Partial Reinforcement on Acquisition

Since extinction weakens a conditioned response, and partial reinforcement, in effect, is the interspersing of extinction with reinforcement, we might expect partial reinforcement to retard acquisition of a conditioned response. Surprisingly, this is not necessarily the case. For both respondent and operant conditioning, partial reinforcement can result in the same rate of acquisition of a conditioned response as continuous reinforcement does. This is not a consistent finding, however. Often, particularly with respondent conditioning, partial reinforcement retards the rate of acquisition. With operant conditioning, partial reinforcement can also lead to a higher level of the conditioned response—for example, a higher rate of pressing a lever or a faster running speed in a runway—after the response has been acquired than continuous reinforcement does.

The degree of partial reinforcement is obviously a factor in whether, and to what extent, it retards acquisition. Clearly, if the percentage of times that the unconditioned stimulus follows the conditioned stimulus or that reinforcement follows an operant response is very low, there is little difference between a conditioning procedure involving partial reinforcement and an extinction procedure (or the absence of conditioning). In this situation acquisition would be greatly retarded if it even occurred at all. Other than this rather self-evident point, however, little is known about the factors determining the effect partial reinforcement has, relative to the effect of continuous reinforcement, on the rate of acquisition of a conditioned response or the final probability or rate of occurrence that it reaches (Mackintosh, 1974, p. 75). In addition, the way in which the rate of acquisition is measured is an important factor. If acquisition is measured not in terms of number of conditioned stimulus presentations, but in terms of the number of times the unconditioned stimulus follows the conditioned stimulus, then there is no retardation of acquisition.

The Partial-Reinforcement Extinction Effect (PREE)

In a phenomenon known as the partial-reinforcement extinction effect (PREE), behavior decreases more slowly during extinction after partial reinforcement than it does during extinction after continuous reinforcement. More generally, the PREE is the tendency for extinction to occur less rapidly after a smaller percentage than after a larger percentage of pairings of the conditioned stimulus with the unconditioned stimulus (in the case of respondent conditioning) or after a lower rather than a higher percentage of instances of the response followed by reinforcement (in the case of operant conditioning). For example, the PREE would be demonstrated in respondent conditioning if extinction occurred less rapidly after 25% of the presentations of a conditioned stimulus had been paired with an unconditioned stimulus (and 75% had not) than after 50% of the presentations of the conditioned stimulus had been paired with the unconditioned stimulus (and 50% had not). Similarly, PREE would be demonstrated if extinction of an operant response occurred more slowly after reinforcement had followed 25% of the responses than if it had followed 50% of the responses.

An overview of the PREE.   The PREE is far from universal: There are many exceptions to it. What is important is the fact that it occurs at all, since there is reason not to expect it. We have seen that, with respondent behavior, conditioned responses are strengthened by pairings of a conditioned stimulus with an unconditioned stimulus, and weakened in extinction by the occurrence of the conditioned stimulus without the unconditioned stimulus; and that, with operant behavior, conditioned responses are strengthened by being followed by reinforcement, and weakened in extinction by occurring without being followed by reinforcement. Why would mixing strengthening and weakening processes prior to extinction lead to more responding in extinction than strengthening alone (i.e., continuous reinforcement)? One way to view the PREE is as an instance of the principle of small increments. The change from continuous reinforcement to extinction is larger than the change form partial reinforcement to extinction, because partial reinforcement contains some extinction-like events (instances of the conditioned stimulus not followed by the unconditioned stimulus or the conditioned response not followed by reinforcement) while continuous reinforcement does not. Therefore, from the principle of small increments, the effect of changing from partial reinforcement to extinction should be less drastic—that is, a slower decrease in conditioned responding—than the effect of changing from continuous reinforcement to extinction.

The principle of small increments is not the only factor affecting the amount of conditioned responding during extinction, however. The strengthening effect of pairing conditioned and unconditioned stimuli and the strengthening effect of following responses with reinforcement are also factors, and they operate against the principle of small increments when the effect of partial reinforcement on conditioned responding during extinction is observed. This opposition of factors provides a general explanation for why the PREE sometimes occurs and sometimes does not.

Factors affecting the PREE.   Having reviewed some general points about the partial-reinforcement effect, we now become a bit more specific. Whether the PREE occurs with respondent behavior seems to depend on the unconditioned stimulus, among other factors (Mackintosh, 1974, pp. 72–75). Whether it occurs with operant behavior is dependent on whether the conditioning and extinction procedures are discrete trials or free operant. The PREE is large and reliable with discrete-trials of operant behavior (Robbins, 1971). It occurs much less reliably, and to a much smaller degree when it does occur, with free-operant behavior. This is particularly true when the measure of amount of responding during extinction is the proportion of responding relative to the rate of responding prior to extinction, because free-operant responding maintained by partial reinforcement is often higher than free-operant responding maintained by continuous reinforcement (Nevin, 1988).

The PREE in operant behavior can be understood as a special case of stimulus control. To see this, note that during operant responding the pattern of occurrence and nonoccurrence of reinforcement is present when responding is reinforced. This pattern therefore acquires stimulus control over responding. In the case of free-operant behavior, the time between occasions in which reinforcement can occur is usually fairly short; in the case of discrete-trials, however, it can be quite long—depending on the amount of separation between trials. It may seem implausible that a pattern spread out over such a long time span can be a controlling stimulus; in later chapters, however, we shall see that under certain conditions there can be long temporal gaps between controlling stimuli and the responses that they control. The stimuli present during extinction are thus more similar to the stimuli present during partial reinforce-ment—where responses *sometimes* occurred without the occurrence of reinforcement—than to the stimuli present during continuous reinforcement—where responses *never* occurred without reinforcement. Thus the stimuli present during extinction should control more re-sponding after partial reinforcement than after continuous reinforcement.

But why is the PREE weak and unreliable with one form of operant behavior—namely, free-operant behavior—yet robust with another type—namely, discrete-trials operant behavior (Nevin, 1988, 1992; Robbins, 1971)? In the case of free-operant behavior, in addition to the inverse effect of rate of reinforcement on later responding during extinction—due either to the principle of small increments or stimulus generalization—the quantity of reinforcement that occurred over time has a direct (i.e., a positive or increasing) effect on the amount of re-sponding during extinction, due to the strengthening effect of reinforcement. In other words, in the case of free-operant behavior, a high rate of reinforcement prior to extinction has two opposing effects on responding during extinction: (1) it tends to decrease responding because it is less simi-lar to extinction than a low rate of reinforcement (i.e., the PREE); and (2) it tends to increase responding because it results in a greater quantity of reinforcement over time prior to extinc-tion. The second effect tends to counteract the PREE, making it appear unreliable and weak when it is tested on free-operant behavior. Intuitively, the existence of this second effect makes sense, because there must (by definition) be at least some reinforcement in order for an operant response to be conditioned prior to extinction, and hence the rate of reinforcement prior to extinction must be larger than zero for the response to show any resistance at all to extinction.

One indication of the existence of these two opposing effects during free-operant extinc-tion is the fact that, with free-operant behavior, the PREE decreases and eventually reverses as the number of sessions (and hence number of reinforcers) prior to extinction increases. Another indication is the fact that if we look just at the amount of the decrease in a free-operant response during extinction relative to the level of the behavior prior to or early in extinction, we find that the PREE tends to reverse—especially when the number of sessions prior to extinction is large (Nevin, 1988).

Although an increased quantity of reinforcement over time prior to extinction tends to offset the PREE in free-operant extinction, it appears not to do so in discrete-trials extinction. The reason for this seems to be that the effects of prior quantity of reinforcement on subse-quent responding during extinction act more on the tendency for a response to be repeated once it starts occurring than on the tendency for the response to be emitted in the first place (Mellgren & Elsmore, 1991). Because free-operant responses can, by definition, be repeated many times in quick succession during extinction, these effects are more evident during free-operant extinction than they are during discrete-trial extinction where the response cannot occur more than once per trial. The principle of small increments and stimulus generalization operate on the tendency of a response to occur when it is not currently being emitted and thus operate equally well during discrete-trials extinction and free-operant extinction. Hence, al-though appearing weak and unreliable in free-operant extinction, the PREE is manifested strongly in discrete-trials extinction.

SCHEDULES OF REINFORCEMENT

Partial reinforcement of operant behavior is commonly called intermittent reinforcement. There exist many possible procedures or rules, called schedules of reinforcement, by which some emissions of a response are reinforced while others go unreinforced.

A term closely related to schedule of reinforcement is contingency of reinforcement, which refers to the specific relationship that exists between responding and reinforcement. The two terms therefore have essentially the same meaning; however, "schedule of reinforcement" is typically used when the emphasis is on the procedure or rule governing the presentation of reinforcement, whereas "contingency of reinforcement" is typically used when the emphasis is on the specific behavior required to produce reinforcement. We have already seen this use of the term "contingency" in Chapter 3.

Basic Types of Reinforcement Schedules

We have already discussed at length two schedules of nonintermittent reinforcement; namely, continuous reinforcement and extinction. Between these two extremes are the schedules of intermittent reinforcement. Four of the most simple of these schedules will now be discussed: fixed ratio, variable ratio, fixed interval, and variable interval. The examples given to illustrate these schedules will involve food-deprived pigeons (usually maintained at 80% of their free-feeding weights) that have been conditioned to peck keys for grain reinforcement (Ferster & Skinner, 1957).

Fixed ratio. In a fixed-ratio (FR) schedule of reinforcement the reinforcement occurs after a fixed number of responses following the previous reinforcement. For example, in an FR 10 schedule every tenth response is reinforced; in an FR 60 schedule every 60th response is

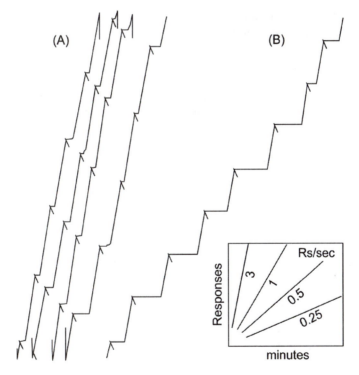

Figure 4.6. Stable fixed-ratio key-pecking performance of two pigeons. One pigeon (A) was on FR 200 and the other (B) was on FR 120 after extensive histories of lower fixed ratios. The downward "pips" or slash marks indicate reinforcements. Note the pause after each reinforcement, followed by high, steady response rates. Also note the similar response patterns despite different overall response rates of the two birds. (From Ferster & Skinner, 1957)

reinforced. Note that we are using the term "response" to indicate the emission of a specific response, such as a key peck or lever press; for example, "four responses" means four emissions of the same response. We follow this convention throughout the rest of this book, unless otherwise indicated.

Figure 4.6 illustrates two examples of the cumulative record pattern of responding that is typically generated by an FR schedule. The records were generated by two pigeons: Bird A was on FR 200 and Bird B was on FR 120. Previously both birds had extensive experience with lower FR schedules, which is necessary in order for their responding to be maintained on the higher FR schedules. To conserve space the record for Bird A has been compressed by cutting out the lines and placing them close to each other, while carefully maintaining the correct angle of each portion of the record with respect to the vertical. The scale of the records is indicated by the small set of coordinates containing some representative slopes in the lower right-hand corner. The slash marks (downward deflections of the pen) indicate reinforcements. Note that responses were emitted at a high, steady rate except for a pause (i.e., period of no responding) after each reinforcement. Both the length of the pause and the rate of responding after the pause differ from one individual to another. In general, however, the length of the pause varies directly with the size of the FR schedule. Response rate after the pause does not seem to depend to any great extent on the size of the FR schedule.

Figure 4.7 shows an example of extinction after FR. (As with the record for Bird A in the previous figure, this record has been compressed by the standard procedure of cutting out excess empty space between the lines.) Note that a high rate of responding alternates with pauses. As extinction progresses the pauses become increasingly longer. Responding still occurs at a high rate, however, during those periods in which it does occur. Eventually it ceases altogether because of the increasing length of the pauses.

Variable-ratio.   In a variable-ratio (VR) schedule reinforcement occurs after a given number of responses where the number varies from reinforcement to reinforcement. In a VR 20 schedule, for example, the number of responses between reinforcements varies unpredictably, but the average over a large number of responses equals 20.

Figure 4.8 shows an example of the type of cumulative record typically produced by a VR schedule. The particular schedule in effect was VR 360. (The bird had had prior experience with a number of smaller VR schedules.) Note that VR generates rapid and fairly steady responding. Unlike the case with FR, little pausing after reinforcement occurs.

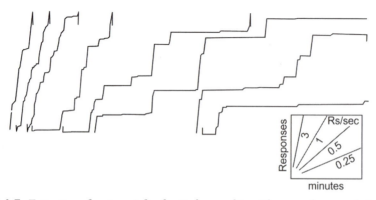

FIGURE 4.7. Extinction of a pigeon's fixed-ratio key pecking. The record was made in a single session following 700 reinforcements on FR 60. (From Ferster & Skinner, 1957)

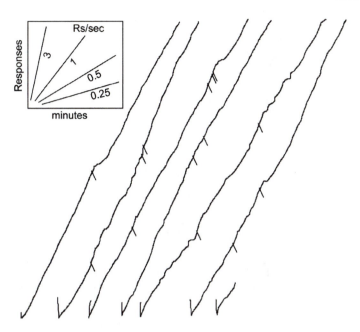

FIGURE 4.8. Stable variable-ratio key pecking by a pigeon. The schedule of reinforcement was VR 60. The bird had previously received reinforcement on lower variable-ratio schedules. Slash marks indicate reinforcements. Note the high steady response rate with no pausing after reinforcement. (From Ferster & Skinner, 1957)

Figure 4.9 shows an example of extinction after VR. The bird was on VR 110 prior to extinction, and a segment of the performance on that schedule appears before the arrow (the short horizontal marks before the arrow indicate reinforcements). Extinction continued at essentially the VR-reinforcement response rate for the first 3000 responses. Although the rate shifted to a somewhat lower value in the fifth segment, the last part of the session shows mainly long pauses separated by brief periods of responding at approximately the original VR response rate. As is the case with FR extinction, in VR extinction the pauses become increasingly longer until responding ceases altogether.

Although the number of responses between reinforcements forms an unpredictable sequence in VR schedules, this sequence is not actually random. This is mainly because the sequence repeats after a while and also there may be more very short segments than would be the case if the sequence were random. If a random sequence is used, the schedule is called a random-ratio (RR) schedule rather than a VR schedule. There is little difference between the effects of VR and RR schedule, however, so in this book RR schedules will be considered to be essentially the same as VR schedules.

Fixed-interval.   In a *fixed-interval (FI)* schedule of reinforcement the first response after a designated interval of time following the previous reinforcement is reinforced. For example, in an FI 1-minute schedule responses occurring during the one-minute interval following reinforcement have no effect. The first response occurring any time after the one-minute interval has elapsed, however, is reinforced and a new one-minute interval begins.

Figure 4.10 shows an example of performance on an FI schedule. After having previously been on continuous reinforcement and then shifted directly to FI 4 minutes, the bird had had 66 hours of exposure to the FI 4-minute schedule at the beginning of the record shown in the figure. Note that, as with high FR schedules, there is a pause after each reinforcement. Unlike

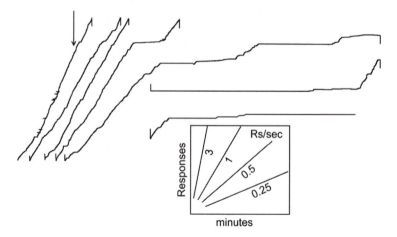

FIGURE 4.9. Extinction of a pigeon's variable-ratio key pecking. Prior to extinction the bird was on variable ratios ranging from 15 to 110. A segment of the performance on VR 100 appears before the arrow. The horizontal pips before the arrow indicate reinforcements. (From Ferster & Skinner, 1957)

the typical FR pattern, however, the FI pattern after the pause often consists of a fairly gradual acceleration to a high terminal response rate prior to the next reinforcement. Such instances of gradual acceleration are called *fixed-interval scallops*. A detailed analysis of the response pattern comprising FI scallops, however, has revealed that the gradual acceleration to a high terminal rate is not as smooth as cumulative records of scallops suggest. Instead, scallops appear to be due to alternating "bursts" of high-rate responding and pauses, with fewer and fewer pauses occurring as the interval progresses (Gentry, Weiss, & Laties, 1983). In addition, with extensive training on an FI schedule the scallop pattern tends to be replaced by a rapid transition from the pause immediately following reinforcement to the high terminal rate that continues to the next reinforcement. Well trained FI behavior therefore resembles FR behavior (Ferster & Skinner, 1957).

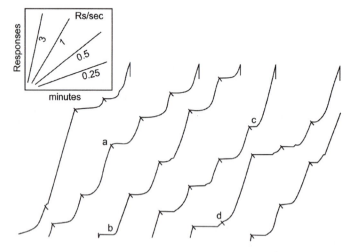

FIGURE 4.10. Stable fixed-interval key-pecking by a pigeon. The reinforcement schedule was FI 4 minutes, which the bird had been on for a total of 66 hours. The slash marks indicate reinforcements. Note the pauses after reinforcement, followed by gradually increasing response rates (scallops).

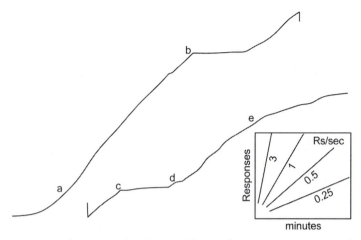

FIGURE 4.11. Extinction of a pigeon's fixed-interval key pecking. Prior to extinction the bird had been on FI 45 minutes. Note the periods of positively accelerated response rate (scallops), such as at "a," and negatively accelerated response rate, such as at "c" and "e." (From Ferster & Skinner, 1957)

Figure 4.11 shows an example of extinction after FI. The bird had been on FI 45 minutes prior to this brief extinction session. The session began with a scallop at *a* and the terminal response rate was held, with only a slight decline, until it suddenly dropped to zero at *b*. The resulting pause initiated another extended scallop which reaches a somewhat lower terminal rate. At *c* response rate fell to zero again, followed by a slow acceleration. After a brief increase at *d*, rate then gradually declined.

Variable-interval.   A variable-interval (VI) schedule is like an FI schedule with the exception that the size of the interval between scheduled reinforcements varies from reinforcement to reinforcement. The schedule stands in the same relation to the FI schedule as VR does to FR. In a VI 1-minute schedule, for example, the time scheduled between reinforcements varies, but the average over a large number of intervals is equal to one minute. Thus, in a VI schedule a reinforcer follows the first response emitted after a variable period of time, measured from the previous reinforcement.

Figure 4.12 shows an example of the type of cumulative record typically produced by a VI schedule. The VI schedule in effect was VI 3 minutes. Note that the bird maintained a constant overall response rate throughout the session with no long pauses after reinforcement. Thus, VI generates a pattern much like that produced by VR. Although differing across individuals, response rates for the same individual are much higher under VR than under VI, even when reinforcement rates on the two schedules are equal (Ferster & Skinner, 1957, pp. 399–407).

Figure 4.13 shows an example of extinction after VI. The bird had been on VI 7 minutes prior to this extinction session. Extinction began at 1.25 to 1.5 responses per second, which was maintained for the first 8000 responses. Then the rate of responding fell fairly continuously, reaching a very low value at the end of the record. Clearly one of the most impressive properties of VI is the huge output of behavior it can generate during extinction.

Although the minimum time intervals between reinforcements form an unpredictable sequence in VI schedules, this sequence is not actually random. This is mainly because—as with the sequence that constitutes a VR schedule—the sequence repeats after a while and also there may be more very short segments than would be the case if the sequence were random. If a random sequence is used, the schedule is called a random-interval (RI) schedule. There is

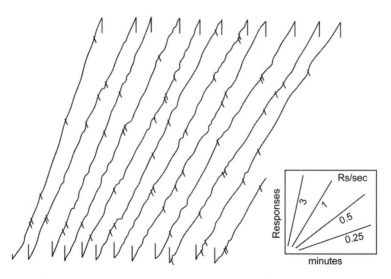

FIGURE 4.12. Stable variable-interval key pecking by a pigeon. The reinforcement schedule was VI 3 minutes, which the bird had been on for a total of 45 hours. Slash marks indicate reinforcements. Note the steady responding with little pausing after reinforcement. (From Ferster & Skinner, 1957)

little difference in the effects of VI and an RI schedules, so in this book we will consider them to be essentially the same.

Basic Schedules With Added Temporal Contingencies

Temporal contingencies may be added to the basic schedules of reinforcement. One type of added temporal contingency is a completion-rate requirement. For example, reinforcement on an FR may occur only if the required number of responses is completed within a given time period. Conversely, a contingency may be added to an FR schedule in which completing the required number of responses must take longer than a given time period. In addition, these

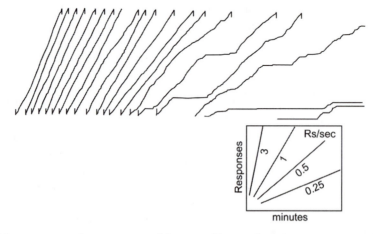

FIGURE 4.13. Extinction of a pigeon's variable-interval key pecking. Prior to extinction the bird had been on VI 7 minutes. Note the high, steady response rate, with little decrease during the first 20 minutes of the session. (From Ferster & Skinner, 1957)

two types of contingencies may be combined, so that reinforcement will occur only if the time taken to complete the required number of responses is between two given values. The more common variations of completion-rate contingencies (i.e., differential reinforcement of high or low response rates) are discussed in Chapter 7.

Another common type of added temporal contingency is termed a *limited hold*. In this type of contingency, the opportunity for a response to produce reinforcement is present only for a given (usually short) amount of time, rather than indefinitely. Thus, if the individual does not respond within the limited-hold time period when the opportunity for reinforcement has been set up by the interval schedule, the opportunity to obtain that particular reinforcement is lost. The typical effect of adding a limited hold to an interval schedule is to increase the response rate (Ferster & Skinner, 1957, pp. 355–360).

Fixed- and Variable-Time Schedules

There are two types of schedules that are similar to FI and VI schedules, but should not be confused with them. These are fixed-time (FT) schedules, in which reinforcement occurs after a fixed period following the previous reinforcement, and variable-time (VT) schedules, in which reinforcement occurs after a variable period following the previous reinforcement independent of responding. Thus, FT and VT schedules are identical to FI and VI schedules except that no response is required in the former in order for reinforcement to occur. Since reinforcement is not contingent on any responses in an FT or a VT schedule, these schedules are called response-independent schedules.

Since no response is required for reinforcement in FT and VT schedules, it might seem odd that they would be included in a book on learning. These schedules can, however, produce superstitious behavior, as described on page 42, and other effects described in Chapter 15. In addition, they are often used as control conditions when studying the effects of response-contingent reinforcement.

Schedule Shaping

Responding can be maintained by infrequent reinforcement on all schedules provided that the value of the schedule has been increased—that is, that the rate of reinforcement has been decreased—gradually. This is another instance of the principle of small increments mentioned in Chapter 1. For example, if one were to introduce FR 100 immediately after FR 1 (continuous reinforcement), extinction would probably occur. If, however, the FR schedule is increased gradually by, say, steps of 5 or 10, with care being taken to give enough reinforcement at each step so that the behavior is not lost, responding can usually be maintained at FR 100. This procedure, called schedule shaping because of its resemblance to response shaping, is especially important in getting behavior to occur on high ratio schedules. It is not quite as crucial with interval schedules because they have a self-corrective feature. On an interval schedule, the lower the response rate, the higher the probability that the next response will be reinforced. For example, if the rate of responding is low enough, every response will be reinforced, which will generate a higher rate of responding. This self-corrective feature whereby a lowering of the response rate leads to an increase in the response rate is lacking in ratio schedules. Hence, behavior is much more easily lost on ratio than on interval schedules when the value of the schedule is increased too quickly.

Even with schedule shaping, there is a response-requirement level beyond which responding on a ratio schedule will not be maintained. Beyond this level pauses on a ratio schedule become extremely long and responding may eventually stop completely (Skinner, 1953, pp. 103–104). The occurrence of extremely long pauses on a ratio schedule due to a high response requirement is called ratio strain.

Human Responding on Reinforcement Schedules

A number of experiments have been conducted to determine whether humans show the same patterns of responding that other animals do when exposed to schedules of reinforcement. A common procedure in these experiments is to seat a human volunteer in front of a lever or key which may be pressed to produce points that can be exchanged for money, a lottery ticket, or some other reinforcing item. In some cases humans have produced cumulative response patterns that are indistinguishable from those produced by animals under the same types of reinforcement schedules. In many other cases, however, human cumulative records have not resembled those produced by animals. In particular, humans often do not show: (1) pauses after reinforcement on FR and FI schedules; (2) scallops on FI schedules; and (3) lower response rates on VI than on VR schedules; (4) reduced responding after long periods of extinction (see reviews by Baron & Galizio, 1983; Lowe, 1979; and Weiner, 1983). Moreover, humans also tend to be insensitive to changes in reinforcement schedules; that is, their responding may not change when the reinforcement schedule is changed (Cerutti, 1991; Harzem, Lowe, & Bagshaw, 1978; Hayes, Brownstein, Zettle, Rosenfarb, & Korn, 1986; Mathews et al., 1977; Shimoff, Catania, & Matthews, 1981).

One reason humans perform differently from other animals on reinforcement schedules in laboratory settings may have to do with previous reinforcements for following instructions. Because of past experience with reinforcement for following instructions, and punishment for not following them, the human subject may simply make the response requested of them (such as press a button) repeatedly at a constant rate, irrespective of the reinforcement schedule the experimenter has programmed. In addition, humans may make statements to themselves and respond to those statements rather than to the schedules in effect. Humans may tell themselves that, for example, the experimenter will be pleased if they respond at a high rate throughout the session (or displeased if they do not). This self-instruction may then act as a stimulus controlling a high rate (see next section on stimulus control) because the experimenter's approval is a reinforcer to them.

The major evidence that following verbal rules is the primary factor responsible for humans responding differently from animals on reinforcement schedules is that: (1) human infants, who have not yet learned to follow instructions, show schedule effects characteristic of other animals (Lowe, Beasty, & Bentall, 1983); (2) instructing an adult human to respond at a particular rate (e.g., telling him or her to press fast or press slow) produces the specified rate but the person will be insensitive to changes in the schedule (Baron, Kaufman, & Stauber, 1969; Buskist & Miller, 1986; Catania, Matthews, & Shimorr, 1982; Cerutti, 1991; Shimoff et al., 1981; Torgrud & Holborn, 1990); however, shaping a high or low rate of responding in a person tends to result in the same schedule effects and sensitivity to schedule changes other animals show (Catania et al., 1982; Shimoff et al., 1981); (3) shaping verbal behavior in adult humans (e.g., shaping the response "press fast" or "press slow") alters the individual's responding in the corresponding direction (i.e., fast or slow, respectively) even when this is not appropriate to the schedule in effect (Catania et al., 1982); and (4) describing the schedule in effect to the individual results in responding similar to that produced by animals (Kaufman, Baron, & Kopp, 1966).

There appear to be several ways to increase human sensitivity to the operative schedules of reinforcement in a laboratory experiment. One method is to focus instruction on some aspect of the task other than rate of responding, thus enabling schedule effects that are independent of instruction to occur. For example, the individual may be told that the task is to detect blips on a radar screen, and that a button must be pressed to make the blips visible. What the individual is not told, however, is that the blips are contingent on button pressing. Presenting the blips on basic schedules of reinforcement produces response patterns that resemble those produced by animals on those schedules (Holland, 1958).

Another method to increase sensitivity to the schedule of reinforcement, relative to sensitivity to verbal control, is to make the response aversive (i.e., punishing) or to increase its aversiveness. For example, the force required to operate the operandum may be increased (Azrin, 1958), a loss of points may be made contingent on each response (Weiner, 1962), or a response more complex than a simple lever or key press may be used (Azrin, 1958; Laties & Weiss, 1963).

Finally, experience that tends to counteract rules or self-generated instructions controlling a particular pattern or rate of responding may be provided. For example, the individual might be given prior exposure to schedules that develop high and low rate responding (Weiner, 1969, 1982). Alternatively, the individual might be given prior exposure to a number of schedules that produce a variety of response rates, with specific instructions appropriate to each schedule. If a test schedule then occurs without instruction on how to respond on it, the behavior that develops tends to be sensitive to the schedule of reinforcement (LeFrancois, Chase, & Joyce, 1988).

Although humans are often insensitive to reinforcement schedules under laboratory conditions when the response is pressing a lever, key, or button, humans typically are strongly affected by reinforcement schedules when reinforcement is contingent on socially significant behavior in more natural settings. The inadvertent scheduling of reinforcement (e.g., attention) has been implicated in the development and maintenance of much behavior that is troublesome or undesirable, and altering the prevailing reinforcement schedules or programming new ones has proven effective in developing socially desirable behavior and eliminating or reducing undesirable behavior in a wide variety of applied settings (see Martin & Pear, 1999).

STIMULUS GENERALIZATION AND DISCRIMINATION: TWO OPPOSING STIMULUS-CONTROL PROCESSES

Two opposing stimulus-control processes—stimulus generalization and discrimination—will be discussed in turn. It is important to understand both of these processes. One reason for understanding stimulus generalization is that learning to respond to a stimulus without it would be useless, because the exact same stimulus never occurs again. One reason to understand stimulus discrimination is that without it learning to respond to a specific stimulus or range of stimuli would be impossible. An individual would emit every response it had ever learned to every stimulus that occurred, regardless of the effectiveness or ineffectiveness of that response to that stimulus. Clearly, an animal that did not show stimulus generalization and stimulus discrimination would have little or no chance of surviving.

Stimulus Generalization

As mentioned in the previous chapter, stimulus generalization is the tendency for a response to occur to stimuli that are different from the stimulus to which it was trained. The phenomenon can be demonstrated with both respondent and operant conditioning. Suppose, for example, that a dog is respondently conditioned to salivate when touched at a particular point on its back. If a point close to that point is then touched the dog will salivate, but to a lesser extent. In general, the conditioned response is weaker the further the test point is from the point corresponding to the conditioned stimulus. The tendency for the strength of the response to decrease as the distance between the test stimulus and the conditioned stimulus increases is called a generalization gradient.

Generalization gradients are also obtained with operant behavior. Suppose, for example, that a pigeon is trained to peck on a VI schedule at a translucent plastic key. Behind the key is a bulb that illuminates the key with a colored light. The wavelength of the light is, let us say, 550 nanometers (nm)—which means that the color of the light (to the human eye) is yellow-green. If the behavior is now extinguished while different wavelengths of light—for example, 490 nm (blue-green), 530 nm (green), 590 nm (yellow), 610 nm (yellow-orange), 650 nm (orange-red), and the original training stimulus (550 nm, yellow-green)—are randomly projected a number of times on the key for 30 seconds each per presentation, the highest rate of responding will typically occur in the presence of the original training stimulus. As the difference between the wavelengths of the test stimuli and the training stimulus increases, the rate of responding generally decreases.

Figure 4.14 shows some generalization gradients obtained from six pigeons in the manner described above. The wavelength of the keylight during training was 550 nm for Birds 130 and 098, 570 nm for Birds 755 and 818, and 530 nm for Birds 951 and 6454. Three generalization tests, in the order indicated by the numbers on the curves, were conducted with each bird. Prior to the first generalization test the birds were reinforced on a VI schedule in the presence of the training stimulus. The use of this schedule ensured that each test stimulus could occur a number of times during generalization testing before responding had decreased substantially due to extinction. Prior to the second and third generalization tests the behavior was reconditioned on VI for two hours at the training wavelengths. There are several things to note about the generalization gradients in Figure 4.14. First, and most important, note that the peak of each gradient usually occurs at the wavelength of the training stimulus. Second, note that the shapes of the gradients are usually not symmetrical. This, however, should not be surprising. The wavelength scale is used by convention, and some other arbitrary scale (e.g., frequency) would yield a different set of shapes. Third, note that although the three gradients produced by each bird are quite similar, they differ markedly from the gradients of the other bird trained at the same wavelength. Clearly, even at a given training wavelength, there is no

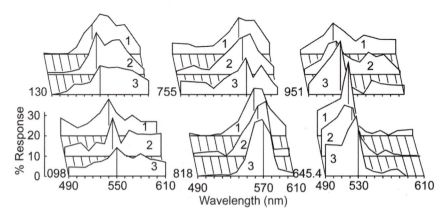

FIGURE 4.14. Successive generalization gradients of three wavelengths-of-light from each of six pigeons. Two birds were trained on a stimulus of 550 nm, two on a stimulus of 570 nm, and two on a stimulus of 530 nm. Reinforcement on VI 9 minutes occurred before each generalization test. (From Blough, 1961)

one curve that could be called the "generalization gradient" for all birds. Fourth, note that the training wavelength also seems to contribute to the shape of the gradient. The gradients centered at 530 nm are high on the left; those centered at 550 nm are high on the right; and those centered at 570 nm tend to be more rounded and symmetrical.

Stimulus Discrimination

Stimulus discrimination is the tendency for a response that has been conditioned to a particular stimulus *not* to occur to other stimuli. It is demonstrated whenever the amount of responding occurring to the training stimulus is greater than that occurring to some other stimulus. That is, stimulus discrimination is the opposite of stimulus generalization. There are procedures for establishing or enhancing stimulus discrimination in both respondent and operant conditioning.

Respondent stimulus discrimination. In respondent conditioning the standard procedure for establishing (or enhancing) a discrimination is to randomly alternate the conditioned stimulus with a stimulus that is not paired with the unconditioned stimulus. For example, touching one point on a dog's back might be randomly alternated with touching another point on the dog's back, with food being presented after the first point is touched and not after the second point is touched. In referring to this type of procedure the first stimulus is often abbreviated CS+ and the second stimulus CS–. The result of the procedure is that the conditioned response occurs to the CS+ and not to the CS–. In addition, the CS– will decrease the response to the CS+ if it occurs at the same time as the CS+. For this reason a CS– is said to be an inhibitory stimulus. The CS+ is called an excitatory stimulus to indicate that it has the opposite effect as an inhibitory stimulus. A stimulus that has been established as an inhibitory stimulus for one excitatory stimulus will also inhibit responding to another excitatory stimulus (Rescorla, 1981, p. 249). The reduction of responding to an excitatory stimulus by an inhibitory stimulus is called conditioned inhibition.

We alluded to conditioned inhibition when referring to trace conditioning and backward conditioning earlier in this chapter. Note that in both of these cases, the conditioned stimulus precedes a period in which the unconditioned stimulus does not occur. This causes the conditioned stimulus to act at least a little like a CS–, which explains why these types of conditioning are less effective than delay conditioning (although, as mentioned, there may be other explanations as well).

Establishing a respondent stimulus discrimination provides evidence that what appears to be respondent conditioning is indeed respondent conditioning, rather than sensitization. If the apparent conditioning was due to sensitization, then we would expect the CS– to be just as likely as the CS+ to elicit the apparent conditioned response. To conclusively rule out sensitization, researchers often counterbalance the CS+ and CS–; that is, they make one of the two stimuli the CS+ for half the individuals in an experiment and the other stimulus the CS+ for the other half of the individuals. Then, if the apparent conditioned response always occurs to the CS+ and seldom to the CS–, regardless of which particular stimulus is the CS+ or the CS–, the researcher can confidently conclude that the result is due to conditioning rather than sensitization.

Operant stimulus discrimination. In operant conditioning, as in respondent conditioning, the standard procedure for establishing a discrimination, called discrimination training, involves alternating two stimuli. In the presence of one of these two stimuli responding is reinforced on some schedule while in the presence of the other responding is not reinforced.

For example, in an experiment with pigeons, key pecking might be reinforced on a VI schedule when the keylight is red and extinguished when the keylight is green. The result is that the pigeon will show the characteristic VI pattern of responding when the keylight is red and respond little or not at all when the keylight is green. The stimulus in the presence of which responding is reinforced is called a discriminative stimulus for responding; the stimulus in the presence of which responding is extinguished is sometimes called a discriminative stimulus for not responding. The discriminative stimulus for responding and for not responding are often abbreviated S^D and S^Δ, respectively (as seen in Chapter 3). They are also commonly abbreviated S+ and S–. Both sets of abbreviations will be used in this book.

Responding to a CS+ or to an S^D increases over what responding to it was prior to discrimination training. For example, a CS+ that has been paired with food will elicit more salivation in a dog than the conditioned stimulus did prior to the introduction of the CS–. Pavlov (1927) called this phenomenon "induction," but the term behavioral contrast has become the standard label for it. Behavioral contrast of operant behavior is discussed in Chapter 8.

Training an operant discrimination has an interesting effect on the generalization gradient. Figure 4.15 shows some generalization gradients obtained from four pigeons after operant discrimination training. Each bird received daily sessions in which key pecking was reinforced on a VI 1 schedule when the key was transilluminated with a wavelength of 580 mμ and extinguished when the key was transilluminated with a wavelength of 560 mμ. As seen in the figure, four generalization tests were conducted with each bird. The first test occurred after the fifteenth discrimination session; each of the other generalization tests occurred after fifteen additional discrimination sessions were conducted following the previous generalization test. No reinforcement occurred during the generalization tests.

There are several points to note in Figure 4.15. First, note that responding in the presence of the S– (or S^Δ) decreased to zero as discrimination training increased (i.e., over succes-

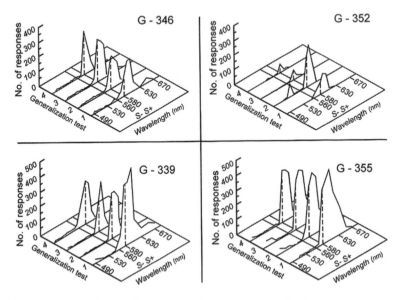

FIGURE 4.15. Prior to each generalization test, the same pigeons (with key pecking reinforced on a variable-interval schedule) received discrimination training in which the S^Δ was 580 mm and the S^Δ was 560 mm. The first generalization test occurred after the 15th discrimination session, and the remaining generalization tests were each separated by 15 discrimination sessions. (From Terrace, 1966a)

sive generalization tests). Second, note that in the first generalization test the peak of the gradient was not at the S+ (or S^D), but was shifted to the side of the S+ away from the S−. This phenomenon is known as the peak shift. Third, note that as discrimination training increased, the peak shift gradually disappeared. The reason for the peak shift and its disappearance with extended discrimination training is, at present, unclear.

While the peak shift has been studied extensively with operant behavior, it has hardly been studied at all with respondent behavior. There is evidence, however, that it does not occur with respondent behavior (Weiss & Dacanay, 1982).

Conceptual Stimuli and Conceptual Behavior

In many examples of stimulus discrimination, the stimuli considered are simple physical properties, that is, properties that can be measured with simple physical instruments. For example, color can be measured by a spectrometer as wavelengths of light, brightness by a photometer as number of photons emitted, force by a strain gauge as amount of pressure applied, and the angle of one line relative to another by a protractor. Discriminations also occur between stimuli that cannot be specified by such simple physical procedures. For example, pigeons readily learn to discriminate between slides that contain a human and those that do not (Edwards & Honig, 1987; Herrnstein, 1979; Herrnstein & Loveland, 1964; Siegel & Honig, 1970), that contain human-made objects and those that do not (Lubow, 1974), that contain a specific person and those that do not (Herrnstein, Loveland, & Cable, 1976), that contain a tree and those that do not (Vaughan & Herrnstein, 1987), and that contain fish and those that do not (Herrnstein & deVilliers, 1980). The proof that the birds learn these discriminations, rather than discriminations between simpler physical stimuli in the slides, is that they continue to discriminate appropriately—with little decrease in accuracy—when presented with new slides containing different scenes in which the discriminated items appear quite different from their appearance in the original slides.

Stimuli that can be described as a category—such as humans, human-made objects, trees, and fish—that cannot be measured by simple physical instruments are called conceptual stimuli or concepts. Discriminating between such stimuli is called conceptual behavior, and developing this type of discrimination is called concept formation.

Concepts are not restricted to categories of similar objects. We have already indicated that a specific person in different clothes, in different poses, and in different situations is a concept. We may also think of a single object or many objects together in a scene as a concept because (1) viewing the object or objects in a scene from different orientations presents different physical stimuli to the eye, and (2) the individual learns to discriminate the presence or absence of that object or objects regardless of orientation. For example, pigeons trained to discriminate between slides of an outdoor location and another location—where each set of slides is taken at different orientations—readily learn the discrimination and continue to discriminate that location from other locations (with very few errors) when presented with new slides taken at different orientations from the slides on which discrimination training occurred (Honig & Stewart, 1988; Kendrick, 1992; Wilkie, Wilson, & Kardal, 1989). Similarly, pigeons discriminate between different computer-simulated three-dimensional geometrical figures when rotated into new orientations (Cook & Katz, 1999).

Another example of a concept that does not consist of a collection of similar objects is number, where the number of objects (but not the specific objects themselves, their arrangement, their combined size, etc.) is the basis for the discrimination. Pigeons, for example, readily learn to discriminate between displays containing 16 and 20 elements and between displays containing 2 and 7 elements, and can sometimes and with more difficulty be taught to discriminate between displays containing 4 and 5 elements (Honig, 1993; Honig & Stewart, 1989). It should be noted that there is no question of the animals counting the elements in order to make the discrimination because, as discussed later in this book, counting is a complex skill that requires special training. Humans also discriminate on the basis of number, without counting, when number stimuli occur too briefly and the discriminative responses occur too rapidly for counting to have occurred (e.g., Klahr, 1973).

It is important to stress that concept formation generally requires discrimination training on more than one instance or exemplar of the concept. If training is given on only one exemplar (e.g., if only one location is used for either the S^D or S^Δ in training an operant location discrimination), the discrimination will likely be based on some simple physical difference rather than the abstract difference that constitutes the concept.

Configural Stimuli

During either operant or respondent conditioning, two stimuli may occur together in what is called a compound stimulus. For example, a tone and a light presented together comprise a compound stimulus consisting of two elements: a tone and a light. Similarly, a red triangle on a green background comprise a compound stimulus; likewise, a tone, a clicker, and a light presented together comprise a compound stimulus.

It is possible to train a discrimination between a compound stimulus and its elements. For example, if we call the elements of a two-element compound stimulus A and B, and the compound stimulus AB, we can readily establish A and B each as an S^D or a CS+ and the compound AB as an S^Δ or a CS–. This is called positive patterning. Conversely, in what is called negative patterning, we can condition the elements each as an S^Δ or a CS– and the compound as an S^D or a CS+ (Rescorla, 1972; Whitlow & Wagner, 1972). Thus the elements together of a compound stimulus may constitute a unique stimulus. When it gains control over a response apart from its elements, we call this unique stimulus a configural stimulus.

RESPONSE GENERALIZATION

We have said that reinforcing a response increases the probability of that response being emitted again. However, the response will not be exactly the same each time it occurs; instead, it may vary along several dimensions. It may vary, for example in:

- magnitude or intensity; for example, the amount of force with which a animal presses down on a lever;
- location; for example, the place where the response occurs, or the position on the operandum at which the response occurs; and
- spatial configuration or topography; for example, pressing a lever with the left paw or snout is a different topography from pressing it with the right paw.

The extent to which successive instances of a response differ is termed response variability, while its opposite—the extent to which they are the same—is termed response stereotypy.

Note that response variability is analogous to stimulus generalization in this respect: with stimulus generalization, we are concerned with the same response occurring when the stimulus varies, whereas with response variability we are concerned with the response varying while the stimulus (or situation) remains constant.

For this reason, another name for response variability is response generalization, and another name for response stereotypy is response discrimination. Thus, response generalization is the tendency for a response other than the conditioned response to occur to the conditioned stimulus or S^D; and response discrimination is the tendency for only the conditioned response to occur to the conditioned stimulus or S^D.

In general, a response becomes less variable (i.e., more stereotyped) the more times it is reinforced. However, both stereotypy and variability can be increased by differentially reinforcing them—reinforcing instances that meet some criterion of stereotypy or variability, while not reinforcing instances that fail to meet that criterion.

For example, if only lever presses with a downward force of between 5 and 10 grams are reinforced, instances of the response will tend to concentrate in that range and hence be more stereotyped than would likely be the case if lever presses with a wider range of forces were reinforced.

Conversely, only reinforcing instances that differ from previous instances of the response increases response variability. In a particularly impressive demonstration of this, porpoises can be conditioned to emit strikingly novel behavior by reinforcing a response in a given session. Porpoises exposed to this procedure eventually begin emitting a wide variety of responses, such as aerial flips, gliding with the tail out of the water, skidding on the floor of the tank, and lying part way out of the water in front of the trainer (Pryor et al., 1969). Similarly, pigeons will come to emit highly variable sequences of pecks on right and left response keys if reinforcement occurs only after sequences of eight pecks on the two keys that differ from any of the previous 50 sequences of eight key pecks (Page & Neuringer, 1985). As a final example, pigeons will learn to increase the variability in the time that elapses between consecutive responses—which probably corresponds to increased variability in the movements between consecutive responses—when reinforcement is contingent on increased variability in the time between consecutive responses (Machado, 1989). Response variability may also come under stimulus control; that is, if an individuals received reinforcement for varying responses in the presence of one stimulus and not in the presence of another, that individual will emit more varied responses in the presence of the former stimulus than in the presence of the latter stimulus (Denney & Neuringer, 1998).

There are important practical implications to the fact that reinforcement can strengthen response variability and bring it under stimulus control. Response variability is often necessary for creativity and problem solving. Bringing it under appropriate stimulus control is, therefore a worthy educational objective. Consequently, learning scientists have researched and developed techniques involving reinforcing response variability to, for example, establish creative play by children (Holman et al., 1977) and reduce behavioral stereotypy by autistic individuals (Miller & Neuringer, 2000).

STIMULUS-STIMULUS AND RESPONSE-RESPONSE INTERACTIONS

The effect of a conditioned or discriminative stimulus may be altered by another stimulus that occurs at the same time. This is called a stimulus-stimulus interaction. Similarly, a response may be altered if there is a tendency for another response to occur at the same time. This is called a response-response interaction.

Stimulus-Stimulus Interactions

Stimulus summation.   If two stimuli that each elicit or evoke the same response (i.e., each stimulus is a conditioned stimulus or an S^D for that response) occur together, the response will tend to be greater or occur at a higher rate than if either stimulus occurs separately (Butter, 1963; Miller & Ackley, 1970; Panlilio, Weiss, & Schindler, 1998; Weiss, 1967; Wolf, 1963), although there are exceptions (Lawson, Mattis, & Pear, 1968; Weiss, 1967). This is called summation of excitation. If two stimuli that inhibit the same response (i.e., each stimulus is a CS– or an S^Δ for that response) occur together, the response will tend to be less or occur at a lower rate than if either stimulus occurs separately (Blough, 1975). This is called summation of inhibition.

Stimulus summation is algebraic—that is, it may be subtractive as well as additive. Thus if a stimulus that elicits or evokes a response occurs in combination with a stimulus that controls the nonoccurrence of that response, the response will be less than it is to the former stimulus alone but greater than it is to the latter alone (Reberg & Black, 1969).

Stimulus-stimulus interference. We have seen that during either operant or respondent conditioning, two stimuli may occur together in what is called a compound stimulus. For example, a tone and light presented together are a compound stimulus consisting of two elements, tone and light, while a red triangle on a green background is a compound stimulus consisting of the elements red triangle and green background. We have also seen that we may condition a discrimination between a compound stimulus and its elements. Suppose, however, that we do not condition a discrimination between the compound and its elements, but simply present the compound followed by an unconditioned stimulus or reinforce a response in the presence of the compound. If a response is conditioned to a compound stimulus, but not the elements separately, both stimulus elements may gain control over the response—as can be demonstrated by testing the two elements separately. Under certain conditions, however, only one element in a compound may gain control over a response even though the second element would have gained control over the response if the other element had not been present. In other words, we may say that one element preempts control from the other.

Overshadowing and blocking. If an element preempts control from another element without any special procedure being carried out to cause this to happen, we say that the former element overshadows the latter. We also may cause a stimulus to preempt control from another stimulus in two ways: (1) conditioning a response to the former stimulus before conditioning the response to the compound consisting of the two stimuli; and (2) making the former stimulus more predictive of the unconditioned stimulus or the reinforcer than the latter stimulus. After the response is then conditioned to the compound, testing the two elements separately will show that the one that was not conditioned prior to conditioning trials with the compound or the one that is less predictive of the unconditioned stimulus or reinforcer will not control the response. This is called blocking, and the stimulus element that preempts control from the other stimulus element in the compound is said to block the that element (Kamin, 1968, 1969; vom Saal & Jenkins, 1970). Thus, blocking is the tendency for one element of a stimulus compound to prevent control of responding by another element of the compound due to conditioning of a response to the aforementioned element.

Interference by context stimuli. A phenomenon called the unconditioned-stimulus-preexposure effect may be a special case of blocking. If the unconditioned stimulus occurs a number of times in the experimental situation prior to conditioning it will retard conditioning (Randich & LoLordo, 1979; Rescorla & Wagner, 1972). What may cause this effect is that stimuli in the experimental situation, called context stimuli, become conditioned stimuli as a result of pairing with the unconditioned stimulus. These context stimuli then form a compound with the conditioned stimulus when it is presented during conditioning trials, and block it because of their prior pairing with the unconditioned stimulus (Rescorla & Wagner, 1972; Wagner, 1981; for an alternative account, see Miller & Matzel, 1988). Because of this theoretical explanation, another name for the unconditioned-stimulus-preexposure effect is context blocking.

Response-Response Interference

It is a fundamental property of the nervous system that the activation of some groups of neurons inhibits other groups. This phenomenon, called reciprocal inhibition, operates throughout all levels of the nervous system (Sherrington, 1906/1961). A particularly clear example of reciprocal inhibition is the relaxing of an extensor muscle that occurs when the antagonistic flexor muscle contracts and vice versa, as when one flexes or extends one's arm. In learning, reciprocal inhibition is manifested in the interference of one learned response by another.

In should be noted that in our discussion of response interference, we are using the term "response" very broadly. Responses that interfere with each other may be skeletal muscle responses, as when a person covers his or her own mouth to keep from laughing out loud. Responses may also interfere at the level of the nervous system before any overt response is manifested (see definition of behavior on p. 12). Thus, in discussing response interference we are not necessarily concerned with the locus of the interference.

Responses interfere most strongly with each other if they are incompatible—that is, if they physically cannot occur at the same time. For example, one cannot turn right and turn left at the same time, so the responses of turning in opposite directions are incompatible. Inadvertently turning in the direction of one's former place of employment when going to work after having just changed jobs is a familiar example of response-response interference, in which a more strongly conditioned response interferes with a less strongly conditioned response with which it is incompatible.

The concept of response-response interference is important for understanding several behavioral phenomena that might superficially seem to have little in common as discussed below.

Counterconditioning. Both respondent and operant extinction take time and may not completely eliminate the response. The elicitation or emission of a given response may decrease more quickly and to a lower level if, at the same time it is being extinguished, conditioning of a response that is incompatible with it occurs. This is called counterconditioning.

Everyone has experienced examples of respondent counterconditioning. One familiar example is that of someone who is anxious in an airplane. That is, the stimuli in the plane elicit in this person an emotional response of anxiety. Given enough uneventful air trips, this emotional response should eventually decrease to zero due to extinction. It will probably decrease more quickly, however, if the stimuli in the plane are paired with good-tasting food, relaxing music, a pleasant conversation, stimuli that have previously been paired with an enjoyable vacation, and other stimuli that elicit positive emotional responses. By being paired with these stimuli, the stimuli in the plane come to elicit positive emotional responses, and these responses tend to interfere with the elicitation of anxiety by the stimuli in the plane. As the novice flyer takes more and more air trips in which stimuli in the plane are not paired with anxiety and are paired with stimuli that elicit positive emotions, the anxiety elicited will become weak enough and the positive emotions elicited strong enough that the latter will completely counteract or overpower the former.

Respondent counterconditioning is used in several behavior therapy procedures. For example, in a procedure called systematic desensitization, which is designed to rid clients of irrational fears and anxieties, the therapist presents anxiety-eliciting stimuli to clients who have been trained to relax their muscles during these stimuli. The reasoning here is that relaxation will become conditioned to the anxiety-eliciting stimuli and interfere with anxiety, because it is impossible to be both anxious and relaxed at the same time. Usually, at least in the initial stages of therapy, the stimuli are private ("mental") images that the client produces, although pictures, video presentations, or real objects or events may also be used. The fear-eliciting stimulus items are arranged from those that elicit the least fear to those that elicit the most (e.g., if the irrational fear is one of heights, the items might be ordered from looking out a first-floor window to leaning over a guard rail on the roof of a skyscraper), and the therapist presents the more intense fear-eliciting stimuli only after having counterconditioned the less intense fear-eliciting stimuli (Wolpe, 1958, 1990, 1995).

Although perhaps the most common, relaxation is not the only behavior used by behavior therapists to inhibit maladaptive respondent behavior. Controlled anger is used in assertiveness training to reduce anxiety involved in standing up for one's rights, sexual arousal is used to overcome anxiety in sexual situations, and verbally elicited pleasant emotions are used to inhibit various other types of maladaptive fear responses (Wolpe, 1995).

Operant counterconditioning likewise is more effective than simple extinction. An operant response that is undergoing extinction or punishment will decrease in frequency more rapidly if an incompatible operant response is reinforced (Azrin, Hake, Holz, & Hutchinson, 1965; Martin & Pear, 1999). Operant response interference is a major component of a treatment called habit reversal, in which the client practices responses that interfere with maladaptive habits, such as depressing one's shoulders while keeping arms close to the body to interfere with shoulder jerking (Azrin & Nunn, 1973, 1977; Azrin, Nunn, & Frantz, 1980).

Retardation of conditioning.   If a response has been conditioned to a given stimulus, conditioning a new response to that stimulus—that is, counterconditioning, as discussed above—may take longer or occur at a lower level than if the original response had not been conditioned to the stimulus. This can occur even when the two responses are not physically incompatible. For example, the blink response (elicited by shock near the orbit of the eye) in rabbits and the jaw-movement response (elicited by water injected into the mouth) are not physically incompatible responses. Nevertheless, conditioning the former will interfere with later conditioning of the latter (Dearing & Dickinson, 1979). In this case, the interference may be due to the two unconditioned stimuli having opposite reinforcement (i.e., motivational) signs; one is a positive reinforcer while the other is an aversive stimulus.

Forgetting.   The word "forgetting" in common, everyday speech (as opposed to behavioral terminology, as used in this book) refers to the temporary unavailability of a response despite the fact that it had been conditioned and has not been extinguished, and its establishing operation is in effect. One reason a response might be unavailable despite these circumstances is that it is being interfered with by another response or responses (Osgood, 1946, 1949; Watkins, 1979). Called response-response interference, this phenomenon is common with verbal responses because there are so many of them and so much overlap in their physical means of production (e.g., the larynx, its associated muscles and nerves, the speech areas of the brain).

Two types of response-response interference that result in forgetting are proactive interference and retroactive interference. In the former, a newly learned response is interfered with by a previously learned response; in the latter, a previously learned response is interfered with by a newly learned response. Thus, when trying to recall the name of either a new or an old acquaintance, many more recently or less recently learned names may "come to mind"— that is, may tend to be emitted, either privately or overtly. The tendency to emit these other names interferes with the name to be recalled, even though that name may be perfectly well conditioned (i.e., learned). Responses that are elicited or evoked by similar stimuli, or by stimuli that have often occurred together, tend to interfere strongly with each other. For example, if two people look alike or are often seen together, we may tend to say the name of one when seeing the other, and thus tend not to "recall" the name of either. Names, or other words that sound similar, may also tend to interfere with each other and thus may be difficult to remember. This is because the similar sound in both names is a stimulus that tends to evoke the rest of both names.

Although forgetting due to response-response interference seems to be most common with verbal responses, it occurs with nonverbal responses as well. For example, when stimuli similar to those of falling forward occur while skiing, one prevents falling by leaning forward. This is exactly the opposite of what one does to prevent falling when those stimuli occur when one is not on skis. When just starting a ski run after having been off skis for a long time, however, the infrequent skier may fall because of "forgetting" to lean forward—that is, because of leaning backwards.

Various formal and informal systems, called mnemonic techniques, have been developed to prevent forgetting (Bellezza, 1987). Essentially, these techniques involve bringing a response to be remembered under the control of distinctive stimulus that will evoke the desired responses without evoking interfering responses. For example, you might remember the name of a Mr. Bush by attending to some distinctive facial feature that he has, such as bushy eyebrows, and imagining the feature sprouting into a bush. The chances will then be good that the next time you see Mr. Bush this facial feature will elicit an image of a bush that will evoke the verbal response "Mr. Bush."

It should be noted that response-response interference is not the only possible reason for what is commonly called forgetting. A conditioned response may be unavailable because the stimuli necessary to elicit or evoke it are not present, because of neurological damage, or because of a combination of factors. We explore the complex topic of memory in greater detail in Chapter 10.

Blends.   Occasionally, two mutually interfering responses may combine in a sort of hybrid called a blend (Skinner, 1957a, pp. 294–299). For example, the word "smog" probably first occurred when the words "smoke" and "fog" both tended to be evoked at the same time in someone. Of course, now that "smog" has become part of the English language, it probably never occurs for that reason again.

Attending.   In Chapter 3 we noted that habituation of attending may explain the phenomenon of latent inhibition, whereby a neutral stimulus that has occurred repeatedly prior to conditioning requires more conditioning trials to become a conditioned stimulus than a neutral stimulus that has not occurred prior to conditioning. Weak or absent attending responses may also partially explain overshadowing and blocking (discussed above), although in these cases the attending response to one stimulus would be weak because it was being interfered with by attending response to another stimulus.

That is, response-response interference may partially account for stimulus-stimulus interference in the following way. Suppose that a stimulus can only become a conditioned stimulus or a discriminative stimulus if that stimulus is first attended to. In other words, in order for a stimulus to become a conditioned stimulus or a discriminative stimulus, that stimulus must first elicit or evoke attending responses. Now if one element in a compound stimulus elicits strong attending responses, those attending responses may interfere with the attending responses elicited by the other elements in the compound. In this interpretation, overshadowing and blocking may be due partly to the failure of conditioning to occur to one element of a compound stimulus because that element's attending responses are being interfered with by those elicited or evoked by another element.

This cannot be the full explanation, however, because overshadowing and blocking can be reduced *after* they have occurred. There are at least two ways to do this. One is to extinguish the conditioned response to the overshadowing or blocking element (Kaufman & Bolles, 1981; Matzel, Schachtman, & Miller, 1985). The other is to condition a new response to the overshadowed or blocked element (Blaisdell, Denniston, Savastano, & Miller, 2000). The fact that these procedures work after the original conditioning has occurred indicates that overshadowing or blocking cannot have been entirely due to lack to attending to the blocked or overshadowed element at the time of conditioning.

Resurgence.   If, after a response has been conditioned and extinguished, another response is conditioned, the first response may reappear if the second response is then extinguished (Hilgard & Marquis, 1935; Pittenger & Pavlik, 1989; Rashoutte & Amsel, 1968; Schreurs, 1993, 1998). This phenomenon, which is called resurgence (Epstein, 1983, 1985), may result from response interference in the following way. Normally the first response would show spontaneous recovery after being extinguished; however, it was prevented from doing so by interference from the second response. This interference is removed when the second response is extinguished, and hence the resurgence of the first response is the spontaneous recovery that would have been seen if the second response had not been conditioned.

SUMMARY AND CONCLUSIONS

Respondent and operant conditioning are the major learning processes for animals with complex nervous systems. The defining difference between respondent and operant conditioning is that the former is produced by the pairing of two stimuli (called a conditioned stimulus and an unconditioned stimulus) whereas the latter is produced by the pairing of a response with an event called reinforcement (which is either the presentation of a stimulus called a positive reinforcer or the removal of a stimulus called a negative reinforcer). The result of respondent conditioning is that the conditioned stimulus comes to elicit a new response (generally similar to the one elicited by the unconditioned stimulus) while the result of operant conditioning is that the response paired with reinforcement occurs more frequently or with a higher probability.

The most effective respondent conditioning procedure is simultaneous conditioning, which consists of the conditioned stimulus occurring slightly before the unconditioned stimulus and overlapping with it. The least effective respondent conditioning procedure is backward conditioning, in which the unconditioned stimulus precedes the conditioned stimulus. Trace conditioning, in which the conditioned stimulus terminates some time before the unconditioned stimulus occurs, is moderately effective.

If, after either respondent or operant conditioning has taken place, the conditioned stimulus occurs repeatedly without being followed by the unconditioned stimulus or the operantly conditioned response occurs repeatedly without being followed by reinforcement, the probability of the conditioned response will decrease to the level it was at before being conditioned. This process is called extinction. If, after extinction has taken place, a stimulus or set of stimuli that were present during extinction reoccur after being absent for a period of time, the probability of the conditioned response will increase. This is called spontaneous recovery.

Maintenance of the conditioned response does not require that all occurrences of the conditioned stimulus be followed by the unconditioned stimulus or that all occurrences of the operantly conditioned response be followed by reinforcement. Following some (but less than 100%) of the occurrences of a conditioned stimulus with the unconditioned stimulus of some (but less than 100%) of the occurrences of an operant response with reinforcement is called partial reinforcement, as opposed to continuous reinforcement in which the unconditioned stimulus follows *all* occurrences of the conditioned stimulus or reinforcement follows *all* occurrences of an operant response. In some cases responding persists longer during extinction after partial reinforcement than after continuous responding. This phenomenon, which is called the partial reinforcement extinction effect (PREE), is common with free-operant behavior—that is, operant responding in which there are no restrictions on when a response can occur—and much less common with respondent behavior and discrete-trials operant behavior. The PREE seems to result from the similarity between extinction and partial reinforcement and stimulus generalization, which is the tendency to respond similarly in similar situations. There seems to be a direct relationship between number of conditioned stimulus-unconditioned stimulus pairings or number of reinforcements and response strength, which tends to override the PREE and thus accounts for the fact that it is sometimes weak or absent.

A schedule of reinforcement is a rule determining which instances of an operant response will be reinforced. Schedules of reinforcement may be based on quantity of behavior (e.g., number of responses) or on time (e.g., time since the previous reinforcement), or both. The basic quantity-based schedules are fixed ratio and variable ratio, in which reinforcement is contingent on a fixed or variable, respectively, number of responses following the previous reinforcement. The basic time-based schedules are fixed interval and variable interval, in which reinforcement is contingent on the first response after a fixed or variable, respectively, time interval following the previous reinforcement. Each schedule of reinforcement produces its own characteristic pattern of responding. Ratio schedules produce higher rates than interval schedules; fixed schedules produce pauses (i.e., periods of no responding) after reinforcement whereas rate of responding tends to be constant throughout on variable schedules.

Respondent behavior is elicited by stimuli. Operant behavior is not elicited in the same sense, and we say that it is evoked (rather than elicited) by stimuli in the presence of which it has been reinforced. We also say that operant behavior is emitted by an animal as opposed to being elicited by stimuli. Control by eliciting (in the case of respondent behavior) or evoking (in the case of operant behavior) stimuli can be sharpened by randomly alternating two stimuli, one that precedes the unconditioned stimulus and one that does not (in the case of respondent conditioning), or one in the presence of which responding is reinforced and one in the presence of which it is not (in the case of operant conditioning). This is called developing a discrimination, and the differential responding that results from this is called a discrimination. In a respondent discrimination the eliciting stimulus is called a CS+ and the stimulus that alternates with it is called a CS–, while in operant conditioning the evoking stimulus is called an S^D (discriminative stimulus) or an S+ and the stimulus that alternates with it is called an S^Δ or S–. Stimuli that elicit or evoke responses are called controlling stimuli.

While stimulus generalization is the tendency for a given response to occur in the presence of stimuli similar to its controlling stimulus, response generalization is the tendency for responses similar to a given response to occur as a result of the conditioning of that response. Stimulus and response generalization are involved in conceptual behavior, various instances of creativity, and both verbal and nonverbal remembering and forgetting. A stimulus generalization gradient is a graph showing how response probability or rate varies as a function of the similarity of a given stimulus with the training stimulus. The shape of a generalization gradient is affected by discrimination training; in particular, the peak of the generalization gradient is shifted away from the stimulus that is paired with nonreinforcement.

5

Derivatives of
Associative Learning

*I*n any science it is desirable to have as few basic terms as possible. In the previous chapters we covered the basic concepts and processes of the two major types of associative learning: respondent and operant conditioning. Other types of associative learning appear to be derivatives of these two basic types. In this chapter we cover some of these derivatives, and indicate how they are reducible to respondent and operant conditioning. By showing how the basic concepts of respondent and operant conditioning form the building blocks, so to speak, of various other concepts, we restrict the number of fundamental phenomena that our science must deal with and thereby (among other things) make it more manageable.

LATENT LEARNING

Early in the history of the experimental study of learning a lively controversy raged over whether or not reinforcement was necessary for the occurrence of operant learning (or instrumental learning, as it was more commonly called). A number of experiments attempted to settle this controversy by showing the existence of a phenomenon called latent learning—that is, learning in the absence of reinforcement (Mackintosh, 1974, pp. 207–211). Typically, these experiments tested the learning by rats of the path from the start box to the goal box in various experimental mazes. Two types of simple mazes—a T-maze and a runway—used in this research are shown in Chapter 4 (Figure 4.1).

Two groups of rats were generally used in a latent learning experiment. Rats in one group, called the "latent-learning group," were first given exposure to the maze. That is, each rat in this group was placed in the start box on a number of occasions and allowed to wander through the maze. The goal box, however, was empty so that presumably there would be no reinforcement during these trials. Rats in the other group, the "reinforcement-only" group, were not given this preliminary exposure to the maze. Then both groups were deprived of food for a number of hours and given trials in the maze with food in the goal box. Often the latent-learning group learned to traverse the maze from start box to goal box more rapidly, and with fewer errors, than did the reinforcement-only group. In order for the latent-learning group to show significantly faster learning in the trials on which food was available in the goal box that group must have learned something about the maze on the trials in which food (and hence reinforcement) was absent.

One problem with many of these studies is that they neglected to control for the possibility that preliminary exposure to the maze may have habituated startle or other "fear-type" responses to the maze in that group. If this were the case, the latent-learning group would have an advantage over the reinforcement-only group in learning the maze simply because the maze was less likely to elicit responses in the latent-learning group that would interfere with learning the maze (Mackintosh, 1974, p. 208). There is, however, a more serious problem with these studies. The fact that there was no food or other obvious reinforcer in the maze when the latent-learning group was first exposed to it does not mean that reinforcers were completely absent. It is difficult, to say the least, to see how all possible reinforcers can be completely eliminated from any situation in which an animal's behavior produces consequences. One may keep obvious reinforcers such as food out of a situation, but less obvious reinforcers will always be present.

For example, merely changing the surroundings can be at least weakly reinforcing. This is clear from the fact that a rat in a dark chamber can be operantly conditioned to press a lever by following lever presses with brief presentations of light (Kish, 1966). This reinforcer is quite weak in that it will not maintain the behavior at a high rate nor for very long; however, the important point is that such reinforcers do exist. Moreover, it appears that the stimuli resulting from exploring or patrolling a maze are reinforcing (Cowan, 1977, 1983; Wilkie, Mumby, Needham, & Smeele, 1992). To see how such reinforcers can account for latent learning, consider an experiment involving a T-maze. On a latent-learning trial the rat is placed in the start box, moves down the main alley, and turns toward and enters, let us say, the right goal box. Since, by assumption, the stimuli in the right goal box are somewhat reinforcing, the behavior of turning toward and entering that goal box will be slightly reinforced. This does not necessarily mean that the rat will go directly to the right box on the very next trial. There are a number of reasons that an animal might not immediately go back to a goal box in which it has just received reinforcement. One possible reason in this case might be that the rat has been temporarily satiated on the reinforcers in that goal box, thus weakening their effectiveness relative to other reinforcers in the maze (just as satiation on food reduces its reinforcing effectiveness). On the next trial, therefore, the rat might go to the left goal box and encounter weakly reinforcing stimuli there. Eventually, over trials, the rat will have sampled both the right and left goal boxes a number of times, although it may have developed a "preference" for one of the boxes—that is, it may go to that goal box more times than to the other box—because, for some reason, the stimuli in that goal box are at least somewhat more reinforcing than the stimuli in the other box.

Now suppose that the rat is deprived of food for a period of time and then food is placed in, say, the right goal box. Because the response of entering each goal box has been previously reinforced (albeit weakly) on a number of occasions, the response of entering the right goal box has been previously reinforced. It is therefore not because of latent learning—that is, learning without reinforcement—that the probability of turning toward and entering the right goal box upon the introduction of the food increases more rapidly than it would have without the latent-learning phase. The effect of putting food in the goal box on the right is simply that of adding a strong reinforcer to the weak reinforcers already present in the situation. It is known that increasing the amount of reinforcement in a situation (e.g., increasing the number of food pellets in the goal box from one to four) can quite suddenly and dramatically increase the probability of the operantly conditioned behavior. (We discuss this phenomenon in Chapter 13.) Latent learning seems to be simply a special instance of this effect.

Thus, it appears that latent learning can be accounted for on the basis of known principles of operant conditioning, and need not be considered to be basic types of learning.

LATENT EXTINCTION

Whereas latent learning refers to learning that appears to occur in the absence of reinforcement, latent extinction is extinction in the absence of the behavior that is being extinguished (Clifford, 1964; Klugh, 1961; Robinson & Capaldi, 1958; Seward & Levy, 1949; Stanley & Rowe, 1954; Thomas, 1958). Suppose that we place a group of rats, one individual at a time, in an empty goal box of a T-maze after the behavior of going to that goal box has been operantly conditioned with food reinforcement. The group is then given extinction trials in the maze and its performance is compared with that of another group that is being given extinction trials in the maze but that did not have previous exposure to the empty goal box. The typical finding is that the group with the previous exposure to the empty goal box shows more rapid extinction than does the group that did not have that previous exposure.

Latent extinction may be due to the weakening of a conditioned reinforcer (Moltz, 1955). Recall that if a stimulus has been paired with a positive reinforcer, that stimulus will acquire positive reinforcing properties. The stimuli in the goal box therefore become conditioned positive reinforcers when an animal is positively reinforced in the goal box. Placing the animal in an empty goal box weakens the conditioned reinforcing properties of the stimuli in the goal box. Weakening of a conditioned reinforcer will weaken responses that have previously been reinforced by that conditioned reinforcer. Therefore, the rat's behavior of going to the goal box will extinguish more rapidly as a result of having been exposed to the empty goal box because the behavior will be starting from a lower level than would be the case if the rat had not had the previous exposure to the empty goal box.

Thus, like latent learning, latent extinction can be accounted for on the basis of principles we have already discussed in this text, and need not be considered to be basic types of learning. Both require sensitive tests to detect because of the procedures they involve. Latent learning involves the use of unspecified weak reinforcers. Naturally, an operant conditioning procedure that uses weak reinforcers will produce weak conditioning. Latent extinction involves the weakening of conditioned reinforcers in the absence of the behavior that is to be extinguished. Extinction proceeds most rapidly, however, when the behavior that is to be extinguished is permitted to occur. Although it is sometimes useful to study weak versions of various procedures, it is generally more informative to study the procedures at their most effective levels. The information covered in this book, therefore, is based mainly on studies in which strong effects on behavior have been demonstrated.

LEARNED HELPLESSNESS

Presenting an aversive stimulus that cannot be terminated or avoided can impair an individual's subsequent learning to terminate or avoid aversive stimuli. This detrimental effect on learning to terminate or avoid aversive stimuli is called learned helplessness.

Learned Helplessness in Animals

Learned helplessness is commonly studied in a two-sided chamber called a shuttle box (see Figure 5.1). The two sides are separated by a barrier over which a test animal can jump to escape from—to terminate—electric shock presented on its side of the chamber. There is typically a warning stimulus such as a flashing light a number of seconds before the shock.

Consider the normal behavior of a dog, for example, when exposed to this situation. Upon

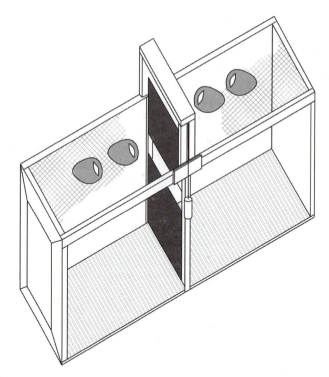

FIGURE 5.1. This apparatus (a shuttle box) is used to study learned helplessness and escape and avoidance conditioning. The animal escapes or avoids an electric shock (delivered through the bars in the floor) by jumping over the hurdle from one side to the other. Lights on top of the apparatus may be used as stimuli correlated with shock. (From Solomon & Wynne, 1953)

the occurrence of the first shock the dog will run about until it accidentally scrambles over the barrier and escapes the shock. With successive trials the dog will escape the shock more and more quickly. Eventually, in fact, in perhaps just a few trials, the dog will consistently avoid shock altogether by jumping over the barrier as soon as the warning stimulus (flashing light) appears. That is the normal pattern.

Quite a different pattern will often occur, however, if the dog has received a number of inescapable and unavoidable shocks (such as while suspended in a restraining harness) prior to its first experience with shock in the shuttle box. On the first trial in the shuttle box the dog will run about, as in the case of the normal dog, but then it may simply lie down and quietly whine. Even if the dog accidentally gets over the barrier, it still may not jump the barrier on the next trial. Instead, it may passively take the shock more and more readily with each successive trial. Such dogs, which constitute about three-fourths of the cases exposed to inescapable and unavoidable shocks, never learn to escape the shock (Maier & Seligman, 1976; Overmeir & Seligman, 1967; Seligman, 1975; Seligman & Maier, 1967). They are said to have learned to be "helpless."

There are several ways in which learned helplessness might be due to one of the more basic types of learning, respondent or operant conditioning, already discussed. One possibility is that exposure to inescapable shock tends to operantly condition immobility in response to shock, and this immobility later interferes with the learning of an escape response to the shock (Glazer & Weiss, 1976 b). Inescapable shock can operantly condition immobility as follows: when inescapable shock first occurs, there is an initial increase in activity that is followed by a decrease in activity as the shock continues. If the duration of the shock is fairly long, activity may be close to zero when the shock stops, and immobility will therefore be reinforced by the termination of the shock (even though it did not turn the shock off). This explanation implies that greater immobility and more impairment of later escape and avoidance learning should be produced by inescapable shocks of long duration than by inescapable shocks of short duration. These results have in fact been obtained, at least with rats (Crowell & Anderson, 1981; Glazer & Weiss, 1976a) and mice (Anisman, DeCatanzaro, & Remington, 1978).

According to the above explanation immobility is reinforced by shock termination even though it does not actually affect the shock. It is also possible, however, that immobility directly reduces the aversiveness of the shock. With the type of shock procedure generally used in learned helplessness studies with rats, at least, the individual can minimize the total amount of electric power going through its body during shock by remaining motionless while touching as few of the floor grids in the chamber as possible (Wilson & Butcher, 1980). Once the individual has thereby been reinforced for immobility in the unavoidable/inescapable shock situation, the behavior would most likely persist when exposed to the avoidable/escapable shock situation. Thus the animal would give the appearance of "learned helplessness," even though closer examination would show that it was not "helpless" at all because it was performing a response that at least reduces the intensity of the shock.

It is also possible that, rather than being operant behavior, learned helplessness is a respondently conditioned defensive response. For example, when under attack by a predator and escape is impossible, many species simply become immobile and cease to resist. This lack of resistance, or "helplessness," may be an unconditioned response to an aversive stimulus which an animal's behavior fails to terminate or prevent. This behavior may well have evolved as a unconditioned defensive reaction to persistent aversive stimulation (Ratner, 1967), for it appears to have the survival value of reducing attack by predators (Thompson et al., 1981). Alternatively, the "helplessness" response may have evolved as submissive behavior—that is, behavior that inhibits attacks by dominant members of one's species (Minor, Dess, & Overmier, 1991). (Chapter 16 discusses submissive behavior in more detail.) In either case, a series of inescapable and unavoidable electric shocks would elicit this "helplessness" as an unconditioned response. Shocks in a different situation, even though now escapable, would then (through respondent conditioning) tend to elicit the "helplessness" response that would then interfere with behavior that would terminate or avoid the shocks.

Evidence for learned helplessness as an unconditioned defensive or submissive response is the fact that (at least in rats) the deficit in learning produced by inescapable shock disappears if the task is automated, so that the animals do not see the experimenter (Minor, Jackson, & Maier, 1984). It is as though the animals are reacting to the experimenter as they would to a predator or a dominant cohort. Further evidence is the fact that there appears to be a close relationship between learned helplessness and the tendency for many species of animals to go into a state called tonic immobility, in which they are motionless after a brief period of physical restraint (e.g., by manually restricting any movement). (This condition has also been called "animal hypnosis," although it has nothing to do with human hypnosis which is simply a heightened state of suggestibility.) The obvious relationship between tonic immobility and defensive immobility of animals in their natural environments clearly points to a similarity with learned helplessness. In keeping with this similarity, inescapable shock facilitates tonic immobility (Maser & Gallup, 1976; Rodd, Rosellini, Stock, & Gallup, 1997). Another piece of evidence suggesting a relationship between learned helplessness and tonic immobility is the fact that both effects seem to be fairly short lived. Learned helplessness is usually undetectable after between 48 and 72 hours following its induction (Maier, 1993), which is a relatively brief time compared to many other learning phenomena.

Note that while the first two explanations of learned helplessness are based on operant conditioning, the second two are based on respondent conditioning in which both the unconditioned stimulus and the unconditioned response are assumed to be rather complex. The unconditioned stimulus is assumed to be an uncontrollable aversive event; the unconditioned response is assumed to be "helplessness"; and the conditioned stimulus is assumed to be electric shock. The above possibilities do not exhaust the ways in which learned helplessness might be due to the basic types of learning already described. They do indicate, however, that there seems to be no reason at present to treat learned helplessness as a special type of learning different from respondent or operant conditioning.

Learned Helplessness In Humans

Humans who have experienced various types of traumatic events, such as homelessness or spousal abuse, often fail to engage in behavior that might remove or ameliorate the aversive stimuli in their situations. This has led to speculation that such individuals are suffering from learned helplessness. There are, however, some critical differences between learned helplessness, as studied in the laboratory, and the plights of humans in distressing social conditions (Flannery & Harvey, 1991). For example, a battered wife may fail to seek help not because of learned helplessness but rather because there are no social agencies or family members who can provide her with any real support and safety. Similarly, a sexually abused child may not report her abuser simply because she has not learned whom she can safely tell about the abuse. In subsequent chapters it will become apparent how principles of operant conditioning and extinction can account for the absence of the escape or avoidance behavior that might be expected in aversive social situations, apart from considerations of learned helplessness as a separate concept.

INSIGHT

When an individual in a given situation suddenly emits new behavior that is appropriate to the situation we frequently call that insight. A classic demonstration of insight in a chimpanzee was conducted in the following manner (Kohler, 1927, pp. 39–40). A banana was nailed to the ceiling in a corner of a room housing six young chimpanzees. A wooden box was located near the center of the room. Immediately after the banana was in place, all six animals began leaping at it, but it was too high for them to reach. Soon one of the apes stopped leaping and began pacing back and forth. Suddenly the animal stood in front of the box and pushed it straight toward the banana. When the box was about one-half meter from directly under the banana, the animal climbed up on the box, sprang toward the banana, and seized it. Insight differs in an important way from other types of learning. Except for insight, all the types of learning discussed in this book are defined by a specific history. In respondent conditioning, for example, the specified history is pairing a neutral stimulus and an unconditioned stimulus; in operant conditioning it is following a response with an event termed reinforcement. No information was given, however, about the history necessary for a chimpanzee to solve the above box-and-banana problem.

A clue as to the type of history necessary for insight comes from the following demonstration (Epstein, Kirshnit, Lanza, & Rubin, 1984): A pigeon is operantly trained to emit two separate behaviors in different situations. One behavior consists of standing on a small box in an operant chamber and pecking at a small plastic banana suspended from the ceiling of the chamber. (The pigeon's wings are clipped so that it cannot reach the plastic banana except by standing on the box.) The other behavior, which is conditioned in a different chamber with no plastic banana present, consists of pecking at the box and moving it to a location corresponding to a dot marked on the floor. The position of the dot is varied over sessions. When these two behaviors are well established, a test is conducted in which the bird is placed in the chamber with the banana. The box, however, is not directly under the banana but some distance from it. Typically, the behavior that results will very much resemble that of the chimpanzee that solved the box-and-banana problem. At first the bird will stretch its neck toward the banana and flap its wings. After these responses prove unsuccessful, the bird will start pacing back and forth, and then move to the box. At this point the bird may stand on the box and make pecking motions toward the banana. Very soon, however, the bird will move behind the box and peck it toward the banana. When the box is near the banana, the bird will jump up on it and peck the banana.

What has clearly occurred in this example is that two behaviors that had been operantly conditioned separately have combined under circumstances in which neither behavior by itself would produce reinforcement. This may be what happens in all cases labeled "insight." In the example in which the chimpanzee solved the box-and-banana problem, the animal may have never before obtained reinforcement by standing on boxes or by moving boxes around. It had probably, however, obtained reinforcement previously by standing on other objects and by moving other objects around. It seems reasonable to assume that these two previously-established operant behaviors somehow combined under a novel condition to produce a new sequence of behavior whose components were similar to the old behaviors. We have already indicated how long behavioral chains can be developed through conditioned reinforcement, and will discuss this in more detail in Chapter 11. For now, however, it is sufficient to note that instances of insight appear to be due to the action of operant conditioning principles; therefore, insight need not be classified as a separate type of learning.

LEARNING BY IMITATION

We may define imitation as the performance of some behavior as a result of observing another individual engage in similar behavior. A great deal of human learning occurs through imitation: an instructor models some behavior that the student imitates, and the student then demonstrates learning by performing the behavior at a later time in the absence of the model. Despite the common perception that imitation is widespread among animals (e.g., note the familiar expression "monkey see, monkey do"), it does not appear to be prevalent in any nonhuman species (Galef, 1988). The limited amount of imitation that does occur in nonhuman animals can generally be accounted for by more fundamental processes. One such process is simple respondent behavior. In what is sometimes called contagious behavior (e.g., Thorpe, 1963, p. 133), some instances of imitation appear to be unconditioned responses in which the elicited responses are similar to the eliciting stimuli (responses by another individual). For example, animals engaging in fear responding, such as, moving in an agitated manner, sounding distress calls, attacking, or fleeing, tend to elicit similar responding in nearby members of their species.

Imitation is not itself a learning process; however, individuals may learn to perform a given response by observing another individual perform that response. This is called imitative learning.

Types of Imitative Learning

Because imitative learning is so common in humans, it is tempting to believe that it must be a fundamental type of learning in its own right. It appears, however, that imitative learning can be accounted for in many cases by respondent and operant conditioning processes. In order to show this, we first consider four types of imitative learning that appear to be accounted for in this way. In addition, we consider a type of imitative learning ("true imitation") that does not appear to be reducible simply to respondent and operant conditioning.

Observational conditioning. As a result of being paired with another individual's responding that (acting as an unconditioned stimulus) elicits unconditioned responding that resembles the other individual's responding, a stimulus may become a conditioned stimulus for conditioned responding that resembles the other individual's responding. This phenomenon is called *observational conditioning.* For example, rhesus monkeys that have not previously been exposed to snakes, and show no fear responding in the presence of snakes, will do so after observing another rhesus monkey show fear responding to a snake (M. Cook et al., 1985; Mineka & Cook, 1988). The conditioned stimulus in this example is snakes, the unconditioned stimulus is another monkey exhibiting fear reactions, and the unconditioned and conditioned responses are fear reactions.

Stimulus enhancement. A stimulus may lose aversive properties or become a reinforcer for an individual as a result of that individual observing another member of its species interact with that stimulus or one similar to it (cf. Galef, 1988, pp. 15–16; Spence, 1937, p. 821). This is termed stimulus enhancement. For example, birds tend to lose their fear of—that is, their tendency to fly away from—railroad trains as a result of observing other birds staying near trains (Thorndike, 1911, p. 77). The stimulus that is enhanced in this example is railroad trains. Another example of stimulus enhancement is the fact that animals seeing a conspecific (i.e., another member of their species) eat a particular food will show a strong increase in their preference for that food (Galef & Wigmore, 1983; Galef, Kennett, & Wigmore, 1984; Posadas-Andrews & Roper, 1983; Richard, Grover, & Davis, 1987; Valsecchi & Galef, 1989). Similarly, a female guppy that sees another female guppy (especially an older one) with a particular male will (other factors being equal) tend to choose that male over a male that she did not see with another female (Dugatkin, 1992; Dugatkin & Godin, 1992, 1993). As another example of stimulus enhancement, consider an experiment in which a pigeon pecks on an extended key—for example, a key with half a Ping-Pong ball rigidly attached to it—in view of another pigeon with access to a similar extended key and separated by a glass partition from the first pigeon (Epstein, 1984). The result is that the second pigeon will start pecking its extended key, even though the second pigeon has never received reinforcement contingent on this behavior. Moreover, the second bird will continue pecking at the key for a number of sessions in which the first bird is absent. The stimulus that is enhanced in this example is the extended key. One interpretation of stimulus enhancement is that the enhanced stimulus is a conditioned reinforcer for an animal due to being paired with another member or members of the animal's species.

A concept that overlaps with stimulus enhancement is social facilitation. This refers to the fact that others engaging in a particular phylogeneitc behavior (or sometimes even simply being present) may act as a stimulus to increase the tendency of an individual to engage in similar behavior (Crawford, 1939; Zajonc, 1965). Examples of social facilitation in humans include "contagious" yawning or laughter (Allport, 1924, pp. 257–258, 300–301; Nice, 1943). A particularly prevalent example of social facilitation is the increased eating that humans (de Castro & Brewer, 1992) and other animals (James, 1966; James & Gilbert, 1955; Harlow, 1932; Harlow & Yudin, 1933; Platt & James, 1966) display when in the presence of conspecifics who are eating. Note that the concept of stimulus enhancement focuses on individual's responses to specific nonsocial stimuli that other individuals are interacting or have interacted with, whereas the concept of social faciliatation focuses on phylogenetic behavior (such as eating) apart from specific nonsocial stimuli (e.g., type of food) controlling the behavior.

Copying. Some responding may produce stimuli that are conditioned reinforcers because of their similarity to the responding of another individual (Galef, 1988, pp. 20–21; Mowrer, 1960, p. 69). This is called copying. It is more likely to occur with vocal than with nonvocal (or motor) behavior because sounds affect hearing in much the same way whether made by another individual or oneself, whereas motor behavior generally affects vision differently when emitted by another individual than when emitted by oneself. An example of copying is a human infant imitating speech sounds made by its parents because those sounds have been paired with the parents who have been paired with reinforcement such as food and cuddling. A similar example is that of a young bird imitating the calls of its parents because those sounds have been paired with the parents which, in turn, have been paired with food and other primary reinforcers.

Matched-dependent learning. Behavior that is similar to that emitted by another individual because it has been reinforced in the presence of that individual emitting that behavior is called matched-dependent behavior. An example of an animal engaging in matched-dependent behavior is a rat turning in the same direction in a maze as a rat directly in front of it as a result of receiving reinforcement contingent on this following behavior (Miller & Dollard, 1941). A clear distinction must be made between matched-dependent behavior and matched-dependently learned behavior. The latter is responding that began as matched-dependent behavior and then came under the control of a new stimulus. Matched-dependently learned behavior is demonstrated when the follower rat in the above example consistently turns in a specific direction when a specific stimulus is present because that stimulus had been present when the leader rat had turned in that direction (Church, 1957). For example, suppose that the leader rat in the previous example received reinforcement in a T-maze for turning in the direction indicated by a black circle (as opposed to, say, a white triangle). The follower rat would be demonstrating matched-dependent learning if after receiving reinforcement for following the leader rat on a number of trials, it then, on its own (i.e., without the leader present), consistently turned in the direction of the black circle.

It is important to note that although we speak of matched-dependently learned behavior as behavior acquired through imitation, it is basically operant responding that has been under the control of one stimulus and then come under the control of a different stimulus.

True imitation. Imitation that does not fall into any of the above categories is called true imitation. To demonstrate true imitation, an individual must make a novel response that could only have been emitted by observing another individual emit a similar response (Thorpe, 1963).

True imitation is a rare and difficult phenomenon to demonstrate, and it is not clear that it occurs in many species. The following appear to be examples of true imitation by several species:

- Budgerigars that observe another budgerigar remove a cap on a container in a particular manner (e.g., pushing it off with the beak, twisting it off with the beak, or grasping it off with the foot) to obtain food will tend to remove caps on similar containers in the same manner when given an opportunity to do so (Dawson & Foss, 1965).
- An African Grey parrot (*Psittacus erithacus*) trained to imitate words also imitated the actions that its trainer made when saying the words; e.g., the bird waved its wing in imitation of the trainer waving his hand when saying the word "ciao" (Moore, 1992).

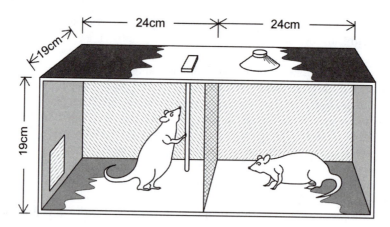

FIGURE 5.2. After observing the rat on the left push the rod in a specific direction and receive food, the other rat will be put on the left side with the identical rod but will receive no food. Statistically, rats that observed another rat push the rod in a particular direction will show a greater tendency to push the rod in the same direction (relative to the demonstrator rat's body) than in the other direction. (From Heyes & Dawson, 1990)

- Rats that observe another rat push a suspended rod in a particular direction (either left or right) and receive reinforcement will tend (with a statistically significant greater-than-chance probability) to push the rod in the same direction when given an opportunity to do so. A particularly remarkable aspect of this phenomenon is that the imitator tends to push the rod in the same direction relative to its body that the demonstrator pushed it relative to its body, regardless of the orientation of the demonstrator and imitator relative to each other during the demonstration (Heyes & Dawson, 1990; Heyes, Dawson, & Nokes, 1992). Figure 5.2 shows a drawing of the apparatus used in these studies.
- Captive dolphins (*Tursiops aduncus*) have been reported to rub various objects against the bottom and windows of their tank in the same manner in which their trainers clean the tank with scrappers and sponges (Tayler & Saayman, 1973).
- A rhesus monkey lapped water in the same manner as a kitten that she kept, although lapping water like a kitten is not normal for rhesus monkeys (Ball, 1938). Another young female rhesus monkey carried a coconut shell next to her body in the same manner that her mother carried a sibling (Breuggeman, 1973).

Despite the fact that "to ape" means "to imitate," there is no evidence that apes naturally engage in true imitation even when conditions for doing so are highly favorable (Tomasello, 1996). However, at least some chimpanzees (Custance & Bard, 1994; Hayes & Hayes, 1952) and an orangutan (Miles, Mitchell, Mitchell, & Harper, 1992) that received reinforcement for imitating (in the sense of matched-dependent behavior, as described above) many different responses following the verbal stimulus "Do this!" eventually imitated novel responses when presented with "Do this!" and shown the new response to be imitated. Imitating new responses after receiving reinforcement for imitating a number of other responses is called generalized imitation.

When generalized imitation exists, imitation is an operant response class in the sense discussed in Chapter 3. Spontaneous true imitation, if the phenomenon exists (which is in considerable doubt given the limited number of apparent instances of it), does not appear to be due to the pairing two stimuli or of a response and a stimulus. It may be that true imitation should be classified as both a type of learning and an operant response category. If this is the case, then we could state the following: As a response category, true imitation has a small but greater-than-zero probability of occurrence in a limited number of species. In those species in which it does occur, however, it can be developed as an operant response class through reinforcement of a number of instances of it (thus producing the phenomenon of generalized imitation in which an individual demonstrates repeated instances of true imitation).

Imitative Learning by Humans

Humans learn by imitation to an astounding degree. Most of informal and formal education involves someone modeling a behavior to be imitated. Much socially desirable and undesirable imitative learning also occurs unintentionally, such as when someone acts as a socially desirable or undesirable role model. Clearly, a huge amount of the behavior any socialized human has learned was initially developed by observing someone else engage in similar behavior.

Imitative learning based on conditioning. Respondent and operant conditioning can explain much imitation in essentially the same manner in humans as in other animals. The following examples illustrate this.

Observational conditioning is readily apparent in children when they learn to fear particular stimuli, such as snakes, spiders, and insects, from a parent who exhibits such a fear. Stimulus enhancement can be seen when toys that resemble objects that adults interact with—vehicles, machinery, and all types of tools—become reinforcing to children. A person's fear of some object or situation decreasing in intensity as a result of that person observing someone else interact with that object or situation is another familiar example, and in fact is the basis of a systematic procedure used to help people overcome irrational fears (Martin & Pear, 1999, pp. 331–332).

Copying occurs when a human infant tends to repeat sounds that resemble speech sounds that are conditioned reinforcers for the infant because they have been paired with primary reinforcers (e.g., food, cuddling) that adults provide while emitting the sounds (Smith, Michaels, & Sundberg, 1995; Sundberg, Michaels, Partington, & Sundberg, 1995). Unlike the case of animals in which copying is mainly limited to vocalizing, humans also copy motor behavior to a remarkable degree of accuracy partly because images in mirrors, photographs, television and movies screens, and so forth have similar stimulus effects on humans as the objects the images represent do. However, infants imitate facial movements before they learn to respond to their images in mirrors and the like. This is explained by the fact that, beginning at about 13 to 15 months of age, infants touch the parts of their parents faces (e.g., eyes, nose, mouth, teeth, tongue) when the parents are emitting various facial movements (Piaget, 1945/1951, pp. 57–58). They then feel the corresponding parts of their own faces, stimulating their hands in the same manner as the parents' facial movements did which is then reinforced by the copying process described above.

Matched-dependent learning depends on matched-dependent behavior, which we have said develops through the reinforcement of responding similar to that emitted by another individual. Yet with humans it frequently appears possible to produce matched-dependent behavior reliably on the first presentation of the modeled behavior, without having to develop it through reinforcing previous instances of it. One way in which this occurs is through the individual learning to imitate the elements that constitute a response, which is possible because many responses are composed of smaller, more elementary responses. For example, a child may imitate the word "alligator" upon hearing it for the first time because the child has previously received reinforcement for imitating the elements "al," "li," "ga," and "tor," although perhaps in separate words (Martin & Pear, 1999, p. 229; Skinner, 1957a, pp. 62–63).

Generalized imitation in humans.   There is research indicating that many imitative responses by humans are instances of generalized imitation, as described earlier in this chapter. Early evidence for generalized imitation in humans came from a study in which a puppet asked normal preschool children to imitate some of its actions and then praised them for doing so. Occasionally, the puppet would press a lever similar to a lever the child had access to. Although the puppet never suggested that the child should imitate this response and never gave the child praise or any other reinforcement for doing so, each child pressed the lever at a high rate as a result of the reinforcement for imitating other actions of the puppet (Baer & Sherman, 1964).

Being performed with normal preschool children, the above study demonstrates generalized imitation in individuals with extensive imitative repertoires. The children in the above study did not learn a new imitation as a result of the imitation training they received in the experiment (i.e., they would readily have imitated pressing the lever if requested to do so without having been reinforced for other imitations in the experiment). Evidence for generalized imitation in the absence of an imitative repertoire comes from studies with developmentally delayed and autistic individuals who are severely deficient in imitation (Baer, Peterson, & Sherman, 1967; Garcia, Baer, & Firestone, 1971; Metz, 1965; Young, Krantz, McClannahan, & Bulson, 1994). To begin learning imitations, these individuals typically require a large number of trials in which a simple response to be imitated occurs along with some instruction such as "Do this," "Say _____," or "Ready," and praise along with a primary reinforcer (e.g., a piece of pretzel or potato chip, a sip of juice, a tickle, a hug) is given contingent on a correct imitations (see Martin & Pear, 1999, p. 221). The results of such studies indicate that generalized imitation tends to occur within certain narrowly defined response categories, but not across these categories. For example, developmentally delayed children taught to imitate small motor responses (e.g., touch knee, clap, move tray) may then imitate other small motor responses (e.g., clap hands, ring bell), but not large motor responses (e.g., touch door, move waste paper basket), short vocal sounds (e.g., "aw" as in "Paul," "oh" as in "Joe"), or long vocal sounds (e.g., "i" as in "it," "uh" as in "but"). As the individuals learn imitations in each of the other categories, however, they begin to make imitations that they have not been taught and have not received reinforcement for making in that category (Garcia et al., 1971). Using categories such as vocal responses (e.g., "my cookie," "I ride a bike"), vocal responses while handling a toy (e.g., picking up toy cat with one hand while petting it with the other and saying "meow"), and playing with a toy (e.g., making, pouring, and drinking motions with a toy tea set), studies with autistic children have produced similar results (Young et al., 1994).

Thus, generalized imitative responses in humans appear to constitute at least several operant response classes. It is possible, however, that a single, broad operant imitation response class emerges with extensive imitation training within a wide variety of response classes. Highly skilled professional mimics and actors may exemplify this level of generalized imitation.

SUMMARY AND CONCLUSIONS

In this chapter we have seen how various types of associative learning appear to be derivatives of respondent and operant conditioning processes. Latent learning can be accounted for on the basis of weak reinforcers. Latent extinction can be accounted for on the basis of the weakening of conditioned reinforcement. We would expect both of these processes to be weak. Weak reinforcers result in weak conditioning. Weakening of the conditioned reinforcer that maintains a response does not eliminate the response as effectively as extinguishing the response itself.

Learned helplessness may be due to a variety of respondent and operant phenomena. Operantly conditioned immobility is one possibility. It may also be a respondently conditioned defensive response. Evidence for learned helplessness as an unconditioned defensive or submissive response is the fact that (at least in rats) the deficit in learning produced by inescapable shock disappears if the task is automated, so that the animals do not see the experimenter. The unconditioned stimulus is assumed to be an uncontrollable aversive event; the unconditioned response is assumed to be "helplessness"; and the conditioned stimulus is assumed to be repitition of the aversive event.

Learned helplessness in humans may be quite different from learned helplessness in animals. It may simply be a regression to previously effective behavior that is now maladaptive, or it may simply reflect the fact that resources that would enable the person to adapt are not available or the individual has not learned to make use of these resources.

Insight appears to consist of previously learned operant responses that have been combined in a way that turns out to be effective in producing reinforcement in a novel situation.

Imitative learning can be broken down into observational conditioning, stimulus enhancement, copying, matched dependent learning, and true imitation. Only the latter meets the definition of occurring as a result simply of making a novel response that could only have been emitted by observing another individual emit a similar response. True imitation is extremely rare, especially in animals other than humans. It is possible that when it does occur, it is due to a history of many reinforced imitative responses. Imitative responding that is due to this is called generalized imitation.

BASIC STIMULUS-STIMULUS AND RESPONSE-STIMULUS CONTINGENCIES

When dealing with respondent and operant conditioning, we are concerned with contingencies—the pairing of events, in which one event depends probabilistically on another. There are two basic types of contingencies: stimulus-stimulus contingencies, in which one stimulus is paired with another; and, response-stimulus contingencies, in which a stimulus is paired with (i.e., follows) a response. Respondent conditioning is the result of stimulus-stimulus contingencies, while operant conditioning is the result of response-stimulus contingencies. There are, however, certain stimulus-stimulus contingencies that affect operant behavior. Theoretically speaking, stimulus-stimulus effects on operant conditioning may be regarded as resulting from respondent conditioning interacting with operant conditioning.

Chapter 6 deals with stimulus-stimulus contingencies in both respondent and operant conditioning. Then, Chapter 7 focuses on the basic response-stimulus (i.e., response-reinforcement) contingencies of operant conditioning.

Stimulus Pairings
Across Response Systems

s we saw in Chapter 3, respondent conditioning is produced by pairing—that is, creating a contingency between—two stimuli. For explanatory purposes, we made the procedure and its effects sound fairly simple. The procedure is simple enough, but the effects are far from simple. Although many experiments have (for the sake of simplicity) examined the effects that pairing stimuli have on just one (or a few) responses, in actuality a stimulus pairing procedure may affect many responses and, indeed, entire integrated systems of responses. These different responses may interact with each other, may interact with operant responses, may be affected differentially by different parameters, and may show different time courses. In short, despite the impression that may have been given by the introductory chapters of this book (and perhaps by other simplifying accounts elsewhere), the effects of pairing two stimuli can be extremely complex. This chapter details the varied effects of stimulus-stimulus contingencies on response categories ranging from internal to external, specific to diffuse, and stimulus-directed to nonstimulus-directed.

The phenomena covered in this chapter are varied and far ranging. What ties them together is the fact that they are all produced by the pairing of stimuli. In addition, although the effects of stimulus pairing are extremely varied when looked at superficially, there is an underlying similarity between them. Each can be seen as an instance or special case of respondent conditioning as described in Part I of this text. The purpose of this chapter is to highlight these similarities across a broad range of phenomena, thereby illustrating the widespread generality of respondent conditioning.

INTERNAL RESPONSES

Many responses that are subject to respondent conditioning occur inside the body. Many of these internal responses, from an evolutionary point of view, have to do with maintaining internal functioning. Others are more related to preparing the individual to engage effectively in external behavior (escape, avoidance, attack, copulation). We consider each of these types of internal responses separately.

Responses Related to Internal Maintenance

Many responses within the body are concerned with homeostasis, or the maintenance of temperature and chemical substances in the body within the ranges necessary for optimal internal functioning.

Digestion and excretion.   Salivation, elicited by either food or acid, is a standard example of an internal response having to do with the maintenance of internal functioning, but there are many others. For example, hydrochloric acid injected into the stomach through a fistula (i.e., a tube inserted into an artificial opening in the body) elicits the secretion of bile by the liver. A neutral stimulus (e.g., a bell) paired with the injection of hydrochloric acid into the stomach will, over trials, come to also elicit the secretion of bile (E. Ivanov; cited in Airapetyantz & Bykov, 1966, p. 145). As another example, injection of water into the stomach elicits the secretion of urine by the kidneys. A neutral stimulus paired with this injection of water will come to also elicit this secretion of urine (Airapetyantz & Bykov, 1966, pp. 145, 149).

Internal sexual responses.   Various internal sexual responses can be respondently conditioned. For example, the secretion of luteinizing hormone by the pituitary and testosterone by the testes in male rats, in response to the presence of a receptive female, has been respondently conditioned to an odor that did not initially elicit these responses (Graham & Desjardins, 1980). In humans, male sexual arousal has been respondently conditioned to slides of neutral objects (a penny jar, a lamp shade, or a coffee table) by pairing them with erotic slides (Plaud & Martini, 1999). Sexual arousal was measured with a device called a penile plethysmograph that continuously measures penis circumference. The evolutionary function of respondently conditioned sexual responses is that they prepare the individual to engage in copulation.

Nausea.   Nausea is a response that can be readily conditioned. For example, experiments on dogs have shown that a neutral stimulus that has been paired a number of times with morphine injections (e.g., the mere sight of the syringe or the prick of the needle in the skin) will produce a sequence consisting of an "uneasy" appearance, licking of chops, copious salivation, frothing at the mouth, vomiting, and sleep (Airapetyantz & Bykov, 1966, p. 149).

To take another example, chemotherapy (i.e., drugs administered to treat cancer) frequently elicits nausea and vomiting in people receiving it. For many patients, stimuli that have been paired with the treatment (i.e. the sights and smells of the clinic) also come to elicit feelings of nausea (Carey & Burish, 1988; Redd & Andrykowski, 1982).

Drug-opponent responses.   Drugs such as opiates (e.g., morphine), alcohol, caffeine, and many others are toxins. As such, the body mobilizes resources to rid itself of these substances. In addition, it produces responses—called drug-opponent responses (also called compensatory responses)—that counteract the effects of toxic substances. Pairing stimuli with the injection or ingestion of various drugs results in conditioned drug-opponent responses that produce the phenomenon known as drug tolerance (Siegel, 1991). For example, the analgesic (i.e., pain-reducing) effect of morphine can be counteracted by respondent conditioning. If a rat is placed on a hot surface at a controlled temperature, the time that elapses until the rat licks a paw will be greater if the rat has been given morphine just before being placed on the hot surface. With repeated daily injections of a specific dose of morphine, however, the time taken by the rat to lick a paw gradually decreases. Called morphine tolerance, this decrease in the analgesic effects of the drug is caused by a morphine-opponent response that counteracts the analgesic and other effects of the drug, and that becomes conditioned through respondent conditioning to various stimuli in the setting in which the drug is administered. (Note that the response that we are concerned with here is the drug-opponent response to the drug, not its analgesic effect.)

The evidence is as follows (Siegel, 1977, 1978, 1979):

- Placebo injections (i.e., injections of saline) given before beginning a series of morphine injections retards the development of tolerance. This is due to latent inhibition, as discussed in Chapter 3 (i.e., repeated presentations of a conditioned stimulus prior to beginning the conditioning procedure will retard conditioning—where in this case the conditioned stimulus is the injection of a hypodermic needle).
- Placebo injections interspersed among injections of the drug retard the development of tolerance. This corresponds to partial reinforcement which, as indicated in Chapter 4, produces less effective conditioning than does continuous reinforcement.
- Presenting a series of placebo injections (i.e., injections of saline, which have no effect) following a series of morphine injections (i.e., extinction trials following conditioning trials) attenuates tolerance. This is due to the extinction of the drug-opponent response, since presenting the placebo amounts to presenting the conditioned stimulus without presenting the unconditioned stimulus.
- Pairing a stimulus (e.g., change in background noise and overhead illumination) with drug-free periods and presenting that stimulus during morphine injection and the subsequent tolerance test attenuates tolerance. This is due to the inhibiting effect of a CS– on a CS+ as described in Chapter 4.
- After tolerance occurs at a particular dosage level of morphine or heroin (a potent derivative of morphine), changing the background stimuli (i.e., administering the drug in a different setting or situation) can be lethal (Siegel & Ellsworth, 1986; Siegel, 1984; Siegel et al., 1982). Changing the background (or contextual) stimuli weakens a conditioned response because some of the stimuli paired with the response are changed or removed, and this is apparently true for the conditioned drug-tolerance response as well. In support of this point, a lethal overdose of heroin sometimes occurs when an addict administers the drug in a different environment from the one in which he or she usually takes the drug, even though the amount of drug may not change (Siegel, 1984; Siegel et al., 1982). The reason is that if stimuli paired with the drug are removed (as would occur if the drug were administered in a new location), the drug-opponent response fails to occur, permitting the addict to be killed by an amount of the drug which he or she had previously been able to withstand because of the drug-opponent response. Changing the context of a drug can also result in a lethal dose of Pentobarbital (Vila, 1989) and alcohol (Melchior, 1990).
- The presentation of a novel stimulus, such as a burst of noise, with the administration of alcohol decreases tolerance to it (Siegel & Larson, 1996). A novel stimulus presented along with a conditioned stimulus is known to inhibit the conditioned response (Pavlov, 1927).

Immunological effects.   There is a delicate balance of immunological effects within the body. To survive the body must maintain defenses against invading organisms, such as bacteria and viruses; it is also important to survival that these defenses not act against the body itself. Certain drugs can facilitate or suppress the body's natural defenses, and stimuli paired with these drugs can take on the corresponding immunological facilitative or suppressive effects (Ader, 1985; Ader & Cohen, 1975, 1982, 1993; Russell et al., 1984; Spector, 1987). Similarly, conditioned changes in the immune system may occur in response to stimuli paired with chemotherapy (Stockhorst, Klosterhalfen, & Steingrüber, 1998). These findings have promising implications for the treatment of diseases of the immune system and for transplant technology, where it is important to suppress the tendency for the immune system to attack a transplant.

Internal Responses Related to Defensive Behavior

Aversive stimuli, particularly those that subjectively we label as "painful," tend to elicit external defensive behavior. In addition, they elicit internal responses that appear to facilitate or enable external defensive behavior. Painful stimulation causes a sharp drop in the resistance of the skin to electricity, as measured by running an imperceptible current between two electrodes placed near sweat glands on the skin. Called the skin conductance response, the electrodermal response, or the galvanic skin response (GSR), this reaction appears to be due to the action of sweat glands. A neutral stimulus paired with a painful stimulus (e.g., an electric shock) will come to also elicit a GSR. This is one of the most frequently studied conditioned responses in humans (Beecroft, 1966, pp. 38–42).

A painful stimulus will also elicit an initial marked acceleration in heart rate. At least with humans, however, a neutral stimulus that has been paired with a painful stimulus will often come to elicit a deceleration in heart rate (e.g., Notterman, Schoenfeld, & Bersh, 1952). The reason for this is not known. Accelatory conditioned heart-rate responses seem to be obtained more reliably with dogs (e.g., Black, Carlson, & Solomon, 1962).

Sensory Responses

Everyone has experienced a sensation for which there is no immediate physical stimulus. For example, try to imagine someone who is familiar to you but not actually present. In doing this you may, especially if you are a "visualizer" (i.e., if the visual sense is dominant for you), have an experience somewhat like that of seeing that person. In everyday speech we call this a "mental image" of that person. If you are an auditory person, you might have an experience similar to hearing that person say something. We might call this a "mental auditory experience," although we do not have such a term in everyday English (probably because the visual sense is stronger than the auditory sense in most people). In this book, as discussed in Chapters 1 and 3, we refer to these types of experiences as covert sensory responses (or simply sensory responses for short).

Conditioned sensory responses.   Sensory responses can be respondently conditioned. One demonstration of this was carried out on a wounded soldier in one of the Leningrad evacuation hospitals during World War II (Airapetyantz & Bykov, 1966, pp. 154–155). During the treatment it was possible to place a small rubber balloon into the bowels without harm or discomfort to the patient due to the nature of the wound. The experiment involved filling the balloon with cold water in the presence of a red flashing light and filling it with warm water in the presence of a blue flashing light. The cold and warm water elicited corresponding sensations of cold and warmth in the patient, and he was also aware of the peristaltic movements of the bowels during these water stimuli. In addition, the red and blue flashing lights came to elicit the corresponding reactions and sensations without the balloon after several pairings with the cold and warm water stimuli.

Somewhat less dramatically, people serving in experiments that involve presenting a conditioned stimulus (such as a tone) followed by an electric shock to the skin report experiencing a mild shock on trials on which the shock actually is omitted (Cole, 1939; Mowrer, 1938; also see Holland, 1990).

Sensory responses as stimuli.   In addition to being able to be conditioned, sensory responses can act as conditioned and unconditioned stimuli for other responses. Moreover, in addition to being respondent responses, sensory responses are also operant. Thus, although they may be elicited, they do not require an eliciting stimulus. A mental image may, for example, occur under the discriminative control of an instruction to produce it. Subjectively, we may feel that mental images sometimes come to us involuntarily but that we can also produce them at will. As far as we currently know, whether a sensory response is elicited or evoked (i.e., whether it is respondent or operant) has no bearing on its properties as a stimulus.

Sensory responses as conditioned stimuli. Privately presenting the sensory stimuli that are elicited by a conditioned stimulus produces the conditioned response. For example, an individual who imagines a conditioned stimulus based on electric shock will show a physiological response similar to, but weaker than, the one the actual conditioned stimulus would elicit (Holzman & Levis, 1991).

As mentioned previously in this chapter, nausea and vomiting elicited by chemotherapy frequently become conditioned to stimuli that have been paired with the treatment. In addition, for many patients, simply imagining the stimuli paired with chemotherapy produces nausea (Redd, Dadds, Futterman, Taylor, & Boubjerg, 1993).

Sensory responses also apparently function as conditioned stimuli when images of a particular type of object or situation to which a person is phobic (e.g., snakes, spiders, airplane rides) elicit physiological fear responses in that person (Lang, 1979). In fact, it is well established that counterconditioning or extinction of phobic responses to images of phobic objects and situations can result in a reduced fear reaction to those objects and situations (Lang, Kozak, Miller, Levin, & McLean, 1980; Wolpe, 1958, 1968, 1990).

Sensory responses as unconditioned stimuli. Under some conditions, it appears that a mental image of an unconditioned stimulus can itself be an unconditioned stimulus. For example, if the unconditioned stimulus consists of rotating an individual (who is strapped to a table-like apparatus) backward a specific amount that produces a decrease in heart rate, having the individual simply imagine the unconditioned stimulus when a new stimulus (to which the response has not been conditioned; e.g., a tone) occurs can cause the new stimulus to become a conditioned stimulus for decreased heart rate (Arabian, 1982).

In addition to producing conditioning, mental images of unconditioned stimuli can also retard extinction. For example, following the conditioned stimulus with a mental image of the unconditioned stimulus after the latter has ceased to occur subsequent to conditioning trials involving tone-shock pairings retards the extinction of the GSR in individuals with good visual imagery skills (Drummond, White, & Ashton, 1978).

Perceptual Responses

Closely related to conditioned sensory responses are conditioned perceptual responses. With conditioned sensory responses a conditioned stimulus elicits a particular sensation; with a conditioned perceptual response a conditioned stimulus causes an individual to perceive some stimulus in the environment in a particular way. A striking example of this is the McCullough effect, whereby an individual who has previously been exposed to a pattern of a particular color will perceive the complementary color on that pattern when it is presented monochromatically (Humphrey, 1998; McCullough, 1965). For example, an individual who stares at red vertical grid lines on a black background and subsequently looks at white vertical lines on the same background will see them to have a greenish tinge. The McCullough effect appears to be a conditioning phenomenon that is completely analogous to the conditioning of drug-opponent responses discussed earlier (Allan & Siegel, 1997a, 1997b; Murch, 1976; Siegel & Allan, 1992, 1998). The conditioned stimulus is the background pattern, the unconditioned stimulus is the color, and the unconditioned and conditioned response is a response that opposes the visual effect of staring at a particular color. This effect is quite strong and can last hours, days, weeks, or even longer (apparently until extinction occurs as a result of viewing the pattern, or similar ones, in the absence of the color).

SPECIFIC MOTOR REACTIONS

In addition to internal behavior, certain fairly specific external muscle responses are also subject to the effects of respondent conditioning. An example that has been studied extensively in humans is the eye-blink response, which is typically elicited by a puff of air to the cornea. A neutral stimulus paired with the air puff will come to also elicit the eye blink. There are, however, two major difficulties in studying eyelid conditioning. One is that the conditioned stimuli typically used in eyelid conditioning, such as buzzers and lights, elicit eye blinks quite apart from being paired with the unconditioned stimulus. It is frequently rather difficult to distinguish these eye blinks from the conditioned eye blinks. Another difficulty is that at least some eye blinks to the conditioned stimulus may be operant responses which are reinforced by the avoidance of the air puff to the cornea (Beecroft, 1966, pp. 27–34).

A more commonly studied conditioned response is that of the nictitating membrane of the rabbit. (In Chapter 3 we spoke of this simply as conditioning the rabbit's eye blink.) The nictitating membrane is an inner eyelid that helps to keep the eye clean. It blinks when a puff of air is applied to the cornea; it does not, however, completely cover the cornea and is thus unlikely to be operantly conditioned as an avoidance response. In addition, the rabbit has a low blink rate so that spontaneous blinks are less likely to be confused with conditioned blinks than is the case with humans. The nictitating membrane also responds to an electric shock delivered near the orbit of the eye, and this unconditioned stimulus is used much more often than the air puff because it produces faster conditioning (Brelsford & Theios, 1965).

Another fairly specific muscle response is finger withdrawal in humans. In experiments on finger withdrawal the finger typically rests on electrodes placed on a table. A neutral stimulus such as a light or buzzer occurs and is followed by electric shock. Conditioning typically does not occur as rapidly or as reliably as it does in eyelid conditioning, possibly because of the instructions that are usually given to minimize "voluntary" (i.e., operant) responding (Beecroft, 1966, pp. 37–38).

Somewhat similar to the finger withdrawal response in humans is the leg flexion response in animals. Electrodes are attached to the leg of an animal such as a sheep, goat, or dog. A neutral stimulus occurs prior to a shock to the leg. The unconditioned response is a flexing of the leg. The conditioned response has been frequently reported as "gross, diffuse excitement" which, over conditioning trials, yields to specific and precise flexion "without accompanying excitement" (Beecroft, 1966, p. 37).

SIGN TRACKING

A localized stimulus (such as a key light) that has been paired with a reinforcer may produce an approach toward the stimulus and often some kind of interaction with it. For example, if the response key in a dimly lighted operant chamber for a pigeon is illuminated for a brief period (e.g., eight seconds) and then grain is delivered noncontingent on responding, the pigeon—even if it has never received reinforcement for approaching or pecking the key—will eventually begin to approach the key and, in most cases, peck it when the key light turns on. Approaching and interacting with a stimulus that has been paired with reinforcement is termed sign tracking (Hearst & Jenkins, 1974).

Autoshaping

Consistent contact with a stimulus paired with a reinforcer (pecking the illuminated key in the above example) is termed autoshaping. The term was coined by the experimenters who discovered it (Brown & Jenkins, 1968) because it seemed to be a way to shape key pecking automatically. The name "autoshaping" has stuck even though it now seems that the process has nothing to do with response shaping (as described in Chapter 4). Instead, it appears that through respondent conditioning the key light becomes a conditioned stimulus for a conditioned peck response similar to the unconditioned peck response elicited by the reinforcer (acting as an unconditioned stimulus).

Autoshaping based on positive reinforcers.   The major evidence leading to the conclusion that autoshaping is respondent conditioning comes from research done with positive reinforcers as unconditioned stimuli. Some of that evidence is as follows: First, autoshaping occurs if and only if the presentation of the grain is contingent on the occurrence of the key light. Random presentations of key light and grain do not produce it, nor does backward pairing (Moore, 1973). Second, the autoshaped response can be maintained indefinitely simply by maintaining the contingency between the key light and the grain. This is called automaintenance. Moreover, the possibility that the conditioned response is maintained as a superstitious response by adventitious pairing of the response with reinforcement is ruled out by omission training, as described in Chapter 3. That is, each response prevents the occurrence of reinforcement at the end of the conditioned stimulus. This procedure, which is also called negative automaintenance when used with an automaintenance procedure, sustains a considerable amount of responding even though it permits no response to be reinforced (Williams & Williams, 1969). Third, when autoshaping is done using water instead of grain as the unconditioned stimulus (and water deprivation instead of food deprivation as the establishing operation), the key pecks resemble the pigeon's drinking movements (as revealed by, for example, high speed photography), whereas autoshaped responses based on grain resemble the pigeon's grain pecking. In the former case the pecks may be described as soft and "sipping"; in the latter they are brief and hard with the beak more closed (Jenkins & Moore, 1973; Moore, 1973).

Autoshaping can be obtained with positive reinforcers other than food and water, although in the case of these other reinforcers the autoshaped responses do not necessarily resemble the unconditioned response. Three-day-old chicks, for example, will peck a key whose illumination always precedes the illumination of an overhead heat lamp (Wasserman, 1973). In some cases the contact with the key is a "snuggling" response. The unconditioned response to the illumination of the heat lamp is a reduction in activity, extension of the wings, and twittering sounds. Thus, the conditioned response does not resemble the unconditioned response. Pecking and snuggling are, however, responses that would be elicited by the mother who is normally a heat source for the young chicks. These responses of the chicks induce the mother to brood them.

Male Japanese quail (*Coturnix japonica*) vigorously approach a stimulus that has been paired with a copulation partner. Interestingly, the female's conditioned response to a stimulus that has been paired with a copulation partner is quite different from the male's: Rather than approaching the conditioned stimulus the female increases her squatting, which is correlated with receptivity to sexual contact (Gutiérrez & Domjan, 1997).

Autoshaping is not limited to birds. It has been demonstrated in several different species of fish (Squier, 1969). Dogs, if they are permitted to reach it, will lick an electric bulb that is a conditioned stimulus for food (Pavlov, 1955). Rats will develop the behavior of licking and gnawing at a retractable lever that is inserted into an operant chamber just prior to food delivery (Peterson, Ackil, Frommer, & Hearst, 1972; Stiers & Silberberg, 1974). Rats also will approach a light that has been paired with food delivery (Cleland & Davey, 1983; Holland, 1980). Rhesus monkeys and squirrel monkeys will press a response key whose illumination precedes food delivery, although the topographies of the responses to the key and to the food are usually quite different (Gamzu & Schwam, 1974; Sidman & Fletcher, 1968). It should be noted, however, that the eating responses of monkeys are generally quite variable compared to those of pigeons.

Autoshaping based on negative reinforcers.   It may seem paradoxical to speak of autoshaping based on negative reinforcers, since by definition animals tend to respond to remove negative reinforcers. However, negative reinforcers also tend to elicit attacking (discussed later in this chapter), and this implies approaching some stimulus. Pigeons exposed to an autoshaping procedure of key light followed by shock, where the key is fitted with a transparent hemispheric extension, will activate the key. Some pigeons peck the key; others slap it with their wings (Rachlin, 1969). An interesting aspect of this example is that the conditioned responses do not resemble any unconditioned response to the shock in this situation.

In what may also be an example of autoshaping based on a negative reinforcer, a stimulus that does not initially elicit mobbing—that is, directing attacks toward the stimulus and producing attack, or mobbing, calls—in blackbirds will come to do so if it is paired with mobbing by another blackbird (Curio, Ernst, & Vieth, 1978; Curio, 1988).

Feature-Positive/Feature-Negative Effects

If in a standard discrimination involving a visual display, the S^D is distinguished from the S^Δ by a small portion (i.e., a feature) of the display, the individual will tend to respond to that feature of the display. For example, if a pigeon's key pecks are reinforced when two circles and a star are projected simultaneously on different parts of the key, and not reinforced when the star is replaced by another circle, the pigeon will not only peck the key only when the star is present but also will concentrate its pecks on the star (Jenkins & Sainsbury, 1969). This effect, which is called the feature-positive effect, also occurs when the distinctive feature is part of a landscape (e.g., a log or a potted plant) displayed on a video screen (Wilkie, Mak, & Saksida, 1994). The feature positive-effect is an example of sign tracking—or more specifically, autoshaping—because the individual contacts the distinctive feature even though reinforcement does not depend on contact with the feature.

If more than one positive feature is used in a discrimination, responses will be concentrated only on one; for example if a log and a potted plant are both positive features presented on a video screen to a pigeon, the pigeon will peck on the log or on the potted plant, but not on both (Wilkie, Mak, & Saksida, 1994). The factors that determine which positive feature will overshadow the other when more than one positive feature is present are not well understood at present.

Complementary to the feature-positive effect is the feature-negative effect. Here, the distinctive feature is on the S^Δ. When the individual responds to the S^Δ responding is concentrated on a common feature of the two displays. Individuals learn feature-positive discriminations more rapidly than feature-negative discriminations (Edwards & Honig, 1987; Jenkins & Sainsbury, 1969), perhaps because of their tendency to peck at the feature on the S^Δ that is the same as the one on the S^D. When reinforcement is discontinued for pigeons that have shown no evidence of forming a feature-negative discrimination during training, however, the discrimination appears while the behavior is decreasing—that is, responding decreases more rapidly in the presence of the negative feature than in its absence during extinction (Hearst, 1984). Although humans also show much poorer learning of feature-negative than feature-positive discriminations, it is not known whether the discrimination would appear during extinction for humans who fail to exhibit it during training.

Although humans normally learn a feature-positive discrimination readily, presenting them first with a feature negative discrimination that they do not learn will retard their learning of the complementary feature-positive discrimination—that is, a discrimination in which the feature that was negative is now positive. Humans who have learned a feature-positive discrimination, however, readily learn the complementary feature-negative discrimination (Hearst, 1984).

Sign Tracking Involving Displays

Sometimes sign tracking involves displays rather than contact with the conditioned stimulus. Two examples, one involving a sexual display and one an aggressive display, are as follows. (1) Male pigeons engage in a complex courting display in the presence of a female pigeon. Repeated pairings of a stimulus light and a female pigeon produces conditioning of the characteristic courting display. The conditioned response is directed toward the conditioned stimulus although it does not make contact with it (Rackham, 1971, cited in Moore, 1973). (2) As suggested by its name, the Siamese fighting fish engages in an aggressive display when confronted by another male of its species. The display consists of (a) fin erection, (b) undulating movements, (c) gill-cover erection, and (d) frontal approach to the other male. Pairing a red light with a mirror presentation (which effectively elicits the display when the fish sees its image) produces conditioning of the display toward the red light. The components condition progressively, with fin erection and undulating movements being conditioned most rapidly and gill-cover erection and frontal approach least rapidly. The components extinguish in the reverse order in which they are conditioned (Thompson & Sturm, 1965).

Sexual conditioning can also result in the interference of certain displays, perhaps through competition of the conditioned response with them. In the male blue gourami fish, for example, presenting a stimulus that has been paired with copulation reduces the aggressive displays that males initially make toward a female and generally increases the speed and effectiveness of mating and other sex-related behavior (Hollis, Cadieux, & Colbert, 1989; Hollis, Pharr, Dumas, Britton, & Field, 1997).

Conditioned Stimulus Effects on Sign Tracking

The occurrence of sign tracking, or the exact form of sign-tracking behavior that develops depends on the type of conditioned stimulus that is used. For example, although a lever that has been inserted into the chamber just before food delivery will come to elicit licking and gnawing in rats, a restrained rat that is similarly inserted prior to food delivery will not do so. Instead, it will elicit social behavior such as pawing and climbing over it and ano-genital sniffing (Timberlake & Grant, 1975). Similarly, a moving ball bearing that is paired with food will elicit in rats the behavior of digging the ball bearing out of an entry hole, carrying it to the end of the conditioning chamber, gnawing on it, and repeatedly dropping and retrieving it

(Timberlake, Wahl, & King, 1982a). The above autoshaped responses of rats to another rat paired with food and to a moving ball bearing paired with food resemble the animal's social behavior and predation of insects, respectively. (Food-deprived rats will seize and manipulate moving ball bearings even if they have not been paired with food, but not to the same extent as after they have been paired with food.)

A rat in a chamber with dirt, wood shavings, or similar loose material will bury an object (e.g., a small thin rod) that had delivered a painful stimulus when introduced into the chamber (Pinel & Mana, 1989; Pinel & Treit, 1978). This phenomenon, called defensive burying, is the same type of behavior that a rat performs in its natural environment when a snake, scorpion, or other potentially harmful small animal enters the rat's burrow.

Conditioned mobbing of a stimulus by blackbirds as a result of pairing the stimulus with another blackbird depends on the nature of the conditioned stimulus. Stuffed birds, whether natural predators (e.g., an owl) or harmless species (e.g., a honey eater), are more readily established as conditioned stimuli for mobbing by blackbirds than is a completely arbitrary stimulus, such as a multicolored plastic bottle (Curio et al., 1978; Curio, 1988).

Visual and auditory conditioned stimuli can also have different effects on sign tracking. For example, rats will approach a light that is some distance away from the food tray if the light has been paired with food; but they will not approach the source of a clicking sound located the same distance from the food tray when the clicking sound has been similarly paired with food. Instead, turning and rearing toward the source of the sound and putting their heads in the food tray are the predominant conditioned responses to the sound (Cleland & Davey, 1983). Cats, however, will readily approach a clicking sound that has been paired with food, even when the source of the sound is some distance from the food site and approaching the conditioned stimulus causes the animal to miss the food presentation on that trial. After approaching the auditory conditioned stimulus, cats sniff and search around it and sometimes also paw and bite in its general region (Grastyan & Vereczkei, 1974). These differences between rats and cats may be related to the fact that cats are carnivorous predators who often locate their prey on the basis of auditory stimuli, while rats are omnivorous foragers that rarely detect food on the basis of auditory stimuli.

The phenomena described above suggest that, at least in many cases, conditioned and unconditioned stimuli interact to cause phylogenetic response systems, rather than single isolated responses, to be elicited by the conditioned stimuli in autoshaping (Timberlake, 1983, 1994). This does not always explain, however, why a particular response or system of responses occurs to a specific localized conditioned stimulus in autoshaping. For example, although pigeons primarily locate food through vision and are nonpredatory, they will (as discussed below) peck in the direction of a speaker emitting a localized auditory conditioned stimulus based on food (Hearst & Jenkins, 1974; Steinhauer, Davol, & Lee, 1977; but see Bilbrey & Winokur, 1973).

Sign Tracking and Non-localized Conditioned Stimuli

In order for sign tracking to occur, by definition the conditioned stimulus must be a localized one. Behavior similar in some ways to sign tracking, however, does occur when the conditioned stimulus is not localized. For example, if a diffuse, nonlocalized tone instead of a key light is the conditioned stimulus in an autoshaping procedure with a pigeon, the animal will develop head bobbing or pecking motions in the presence of the tone. These head movements will not, however, be directed toward the tone because of its diffuse or nonlocalized nature. The terminal response of pecking by pigeons that sometimes occurs in the superstition experiment (Staddon & Simmelhag, 1971), described in Chapter 3 (p. 42), may also be an example of a gross motor conditioned response that is not directed toward the conditioned stimulus. That is, it may be a temporally conditioned respondent response as described in Chapter 4 (p. 57).

Similarly, courting behavior can be respondently conditioned to diffuse or nonlocalized stimuli. For example, the courting behavior of the male Japanese quail involves a complex sequence consisting of (a) stiffening and thrusting forward of the head and neck, (b) straightening and stiffening of the legs, (c) toe walking, (d) emission of a two-syllable squawk sound lasting for several seconds, and (e) feather puffing. Pairing of an overhead buzzer with the presentation of a female quail will result in the buzzer eliciting this characteristic courting display. As with the conditioned aggressive display of the Siamese fighting fish described earlier, the individual components of the display condition progress over trials and extinguish in the reverse order to that in which they condition (Farris, 1967).

Sign Tracking versus Goal Tracking

In some cases, rather than moving toward the conditioned stimulus, individuals move toward the site of the reinforcer when the conditioned stimulus occurs. This is termed goal tracking (Boakes, 1977). The following factors determine whether sign tracking, goal tracking, or some combination of both occurs.

One factor is whether the type of conditioning used is delay or trace. Recall from Chapter 4 that with trace conditioning the conditioned stimulus terminates before the beginning of the unconditioned stimulus, whereas with delay conditioning the conditioned stimulus continues until the start of the unconditioned stimulus. In a sign-tracking procedure with trace conditioning, the individual tends to goal track during the period between the termination of the conditioned stimulus and the start of the unconditioned stimulus (Brown, Hemmes, Cabezade, Vaca, & Pagano, 1993). It is easy to see why this would be the case: When the conditioned stimulus is absent, stimuli at the site of the unconditioned stimulus are the only ones present that have been consistently paired with the unconditioned stimulus.

Another factor is whether the intervals between presentation of the unconditioned stimulus are random or fixed. Individuals are more likely to sign track in the former case because temporal stimuli correlated with the unconditioned stimulus tend to override the conditioned stimulus (van Hest, van Haaren, Kop, & van der Schoot, 1986).

The ratio of the duration of the unconditioned stimulus to the length of the interval between instances of the unconditioned stimulus is a factor. The smaller this ratio (within limits), the more likely it is that sign tracking will occur because the stronger the contingency between the conditioned stimulus and the unconditioned stimulus will be (van Hest et al., 1986).

The shape of the chamber may be a factor. A few studies using a chamber much longer than it was wide (a "long box") with the conditioned stimulus at one end and the feeder at the other found that pigeons sign tracked even though this made them miss reinforcers because (as is commonly the case in learning experiments with pigeons) the food hopper remained accessible for only several seconds (e.g., Hearst & Jenkins, 1974; Peden, Browne, & Hearst, 1977).

The distance between the conditioned stimulus and the site of the reinforcer seems to be a major factor determining whether the conditioned stimulus elicits sign tracking or goal tracking. For example, pigeons always sign track when the conditioned stimulus and feeder are both at the front of a standard operant chamber for pigeons, but they typically goal track when the conditioned stimulus is moved to the back of the chamber (Boakes, 1977; Silva, Silva, & Pear, 1992). Pigeons engage in behavior that is intermediate between sign and goal tracking— for example, they may sign track at the beginning of the conditioned stimulus presentation and goal track near the end of the conditioned stimulus presentation, or they may sign track on some conditioned stimulus presentations and goal track on others—when the conditioned stimulus is on the side of the chamber, somewhere intermediate between the front and back (Silva et al., 1992). Rats often sign track during the first part of the conditioned stimulus presentation and goal track during the latter part in a standard operant chamber in which the conditioned stimulus and feeder are at the front of the chamber (Davey & Cleland, 1982; Davey, Oakley, & Cleland, 1981). Like pigeons, rats goal track less and sign track more as the conditioned stimulus is moved closer to the feeder (Holland, 1980). The fact that rats tend to goal track at shorter distances between the conditioned stimulus and feeder than pigeons do may be related to the rat's extremely limited distance vision compared to the pigeon's.

At least part of the reason that distance between the conditioned stimulus and reinforcer site may be an important determinant of whether sign or goal tracking occurs is probably that an individual that travels too far from the site of the reinforcer will be delayed in getting to it or, if reinforcer presentation is timed (which, as already mentioned, it usually is in pigeon studies), may miss some or all of the reinforcer. Thus, there is a built-in avoidance contingency in sign tracking experiments in which the conditioned stimulus and reinforcer site are far apart. Offsetting this contingency for pigeons by allowing a set amount of time for them to eat the reinforcer (van Hest et al., 1986) regardless of how long it takes them to get to it accordingly may increase the distance between conditioned stimulus and reinforcer site at which sign tracking occurs.

Finally, species may to be a factor determining whether sign tracking or goal tracking will occur. For example, male Japanese quail sign track and do not goal track during delay conditioning when the conditioned stimulus is quite far from the unconditioned stimulus and the unconditioned stimulus is either food (Burns & Domjan, 2000) or a receptive sex partner (Burns & Domjan, 1996, 2000).

DIFFUSE MOTOR RESPONSES

Earlier we saw numerous examples of conditioned stimuli eliciting specific motor responses toward themselves (sign tracking) or toward the site of the unconditioned stimulus (goal tracking). We have also seen that one factor determining whether sign tracking or goal tracking takes place is the time between the conditioned stimulus and the unconditioned stimuli. The time between the conditioned and unconditioned stimuli will also affect whether the conditioned stimulus will elicit a specific goal tracking response or a more diffuse or nonspecific motor response.

For example, if a nonlocalized stimulus, such as a tone, is paired with food, and is then presented in combination with a noisy moving object, such as a ball bearing rolling down a track or a lever inserted into the experimental space, rats may either approach the noisy moving object and manipulate it or approach the food trough and poke their noses in it. They will do the former if the time between the conditioned and unconditioned stimuli is relatively long; they will do the latter if it is relatively short (Silva & Timberlake, 1997; Silva, Timberlake, & Cevik, 1998; Silva, Timberlake, & Koehler, 1996). The amount by which the animals will manipulate the object in the former case will be greater than it would be if the tone had not been paired with food.

Interestingly, an effect similar to the above occurs even if the unconditioned stimulus precedes the conditioned stimulus (which as we saw in Chapter 4 is called backward conditioning, and is not a generally effective procedure). With the backward procedure, nosing the food trough quickly drops off while manipulating the moveable object quickly increases above nosing the food trough as time between the food and tone increases (Silva et al., 1996; Silva et al., 1998). That is, the forward and backward procedures show some asymmetry in the effects of time between the conditioned and unconditioned stimuli on the effect of the conditioned stimulus on behavior in the presence of a moveable object.

Results such as the above seem to indicate that particular states (or dispositions to respond in particular ways), in addition to specific responses, may be elicited. When the unconditioned stimulus is some temporal distance away from the conditioned stimulus, the conditioned stimulus elicits a diffuse state called a general search mode; when the unconditioned stimulus is close in time to the conditioned stimulus a focal search mode is elicited. This is consistent with the fact that reinforcement of response variability in a sequence of responses more readily increases the variability of responses early than those late in the sequence (Cherot et al., 1996). The general and focal search modes for each primary reinforcer constitute a behavior system (Timberlake, 1983, 1994; Timberlake & Fanselow, 1994; Timberlake & Lucas, 1989; Timberlake & Silva, 1995).

CONDITIONED EMOTIONAL RESPONSES

We have seen how stimulus-stimulus pairings can produce specific responses directed at the conditioned stimulus and diffuse (search-type) responses that make the animal (at least in its natural environment) more likely to encounter and successfully interact with a positive reinforcer. Stimulus-stimulus pairings also can produce fairly diffuse responses that are directed toward or away from the conditioned stimulus or some other specific (present) stimulus. These reactions might be considered as "emotional," in that certain words—for example, "anger," "fear," "anxiety," "joy"—in the language of emotion seem to apply to them.

Conditioned Aggression

As mentioned earlier in this chapter, aversive stimuli elicit attack. In addition, as also mentioned earlier in this chapter, components of aggressive displays can be respondently conditioned. When they are directed toward the conditioned stimulus, they are examples of sign tracking. Conditioned aggressive responses not directed toward the conditioned stimulus can also be established through respondent conditioning. For example, shocking a restrained squirrel monkey will cause it to bite a rubber tube placed in front of it. If a tone is turned on ten seconds before each shock, eventually the tone will come to elicit biting of the tube by the monkey (Hutchinson et al., 1971). Fighting by rats also can be repondently conditioned. It can be elicited as an unconditioned response by delivering foot shock to two rats in the same chamber. An auditory stimulus paired with the shock over a number of trials will come also to elicit fighting (Vernon & Ulrich, 1966). Similarly, pairing a tone with a shock to a specific region of the brain (the posteroventral nucleus of the thalamus), where the application of shock elicits aggression, causes the tone to elicite aggression in monkeys (Delgado, 1963).

From the above and from the section on autoshaping, we may conclude that in the presence of a conditioned stimulus that has been paired with an aversive stimulus, animals will tend to either (a) attack the conditioned stimulus or (b) attack other animals (if any) in the vicinity.

Conditioned Aversion

If a neutral stimulus such as a tone is paired with an aversive stimulus such as a shock, the neutral stimulus will also become aversive. That is, the formerly neutral stimulus will be both a negative reinforcer and a punisher. For example, it will reinforce lever pressing if its removal is contingent on a lever press. Alternatively, it will punish lever pressing if its presentation is contingent on a lever press. The process by which a neutral stimulus becomes aversive through pairing with an aversive stimulus is called aversive conditioning. Several terms used to describe the previously neutral stimulus are conditioned negative reinforcer, conditioned punisher, and conditioned aversive stimulus.

One way to explain aversive conditioning is to assume that an aversive stimulus elicits an internal response that is an aversive stimulus (since a response is also a stimulus; or, to be more precise, produces stimuli). Two types of internal responses/aversive stimuli that have been postulated are fear and nausea.

Conditioned responses based on fear.

Some learning scientists postulate that certain (usually painful) stimuli, such as shock, elicit an internal response that we may call "fear." They also postulate that a neutral stimulus paired with the unconditioned stimulus will come to elicit this response called "fear," or "anxiety," which is both a response and an aversive stimulus. According to this interpretation, the reinforcement of turning off the conditioned aversive stimulus is due to the fact that this turns the aversive response off. Similarly, the punishment of a response by a conditioned aversive stimulus is assumed to be due to the elicitation of the aversive response by the conditioned aversive stimulus (e.g., Mowrer, 1960; Dinsmoor, 1954; Mowrer & Lamoreaux, 1942).

Some stimuli are more readily made into conditioned aversive stimuli based on fear than others. For example, snakes and spiders that are paired with shock become conditioned aversive stimuli for humans more readily than do flowers, mushrooms, and even electric outlets that are paired with shock (Öhman, Ericksson, & Olofsson, 1975; Öhman, Fredrikson, Hugdahl, & Rimmo, 1976; Hugdahl & Kärker, 1981). In addition, the aversive response (as indicated by the GSR) takes longer to extinguish to the former conditioned stimuli than to the latter when the conditioned stimulus occurs without the unconditioned stimulus. Similarly, rhesus monkeys develop snake fear—as measured by their latencies in reaching for food in the presence of a real or toy snake—as a result of observing videotapes of other monkeys showing fear reactions to snakes, but do not develop fear of flowers as a result of observing videotapes portraying other monkeys showing fear reactions to flowers (Cook et al., 1985; Cook & Mineka, 1990). The tendency for snakes and spiders to become aversive conditioned stimuli more readily than flowers, mushrooms, and electric outlets probably results from an evolutionary history in which snakes and spiders were dangerous, but the other objects mentioned were not.

The differential ability of certain stimuli to become conditioned aversive stimuli is not a phenomenon that is limited to vertebrates. Foraging honeybees readily learn to avoid shock when it is preceded by an air steam or by vibration of the object on which they are feeding, but not when either lights or changes in the magnetic field precede it—despite the fact that honeybees respond well to lights and changes in the magnetic field in other kinds of situations (Bitterman, 1996, pp. 125–126; Walker, Baird, & Bitterman, 1989).

Conditioned responses based on nausea.

Earlier in this chapter (p. 106) we discussed how stimuli that are paired with nausea-eliciting stimuli can come to elicit nausea. We now discuss nausea as an internal aversive response. Taste stimuli are particularly susceptible to becoming conditioned stimuli for nausea. Thus, a type of conditioned aversion of special interest is conditioned taste aversion.

If an animal eats a substance with a distinctive or novel taste and later becomes ill, the animal will subsequently show a reduced tendency to consume that particular substance. For example, suppose that rats are permitted to drink some saccharin-flavored water and are then made ill (e.g., by being exposed to x-rays). The result will be a considerable suppression of drinking saccharin-flavored water. This can be understood in terms of respondent conditioning by assuming that the taste of the food becomes a conditioned stimulus for nausea, which is assumed to be aversive. Essentially, this is the same explanation as that given for conditioned aversiveness based on shock (with nausea being substituted for fear in the explanation).

Comparisons between conditioned aversions based on fear and nausea. There are, however, some interesting differences, as well as similarities, between conditioned taste aversions and conditioned aversions based on fear.

Differences. Suppose that in place of saccharin-flavored water in the above example of conditioned taste aversion, there is a distinctive audiovisual stimulus (e.g., gurgling noises and flashing lights) with each lick of plain water. As above, the rats are made ill after licking the water and experiencing the distinctive stimulus (which is auditory and visual rather than gustatory). In this case, the distinctive stimulus will cause little or no suppression of the water-licking response that produces it. The results would have been quite different, however, if the rats had been shocked rather than made ill after drinking the water. Had they been shocked after drinking the saccharin-flavored water, the taste of saccharin would have little or no suppressive effect on subsequent drinking. Had they been shocked after drinking the water that produced the distinctive audiovisual stimulus, however, the audiovisual stimulus would have suppressed subsequent drinking (Garcia & Koelling, 1966). This is because the extent to which

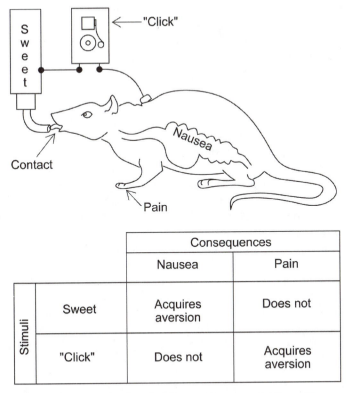

FIGURE 6.1. The figure illustrates the fact that (for a rat) a taste stimulus will more readily become a conditioned aversive stimulus if it is paired with nausea than if it is paired with shock; whereas the opposite is true for an auditory stimulus. (From Garcia et al., 1973)

a particular stimulus will become a conditioned aversive stimulus depends on the type of unconditioned aversive stimulus that it is paired with. Figure 6.1 illustrates this differential conditionability to aversion of different types of stimuli when paired with different types of aversive stimuli.

Whether taste stimuli more readily condition than visual stimuli to nausea, however, depends on the species being considered. For example, conditioned aversions based on nausea in quails are more readily established to visual (e.g., color) than to taste properties of water (Wilcoxon, Dragoin, & Kral, 1971). The evolutionary reason for this difference between rats and quails is that taste is a more salient property of food for the former (because rats are color blind) whereas color is a more salient property for the latter—and the bird can respond to it without having to risk swallowing even the slightest morsel. Rats have evolved to depend largely on taste and smell in discriminating food from nonfood; whereas, birds have evolved to depend on vision for this purpose, probably because vision is critical to their being able to fly. The salient properties of food for a given species more readily become conditioned aversive stimuli based on nausea because in an animal's natural environment illness is more likely to follow eating poisonous substances than other behavior by the animal.

In addition to the differences in the conditionabilities of different types of stimuli, there are two other interesting differences between conditioned taste aversions and conditioned aversive stimuli based on shock. One is that conditioned taste aversions occur surprisingly fast, generally in a single trial. The other is that they can occur despite intervals of several hours between the conditioned stimulus (the taste of a particular food) and the primary aversive event (nausea). In fact, effective conditioning has been reported with intervals up to 24 hours (Etscorn & Stephens, 1973). In contrast, trace conditioning intervals greater than a few seconds are usually ineffective in establishing a conditioned aversive stimulus based on shock.

The differences between conditioned taste aversions and other types of conditioned aversions probably have a strong evolutionary basis. When an animal has eaten a poisonous substance, the effects of being poisoned usually do not occur until a fairly long time has passed. Hence, from an evolutionary point of view, it is important that conditioning be susceptible to a fairly long interval between the occurrence of the substance and the aversive effects of the substance. Moreover, since poisoning is often fatal, it is adaptable for an animal to acquire a conditioned taste aversion rapidly, since the animal may not get more than one trial in its natural environment. Finally, among the various stimuli present when poisoning occurs, the ones on which the poison is most likely to be contingent are those involving the taste, texture, and color of the substance rather than auditory and complex visual stimuli. Considering that one-trial conditioning of taste aversions was selected because of its high survival value, the stimulus that becomes the conditioned aversive stimulus should be one (e.g., taste) that is likely to be present on the next occasion that the poison is encountered in the animal's natural environment.

Because of the differences between conditioned taste aversions and conditioned aversions based on shock, some learning scientists have argued that different behavioral laws are required to account for the two processes (e.g., Seligman, 1970). Others have suggested that the differences thus far observed are merely quantitative (e.g., one-trial learning versus many-trial learning, 2-second effective trace conditioning interval versus 24-hour effective interval) and that therefore different laws need not be postulated (e.g., Domjan, 1980, 1983; Logue, 1979; Spiker, 1977). For example, objects fall at different rates on the earth and moon, but this fact does not require two different laws of gravitation on the earth and moon.

Similarities.   In addition to differences, conditioned aversions based on nausea shares important features with those based on fear (Schafe & Bernstein, 1996). Both types of conditioned aversions show:

1. extinction (p. 26)
2. stimulus generalization (p. 27)
3. latent inhibition (p. 47)

With regard to extinction, it should be noted that reduction of a conditioned aversive response through extinction takes a long time if the individual is able to avoid the conditioned aversive stimulus. This is because a conditioned response must occur in order to be extinguished.

Conditioned taste aversions in humans. Conditioned taste aversions occur in humans as well as other animals. Most of us probably have had the experience of developing a dislike for a particular food as a result of becoming ill after eating it, even if the food did not cause the illness. As mentioned earlier in this chapter, one of the problems faced by cancer patients undergoing chemotherapy, which has nausea and vomiting as side effects, is that of developing conditioned taste aversions to foods (Bernstein, 1978, 1991; Bernstein & Webster, 1985; Jacobsen et al., 1993; Stockhorst et al., 1998). This can happen to any food that the patient happens to eat some time before a treatment. It should be noted that, as with all respondent conditioning, the effect is automatic and cannot be counteracted by simply telling the patient that the food did not cause the nausea and vomiting (Redd, 1989, p. 426). However, since conditioning occurs more readily to novel than to familiar stimuli, a novel food eaten prior to treatment can prevent (or reduce) conditioning of nausea to a familiar food that is also eaten prior to treatment (Andresen et al., 1990; Broberg & Bernstein, 1987). That is, through latent inhibition (Chapter 3, p. 47) conditioning of nausea occurs to the novel food rather than to the familiar food. Called the scapegoat technique, this method may prove to be a practical and effective means for reducing the risk of forming conditioned taste aversions to routine dietary items as an undesirable side effect of chemotherapy.

Conditioned suppression. Suppose that a lever-press response by a rat is being maintained on a VI 1 schedule. Occasionally a tone lasting three minutes occurs. Although when first introduced the tone disrupted the behavior somewhat, this no longer occurs due to habituation (see Chapter 2). Now assume that a brief electric shock occurs at the end of the tone. After several exposures to this procedure, lever pressing will be suppressed in the presence of the tone (Estes & Skinner, 1941). This is termed conditioned suppression. Figure 6.2 shows how conditioned suppression appears on a cumulative record. It is important to note that conditioned suppression of a response *is not* punishment of that response, because the response does not produce the primary aversive stimulus (i.e., the shock in this example). (See the definition of punishment in Chapter 3.)

The reason that conditioned suppression occurs is not known. It is generally assumed, however, that it is probably due to some sort of respondently conditioned behavior that interferes with the operant behavior under observation. One possibility is that it reflects freezing or cowering elicited as a conditioned response to a conditioned aversive stimulus (e.g., Bouton & Bolles, 1980).

The amount of conditioned suppression that occurs to the conditioned aversive stimulus relative to baseline responding in the absence of the stimulus depends on a number of factors (Blackman, 1977) including that: (1) more conditioned suppression is produced by a strong primary aversive event than by a weak one; and (2) more conditioned suppression occurs on a schedule with a low rate of reinforcement than on one with a high rate of reinforcement.

Backward aversive conditioning. In Chapter 4 we saw that backward conditioning—that is a pairing procedure in which the unconditioned stimulus precedes the conditioned stimu-

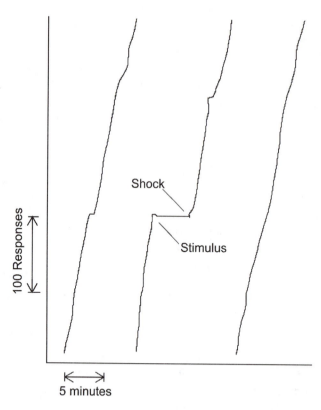

FIGURE 6.2. Conditioned suppression. The cumulative record in the figure shows the disruption of a monkey's lever pressing by a stimulus (a series of rapid clicks) that preceded a brief, unavoidable shock. The monkey was responding on a variable-interval schedule of food reinforcement. (The reinforcements are not shown.) The downward displacement of the pen indicates the start of the clicking sound, and the rectification of the pen ndicates the termination of the clicking sound and presentation of the shock. Note that the animal resumed normal responding immediately after the shock. (From Sidman, 1960)

lus—is not an effective conditioning procedure. With backward conditioning, rather than becoming excitatory, the conditioned stimulus becomes an inhibitory stimulus (a CS−). Thus, if it is presented in conjunction with a conditioned stimulus that has been established through forward conditioning, the conditioned response will be decreased. Moreover, if backward conditioning is carried out with a particular stimulus and then forward conditioning is carried out with that same stimulus, acquisition will not occur in the first phase and will be retarded in the second phase due to the inhibition that built up during the first phase (Hall, 1984; Plotkin & Oakley, 1975; Siegel & Domjan, 1971).

Nevertheless, a stimulus can become a conditioned aversive stimulus through a backward pairing procedure (Burkhardt, 1980; Mowrer & Aiken, 1954; Williams et al., 1986). In fact, a stimulus may be both a conditioned inhibitory stimulus for respondent conditioning and, at the same time, a conditioned aversive stimulus. For example, if a shock near the orbit of a rabbit's eye is followed by a tone, that tone presented along with a conditioned stimulus that elicits the nictitating membrane response will decrease the conditioned response. Moreover, forward conditioning of the nictitating membrane to the tone will be retarded as a result of the previous shock-tone pairings. That same tone, however, will suppress licking on a water tube when presented following water-tube licks (Tait & Saladin, 1986). In addition, if it is presented just before a stimulus that produces a startle response—for example, a puff of air to the ear—that startle response will be enhanced (McNish, Betts, Brandon, & Wagner, 1997).

Suppose that a conditioned stimulus overlaps the unconditioned stimulus. That is, part of the conditioned stimulus occurs *before* the onset of the unconditioned stimulus and part of the conditioned stimulus occurs *after* the termination of the unconditioned stimulus. In a sense, we may say that this conditioned stimulus is both a forward conditioned stimulus and a backward conditioned stimulus. The result is that the forward and backward parts of the conditioned stimulus sum algebraically. Thus the stimulus is less effective in the conditioning of a motor response, such as the nictitating membrane response, than a stimulus that is paired with the unconditioned stimulus in a forward manner (Barnes, 1956; McNish et al., 1997; Schneiderman, 1966). The reason is that the inhibitory (i.e., backward) component of the stimulus overlapping the unconditioned stimulus subtracts from the excitatory (i.e., forward) component. The result is quite different with regard to aversive conditioning, however. In that case the overlapping stimulus is a stronger conditioned stimulus than one that is simply paired in a forward manner (McNish et al., 1997). The reason is that both the forward and backward parts of the overlapping conditioned stimulus are excitory, so that the net effect is a greater amount of excitation in comparison with a stimulus that received only forward pairing with the unconditioned stimulus. This result will, however, depend on how long the backward part of the conditioned stimulus lasts. As this time increases, we would expect the conditioned stimulus to eventually become neutral or even inhibitory for the conditioned aversive response.

Indeed, backward aversive conditioning in rats can produce a stimulus that inhibits, not excites, aversiveness. A stimulus paired in a forward manner with this inhibitory stimulus may, however, become a higher-order conditioned aversive (not inhibitory) stimulus (Barnet & Miller, 1996).

Blocking and unblocking of aversive conditioning.

As seen above, there is an important difference between respondent conditioning of specific responses and aversive conditioning: Although backward conditioning of specific responses typically is inhibitory, with aversive conditioning it is excitatory. Another important difference between respondent conditioning of a specific response and aversive conditioning is the fact that a procedure that unblocks the former does not unblock the latter.

Consider the following experiment. A tone is presented to a rabbit followed by a shock near the orbit of one eye. This is repeated until the conditioned blink response occurs to the tone. Next, a light is presented in combination with the tone, again followed by shock near the orbit of the other eye. Note that this is a standard blocking procedure except the location of the unconditioned stimulus (and hence the blink response) has changed. If the standard blocking procedure had been used—that is, had the location of the shock not been changed—the light would have been blocked from becoming a conditioned stimulus for the blink response. Changing the location of the shock prevents the light from being blocked as a conditioned stimulus for a blink response—it unblocks the light. Nevertheless, the light is still blocked from becoming a conditioned aversive stimulus. As in the case of backward inhibitory conditioning of a stimulus to a specific response and backward excitatory conditioning of the same stimulus to aversiveness describe above, the same stimulus may be unblocked for a specific response and blocked for aversiveness (Betts, Brandon, & Wagner, 1996). Why these differences between respondent conditioning of specific responses and conditioned aversiveness occur is not currently known.

Conditioned Value

We have seen that a stimulus that has been paired (at least in a forward manner) with an aversive stimulus will become aversive, in that it will be both a punisher and a negative reinforcer. As we have said, this is apparently because it has come to elicit an internal aversive response (e.g., fear, nausea). Similarly, a stimulus that has been paired with a positive reinforcer will become a positive reinforcer. We postulate that this is because it has come to elicit an internal reinforcing response, that we might call "pleasure," "joy," or some such. Somewhat more objectively, the internal reinforcing and aversive responses elicited by conditioned positive and negative reinforcers are called conditioned evaluative responses. The internal reinforcing responses elicited by conditioned positive reinforcers are conditioned positive evaluative responses, and the internal aversive responses elicited by conditioned aversive stimuli are conditioned negative evaluative responses. Correspondingly, we may say that a conditioned positive reinforcer has conditioned positive value and a conditioned aversive stimulus has conditioned negative value. (Theories that postulate respondently conditioned responses to account for conditioned aversion or conditioned reinforcement are called two-factor theories, and are discussed further in Chapter 13.)

Conditioned positive reinforcement.   A neutral stimulus that is paired with a positive reinforcer will become a positive reinforcer. The previously neutral stimulus is then called a conditioned (positive) reinforcer, as opposed to a primary reinforcer which is a stimulus (e.g., food) that is reinforcing without having been paired with another reinforcer.

Measurement of Conditioned Reinforcement.   There are several ways to demonstrate or measure conditioned reinforcement. We may measure it by using it to condition a new response, by testing it in extinction, and by testing preference for it over some other stimulus. We detail each of these measurement methods below.

Conditioning a new response.   The clearest demonstration of conditioned reinforcement is showing that a stimulus that has been paired with a positive reinforcer can be used to reinforce a new response—that is, a response that the individual does not already emit. Such a demonstration is often difficult because it requires presenting the conditioned reinforcer without presenting the primary reinforcer on which it is based. This may result in the extinction of the conditioned reinforcer before the new response can be conditioned.

Extinction test.   Another way to demonstrate conditioned reinforcement is to make a conditioned reinforcer contingent on a response that is being extinguished. This will result in a temporary increase in the rate of the response. For example, a lever-press response may be extinguished by disconnecting the feeder mechanism. When the response rate has decreased to a low level, the feeder mechanism is reconnected although the feeder is empty. Although no food is delivered, the sound of the feeder mechanism, having been previously paired with food, will reinforce the lever-press response causing an increase in its rate. (Chapters 11 and 12 describe several other response-contingent ways of demonstrating conditioned reinforcement.)

Preference test.   A preference test consists of giving an individual a choice between two stimuli, one of which is a neutral stimulus and the other a putative conditioned reinforcer. For example, a rat that has drunk a saccharin solution (which is reinforcing because of its sweet taste) containing an aqueous odor (i.e., an odor that is soluble in water) may receive a choice between plain water and water containing only the aqueous odor. Strong evidence that the odor is a conditioned reinforcer due to its pairing with saccharin occurs if the animal consistently drinks more of the liquid containing the previously neutral odor than the plain water (Fanselow & Birk, 1982; Holman, 1975).

Blocking of a conditioned reinforcer. A conditioned reinforcer may be blocked with procedures completely analogous to those that block a conditioned response or conditioned aversiveness. For example, a rat will not acquire a preference for an odor presented in a sucrose solution (i.e., sugar water) if that solution also contains another odor that the rat had previously experienced in solution with sucrose (Holder, 1991). Similarly if water containing only sucrose is presented to a rat prior to, or in alternation with, trials in which the rat receives a solution containing sucrose along with an almond odor, the almond odor will not become a conditioned reinforcer (Harris, Gorissen, Bailey, & Westbrook, 2000). In the former case, the neutral odor is blocked by the odor that had been previously paired with sucrose; in the latter case it is block by context stimuli (see Chapter 4, p. 82).

Effect of satiation on a conditioned reinforcer. Satiation of the primary reinforcer on which a conditioned reinforcer is based weakens the conditioned reinforcer. The conditioned reinforcer may, however, maintain some of its effectiveness for responses that are not close in time to the consumption of the primary reinforcer (Morgan, 1974; Rescorla, 1977). For example, a food-satiated rat running a complex maze it has learned for food reinforcement will make fewer errors at the beginning of the maze than at the end, due to the fact that the stimuli near the end are more closely paired with primary reinforcement.

Evaluative conditioning and testing. In humans conditioned value (either positive or negative) is frequently studied by pairing a number of different originally neutral stimuli (i.e., stimuli that have neither positive nor negative value) with stimuli that have either positive or negative value (as determined by ratings or in some other way). This process is called evaluative conditioning, and is assumed to be an analogue of a similar process of evaluative conditioning that occurs naturally in one's social environment. Then, in a test phase, individuals who underwent evaluative conditioning rate the originally neutral stimuli on one or more scales (e.g., a scale ranging from "strongly like" to "strongly dislike") or in some other way verbally indicate the conditioned value of the stimuli. For purpose of comparison, the individuals also rate stimuli that were not paired (or that received random pairings) with stimuli that have either positive or negative value.

Note that this procedure makes use of humans' ability to describe private (i.e., internal or covert) stimuli in this case, stimuli produced by internal evaluative responses. The internal evaluative responses of nonverbal animals cannot be studied in this way. Even in the case of humans, it is not completely clear how accurately they can describe internal stimuli. The problem becomes evident when one considers that no one is ever able to reinforce our accurately describing private stimuli because (by definition) no one other than ourselves has access to our private stimuli. So how is it that we apparently do learn to describe them at least somewhat accurately? There are processes that explain how it is that we learn with at least a minimal degree of accuracy to describe private stimuli; however, we must defer discussion of these processes to Chapter 17.

Use of the above general method shows that previously neutral flavors will take on positive or negative value if they are presented in simultaneous combination with a good (Zellner, Rozin, Aron, & Kulish, 1983) or bad (Baeyens, Crombez, De Houwer, & Eelen, 1996; Baeyens, Crombez, Hendrickx, & Eelen, 1995; Baeyens, Eelen, Van den Bergh, & Crombez, 1990) tasting substance, respectively. Similarly, slides of neutral pictures (e.g., ordinary human faces) that have been paired with slides of aversive stimuli (e.g., unattractive faces) may take on negative value (Levey & Martin, 1975; Martin & Levey, 1978). The results of these studies are in doubt, however, because of problems replicating them under conditions that explicitly control for perceptual similarity between the conditioned-stimulus pictures and the unconditioned-stimulus pictures (Field & Davey, 1999).

It has long been known that conditioned evaluative responses are important in the formation of attitudes (Staats & Staats, 1969). To take an example from the field of advertising, neutrally valued (fictitious) brand names take on positive value after being paired with pleasant images (Grossman & Till, 1998; Shimp, Stuart, & Engle, 1991; Stuart, Shimp, & Engle, 1987). Conversely, brand names that have been paired with negatively valued stimuli, such as music made aversive by being paired with an arduous task (Blair & Shimp, 1992), take on negative value.

MEDIATED PAIRINGS

There are phenomena that at first do not appear to be due to stimulus pairing even though stimulus pairing has in fact produced them. On closer inspection of such cases we find that stimulus pairing has occurred vicariously. That is, we find that two stimuli have been paired indirectly through the pairing of each with a third stimulus. In a sense, we may say that any stimulus that has been paired with another stimulus has been paired with every stimulus that other stimulus has been paired with. To fully understand phenomena produced by stimulus pairings, then, we need to examine the effects of indirectly pairing stimuli through intermediate stimuli.

The indirect pairing of one stimulus with another through an intermediate stimulus is referred to as mediated pairing.

Effects of Mediated Pairings

Mediated pairings produce results that, except for being weaker, are the same as those produced by nonmediated, or direct, pairings. For example, in sensory preconditioning (described in Chapter 3) stimulus A is paired with stimulus B which is then paired with an unconditioned stimulus. The result is that A elicits a conditioned response as though it had been directly paired with the unconditioned stimulus (although the conditioned response it elicits will be weaker than would be the case if A had been directly paired with the unconditioned stimulus). We call this a mediated pairing because B mediates the pairing of A with the unconditioned stimulus.

This is similar to higher-order conditioning as described in Chapter 3, except that in higher-order conditioning B is paired with the unconditioned stimulus before A is paired with B. In Chapter 3 we spoke of this as a conditioned stimulus (namely, B) becoming an unconditioned stimulus that is paired with another conditioned stimulus (namely, A), but we could also have described B as mediating the pairing of A with the (actual) unconditioned stimulus.

Devaluing the connection between stimulus B and the unconditioned stimulus in some way—either by extinguishing stimulus B or by satiation of the individual with the unconditioned stimulus—has little effect on the mediated conditioned response to stimulus A (Holland & Rescorla, 1975; Morgan, 1974; Rescorla, 1980) unless stimulus A and stimulus B are very similar (Nairne & Rescorla, 1981). The connection between stimulus A and its conditioned response does not depend on further mediation, and is said to be autonomous. Of course, the connection can be broken through an extinction procedure in which stimulus A is presented repeatedly without being followed by stimulus B.

Pairings Within Compound Stimuli

The elements of a compound stimulus are paired by definition. It is therefore not surprising that sensory preconditioning (pp. 29–30) occurs with compound stimuli. For example, suppose that sometimes a black line at a +45° angle on a green background is projected on a key that a pigeon is attending to for some reason (e.g., presentations of a white light on that key may be followed by food), and sometimes a black line at a –45° angle on a red background is projected on the key (the colors and line angles are arbitrary, and may be changed around without affecting the result described below). Suppose that after this the +45° line is presented on a white background and paired with food, and the –45° degree line is presented on a white background and not paired with food, so that the pigeon eventually pecks at the former and not the latter (autoshaping). If a test now is conducted in which a green light is sometimes projected on the key and at other times a red light is projected on the key, the pigeon will tend to peck more at the green light than at the red light (Rescorla, 1981). This, then, is simply a variation of sensory preconditioning (i.e., the green light elicits more pecking than the red light because of the former's pairing with the line that was later paired with food) involving a compound stimulus. A compound-stimulus variation of higher-order conditioning would show a similar result.

Several other compound-stimulus variations of mediated pairings, however, produce results that are a bit more surprising (Rescorla, 1981; Speers, Gillan, & Rescorla, 1980).

Mediated pairings and inhibitory stimuli.   Let A_1 and A_2 be two single stimuli, such as two line orientations, and B_1 and B_2 be two single stimuli, such as two colors, that can be combined with A_1 or A_2 to make compound stimuli. Let A_1B_1 be the compound stimulus consisting of the stimulus elements A_1 and B_1, and A_2B_2 be the compound stimulus consisting of the stimulus elements A_2 and B_2. Now consider the following sequence of events:

1. We pair A_1 and A_2 with an unconditioned stimulus when they occur by themselves, but with nothing when they occur in combination with B_1 and B_2, respectively. That is, we make A_1 and A_2 each a CS+ when they appear by itself and CS– when they appear in the compound stimuli A_1B_1 and A_2B_2. We abbreviate this arrangement as: A_1+, A_2+, A_1B_1-, and A_2B_2-. Thus B_1 and B_2 are inhibitory stimuli (see Chapter 4, p. 77).
2. Next we establish A_1+ and A_2-(i.e., we continue to pair A_1 with the unconditioned stimulus but we now extinguish A_2; or, in other words, present it without the unconditioned stimulus).
3. Finally, as a test, we establish B_1+ and B_2+; that is we pair both B_1 and B_2 (separately) with the unconditioned stimulus. The question we are asking in this test is whether B_1 or B_2 elicits more responding. The answer is that there will be a small, but statistically significant, difference in favor of more responding to B_1. This result indicates that even stimulus elements that are inhibitory within their compound stimuli (as B_1 and B_2 are in the above example) will, due to their pairing with other elements of the compound, take on either excitatory or inhibitory functions present in or later established to those other elements. Mediated pairing thus occurs between excitatory and inhibitory stimulus elements within a compound stimulus.

Pairings within positive and negative compound stimuli.   Now consider the following sequence of events (using the same notation as above):

1. We condition A_1B_1+, A_2B_2+, A_1B_2-, and A_2B_1-.
2. Next we condition B_1+ and B_2-.

3. Finally, as a test, we extinguish A_1 and A_2 to determine which of these two stimuli elicits more responding during extinction.

Note that both A_1 and A_2 are paired equally with B_1 within compound stimuli. However, the compound stimulus is positive in the case of A_1 and negative in the case of A_2. The question we want to answer is: will B_1 mediate more strongly with its co-member in the positive compound stimulus or with its co-member in the negative compound stimulus? If the former, then we would expect A_1 to tend to elicit more responding in the test; if the latter, we would expect A_2 to tend to elicit more responding in the test. Note also, that both A_1 and A_2 are paired equally with B_2 within compound stimuli. However, the compound stimulus is negative in the case of A_1 and positive in the case of A_2.

Again, the question we want to answer is: will B_1 mediate more strongly with its co-member in the positive compound stimulus or with its co-member in the negative compound stimulus? If the former, then we would expect A_1 to tend to elicit more responding in the test; if the latter, we would expect A_2 to tend to elicit more responding in the test.

Thus, the considerations in both of the above two paragraphs lead us to predict that during the test A_1 will elicit more responding if mediation between the elements of a compound stimulus is stronger within a positive compound stimulus than within a negative compound stimulus. The result, however, is the opposite: There is a small but statistically significant difference in favor of A_2, indicating that mediation between elements is stronger within a negative stimulus compound. Thus, we may conclude that an unconditioned stimulus following a compound stimulus tends to interfere with mediated pairing between the elements within that compound stimulus. It is not clear at present why this is the case.

Pairings within compound stimuli and blocking. Consider the following sequence of events (again using the same notation as above):

1. First condition A+ in one group of individuals but not in a second group.
2. Next condition AB+ in both groups.
3. Finally, conduct a test to determine in which group B elicits more responding.

The typical result is that B elicits more responding on average in the second group than in the first group because the prior conditioning of A in the first group tends to block the conditioning of B as a co-member of A in a compound stimulus (see Chapter 4, p. 80). Another way to demonstrate blocking is as follows:

1. Instead of using two groups as in the above demonstration, we condition A_1+ and A_2– in the same individuals.
2. Next we condition A_1B_1+ and A_2B_2+.
3. Finally, as a test, we compare the responding elicited by B_1 and B_2.

The typical result is that B_1 tends to elicit significantly less responding than B_2. The reason is that the prior conditioning of A_1 as a CS+ tends to cause that stimulus to block the conditioning of B_1 when the two stimuli are co-members of a compound stimulus. In comparison, not being a CS+ prior to being paired with B_2 in a compound stimulus, A_2 tends not to block (or to block less) the conditioning of B_2 when these two stimuli are co-members of a compound stimulus.

There are other, more precisely controlled experimental demonstrations of blocking, but the two outlined above suffice to illustrate the general point to be made here. Note that in a demonstration of blocking, the blocked stimulus (B in Group 1 in the first blocking demonstration above and B_1 in the second) has been paired with a blocking stimulus (A in Group 1 in the first blocking demonstration above and A_1 in the second). The blocking stimulus has been previously paired with an unconditioned stimulus. Thus, from what we have said about mediated pairings, the blocking stimulus mediates pairings of the blocked stimulus with the unconditioned stimulus. This increases the responding the blocked stimulus elicits, and so tends to oppose blocking. Under certain circumstances, this can even result in elevated responding to a blocked stimulus in comparison to a nonblocked control stimulus (e.g., B in Group 2 in the first blocking demonstration above or B_2 in the second). In such cases, "blocking" is a misnomer; the term potentiation is used instead. The important thing to note, however, is that the occurrence of potentiation does not contradict blocking; rather, it is just an outcome of the mediated pairings that occur in the situation that produces blocking (Durlach & Rescorla, 1980).

SUMMARY AND CONCLUSIONS

A stimulus-stimulus contingency is the pairing of two stimuli. Stimulus-stimulus contingencies result in respondent conditioning of a wide variety of internal and external responses. The effects of stimulus-stimulus contingencies may be seen in the conditioned responses they produce or in the effects those conditioned responses have on other behavior.

Sign tracking is the result of a stimulus-stimulus contingency in which a freely moving individual approaches a conditioned stimulus based on (i.e., established through pairing with) a positive or a negative reinforcer. Autoshaping is said to occur if the individual interacts physically with the conditioned stimulus, such as manipulating or attacking it. Goal tracking is said to occur if the individual approaches the location of the unconditioned stimulus rather than the conditioned stimulus. The tendency for goal tracking to occur, rather than sign tracking, increases with the spatial distance between the conditioned and unconditioned stimuli.

Pairing a stimulus with an aversive event (i.e., a negative reinforcer) causes it to become a negative reinforcer; that is, individuals will respond to remove it (escape behavior) or to prevent it from occurring (avoidance behavior). This may be because, through respondent conditioning, stimuli paired with aversive events elicit internal responses that produce aversive stimuli. Examples include fear and nausea. Conditioned stimuli based on stimuli, such as electric shock, that excite pain receptors may elicit fear; conditioned stimuli based on toxins may elicit nausea. The type of conditioned stimuli that is most readily based on pain-exciting stimuli differs from the type of conditioned stimuli that is most readily based on nausea-exciting stimuli. Food-related stimuli (e.g., taste) are more effective as conditioned stimuli based on nausea, whereas auditory, visual, and tactile stimuli are more effective as conditioned stimuli based on pain. Moreover, conditioning an aversion based on nausea, relative to conditioning one based on pain, may be effective when there is a long time period between the conditioned and unconditioned stimuli.

A stimulus that has been paired with an aversive event and that then occurs when operant responding is occurring will tend to suppress that operant responding. This phenomenon, which is called conditioned suppression, is not to be confused with punishment because it does not depend on either the conditioned aversive stimulus or the unconditioned aversive stimulus on which it is based being presented contingent on responding. Conditioned suppression appears to be due to immobility (freezing or general lack of activity) that occurs during the conditioned aversive stimulus as a conditioned response to it.

Conditioned positive reinforcers are stimuli that are positive reinforcers because they have been paired with other positive reinforcers. They are to be distinguished from primary reinforcers, which are stimuli that are reinforcing without having been paired with other reinforcers. Just as conditioned negative reinforcers may elicit internal aversive stimuli, conditioned positive reinforcers may elicit internal positive reinforcing stimuli. Thus, respondent conditioning may account for both conditioned positive and conditioned negative reinforcement.

7

Basic Operant Behavior

*B*y definition an operant response must occur in order to be reinforced, but in order to occur it must be reinforced. If the second part of this statement were strictly true, it would be a logical contradiction for operant responses ever to occur. There are, however, ways for an operant response to occur prior to its first reinforcement.

At first blush, the issue of getting an operant response to occur before it has received its first reinforcement may not seem to be a problem. When considering ways in which to get someone to make a response, most people probably think immediately of just telling the person what to do, or showing the person what to do if that does not work, or physically putting the person through the motions as a last resort. But these methods all assume prior learning. To successfully tell a person what to do, the person must first have learned to follow instructions. To successfully demonstrate to an individual what to do, the individual must first have learned to imitate. To successfully guide an individual through the motions of an action, the individual must first have learned to yield to physical manipulation in a training situation. Thus, none of these methods can be used to teach someone anything until prior learning has occurred. Specifically, the prior learning that is required involves behavior coming under stimulus control, as will be discussed in detail in Chapter 8. As we have already seen, however, an operant response cannot come under stimulus control until it has occurred (Chapter 3). Thus, we are back to the original problem: How can an operant response occur before it is reinforced?

Another way to see the problem is to think of teaching a pigeon to turn around in circles or a preverbal infant to say the word "chair." Clearly instruction, demonstration, and guidance would not work in such cases. To see the problem in even sharper relief, think of how a new response might occur in a situation in which there is no trainer.

In this chapter we examine how new responses occur for the first time without instruction, demonstration, or guidance. Once a new response occurs, schedules of reinforcement come into play to determine the rate at which it occurs and its rate patterns and variations. Thus, this chapter examines ways in which an operant response first comes to be generated and how subsequent patterns of reinforcement affect its overall and moment-to-moment probability of occurrence.

RESPONSE GENERALIZATION AND SHAPING

Logically there have to be some operant responses that occur prior to reinforcement because reinforcement cannot work until there is at least one response for it to work on. This initial behavior, which must be phylogenetically determined, probably occurs soon after birth if not earlier. It is possible that there are many phylogetically determined operant responses that occur throughout an individual's lifetime; however, we have no evidence to support this and it serves no useful scientific purpose to assume it. There is another way, which does have empirical support, for new operant responses to occur for the first time. Once a response occurs, reinforcement strengthens (i.e., increases the probability of occurrence of) that response *and* similar responses. For example, suppose that reinforcement occurs after a rat presses a lever with its right front paw. As a result, pressing the lever with the right front paw will have been strengthened. In addition, pressing the lever with the left front paw, with both paws, and perhaps even with the snout also will have been strengthened. The occurrence of responses that differ from the reinforced response is, as we have seen (Chapter 4), called response variability or response generalization. Response generalization is to be distinguished from stimulus generalization, which is the process whereby reinforcing a response in the presence of a particular stimulus increases the probability that the same response will occur in the presence of similar stimuli. Note that in response generalization the response varies while the stimulus remains constant, whereas in stimulus generalization the stimulus varies while the response remains constant.

One way to illustrate response generalization (or response variability) involves using a long horizontal strip or key as the operandum with an animal such as a rat or pigeon (see Figure 7.1, picture). Nose-poking responses on the strip by rats or pecking responses on the key by pigeons are reinforced, and the location of each response is recorded. The typical findings are that: (1) variability in response locus decreases to a low value with increased exposure to continuous reinforcement; and (2) variability in response locus increases when rate of reinforcement is decreased by introducing either extinction, a fixed-interval schedule, or a variable-interval schedule (Antonitis, 1951; Eckerman & Lanson, 1969; Millenson & Hurwitz, 1961; Morgan & Lee, 1996). The increase in response variability that occurs when reinforcement rate decreases may be a return toward the response variability that existed prior to reinforcement (Margulies, 1961). Response generalization is one of two essential ingredients of response shaping (the other essential ingredient being reinforcement).

Types of Response Shaping

From the above we see that new operant responses occur through responses generalization. They do not typically, however, differ very much from the response initially reinforced. Therefore, response generalization alone cannot account for the occurrence of responses that differ greatly from the response originally reinforced. Response shaping, however, which we discussed in Chapter 4, can account for this. Response shaping depends on response generalization. Some of the responses that are strengthened by reinforcement of a particular response are closer to a target response than is the response that is being reinforced. Reinforcing one of these responses will strengthen, through response generalization, responses that are still closer to the target response. Reinforcing one of these responses will provide even closer approximations to reinforcer; and so on, until the target response occurs and is reinforced. It should be pointed out that this process does not necessarily require someone doing the shaping; the environment may shape behavior.

There are perhaps an uncountable number of different types of shaping; we discuss some of them now.

Position shaping. The process of shaping can be illustrated with the long key described above. First the position of the response (or *position shaping*) reinforcement might be given for pecks on the right 1/2-inch region of the key. Then the reinforced area might be moved 1

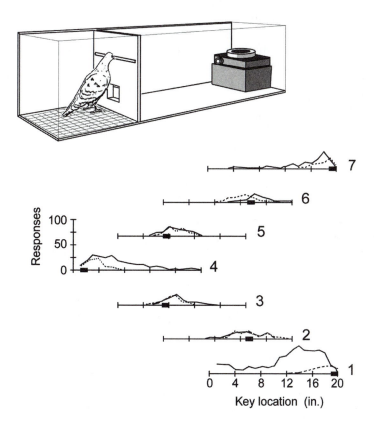

FIGURE 7.1. Shaping pecking location along a "long key." Top: An operant conditioning apparatus containing a long key consisting of 20 one-inch plastic plates, with a microswitch behind each for recording pecks. A slide projector illuminates the long key uniformly from behind. Bottom: Pecks at various locations on the long key during seven consecutive sessions of 100 reinforced responses each. The dark bars along the horizontal axes indicate the locations on the key at which responding was reinforced. Dotted lines plot the first 75 responses in each session; solid lines plot the last 25 responses in each session. Note that the latter responses tended to peak at the reinforced locations, and that the response distribution shifted as the reinforced location changed systematically first to the left (sessions 1 to 4) and then to the right (session 5 to 7). (From Eckerman et al., 1980)

inch to the left; then another 1 inch to the left; and so on, until the bird is pecking at the left 1.5 inch region of the key. Results from a study (Eckerman, Hienz, Stern, & Kowlowitz, 1980) involving such an experiment are shown in Figure 7.1.

The series of graphs in Figure 7.1 is from a bird whose pecking on the right 1.5 inch region of the key first received 100 reinforcements. Then the reinforced area was moved 3 inches to the left where it remained for another 100 reinforcements; then the reinforced area was moved another 3 inches for another 100 reinforcements; and so on. After the reinforced region reached the left end of the key, it was shifted back in the same manner to the right end of the key.

The same pigeon was exposed to two other series in the same way, except that the sizes of the shaping steps were different. The step size for one of these series was 1.5 inches; the step size for the the other as 1 inch. Other pigeons exposed to the same three series in different orders gave the same results. The largest shaping step produced faster shaping than the smallest one. Thus, large shaping step can be more efficient than small ones. Much more research on shaping is required, however, before we make definite statements about optimal step size. Large shaping steps may be effective with a long key because once a pigeon has learned to peck on one side of the key, pecking on the other side may not involve much more new learning.

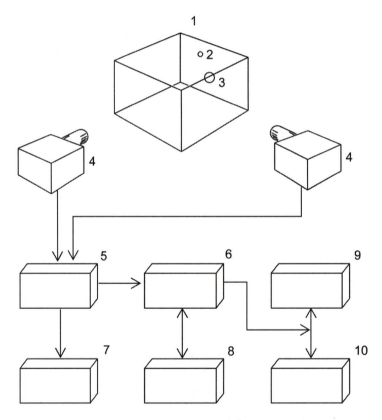

FIGURE 7.2. The behavioral tracking system tracks in real-time 3-dimensional space the head movements of a pigeon in an operant conditioning chamber. The parts of the apparatus are: (1) operant conditioning chamber; (2) response key; (3) feeder; (4) video cameras; (5) video acquisition module; (6) computer; (7) video monitor; (8) data storage; (9) computer monitor; (10) printer. (From Pear & Eldridge, 1984)

Shaping may also be examined with a procedure that looks at the individual's position continuously rather than just at discrete points in time (i.e., when responses, such as pecks, occur). Figure 7.2 shows a diagram of an apparatus developed for this purpose. As can been seen from the figure, the main components of the system are an operant conditioning chamber, two TV cameras, a video acquisition module, and a computer. The two TV cameras are directed toward the front and back walls of the chamber, which are made of transparent glass. A pigeon with a dark head, or one whose head is painted black, is studied with this apparatus so that the computer can track the bird's head. In order to study shaping, a target region is defined such that reinforcement will occur when the bird contacts that region. The target might be the key, but it might also be defined as a region in space that is not even visible to the bird.

A general shaping procedure that has been used with this apparatus is one in which the target is a sphere located in a part of the chamber that is seldom visited by the bird, so that contact with the target is unlikely to occur in the absence of shaping. Concentric with the target is another computer generated sphere, called the shaping sphere, that can be programed to expand at a set rate and to contract a set amount when "contact" occurs between it and the bird's head. (Of course the shaping sphere, like the target sphere, is invisible to the bird.) Reinforcement occurs whenever contact occurs between the bird's head and the shaping sphere. Since the shaping sphere expands gradually, eventually the bird will need to make only a slight movement in the direction of the target in order to receive reinforcement. Since the shaping sphere contracts a set amount after each contact, a larger movement toward the target must then occur in order for reinforcement to occur prior to the expansion of the shaping sphere to the size at which reinforcement had just occurred. In this way, contacting the target is shaped automatically by the computer.

Figure 7.3 shows data from three pigeons for which the radius of the shaping sphere decreased 1 cm each time the bird contacted the shaping sphere, and increased 0.25 cm every 10-second period in which the bird did not contact the shaping sphere. The target was located toward the back of the chamber, slightly lower than the birds normally held their heads so that they had to crouch in order to contact it. The top set of graphs plots the radius of the shaping sphere over the shaping sessions, while the bottom set of graphs plots the distance of the bird

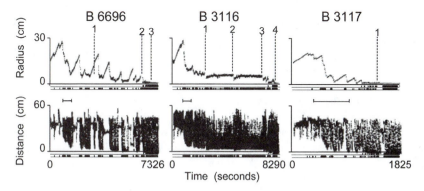

FIGURE 7.3. Automated shaping of contact with virtual target sphere. The radius of a shaping sphere (top graphs) and distance from the center of the target sphere (bottom graphs) for three pigeons are plotted over sessions. Each contact of the pigeon's head with the shaping sphere produced reinforcement. All shaping sessions and the session following shaping are shown. The dashed vertical lines indicate the end of each shaping session. The vertical marks in the top band below each graph indicate target contacts; those in the bottom band indicate reinforcements. (From Pear & Legris, 1987)

from the target. Data for the session following shaping (session 4 for B6698, session 5 for B3116, and session 2 for B3117) are also shown for each bird. The important thing to note about these data is the abruptness with which moving close to the target was shaped (see the regions under the horizontal bars in the bottom set of graphs). Actual contact with the target took a little longer, apparently because it required the bird to lower its head from the position it normally held it. These data, like those in Chapter 4 (Figure 4.3), demonstrate the abruptness with which operant conditioning can occur.

Topography shaping.   We saw above that position shaping involves moving, by reinforcing successive approximations, a small set of points on an individual (e.g., the beak of a pigeon) to a small set of spatially defined points (e.g., a particular region of a response key). Topography shaping is similar, but more complex. The topography of a response is the form of the response or the way in which it is configured in space and time. Mathematically speaking, we could say that the topography of a response is the collective path described by a set of points on an individual that result in a response by that individual. Rather than simply making a particular set of points on an individual more likely to come in contact with a particular set of spatial points (as in position shaping), topography shaping alters the collective paths that a given set of points on an individual describe. (These paths may be relative to some feature of the individual or the environment). It does this by reinforcing paths that are increasingly different from the original path until eventually the points describe completely new paths. Put more simply, topography shaping involves reinforcing increasingly different response forms until eventually the individual emits a response with a completely new (to that individual) form.

An example of topography shaping is developing in a rat the response of depositing a ball bearing into a hole in the floor of an experimental chamber. The successive approximations toward this target response might be: approaching the ball bearing, touching it, grasping it, picking it up, and picking it up and dropping it in locations increasingly closer to the hole. After a given approximation had occurred a certain number of times, it would be extinguished and reinforcement would be made contingent on the next closer approximation. If the approximation currently set for reinforcement fails to occur, the criterion for reinforcement is relaxed in that reinforcement is made contingent on the previous approximation.

Computer technology has not yet developed to the point that topography shaping can be, in general, completely automated. Human observation is necessary to discriminate successive topographical approximations toward a target response. Topographical shaping can be enhanced, however, by a person-computer interaction in which a human observer enters coded topographical observations into the computer and the computer decides, on the basis of a specific shaping program loaded into it, whether or not to present reinforcement when a response occurs (Midgely, Lea, & Kirby, 1989).

Other types of shaping.   Position and topography shaping are only two of many different kinds of shaping. In fact, probably any behavior that can be ordered along a continuum of similarity can be shaped. Examples include response force, response duration, distance traveled, amount of responding, and (as we shall see) time between successive responses or response rate.

Shaping Algorithms

Shaping is generally done in an intuitive manner; hence, shaping is frequently said to be an art rather than a science. With the development of computer technology, however, implementing precisely defined shaping procedures has become more feasible (Midgely et al., 1989). A shaping algorithm is a sequence of shaping steps so precisely specified that a program could be written for a computer to carry them out. The algorithm specifies the shaping approximations to be reinforced, the step size (i.e., distances between the approximations to be reinforced, according to some metric of similarity), a shaping criterion for advancing reinforcement from one approximation to the next, and a backstep criterion for revisiting an earlier approximation if the current to-be-reinforced approximation fails to occur.

The shaping sphere procedure used with the continuous tracking system described above is an example of a shaping algorithm. The approximations are measured as the spatial distance from the target location to be contacted, the criterion for advancing reinforcement from one approximation to the next is contact with the shaping sphere, the step size is the distance the radius of the shaping sphere contracts when it is contacted, and the criterion for returning to previous approximations is failure to contact the shaping sphere within a set period of time. Another example of a shaping algorithm is called percentile reinforcement (Galbicka, 1994; Platt, 1973). This algorithm involves taking successive samples of the behavior being shaped, determining the level (the percentile) at which a set percentage of the responses fall above or below in the preceding sample of behavior, and reinforcing only those responses that fall above or below (depending on the direction of shaping) that level (while simultaneously recording the current sample of behavior). Note that with this procedure the criterion for reinforcement automatically shifts in the direction of shaping when the percentage of responses in that direction (as defined by the percentile) in the current sample is greater than the percentage of responses in that direction in the preceding sample. Similarly, the criterion for reinforcement stays the same when the two percentages are equal, and shifts in the direction away from shaping when the percentage of responses in that direction in the current sample is less than the percentage of responses in that direction in the preceding sample.

Applications of Shaping

Shaping is an important tool in many applied situations. It has been used in psychiatric hospitals and rehabilitative settings, for example, to establish or reestablish verbal responding (e.g., Isaacs, Thomas, & Goldiamond, 1960) and movement of the upper extremities (Taub, 1994). It is also a part of normal social learning, as when, for example, children progress from babbling the sounds in their native language, to baby talk, and finally to adult speech. These transitions occur because of increasingly stricter reinforcement criteria members of a culture impose on the topography of an individual's verbal responses as he or she matures.

Sources of Response Variability

As we have seen, in order for response shaping to occur there must be response variability. Therefore, a question of considerable theoretical interest is: Where does response variability come from? There are four possibilities (Neuringer, Deiss, & Olson, 2000, pp. 98–99), which are not necessarily mutually exclusive.

One possibility is that response variability is simply an inherent property of behavior. That is, behavior by its very nature, perhaps due to the organization of the nervous system, is variable (Freeman, 1990; Neuringer et al., 2000).

A second possibility is what engineers call noise in the environment (Bandura, 1982). That is, the continuous variable flux of stimuli (such as changes in light, sounds, temperature, smells) in the environment causes continuous changes in responses.

A third source of variability is low frequencies or amounts of reinforcement (Antonitis, 1951; Balsam, Deich, Ohyama, & Stokes, 1998; Boren, Moerschbae-Cher, & Whyte, 1978;

Lachter & Corey, 1982; Tatham, Wanschisen, & Hineline, 1993). For example, when the rate of reinforcement decreases, the variability of responding increases. An evolutionary reason for this is easy to see. When a response that once produced reinforcement is now less effective or ineffective in producing reinforcement, the response requirement for reinforcement may have changed. An increased variety of responses increases the chances that the new response required for reinforcement will occur. Response shaping makes use of the increased variability produced by extinction, because shaping consists of extinguishing previously reinforced approximations to the target behavior. Shaping may fail, however, if new approximations are not reinforced before extinction eventually leads to the cessation of all responding.

As we saw in Chapter 4, another source of response variability is reinforcement of it (Machado, 1989, 1994; Neuringer, 1992; Page & Neuringer, 1985). It appears that directly reinforcing response variability prior to attempting to condition an operant response that is difficult to learn will increase the probability that an animal will learn it (Neuringer et al., 2000). Prior exposure to response-independent reinforcement may also increase the probability of an animal learning a difficult response. The reason appears to be that, because any response can occur just prior to an instance of it, response-independent reinforcement results in the reinforcement of a variety of different responses (i.e., it reinforces responses variability). It is also possible that apparent reinforcement of variability is actually reinforcement of certain behavior patterns that, due to their complexity, appear variable, but would be quite predictable if we knew the laws under which they operated (Machado, 1999).

DIFFERENTIAL CONDITIONABILITY OF OPERANT RESPONSES

Just as not all respondent responses are equally conditionable to all stimuli, neither are all operant responses equally conditionable by all reinforcers. For example, access to the image of another male stickleback can be used to reinforce biting a glass rod by a male stickleback, but it will not readily reinforce swimming through a ring. Conversely, the image of a female stickleback will not readily reinforce biting a glass rod, but it will reinforce swimming through a ring (Sevenster, 1973).

Similarly, it appears to be extremely difficult to increase a cat's grooming by reinforcing it with food (Thorndike, 1911). Likewise, although a pig or a raccoon may be operantly trained with food reinforcement to carry a token, as the distance to carry the token is increased the pig may drop its token and start rooting it while the raccoon may begin washing its token (Breland & Breland, 1961, 1966). Moreover, a chimpanzee presented with food reinforcement for an operant response may begin making food calls that interfere with the response (Gardner & Gardner, 1988). In all these cases, phylogenetic behavior appears to be intruding into the operant conditioning situation and detracting from the conditioning. In at least some of these cases, the interfering phylogenetic behavior is actually respondent behavior that has been conditioned to stimuli in the operant conditioning situation. For example, a raccoon may wash a token because the token has been paired with food-in-paws, which is an unconditioned stimulus for the raccoon washing what is in its paws.

SCHEDULE EFFECTS ON RESPONSE RATE

Once established, a response can be maintained by various intermittent reinforcement schedules. As we saw in Chapter 4, each of these schedules has a characteristic effect on both rate and patterning of responding. Ratio schedules (VR and FR) produce higher rates of responding than do interval schedules (VI and FI), even when rate of reinforcement is held constant. This can be demonstrated by what is called a yoked-control experiment. To take an example involving VR and VI, suppose that a pigeon is on a VR 100 schedule in an operant conditioning chamber that is "yoked" to a chamber containing another bird. Every time the bird in the first chamber emits a reinforced response, reinforcement becomes available for the "yoked-control" bird in the second chamber. Thus the yoked-control bird will be on a VI schedule whose reinforcement rate equals that of the VR schedule of the first bird. Typically, the bird on the VR schedule will respond at a higher rate than the bird on the VI schedule (Ferster & Skinner, 1957).

Rate of responding also depends on the rate of reinforcement on a single type of reinforcement schedule. For example, Figure 7.4 shows how rate of key pecking varied as a function of rate of reinforcement on VI schedules for six pigeons. Note that rate of responding increased in a negatively accelerated fashion as rate of reinforcement increased (Catania & Reynolds, 1968).

High or low response rates can also be reinforced directly. For example, imagine a schedule in which a response is reinforced only if it occurs at least t seconds after the previous response. This is called a differential-reinforcement-of-low-rates t (DRL t) schedule. If $t = 5$, for example, the schedule would be called a DRL 5-seconds schedule. The effect of a DRL schedule, as its name suggests, is to produce a low rate of responding.

Similarly, a differential-reinforcement-of-high-rates t (DRH t) schedule is one in which a response is reinforced only if it occurs no more than t seconds after the previous response. If $t = 2$, for example, the schedule would be called a DRH 2-seconds schedule. This type of schedule produces a high rate of responding.

LEVELS OF ANALYSIS

Note that each data point in Figure 7.4 was obtained by summing all the responses that occurred during an entire session. Consequently, the figure tells us little about the individual responses that make up the figure. There are two general levels which we may examine or try to explain data like that in Figure 7.4: (1) molar analyses, and (2) molecular analyses (Baum, 1989). The former corresponds to the larger (analogous to looking at matter as a whole in physics), the latter to the small (analogous to elementary particle physics).

Molar Analyses

A molar analysis takes overall response rate data such as that in Figure 7.4 as fundamental, and attempts to give some sort of mathematical description of those data without regard to the individual responses that go to make up the data. One of the most influential molar theories is that devised by R. J. Herrnstein.

Herrstein's Formula. To account for the data in Figure 7.4, Herrnstein (1970) proposed the following equation:

$$B = \frac{kr}{r + r_0} \tag{7.1}$$

where B is the behavior or number of responses (key pecks) that occurred during the session, R is the number of reinforcements received for responding, k is a constant (which may differ

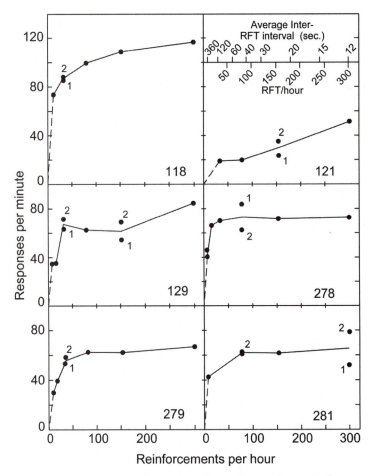

FIGURE 7.4. Key pecking as a function of rate of reinforcement. Each point is the mean response rate over the last five sessions of a given variable-interval schedule for each of six pigeons. Sessions were conducted daily and ranged from about 16 to 430 minutes long. The numerals "1" and "2" indicate first and second determinations. (From Catania & Reynolds, 1968)

for different individuals), and r_0 is the reinforcement for behavior other than that reinforced by the experimenter. r_0 represents reinforcements that are usually not under experimental control, such as those for scratching, preening, resting, and walking around. (See Appendix C for a mathematical treatment of Herrnstein's equation.)

Note that when the total number of reinforcements for responding is zero ($r = 0$), the total number of responses will be zero ($B = 0$). Thus, Herrnstein's equation accurately describes the results of extinction. In addition, note that B increases to a maximum of $B = k$ as r increases to a theoretical maximum of infinity. Thus, Herrnstein's equation describes the increase in responding that occurs as reinforcement rate increases, as shown in Figure 7.4. Finally, note that according to Herrnstein's equation another way to increase B to its maximum of $B = k$ is to reduce r_0 to $r_0 = 0$ by eliminating all reinforcement from the situation except that for the experimentally reinforced response.

Herrnstein's equation is relevant to behavior of social significance. For example, engagement by children in academic tasks conforms to the equation when teachers reinforce the behavior with praise on VI schedules (Martens, Lochner, & Kelly, 1992). Behavior inadvertently reinforced by adult attention (e.g., reprimands), such as self-injurious scratching by a retarded child (McDowel, 1981), also conforms to the equation. Reduction of socially significant behavior by reinforcement of alternative behavior also occurs in conformity with Herrnstein's equation. For example, the undesirable behavior, which included noncompliance, argumentativeness, and temper tantrums, of a mildly retarded 22-year-old male was decreased by providing token reinforcement (in the form of points which could be exchanged for money) for behavior that was unrelated to the undesirable behavior (McDowell, 1981). According to the equation, this intervention decreased the frequency of the undesirable behavior (B in the equation) by increasing the total amount of reinforcement in the environment (the denominator of the right side of the equation), even though the reinforcement (r in the equation) for the undesirable behavior did not change.

There are some problems with Herrnstein's equation. One problem is in regard to the parameter k which should be a constant across all situations (especially since in Herrnstein's theory, k represents the total amount of all behavior that an individual could engage in). However, research shows that k varies under certain conditions (Williams, 1988), such as when reinforcement magnitude or amount varies (Dallery, McDowell, & Lancaster, 2000).

In addition, Herrnstein's equation does not seem to work very well for ratio schedules. As the response requirement on ratio schedules increases above continuous reinforcement, response rate increases even though reinforcement rate decreases (or, at least, does not increase proportionately as required by the equation; Pear, 1975; Timberlake, 1977; see Appendix C). As the response requirement increases further, and reinforcement rate decreases, response rate then decreases steadily (which is more in accordance with Herrnstein's equation). Another way of stating this same relationship is that as reinforcement rate increases on ratio schedules, response rate increases and then decreases (instead of increasing monotonically as predicted by Herrnstein's equation). This curvilinear relationship between response rate and reinforcement rate on ratio schedules has been found consistently in numerous experimental arrangements. These have ranged from mice, rats, and pigeons pressing levers or pecking keys for food (Barofsky & Hurwitz, 1968; Greenwood, Quartermain, Johnson, Cruce, 1974; Kelsey & Allison, 1976; Mazur, 1982) to developmentally disabled humans pressing buttons for auditory and visual stimuli (Tustin, 1994).

Although FR schedules seem especially problematic for Herrnstein's equation, there is considerable evidence that other schedules also show a decrease in response rate that cannot be accounted for by satiation, eating time, or other obvious variables, as reinforcement rate becomes very high (e.g., Baum, 1981, pp. 395–397; Dougan & McSweeney, 1985; McSweeney & Melville, 1991). Nevertheless, Herrnstein's equation does provide a reasonable description of response rate over a wide range of reinforcement rates on various reinforcement schedules. In addition, although response rate may not decrease monotonically on ratio schedules as reinforcement rate decreases, the postreinforcement pause of FR schedules increases in a consistent manner as the size of the ratio (i.e., the number of responses required for reinforcement) increases (Powell, 1968). Thus, in FR schedules, the time spent responding shows the relationship to reinforcement rate that Herrnstein's equation predicts response rate should, even if response rate itself does not.

Other molar formulations. Because it is both simple and reasonably predictive of data, Herrnstein's equation has been extremely influential. There are alternative formulations that are more accurate in their predictions; however, they are also more complex and it is not clear which if any of them will prove to be more fundamentally correct in the long run.

Killeen's model. One alternative formulation is a model proposed by P. R. Killeen (1994) that uses Herrnstein's equation as its starting point. Killeen's model goes on to assume that each reinforcement not only strengthens the response that it follows, but also has weakening effects on earlier reinforced responses (or, as Killeen [p. 105] puts it, "incentives displace memory for responses that occur before them"). The mathematics that Killeen develops from this assumption is too complex to present here. One consequence of the assumption, however, is that (contrary to Herrnstein's formulation, but consistent with experimental findings described above) response rate will first increase and then decrease as the response requirement on ratio schedules increases (because increasing the response requirement removes some of the reinforcement-produced inhibition on responding). In other words, increasing the response requirement on an FR or VR schedule will cause an initial increase (not a decrease) in response rate. Response rate will then start to decrease as the response requirement continues to increase. Similarly, response rate will first increase and then decrease as the rate of reinforcement decreases in an interval schedule.

Economic models. Economists have developed sophisticated models to describe how individuals allocate their resources—such as labor, time, or money—to obtain various goods. Some learning scientists have argued that economic models should be extended to schedules of reinforcement (Hursh, 1980, 1984; Kagel et al., 1995). The rationale for this viewpoint is that an individual's operant responses (e.g., key pecks or lever presses) or time spent responding is analogous to the resources of a worker or consumer in an economy. There are two basic goods that are available in the operant responding situation: the reinforcer (e.g., food) and leisure (i.e., whatever the individual does when not responding for the reinforcer). (Note that leisure in economic models corresponds to r_0 in Herrnstein's formulation.) In the economic analogy of operant responding, increasing the response requirement on a ratio schedule corresponds to increasing the cost of a good or the amount of work the individual will expend for that good. Economic models deal with these kinds of situations. The mathematics involved in these models is too complex to describe here; however, the basic concepts behind the models are fairly simple. As the amount of time or effort required to obtain a good increases, the first effect may (depending on a variable called the elasticity of the good) be an increase in the time or effort expended to obtain that good. The less elastic the good, the more time and effort the individual is willing to put into continuing to obtain the same amount of the good obtained before the price increase. As the price increases further, however, a point is reached at which the individual no longer is willing expend enough resources to obtain the same amount of the good. At that point, further price increases result in the individual's expenditures for the good failing to keep track with the increased cost and the individual opts increasingly for more leisure. A reinforcer such as food, being a necessity of life, is fairly inelastic. Thus, as with Killeen's model (but unlike Hernstein's) economic models predict (or, more precisely, allow for the possibility) that at least with some reinforcers response rate may initially increase as the response requirement increases (Kagel et al., pp. 86–87). The less elastic the reinforcer, the more responses will track increases in the response requirement for that reinforcer.

Molecular Analyses

A molecular analysis focuses on individual responses in accounting for changes in overall response rate. This type of analysis is usually based on the fact that when a response such as a lever press or a key peck is reinforced, more than just the isolated press or peck is reinforced. Rather, the behavior that immediately preceded the response is also reinforced. This is the behavior that occurs between successive lever presses or key pecks, and hence it will affect the amount of time between successive responses. The time between two successive responses is called an interresponse time (IRT).

As we have seen (p. 139), DRH and DRL schedules produce high or low response rates by selectively reinforcing short or long IRTs, respectively. It may be that other schedules produce their effects on response rate in a similar manner, even though these schedules are not explicitly programmed to reinforce short or long IRTs. On a VI schedule, for example, long IRTs have a greater probability of being reinforced than do short IRTs. Therefore, a VI schedule might tend to differentially reinforce long IRTs. Moreover, the higher the VI schedule the more it would tend to differentially reinforce long IRTs, and hence the lower one would expect response rate to be.

Several lines of evidence support this view that VI schedules differentially reinforce long IRTs. One line of evidence is that if the availability of reinforcement on a VI schedule is limited to brief durations, so that long IRTs are much less likely to be reinforced, response rate will increase considerably (Morse, 1966). Another line of evidence comes from studies in which differential reinforcement of certain IRTs is explicitly programmed to mimic the differential reinforcement of IRTs that is thought to occur on VI schedules.

For example, consider a schedule that reinforces IRTs according to the following equation:

$$p(\mathbf{S}^\circ) = IRT/T, \qquad\qquad (7.2)$$

where $p(\mathbf{S}^\circ)$ is the probability that the IRT will be reinforced, and T is a constant. This schedule is called a stochastic reinforcement of waiting (SRW) schedule. Note that the greater the IRT in a SRW schedule, the greater the probability of reinforcement, which is similar to the case in a VI schedule. Thus, when IRT $\geq$ T the probability of reinforcement is $p(\mathbf{S}^\circ) = 1.00$ (since probability can never be greater than one). Also note that increasing T in an SRW schedule both increases the length of the IRTs that tend to be differentially reinforced and decreases the rate of reinforcement. Increasing T in an SRW schedule thus duplicates what is assumed to occur in a VI schedule when reinforcement rate is decreased. Increasing T does result in a decrease in response rate, just as decreasing reinforcement rate does in a VI schedule.

More definitive evidence on this score is obtained by removing the contingency between IRTs and reinforcement while holding other variables constant. This can be done by using an earlier IRT rather than the current IRT to determine the reinforcement probability for the current IRT (Platt, 1979). For example, the fifth IRT preceding the current IRT might be used to compute the reinforcement probability for the current IRT. This schedule, which is called an SRW/lag = 5 schedule, results in an increase in response rate, indicating that the differential reinforcement of long IRTs is a factor determining response rate in SRW schedules and hence in VI schedules as well. It is also found, however, that response rate decreases as reinforcement rate is decreased (by increasing T) in an SRW/lag = 5 schedule. Hence, the decrease in response rate that occurs when reinforcement rate is decreased in SRW schedules and, by implication, in VI schedules (Figure 7.4) is not entirely due to the differential reinforcement of long IRTs (Platt, 1979).

It should be noted that an IRT is actually an interval of time, not a response. A period of time cannot be reinforced; thus, it is technically incorrect to speak of the reinforcement of an IRT as we have been doing. When we set up a contingency to reinforce certain IRTs we ensure that the reinforcement of behavior that produces the appearance that IRTs corresponding to the time taken by this behavior is reinforced. We return to this point later in this chapter. First, however, we look at another type of time period that occurs in reinforcement schedules; namely, pausing.

SCHEDULE EFFECTS ON PAUSING

Thus far our discussion has been concerned with the effects of rate of reinforcement and IRT reinforcement on response rate under various schedules of reinforcement. Pausing is another variable that is influenced by schedules of reinforcement. As described in Chapter 4, the fixed schedules (FR and FI) produce rather long pauses right after reinforcement, whereas postreinforcement pauses on the variable schedules (VR and VI) are much shorter. The reason for this difference in postreinforcement pausing between the fixed and the variable schedules is not fully understood. It is likely, however, that since reinforcement on fixed schedules is followed by a period of time in which the probability of reinforcement is zero, the occurrence of reinforcement on a fixed schedule is an S^Δ. Thus, responding is absent right after reinforcement because of the occurrence of an S^Δ. This S^Δ does not, however, have exactly the same effect in FR and FI schedules. Longer postreinforcement pauses occur on low FI schedules than on low FR schedules when the time between reinforcements is equated for the two types of schedules (Capehart, Eckerman, Guilkey, & Schull, 1980). As the size of the schedule increases this difference becomes smaller, and may even be reversed so that large FR schedules may generate longer postreinforcement pauses than do large FI schedules. The reason for these differences between FR and FI is not known at present.

In addition, as mentioned in Chapter 4, renewed pausing also tends to occur after responding begins following the postreinforcement pause in FI schedules. The amount of this renewed pausing tends to decrease as the interval progresses, which appears to account for the scallops that occur in FI schedules (Gentry et al., 1983).

SPATIOTEMPORAL PATTERNS OF BEHAVIOR

None of the experiments described thus far have recorded the behavior that occurs between responses. Yet this behavior may be important in understanding why these responses are spaced in time the way they are. The behavioral tracking system described earlier in this chapter (see Figure 7.2, p. 134) has therefore been used to study behavior that occurs between responses. Figure 7.5 presents an example of some variable-interval-schedule data collected with the behavioral tracking system. The data are from a bird on one 3600-seconds session of VI 5 minutes for key pecking after 42 sessions of exposure to that schedule. The data on the left side of the figure are from the first 1200 seconds of the session, while the data on the right side are from the last 1200 seconds (the middle 1200 seconds have been omitted to conserve space).

The top row of the figure shows the first and last 1200 seconds of the cumulative record (which was drawn by the computer) of the session. The vertical lines between the upper and lower horizontal bands below the records indicate responses and reinforcements, respectively. Responding was fairly steady throughout the session, as is typical with VI schedules.

In the second row the distance of the bird's head from the key is plotted over time. A key peck occurs when this distance is zero (or near zero). Note that the schedule has generated a fairly constant range of moving to and from the key, extending out to about 30 cm from the key.

The third row shows the expansions of the regions between a and b, and between c and d in the second row. These graphs document a rather complex, but regular, pattern of behaving between key pecks. The pattern consisted of several pecking motions close to the key, followed by two rather long excursions away from the key. The first of these excursions (labeled r in the figure) was a clockwise circle to the right of the key; the second (labeled l) was a counterclockwise circle to the left of the key.

The two boxes in the bottom row show the pattern as it was traced out during the time periods between a and b, and between c and d, respectively, from an overhead view of the chamber. K and F in the figure indicate the positions of the key and feeder. Note the high degree of regularity of the pattern.

A different, but equally regular, pattern (an elongated figure "8" with some occasional overlapping, alternating circles) has been obtained with another pigeon (only two have thus far been studied using this system with VI schedules). The results from both of these birds indicate that elaborate patterns such as these are developed on high VI schedules, but not on low ones. A logical conclusion of this research seems to be that the long IRTs produced by high VI schedules reflect these elaborate, highly regular, behavior patterns. The results also indicate that the behavior patterns, along with the operant response, have been shaped by the reinforcement contingency. These elaborate patterns would appear to be superstitious behavior (see p. 42).

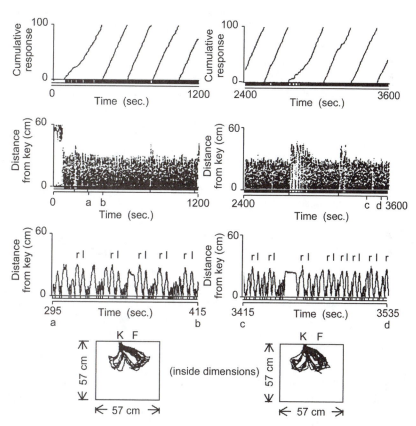

FIGURE 7.5. A pigeon's spatiotemporal behavior pattern on a variable interval schedule. The two graphs in the top row are cumulative records from the first and last 1200 seconds of a 1-hour session. The two graphs in the next row show head movement, in terms of distance from the key, of the birds during the same time period as in the above graphs. The graphs in the third row show distance from the key during the time periods between a and b and c and d in the graphs above them. The vertical lines in the upper horizontal bands below each of the graphs indicate key pecks; those in the lower horizontal bands indicate reinforcements. Each of the graphs in the bottom row shows an overhead view of the pattern traced by the movement indicated in the graph just above it. Clockwise and counterclockwise circles are indicated by r and l, respectively, in the graphs in the third row. (From Pear, 1985)

WITHIN-SESSION CHANGES IN RESPONSE RATE

Thus far we have talked about responding as though it were uniform, or at least shows no systematic changes, within a session. Under a wide variety of reinforcement schedules and other conditions, however, responding tends to first increase to a maximum or peak near the beginning of a session, and then decline throughout the remainder of the session (McSweeney & Hinson, 1992; McSweeney, Hinson, & Cannon, 1996; McSweeney & Roll, 1993).

Respondent as well as respondent behavior may show this pattern (Siegel & Domjan, 1971). For example, it occurs in both autoshaping and automaintenance (McSweeney, Swindell, & Weatherly, 1996a). It is also observed in locomotor and manipulatory behavior (Montgomery, 1953; Schoenfeld, Antonitis, & Bersh, 1950), and in the phenomenon of spontaneous recovery—that is, the tendency for an extinguished response to be higher at the beginning of an extinction session than it was at the end of the previous extinction session (see Chapter 4, Figure 4.5, p. 63).

Research has eliminated a number of potential explanations for both the early increase and later decrease in response rate over a session, for example, recovery from being taken from the home cage to the conditioning chamber (McSweeney & Johnson, 1994), factors such as feeding that often reliably follow a session (McSweeney, Weatherly, & Swindell, 1995); and muscle warm-up and fatigue (McSweeney & Johnson, 1994; McSweeney, Weatherly, & Roll, 1995; McSweeney, Weatherly, Roll, & Swindell, 1995; Weatherly, McSweeney, & Swindell, 1995). Satiation due to factors such as stomach distension and increased blood glucose level also does not seem to account for the pattern, because the pattern is not affected by varying the size of the food reinforcer, its caloric content, and the deprivation for it within a wide range (McSweeney & Johnson, 1994; Roll, McSweeney, Johnson, & Weatherly, 1995; Weatherly et al., 1995). (This point is somewhat controversial, however; Bizo et al., 1998).

Recall from Chapter 2 that sensitization and habituation act in opposition to each other: When a strong stimulus occurs repeatedly, sensitization occurs first followed by habituation (Groves & Thompson, 1970). A plausible explanation of the pattern of within-session responding shown by operant responding, therefore, is that it reflects sensitization to the reinforcer (and, especially during extinction, other stimuli in the situation) followed by habituation (McSweeney, Hinson, & Cannon, 1996; McSweeney & Swindell, 1999). According to this explanation, a sensitized reinforcer is more effective than normal and hence generates a higher response rate, whereas a habituated reinforcer is less effective than normal and hence generates a lower response rate. We may summarize the evidence that sensitization followed by habituation accounts for the within-session increase and subsequent decrease in response rate across a session examining operant responding as follows:

1. The pattern tends to be steeper and have an earlier peak when reinforcement rate is high than when it is low (McSweeney, 1992; McSweeney et al., 1994). This could be because sensitization followed by habituation to a stimulus (the reinforcer in this case) occurs more rapidly when the stimulus occurs more frequently (Thompson & Spencer, 1966).

2. If an S^D correlated with a different kind of reinforcer (e.g., wheat when mixed grain is the reinforcer during most of the session) is presented late in the session, response rate increases to the level at which it would have been earlier in the session if the different reinforcer had been used throughout the session (McSweeney, Weatherly, & Swindell, 1996). According to the sensitization-habituation explanation of the within-session increase-and-decrease in response rate, this would be because infrequent re-

inforcer had not habituated. (Note that this point also appears to rule out fatigue as an explanation for the decrease in response rate over the session.)

3. When a variable-interval schedule is changed to a variable-time schedule (i.e., reinforcement occurs randomly, independently of responding), the within-session pattern of responding is similar to (although lower than) the pattern on the variable-interval schedule and differs from the pattern that occurs when a variable-interval schedule changes to extinction (McSweeney et al., 1999). Specifically, more of the total occurs earlier in the session during extinction than during variable-interval and variable-time schedules. According to the sensitization-habituation explanation of the within-session increase-and-decrease in response rate, this is because sensitization and habituation to the reinforcer depend only on its on its occurrence, not on whether it is contingent on responding.

OPEN VERSUS CLOSED ECONOMIES

In the vast majority of the research described in this chapter, sessions occur under a constant state of food deprivation. Animals typically have been maintained at a fixed percentage (typically 80%) of their free-feeding body weights to ensure that the reinforcer is strong (i.e., motivation for it is high) and relatively constant. This is accomplished by providing only a small amount of the reinforcer after each reinforced response, so that the animal does not receive enough food during the session to cause it to exceed the designated body weight. After each session, the experimenter provides the animal with the balance of the food required to maintain the animal's body weight at the desired level. Borrowing a term from economics, this arrangement is called an open economy because "goods" (the reinforcer) are available from outside as well as from within the "economy" (the experimental situation). In a closed economy, in contrast, goods are available only from within the economy (Hursh, 1980).

Although in the minority, learning experiments with closed economies have been done. In these experiments, the animal receives all of its food in the experimental situation. In addition, typically there is no restriction on the amount of food that the animal eats when reinforced: The food is available until the animal stops eating for a specified period. Results obtained with closed economies are strikingly different from those obtained with open economies (Collier et al., 1972; Hall & Lattal, 1990; Hursh, 1978; Kanarek, 1975; Timberlake & Peden, 1987; Zeiler, 1999).

In open economies (as discussed on pp. 139–141 of this chapter) response rate either first increases and then decreases or steadily decreases as reinforcement rate decreases. In closed economies response rate steadily increases as reinforcement rate decreases (as long as reinforcement rate does not decrease to the point that the animal's body weight drops substantially below its free-feeding weight). In addition, responding may be maintained with much less frequent reinforcement in a closed than in an open economy. For example, with pigeons key pecking for food, fixed-ratio schedules as high as FR 10,000 may maintain responding in a closed economy whereas the maximum fixed-ratio schedule that can do so under comparable conditions in an open economy is FR 400 (Zeiler, 1999).

The difference between responding in open and closed economies is consistent with the economic models of behavior discussed earlier in this chapter. Goods are less elastic in a closed economy than in an open economy. This is because in a closed economy, an individual receives only the goods for which he or she works. Therefore, to continue receiving the same amount of goods when there is a price increase, an individual must increase his or her work output. In an open economy, however, one eventually receives the same amount of goods regardless of the amount of work done. Therefore, when the price increases the individual is more likely to opt for increased leisure rather than working to obtain goods in the immediate future that will eventually be available regardless of the amount of work done (Hursh, 1980, 1984; Kagel et al., 1995, p. 91).

There is also a plausible evolutionary explanation for the difference between responding as a function of reinforcement rate in open versus closed economies. Because they typically involve rather severe food deprivation with small amounts of the reinforcer per reinforcement, open economies in animal experiments with food reinforcement mimic conditions in nature in which food is in short supply and energy conservation is critical. Because the amount of reinforcement the individual receives per reinforcement is much greater in a closed than in an open economy, closed economies mimic conditions in which food is abundant and expending energy to obtain it is more beneficial to survival (Zeiler, 1999). To continue with an economics analogy, investing a great amount of energy (calories) to obtain more calories (from food) makes sense when the economy is good (i.e., when food is plentiful), but makes less sense when the economy is poor and expending calories is less likely to pay off. Of course, this is not to imply that animals reason as a sensible consumer, worker, or investor would, but only that mechanisms may have evolved to make them behave (in some respects, at least) in that way. What these mechanisms might be is a matter for speculation that is beyond the scope of this book.

Because an animal's deprivation state and reinforcer amount is generally much better controlled in an open economy than in a closed economy, research on learning is much more common in open economies. Throughout this book we assume open economies unless otherwise specified.

SUMMARY AND CONCLUSIONS

The process of behavioral shaping a simple operant response consists of reinforcement of closer and closer approximations to the response while extinguishing previously reinforced approximations. The process proceeds through reinforcement of an approximation to the target response, followed by extinction of that (and previous) approximations, and combined with reinforcement of a closer approximation that appears as a result of response generalization from reinforcement of the preceding approximation. The process continues until the target response occurs. Thus, another name for behavioral or response shaping is the method of successive approximations.

A simple operant response may be established by behavioral shaping, by autoshaping, or by straight reinforcement (i.e., just making reinforcement contingent on the response). Behavioral shaping and autoshaping, however, generally work much faster than straight reinforcement. Once an operant response is occurring with a high probability, it will come under the control of the prevailing schedule of reinforcement. Different schedules of reinforcement produce different rates and patterns of responding.

There are two general approaches to analyzing the effects of schedules of reinforcement on responding: molar analysis and molecular analysis. The former looks at overall rate of responding whereas the latter breaks rate of responding into its smallest unit, the interresponse time (IRT). An example of a molar approach is Herrnstein's hyperbola, which is an equation that states that response rate increases in a negatively accelerated manner toward an asymptote as the reinforcement rate of the response increases relative to total reinforcement rate (i.e., the rate of reinforcement for all behavior). The molecular approach accounts for the effects of different reinforcement schedules by pointing to the differential reinforcement of IRTs of varying lengths that occurs on different schedules. Combining both approaches leads to fairly accurate predictions with regard to response rate.

Although the characteristic patterns of responding that they produce is perhaps the most striking difference between different schedules of reinforcement, little is known about why they produce their characteristic patterns. The postreinforcement pause (i.e., the pause after reinforcement) that is much shorter on VR and VI schedules than on FR and FI schedules is an important feature of the patterns of responding in reinforcement schedules. One way to think about the postreinforcement pause is that in the fixed schedules (FR and FI) reinforcement is an S^Δ because it is followed by a period in which no reinforcement will occur, whereas in the variable schedules (VR and VI) reinforcement is just as likely to occur after a reinforcement as at any other time. This explanation, however, does not account for the differences in the lengths of the postreinforcement pauses in FR and FI schedules that are matched for reinforcement rate.

Most studies of operant behavior do not record the entire trajectory of a response (that is, the entire path of movement involved in making the response), but only the endpoint of that trajectory. The part of the trajectory preceding the endpoint, however, is also important. For example, the patterns that develop in the movements of pigeons pecking response keys on various reinforcement schedules correlate with the lengths of the IRTs that develop on those schedules. Thus, examining how different movement patterns develop under different reinforcement schedules can help us understand how these schedules generate their characteristic rates and patterns of responding.

Many studies of operant behavior look at overall response rate across sessions without considering systematic changes in response rate within sessions. These patterns occur reliably under a wide variety of conditions, and could be important to our understanding of how several learning processes (specifically, operant conditioning, sensitization, and habituation) interact.

All of the preceding studies assume an open economy in which animals are maintained in a constant state of deprivation. Quite different results are obtained when animals are not deprived and receive all their reinforcement in the experimental situation.

PART III

COMPLEX CONTINGENCIES

*H*aving discussed simple stimulus-stimulus and response-reinforcement contingencies in Part II, we now examine ways in which these contingencies may become more complicated.

Chapter 8 details how stimuli that alternate with stimuli that are paired with unconditioned stimuli (in the case of respondent conditioning) or that alternate with stimuli in the presence of which responses are reinforced (in the case of operant conditioning) sharpen stimulus control over responding (i.e., produce or strengthen stimulus discriminations). Chapter 8 also describes the interactions that occur between different contingencies of reinforcement operating in the presence of different stimuli that alternate. Furthermore, in addition to describing successive discriminations (i.e., stimulus discriminations in which the stimuli that are discriminated alternate), the chapter discusses simultaneous discriminations (in which the stimuli that are discriminated are present simultaneously) and shows how these two types of discriminations are related.

Chapter 9 delves further into the topic of stimulus discrimination by considering situations in which whether a stimulus is an S+ (i.e., either a CS+ or an S^D) or an S– (i.e., either a CS– or an S^Δ) is conditional on another stimulus.

Chapter 10 considers the problem of memory by focusing on situations in which a stimulus that is no longer present exerts, or fails to exert, control over behavior. In addition, the chapter considers situations in which stimuli fail to exert control over responses due to interference from other responses.

Chapter 11 turns from the antecedent stimulus in an operant discrimination to the consequent stimulus, the reinforcer, and considers how new reinforcers come about through the process of conditioned reinforcement. The chapter also discusses how conditioned reinforcers enable the development and maintenance of long stimulus-response chains of operant behavior and enable behavior to develop and persist when there are long delays in primary reinforcement.

Finally, Chapter 12 considers different ways in which several schedules of reinforcement may be programmed concurrently, and describes the interactions that occur between variously programmed concurrent schedules of reinforcement. In this chapter we also see that concurrent schedules are present (at least in a theoretical sense) even in relatively simple cases that superficially seem to involve only single schedules.

8

Stimulus Control
Discrimination and Generalization

When a stimulus exerts control over a response we say that the individual is showing a discrimination or that the individual is discriminating between that stimulus and other stimuli. Stimulus discriminations vary in sharpness and breadth; that is, they may range from fine to gross discriminations between stimuli. Stimulus generalization is the opposite of stimulus discrimination in the sense that the less sharp or fine a stimulus discrimination is, the more generalization there is.

We have already indicated how important stimulus discrimination and generalization were in evolution (Chapter 4). They also are of great social and practical significance—it is important to generalize across stimuli that are irrelevant and to discriminate between stimuli that are relevant to particular objectives. For example, it is socially important to generalize across skin colors when hiring people but to discriminate between different colored traffic signals when driving.

It is important to study stimulus discrimination and generalization because they are fundamental processes in all learning. In addition, techniques that learning scientists have developed for studying these processes are valuable for answering various practical and scientific questions. For example, specialists can use these methods to detect sensory deficits, such as in vision and hearing, in preverbal infants and other nonverbal humans (Macht, 1971; Meyerson & Michael, 1964; Reese, Howard, & Rosenberger, 1977; Rosenberger, 1974). Similarly, scientists interested in the sensory capabilities of animals can use the techniques to determine, for example, the ranges of frequencies and intensities of colors that pigeons can see or sounds that rats can hear (Blough, 1958; Gourevitch & Hack, 1966). Another example of the value of stimulus control techniques is their use in objectively determining whether nonverbal animals are subject to the same perceptual phenomena, such as visual aftereffects, that humans are (Scott & Powell, 1963). This can provide information about possible similarities and differences between the nervous systems of humans and other animals.

MULTIPLE SCHEDULES

A standard way to study the discrimination process is with multiple schedules, which are schedules in which two or more stimuli alternate and a specific reinforcement schedule is in effect in the presence of each stimulus. The result is that each discriminative stimulus (i.e., the stimulus paired with each component of the multiple schedule) comes to control a pattern of responding similar to that which the schedule in that component would produce in isolation (i.e., if it were not in a multiple schedule). For example, suppose that the key light in an operant chamber for pigeons alternates between red and green every five minutes. In the presence of the red key light an FI 1 schedule is in effect and in the presence of the green key light an FR 30 is in effect. This would be called a multiple fixed-interval 1-minute fixed-ratio 30 schedule of reinforcement (abbreviated mult FI 1-min FR 30). The effect of such a schedule is that the red key light will come to control typical FI 1-minute performance and the green key light will come to control typical FR 30 performance. Thus, each stimulus in a multiple schedule will come to control behavior that is appropriate to the schedule that is in effect when that stimulus is present.

If two component schedules alternate, as in a multiple schedule, but different stimuli are not correlated with the two component schedules, the schedule is called a mixed schedule. The purpose of studying mixed schedules is typically to determine the importance of the stimuli correlated with the component schedules in multiple schedules. For example, mult FI 1-min FR 30 may be compared with mixed FI 1-min FR 30 to determine whether the change in behavior patterns that occurs when the component schedules change is in fact controlled by the change in the stimulus that occurs from one component to the next. Mixed schedules are also used to study the extent to which an individual's previous behavior can come to act as a discriminative stimulus controlling subsequent behavior. For example, if an individual eventually ceases to respond after about 30 responses in the extinction component of a mixed FR 30 Ext schedule (i.e., a schedule in which FR 30 alternates with extinction for a given period of time, with no specific stimuli correlated with the two components), this would indicate that the individual's own behavior of making about 30 responses with no reinforcement has come to act as an S^Δ for that individual (Ferster & Skinner, 1957).

STIMULUS DISCRIMINATION AND BEHAVIORAL CONTRAST

Suppose that a pigeon is placed on a multiple VI 3-min VI 3-min schedule in which a red key light is associated with the first component and a green key light is associated with the second component. Since the same schedule (i.e., VI 3 minutes) is in effect in both components, response rate should be about the same in the two components. Now, however, suppose that the multiple schedule is changed to multiple VI 3-min Ext, which means that the second component is changed to extinction. This, it will be noted, is simply another way of describing the training of a stimulus discrimination between an S^D or S+ (the red key light) and an S^Δ or S− (the green key light). As was explained in Chapter 4, responding in the second or extinction component will decrease to (or close) to zero. But, in addition, responding in the first or VI 3-minute component will increase above its rate during the previous multiple VI 3-min VI 3-min schedule. If the multiple schedule is then changed from multiple VI 3-min Ext back to multiple VI 3-min VI 3-min, responding during the second component will increase back to its level during the original exposure to multiple VI 3-min VI 3-min. In addition, responding during the first component will decrease to its level during the original exposure to multiple VI 3-min VI 3-min. This illustrates a phenomenon called behavioral contrast which is defined as:

a change in the rate of responding in an unchanged component of a multiple schedule that is in the direction opposite to that of the change in the rate of responding in a changed component (Reynolds, 1961a).

Thus, the preceding two examples of changes in multiple schedules are examples of behavioral contrast. If the rate of responding in the unchanged component increases, as in the first example of behavioral contrast above, the effect is termed positive behavioral contrast; if it decreases, as in the second example, the effect is termed negative behavioral contrast.

It is not necessary to change reinforcement rate in one component to or from zero to obtain behavioral contrast. For example, positive behavioral contrast may be obtained by shifting from multiple VI 2-min VI 2-min to multiple VI 2-min VI 4-min. Negative behavioral contrast may be obtained by shifting from multiple VI 2-min VI 2-min to multiple VI 2-min VI 1-min.

Note that the change in response rate in the unchanged component has no effect (or practically no effect) on reinforcement rate in that component when a variable-interval schedule is in effect in that component. Therefore, change in reinforcement rate in the unchanged component is not a factor in behavioral contrast. The causes of behavioral contrast are complex and appear not to be unitary. There are several factors that may contribute to behavioral contrast.

Habituation and Behavioral Contrast

We saw in Chapter 7 that over a session a reinforcer that is repeatedly presented appears to habituate, thus decreasing their response rate for that reinforcer. When reinforcement is reduced in one component of a multiple schedule, habituation to the reinforcer decreases. This makes the reinforcer in the unchanged component more effective, resulting in an increase in response rate in the unchanged component (McSweeney & Weatherly, 1998).

The major evidence for the contribution of habituation to behavioral contrast is as follows:

1. Presenting strong stimuli in one component of a two-component multiple schedule may produce an effect similar to positive contrast in the other component. For example, adding punishment (Brethower & Reynolds, 1962; Crosbie et al., 1997), stimuli paired with reinforcement (Brownstein & Hughes, 1970; Brownstein & Newsom, 1970; Hughes, 1971; Reynolds & Limpo, 1968; Wilkie, 1973, 1977), or randomly presented stimuli in one component may cause responding to increase in the other component. These findings could be due to dishabituation (see Chapter 2) of the reinforcer (supporting the idea that positive contrast is due to a decrease in the habituation of the reinforcer).

2. The size of the positive-contrast effect may decrease over sessions (Bloomfield, 1966; Pear & Wilkie, 1971; Sadowsky, 1973; Selekman, 1973; Terrace, 1966). This could be a result of long-term habituation (Chapter 2) to the general change that occurred in the conditions of reinforcement when the multiple schedule was changed (McSweeney & Weatherly, 1998, p. 208).

3. The size of the behavioral contrast effect seems to vary directly with the duration of the changed component and inversely with the duration of the unchanged component (Williams, 1983). This could be because the longer the duration of the changed component, the stronger effect it should have on the changed component; whereas, the

shorter the duration of the unchanged component, the less time available for the individual to recover (e.g., for habituation to occur if the preceding component had a lower reinforcement rate, or habituation to dissipate if the preceding component had a higher reinforcement rate).

4. While behavioral contrast occurs across session, analogous effects known as local contrast[1] often occur within sessions (Bernheim & Williams, 1967; Freeman, 1971; Nevin & Shettleworth, 1966). Positive local contrast is an increase in response rate at the beginning of a component following a component with a lower reinforcement rate, and negative local contrast is a decrease in response rate at the beginning of a component following a component with a lower reinforcement rate. Response rate then decreases, in the case of positive local contrast, or increases in the case of negative local contrast, over the duration of the component. Both positive and negative local contrast are consistent with the habituation explanation of behavioral contrast because there should be less habituation of the reinforcer after exposure to a low reinforcement rate and more habituation of the reinforcer after exposure to a high reinforcement rate.

5. Local contrast occurs with respondent as well as operant behavior. The magnitude of the conditioned response on a given CS+ trial will be greater if the CS+ trial has just been preceded by a CS– trial than if it had just been preceded by a CS+ trial (Pavlov, 1927).[2] This could be due to habituation to the CS+ or the unconditioned stimulus if the former or both had occurred on the preceding trial.

Not all local contrast effects are compatible with the above habituation explanation of behavioral contrast. For example, both positive and negative local contrast dissipate over time as discrimination training progresses (Gonzalez & Champlin, 1974; McLean & White, 1981; Nevin & Shettleworth, 1966). While long-term habituation might explain the dissipation of positive local contrast, it does not explain the dissipation of negative local contrast. Moreover, both positive and negative local contrast take longer to dissipate when the stimuli in the standard and variable components are quite similar than when they are quite different (P. Blough, 1983; Hinson & Malone, 1980; Malone, 1976). It is not clear how this fact fits in with the habituation explanation. Further, local contrast effects do not always occur and sometime a pattern opposite to that of local contrast occurs (Buck et al., 1975; Freeman, 1971; White, 1995).

Autoshaping and Behavioral Contrast

The procedure that produces positive behavioral contrast is similar to the autoshaping procedure (Chapter 6, pp. 111–112). Like autoshaping, the procedure that produces positive behavioral contrast involves a stimulus paired with a relatively high rate or probability of reinforcement alternating with a stimulus paired with a relatively low rate of reinforcement. Some of the responses that occur during the unchanged mulitple-schedule component during positive behavioral contrast could therefore be autoshaped rather than operant responses. It would be difficult to tell which responses are operant and which are autoshaped (e.g., an autoshaped key peck is very similar to an operant key peck). If the same number of operant responses occurred in the unchanged component of the multiple schedule after the change in the other

---

1. Because of its tendency to dissipate, Nevin and Shettleworth (1966) originally called local contrast transient contrast.
2. Pavlov (1927, pp. 189–196) called this effect induction, a term that now has the opposite meaning.

component as before the change, the added occurrence of autoshaped responses would be seen as an increase in response rate. Thus, according to this explanation which is called the additivity theory of behavioral contrast, positive behavioral contrast occurs because the procedure produces autoshaped responses that add to the responses being maintained by reinforcement in the unchanged component (Gamzu & Schwartz, 1973; Hearst & Jenkins, 1974; Rachlin, 1973). This explanation accounts for negative behavioral contrast as the reversal of positive behavioral contrast (although this does not fit all instances of negative behavioral contrast).

Two pieces of evidence in support the additivity theory are that, while behavioral contrast is quite reliably obtained when pigeons peck a key whose light is correlated with food reinforcement, it appears to be much less easily obtained (1) when rats press a lever for food reinforcement (e.g., Pear & Wilkie, 1971), and (2) when pigeons press a foot treadle for food reinforcement (e.g., Westbrook, 1973). According to the additivity theory, this is because these responses also do not autoshape as readily as key pecking by pigeons does (although as mentioned in Chapter 6, licking and gnawing at a lever can be autoshaped in rats).

However, behavioral contrast can occur with the lever pressing of rats if the S+ and S− are made extremely distinct (e.g., by using a light as the S+ and a tone as the S− (Gutman, 1977); and it can occur with the treadle pressing of pigeons if a low VI schedule is used (e.g., VI 15 seconds instead of VI 30 or VI 60 seconds; McSweeney, 1983). Moreover, behavioral contrast is not limited to arbitrary behavior such as key pecking by pigeons or lever pressing by rats; it also occurs with humans in socially significant situations where autoshaping does not seem to be a factor. For example, it occurs when children are reinforced with tokens for correct academic responses in several different learning situations, and reinforcement is then varied in some of the learning situations while continuing as before in others (Simon, Ayllon, & Milan, 1982). (As indicated earlier, tokens are conditioned reinforcers because they can be exchanged for reinforcing items periodically.) The different settings are like the components of a multiple schedule, and changing the reinforcement rate in one or more of these components causes responding in those components to vary in the same direction as reinforcement rate while responding in the unchanged components varies in the opposite direction as reinforcement rate. Likewise, autistic and handicapped children who receive reinforcement in two different settings for desirable behavior (e.g., compliance), show an increase in that behavior in one setting when reinforcement for it is eliminated in the other setting (Koegel et al., 1980).

Therefore, it appears that behavioral contrast does not depend entirely on the occurrence of autoshaped responses produced by the alternation of an S+ with an S− (although under some conditions autoshaped responding may contribute to the effect).

The Following-Schedule Effect

We have seen that although autoshaping may contribute to behavioral contrast it cannot completely account for it. We shall see in this section that habituation also (either by itself or in combination with autoshaping) is insufficient to account for behavioral contrast. When a changed component of a multiple schedule alternates with an unchanged component, the former both precedes and follows the latter. If habituation caused it, behavioral contrast should be due to the changed component preceding the unchanged component rather than following it (because as we saw in Chapter 2, habituation is an accumulative, not an associative, process). In what is called the following-schedule effect, however, it is the changed component following the unchanged component that produces stronger behavioral contrast (Williams, 1979; 1981). This cannot be seen with a two-component multiple schedule. Consider, however, a three-component multiple schedule consisting of the components A, B, and C that always occur in that order. The order is repeated throughout the session, so that B follows A, C follows B, and A follows C. Suppose that initially each component contains a VI 3-min schedule. Then, when responding has stabilized (and is about equal) in the three components, the schedule in component B is changed to VI 6 min. Naturally, responding will decrease in component B. In addition, responding will increase in both components A and C. The increase in component A, however, will generally be larger than that in component C, and will not dissipate over sessions as that in component C will tend to do. Thus, changing the reinforcement rate in a component of a multiple schedule has a greater effect on responding in the component that it follows than in the component that it precedes. In the typical behavioral contrast study that uses a two-component multiple schedule, the changed component both precedes and follows the unchanged component and the behavioral contrast that is observed probably stems from both local contrast and the following-schedule effect. The latter, however, appears to be the more effective source.

Like habituation and autoshaping, the following-schedule effect does not by itself fully account for all behavioral contrast effects. In particular, it does not account for local contrast. It therefore appears that behavioral contrast is the product of several mechanisms, including (but not necessarily limited to) habituation, autoshaping, and an unknown factor that is responsible for the following-schedule effect.

STIMULUS GENERALIZATION

Stimulus generalization is the tendency for stimuli that are close on some physical dimension of similarity to control the same response or, conversely, to control the absence of that response. The function showing the change in responding as the physical differences between a conditioned or discriminative stimulus and other stimuli increases is called a stimulus generalization gradient. There are two types of stimulus generalization gradients: excitatory and inhibitory. Stimulus generalization gradients are typically studied by measuring responding to various stimuli during extinction.

Excitatory Gradients

As described in Chapter 4, stimulus generalization occurs when responding that is reinforced in the presence of one stimulus (the S+) occurs in the presence of other stimuli. An excitatory stimulus generalization gradient depicts the tendency of other stimuli to control responding as a function of their distance from the S+ along some continuum (e.g., wavelength of light). Typically, the more distant a stimulus is from the S+ the less will be that tendency.

A question of interest is whether rate of reinforcement and type of schedule affect the shape of the generalization gradient. Figure 8.1 shows data obtained from one study that looked at the effect of reinforcement rate on the excitatory stimulus generalization gradient. The generalization gradients in this study (Heast et al., 1964) were obtained by exposing pigeons to various stimuli during extinction after training the birds on several different VI schedules. The S+ was a vertical line (labeled "0 degrees" in the figure) projected on the response key, and the test stimuli were lines tilted various degrees from the vertical. The amount of generalization to each test stimulus is shown as the number of responses that occurred in the presence of that test stimulus relative to the number that occurred to the S+ during testing. Hence, the vertical axis in the figure is labeled "Relative Generalization." Note that the higher the VI schedule the less steep (or more flat) the generalization gradient. Thus, it appears from this study that schedules with low reinforcement rates produce more generalization than do schedules with high reinforcement rates. A more recent study, however, failed to replicate this flattening of the generalization gradient as reinforcement rate decreased (Walker & Branch, 1998). Instead, with the exception of more responding to the training stimulus that had been paired with the higher reinforcement rate, both absolute and relative generalization gradients in the more recent study were similar regardless of reinforcement rate. The reason for the discrepancy between these two studies is unknown. One possibility is that the training stimuli used in the later study may have been more salient than those in the earlier study; that is, the training stimuli may have contrasted more with the background stimuli in the later study (Dinsmoor, 1995).

Regarding the effect of type of schedule on the generalization gradient, it appears that DRL schedules produce flatter relative gradients than VI schedules do (Hearst, Koresko, & Poppen, 1964). In addition, VR schedules produce slightly flatter generalization gradients than VI schedules do when reinforcement rate for the two types of schedules is equated through a yoked-control procedure (Thomas & Switalski, 1966). External stimuli may therefore show less control over behavior when correlated with DRL and VR schedules than when correlated with VI schedules, possibly because stimuli arising from the individual's own behavior are more critical in the former schedules. This is because both of these schedules tend to strongly reinforce specific IRTs.

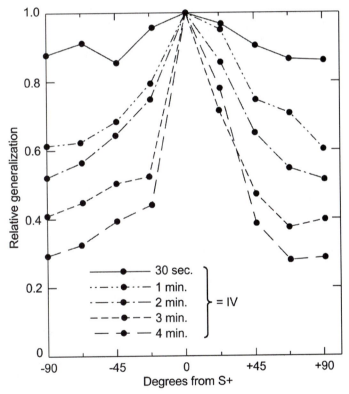

FIGURE 8.1. Effect of reinforcement schedule on stimulus generalization. Each group of five pigeons received training on a different variable-interval schedule prior to the generalization test. The S+ was a vertical line (orientation = 0°) for all birds. The data are averaged over the five members of each group. In general, as the value of the VI schedule increases the gradients become flatter. (From Hearst et al., 1964)

The steepness of a generalization gradient can also be affected by discrimination training. In one study with two groups of pigeons the S+ was a particular frequency (i.e., pitch) of tone. No S– was used with one group and the generalization gradient was found to be rather flat during subsequent testing. An S– of silence (no tone) was used with the other group. This was found to produce a steep generalization gradient (Jenkins & Harrison, 1960). Hence, less generalization occurs when discrimination training is given than when it is not given.

In the above study S– (no tone) was not on the same continuum or dimension as that on which generalization was tested (tones with different frequencies). This type of discrimination procedure is called extradimensional training (also known as interdimensional training). If the S– is on the same continuum as that on which generalization is tested (e.g., if S- in the above study had been a tone of a particular frequency) the discrimination procedure would have been referred to as intradimensional training. Intradimensional training produces steeper generalization gradients than does extradimensional training (Jenkins & Harrison, 1962). In addition, as described in Chapter 4 (pp. 78–79), intradimensional training produces a peak shift—that is, the peak of the generalization gradient occurs on the side of the S+ away from the S– (see Figure 4.15, p. 78). Training with no S- and interdimensional training does not produce a peak shift—the peak of the gradient occurs at the S+.

As mentioned, generalization gradients are usually studied during extinction. This is done to avoid conditioning responding to the test stimuli, thereby contaminating the measure of generalization. A problem with this is that the behavior being measured will decrease during the test. A way to offset this is to intersperse test trials with brief conditioning trials with the S+ (D. Blough, 1969, 1975; P. Blough, 1972; Pierrel, 1958). A disadvantage of this method is that it develops a discrimination between the S+ and the test stimuli, thus tending to obscure generalization. It seems that it is impossible to obtain a pure measure of generalization. Reinforcing responding on a low-reinforcement VI schedule prior to obtaining an operant excitatory generalization gradient, however, tends to ensure that responding will not decrease substantially due to extinction during the test stimuli (and thus that any decrement will be mostly due to a decrease in generalization).

Inhibitory Gradients

The stimulus generalization gradients discussed above are called "excitatory" because they demonstrate control of responding by stimuli along a continuum. There are also gradients that demonstrate control of nonresponding across a continuum. Since inhibition is the opposite of excitation, these gradients are called inhibitory gradients. The clearest way to see an inhibitory gradient is to use extradimensional training in which the S– is on a continuum along which stimuli occur during generalization testing. For example, suppose that in a study with pigeons the S+ is a white key light and the S– is a black vertical line bisecting the white key. During generalization testing stimuli around S–, rather than S+, are varied by presenting lines with different degrees of tilt. The result is an inhibitory gradient which is, essentially, an inverted excitatory gradient. The lines connected by circles in Figure 8.2 show an example of two such inhibitory gradients from two studies using the procedure just described. For the purpose of comparison the figure also shows two excitatory gradients obtained by training the vertical line as the S+ and the white key light as the S–.

In Chapter 7 it was mentioned that the postreinforcement pause in fixed schedules may be due to reinforcement, or stimuli occurring right after reinforcement, acting as an S–. This view has been supported, at least for FI schedules, by a study in which a vertical line appeared on the key during exposure of pigeons to an FI schedule. After FI performance was well developed the angle of the line was varied randomly during different intervals. The result was that an inhibitory gradient was obtained during the first part of the FI intervals and an excitatory gradient was obtained during the last part of the intervals (Wilkie, 1974). Therefore, stimuli occurring right after reinforcement on FI seem to acquire inhibitory control over responding.

If we think of inhibitory gradients as inverted excitatory gradients, it should be possible to obtain an inverted or negative peak shift following procedures analogous to those used for obtaining a positive peak shift. This can be done by first reinforcing responses to a number of stimuli along a continuum. Then intradimensional discrimination training is given as described above; that is, responses are reinforced in the presence of one of the stimuli on the continuum and extinguished in the presence of another stimulus on the continuum. If care is taken not to eliminate responding in the presence of the second stimulus, subsequent generalization testing will reveal a negative as well as a positive peak shift, as shown in Figure 8.3.

Like excitatory gradients, inhibitory gradients are usually studied during extinction. Thus that inhibition is being developed to the test stimuli during testing, thereby contaminating the measure of inhibitory generalization. Conditioning or presenting reinforcement in the presence of the test stimuli would produce the opposite problem. As with excitatory stimulus generalization, it seems impossible to obtain a pure measure of inhibitory stimulus generalization.

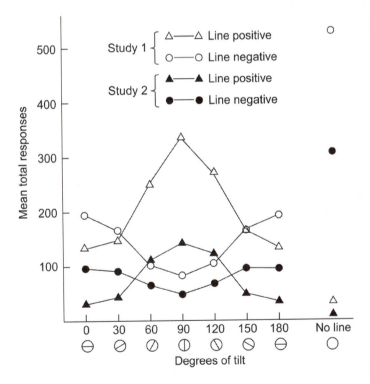

FIGURE 8.2. Excitatory and inhibitory stimulus generalization gradients. The gradients with triangles were obtained following extradimensional discrimination training between a vertical line as S+ and no line as S−, and demonstrate excitatory stimulus control. The functions with circles were obtained following extradimensional discrimination training between a vertical line as S− and no line as S+, and demonstrate inhibitory stimulus control. (From Honig, 1963)

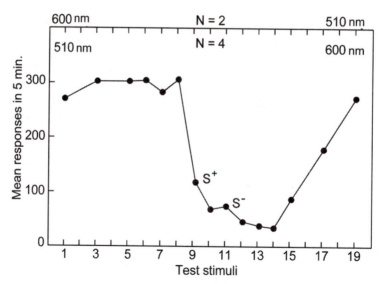

FIGURE 8.3. A generalization with positive and negative peak shift. Key pecking to all test stimuli was first reinforced. Then intradimensional discrimination training occurred: pecking to the S+ was reinforced and pecking to the S– was extinguished. For four pigeons the S+ was 550 nm and the S– was 560nm; and for two pigeons the reverse was the case. The generalization-test data were averaged across the six pigeons. Note that maximum responding is shifted to the side of the S+ away from the S– and that minimum responding is shifted to the side of the S– away from the S+. (From Guttman, 1965)

SIMULTANEOUS DISCRIMINATIONS

As we have seen, we can obtain differential responding to two stimuli—that is, a discrimination between the two stimuli—by reinforcing responses in the presence of one stimulus and extinguishing them in the presence of a stimulus that alternates with that stimulus. This multiple-schedule procedure is sometimes called successive-discrimination training, since the two stimuli occur successively. Another possibility is to teach a discrimination between two stimuli that occur simultaneously. This, appropriately enough, is called simultaneous-discrimination training. For example, in training a simultaneous red-green discrimination in pigeons, a red key and a green key may be present simultaneously, and responding to one of the colors (the correct stimulus) is reinforced while responding to the other color (the *incorrect stimulus*) is extinguished. The positions of the correct and incorrect stimuli change frequently and unsystematically so that position, rather than the correct stimulus, does not acquire control over responding.

Note that a simultaneous discrimination is actually two (or more) successive discriminations operating simultaneously. For example, consider a procedure in which one of two keys is red or green in random alternation while the other is green when the first key is red and red when the first key is green. If responding on a red key is reinforced and responding on a green key is not, then this procedure is a simultaneous discrimination. It is also, however, two successive discriminations in which red and green alternate on each key and responding on each key is reinforced when that key is red and extinguished when that key is green. Thus, we can consider simultaneous discriminations to be a special case of successive discriminations. It should not be surprising, therefore, that much of what we have said about successive discriminations is applicable to simultaneous discriminations.

Simultaneous Discrimination Methods

Both successive and simultaneous discriminations may employ either a free-operant or a discrete-trials method (see Chapter 4, pp. 58–59). The former is more commonly used with successive discriminations, however, while the latter is more commonly used with simultaneous discriminations. Discrete trials may be conducted in mazes, as illustrated in Chapter 4 (Figure 4.1, p. 58), or in operant conditioning chambers. In the discrete-trials method in an operant conditioning chamber, each response (correct or incorrect) turns off the stimuli-to-be-discriminated for a brief period of time (e.g., five seconds) during which responses have no effect. This period is called the intertrial interval. Usually the amount of time the stimuli are available per trial, called the trial interval, is also limited. A variation on the discrete-trials method is a correction procedure, in which only correct responses initiate the intertrial interval. Thus, if an animal emits an incorrect response, it must correct itself by emitting a correct response before the trial will terminate. In the free-operant method, there is no intertrial interval and the correct and incorrect stimuli are continuously available.

A particularly interesting measure in both discrete-trial and free-operant simultaneous discriminations is the accuracy of the behavior, defined as the percent of responses to the correct stimulus. Another measure of interest in the discrete-trials method is the probability that a correct or incorrect response will occur during a trial (computed as the percent of trials in which a response occurred in experiments where trial length is limited). A measure of interest in the free-operant method is rate of responding, just as it is in studies involving only one operandum.

Experiments on simultaneous discriminations show that accuracy of responding varies directly with the physical similarity between the stimuli to be discriminated. For example, if pigeons learn a simultaneous brightness discrimination (e.g., the brighter of two keys is designated as correct), accuracy will decrease as the difference between the brightness of the two keys decreases. Thus, by appropriately adjusting the relative brightness of the two stimuli it is possible to set accuracy at any desired level (e.g., 85%) for the purpose of studying the effects of other variables on accuracy (e.g., Nevin, 1967).

Probability Learning

Although usually in a simultaneous discrimination 100% of the reinforcements occur to one alternative, this is not necessarily the case. In a discrete-trials procedure called probability learning one alternative is correct (i.e., reinforcement occurs if that alternative is chosen) on a certain percentage of trials while another alternative is correct on the remaining trials. For example, in a T-maze (see Figure 4.1) reinforcement may be in the left goal box on 70% of the trials and in the right goal box on 30% of the trials, with the sequence of which goal box contains the reinforcement varying randomly from trial to trial. Some early research seemed to indicate that individuals in a probability learning situation would tend to match their choices to the reinforcement probabilities. For example, if alternative A is correct on 25% of the trials and alternative B is correct on the other 75%, individuals would choose the latter 75% of the time and the former the other 25% of the time. If it held up, this result would be surprising because it would mean that the individual was consistently getting less than the maximum amount of reinforcement available. In the 75% versus 25% case, for example, always choosing the alternative that was most often correct will result in reinforcement 75% of the time ($1.00 \times 0.75 + 0.0 \times 0.25 = 0.75$), whereas choosing it only 75% of the time will result in reinforcement only 62% of the time ($0.75 \times 0.75 + 0.25 \times 0.25 = 0.56 + 0.06 = 0.62$). Subsequent studies, however, indicate that individuals do tend to consistently choose the alternative with the higher probability of reinforcement (Mackintosh, 1974, pp. 191–192). Failures to do so point to a lack of discrimination between stimuli correlated with the alternatives, just as when performance is less than perfect in a simultaneous discrimination in which one alternative is correct 100% of the time. In our subsequent discussion of simultaneous discriminations, we focus on cases in which just one alternative is always the correct one.

Schedule Variables on Simultaneous Discriminations

We have seen that schedules of reinforcement have powerful effects on response rate. This raises the question of whether schedules of reinforcement affect accuracy of responding in a simultaneous discrimination in the same way that they affect response rate. For example, we know that the period just after reinforcement on a high FR or FI schedule is characterized by a low probability of responding (the postreinforcement pause). Is accuracy also reduced at or shortly after this period?

When reinforcement is scheduled after every N trials containing correct responses in a discrete-trials procedure, the schedule is similar to an FR schedule in a free-operant procedure; when reinforcement is scheduled after a trial containing a correct response following N trials (both correct and incorrect), the schedule is similar to an FI schedule in a free-operant procedure. In both of these types of discrete-trials schedules, response probability is low just after reinforcement. Nevertheless, accuracy is fairly constant across trials (Nevin, 1967). In other words, accuracy is about the same just after reinforcement as it is just before reinforcement.

The results with free-operant simultaneous discriminations seem to be similar to those found with the discrete-trials procedure—that is, accuracy is constant across ratios and intervals—although there is little direct evidence on this point. A schedule similar to an FR schedule has produced some interesting results, however. In this schedule, incorrect as well as correct responses advance the ratio, although (as in a regular FR schedule) only a correct response is reinforced each time the ratio is completed. The one experiment studying this procedure found that practically all responses occurred to the correct stimulus. The relatively few incorrect responses that did occur usually occurred immediately after the postreinforcement pause (Zeiler, 1968). Thus, factors that produce pausing in FR schedules also may tend to decrease accuracy, but the effect seems to be slight.

Another question we might ask is whether accuracy is affected by the overall rate of reinforcement. We know that, on various schedules of reinforcement, rate of responding decreases as reinforcement rate decreases. Is this also true for accuracy? The answer seems to be no. In both discrete-trials and free-operant procedures, increasing the number of trials or correct responses required for reinforcement does not appear to change accuracy in any systematic way. In fact, accuracy in simultaneous discriminations remains fairly constant even during extinction when rate of responding is, of course, decreasing (Nevin, 1967; Zeiler, 1968).

STIMULUS CONTROL AND ATTENTION

When an S^D is a compound stimulus, one element in the compound may gain or demonstrate control to the apparent exclusion of another member. This may be the result of lack of attending to one member either during conditioning of the compound or testing of the elements.

Overshadowing

As mentioned in Chapter 4, one stimulus element in a compound stimulus may overshadow another stimulus element in the compound. Consider a discrimination in which the S^D and S^Δ

each consist of more than one stimulus. For example, suppose that sometimes a white triangle on a red background is projected onto a response key for pigeons, and that at other times a white circle on a green background is projected onto the key. In the presence of the white triangle on the red background a VI 1 schedule is in effect, while in the presence of the white circle on the green background extinction is in effect. Thus, the white triangle on the red background is an S^D and the white circle on the green background is an S^Δ. Eventually the pigeon will respond at a high rate in the presence of the S^D and will emit few or no responses in the presence of the S^Δ.

Both the S^D and the S^Δ in this example are compound stimuli. One of the stimulus elements in the S^D is a white triangle and the other is the color red. The question therefore arises as to whether, as a result of discrimination training with the compound stimuli, either or both of these elements will control responding. The answer can be obtained by conducting a test in which the elements of both the S^D and the S^Δ occur separately during extinction. If this is done some pigeons will respond only in the presence of the color element of the compound S^D (red in this example), while others will respond only in the presence of the shape element (the white triangle) (Reynolds, 1961b).

It is as though the birds in the above experiment attend to only one stimulus dimension—color or shape—of the compound stimuli during discrimination training. In Chapter 3, we said that attending to a particular stimulus means that that stimulus is eliciting or evoking a particular type of response called an attending response. In order for a stimulus to become a conditioned stimulus or a discriminative stimulus, that stimulus must first elicit or evoke an attending response (i.e., it must first be attended to). One reason for a particular stimulus element in a compound stimulus not to gain control over responding, then, is that the attending responses it elicits or evokes are being interfered with by the attending responses elicited or evoked by another stimulus element in the compound. In any case, testing the elements separately in extinction—as was done in the experiment described above—is one way to determine which stimulus dimension the individual was attending to during discrimination training.

In Chapter 4 (pp. 85–86) we also indicated that this can not be the full explanation for overshadowing, however, because it is possible to reduce overshadowing *after* it has occurred. If overshadowing was caused by lack of attending at the time that it occurs, this would not be possible because attending to a stimulus that is no longer present cannot occur retroactively. Lack of attending to an overshadowed element of a compound S^D during conditioning also cannot explain why that element will exert control over responding under certain conditions. For example, in a multiple VI VI schedule in which the stimulus coupled with one component is the overshadowed element and the stimulus coupled with the other is the corresponding element of the compound S^Δ, more responding will initially occur to the overshadowed element (Wilkie & Masson, 1976). Hence, it appears that both elements of a compound S^D may affect behavior, although a special test is sometimes required to detect the effect of one of the elements.

Blocking

As also mentioned in Chapter 4, prior discrimination training with one element of a compound stimulus may block (i.e., prevent or hinder) another element from acquiring control during discrimination training with the compound stimulus. Consider the following sequence of events: (1) pigeons are first given simple stimulus discrimination training with a vertical line on the key as the S^D and a horizontal line as the S^Δ; (2) the birds are then given compound discrimination training in which a vertical line on a green background is the compound S^D and a horizontal line on a red background is the compound S^A; (2) finally, a test is given in which the elements (vertical line, horizontal line, green background, red background) of the compound S^D and S^A are alternated separately during extinction. Very little responding will occur to the color element of the compound S^D during the test, even though pigeons given only the second and third stages usually respond exclusively to the color element (Johnson & Cumming, 1968; vom Saal & Jenkins, 1970). This may happen in part because the initial training with one element strengthens an attending response to that element such that it interferes with the attending response to the other element. Of course, as with overshadowing, lack of attending to one of the stimulus elements during conditioning may not be a complete explanation of blocking.

Generalization Testing

Up to this point we have spoken of control by a particular stimulus in terms of the amount of responding that occurs in the presence and absence of that stimulus. Another way to assess stimulus control is by the steepness of the generalization gradient on a particular stimulus dimension. For example, a flat generalization gradient on the dimension of frequency of tones would indicate that tone frequency (i.e., pitch) does not control responding. Blocking has also been observed with this test of stimulus control.

For example, pigeons trained on a vertical-horizontal discrimination and then given compound discrimination training with the vertical line superimposed on one color and the horizontal line superimposed on another color show, on average, flatter gradients on the color dimension (i.e., wavelengths of light) than do pigeons not trained on the vertical-horizontal discrimination prior to compound discrimination training (Johnson, 1970). (In comparing the steepness of generalization gradients, calculations are usually based on the percent of total responses to the test stimuli rather than the absolute number of responses.)

Blocking, by definition, refers to a very clear procedure: An element of a compound stimulus prevents or hinders another element from gaining control over responding due to prior discrimination training. Often, however, we do not know why some stimuli tend to overshadow others. For example, it is not known why a stimulus with a particular geometrical form overshadows a color stimulus for some pigeons while the opposite is true for other pigeons. It appears, however, that for most pigeons color overshadows form. This may be a phylogenetic characteristic with survival value, in that color is probably more relevant than shape to the pigeon's food-seeking behavior in the natural environment. This possibility is supported by the fact that the nature of the reinforcer can determine which element of a compound stimulus will overshadow another element. For example, if a compound stimulus consisting of a red light and a tone is used as the S^D for a pigeon's treadle pressing response with food as the reinforcer, the light will tend to gain more control than the tone over responding; whereas, if the compound stimulus is used as the S^D for shock-avoidance responding, the tone will tend to gain more control over responding (Foree & LoLordo, 1973). Possibly this is because visual stimuli are more important to a pigeon's food seeking, whereas auditory stimuli are more important to it in avoiding or escaping predators. Hence, when pigeons are food deprived visual stimuli tend to elicit attending responses, whereas when aversive stimuli are present auditory stimuli tend to elicit attending responses in pigeons. In any case, this relationship between the reinforcer and the controlling element in a compound stimulus is so strong that it is difficult to block it by prior discrimination training with the tone when food is the reinforcer or with the light when shock is the reinforcer (LoLordo, Jacobs, & Foree, 1982).

Thus, it appears that phylogenetically determined overshadowing can be more powerful than blocking. Nevertheless, if unrelated stimuli and other procedural factors are carefully controlled, prior training on a visual discrimination with rats and pigeons responding to avoid shock and prior training on an auditory discrimination with rats and pigeons responding for food (Schindler & Weiss, 1985; Weiss & Panlilio, 1999) can effectively block the other, phylogenetically advantaged stimulus element in a compound auditory-visual stimulus.

Masking

Overshadowing and blocking are important concepts in our understanding of how stimuli may gain or fail to gain control over behavior. A related concept is that of masking, which occurs when a stimulus gains control over behavior but this control is hidden or "masked" by another stimulus that is present during testing. For example, suppose that a pigeon has been trained on a line orientation discrimination and then tested with various line orientations when a particular color is also projected on the key. If a steeper generalization gradient is obtained when color is absent than when it is present during testing, regardless of whether it was present or absent during training, then we would say that the color masks the control acquired by the line orientation (Farthing, 1972). One possible explanation of masking is that a masking stimulus elicits or evokes attending responses that interfere with the attending responses evoked by an S^D.

RESPONSE COUNT AND DISCRIMINATIVE CONTROL

We have seen in discussing mixed schedules at the beginning of this chapter that an individual's response count, or the number of responses the individual has made, can be a discriminative stimulus for that individual. Another way to demonstrate this is to modify an FR schedule so that reinforcement is contingent on a terminal response that is different from the response that advances the count toward reinforcement. For example, after emitting the number of presses specified by an FR schedule on a given lever, a rat receives food or water for ceasing to press that lever and either presses another lever (Mechner, 1958) or enters a reinforcement area monitored by a photocell (Platt & Johnson, 1971). The result of this procedure is that as the FR schedule increases, there is a corresponding increases in the number of responses the rat emits on the FR schedule before emitting the terminal response, with the mean number of responses prior to the terminal responses being slightly greater than the number specified by the FR schedule.

The evidence also indicates that the S^D for emitting the terminal reinforced response is the response count rather than some other stimulus correlated with time. Decreasing response rate by, for example, decreasing the level of deprivation, thus resulting in a longer time to complete the specified number of responses, does not affect the discrimination (Mechner & Guevrekian, 1962).

BEHAVIORAL MOMENTUM

The term behavioral momentum is used in two senses which, unfortunately, are easily confused:

- the tendency for behavior that is currently occurring to continue occurring despite various disruptive factors; or
- the tendency for behavior to occur in the presence of a particular stimulus despite various disruptive factors.

The first meaning translates into what in less technical, everyday language we frequently refer to as "being on a roll." For example, you might say you had built up momentum (or were "on a roll") in a particular activity if you (although perhaps reluctant to start) were reluctant to stop in the face of some potential disruption (such as being called to lunch). The second meaning refers to the tendency to emit behavior in the presence of a given stimulus despite various factors that may tend to decrease the probability of that behavior occurring. For example, we might say that someone has a high party-going momentum if he or she often responds positively to party invitations even at the expense of not completing important tasks (such as studying for exams) that might ultimately be more reinforcing. The difference between the two meanings of behavioral momentum may not be as great as it first seems. Note that the first meaning is a special case of the second, given that behavior itself may be an S^D for subsequent behavior. The following discussion deals with the second meaning unless otherwise indicated.

Behavioral and Physical Momentum: An Analogy

Nevin and his associates (Nevin, 1992; Nevin, Mandell, & Atak, 1983) have drawn an analogy between momentum in physics and behavioral momentum. In physics, momentum is the product of velocity and mass. The greater an object's momentum, the greater the force required to slow it down. Thus, the momentum of a heavy (i.e., massive) object moving at a low velocity and that of a light (i.e., less massive) object moving at a high velocity may be identical, in that equivalent forces applied to the objects against the directions in which they are moving may slow them down the same amount. Nevin suggests that response rate corresponds to velocity in physics, resistance of responding to change in the presence of a stimulus controlling the response corresponds to mass, and various events that tend to disrupt or slow responding down correspond to the external forces that slow physical objects down. Numerous experiments lend support to this analogy and tend to indicate, moreover, that resistance of responding to change in the presence of a given stimulus is a direct function of the rate or amount of reinforcement occurring in the presence of that stimulus.

Consider a multiple VI 60-seconds VI 120-seconds schedule for key pecking by pigeons for food reinforcement, where the keylight is red during the VI 60 component and green during the VI 120 component. Suppose that between each VI component, which lasts for 60 seconds, there is a 30-second period in which the key is dark and key pecks are not reinforced. When responding has stabilized on this procedure, it will be higher in the VI 60-seconds component than in the VI 120-seconds component (and zero when the keylight is dark because key pecks are not reinforced then and also because pigeons tend not to peck at dark keys). Now we present reinforcement independently of responding—for example, on a VT schedule—when the key is dark. Due to behavioral contrast, this will cause responding to decrease in both the red-keylight and green-keylight components. It will decrease less in the presence of the red keylight (the keylight component with the higher reinforcement rate), however, than in the presence of the green keylight (the keylight component with the lower reinforcement rate). By definition, we say that responding in the presence of the red keylight has more momentum than responding in the presence of the green keylight, since presenting reinforcement when the key was dark disrupted responding less in the red-keylight component than in the green keylight component.

With reference to our physics analogy, the above result was obtained because both velocity (response rate) and mass (resistance to change) were higher in the red-keylight component than in the green-keylight component. As in the physics analogy, however, it is possible to vary these two ingredients of behavioral momentum independently of each other. Suppose, for example, that we vary response rate while holding reinforcement rate constant. One way to do this is to use identical VI schedules in the two reinforced-responding components of a multiple schedule similar to the one in the previous experiment, but to add a short DRL schedule to the VI schedule in one component and a short DRH schedule to the VI schedule in the other component (Fath, Fields, Malott, & Grossett, 1983). For example, beginning with a two-component multiple schedule as in the above experiment, one component might be a VI 60-seconds schedule with an added DRL 2.5 seconds, while the other component might be a VI 60-seconds schedule with an added DRH 1.5 seconds. What this means is: (1) responding will be reinforced in one component only if the VI 60-seconds schedule has made a reinforcer available in that component and the response occurs at no less than 2.5 seconds after the previous response; and, (2) a response will be reinforced in the other component only if the VI 60-seconds schedule in that component has made a reinforcer available and the response occurs no more than 1.5 second after the previous response. As in the above experiment, between each of the two components in which key pecking is reinforced, we include a short period in which the key is dark and key pecking is not reinforced. After a number of sessions, responding will be higher in the component with the added DRH than in the component with the added DRL, yet reinforcement rate will be nearly equal in the two components. Now, as in the preceding experiment, we introduce response-independent reinforcement when the key is dark. As in the preceding experiment, responding will decrease in both components in which responding is reinforced. Likewise, as in the preceding experiment, it will decrease more in the component with the lower response rate because that component will have the smaller behavioral momentum.

Suppose that instead of looking at absolute decreases in responding in the above two experiments, however, we look at proportionate decreases—that is, the decrease in each component relative to the level of responding in that component prior to the introduction of response-independent reinforcement when the key was dark. Now we find something very interesting: The proportionate decrease in responding is greater in the green-keylight component than in the red-keylight component in the first experiment, but is equal in both reinforced-responding components in the second experiment. This tells us that resistance to change was greater in the component with the higher reinforcement rate in the first experiment, but is the same in both reinforced-responding components in the second experiment despite the different response rates between these components in the second experiment. It seems clear, therefore, that different reinforcement rates produce different resistances to change—with larger reinforcement rates producing more than smaller reinforcement rates—in the presence of different stimuli.

The outcome is similar if two reinforced-responding components of a multiple schedule contain different amounts—instead of different rates—of reinforcement. For example, a pigeon responding on a multiple schedule will show greater resistance to change in a component in which grain is presented for six seconds on a VI 60-seconds schedule than in a component in which grain is presented for three seconds on a VI 60-seconds schedule (Harper & McLean, 1992; Nevin, 1974).

Presenting response-independent food between components of a multiple schedule is but one way to probe responding for resistance to change. There are numerous other ways. For example, responding may be reduced by reducing deprivation level prior to an experimental session, by punishment, by presenting a stimulus paired with an aversive stimulus (i.e., conditioned suppression), and by providing an alternative source of reinforcement. All of these methods generally support the following rule:

> To increase the resistance of responding to change in the face of any type of disruption in the presence of a given stimulus, increase the rate or amount of reinforcement occurring in the presence of that stimulus.

Despite the wide generality of this rule, however, it may not hold for all stimuli. Auditory stimuli appear to be an exception with rats, for example, although the rule holds for visual stimuli with rats as it does with pigeons (Mauro & Mace, 1996).

Surprising as it might seem, reinforcement can increase the resistance of responding to change even when it is not contingent on that responding. Consider, for example, a multiple schedule with two VI x-seconds components (i.e., two components containing identical VI schedules), where x may be any value. Suppose we add a VT y-seconds (a schedule in which reinforcement occurs every y seconds, on average, regardless of responding) to one of these VI x-seconds components. This will clearly result in a higher reinforcement rate in that component, but also a lower response rate. Nevertheless, despite the lower response rate, the resistance to change in that component will be greater than in the other VI x-seconds component. This result has wide generality: it has been demonstrated not only with pigeons pecking response keys for food (Nevin, Tota, Torquato, & Shull, 1990), but also with developmentally disabled humans sorting dinnerware on multiple VI 60-seconds VI 60-seconds schedules for popcorn or coffee (Mace et al., 1990). In the latter case, additional reinforcers in one component occurred on a VT 30-seconds schedule and the behavioral disrupter was a video music/dance program playing at the same time that the individuals sorted the dinnerware.

Additional reinforcement during a component of a multiple schedule will increase resistance of responding to change in that component even if the added reinforcement is for another response, such as responding on a different operandum (McLean & Blampied, 1995; Nevin et al., 1990). The results that occur when another response is reinforced, however, are somewhat difficult to fit into the simple model of behavioral momentum thus far presented. Consider, for example, a multiple schedule in which reinforcement is programmed on a VI 40-seconds schedule in one component and a VI 360-seconds schedule in another component for response A (e.g., a peck on one key), and on a VI x-seconds schedule during both of these components for response B (e.g., a peck on a different key) where the two responses cannot be emitted simultaneously. We would expect both response A and response B to show greater resistance to change in the VI 40-seconds component because reinforcement rate is greater in that component than in the VI 360-seconds component. This is, in fact, the case when responding is disrupted by changes that do not involve changing the schedule of reinforcement for either response in either component of the multiple schedule. But suppose that the value of x is changed, which of course means changing the reinforcement schedule for response B in both the VI 40-seconds and VI 360-seconds components. This will cause the rate of response A to decrease proportionately more in the VI 360-seconds component of the multiple schedule than in the VI 40-seconds component. That is, response A will show greater resistance to change in the component with the higher reinforcement rate than in the component with the lower reinforcement rate. This is consistent with the rule given previously for increasing resistance of responding to change. Response B, however, will show greater resistance to change in the component with the lower reinforcement rate than in the component with the higher reinforcement rate (McLean & Blampied, 1995). This seems inconsistent with the rule, and the reason for this apparent exception is not known at present. Perhaps, however, it is explainable by interactions between the schedules for responses A and B and between the responses themselves.

Behavioral Momentum and the PREE

Because responding with a high reinforcement rate (or with a high probability of reinforcement) has a large momentum, we might reasonably expect it to persist longer after the introduction of extinction than responding with a low reinforcement rate (or with a high probability of reinforcement). But this is often not the case. Recall from the discussion of the partial-reinforcement-extinction effect (PREE) in Chapter 4 (pp. 64–66) that resistance to extinction is often greater after a lower rather than a higher rate of reinforcement prior to extinction. We discussed in Chapter 4 how this example of the principle of small increments appears to be due to stimulus generalization, because the rate at which a particular stimulus occurs may itself be a stimulus. Thus, at least one stimulus (i.e., a zero rate of reinforcement) present during extinction is more similar to a stimulus (i.e., a low rate of reinforcement) present during a low rate of reinforcement than to a stimulus (i.e., a high rate of reinforcement) present during a high rate of reinforcement. On the basis of stimulus generalization, then, responding should persist longer during extinction after a low rate of reinforcement than after a high rate of reinforcement.

Hence, a given rate of reinforcement has opposing effects on behavioral momentum during extinction. On the one hand, a high rate of reinforcement contributes more to momentum during extinction than a low rate of reinforcement because it contributes more to the resistance of responding to change. On the other hand, a high rate of reinforcement contributes less to momentum during extinction than a low rate of reinforcement because it contributes less similarity to the stimuli present during extinction. Whether a higher or lower rate of reinforcement produces more responding during extinction thus depends on an interaction between resistance of responding to change and stimulus generalization.

Examining resistance of responding to change, rather than simply amount of responding, in numerous experiments on the PREE confirms the above interpretation for free-operant behavior (Nevin, 1988). This picture is incomplete, however, because numerous experiments show that the PREE is extremely robust in discrete-trial experiments, and does not appear to be opposed by resistance of responding to change as it is in free-operant experiments (Nevin, 1988, 1992). For example, the speed with which a rat runs toward the goal box in a runway (see Figure 4.1, p. 58) during extinction (i.e., no food in the goal box), relative to the speed with which it ran prior to extinction, decreases much more slowly if running had been reinforced with a low probability than a high probability.

What accounts for this difference between free-operant and discrete-trials behavior during extinction after high-rate (or high-probability) versus low-rate (or low-probability) reinforcement? The answer seems to be that the frequent interruptions in responding during discrete-trials decrease behavioral momentum (in the first sense of the term given at the beginning of this section). That is, one factor that contributes to behavioral momentum in the second sense (at least during extinction) is the tendency for responding to continue once it has begun (Mellgren & Elsmore, 1991), which is behavioral momentum in the first sense. Perhaps, therefore, a single definition of behavioral momentum that combines both meanings would resolve the apparent inconsistency between the effects of varying rates or probabilities of reinforcement on subsequent free-operant and discrete-trials extinction.

Extensions of Behavioral Momentum to Applied Settings

A problem often faced in applied settings is that of generating a high rate or probability of a particular response. The first meaning of behavioral momentum suggests that to do this, all we have to do is to start the response occurring at a high rate or probability and ensure adequate reinforcement. Behavioral momentum will keep the response occurring as long as it continues to receive adequate reinforcement. This application of behavioral momentum may not sound like a solution to the problem, because it still leaves us with the problem of getting the response to occur with a high rate or probability to begin with. It can be a solution, however, if the response already occurs with a high rate or probability in the presence of certain stimuli and our problem is to get it to occur with a high rate or probability in the presence of other stimuli. Let's call the first type of stimuli HP stimuli and the second type LP stimuli. The first meaning of behavioral momentum suggests that to get the response occurring with a high rate or probability to an LP stimulus, we should present that stimulus within a short time after the response has occurred to several of the HP stimuli. For example, a child who does not comply with certain requests or instructions might be given several instructions consecutively that are effective with that child—that is, requests or instructions with which the child is likely to comply—and reinforce his or her compliance. Immediately after the child has complied with these instructions and received reinforcement for doing so, the teacher gives the child an instruction with which he or she is less likely to comply. The typical result is that the child then complies with the previously ineffective instruction.

Increasing the momentum of responding to particular target stimuli by immediately preceding those stimuli with reinforcement of high-probability responding to other stimuli is effective in increasing appropriate behavior during transitions to recess time (Singer, Singer, & Horner, 1987), performance of self-care routines (Mace et al., 1988), appropriate self-administration of medicine (Harchik & Putzier, 1990), task completion (Horner, Day, Sprague, O'Brien, & Healthfield, 1991; Mace & Belfiore, 1990), social interactions (Davis, Brady, Hamilton, McEvoy, & Williams, 1994), and compliance with parental requests in the home (Ducharme & Worling, 1994). The increased responding to the target stimuli may be maintained if the stimuli that reliably evoked the responses are faded out (i.e., removed gradually over trials) and if reinforcement for appropriate responding to the target stimuli continues.

Note that the above "HP-LP" procedure for increasing the momentum of responding to target stimuli differs in several respects from the multiple-schedule procedure for varying behavioral momentum. In fact, the variable the HP-LP procedure deals with is more analogous to inertia (the tendency of an object to remain either at rest or in motion) than to momentum, and it has therefore been suggested that the variable the procedure increases should be given another name (e.g., behavioral motion) to reflect this and to distinguish it from behavioral momentum as studied in multiple schedules (Plaud & Gaither, 1996).

Implications of Behavioral Momentum

Although we have seen elsewhere in this book that responding can be maintained at a high rate with little reinforcement, research on behavioral momentum indicates that responding is more susceptible to disruption when reinforcement rate is low. This implies that in applied settings, one should ensure that desired response receives plenty of reinforcement even when that response has a high probability of occurring. If the desired response is occurring in the presence of a particular stimulus, reinforcement delivered noncontingent on responding in the presence of that stimulus will also help increase the resistance of the behavior to disruption. Enough reinforcement should be contingent on responding to maintain it at a high level, however, because momentum is a product of both resistance of responding to change and response rate.

LANDMARK LEARNING

Successive and simultaneous discriminations are involved when an individual learns to go to a particular location. A child walking toward two similar houses to visit a friend may learn, for example to go toward the house with a large tree instead of a small bush in front. If the first house is visible before the second, this is a successive discrimination; if both houses are visible at the same time, it is a simultaneous discrimination. Stimuli (the tree and bush in the above example) that are correlated with the location in which a particular response (e.g., ringing a doorbell) will be reinforced are called potential landmarks. Stimuli that control responding that is reinforced at a particular location are called effective landmarks. In the above example, both the tree and the bush are potential landmarks but it is not easy to tell which (if either) is an effective landmark. Asking the child is one possibility, but verbal behavior is not necessarily correlated with other behavior. A more direct way to tell is to move (or remove) either the bush or the tree, and note whether the child's going to the friend's house as opposed to the other house is affected. If it is, then the object that was relocated was an effective landmark.

One way in which landmarks have been studied is by burying food in a large flat boxed-in area (called an open field) and using as potential landmarks various objects placed in fixed locations in the field (Cheng, 1988, 1989). An alternative to the open field method is a touch-screen video monitor on which responses (e.g., pecks by a pigeon) at an unmarked location on the monitor are reinforced, and stimuli such as geometric shapes (Spetch, Cheng, & Mondloch, 1992; Spetch & Mondloch, 1993) or objects in a picture of an outdoor scene (Spetch & Wilkie, 1994) serve as potential landmarks. Similar to the method described in the above example, after the animal responds consistently on the reinforced location (i.e., location on which re-sponding is reinforced), effective landmarks are determined by shifting potential landmarks and noting whether there is a corresponding shift in the location of the responses. Typically, landmarks closer to the location at which responding is reinforced tend to be more effective than those that are more distant.

Processes that apply to other discrimination learning appear to apply to the learning of landmarks. For example, if a rat receives training on one landmark (with special procedures employed to ensure that the landmark controls responding on the hidden reinforcer or rein-forced location) and a second landmark is introduced (without removing the first), responding will not come under the control of the second landmark (Biegler & Morris, 1999). This is shown by the fact that if the first landmark is then removed, performance will be the same as if no landmark were present (even though the rat may have investigated the second landmark when it was introduced). In other words, training on the first landmark will have blocked stimulus control by the second landmark (see Chapter 4 and earlier in this chapter).

CONTROL BY SOCIAL BEHAVIORAL STIMULI

Up to now this chapter has dealt with the stimulus control of behavior by inanimate objects and events, as represented in experiments by stimuli such as lights and tones. Stimulus control over an individual's behavior can also be acquired by the behavior of another individual. Three major categories of behavior under the control of social behavioral stimuli in human societies are following instructions, imitation, and cooperation. Following instructions for example, is a behavior that is reinforced in the presence of (or just after) the behavior of another individual giving instructions; imitation is behavior that is reinforced in the presence of someone engag-ing in similar behavior; and, cooperation is behavior that is both controlled by and controls the behavior of another individual by virtue of the fact that both behaviors are reinforced when they occur at the same time.

Both successive and simultaneous discrimination training have been used in studying the control acquired by social behavioral stimuli. In a successive-discrimination procedure, for example, a particular rate of responding by a stimulus individual might be a social behavioral S^D and another rate a social behavioral S^Δ in a multiple VI Ext schedule for another individual. The use of this type of procedure with monkeys (Danson & Creed, 1970) and with pigeons (Millard, 1979) has shown that the rate of responding of another individual can control the responding of an animal in essentially the same way that inanimate discriminative stimuli can control behavior, including the type of generalization data that are obtained when the stimulus individual's rate of responding is varied during extinction.

In a well-known simultaneous-discrimination procedure involving social behavioral stimuli, a "follower" rat placed immediately behind a "leader" rat in a T-maze receives reinforcement for turning in the same (or different) direction from that in which the leader turns at the choice point of the maze (Miller & Dollard, 1941). A refinement of this procedure uses an operant chamber divided into two compartments by a transparent partition, with two response keys and a food cup in each compartment. The leader animal is in one compartment and receives reinforcement for pressing one key on some trials and the other key on other trials; the follower animal is in the other compartment and receives reinforcement for pressing the key corresponding to the one just pressed by the leader (Hake, Donaldson, & Hyten, 1983). As with successive discrimination procedures involving social behavioral stimuli, the results of these experiments indicate that social behavioral discriminative stimuli function in much the same way as do inanimate discriminative stimuli. This conclusion is an important one to be able to make, for it permits us to more confidently extrapolate the results of learning experiments involving inanimate discriminative stimuli to social situations. (See Chapter 17.)

FACILITATING STIMULUS DISCRIMINATION TRAINING

Stimulus discrimination training may be facilitated by procedures that are done during or before discrimination training.

Procedures During Discrimination Training

Procedures done during discrimination training involve the manner in which the S+ and S– (particularly the latter) are introduced.

Time of introduction of the S–. In developing either a successive or simultaneous discrimination one might proceed in one of two ways:

- First reinforce the response to the S+ and then—when responding to the S+ is well conditioned—introduce the S–, either in alternation with the S+ (successive discrimination) or at the same time as the S+ (simultaneous discrimination).
- Introduce the S– early, before the response to the S+ is well conditioned. Naturally, a number of errors—defined as responses to the S– or incorrect stimulus—will occur, and the discrimination will take some time to develop. The discrimination will occur faster and with fewer errors, however, if we introduce the S– early rather than late.

Transfer along a continuum.   If the S+ and S- are close together on a continuum—for example, if they are two shades of gray—the discrimination may be facilitated by first training a discrimination in which the S+ and S– are further apart on the continuum—for example, train a black-white discrimination. This procedure, called transfer along a continuum, can result in a difficult discrimination being learned more rapidly even when we include the time taken to learn the easier discrimination. The procedure is effective for developing respondent as well as operant discriminations (Mackintosh, 1974, pp. 593–594; Pavlov, 1927, p. 121).

Fading.   A successive application of transfer along a continuum involves applying the principle of small increments, mentioned in Chapter 1, by changing either the S+ or the S–, or both, gradually rather than abruptly. In this method, which is called fading, the S– might at first occur either very briefly (e.g., a few seconds) and/or at a much lower intensity than the S+, which might occur at its full intensity at the very beginning. The duration and intensity of the S– would then be gradually increased, in a systematic step-by-step fashion, until they equal the duration and intensity of the S+. Early introduction of the S– combined with fading can result in the formation of an "errorless discrimination," a discrimination in which practically no errors have been emitted during training (Terrace, 1963, 1964).

In the fading procedure described above, we would say that the S– is faded in. Another fading procedure gradually reduces the intensity or duration (or both) of the S+ in the presence of another stimulus that does not presently control the behavior, so that this second stimulus eventually comes to control it. In this procedure we say that the original S+ has been faded out. Both these procedures—fading in and fading out—may be combined, as in the following example.

Some developmentally disabled individuals engage in behavior called echolalia, which consists of repeating words that they hear. For example, when asked "What's your name?" an echolaic child named Peter would simply repeat some part of the question, such as "name." To teach the child to say his name when requested, a teacher conducted trials with Peter in which she at first said "What's your name?" very softly and quickly, and then immediately shouted "PETER!" On the first trial, Peter repeated his name and received a small treat as reinforcement. A stimulus that is presented to evoke a response in a training situation is called a prompt. Over trials, the teacher gradually reduced the intensity and duration of the prompt "Peter" and increased the intensity and duration of the question "What's your name?" Eventually Peter answered with his name, and did not echo words in the question, when the student asked it in a normal voice without saying "Peter" (Martin, England, Kaprowy, Kilgour, & Pilek, 1968; Martin & Pear, 1999, p. 112).

Fading is useful in teaching echolalic individuals (or, for that matter, nonecholalic individuals who readily imitate speech but have little speech-production capability) to answer a wide variety of questions. For example, when taking the child outside, the teacher might say "Where are you going" and then, before the child has a chance to imitate the question, the teacher says "out the door." If the child repeats this prompt reinforcement is given, and on the next occasion the teacher may delete the last word of the prompt by simply saying "out the ____." If the child says the complete phrase to the shortened prompt, it is shortened still further over trials until eventually the child is correctly answering the question without benefit of any prompt (Risley & Wolf, 1964/1966). As an echolalic child learns more and more correct responses to questions, it appears that less and less fading is necessary and the echolia tends to disappear. Procedures that use fading combined with prompts, as in the preceding two examples, are called prompting-fading procedures.

The above examples of fading involved successive discriminations. Fading may also be used to teach simultaneous discriminations. Suppose, for example, we wish to teach a simultaneous circle-ellipse discrimination to a developmentally disabled or very young child. We might begin by presenting a black circle on a bright yellow background on one key in an array of eight keys while the other keys in the array remain dark (Sidman & Stoddard, 1966, 1967). The reason for using an array of eight keys, rather than just two, is to help ensure attending to the choices. The key on which the circle occurs changes randomly from trial to trial. The child must press the key on which the circle appears to obtain reinforcement. This discrimination, which at this stage is simply between a bright key and dark keys, is easily taught. When the child is consistently pressing the key with the circle, the illumination is gradually increased on the other seven keys over trials. (See Figure 8.4, top row.) Then very faint ellipses are introduced on the incorrect keys, and gradually made more distinct over trials (see Figure 8.4, bottom row). If an error occurs—although this will be rare if the procedure is carried out properly—the child is returned to the previous step for one trial. Correct responses are reinforced with treats or tokens which may be exchanged later for a toy or other reinforcing item. Once the child is discriminating between a circle and an ellipse, it is then possible to make the discrimination finer and finer by gradually reducing the difference between the major and minor axes of the seven ellipses (i.e., making the ellipses more and more similar to a circle) over trials, until eventually the target discrimination is taught.

If carried out properly, fading produces a discrimination in which no (or practically no) errors have occurred. It was once thought that there were major theoretical differences between errorless and nonerrorless discriminations (Terrace, 1966b), but it now appears that the discriminative behavior of individuals with few or no errors in learning a discrimination is not fundamentally different from the discriminative behavior of individuals who have made many errors (Rilling, 1977, p. 475). For example, behavioral contrast occurs with errorless as with nonerrorless discriminations. Of course, one cannot demonstrate behavioral contrast with a nonerrorless discrimination by first establishing a baseline for responding to the S+ prior to extinguishing responding to the S–. Thus, in an errorless discrimination, behavioral contrast is demonstrated by first establishing the discrimination, then presenting S+ alone for a number of sessions to establish a baseline of responding to it in isolation from the S–, and then alternating the S+ and S– (Kodera & Rilling, 1976). Inhibitory gradients have also been found around the S– of an errorless discrimination (formed, of course, through extradimensional training). Because so few responses occur during the presentation of S– and other test stimuli on the same continuum, however, it is necessary to reinforce responses in the presence of the test stimuli in order to have sufficient responding during the inhibitory generalization test.

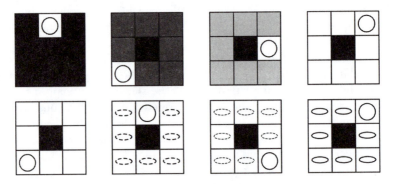

FIGURE 8.4. The top row illustrates early fading steps in teaching a discrimination between a circle and ellipse; the bottom row illustrates later fading steps. (From Sidman & Stoddard, 1967)

When this is done an inhibitory gradient with a minimum at S– is obtained (Rilling, Caplan, Howard, & Brown, 1975).

The only phenomenon of stimulus control that occurs with nonerrorless discriminations but has not been observed with an errorless discrimination is the peak shift. This may be because experimenters, in order to more readily obtain errorless discriminations, have used values of S+ and S– that are too far apart to permit the peak shift to be observed (Rilling, 1977, p. 471).

Intradimensional versus extradimensional shifts.

Transfer along a continuum and fading (above) are particularly effective in facilitating the formation of difficult discriminations. Note that in these two methods, the discrimination to be established is easier than the discriminations leading up to it, in the sense that the S+ and S– in the earlier discriminations are farther apart than the S+ and S– in the discrimination to be established. In addition, the stimuli between the S+ and S– of the earlier discriminations include the S+ and S– in the discrimination to be established. For example, black and white are farther apart on the dark-light continuum than two shades of gray are, and the latter fall somewhere between the former on that continuum. We might say that a black-white discrimination "encompasses" a two-shades-of-gray discrimination.

In what is called an intradimensional shift, a discrimination can also be facilitated by first training a discrimination on the same continuum as the one ultimately to be trained but that does not encompass it. For example, training a discrimination between two light shades of gray will be facilitated by the prior training of a discrimination between two dark shades of gray, in comparison with the prior training of, for example, an auditory discrimination. The shift from an auditory discrimination to a shades-of-gray discrimination would be called an extradimensional shift.

The facilitative effect of an intradimensional shift can be nicely demonstrated in a controlled experiment involving compound stimuli. Consider a simultaneous discrimination in which two wooden stimuli cover two food wells drilled into a board. There are two pairs of stimuli that may cover the food wells: (1) a circle painted with black horizontal stripes and a square with black vertical stripes; and (2) a circle with black vertical stripes and a square with black horizontal stripes. Note that there are two stimulus dimensions in this discrimination: shapes and stripes. Suppose that, in a discrete trials procedure, the two sets of stimuli vary randomly across trials and the positions of the circle and square (and hence of the horizontal and vertical stripes) likewise varies randomly. Suppose, moreover, that food is always under one of the shapes—say, the circle—and never under the other shape—the square. In this case, shape would be the relevant dimension and stripes would be an irrelevant dimension. If, however, food was always under one striped pattern—say, the vertical stripes—and never under the other—the horizontal stripes—then stripes would be the relevant dimension and shape would be an irrelevant dimension. The test animal (a rat for example) will quickly learn to push aside the correct stimulus to get the food on each trial.

Now suppose that we teach a new discrimination using two new sets of stimuli: (1) a triangle with thick black diagonal stripes on it and a cross with thin black diagonal stripes; and (2) a triangle with thin black diagonal stripes and a cross with thick black diagonal stripes. This new discrimination may be either an intradimensional shift or an extradimensional shift. If shape was the relevant dimension in the first discrimination, then teaching the triangle-cross discrimination would be an intradimensional shift and teaching the thick-thin stripe discrimination would be an extradimensional shift. If stripes were the relevant dimension in the first discrimination, the teaching the thick-thin stripe discrimination would be an intradimensional shift and teaching the triangle-cross discrimination would be an extradimensional shift. Experiments along the lines indicated above have demonstrated that intradimensional-shift discriminations are learned more rapidly than extradimensional shifts (Shepp & Eimas, 1964).

Facilitating discriminations and attention.   All of the methods done during discrimination training that facilitate the discrimination may work, at least in part, because they develop attending responses to stimuli and stimulus dimensions that are relevant to the discrimination. For example, developing a prior discrimination between two shades of gray establishes shades of gray as a stimulus dimension toward which to direct attending responses. Evidently, starting with a large difference between stimuli in transfer along a continuum and in fading is effective because it causes the individual to attend to the appropriate stimuli when the discrimination is easily learned (Stoddard & Sidman, 1967).

Prior Stimulus Discrimination Training

Procedures done before stimulus discrimination training to facilitate discrimination training involve prior discrimination training.

Stimulus discrimination reversals.   If the positive and negative discriminative stimuli in a simultaneous discrimination are reversed a number of times, the altered discriminative contingencies will be learned more and more rapidly. For example, stimulus A and stimulus B may occur simultaneously on trial 1, with a response to A being reinforced on trials 2 to n (where n is some arbitrary integer greater than 1) if a response to A was reinforced on trial 1, and a response to B being reinforced on trials 2 to n if a response to B was reinforced on trial 1. In what is referred to as a discrimination reversal problem, if responses to A are reinforced over one or more blocks (or sessions) of n trials, then responses to B are reinforced for one or more blocks of trials, followed by responses to A being reinforced for one of more blocks of trials, and so on. When exposed to a discrimination reversal problem, many species of animals gradually increase their percentage of reinforced responses after shifts in the discriminative reinforcement contingency. In other words, successive discrimination reversals are learned more and more rapidly (Mackintosh, 1974, pp. 608–610).

Learning sets.   Now suppose that instead of reversed discriminations, new discriminations are presented at the beginnings of successive blocks of trials. This type of situation is called a learning-set problem, and individuals that learn the new discriminations more and more rapidly (according to some criterion based on percentage of reinforced responses) are said to have acquired a learning set (Harlow, 1949). Learning sets have been most clearly demonstrated with primates by presenting the animal with two stimulus objects covering food wells on each trial, with food consistently under one of the two (which changes position randomly) over a block of trials. The animal selects one of the objects and receives the food if it is under that object and no reinforcement if it is not. Objects such as small toys and knick-knacks provide a wide variety of new discriminations for the animal to learn over numerous blocks of trials. Over several hundred trials, monkeys eventually respond with almost 100% accuracy on the second trial of each new discrimination.

The process of acquiring learning sets is called "learning-to-learn." Why this process occurs is not known. One likely explanation involves attention: over successive discrimination problems an individual learns to attend to the stimuli that are relevant to the discriminative contingencies presented to it. For example, an animal that is attending to the position of the previous reinforcer will make many errors in a learning-set problem in which position is irrelevant. As the animal begins to attend less to position and more to stimuli such as the color and shape of the objects, it will begin to make correspondingly fewer errors on successive discriminations and will thus exhibit learning to learn.

TRANSITIVE INFERENCE

Consider five arbitrary stimuli which we will call A, B, C, D, and E. Suppose that in a given individual we condition the following simultaneous discriminations:

- A correct and B incorrect;
- B correct and C incorrect;
- C correct and D incorrect;
- D correct and E incorrect.

When the individual has learned these discriminations, we then present two stimuli that the individual has never experienced together: B and D. Both of these stimuli have been the correct stimulus and the incorrect stimulus an equal number of times; that is, responses have been reinforced and gone unreinforced an equal number of times to both stimuli. Nevertheless, individuals consistently tend to respond to B rather than D. This phenomenon is called transitive inference, because it is as though the individual is using the deductive process that is known in logic by this name. In other words, it is as though the individual is inferring that because B is "better than" C and C is "better than" D, therefore B must be "better than" D. Yet the phenomenon occurs in animals, such as chimpanzees (Gillian, 1981) and pigeons (von Fersen, Wynne, Delivs, & Staddon, 1991), that have no facility with the use of logical rules.

To account for this phenomenon, one need not assume that the individual is following logical rules. What appears to be happening is that the strength of the conditioned response to B is greater than the strength of the conditioned response to C, which is greater than the strength of the conditioned response to D; and *response strength is a transitive phenomenon.* The reason the strength of B is greater than that of C is that responding to B was extinguished in the presence of a stronger stimulus (one that did not receive extinction trials), namely A. Because B is weak, many errors are made to C when it is the negative stimulus and B is the positive stimulus. But this makes C weaker than B, so that even more errors are made to D when it is the negative stimulus and C is the positive stimulus. Thus, D is weaker than C which is weaker than B, and so D is weaker than B.[3] An analogous situation would be the case in which an object, say object B, is heavier than object C which is heavier than object D. Since weight is a transitive property, it follows that object B is heavier than object D. No one would argue that these inanimate objects are engaging in logical reasoning to produce this result. Similarly, the transitive-inference behavior described in the above experiment can be explained by basic conditioning principles without assuming logical reasoning on the part of individuals engaging in the behavior. Of course, logical reasoning does exist in humans, but processes in addition to discrimination learning are involved in this type of behavior. We elaborate on these processes in the next and later chapters.

---

3. See Wynne et al. (1992) for a more detailed explanation, and Couvillon and Bitterman (1992) for a mathematical derivation of this result using the model of Bush and Mosteller (1951), or alternatively, the model of Rescorla and Wagner (1972; described in Appendix A), which is based on the Bush-Mosteller model.

SUMMARY AND CONCLUSIONS

To discriminate between two stimuli is to respond differentially in their presence—that is, to respond differently in the presence of one than in the presence of the other. A discrimination (the behavior of discriminating between stimuli) may be either successive or simultaneous, depending on whether the discriminated stimuli are present successively or simultaneously, respectively. Successive discriminations are produced by multiple schedules. In a multiple schedule, two or more schedules alternate, either strictly or randomly, in conjunction with distinctive stimuli. The schedule operating during each stimulus in a multiple schedule controls a rate and pattern of responding that is characteristic of that schedule operating in isolation, or as a single (as opposed to multiple) schedule. A mixed schedule is like a multiple schedule, except that distinctive external stimuli are not coupled with the schedule components. In mixed schedules, however, aspects of the individual's own behavior may acquire stimulus control over responding in a manner similar to that in which the external stimuli coupled with the components of multiple schedules do.

A strong interaction called behavioral contrast develops between the components of multiple schedules. This is a tendency for response rate in one component of a multiple schedule to increase when reinforcement rate in another component decreases (positive behavioral contrast) or, conversely, for response rate in one component of a multiple schedule to decrease when reinforcement rate in another component increases (negative behavioral contrast). Although there are probably several distinct causes of behavioral contrast, its occurrence in a particular component appears due to more changes in the reinforcement rate in the component that follows, the one that precedes, it. This is called the following-schedule effect.

A stimulus generalization gradient is a functional relationship between the strength or probability of a response to a given stimulus and the similarity (along some physical dimension) of that stimulus to a stimulus to which an individual was exposed during either operant or respondent conditioning. There are two types of stimulus generalization gradients. An excitatory stimulus generalization gradient is a functional relationship between the strength or probability of a response to a given stimulus and the similarity (along some physical dimension) of that stimulus to an S^D or other stimulus that controls a relatively high response rate (in operant conditioning) or a CS+ (in respondent conditioning). An inhibitory stimulus generalization gradient is a functional relationship between the strength or probability of a response to a given stimulus and the similarity (along some physical dimension) of that stimulus to an S^Δ or other stimulus that controls a relatively low response rate (in operant conditioning) or a CS– (in respondent conditioning). Tests in which stimuli are varied (generalization tests) after exposure of an individual to a multiple schedule can reveal both excitatory and inhibitory stimulus generalization gradients. A multiple schedule component whose stimulus controls a relatively high response rate will produce an excitatory stimulus generalization gradient that peaks (i.e., has its high point) at that stimulus and tapers off as stimuli become increasing dissimilar to that stimulus. A multiple schedule component whose stimulus controls a relatively low response rate will produce an inhibitory stimulus generalization gradient that has its low point (an inverted peak) at that stimulus and tapers off as stimuli become increasing dissimilar to that stimulus. Excitatory and inhibitory stimulus generalization gradients are most clearly differentiated when the stimulus controlling the high response rate and the stimulus controlling the low response rate are on different stimulus dimensions. If they are on the same stimulus dimension, there will be an interaction between the two gradients—as manifested in the peak shift, in which the peak of the excitatory gradient and the inverted peak of the inhibitory gradient are displaced away from each other.

Behavioral momentum, or the momentum of a given response in the presence of a given stimulus, is one way of describing the control that a given stimulus has over a given response. Behavioral momentum (roughly analogous to momentum in physics) is the product of response rate (roughly analogous to velocity in physics) and resistance to change (roughly analogous to mass in physics). Resistance to change is measured as the relative amount of change in response rate that occurs when the contingencies of reinforcement change or responding is disrupted in some other way, whereas behavioral momentum is the absolute amount of change in response rate. The rate of a given response in the presence of a given stimulus is a function of the reinforcement rate for that response in the presence of that stimulus. Resistance to change of a given response in the presence of a given stimulus is a function of the amount of reinforcement that has occurred in the presence of that stimulus, regardless of whether the reinforcement was contingent on the response. These functional relationships allow one to predict the amount of behavioral momentum in a given situation, just as physical momentum can be predicted from velocity and mass.

The use of the term behavioral momentum has not been totally consistent in the literature. In addition to the meaning of the term defined above, another meaning has emerged. In this new meaning, behavioral momentum is the tendency of a given response or response class to continue occurring once it has started occurring (for whatever reason). Whether this second meaning follows from the first is not entirely clear. It might, however, do so in combination with the fact that a response may itself be an S^D for subsequent responses.

In a simultaneous discrimination, two stimuli are present at the same time, and responding on one (the S+) is reinforced while responding on the other (the S–) is not. Responses to the S+ are designated as correct whereas responses to the S– are designated as incorrect. Although response rate on the S+ in simultaneous discriminations shows the characteristic effects found in single and multiple schedules, accuracy (the percentage of correct responses) tends to be fairly constant regardless of the schedule of reinforcement for correct responses.

Discrimination training can be enhanced by procedures that occur before or during it. For example, an individual will learn discriminations increasingly more rapidly as a function of number of prior discriminations learned. This process is called learning-to-learn. With both successive and simultaneous discriminations, a process of fading minimizes errors and facilitates rapid development of the discrimination. Fading consists of gradually changing (either in appearance or duration) or gradually replacing stimuli that control responding or nonresponding while continuing to reinforce or extinguish, respectively, responding in the presence of the altered or new stimulus.

Conditional Discriminations

*I*n a standard discrimination (of either the successive or simultaneous type), as we saw in the previous chapter, responses to one stimulus are reinforced and responses to another are not. In a conditional discrimination the S+ varies, depending on the presence or absence of another stimulus (Carter & Werner, 1978). For example, in a conditional red-green discrimination, green may be the S+ if a particular tone is sounded and red the S+ if a different tone is sounded.

We have discussed standard discriminations at length because they are relatively simple and help us understand more complex discriminations. There are probably very few, if any, standard discriminations in natural settings however. Clearly, many familiar discriminations are conditional discriminations. To take a simple example, suppose that a child is playing with a red ball and a green ball. An adult who says to the child, "Please hand me the green ball," will probably praise the child if he gives the adult the green ball but not if he gives the adult the red ball. The converse will be the case if the adult says "Please hand me the red ball." This is a conditional discrimination in that the discriminative stimulus (red or green ball) that is correct is conditional on another stimulus (the instruction that is given to the child).

Note that we have encountered conditional discriminations earlier in this book, although we used a different term for them. We called the stimuli involved in conditional discriminations compound stimuli, and we used the term configural stimulus to refer to that property of a compound stimulus that gains control over behavior when a compound stimulus discrimination develops.

Although conditional discriminations may be either successive or simultaneous, the following discussion focuses on simultaneous conditional discriminations except where otherwise indicated.

BASIC TYPES OF CONDITIONAL DISCRIMINATIONS

Another name for conditional discrimination is matching to sample. We distinguish three main types of conditional discriminations or matching-to-sample procedures: identity matching, oddity matching, and symbolic matching. Each will be discussed in turn.

Identity Matching

In identity matching the S+ is conditional on the presentation of a stimulus that is identical to it. We distinguish two types of identity matching: explicit and implicit.

Explicit identity matching. An example of explicit identity matching is illustrated in Figure 9.1. The top row of panels illustrates a correct sequence of responses in a explicit identity matching procedure. In the first panel in the top row the center key of a three-key array has projected on it a stimulus called the sample. When the pigeon pecks the sample (shown in the first panel), stimuli called the comparison stimuli are projected onto the two side keys. One of the two comparison stimuli is identical to the sample. If the pigeon pecks that comparison stimulus (as shown in the second panel), and thus "matches-to-sample," the keys are darkened and the feeder operates for three seconds (shown in the third panel). The reinforcement cycle is followed by a 15-second intertrial interval in which all three key lights are dark (shown in the fourth panel) and key pecks have no scheduled effect. After the intertrial interval the next trial begins (shown in the fifth panel). Note that at the beginning of each trial the pigeon must peck the sample before the comparison stimuli appear. The reason for this requirement is to help ensure that the pigeon attends to the sample. Indeed, accuracy generally is poorer if this attending response is not required (Eckerman, Lanson, & Cumming, 1968; Zentall, Hogan, & Holder, 1974). Note also that the observing response is maintained by the presentation of the correct comparison stimulus, not by primary reinforcement. The correct comparison stimulus is a conditioned reinforcer because a response to it produces primary reinforcement. (Sequences of stimuli and responses such as this, in which each response in the sequence except the last is maintained by conditioned reinforcer which is also the S^D for the next response, are dealt with in detail in Chapter 11.)

The bottom row of panels in the figure illustrates an incorrect sequence of responses. Note that a peck on the incorrect comparison stimulus produces a 3-second timeout, called a blackout, during which the chamber is totally dark and reinforcement is not available. The purpose of this timeout or blackout is to prevent the adventitious reinforcement of incorrect responses (which could happen if a correct response was followed closely in time by a correct response) and to punish incorrect responses.

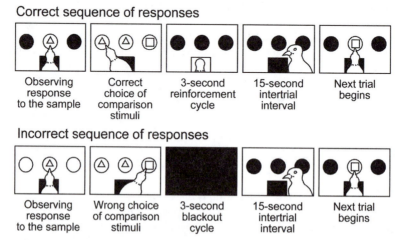

Figure 9.1. Schematic representation of matching-to-sample. The top row of panels shows what happens when the pigeon responds to the correct comparison stimulus; the bottom row illustrates the consequence of an error. (From Carter & Werner, 1978)

Implicit identity matching.   As with explicit identity matching, in implicit identity match-ing a response to a particular stimulus is reinforced only if an identical stimulus is present. In explicit identity matching, however, the individual is required to look at a specific sample stimulus prior to making a matching response. In implicit identity matching there is no explicit sample stimulus. Implicitly, the individual must look at each stimulus at least once in order to make a correct matching response, and whichever is looked at first is functionally the sample stimulus. Typically, however, it would not be known which one this was. An example of implicit identity matching is a procedure in which a lever is positioned below two lights, each of which can be illuminated red or green. Lever pressing is reinforced according to some schedule when both lights are red or both lights are green, but not when one is red and the other green. Note that the conditional discrimination in this example is successive rather than simulta-neous; implicit identity matching is not, however, restricted to successive discriminations. An example of implicit identity matching using a simultaneous conditional discrimination would be one in which there were two pairs of lights with a lever below each pair. On each trial the two lights are the same color for one pair (at random, of course) while being different colors for the other pair, and reinforcement is contingent on responses on the lever below the iden-tical pair.

Generalized identity matching.   A question of considerable interest regarding identity matching is whether these procedures teach the concept "same/different." This cannot be answered simply by noting whether the individual performs correctly with stimuli it has al-ready been trained on in a matching task. The clearest demonstration of generalized identity matching is that the individual responds correctly on the first trial when presented with new matching stimuli. For example, if a pigeon has learned to match red to red and green to green, will it then match yellow to yellow when first given this matching problem (i.e., before it has been reinforced for doing so)? If it consistently performs new matches such as this correctly it would be said to be exhibiting generalized identity matching, which is defined as matching new items that have not been learned as a result of having received identity matching training.

As you can verify by testing your own understanding of the concept "same/different," generalized identity matching is a common, everyday occurrence in human adults. It has also been demonstrated experimentally with human children (Levin & Mauer, 1969; Scott, 1964; Sherman, Saunder, & Brightman, 1970). In addition, there is evidence that it occurs with dolphins when auditory sample and comparison stimuli are used (Herman & Gordon, 1974), and with nonhuman primates such as chimpanzees (Nissen, Blum, & Blum, 1948; Oden, Thompson, & Premack, 1990; Robinson, 1955, 1960; Thompson, Oden, & Boysen, 1997), orangutans (King, 1973), rhesus monkeys (Mishkin, Prockop, & Rosvold, 1962; Sands, Lincoln, & Wright, 1982), and some Japanese monkeys (Fujita, 1983) when visual stimuli are used.

Although there is evidence of generalized identity matching in a parrot (Pepperberg, 1987a, 1988) as we shall see later, clear demonstrations of it in the more commonly studied bird, the pigeon, have been difficult to obtain (Carter & Werner, 1978). Nevertheless, pigeons do appear to show transfer from one color-matching task to another (Zentall, Hogan, & Edwards, 1984). Specifically, a pigeon that has learned to match red to red and green to green will learn more readily to match yellow to yellow and blue to blue than it will to match red to green and green to red. In addition, it appears that pigeons will learn the concepts "same" and "differ-ent" if given training on complex displays in which "same" is represented by displays contain-ing the same element repeated a number of times or a repetitious pattern and "different" is represented by displays containing a region in which a different element is present or in which the pattern is broken (Cook, Katz, & Cavoto, 1997; Wasserman, Hugart, & Kirkpatrick-Steger, 1995; Young, Wasserman, & Garner, 1997). The fact that such highly complex displays are necessary to teach generalized identity (or oddity; see below) matching to pigeons suggests a limitation in the animal's capacity to learn the concepts of "same" and "different." It seems that pigeons have great difficulty learning identity or oddity matching when only two comparison stimuli are presented at the same time (Zentall, Hogan, Edwards, & Hearst, 1980).

Relational concepts and configural stimuli. An individual who exhibits generalized identity matching has learned a relation or a relational concept. What this means is that the individual is not responding to any specific stimulus, but rather to a relation between stimuli. Procedures analogous to identity matching can be used to teach and test for any relational concept. For example, to teach the relational concept "larger than," the sample stimulus might be a geometrical figure such as a circle, the incorrect comparison stimulus might be a smaller figure of the same shape, and the correct comparison stimulus a larger figure of the same shape. To ensure that the individual is learning the concept, one would vary the size and shape of the comparison stimuli over trials. If eventually the individual consistently responds correctly on the first trial when the comparison and sample stimuli have new shapes and sizes, we would conclude that the individual has learned the relational concept "larger than."

In a conditional discrimination, the comparison stimulus and the correct sample stimulus are the elements of a compound stimulus. When a conditional discrimination is learned, these elements form a configural stimulus, as mentioned in Chapter 4 (p. 80) when we discussed compound stimuli. Thus, when a relational concept is learned, the relation is a configural stimulus. Relations such as "same as," "larger than," "above," and many others, quickly become configural stimuli for all normal humans. The full extent or limits to which they can become configural stimuli for other species has yet to be determined.

Oddity Matching

In oddity matching the S+ is conditional on the comparison stimulus being different from the sample stimulus, although both stimuli are usually on the same stimulus dimension (e.g., both colors, both geometrical shapes). As with identity matching, there are two general types of oddity matching: explicit and implicit.

Explicit oddity matching. Explicit oddity matching differs from explicit identity matching in that reinforcement is contingent on choosing the comparison stimulus that is different from the sample. (Explicit oddity matching is sometimes called mismatching to sample.) Figure 9.1 would illustrate an explicit-oddity-matching procedure if the second panels of the top and bottom rows were interchanged.

Implicit oddity matching. In implicit oddity matching, as with implicit identity matching, there is no explicit sample stimulus. An example would be one in which two identical and one nonidentical objects are presented at the same time, and reinforcement is contingent on responding to the "odd" or nonidentical object Note that there is no explicit sample stimulus because either of the two identical objects might be functioning as either a sample or comparison stimulus, depending solely on the looking behavior of the individual.

Generalized oddity matching. Generalized oddity matching is completely analogous to generalized identity matching, and in fact is simply an alternative way of demonstrating the concept "same/different." This is because when we have taught generalized identity matching, we have conditioned the configural stimulus "same" as the S+ and the configural stimulus "different" as the S–. Teaching generalized oddity matching is simply the reverse of this; it conditions the configural stimulus "same" as the S– and the configural stimulus "different" as the S+. In both cases, it is the same discrimination that has been conditioned. This is true for other relational concepts; for example, when we have established the concept "larger than" we have also established the concept "smaller than"—regardless of which of these configural stimuli is the S+ and which is the S–.

Generalized oddity matching has thus far been demonstrated mainly with primates (e.g., Levine & Harlow, 1959; Shaffer, 1967; Thomas & Boyd, 1973; Thomas & Kerr, 1976). Pigeons, however, apparently show transfer from one oddity matching task to another in the same manner that they show transfer from one identity matching task to another (Zentall et al., 1984). In addition, as already indicated, they can learn complex displays containing a region in which another element is substituted for an element repeated elsewhere throughout the display or there is a break in the pattern in the display.

Symbolic Matching

Symbolic matching (sometimes also referred to as arbitrary matching) is a variation of explicit identity or oddity matching in which the sample stimuli and the comparison stimuli are not related in any physical way, and are usually on different stimulus dimensions. For example, a red key light might be the sample stimulus for which a triangle is the correct comparison stimulus, and a green key light the sample stimulus for which a square is the correct comparison stimulus. To an animal trained in this way, red in a sense means "triangle" and green means "square," which is why the procedure is called symbolic matching.

Symbolic matching and logic.   For the purpose of exposition, let A_1 and A_2 be two sample stimuli, and B_1 and B_2 be two comparison stimuli. Let $A_1(B_1,B_2)$, $A_2(B_1,B_2)$ indicate that B_1 is the correct comparison stimulus when A_1 is the sample and B_2 is the correct comparison stimulus when A_2 is the sample. In other words, samples are designated outside the parentheses, comparisons within, and the correct comparison stimulus is the one whose number matches that of the sample. Furthermore, let the above matching-to-sample task be designated A-B training.

Suppose now that a child is taught the conditional relation A-B, where A_1 and A_2 are, for example, printed words, and B_1 and B_2 are pictures corresponding to those words. If we then test for the relation B-A, we find that the child makes the appropriate choices; in other words, if we present $B_1(A_1,A_2)$ and $B_2(A_1,A_2)$, the child will choose A_1 in the first case and A_2 in the second. Thus, by having learned A-B, the child has also learned B-A.

Suppose after teaching A-B we teach B-C, where C represents, for example, arbitrary Greek letters. In other words, we teach $A_1(B_1,B_2)$ and $A_2(B_1,B_2)$, then we teach $B_1(C_1,C_2)$ and $B_2(C_1,C_2)$, and finally we test $A_1(C_1,C_2)$ and $A_2(C_1,C_2)$. It turns out that on the test the child chooses C_1 when A_1 is the sample and C_2 when A_2 is the sample. Thus by teaching A-B and B-C, we have also indirectly taught A-C.

The rule "If A-B, then B-A" is known in logic as symmetry; the rule "If A-B and B-C, then A-C" is known in logic as transitivity. In some studies symmetry and transitivity have been tested for simultaneously by first teaching A-B and C-B, and then testing for A-C. Both symmetry and transitivity have been found in normal children, developmentally delayed but verbal teenagers, and normal adults (Dixon, 1978; Dixon & Spradlin, 1976; Sidman, 1971; Sidman & Cresson, 1973; Sidman, Cresson, & Wilson-Morrison, 1974; Sidman & Tailby, 1982; Sidman et al., 1982; Spradlin, Gotter, & Baxley, 1973; Spradlin & Dixon, 1976; Stromer & Osborne, 1982). In addition, with humans, symmetry and transitivity can extend matching relations over a surprisingly broad range. For example, if normal preschool children are taught the matching relations A-C, A-D, and B-C, using completely arbitrary visual stimuli, subsequent testing will show that they will have indirectly acquired the matching relations A-B, B-A, C-A, C-B, C-D, D-A, D-B, and D-C (Wetherby, Karlan, & Spradlin, 1983).

Most attempts to find symmetry and transitivity in nonverbal (e.g., language-disabled) humans (e.g., Devany, Hayes, & Nelson, 1986) and nonhuman animal species (e.g., Hogan & Zentall, 1977; Holmes, 1979; Rodewall, 1974; Sidman et al., 1982) have thus far been unsuccessful. Whether this is due to experimental factors or represents a true species difference between humans and other animals is not clear. Even attempts to demonstrate symmetry in chimpanzees have failed (Dugdale & Lowe, 2000), despite the fact that these chimpanzees had extensive experience with conditional discriminations and language training (see later in this chapter).

There is one report, however, demonstrating symmetry and transitivity in a 7-year-old female sea lion (*Zalophus californianus*) using 2-dimensional and 3-dimensional objects as stimuli (Schusterman & Kastak, 1993). This was accomplished by first reinforcing the animal on many different transitivity and symmetry problems, with the apparatus shown in Figure 9.2, before testing the animal on completely new transitivity and symmetry problems. Thus, the training of many exemplars may be necessary to establish this behavior. Typically humans receive this training when they learn verbal behavior in their culture, whereas other animals do not receive such training. However, as mentioned above, even language-trained chimpanzees do not show symmetry. In addition, the study with the sea lion has been criticized on methodological grounds (Horne & Lowe, 1996, 1997; Lowe & Horne, 1996).

Symbolic matching and equivalence relations.   A relation r is called an equivalence relation if, for any given set of three stimuli denoted by A, B, and C, the following conditions are true:

- A r A; this is called reflexivity.
- If A r B then B r A; this, as seen above, is called symmetry.
- If A r B and B r C, then A r C; this, as seen above, is called transitivity.

The stimuli that form an equivalence relation are said to be members of an equivalence class. Generalized identity matching, which may be said to indicate reflexivity (A r A), has been demonstrated strongly in only a few nonhuman species. We have seen in the previous section, however, that both symmetry (if A r B then B r A) and transitivity (if A r B and B r C, then A r C) have been demonstrated unequivocally thus far only in verbal humans. Thus, equivalence relations may be restricted to individuals possessing verbal behavior. Rather than verbal behavior being required for the formation of equivalence classes, however, it may be that the learning of verbal behavior that occurs in humans involves the learning of many equivalence classes. That is, it is not clear whether verbal humans are particularly adept at learning equivalence classes because they are verbal or whether humans are verbal because they are adept at learning equivalence classes. If the former is the case, it is not clear exactly what it is about being verbal which enables people to learn equivalence classes. If the latter is the case, it is not what it is about humans that makes them so unique in their ability to learn equivalence classes. (For theoretical discussion of these issues, see Clayton & Hayes, 1999; Commentary, 1997; Horne & Lowe, 1996; Sidman, 1990, 1994, 1997, 2000.)

Regardless of whether human verbal ability causes us to be more proficient at learning equivalence relations or our ability to learn equivalence relations is what makes us verbal, the ability to form equivalence relations seems to be critically related to our use of language. A great deal of language involves reading different symbols as equivalent to each other in the

FIGURE 9.2. Matching-to-sample apparatus for sea lion. Trainers behind the screen change the stimuli and provide a fish through the correct window when the animal makes a correct match. (From Schusterman & Kastak, 1993)

sense of being interchangeable in various situations—for example, a picture of a table, the spoken word "table," and the printed word "table" will each act as an S^D for some responses for which any of the others is an S^D. Language also involves treating symbols as equivalent in some respects to what they denote, which can cause problems for individuals and their social groups. (We shall say more about the relationship between language and conditional discriminations later in this chapter.)

An important property of equivalence classes is what is called transfer of function (or transformation of function). This refers to the fact that any function established for one member of an equivalence class automatically transfers to the other members of that class. For example, if one member is established as a conditioned stimulus (Dougher et al., 1994; Roche & Barnes, 1997) or as a discriminative stimulus (Lazar, 1977; Lazar & Lotlarchyk, 1986) for a particular response, or as a conditioned reinforcer or punisher (Hayes et al., 1991; Greenway et al., 1992), then other members of the equivalence class will take on that same function in the absence of specific training. The sea lion mentioned above has shown transfer of function. When one member of an equivalence class it acquired became a discriminative stimulus in a simple discrimination, the other members of that equivalence class immediately could be substituted for that stimulus in that discrimination (Schusterman & Kastak, 1998).

Training structures for establishing equivalence classes. In the previous section we pointed out that after teaching first $A_1(B_1,B_2)$ and $A_2(B_1,B_2)$ and then $B_1(C_1,C_2)$ and $B_2(C_1,C_2)$, we can then test for transitivity by presenting $A_1(C_1,C_2)$ and $A_2(C_1,C_2)$. We can test for symmetry by presenting $B_1(A_1,A_2)$ and $B_2(A_1,A_2)$, or by presenting $C_1(B_1,B_2)$ and $C_2(B_1,B_2)$. We can save a step by testing for symmetry and transitivity together by presenting $C_1(A_1,A_2)$ and $C_2(A_1,A_2)$. In effect this also tests for equivalence, because an individual who shows both transitivity and symmetry will almost surely show reflexivity. An individual who demonstrates equivalence on the above will have learned two equivalence classes consisting of three members each:

- A_1, B_1, C_1
- A_2, B_2, C_2

By increasing the number of sample and comparison stimuli we can increase the number of equivalence classes taught, and by increasing the number of matching tasks we can increase the number of members in each equivalence class. However, the basic principle remains the same as for the two-classes-three-members-each case. For simplicity, therefore, we confine our discussion to this case.

The training arrangement described above is called a linear training structure. Two other major procedures for establishing equivalence classes are the sample-as-node training structure and the comparison-as-node training structures (Fields & Verhave, 1987). We consider each in turn.

In the sample-as-node training structure (also known as the one-to-many training structure), we train the following: $A_1(B_1,B_2)$ and $A_2(B_1,B_2)$, then $A_1(C_1,C_2)$ and $A_2(C_1,C_2)$. We can test for symmetry by presenting $B_1(A_1,A_2)$ and $B_2(A_1,A_2)$, or by presenting $C_1(A_1,A_2)$ and $C_2(A_1,A_2)$. We can test for symmetry and transitivity together (and hence equivalence, as mentioned above) for the sample-as-node training structure by presenting $B_1(C_1,C_2)$ and $B_2(C_1,C_2)$ or by presenting $C_1(B_1,B_2)$ and $C_2(B_1,B_2)$.

In the comparison-as-node training structure (also known as the many-to-one training structure), we train the following: $A_1(B_1,B_2)$ and $A_2(B_1,B_2)$, then $C_1(B_1,B_2)$ and $C_2(B_1,B_2)$. We can test for symmetry by presenting $B_1(A_1,A_2)$ and $B_2(A_1,A_2)$, or by presenting $B_1(C_1,C_2)$ and $B_2(C_1,C_2)$. We can test for symmetry and transitivity together (and hence equivalence) by presenting $A_1(C_1,C_2)$ and $A_2(C_1,C_2)$ or by presenting $C_1(A_1,A_2)$ and $C_2(A_1,A_2)$.

One might think that which structure is used would not matter, but in fact the comparison-as-node structure often appears to be superior to the other two major structures. The reason for this is not completely clear. A plausible factor, however, is the generalization between the discriminations that are trained and those that are tested for in each of the training structures (K. J. Saunders & Spradlin, 1993; R. R. Saunders & Green, 1999; Sidman, 1994; Spradlin & Saunders, 1986). We may think of a matching-to-sample task as consisting of a combination of successive and simultaneous discriminations (see Chapter 8). For example, the symbolic matching task $A_1(B_1,B_2)$ and $A_2(B_1,B_2)$ conditions a successive discrimination between A_1 and A_2 and simultaneous discriminations between A_1 and B_1, A_1 and B_2, A_2 and B_1, A_2 and B_2, and B_1 and B_2. With this in mind, note that the linear training structure described above conditions the following successive and simultaneous discriminations:

Successive: A_1A_2; B_1B_2
Simultaneous: A_1B_1; A_1B_2; A_2B_1; A_2B_2; B_1B_2; B_1C_1; B_1C_2; B_2C_1; B_2C_2; C_1C_2

The test for symmetry following training with the linear structure involves the following successive and simultaneous discriminations:

Successive: B_1B_2; C_1C_2
Simultaneous: A_1B_1; A_2 B_1; A_1B_2; A_2B_2; A_1A_2; B_1C_1; B_2C_1; B_1C_2; B_2C_2; B_1B_2

The test for symmetry and transitivity together (hence, the test for equivalence) involves the following successive and simultaneous discriminations:

Successive: C_1C_2
Simultaneous: A_1C_1; A_2C_1; A_1C_2; A_2C_2; A_1A_2

Note that all of the discriminations in the above test for symmetry are present in the linear training structure; however, four of the discriminations (A_1C_1; A_2C_1; A_1C_2; A_2C_2) in the test for equivalence are absent in the linear training structure. This would hinder performance on the test for equivalence following conditioning on the linear training structure.

Conducting the above same analysis with the sample-as-node training structure will reveal that it also has the problem that not all discriminations in the tests are present in the original conditioning. The problem does not exist with the comparison-as-node training structure; instead, with that structure, all discriminations in the tests are present in the training structure (Saunders & Green, 1999).

Generality of symbolic matching across species. Interestingly, symbolic matching is not limited to vertebrates. Honeybees, for example, readily learn to land on a blue rather than a green target when both targets have a peppermint scent but to land on the green target when both targets have a geraniol scent, if the bees have consistently experienced a sucrose solution on the blue target in the former case and on the green target in the latter case (Couvillon & Bitterman, 1988). There is no evidence, however, that they can engage in any of the logical relations described above.

DISCRIMINATION LEVELS

As one might expect, conditional discriminations are more difficult to learn than simple discriminations. In fact, there is a hierarchy of discrimination levels in that ability to readily learn discriminations at one level is dependent on the ability to learn lower-level discriminations. The following six levels of discrimination learning have been identified with humans (Casey & Kerr, 1977; Kerr & Meyerson, 1977; Kerr, Meyerson, & Flora, 1977; Martin, Yu, Quinn, & Patterson, 1983; Wacker Kerr, & Carroll, 1983; Wacker, Steil, & Greenbaum, 1983):

Level 1. Simple imitation. Example: the individual consistently imitates the simple action of putting an object (e.g., a piece of foam) into a container (e.g., a yellow can).

Level 2. Simple positional discrimination. Example: the individual consistently places an object into one of two containers of different shapes and colors (e.g., a yellow can and a red box). The correct container (e.g., the yellow can) and its position remain constant over trials.

Level 3. Simple visual discrimination. Example: same as Level 2 except that the positions of the containers are randomly alternated over trials.

Level 4. Identity matching. Example: on some trials the individual is given an object (e.g., a yellow cylinder) that is similar to one of the containers (the yellow can) and one other, randomly alternating, trials the individual is given an object (e.g., a red cube) that is similar to the other container (e.g., the red box). The positions of the containers alternate randomly over trials. The correct response is placing the object in the container that it resembles.

Level 5. Auditory-positional symbolic discrimination. Example: the individual consistently puts an object into one of two containers (e.g., either a yellow can or a red box) when requested to do so. The positions of the two containers remain fixed, but the instructions specifying the correct container (e.g., "Put the piece of foam into the yellow can" and "Put the piece of foam into the red box") alternate randomly.

Level 6. Auditory-visual symbolic discrimination. Example: same as Level 5 except that the positions of the two containers alternate randomly.

Normal children generally reach Level 6 with no special systematic training by the time they are about 27 months of age (Casey & Kerr, 1977). Developmentally delayed individuals, however, take longer and in some cases may never reach Level 6. The hierarchy is useful in predicting, with a high degree of accuracy, the discrimination types (and hence classroom, prevocational, and vocational tasks involving those discrimination types) that developmentally delayed students will be able to learn without much difficulty (Martin et al., 1983; Stubbings & Martin, 1995; Tharinger, Schallert, & Kerr, 1977; Wacker et al., 1983; Wacker, Steil, et al., 1983; and Witt & Wacker, 1981). In fact, the examples given above form the basis of a procedure called the Assessment of Basic Learning Abilities (ABLA) that is used with developmentally delayed individuals to determine at what level a teacher should begin teaching discriminations to a particular student. Taking about 30 minutes to administer, the ABLA involves systematically attempting to teach a discrimination at each level sequentially—using standard discrimination-training procedures described in this and the previous chapter—until the individual fails to learn a discrimination to a set criterion with a set number of trials. The student's level is the highest one he or she can reach to a set criterion based on number of consecutive correct trials within a set number of trials.

A student at a particular level can readily learn other discriminations at that or lower levels, but will have considerable difficulty learning higher-level discriminations. For example, an individual at Level 6 will probably be able to readily learn to place a block on the printed letter "A" or "B" when requested to do so, when the two letters occur together and alternate positions randomly from trial to trial; whereas, a student at a lower level would have considerable difficulty learning this discrimination even with the use of optimal training procedures (Stubbings & Martin, 1998).

CONTROL BY S+ OR S– IN CONDITIONAL DISCRIMINATIONS

From simple observation of accurate performance of a conditional discrimination it is impossible to tell whether the behavior is under the control of the correct comparison (the S+), the incorrect comparison (the S–), or both. Suppose, however, that ambiguous stimuli are substituted for the S+ on some trials and for the S– on other trials, where an ambiguous stimulus is one that is neither an S+ nor an S– (it may, for example, be a completely new stimulus or one that the individual has never experienced in the context presently being considered). If the individual responds to the S+ when an ambiguous stimulus is substituted for the S–, this indicates that the behavior is under the control of the S+; if the individual responds to the ambiguous stimulus when it is substituted for the S+, this indicates that the behavior is under the control of the S–. Using this type of analysis, researchers have found simultaneous control by both the S+ and the S– with children's identity matching (Dixon & Dixon, 1978), and with the symbolic matching of pigeons (Meltzer, 1983) and of developmentally delayed adolescents (Stromer & Osborne, 1982). With pigeons the S– in conditional discriminations seems to exert much stronger control than does the S+ relative to ambiguous stimuli, although the reason for this is not known.

In addition to control by S+ and S– with developmentally delayed adolescents performing conditional discriminations, similarly strong control by the positive and negative stimuli in tests for symmetry and transitivity has been found with these individuals (Stromer & Osborne, 1982). This indicates the view that these individuals form solid equivalence relations.

SCHEDULE EFFECTS IN MATCHING-TO-SAMPLE

There are several ways in which schedules of reinforcement are involved in matching-to-sample procedures. These can be considered under the following main categories:

- *Sample-stimuli schedules*: The comparison stimuli are contingent on a response to the sample stimulus according to some schedule of reinforcement;
- *Trialwise reinforcement schedules*: Termination of the trial is contingent on a response to the correct comparison stimulus according to some schedule of reinforcement;
- *Free-operant reinforcement schedules*: Reinforcement is contingent on correct responses according to some schedule of reinforcement when more than one response to the correct comparison stimulus can be reinforced during the same trial.

With regard to sample-stimuli schedules, matching-to-sample accuracy is much greater when responses to the sample key are required to produce the comparison stimuli than when such responses are not required (Eckerman et al., 1968). Increasing the FR schedule on the sample key further increases matching accuracy (Sacks, Kamil, & Mack, 1972; Wilkie & Spetch, 1978). The fact that requiring responses on the sample key increases matching accuracy is likely because this procedure ensures that the animal attends to (i.e., makes attending responses to) the sample. An animal cannot respond to a stimulus without first attending to it.

With regard to trialwise schedules in matching-to-sample, contradictory results have been obtained in the two studies investigating this type of schedule: One study found that increasing the trialwise FR value increases the matching accuracy (Ferster, 1960), while the other found the opposite effect (Nevin, Cumming, & Berryman, 1963). The reason for these differences is not known.

With regard to free-operant schedules in matching-to-sample, there is evidence that increasing the value of an FR schedule lowers matching accuracy (Lydersen, Perkins, & Chairez, 1977). Matching accuracy is increased, however, if different schedules are used following different sample stimuli (Cohen, Brady, & Lowry, 1981; Cohen, Looney, Brady, & Avcella, 1976; Lydersen & Perkins, 1974; Paul, 1983; Urcuioli & Honig, 1980). For example, in a green-orange matching task, a DRL 3-second schedule might be in effect in the presence of the green sample and an FR 16 schedule might be in effect in the presence of the orange sample. Matching accuracy will be better than if either the DRL 3-second schedule or the FR 16 schedule had been in effect in the presence of both sample stimuli. Apparently the reason for this is that the response-produced stimulation from the behavior produced by each schedule acts as a strong source of stimulus control for the subsequent response to the comparison stimuli. This explanation is particularly convincing in view of the evidence, as discussed earlier (e.g., p. 167), that behavior itself can be a stimulus controlling subsequent behavior.

CONDITIONAL DISCRIMINATIONS AND LANGUAGE

As indicated elsewhere in this chapter, conditional discriminations are extremely important in human languages. Any utterance (i.e., any occurrence or instance of language), whether spoken, written, or made in some other way, is both a response and a stimulus. It is a response for the person who generates it, and it is a stimulus for anyone who hears, sees, or otherwise comes into contact with it. As a response, an utterance is under the control of a specific stimulus. We are not, however, continuously emitting every verbal response that has been conditioned to every stimulus that is present. Instead, we emit a specific verbal response to a specific stimulus only when some other stimulus, correlated with reinforcement for a specific verbal response to that stimulus, is present. Thus, utterances are under conditional stimulus control.

As a stimulus, any utterance is a comparison stimulus in a conditional discrimination. That is, any utterance is correlated with reinforcement for emitting some specific verbal or nonverbal response, among many possible responses, to a specific stimulus that is present.

Keeping with the above distinction between an utterance as a response and as a stimulus, it is useful to distinguish between productive or (generative) and receptive language. The former refers to language as a particular class of responses emitted by an individual, while the latter refers to language as a particular class of stimuli controlling an individual's behavior. In Chapter 17 we discuss language in humans. In this section we focus on efforts to teach human-type (or artificial) languages to nonhuman animals. The involvement of conditional discrimination training in the examples presented below is particularly noteworthy from the perspective of this chapter.

Features of Language: Communication and Syntax

An important property of language—some might even consider it a defining property—is that it can be used in communication to transfer information from one individual to another. Another important property of all languages is that their units (e.g., words) combine according to specific rules. Consider, for example, the following:

- Mary hit the ball.
- The ball hit Mary.
- Hit Mary the ball.
- Ball Mary the hit.

Note that while each of the above contains the same words, we respond very differently to them. The first two correspond to different events or situations, whereas the third and fourth are unintelligible. The rules by which the symbols of a language combine are called the syntax of that language. Syntax is similar to grammar, although the latter word often connotes specific language rules that are taught in school. Children learn to speak syntactically long before they are taught the formal rules of grammar; in fact speakers of every human language speak syntactically whether or not they are ever taught grammar and even when their speech violates the rules that grammarians have formulated. Note that syntax not only reduces the ambiguity in human speech (as seen from the sentences listed above), but also enables human speakers to respond in linguistically appropriate ways to novel situations by uttering novel combinations of words that can, in turn, be responded to appropriately by human listeners. Thus, syntax is responsible for much of what is often called "creativity." Syntax is discussed more extensively in Chapter 17.

Language Learning in Different Species

There are a number of reasons for studying language learning in nonhuman species. One is that it might help us learn more about human language learning, because many or all of the same principles may be involved. It may also help us learn how to more effectively teach language to people with communication disorders. In addition, there could be many benefits to having another species with which we could communicate. It could, for example, give us another perspective that could help in our scientific and practical understanding. In this section, therefore, we examine the progress that has thus far been made in the language training of other species.

Birds. Processes related to language have been studied in at least two species of birds. One is, perhaps not surprisingly, a standard learning research subject. The other is well known for its excellent vocal mimicry.

Pigeons. By means of conditional discrimination procedures, two pigeons separated by a glass partition in an experimental chamber learned to engage in the following sequence (Epstein, Lanza, & Skinner, 1980):

1. One pigeon, Jack, would peck a key that would light up with the words "What color?"
2. This would act as an S^D for the other pigeon, Jill, to look into a small opening, covered by a curtain so that Jack could not see into it, on her side of the chamber.
3. Depending on whether a light in the opening was red, green, or yellow, Jill would peck and illuminate one of three keys labeled with a black "R," "G," or "Y."
4. The letter that Jill pecked was an S^D for Jack to perform two responses in sequence:
   a) Peck a key containing the words "Thank you."
   b) Peck one of three keys that were colored red, green, or yellow.

Jill received a few seconds access to mixed grain when Jack pecked the "Thank you" key; Jack received access to mixed grain if he pecked the key that was the same color as the key behind the curtain on Jill's side of the chamber. Any incorrect response in the sequence produced a brief darkening of the chamber and the loss of the opportunity to obtain reinforcement on that trial for both birds. A diagram of the apparatus used is shown in Figure 9.3.

Although a far cry from what we would reasonably call language, the two-way communicative behavior Jack and Jill learned captures processes involved in productive and receptive language. Jack was asking Jill for information concerning what color he should peck to match the color of the light that was hidden from him. Jill was cooperating by providing the information he requested, and he in turn thanked her. Note that the term "information" as used here is synonomous with "discriminative stimulus."

Any organism that can communicate can lie as well as tell the truth. Lying has been demonstrated in the pigeon by the following slight modification of the above procedure (Lanza, Starr, & Skinner, 1982). Jill's mixed-grain reinforcement occurred for less time after the hidden light was green or yellow than it was after the hidden light was red. As a result, she went through a phase in which she "lied" about one of the colors—yellow—reporting it as red. When Jack was trained on Jill's side of the chamber to report the hidden color to her, and then also given more generous reinforcement when the hidden color was red, he lied even more than Jill had done—reporting both green and yellow as red.

Parrot. An African gray parrot (*Psittacus erithacus*) has learned to vocally identify various objects and a number of their properties, including what they are made of (wood, metal, hide), their shapes ("two-corner" or football shape, "three-corner" or triangular, "four-corner" or rectangular), and their colors ("rose" or red,) (Pepperberg, 1981, 1983). The training procedure involves two teachers putting questions to each other and answering them before putting similar questions to Alex. The rationale for this procedure, which is called a model/rival system, is that it is similar to the dueting of parrots in their natural environment. Presumably

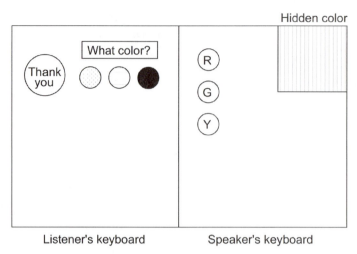

FIGURE 9.3. Diagram of apparatus used to teach verbal interaction between two pigeons. The pigeon on the left (the "listener") cannot see the color hidden behind the curtain in the upper right side of the chamber. The pigeon on the right (the "speaker") responds to the listener's peck on the "WHAT COLOR" key by looking behind the curtain and pecking the key labeled "R," "G," or "Y" — depending on whether the light behind the curtain is red, green, or yellow. The listener pecks the "THANK YOU" key, causing food to be delivered to the speaker, and then pecks the key whose color corresponds to the color indicated by the speaker. The listener's correct responses are reinforced so that the entire sequence is maintained. (From Lanza et al., 1982)

dueting is an important factor in young parrots learning the songs of the adults in their regions, and thus a language training procedure that resembles dueting might have more chance of success than one that consists simply of a single teacher reinforcing specific responses in the presence of specific stimuli.

A partial transcript from a training session illustrating how the model/rival system is used with Alex is shown in Table 9.1. In the early stages of training, reinforcement consisted of the objects that Alex was asked questions about. For example, note from Table 9.1 that Alex earned the green wooden triangle when he correctly identified its color.

The initial objects Alex was trained on were ones that appeared to be positively reinforcing to him; and, perhaps one reason for the success of his training program was that there were a large number of such objects. The consummatory behavior Alex engages in with the objects includes chewing on them, scratching himself with them, and playing with them. As Alex's vocabulary was extended to objects that tended not to be reinforcing to him, he learned to request alternative objects as reinforcers (Pepperberg, 1987a, b). For example, Alex might say "I want cork" after correctly identifying the material a key is made out of as metal. He would then receive a piece of cork as reinforcement for the correct response.

Over several years, Alex has learned to vocally identify more than 30 objects, six colors, and five shapes, and to request not only objects (e.g., "I want X"), but also to be taken to specific locations (e.g., "Wanna go X.") In addition, Alex says "No" to refuse items he did not request or that are not reinforcing to him. In a combination of symbolic and implicit identity and oddity matching, Alex has also learned to respond with a high degree of accuracy when presented with two objects that differ in shape, color, or material and asked "What's same?" or "What's different?" Moreover, Alex shows generalized identity and oddity matching in that his accuracy to "What's same?" and "What's different?" remains high even when presented with objects he has not previously been trained or tested on (Pepperberg, 1987a, 1988).

TABLE 9.1. Except from a verbal training session with an African gray parrot.[a]

Irene:	Kim, what color? [Holds up a green triangular piece of wood].
Kim:	Green three-corner wood.
Irene:	[Briefly removes object from sight, turns body slightly away.] No! Listen! I just want to know color! [Faces back toward K; represents object.] What color?
Kim:	Green wood.
Irene:	[Hands over exemplar.] That's right, the color is green; green wood.
Kim:	OK, Alex, now you tell me, what shape?
Alex:	No.
Kim:	OK, Irene, you tell me what shape.
Irene:	Three-corner wood.
Kim:	That's right, you listened! The shape is three-corner; it's three corner wood [Hands over exemplar.]
Irene:	Alex, here's your change. What color?
Alex:	Wood.
Irene:	That's right, wood; what color wood?
Alex:	Green wood.
Irene:	Good parrot! Here you go. [Hands over exemplar.] The color is green.

[a]Irene and Kim are trainers, and Alex is the parrot. (From Pepperberg, 1983).

Primates. Because humans are primates, it is reasonable to ask to what extent other primates can learn a human-like language. A natural starting point is our closest evolutionary relative, the apes (see Figure 1.1, p. 9).

Apes. Although they are our closest phylogenetic relatives, apes are physiologically incapable of producing the range of speech sounds that humans do. Specifically, unlike that of humans, their vocal tracts are unsuited to switching rapidly between vowel sounds and to producing consonants to break up vowel sounds (Crelin, 1987, p. 87), and thus they cannot vocally produce the large number of words that humans can (see Chapter 17, Figure 17.2, p. 373). To get around this problem, researchers interested in the ability of apes to learn language have focused on nonvocal modalities. For example, chimpanzees (Gardner & Gardner, 1969), an orangutan (Miles, 1983), and a gorilla (Patterson, 1978) have learned to identify objects and make requests by forming hand signs similar to those of American Sign Language (a form of communication used by deaf people).

Perhaps the most impressive work on teaching language to apes, however, has been done using computer lexigrams—that is, geometric symbols connected to a computer — with two species of chimpanzee: the common chimpanzee (*Pan troglodytes*) and the pygmy chimpanzee or bonobo (*Pan panicus*).

Figure 9.4 illustrates the keyboard used with two chimpanzees named Sherman and Austin (Savage-Rumbaugh & Lewin, 1994, p. 62). The geometric symbols are lexigrams corresponding to objects and activities that Sherman and Austin learned, or were learning, to identify, and the blank keys are available for adding new lexigrams as the animals' learning progresses. Pressing a key causes it to light up and also causes the lexigram on it to be projected in a region at the top of the keyboard, so that the lexigram selected is a distinct stimulus for the chimpanzee and anyone else viewing the keyboard. At the beginning of training there were only a few

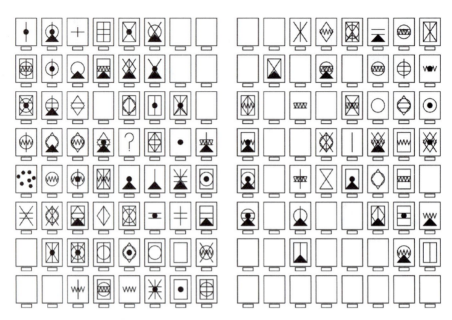

FIGURE 9.4. Keyboard used in language training with chimpanzees. The chimpanzees press the symbols to make requests, identify objects, and transmit information. (From Savage-Rumbaugh & Lewin, 1994)

lexigrams on the keyboard, and as the chimpanzees learned to press these appropriately more were added.

In an early stage of training, Sherman and Austin learned to request a food item the teacher showed them by pressing the lexigram corresponding to that item. At a later stage, they began to request items before being shown them. The teacher reinforced these spontaneous requests with the requested item even if it was not the one she was going to present. In addition, the teacher began adding nonfood items, such as "tickle" (meaning for the teacher to tickle the animal) and "out" (meaning for the animal to be taken outside), to the keyboard.

After they had become proficient at requesting, Sherman and Austin next learned to identify objects. To ensure that they were identifying rather than requesting an item, the teacher used a different item as a reinforcer. Learning to label food items, however, did not follow immediately from the fact that the animals had learned to request those same food items (Savage-Rumbaugh & Lewin, 1994, pp. 67–68). Instead, labeling appeared to be a distinct behavior that had to be learned separately. (The fact that different functions, such as requesting and naming, of the same linguistic element may be learned separately will be taken up again in Chapter 17.) Because introducing the identification task abruptly disrupted the behavior, the task was reintroduced gradually. Correct responses were initially reinforced with a large amount of the item to be identified and a small amount of a different item, and over trials the teacher gradually decreased the amount of the former while gradually increasing the amount of the latter until the chimpanzees eventually identified items they were shown and accepted different items as reinforcement (Savage-Rumbaugh & Lewin, 1994, pp. 68–69).

As mentioned above, an important property (perhaps the defining property) of language is that it can be used in communication or the transfer of information from one individual to another. That this property could be manifested in as primitive an animal as the pigeon was demonstrated in the experiment with Jack and Jill described previously. In a manner somewhat similar to that in which the pigeons learned to communicate the color of a light, Sherman and Austin learned to communicate what food item was hidden in an opaque container. (In fact, the study with the pigeons Jack and Jill was based on the procedure used with Sherman and Austin.) First, because the animals' productive language did not (at least initially) transfer readily to receptive language—that is, a chimp that would request an item would not initially provide that item when it was requested from the animal—the animals were explicitly taught receptive language using the same symbols that they used in their productive language (Savage-Rumbaugh & Lewin, 1994, pp. 70–71, 126–127). Each chimp next learned to press the lexigram corresponding to a food item that it had seen the teacher put in an opaque container. Then both chimps were tested together in a situation in which only one (sometimes Sherman and sometimes Austin) had seen the teacher put a food item in the chamber, and the teacher let the two chimps share the food in the container only if both pressed the lexigram for that food on their respective keyboards. Within a few trials the chimp that had not seen food put in the container learned to attend to the request of the chimp that had, who in turn learned to press the correct lexigram in clear view of the other chimp. As a by-product of this phase of the experiment, the two chimps learned to share food, which is something these animals do not do in the wild (Savage-Rumbaugh & Lewin, 1994, pp. 69–78).

In the next phase of the experiment, Sherman and Austin learned to request from each other specific tools that would give them access to sites in which they had seen the teacher place food. Each chimp had six such food sites located in a room adjoining the other chimp's room, and connected to it by a large window. On any given trial the food was in one room and the tools in the other, and the chimpanzee in the room containing the food saw where it was placed while the other chimp did not. Each chimp learned to request the appropriate tool from the other, who in turn learned to hand him the requested tool through the window. After the chimpanzee requesting the tool had used it to obtain the food, he returned to the window and shared the food with the other chimp (Savage-Rumbaugh & Lewin, 1994, pp. 79–82). Thus, like humans, chimpanzees that have learned productive and receptive language can learn to cooperate by requesting, providing, and using tools to achieve a common goal.

There is considerable interest in whether language-trained animals exhibit syntax, as this relates to whether syntax is unique to humans. To date there is considerable controversy regarding whether any nonhuman animal has learned to consistently produce even the simplest syntactical structures (Kato, 1999a, b). Perhaps the animal for which the best documented evidence for productive syntax exists is Kanzi, a male bonobo (pygmy chimpanzee) who was trained on a lexigram keyboard similar to that used by Sherman and Austin. Kanzi started learning to use lexigrams when he was six months old. By the age of seven years, he had a vocabulary of about 125 words (i.e., lexigrams). The vast majority of his utterances, that is, a single request or identification, consist of single words, and few consist of more than two words. Some of his two word utterances show a particular ordering, perhaps indicating some degree of productive syntax. One apparent syntactical rule Kanzi follows is that when commenting on some action he has performed on an object, such as hiding a peanut or biting a tomato, Kanzi typically utters the action word before the object word ("hide peanut," "bite tomato"; Savage-Rumbaugh & Lewin, 1994, p. 160). He may have learned this as a result of reinforcement from his trainers and caretakers who, being speakers of English, tended to respond more readily to a verb-before-object than to an object-before-verb combination. Another rule Kanzi seems to follow is when requesting someone to perform an action, he indicates through pointing or touching the person who is to perform the action after first pressing the lexigram for the action (e.g., pressing the lexigram for tickle and then pointing to or touching his teacher; Savage-Rumbaugh & Lewin, 1994, p. 161). A final rule Kanzi tends to follow is that when pressing lexigrams corresponding to a sequence of actions, he tends to follow the order in which the actions occur (or occurred), for example, "tickle bite" for the sequence of someone tickling him followed by play-biting him, and "chase-hide" for the sequence of Kanzi running a short distance from someone and then hiding (Savage-Rumbaugh & Lewin, 1994, p. 162).

While there is little evidence that Kanzi can produce syntax (i.e., follow syntactical rules in his productive language), it appears that he has acquired receptive syntax from interacting with his English-speaking trainers and caretakers. When Kanzi was eight years old, his responding to oral instructions in English was compared with that of a 1 1/2- to 2-year-old girl named Alia (Savage-Rumbaugh et. al., 1993). Kanzi and Alia were tested separately in different locations with identical or comparable instructions. Many of the instructions in this test were ones that Kanzi and Alia would never have heard before to ensure that they had not simply learned to respond to those specific instructions. Both Kanzi and Alia demonstrated syntactical receptive behavior in that they made substantially more correct than incorrect responses when instructions varied in the following ways: (1) the order of key words changed (e.g., "Pour the Coke in the lemonade" versus "Pour the lemonade in the Coke"), (2) the verb

---

TABLE 9.2. Some of Kanzi's and Alia's Instructions and Responses.[a]

Instructions 288: Put the monster mask on your head.

→   Kanzi drops the orange that he is eating into the monster mask and then puts the mask on his head.
→   Alia does so.

Instruction 321: Take the potato to the bedroom.

→   Kanzi does so.
→   Alia does so.

Instruction 407: Take the potato outdoors and get the apple.

→   Kanzi picks up the potato and the knife and heads toward the door. . . . Kanzi gets out and stands looking around. Since he seems to be hesitating and not coming back, E says "Now bring the apple back." Kanzi picks up the apple and brings it back but also carries the potato with him.
→   Alia gets up and gets the potato. . . . Alia takes the potato outside, sets it on the bench, but keeps her hand on it. She then picks up the apple and the potato and brings them both inside.

Instruction 414: Bite your ball.

→   Kanzi bites the ball and shakes it hard while holding the handle in his mouth.
→   Alia does so.

Instruction 450: Go outdoors and get the milk.

→   Kanzi starts to take the milk that is in the group room. E says "No, not that milk. Go outdoors and get the milk." Kanzi goes to the refrigerator and gets a banana.
→   Alia does so.

Instruction 541: Take the banana outdoors.

→   Kanzi makes a sound like "banana," then does so.
→   Alia says, "OK, banana, banana, you can eat banana," then shows the banana to the camera person on the way outdoors.

---

[a]Kanzi is a chimpanzee, Alia is a 1½–2 year old girl. "E" refers to the experimenter. (From Savage-Rumbaugh et al., 1993, Appendix, pp. 111–210).

changed (e.g., "Take the rock outside" versus "Get the rock that's outside"), and (3) both the order of key words and the verb changed (e.g., "Take the potato to the bedroom" versus "Go to the bedroom and get the potato"). Table 9.2 shows some selected test instructions and the responses of both individuals, illustrating the similarity of their receptive language.

Humans. Humans of course exhibit both the communication and syntax properties of language to an extreme degree. We discuss humans and language in some detail in Chapter 17.

Other species. There is no doubt that many species can learn two-way communication in the same way that the pigeons Jack and Jill did. The extent to which other species could develop the productive language capabilities of the African gray parrot and ape, however, is not known.

There is also no doubt about the fact—well known to pet owners and anyone who has watched performances by trained animals—that many species can learn receptive language, in the sense of responding to words as stimuli. Learning of receptive syntax by nonhuman animals, however, is a matter about which little is known.

Bottlenosed dolphins can learn to respond appropriately to an artificial language delivered auditorily (Herman, 1986). For example, a dolphin learned to carry out commands such as "pipe fetch gate," meaning to take a piece of pipe to the pool gate, and "surface pipe fetch bottom hoop," meaning to take the pipe that is on the surface to the hoop that is on the bottom. Tests with novel sentences demonstrated that the animal was responding to syntax rather than simply to learned sequences.

CONDITIONAL DISCRIMINATIONS AND NUMEROSITY BEHAVIOR

Conditional discriminations are an important aspect of numerosity behavior, which can be defined as responding to number (e.g., the number of objects in a particular class that is present). We have seen that correctly labeling different colors when they occur successively, or emitting other responses corresponding to those colors (e.g., pressing keys containing symbols corresponding to the colors), is an example of a conditional discrimination. Similarly, correctly labeling a number of objects with a vocal response or symbol that corresponds to the number of objects present is a conditional discrimination. In the case of humans who have learned to count, processes discussed in Chapter 11 are also involved. As a brief preview, however, note that counting objects or other items involves at least the following:

- There exists a set of unique tags or labels—technically called *numerals*—that the individual has learned to emit as a fixed sequence of responses (e.g., the numerals 1, 2, 3 . . .).
- Each of the items to be counted is a stimulus for the emission of one and only one tag in the sequence, with the name of the last tag emitted being the name of the number of items counted.

Likewise, other formal numerical operations that humans engage in, such as adding, subtracting, multiplying, and dividing, also involve processes to be discussed in Chapter 11.

Animals that have not learned formal numerical operations such as counting, however, can engage in numerosity behavior to a limited degree. The items to which numerosity behavior applies can be either distributed in space or in time. In the former case, we refer to the collection of items as *spatial arrays*, while in the latter the items are simply called *events*.

Spatial Arrays

A spatial array consists of a number of items present simultaneously in some sort of spatial arrangement. Numerals may be assigned to the number of items in the array, or the numbers of items in more than one array may be compared in some way.

Assigning numerals. An African gray parrot, Alex (mentioned in the previous section), has learned to vocally emit the English numerals 1 to 6 to corresponding arrays of various objects (Pepperberg, 1987a). Table 9.3 shows a partial transcript from one of Alex's training sessions in which he was learning to identify the number of objects of a particular class within a collection of two classes of objects.

Chimpanzees have learned to press keys representing or containing either binary or Arabic numerals corresponding to up to seven items (Ferster, 1964; Matsuzawa, 1985). Moreover, the number discriminations of both the parrot and the chimpanzees transferred to new instances; that is, the animals responded correctly above chance to sets of objects on which they had not been trained. For example, if five red pencils were used during training, the animal responded correctly at an above-chance level when tested with five blue gloves.

Chimpanzees have also learned to select among arrays of one, two, and three items when the numeral 1, 2, or 3 is projected on a monitor screen (Boysen, 1993). An interesting aspect of the behavior of chimpanzees in the above experiments is that before selecting an array the chimps will often point to and even manipulate the items in the arrays, thus giving the appearance of counting the objects. Since the chimpanzees had not been taught to count according to the procedures to be described in Chapter 11, this behavior was certainly not counting in the formal sense defined above. By providing distinct tactile and proprioceptive stimuli, however, it may have helped them discriminate between the arrays.

Teaching the above behavior is difficult, however, if the array consists of food items because the chimpanzee has a strong tendency to select the array with the largest number of food items regardless of the numeral on the screen.

Relating sizes of arrays. Numerosity behavior includes not just operations that resemble counting, but also operations that involve relating numbers in some way.

Selecting the smaller or larger of two arrays. A simple numerical operation is discerning that a given number is less than or more than another number. This operation involves a conditional discrimination in which the correct response is to select, depending on the relation specified, the smaller or the larger of two simultaneously presented numbers.

In this regard, pigeons can learn to peck the smaller or larger of two arrays of dots, and this behavior generalizes to novel array pairs (Emmerton, 1998). Squirrel monkeys can learn to select the smaller (or larger) of two displays containing up to eight filled circles (Thomas, Fowlkes, & Vickery, 1980).

Chimpanzees have also learned to select symbols (e.g., colored boxes, Arabic numerals that they have been taught) corresponding to the larger of two numbers, and have subsequently responded appropriately when symbols occurred together that had not occurred together during training (Boysen, 1992, 1993; Gillan, 1981). As described in Chapter 8 (p. 179), this is the phenomenon of transitive inference and it is not limited to chimpanzees: pigeons also exhibit it (von Fersen et al., 1991).

TABLE 9.3. Partial Transcript from a Quantitative Training Session
with an African Gray Parrot.[a]

---

1) 3 wood, 4 metal washers [popsicle sticks, contiguous groupings]
T: How many washers?
A: [Grabs a piece of wood and tears it apart. It is not replaced.]
T: Alex, how many washers?
A: Sih [six].
T: That's the number of toys, how many washers?
A: Sih, sih.
T: That's how many toys, how many washers?
A: Four [Alex takes washer momentarily, drops it, and requests pasta].

2) 2 thimbles, 4 wood [plant stakes, contiguous groupings]
T: Alex, look! How many wood?
A: Four
[Alex is given a stake, which he chews. It is replaced and the tray presented again.]
T: Alex, how many thimbles?
A: Sih.
T: That's how many toys; how many metal toys? ["Metal" is a label that he has not yet
acquired, but on which he is being trained.]
A: Two. [He is given a thimble, which he manipulates in his beak.]

3) 3 jacks, 2 bobbins [contiguous]
T: Alex, how many bobbins?
A: Five.
T: Well, that's the number of toys. [Goes on to work with photos.]

4) 4 wood, 2 hearts [rubber heart-shaped 1-inch magnets, contiguous]
T: Alex, how many hearts?
A: Sih.
T: Well, that's the number of toys; how many hearts?
A: Two.
T: You're right. [Gives heart, which Alex immediately drops.]

5) 4 wood, 2 plastic hair clips [interspersed]
T: How many plastic?
A: Two.
T: That's right, two. [Gives plastic pieces. Alex chews one apart.]

---

[a]"T" refers to the trainer, "A" to Alex (the parrot). (From Pepperberg, 1987a)

When two different-size arrays both consist of food items, it is extremely difficult for primates such as squirrel monkeys (Anderson, Awazu, & Fujita, 2000) or even chimpanzees (Boysen, 1993) to learn to reach for the smaller number of items. Even when they receive the larger number contingent on reaching for the smaller number and vice versa, they consistently reach for the larger number. With special training procedures involving a timeout for incorrect responses and a correction procedure, squirrel monkeys are able to learn this discrimination. Chimpanzees can learn to reach for the array containing the smaller number of food items when the larger number of food items is represented numerically (Boysen, Mukobi, & Bemtson, 1999). However, extensive numerical training seems to hinder rather than aid chimpanzees learning to make this discrimination. It is interesting that despite their close relationship to humans, chimpanzees have great difficulty learning not to reach for the larger of two reinforcers or a stimulus associated with the larger reinforcer.

Simple arithmetic: addition and subtraction. Other relational operations include those of simple arithmetic, such as adding or subtracting numbers. In this regard, chimpanzees have learned to select a pair of trays containing chocolates over another pair that contained fewer chocolates in total, where the total in each pair of trays might be as many as ten. Successive trials with different combinations of chocolates in the two trays of each pair demonstrated that the chimpanzees were not selecting the pair that contained the single tray with the most chocolates or avoiding the pair that contained the single tray with the fewest chocolates (Rumbaugh, Savage-Rumbaugh, & Hegel, 1987; Rumbaugh & Washburn, 1993). In another type of summation task involving a delay, a chimpanzee learned to select the Arabic numeral corresponding to the total number of oranges the animal had seen at three different sites it had recently visited, where one or two of the sites contained oranges and the total number of oranges could be as high as four. Subsequently, when Arabic numerals instead of oranges were present at the sites, the animal selected the Arabic numeral corresponding to the sum of the numbers at the sites with a much greater than chance probability (Boysen, 1993; Boysen & Berntson, 1989). (In the next chapter we will consider how it is possible for an animal to respond after a delay to a stimulus that is no longer present.)

Variables affecting numerosity behavior for spatial arrays. Several points should be noted regarding the experiments referred to above:

- Many of the experiments involved stringent controls to reduce or eliminate responding on the basis of any stimulus—for example, pattern, area, brightness—other than number. Thus, the experiments provide strong evidence for numerosity behavior in animals.
- Many of the animals in these experiments have had language training, which could be an important factor in their development of numerosity behavior.
- Training numerosity behavior in animals—even chimpanzees—requires a great deal of time and many training trials, and typically the animals' performances, while greater than chance, are far from perfect.
- There is no evidence that the animals in the above experiments are counting in the sense defined at the beginning of this section. (In Chapter 11 we look at a method to teach an animal to count in the sense defined above.)

Numerosity Behavior for Events

We have already seen that one type of event that may control an animal's numerosity behavior is the animal's behavior itself. In a mixed FR x FR y schedule where x is less than y, for example, an animal will pause if it does receive reinforcement after emitting slightly more y than x responses (Ferster & Skinner, 1957). In addition, animals can learn to emit a distinct terminal response for reinforcement after they have emitted a set number of other responses (Mechner, 1958; Platt & Johnson, 1971). Number discriminations for an animal's own responses have also been studied using conditional discriminations. For example, a pigeon may peck a center key to illuminate two side keys, whereupon pecking the right key is reinforced if 50 responses were emitted on the center key before the side keylights turned on and pecking the left key is reinforced if less than 50 responses were emitted. Pigeons are extremely accurate at this task when the number being compared with 50 is 37 or less, and their accuracy does not fall below 60% until the alternative is increased to 47 (Rilling & McDiarmid, 1965).

Similarly, rats can learn to press one of two levers if they hear a sequence of two sounds and the other lever if they hear a sequence of four sounds (Fernandes & Church, 1982). The animals can learn the discrimination based on either the number of the sounds or on their durations, as can be demonstrated by varying either of these variables independently of each other (Meck & Church, 1983). In addition, the animals' number (and duration) discriminations transfer readily from sounds to lights, and even to mild "tingling" electric shocks (Church & Meck, 1984; Meck & Church, 1983). That is, when new stimuli are substituted for the sounds used in training, the animals quickly learn to respond in the same manner that they did to the sounds.

SUMMARY AND CONCLUSIONS

A conditional discrimination is one in which the S+ and S– are conditional on another stimulus. The potential S+ and S– are called the comparison stimuli, and the stimulus on which they are conditional is called the sample. Hence, another name for a conditional discrimination is matching-to-sample.

There are three types of conditional discriminations: (1) identity matching, in which the S+ is the same as the sample and the S– is different; (2) oddity matching, in which the S– matches the sample and the S+ is different; and (3) symbolic matching, in which the relation between the comparison and sample stimuli is arbitrary. The ability to learn generalized identity or oddity matching, in which the sample and comparison stimuli are novel, may be present to a significant degree only in the higher primates. Generalized identity and oddity matching correspond to the concepts "same" and "different," respectively.

Through symbolic matching it is possible, at least in humans, to develop equivalence relations. These are logical connections in which, without direct training, some sample stimuli come to substitute for others—that is, to function in the same way that other sample stimuli have been conditioned to do—in a symbolic matching procedure. An equivalence relation consists of the relations of reflexivity, symmetry, and transitivity. If A, B, and C are sets of different stimuli, individuals who have learned to match B with A and C with B will demonstrate an equivalence relation (with respect to these sets of stimuli) if they then match A with A, B with B, and C with C (reflexivity), A with B and B with C (symmetry), and C with A (transitivity).

Some have suggested that having language is a prerequisite to forming equivalence relations, and that this is the reason that animals lacking language do not appear to form equivalence relations. However, this suggestion can lead to a circular argument; namely, that it is necessary to have equivalence relations in order to form equivalence relations—which, contrary to fact, would imply equivalence relations could never be formed by any individual. This is because a language consists of a large set of equivalence relations in that, through the complex structure of any human language, words are matched with objects, events, and other words. The reason that only individuals having language have thus far learned equivalence relations in the laboratory may be because having learned a number of equivalence relations (e.g., through language learning) may facilitate learning others in a learning-to-learn fashion.

Because languages consist of conditional discriminations and animals readily learn conditional discriminations, it seems that it should be possible to teach linguistic behavior to animals. There has been some success in teaching rudimentary productive and receptive language to animals such as pigeons, a parrot, an orangutan, a gorilla, and chimpanzees. There has also been success at teaching animals some conditional discriminations involving number. Thus humans are not unique in their ability to learn language and number concepts, although no nonhuman animal has approached the complexity of human language. As indicated above, this may be because nonhuman animals are limited in their capacity to acquire equivalence relations.

10

Memory
Stimulus Discrimination Across Time

*S*timulus discrimination is related to what in common, everyday speech we refer to as "memory" or "remembering" (the active form of the word "memory"). It is important for us to examine the issue of memory in our study of learning because, from a commonsense point of view, learning is of little use unless at least something of what was learned is remembered at a later time. In order to examine this, we must translate some common everyday-expressions about memory into the scientific language of learning that we have been developing in this text up to now. If a discrimination is performed some time after it was learned, we generally say in common, everyday speech that it is "remembered." If learned but not performed, even though a sufficiently strong establishing operation (e.g., deprivation of the reinforcer) has occurred, we say that it is not remembered or that it is "forgotten." Simple discriminations that have been well learned are not forgotten over long time periods. For example, pigeons that have learned to peck a particular location on a complex stimulus for food will emit that precise response four years later even when they have had no opportunity to do so during those four years (Skinner, 1950, pp. 200–201).

There are, however, more complex cases in which a learned response may not occur, despite apparently favorable conditions for it to occur. There are at least three types of these cases: (1) an individual fails to respond correctly to the correct comparison stimulus in a conditional discrimination when the sample stimulus is present; (2) an individual fails to respond correctly in a conditional discrimination in which the same stimulus is no longer present; and (3) an individual fails to emit a particular response at a particular time following a given stimulus after having a history of reinforcement contingent on that response occurring after that time following the stimulus.

An example of a non-delayed conditional discrimination that is unlikely to be forgotten is replying correctly to the question "What is a common food that is often served with bacon for breakfast?" An example of the second complex case, a delayed conditional discrimination, would be replying correctly to the question, "What did you have for breakfast this morning?" That individual's breakfast earlier in the day would be the sample stimulus and the question would be a comparison stimulus. This is, in essence, a symbolic-matching-to-sample task in which the response "eggs" (or the verbal response corresponding to whatever the individual had for breakfast) is matched to the individual's breakfast some time after the breakfast has been eaten. An example of the third case above would be "remembering" (i.e., responding without being prompted by any current external stimulus) to take food out of the oven a certain amount of time after putting the food into the oven.

A technical term for memory for the first case—non-delayed conditional discriminations—is semantic memory (Tulving, 1972). A technical term for the second case—delayed conditional discriminations—is episodic memory (Tulving, 1972; Tulving, 1983; pp. 34–57). A technical term for the third case is time-place memory. In this chapter we focus mainly on the latter two types of cases, including discussion of how it is possible for a response to come under the control of an absent stimulus. Toward the end of the chapter we also consider how memory failures or lapses can result from intruding responses interfering with correct responses to prevent the latter from occurring. First, however, we briefly consider an influential theoretical approach to memory.

THE COMPUTER ANALOGY

It has always been advantageous for humans to respond to stimuli that are no longer present, and early in recorded history some cultures developed a highly effective means of doing so: writing. (In fact, writing is what made recorded history possible.) Record keeping and the processing of records proved to be extremely useful in enabling people to respond to absent stimuli. Maintaining inventory of one's domestic animals, for example, would have been important in keeping track of them and in making a number of decisions regarding them, such as how much feed to procure, how many to trade for other commodities and services, and so on. Our standard folk theory of memory seems to be based to a large extent on the analogy of recording and storing information. Just as people record information on some sort of medium (e.g., stone tablets, paper, film, auditory or video tape, computer discs) and store it in a special location (e.g., library, filing cabinet, computer), animals and people are said to record and store information in their brains. Just as there are temporary and permanent records, so it has been asserted that there are short-term and long-term memories. Just as we search our records to locate specific information, so we seem to "search our memories" for material we wish to recall.

Some see the development of computer technology as support for this general theory of memory. Information, or data, that we put into a computer often first goes into a temporary storage area where we can work on it, as in doing word processing, drawing pictures, making charts or graphs, or performing computations. When we finish working on our records (or files or data), we can store them in a more permanent form by "saving" or "writing" them to disk. Because this is how computers work, it seems to some that the brain must also work this way.

Computer Memory and Animal Memory

The analogy between the brain and a computer suggests that animal and human memory is similar to computer memory. What is often overlooked, however, is the fact that the computer is simply an electronic device for keeping and processing records. The computer functions the way it does simply because it was modeled after the methods that humans have used to keep and process records (both textual material and numerical data) for thousands of years.

Computers differ from earlier methods of keeping and processing records only in that they permit us to store and work on more information more efficiently. Instead of chisel marks on stone or ink on paper, computer records are written with electrons on a magnetic surface. The computer also carries out certain processing tasks automatically, but the way in which it does so is no different in principle from the way in which these tasks could have been done by hand using other media, such as pencil and paper. The fact that humans have found a particular way of keeping and processing records to be highly effective in responding to absent stimuli does not imply that this is the method by which the brain enables us to respond to absent stimuli when we are not working with recorded data. Nevertheless, the analogy is popular with many learning scientists specializing in the study of memory. The analogy between the computer and the brain seems natural to us because the brain consists of chemo-electrical connections that somewhat resemble the electrical connections in a computer and because, through our educational system and general culture, we have learned to keep and process records to enable us to better respond to absent stimuli. However tempting the computer analogy of memory is to us, it does not follow that it is necessarily the best way to describe either animal or human memory. We shall see below, however, that the analogy does have some merit if we are careful not to stretch it too far.

The way in which the analogy can be stretched too far is as follows. Computers belong to a class of objects like automobiles, pianos, and bathtubs that, by definition are made and used by humans. If we were to say that something is analogous to an automobile, piano, or bathtub, we also should say what corresponds to the driver, player, or bather, respectively. Likewise, if we say that the brain or some part of the brain is analogous to a computer, then we also should say what corresponds to its user. If we say that it is something else inside the individual (such as a part of the brain that is not included in the computer analogy), then to be scientifically complete and consistent, we now have to account for this inner computer user. Specifically, we have to say whether this inner computer user is also a computer; and if so, what it corresponds to its user. This line of inquiry leads to an infinite regress—an explanatory "black hole" that, in the end, explains nothing. Essentially, this is a version of the "homunculus" theory of behavior—that there exists an inner individual (the inner computer user in this version of the theory) whose behavior accounts for the behavior of the actual individual. This and other versions of the homunculus theory have been strongly criticized by several cognitive and behavioral scientists (Edelman, 1992, pp. 79–80, 237–238; Searle, 1994, pp. 212–214; Skinner, 1963, p. 951; Skinner, 1974, p.130).

Figure 10.1 shows a diagram of a well-supported contemporary theory of human memory (based mainly on the work of Baddeley, 1986, 1991, 1992) that employs a computer analogy. Note that the figure shows three main areas of memory: sensory storage, working memory (which replaces the concept of short-term memory), and long-term memory. Information from an external stimulus enters through vision, audition, or other senses that are not shown in the figure. The sensory effect (e.g., an "image" of the stimulus) persists for a very brief period after the stimulus has terminated. This sensory memory, as it is sometimes called, most likely occurs in all sensory modalities. In humans, however, it is most evident in vision and hearing, where it has been called iconic memory and echoic memory, respectively (Neisser, 1967). Because sensory memory—at least the iconic (Sperling, 1960) and echoic (Darwin et al., 1972) types— is extremely brief, it cannot account for short-duration memory of longer than a few seconds at most. Working memory contains the central executive, which is involved in developing and implementing strategies for remembering information and processing it. The central executive draws upon the output of slave systems, two of which are shown in the figure: the visuo-spatial sketch pad and the phonological loop. The former is the process called "forming a mental image" in common, everyday speech, while the latter consists of repeating a verbalization covertly in order to retain it in working memory while processing it. The central executive may put information into long-term memory for more permanent storage, and draws upon information in long-term memory when needed for processing new information at a later time.

In the following we integrate the material on standard and conditional discrimination

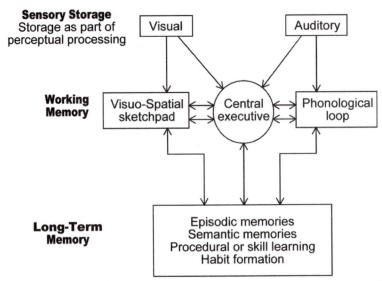

FIGURE 10.1. A diagram of human memory. Information proceeds from the environment through the senses to sensory memory, to working memory (where the central executive may use it in performing various tasks), and finally to long-term memory (where the central executive may draw upon it at a later time). Episodic memories are of specific events ("episodes") that individual has experienced. In general, semantic memories pertain to meaning and knowledge, and procedural, skill, and habit memory pertain to stimulus-response chains the individual has learned (as described in Chapter 11). (From Torgesen, 1996)

learning discussed in previous chapters with the above view of memory, while attempting to avoid the homunculus fallacy outlined above.

Encoding and Retrieval

When we input information (i.e., words or numbers) into a computer, it is "encoded" in the computer's memory as a particular pattern of electricity. Later, when we wish to view the information, it is "retrieved" from memory and printed out (in a "decoded" form; i.e., in the form in which we originally stored it) on a monitor screen or on paper. Somewhat analogues to encoding and retrieval by a computer, learning processes discussed in earlier chapters can also result in the conversion of information from one form to another.

The learning of a stimulus discrimination must by logical necessity be represented by some change in the nervous system. We currently do not know what this change is, however. There are numerous theories that attempt to describe or characterize it in some way, but definitive tests of these theories may be impossible given the current limits of physiological technology and knowledge (Watkins, 1990). Regardless of what the physiological change is that accounts for memory of a stimulus discrimination, we may speak of this change as the encoding of the discrimination. When a conditioned stimulus or S^D occurs and elicits or evokes the conditioned response, we call this the process of retrieval, and we may say that the conditioned response has been retrieved.

Consider a conditional discrimination in which the sample stimulus is absent at the time that the response that matches it occurs. Here the concept of encoding is used in two ways to help us to understand how an individual can respond to an absent stimulus. First, two or more discriminations are encoded, as in a standard discrimination. Second, the absent stimulus is

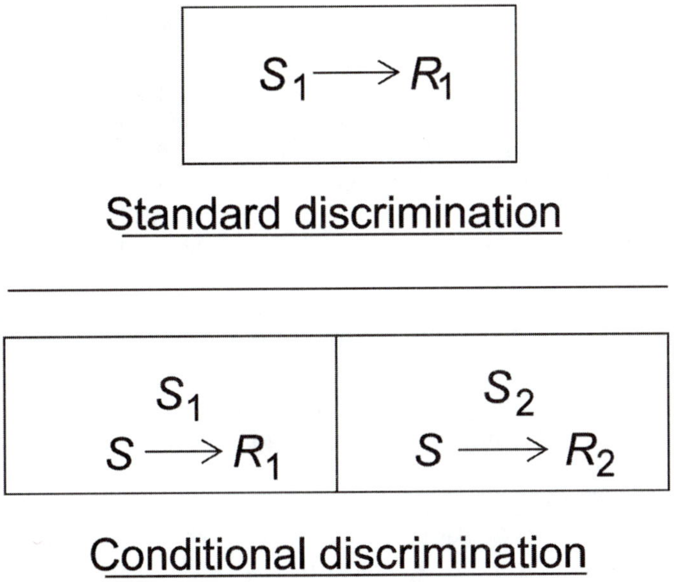

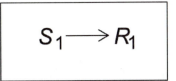

Standard discrimination

Conditional discrimination

FIGURE 10.2. The top part of the figure represents a standard discrimination in which no encoding is assumed. The bottom part represents a delayed conditional discrimination in which the prior encoding of S_1 or S_2 determines whether R_1 or R_2, respectively, occurs when S occurs.

encoded. This difference between encoding in a standard discrimination and encoding in a conditional discrimination in which the sample stimulus is absent is illustrated in Figure 10.2.

The top part of the figure represents the stimulus-response relationship in a standard discrimination. Note that the bottom diagram, representing the stimulus-response relationship in a conditional discrimination, differs from the top in that two stimulus-response relationships are represented. The stimulus (S) is identical in both of these two stimulus-response relationships, but the responses are different. Which response, R_1 or R_2, is likely to be retrieved when S occurs will depend on whether S_1 or S_2, respectively, has been encoded.

Technically, to be more precise, one should say that information, rather than stimuli and responses, is or has been encoded and retrieved.

As mentioned, stimulus-response encoding occurs entirely in the nervous system. Stimulus encoding in conditional discriminations in which the sample stimulus is absent may occur in several other ways as well. We discuss these below.

STIMULUS ENCODING AND RETRIEVAL IN CONDITIONAL DISCRIMINATIONS

The way in which a stimulus is encoded in conditional discriminations seems to depend on the amount of time between the sample stimulus and the comparison stimulus or stimuli. That is, it seems to depend on the amount of time that the sample stimulus needs to be encoded before the occasion for the response to be reinforced occurs.

Short-Duration Memory

The capacity of a recent event that is no longer present to affect behavior is referred to in this book as short-duration memory. It is important not to confuse short-duration memory with what has been called "short-term memory"; the latter is a theoretical construct which has fallen into disfavor among a number of learning scientists.

Matching-to-sample tasks, such as those described in Chapter 9, are commonly used to study short-duration memory (D'Amato, 1973; Grant & Roberts, 1976; Maki, 1979; Medin, Reynolds, & Parkinson, 1980; Moise, 1970; Roberts, 1972; Roberts & Grant, 1976, 1978; Shimp & Moffitt, 1974; Tranberg & Rilling, 1980; Zentall, 1973; Zentall, Hogan, Howard, & Moore, 1978). In a procedure called delayed matching to sample (DMTS), the sample is removed before the presentation of the comparison stimuli. The interval of time between the termination of the sample and the presentation of the comparison stimuli is called the retention interval. Explicit-identity, explicit-oddity, or symbolic-matching procedures may be used. Some of the stimuli that have been used as samples and comparisons are colors, line tilts, the presence or absence of food, and durations of lights or food presentations (e.g., Carter & Eckerman, 1975; Spetch & Wilkie, 1981; Wilkie, 1978). Two typical findings are that memory for a recently presented sample varies directly with the length of time the sample was present and inversely with the length of the retention interval.

Encoding in short-duration memory.

The phenomenon of short-duration memory implies that a stimulus can exert control over a specific response for a short time after the stimulus is removed. There are two major ways in which this occurs. One way is that the neural effects of the stimulus persist for a short time after the physical stimulus disappears. We can observe this phenomenon introspectively as an "image" of the stimulus that persists for a very brief time after the stimulus has terminated. This phenomenon is also responsible for the fact that we perceive continuous motion rather than a sequence of still pictures when we watch movies and TV programs. A sensory impression of each still image remains until the next frame appears. This is the "sensory storage" that is illustrated in Figure 10.1.

The second major way in which a stimulus that is no longer present can be encoded is in behavior that produces a surrogate stimulus for the matching response. This encoding behavior is generally called mediating behavior. To clarify how mediating behavior works, consider the problem of remembering a telephone number after having just looked it up some distance from the phone. Essentially, this is a DMTS task in which the sample stimulus is the number in the phone book, the retention interval is the time it takes to get to the phone and begin dialing, and the comparison stimuli are the digits on the dial on the phone. One way to keep from forgetting the number before dialing it is to keep repeating it, either covertly or overtly (i.e., either silently or aloud). This is an example of mediating behavior in that it is produced by the printed number in the phone book and in turn controls dialing the correct sequence of numbers on the phone. Of course, the procedure is somewhat more complex than the standard DMTS procedure in that a sequence of responses to different stimuli (i.e., the numbers on the dial), rather than just one response to one stimulus, is required for reinforcement (i.e., getting the appropriate person on the line). Nevertheless, it serves to illustrate not only the role mediating behavior can play in short-duration memory, but also how the DMTS procedure relates to problems of everyday life.

Repeating some verbal response in order to keep a verbal stimulus present is an example of the "phonological loop" illustrated in Figure 10.1. The verbal response produces a stimulus that elicits a sensory response called an echoic memory, which acts as a stimulus for the next repetition of the verbal response, which produces a stimulus that elicits an echoic memory, which acts as a stimulus for the next repetition of the verbal response, and so on. Note that the phonological loop depends on echoic memory, which is a form of sensory memory, as well as on mediating behavior (i.e., the verbal response, in this example).

A type of visual mediating behavior that is analogous to the phonological loop keeps the sensory effects of a visual stimulus present until a desired response can be made to that stimulus. This is the "visuo-spatial" sketch pad illustrated in Figure 10.1, also called "forming a mental image" in everyday speech. Although the words phonological loop, visuo-spatial sketch pad, and mental image may sound static, it is important to realize that they refer to behavior that, presumably, is no different in principle from, and hence subject to the same laws, as other behavior (Dadds, Bovbjerg, & Redd, 1997; Skinner, 1953, 1974).

Mediating behavior can take on many forms. In a DMTS task with pigeons, for example, some birds will develop different behavior following different sample stimuli (Blough, 1959; Eckerman, 1970), probably initially as superstitious behavior produced by adventitious reinforcement (p. 42) of these different patterns following different sample stimuli (cf. Morse & Skinner, 1957). In any case, these birds generally show high matching accuracies (i.e., above 90%) for retention intervals at least up to 10 seconds, while pigeons that do not develop differential behavior following different sample stimuli have matching accuracies at about chance levels at delays as short as five seconds. Moreover, any disruption of the differential behavior during the retention interval tends to decrease matching accuracy, thus further supporting the idea that the differential behavior is indeed mediating behavior. Perhaps similarly, preschool children do better at DMTS tasks when they know the names of the stimuli involved than when they do not (Spiker, 1956), suggesting that the children's overt or covert verbalizations of the names of the sample stimuli during the retention interval function as mediating behavior.

Mediating behavior appears to be important in situations other than DMTS. For example, it seems to play an important role in DRL schedules in timing the occurrence of successive responses so as to increase the rate of reinforcement. Much of what we call "thinking" is also mediating behavior, as when a problem produces a sequence of verbal behavior (e.g., performing numerical calculations) that leads to the solution of the problem.

The term precurrent behavior is sometimes used to refer to behavior that makes subsequent behavior more effective (e.g., Skinner, 1968, pp. 120, 124). Thus, mediating behavior is one type of precurrent behavior, but it is not the only type. Another type of precurrent behavior, for example, makes subsequent behavior more effective by increasing the probability that the individual will make contact with an S^D controlling that behavior. Examples of this type of precurrent behavior would be shining a flashlight to find a missing article and sniffing to detect an odor. Other examples are the private or covert attending responses discussed in Chapter 3.

DMTS studies on mediating behavior.   In many DMTS studies the mediating behavior (if any) that develops is left purely to chance. In others, however, specific responses have been deliberately conditioned as mediating behavior in order to better study mediating behavior. For example, keys other than those for the sample and comparison stimuli have been placed in the chamber for the individual to respond on during the retention interval. In one type of experiment, responding on these secondary keys produces the comparison stimuli on an FI schedule (in which the value of the FI is the length of the retention interval). Experiments have shown that kindergarten children perform much better on DMTS tasks if responding on different secondary keys corresponding to different sample stimuli that is required to produce the comparison stimuli (Parsons & Ferraro, 1977; Parsons, Taylor, & Joyce, 1981). These experiments demonstrate how mediating behavior of an arbitrary nature can act as an S^D controlling correct responses in a DMTS task.

Short-duration memory for behavior.   In all human societies it is important for people to be able to answer questions such as "What did you just do?" and, of course, most humans do learn to describe their own recent behavior. It is therefore of interest to know whether other animals can also learn to do so, since this could provide information about this ability and how it develops. One approach to this question has been to use a symbolic DMTS task in which the sample is the number of responses made to the center key. A trial begins with the center key lit and a specified number of responses (say N_1 or N_2) must be made in order for the rest of the trial to occur. On half of the trials at random the specified number is N_1 and on the other half it is N_2. If too few or too many responses are made during the time the key is lit, the key light turns off for a brief period and the trial is then restarted from the beginning. If the designated number of responses occurs the key light turns off and the retention interval begins. At the end of the retention interval the two side keys are lit, one red and the other green. If N_1 had been the number of responses to the center key, a response to the red key is reinforced; if N_2 had been the number of responses to the center key, a response to the green key is reinforced. Using this procedure with $N_1 = 0$ and $N_2 = 2$, it has been shown that a pigeon's memory for its recent behavior may last as long as one minute or more (Kramer, 1982).

Memory for recently emitted interresponse times (IRTs) has also been studied using a DMTS procedure. For example, in one procedure a VI 60-second schedule is programmed for responses terminating two classes of IRTs: short IRTs (e.g., between 1.5 and 2.0 seconds) and long IRTs (e.g., between 10.0 and 12.5 seconds). The individual responds on the center key which is transilluminated with white light. Half of the times at random that the schedule times out, any member of the short IRT class will be reinforced; on the other half any member of the long IRT class will be reinforced. Instead of primary reinforcement occurring when a member of the specific IRT class occurs, however, the center key is darkened and, after a retention interval, the two side keys are lighted. (This acts as conditioned reinforcement for the behavior of responding on the center key, as indicated in the previous chapter and as will be discussed in greater detail in the next chapter.) One of the side keys is green, the other red. A response to the green side key is reinforced if the most recent IRT was in the short IRT class; a response to the red side key is reinforced if the most recent IRT was in the long IRT class. Pigeons are often extremely accurate on this task with retention intervals a few seconds long, but their accuracy quickly decreases to chance levels as the retention interval is increased to eight seconds (Shimp, 1981).

Even when the retention interval is zero (i.e., when there is no retention interval), however, pigeons' accuracy on this task may be low. This can happen, of course, when the difference between the two IRT classes is so small that the bird cannot readily distinguish between them. But it can also occur when the two classes are quite distinct and the bird is accurately emitting IRTs in either or both classes. In these cases, therefore, the bird's accuracy in emitting the specified IRTs implies that it distinguishes between the two classes, but its behavior of matching the correct comparison stimulus to its IRTs suggests that it does not distinguish between the two classes. It is as though the bird "knows how" to emit IRTs of a specified length, but does not "know that" it has done so (Shimp, 1983). This may be related to the distinction some philosophers have made between "knowing how" and "knowing that" (e.g., Wittgenstein, 1953), and may therefore provide a way to experimentally study this interesting philosophical issue.

Short-duration memory for location. Animals in their natural environments do not typically encounter the types of stimuli (e.g., colored lights) used in many DMTS studies. Natural selection may not, therefore, have operated to enable animals to remember such stimuli well, but may have done so for stimuli occurring more commonly in the animals' natural environments. In particular, consider the survival value short-duration memory for specific locations would seem to have. It is advantageous to a fox that sees a rabbit jump into a bush, for example, since its chance of catching the rabbit depends on the fox remembering which bush the rabbit went into. Similarly, if the rabbit survives being chased by the fox, it would probably be to its advantage to remember where it has seen some tasty morsels of food just prior to being chased.

A number of techniques have been used to study short-duration memory for spatial cues or location (e.g., Kamil & Sargent, 1981; Olton, 1978). We can conceptualize all of these techniques essentially as DMTS tasks in which the sample is a particular location, and the comparison stimuli are that location in combination with other locations. The standard operant chamber for pigeons has been used to study DMTS of key location. At the beginning of a trial one of several keys is turned on as a sample. This is followed by a retention interval, after which the former sample key and another key are turned on. These keys remain lit until the bird pecks one of them. If the bird pecks the key that had been the sample, reinforcement occurs; if the bird pecks the other key, the trial terminates without reinforcement.

This procedure produces similar results with DMTS of key location as have been found with other types of sample stimuli (e.g., key color). For example, as with other sample stimuli, accuracy is a direct function of sample-presentation time and an inverse function of the length of the retention interval (Wilkie & Summers, 1982). Interestingly, sample-presentation times as low as 0.2 seconds produce above-chance matching accuracy in the pigeon, although the birds remember key location for only about four seconds. This fact should not be taken to mean, however, that their memory for location in their natural environments is necessarily that short. Significant locations to be remembered in the natural environment are typically larger and farther apart than are keys in an operant conditioning chamber; in addition, the animal can move around in the locations to be remembered in the natural environment.

There is an obvious mediating response that could account for pigeons' short-duration memory for key location: perhaps the birds simply orient toward the sample key (i.e., stare at it or keep some part of their body directed toward it) throughout the retention interval. Suppose, however, that in a chamber with four (or more) keys, two keys are lit simultaneously as the sample. Suppose further that at the end of the retention interval one of the keys that was part of the sample is lit along with a key that was not part of the sample. The correct response is, of course, a peck on the key that was part of the sample. Since the bird could have oriented toward only one of the two sample keys, there would be only a 50% chance that the one it oriented to was the one that occurred as a comparison stimulus. When this experiment is done, the results show that although accuracy is below the level obtained when only one sample stimulus is used, it is above the level that would be expected if the birds were orienting to one of the sample stimuli during the retention interval. In addition, the birds in this experiment have not been observed to engage in any orienting or other obvious overt mediating behavior (Smith, Attwood, & Niedorowski, 1982; Wilkie & Summers, 1982).

What appears to be an example of generalized identity matching in pigeons occurs in a DMTS procedure for key location. In one experiment the chamber contained nine keys (in a 3 × 3 matrix), but only four were used to teach the DMTS task. Then, after the birds were performing at a high level of accuracy with these keys, the other five keys were introduced. Most of the birds performed considerably above chance levels with the new sample stimuli the first time they occurred, suggesting that the pigeons had learned the concept "same key location" (Wilkie, 1983). This raises the possibility that it is easier for pigeons to learn the concept "same location" than it is for them to learn the concepts "same color," "same shape," and so forth.

Short-duration memory for events in a sequence. A DMTS procedure can also be used to, in effect, ask an individual about a specific event among several events that have just occurred in a sequence. Consider, for example, the following DMTS task. In a three-key operant conditioning chamber either the left, center, or right key is lit red. When a response occurs to that key the red light goes off and, after a brief interstimulus interval (ISI), either the left, center, or right key is lit green. A response to that key produces the retention interval, after which all three keys are lit either red or green. If they are red a response to the key that had previously been red is reinforced; if they are green a response to the key that had previously been green is reinforced. In effect, the individual is being asked "Which key was recently red?" or "Which key was recently green?" With pigeons, when the ISI is one second, accuracy for both questions is above chance for retention intervals up to three or four seconds (Jitsumori & Sugimoto, 1982). Accuracy for the first question is lower than that for the second question, but this appears to be because of the longer period between the presentation of the first sample and the comparison stimuli (i.e., the ISI plus the retention interval). The presentation of the second item does not appear to affect short-duration memory for the first item. Likewise, the presentation of the first item does not appear to affect short-duration memory for the second item.

A variation of the above procedure has been used to test a pigeon's memory for its own behavior with respect to specific stimuli that have occurred in a sequence. In this procedure the sample key is first red and turns off only after the pigeon pecks it either one or three times (the requirement varies randomly between the two numbers). After a brief ISI the sample key turns green and either one or three pecks (again, randomly determined) turns off the green stimulus light. After a retention interval, two comparison stimuli are turned on which are both the same color as one of the sample stimuli (i.e., either red or green). If one peck had been emitted to this sample stimulus, a response to the right comparison stimulus is reinforced; if three pecks had been emitted to this sample stimulus, a peck to the left comparison stimulus is reinforced. Thus the comparison stimuli probe an individual's memory for the number of responses emitted to the first or second sample stimulus in a sequence. Pigeons can remember up to several seconds the number of pecks recently made to each of the two different stimuli presented in succession. As might be expected, the more recent number of pecks is remembered better. In addition, retention is longer and more accurate when a number of responses is preceded or followed by the same number of responses than by a different number (Kramer, 1982).

Short-duration memory and directed forgetting.

There are a number of experiments purporting to show that humans can intentionally forget material they have recently learned (e.g., Bjork, 1972; Epstein, 1972; Johnson, 1994). These experiments generally involve giving individuals a list or lists of items (e.g., words or phrases) to recall later. At some point in the procedure an instruction or other stimulus is presented directing the individual to forget certain items. The stimulus might, for example, be a statement or cue indicating that the individual will not be tested on the designated items or that the designated items are unimportant to the task at hand. The details vary with the procedure being used. After the exposure to all the items, however, the individual is tested on all items—those designated to be forgotten as well as the other items. The typical result is that, on average, the items designated to be forgotten are recalled less well than the other items are. This phenomenon is called directed forgetting.

The simple explanation of directed forgetting is that humans engage in a form of mediating behavior called rehearsal, whereby they covertly and repetitively verbalize or visualize (i.e., image) items to be remembered. Rehearsal does two things: (1) as with all mediating behavior, it provides a surrogate stimulus for a response when the original stimulus (e.g., printed words, numbers, etc.) is no longer present; (2) it tends to cause the response to be learned through covert repetition and self-reinforcement. When given a stimulus indicating that they do not need to remember particular items (i.e. that they will not receive reinforcement for recalling those items), people stop rehearsing them or rehearse them less intensively; hence they reproduce them less well because they have been learned less well and mediating behavior that might provide a surrogate stimulus for them is not occurring. Thus, according to this explanation, directed forgetting is not really "forgetting" (at least not in the sense of a response that had once been learned being currently unavailable); instead, it is simply the unavailability of a response due to a failure to rehearse certain material.

There have been attempts to rule out this rehearsal explanation by giving individuals activities (e.g., counting backwards from a large number) designed to prevent rehearsal during the interval between the presentation of the learning items and the testing of them, and by giving the items in an incidental manner to disguise the experimenter's interest in having the individual learn them. It is unclear that these controls can be totally effective, however, because of the strong reinforcement most members of our culture have experienced for recalling verbal material, and hence for rehearsing it under a wide variety of conditions.

There are animal analogues—that is, animal experiments analogous to a human situation—of directed forgetting (Grant, 1981, 1982; Maki & Hegvik, 1980; Maki, Olson, & Rego, 1981; Roberts, Mazmanian, & Kraemer, 1984; Santi & Savich, 1985). The following summarizes an example from a pigeon experiment. In an otherwise standard DMTS task a second stimulus occurs immediately after the sample stimulus, and the comparison stimuli do not occur on all trials. The stimulus that occurs immediately after the sample stimulus is correlated with whether or not the comparison stimuli occur at the end of the retention interval, and hence whether there exists an opportunity for a correct matching response to be reinforced at the end of the retention interval. For example, in a red-green DMTS task a white circle or a white triangle might be projected onto the center key after the termination of the red or green sample stimulus. If the white circle has been presented, the red and green comparison stimuli occur at the end of the retention interval. If the white triangle has been presented, the comparison stimuli do not occur at the end of the retention interval. Since the white circle indicates the future occurrence of an opportunity to be reinforced for emitting a correct matching response, it should act as an instruction to "remember" the sample stimulus and hence perform well when the comparison stimuli occur; conversely, the white triangle, indicating that such an opportunity will not be forthcoming, should act as an instruction to "forget" the sample stimulus. To test whether or not directed forgetting has occurred, occasionally the comparison stimuli occur at the end of the retention interval when the retention interval was preceded by the "forget" stimulus. The percentage of correct responses on these probe trials is compared with the percentage when the "remember" stimulus occurs, and a significantly lower percent on these probe trials with the "forget" stimulus is taken as evidence for directed forgetting.

There is, however, a problem with the above experiment. The decrease in correct responding that occurs after the "forget" stimulus on probe trials appears to be due to the lack of reinforcement that typically occurs after the "forget" stimulus (Roper & Zentall, 1993). When reinforcement for some behavior unrelated to the conditional discrimination typically follows the "forget" stimulus, decreased correct responding on DMTS task does not occur (Kendrick, Rilling, & Stonebraker, 1981; Maki & Hegvik, 1980; Maki et al., 1981; Zentall, Roper, & Sherburne, 1995). It appears that when no reinforcement typically occurs after the "forget" stimulus, a discrimination develops whereby mediating behavior occurs after the "remember" stimulus but not after the "forget" stimulus. When, however, reinforcement typically occurs after the "forget" stimulus the mediating behavior is reinforced adventitiously, and so maintained—that is, a discrimination between the "remember" and "forget" stimulus with regard

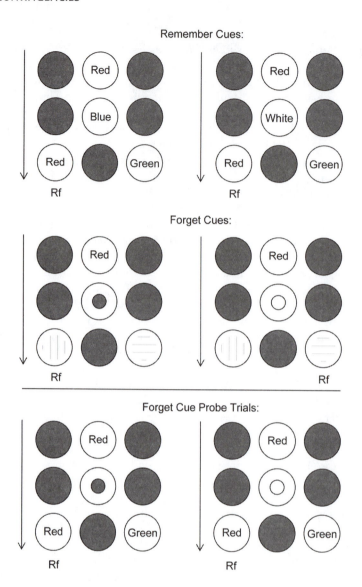

FIGURE 10.3. Experimental design for studying directed forgetting in the pigeon. The two sections above the horizontal line illustrate the sequence of events on "remember" trials and "forget" trials. On a remember trial the center key is first either red or green and the two side keys are dark. During a delay interval, the center key is either blue or white. Finally, the center key is dark, and one side key is red and the other is green. Reinforcement occurs if the bird responds on the key that matches the original sample. A forget trial starts out exactly like a remember trial. During the delay interval, however, the center key has either a dot or a circle on it. After the delay, vertical lines appear on one key and horizontal lines appear on the other key. If the dot was present during the delay interval, reinforcement occurs following a response on the key with the vertical lines, while if the circle was present reinforcement occurs following a response on the key with the horizontal lines. Probe trials, illustrated below the horizontal dividing line, are like forget trials except that the red and green key lights are presented instead of the vertical and horizontal lines. (From Roper et al., 1995)

to mediating behavior does not develop. This is not to say that the animals do not discriminate between the "remember" and the "forget" stimuli; they do, because they respond more on the "forget" stimulus than on the "remember" stimulus when the forget stimulus is followed by a simple simultaneous discrimination involving stimuli other than those used in the DMTS task (Zentall et al., 1995).

Figure 10.3 diagrams an experimental arrangement involving reinforcement after a "forget" stimulus that does, however, result in a decrease in correct DMTS performance by pigeons on probe trials after the "forget" stimulus (Roper, Kaiser, & Zentall, 1995). As the figure shows, this arrangement involves two—rather than one—forget stimuli that are comparison stimuli for a second conditional discrimination (i.e., a second matching task). The second conditional discrimination is not a delayed one, and therefore should not produce mediating behavior that competes with the mediating behavior for the DMTS task. Nevertheless, as mentioned, the second conditional discrimination does produce the directed-forgetting effect and thus must in some way prevent or suppress the mediating behavior involved in the DMTS task. Exactly how it does this is not known; one possibility, however, is that the behavior of attending to the sample stimulus (i.e., either of the two "forget" stimuli) in the second matching task is incompatible with the mediating behavior in the DMTS task.

Species differences in DMTS.

DMTS seems related to our intuitive notion of "intelligence." Matching problems, often in the form of multiple-choice questions, are common on academic and intelligence tests. Moreover, memory is often regarded as an important component of intelligence. Thus, there is considerable interest in how different species perform on DMTS tasks. We are naturally curious as to whether species that are related to us or resemble us in some way, such as in the sizes and structures of their brains, are more intelligent than other species are.

For many learning scientists, intelligence is too vague a concept to be of any scientific use. These scientists are still interested in how different species compare in DMTS tasks, however, for the simple reason that it is important to test the generality across species of all learning phenomena. Because of its complex nature and the reliable results DMTS produces with at least some species, the question of the species generality of DMTS is particularly interesting. It should be kept in mind, however, that it is very difficult to compare species on DMTS tasks partly because of the problem of equating stimuli and responses and behavior during the delay interval across species. For example, the capability of a given species on DMTS will be underestimated if matching stimuli are used that are not ideally suited to the animals' sense receptors, of if matching responses are used that are not ideally suited to the animals' motor responses.

Keeping the above caution in mind, there is evidence that primates and dolphins can maintain accurate DMTS performance over longer retention intervals than pigeons can. As mentioned earlier, pigeons that do not engage in obvious mediating behavior during the retention interval do not exhibit above-chance matching accuracy at retention intervals much above 5 seconds. Some capuchin monkeys, on the other hand, have exhibited high matching accuracies at retention intervals as great as 120 seconds (D'Amato & O'Neill, 1971); and, in one case, even up to 180 seconds (D'Amato & Worsham, 1972). Moreover, a bottlenose dolphin exhibited a high DMTS accuracy at a retention interval of 120 seconds (Herman & Gordon, 1974). Interestingly, while visual sample and comparison stimuli were used in the procedures with the pigeons and monkeys, auditory stimuli were used with the dolphin because of its highly developed auditory sensory system. When the dolphin moved into a region between two speakers in its tank and pressed a start paddle, the sample stimulus was projected simultaneously through both speakers. Following the retention interval, two comparison stimuli were projected sequentially through the two speakers, with the correct stimulus appearing first or second and on the right or left speaker randomly. The correct response was pressing a paddle located next to the speaker at which the correct stimulus had occurred.

While it is tempting to attribute the superior DMTS performances of monkeys and dolphins over that of pigeons to the differences in the complexities of their nervous systems, other possible explanations should not be ruled out. In particular, we do not know the extent to which mediating behavior may have contributed to these superior performances. It is known, however, that mediating behavior can increase the length of the retention interval over which pigeons show accurate DMTS performance to 10 seconds (Blough, 1959). Whether it can increase it to the level achieved by some monkeys and dolphins remains to be determined. It should also be noted that, as mentioned earlier, when the bird's own behavior is the sample stimulus, pigeons' DMTS accuracies are above chance levels at retention intervals up to at least 60 seconds. Therefore, the complexity of the nervous system per se may not be a factor in determining the maximum possible interval over which short-duration memory operates— except insofar as animals with more complex nervous systems may be able to engage in more complex mediating behavior.

Long-Duration Memory

Standard matching-to-sample procedures, as illustrated above, indicate that stimulus control is quickly lost as the interval between comparison and sample stimuli increases. Yet under some conditions animals show remarkable memory—that is, conditional control by stimuli— over long durations in which those stimuli, and any apparent mediating behavior initiated by them, are absent.

Memory of previous trials.   In discrete-trials situations, animals indicate memory for outcomes of earlier trials. A fairly simple demonstration of this uses a runway (see Figure 4.1, p. 58). The measure of interest is the time for an animal to go from the start box to the goal box which may or may not contain a reinforcer. If a stimulus reliably correlated with food in the goal box is present in the start box, a food-deprived rat will leave the start box and traverse the runway more quickly than if a stimulus correlated with the absence of food is present. Interestingly, the outcome of the previous trial can serve as such a stimulus. For example, if a laboratory rat is exposed to a sequence of trials in which the presence and absence of reinforcement alternates, the rat will alternate its running speed between fast and slow, accordingly, on successive trials. That is, the rat will tend to run more rapidly on trials in which food is in the goal box and more slowly on trials in which it is not. Moreover, rats will come to do this even if the time between successive trials is as much as 24 hours (Capaldi, 1985; Capaldi & Lynch, 1966).

Rats exposed to runway trials also can learn sequences of reinforcement and nonreinforcement that are more complex than simple alternation (although apparently not when the intertrial interval is as long as 24 hours). For example, consider the sequence FFFN, where F indicates a trial in which the goal box contains food and N indicates a trial in which it does not. Although trials may be separated by as much as 30 seconds, and there is no stimulus correlated at the beginning of each trial with the presence or absence of food in the goal box, rats learn to run rapidly during the first three trials but run slowly during the last trial. If sessions of FFFN trials alternate irregularly with sessions of NFFFN trials (with sessions separated by 20 minutes), rats still run slowly on the last trial relative to the previous F trials, demonstrating that the number of prior F trials can exert discriminative control in a runway.

This conclusion is supported further by the fact that this behavior pattern persists even when the type of food in the goal box and the length of the intertrial interval vary (Capaldi, 1993; Capaldi & Lynch, 1966; Capaldi & Miller, 1988).

To take another example, consider the sequences FNNNN and NNNNF, which are alternated irregularly over successive sessions with 20 minutes between sessions and 30 seconds between trials. The only stimulus correlated with the presence of food on the last trial in a session is whether or not food was present on the first trial. Nevertheless, rats learn to run rapidly on the last trial of a session beginning with no food and to run slowly on the last trial of a session beginning with food. In an effect similar to an FI scallop, running speed gradually increases over the N trials, but more so over the N trials preceding sessions ending in reinforcement than in sessions ending in nonreinforcement (Capaldi & Verry, 1981).

Moreover, not only can the outcomes of previous trials control running speeds on current trials, but previous sequences of outcomes apparently can control how the outcomes of previous trials control running speeds on current trials. For example, if specific sequences given as much as 20 minutes earlier are correlated with specific subsequent sequences, the earlier sequences will control running speeds on trials within the current sequence (Capaldi, 1992; Capaldi, Miller, Alprekin, & Barry, 1990; Haggbloom, Birmingham, & Scanton, 1992).

Hidden reinforcers. An animal that sees food being hidden in a particular location may go back and obtain the food long after the event. This situation can be classified as a spatial DMTS task in which viewing the food being hidden in a given location is the sample stimulus, and that same location at a later time is the correct comparison stimulus among a large number of incorrect comparison stimuli (i.e., other locations).

The capacity of some animals to come under the conditional control of spatial stimuli over extremely long time intervals has been studied in several types of experimental arrangements. In one procedure, a bird such as a marsh tit or chickadee is allowed to store a few seeds behind opaque flaps covering holes drilled into a vertical board. Each hole holds only one seed, and some of the holes already have seeds in them. Several hours after the bird has stored its seeds, it is allowed to retrieve them. The typical result is that the bird shows a greater-than-chance probability of first checking holes in which it stored or encountered seeds, with no difference between the probabilities of checking holes with stored or encountered seeds (Shettleworth & Krebs, 1986). Thus, marsh tits and chickadees are able to retrieve seeds that they have hid or merely encountered several hours prior to retrieving them.

In another laboratory procedure for studying long-duration memory, a marsh tit or chickadee is allowed to store seeds in a tray of moss that is divided into sectors. At the end of a 24-hour delay interval, the bird shows a greater-than-chance probability of searching sectors in which it stored seeds (Sherry, 1987; Sherry, Krebs, & Cowie 1981). In addition, chickadees that store preferred (sunflower) and less preferred (safflower) seeds in the moss show a greater-than-chance probability of searching in sectors that the former but not the latter are stored (Sherry, 1987). Apparently, chickadees remember over a long delay not only where they stored food, but also what kind of food they stored.

The radial maze. Another procedure demonstrating long-duration memory might be classified as a type of delayed oddity-matching procedure, in that the individual receives reinforcement for going to a location in which food has not been encountered previously. An apparatus widely used in this type of procedure is called a radial maze, which consists of eight or more straight arms (or alleys) extending radially, like the spokes of a wheel, from a central platform. A reinforcer is placed at the end of each arm prior to each trial, and the trial ends when the animal has found and consumed all the reinforcers (see Fig. 10.4). A rat given sev-

(A) (B)

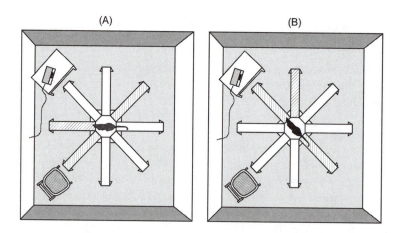

Figure 10.4. An eight-arm radial maze. A) The shaded areas indicate arms the rat has entered. B) The maze has been rotated, and the rat re-enters an arm (the one going toward the radio, lower left) it entered previously, even though it would not have done so if the maze had not been rotated—indicating that the position of the arm, not scent, is the stimulus controlling entry into the arm. (From Olton, 1977)

eral trials in this apparatus will soon start entering arms in which it has not yet obtained reinforcement and avoiding arms in which it has obtained reinforcement (Olton & Samuelson, 1976; Olton & Collison, 1979; Olton, Handelman, & Walker, 1981), even if a delay is interpolated during a trial (Cook, Brown, & Riley, 1985). The animal does not require smell or any other immediately present stimulus when choosing arms in which it has not obtained food. If the arms of the maze are rotated between choices, the animal will enter arms that are in different positions than arms it has previously entered even though this means that it now enters arms that it previously entered (note in Fig. 10.4 the prominent stimuli outside the maze that are correlated with position).

The rat performing in this type of maze is clearly showing memory for location, but not necessarily memory for the location of food per se. Rats that are not food deprived and that have never found food in a radial maze also show a strong preference for entering arms that they have not recently visited (Wilkie et al., 1992), although this preference may be stronger for rats that are food deprived (Timberlake & White, 1990) or that have received food at the ends of the arms (FitzGerald, Isler, Rosenberg, Oettinger, & Bättig, 1985). It appears that the rat in the radial maze is engaging in the phylogenetic behavior of "exploring its surroundings" or "patrolling its territory." Clearly the survival and propagation of animals that explore or patrol depends on stimuli paired with places the animal has recently been becoming aversive and stimuli that have been paired with places it has not recently been being reinforcing. (Chapter 16 contains a more detailed treatment of the evolution of phylogenetic behavior in the natural environment.)

TIMING

Timing is another way that an absent event can control behavior. Consider the following situation. You have put food in the oven to cook, the stove timer is broken, you have no watch, and there are no functional clocks in the house. With no external stimulus to rely on, you must take the food out only after it is cooked but before it is overcooked. In this situation an event has occurred (you have put food in the oven), and some specific time after the event reinforcement (properly cooked food) occurs contingent on responding to the event (taking food out of the oven) at the right time (after the food is properly cooked but before it is overcooked). The original stimulus (food being placed in the oven) is absent—so how does responding to that stimulus occur with a high probability (i.e., with a high degree of consistency) at the right time? To put the question another way, how is it that time appears to act as an S^D in situations such as this?

Since time is not a stimulus, there must be stimuli that change in a fairly regular manner such that a functional S^D for the response occurs at about the time that the response is typically reinforced. Humans have constructed many types of artificial clocks—for example, sundial, sand, water, candle, pendulum, spring, electric, quartz crystal, and atomic clocks (Barnett, 1998)—to provide temporal stimuli that regulate the times at which particular behavior occurs. There are also natural clocks, such as the position of the sun, that control behavior in much the same way that artificial clocks do. Using the "encoding" terminology introduced earlier in this chapter, we might say that when a response is reinforced this event and the time indicated by some artificial or natural clock are encoded. When a response occurs under temporal control we may say that the response has been retrieved by a clock displaying a time that has been paired with the reinforcement of that response.

Endogenous Clocks

Although timing may be more precise in the presence of external clocks, it also occurs in their absence (as in the above hypothetical example of taking food out of the oven at the right time without the assistance of any external timing device). In order for timing to occur in the absence of an external clock, there must be clocks either within the individual or as part of its behavior. Such clocks are called endogenous clocks.

Behavioral clocks. Mediating behavior, similar to mediating behavior that acts as an S^D for a correct response in DMTS (as described earlier in this chapter), can act as a clock. A familiar example is slowly reciting "one thousand and one, one thousand and two, one thousand and three . . . " to count off some specified number of seconds before emitting a response (e.g., to count off 10 seconds before pulling the rip cord of a parachute). The people in this example learn a verbal rule to perform this counting behavior when it is necessary to measure seconds and a suitable external timer is unavailable. Individuals may also engage in mediating behavior that does not stem from a verbal rule. This type of mediating behavior often takes on an idiosyncratic form. Between responses on a DRL schedule, for example, a monkey was observed to regularly jerk its head from side to side; another monkey rhythmically licked at its water bottle (Hodos, Ross, & Brady, 1962); and a rat was observed to nibble at its tail while holding it in its front paws and moving its mouth along the surface of the tail (Laties, Weiss, Clark, & Reynolds, 1965). Repetitive behavior that occurs between responses on DRL schedules seems to be acting as a clock because interfering with the behavior—for example, suppressing the rat's tail nibbling in the above example by coating the tail with a substance put on wires to keep rats from chewing them—disrupts the timing behavior, in that interresponse times (IRTs) tend to shorten so that fewer reinforcements occur.

It is easy to see how mediating behavior is shaped automatically on a DRL schedule. Mediating behavior tends to cause IRTs to be longer, thus increasing the probability of reinforcement on DRL. A chain consisting of mediating behavior followed by the response that produces reinforcement on the DRL schedule tends to be reinforced, whereas responses that are not preceded by mediating behavior tend not to be reinforced.

Physiological clocks.   Mediating behavior is effective for timing short intervals, but decreases in effectiveness as the length of the interval to be timed increases (as will be discussed in Chapter 11, long chains of behavior are maintained less effectively than short chains). Within the body there are physiological processes that act as clocks and that are responsible for timing long intervals. There appear to be two types of physiological clocks: interval and phase (Carr & Wilkie, 1997; Gallistel, 1990, pp. 240–241).

Interval timing.   Interval timing is involved when responding varies as a function of the time between two events, such as the time between two reinforcements on an FI schedule. We can see the effect of some sort of interval physiological clock in the FI scallop (i.e., the tendency for responding to be low after reinforcement and then to gradually increase as the time remaining to the next reinforced response decreases [see Chapter 4]). Two pieces of evidence support the operation of a physiological clock in timing responding on an FI schedule.

- A brief timeout introduced right after reinforcement on an FI schedule will eliminate the postreinforcement pause; that is, after the timeout, responding starts at about the rate it would have been at if the timeout had not occurred (Ferster & Skinner, 1957, pp. 221-222). This suggests that some time-correlated stimulus is an S^D for responding to resume following reinforcement on an FI schedule.
- If an external clock is provided during an FI schedule— for example, by projecting through the response key a horizontal slit that gradually increases in length, reaching its maximum when the next reinforcement is set up—a more uniform scalloped response pattern develops (Ferster & Skinner, 1957, pp. 266–274). This suggests that in the absence of an external clock, an internal (physiological) clock accounts for the scalloped response patterns typical of FI performance. The irregular shape of most scallops during FI in the absence of an external clock indicates that the physiological clock does not keep perfect time.

An interval physiological clock is similar to a stopwatch in that it is resettable. The interval physiological clock operating during an FI schedule, for example, resets after each reinforcement.

Phase timing.   While interval physiological clocks act like stopwatches, there are other types of physiological clocks that cycle continuously, much like a standard clock that keeps track of the time of day (Aschoff, 1981). A physiological clock called a circadian clock cycles approximately every 24 hours. The circadian clock regulates the sleep-wake cycle, daily eating patterns, and other behavior that occurs on a daily basis. Many animals tend to show a large peak in their activity levels about every 24 hours. The proof that this periodicity in activity level is regulated by a physiological clock is that it occurs even in the absence of any periodic external stimulus, such as a light that turns on every 12 hours and off every 12 hours. In the absence of a periodic external stimulus, however, the circadian clock is not a precise 24-hour clock, but is more like a clock that runs a little too fast or a little too slow. Thus, in the absence of a periodic external stimulus, a circadian clock will tend to gradually lose time or gradually gain time relative to a 24-hour clock. If an animal is presented with a light-dark cycle of 24-hours, however, that animal's circadian clock appears to adjust to that cycle; or, at least, the animal's activity level fluctuates more precisely on the basis of a 24-hour clock. When a physiological clock becomes synchronized to an external periodic stimulus, we say that that external periodic stimulus has entrained that physiological clock. Thus, a 24-hour light-dark cycle will entrain an animal's circadian clock (Gallistel, 1990, pp. 223–231).

Circadian clocks produce internal temporal stimuli that acquire control over responding in the same way that external stimuli do. For example, if food is available daily at a particular time, animals will become active shortly before that time every day even if there are no external stimuli present that have been paired with food delivery. Suppose that instead of being made available every 24 hours, however, food is made available every 19 hours—again, with no external food-correlated stimulus present. In this case, each time food occurs there is a different stimulus present on the circadian clock. The result is that animals will not show a peak in activity just before reinforcement is due; rather, if there is a peak at all, it will be small and will tend to occur before the position on the circadian clock at which food previously occurred; that is, it will tend to occur in the presence of a temporal stimulus similar to the one most recently paired with food (Gallistel, 1990, pp. 274).

The operations of interval and phase physiological clocks lead to interesting results. Interval clocks produce timing of events that are separated by perhaps about an hour or less. Circadian clocks produce timing of events that are separated by about 24 hours, give or take 2 hours or so. In addition, there may be other physiological phase clocks that have even longer cycles (e.g., monthly) and that provide distinctive stimuli for timing events that occur regularly but less frequently than once a day.

Time-Place/Response Learning

Just as individuals may learn to make different responses in the presence of different external stimuli, individuals may also learn to make different responses to different times on an endogenous clock. Often making different responses involves going to different locations. We refer to learning to go to different places at different times as time-place learning. For example, if reinforcement is made contingent on responding on one operandum at one particular time and on another operandum at another time, animals will tend to respond more on each operandum at the time that reinforcement has previously been available for responding on that operandum (Wilkie, Mak, & Saksida, 1994). This is an example of time-place learning, as well as time-response learning, because the operandums are located at different positions in the experimental chamber (see Figure 10.5).

MEMORY OF MULTIPLE STIMULUS DISCRIMINATIONS

Barring brain disease or trauma, we do not forget our own names or those of close relatives and friends. We have had too many conditioning trials for such forgetting to occur. It is common, however, to fail to recall the name of someone we have met only recently. The reason for this appears to be response competition or response interference—the tendency for some responses that have been conditioned to a particular stimulus to suppress or interfere with other responses that have been conditioned to that or similar stimuli (Osgood, 1946, 1949; Watkins, 1979).

To learn the name of a new acquaintance, for example, means learning to say that person's name when seeing his or her face. We have learned to say different names to many faces, however, and there is considerable stimulus generalization among faces. Thus, the face of a new acquaintance tends to evoke not only his or her name, but also other names that have generalized to his or her features. These other names tend to compete with and suppress the name of the new acquaintance. Subjectively, we may literally feel that the response is "on the tip of our tongue"—about to be emitted, but for some reason cannot be emitted. The reason it cannot be emitted is that other verbal responses are interfering with and suppressing it.

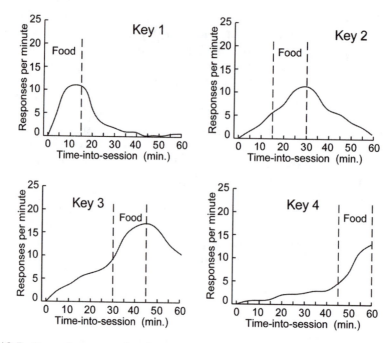

FIGURE 10.5. Time-place responding by a pigeon. Different keys labeled sequentially provide food on a variable-interval schedule at different times, as indicated. (From Wilkie et al., 1994; Carr & Wilkie, 1997)

Numerous experiments have provided evidence for the role of response competition in the forgetting of verbal material. These experiments generally involve having people learn lists of verbal responses and then attempt to recall them.

Retroactive and Proactive Interference

One type of list that people learn in memory experiments consists of paired associates—two verbal paired items in which one item (e.g., a word) is a response to be learned to the other item that is the stimulus for that response. Consider the following two lists of paired associates (in which the item on the left is the stimulus and the item on the right is the response):

LIST 1
      Cake - Door
      Book - Road

      . . .

      Sand - Milk

LIST 2
      Cake - Ball
      Book - Goat

      . . .

      Sand - Rope

Suppose that a person learns List 1 (i.e., learns to emit the verbal response "door" when presented with the verbal stimulus "cake," etc.), and then learns List 2 (i.e., learns to emit the verbal response "ball" when presented with the verbal stimulus "cake," etc.). If we then ask the individual to emit the List 1 responses to the stimuli that they had been paired with, the List 2 responses will tend to interfere with the occurrence of the List 1 responses. Thus the List 1 responses will be recalled less well than they would have if the individual had not learned List 2. This tendency for subsequent learning to interfere with the emission of previously learned responses is called retroactive interference (or retroactive inhibition). Similarly, if we ask the individual to emit the List 2 responses to the stimuli they had been paired with, the List 1 responses will tend to interfere with the occurrence of the List 2 responses. Thus, the List 2 responses will be recalled less well than they would have if the individual had not learned List 1. This tendency for prior learning to interfere with the emission of subsequently learned responses is called proactive interference (or proactive inhibition).

We sometimes experience response interference in the form of intruding responses. When we attempt to remember an item—the name of a particular person—we are frequently aware of other items intruding (e.g., when we engage in a soliloquy of the following sort: "His name is 'Bob,' no, not 'Bob,' 'Jack,' no, not 'Jack' . . . [etc.]"). These intruding names probably interfere with emitting the correct name. It is perhaps only when these responses extinguish, through being emitted without being reinforced, that the correct response can finally emerge.

Retroactive and proactive interference have been demonstrated in numerous experiments. In addition to occurring in paired associate tasks as described above, they also occur when individuals learn serial lists (Underwood, 1945, 1957). For example, the learning of one list of words will interfere with the learning and recall of a new list of words, which in turn will interfere with the recall of previously learned lists. The build up of proactive interference can cause increasing difficulty in learning and remembering new material (Underwood, 1957). It should be noted, however, that this statement applies to the learning of arbitrary responses— that is, what in everyday speech we call rote learning. Most meaningful material to be learned—as in a university course—is interconnected logically, so that the equivalence-class processes described in Chapter 9 should enable previous learning to benefit subsequent learning and remembering (provided, of course, that the logical connections are emphasized or made distinct).

In addition to occurring between lists of items, interference also occurs within lists as will now be discussed.

The Serial-Position Curve

If an individual is presented with a sequence of items to learn, the first few items and the last few items will tend to be remembered better than the middle items. The tendency to remember the first few items better than the middle items is called the primacy effect, and the tendency to remember the last few items better than the middle items is called the recency effect.

Primacy and recency effects are commonly demonstrated by presenting a list of words (or made-up words called nonsense syllables; e.g., "wog") to an individual, and then testing his or her memory of those items. There are several ways to conduct the test. One is the repetition method: the list is cycled through repeatedly at a fixed rate with the individual trying to vocally anticipate each item before it appears. Another procedure, called the free-recall method, involves presenting the list only once and then asking the individual to try to recall the items in any order. In what is called the serial-position curve, the function relating the probability of getting an item correct to the position of that item on the list is U-shaped; that is, the function starts high, decreases, and then increases.

One of the earliest scientific findings about learning (Ebbinghaus, 1902), the serial-position curve has been replicated in numerous experiments (Underwood, 1966, pp. 490–491). In addition to the standard experimental demonstrations described above, the curve is readily apparent in common memory tasks such as the spelling of long words (Jensen, 1962), reciting the names of United States presidents (Roediger & Crowder, 1976), and recalling scores of sports figures (Baddeley & Hitch, 1977). Typically studied using verbal stimuli with humans, the curve has also been found using visual and auditory stimuli with animals (Buchanan, Gill, & Braggio, 1981; Kesner & Novak, 1982; Sands & Wright, 1980; Wright, 1999; Wright &

Rivera, 1997; Wright, Santiago, Sands, Kendrick, & Cook, 1985). In these studies a series of arbitrary visual or auditory stimuli are followed by a test in which the animal receives reinforcement for responding to stimuli that were in the sequence and no reinforcement for responding to stimuli that were not in the sequence. Figure 10.6 illustrates the use of this procedure with a monkey receiving a series of auditory stimuli followed by a test for the monkey's memory of the stimuli in the sequence. Figure 10.7 shows typical data from this experiment.

No definitive explanation for the serial position curve has emerged. It appears to be at least partly due to distinctive stimuli present at the beginning and end of a list (Ebenholtz, 1972; Murdock, 1960) and the occurrence of proactive and retroactive interference between responses to stimuli within a list (Wright & Rivera, 1997).

Retrieval-Induced Forgetting

Responses do not have to intrude in order to interfere with other responses. In what is called retrieval-induced forgetting, a response suppresses a target response simply by being emitted some time earlier than the presentation of the stimulus for the target response. Suppose that individuals are first presented with category names (e.g., "Fruit") and, for each category, they are asked to generate exemplars beginning with certain letters (e.g., "O," "P"). Then they are presented with the same categories, but new letters (e.g., "A," "B"). The result is that if the individuals had to generate only one exemplar for each category in the first task, their performance on the second task is improved (i.e., they generate correct exemplars more rapidly) over what it would have been had they not been given the first task (or had been given a control task instead); but if they had to generate as many as four exemplars per category in the first task, their performance in the second task is impaired (Blaxton & Neely, 1983). Exemplars must actually be generated, not merely emitted under textual control (e.g., read), in order to interfere with the generation of subsequent exemplars.

Retrieval-induced forgetting can also be demonstrated using a paired-associates procedure and using a free-recall procedure. We will consider each in turn.

A paired-associates procedure. Suppose that instead of the procedure outlined above, individuals are first given a paired-associates task in which the stimulus items are category names and the response items are exemplars of the categories (e.g., fruit-orange, fruit-ba-

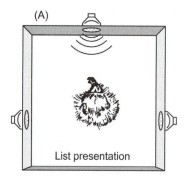 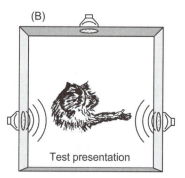

FIGURE 10.6. Test of the auditory serial-position effect in a rhesus monkey. A) A sequence of sounds (e.g., ping pong, walking on gravel, Big Ben, rooster, busy signal) is presented through the center speaker. B) One sound at a time is presented through both side speakers, and reinforcement occurs if the monkey touches either side speaker when a sound from the original list occurs. (From Wright & Rivers, 1997)

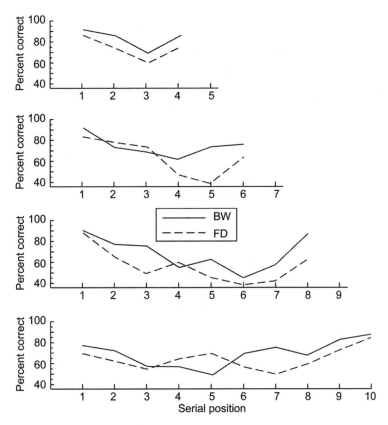

FIGURE 10.7. Serial-position curves from two monkeys (BW and FD). The mean percentage of correct responses at each serial position from lists of sizes 4, 6, 8, and 20 are shown for each of two monkeys that participated in the experiment illustrated in Figure 10.6. Note that both primacy and recency effects occur with each list size. (From Wright & Rivera, 1997)

nana, . . . , animal-sheep, animal-giraffe. Next they are presented with some of the category names with a partial prompt (e.g., the first two letters) for one of the exemplars that had been paired with each presented category name (e.g., fruit-or). Finally, after a "retention interval" during which they engage in a task designed to prevent rehearsal of the learned material, they are presented with all the category names and asked to recall as many exemplars as they can that had been paired with the presented category names during the initial learning task. The result is that (assuming a 20-minute retention interval) they will generate about 11% fewer of the exemplars that had not been practiced in the second task than corresponding exemplars in categories that were not included in the second task (Anderson, Bjork, & Bjork, 1994; Anderson & Spellman, 1995). Thus, practicing a response to a stimulus in a given category can inhibit or interfere with other responses to stimuli in that category.

Even more remarkable, practicing a response in a given category can inhibit a response in a category different from that of the practiced response (Anderson & Spellman, 1995). That is, inhibition caused by practicing a stimulus-response relation in one category can spread across categories. This phenomenon is illustrated in Figure 10.8. The top part of the figure, labeled the "Related Condition," illustrates two stimulus categories, "green" and "soups," along with two responses that are taught to each of these stimulus categories. (In an actual experiment there would be a more than two stimulus categories, and more than two responses to be learned in each category.) The response "emerald" is then practiced to the stimulus "green." This results not only in the inhibition of "lettuce," but also in the inhibition of "mushroom" because it belongs to the same category as "lettuce," namely, "vegetable," even though "vegetable" was not one of the stimulus categories taught. The response "chicken" is not inhibited, however, because it does not belong to a category that is related closely enough to "lettuce."

The bottom part of Figure 10.8 illustrates a control condition called the "Unrelated Condition." As with the Related Condition, the bottom part shows two stimulus categories, "loud" and "soups," along with two responses that are taught to each of these stimulus categories. Following the initial training, the response "siren" is practiced, resulting in the inhibition of "grenade." Unlike the case in the "Related Condition," however, "mushroom" is not inhibited. The reason for this difference between the two conditions is that "mushroom" is related to "lettuce" (through the category "vegetable") but not to "grenade."

One point to note in examining Figure 10.8 is that retrieval-induced forgetting tends to spread across equivalence classes as defined in Chapter 9 (p. 188). Note that, for example, the words "green," "lettuce," "vegetable," "mushroom" form an equivalence class for anyone who has learned a language (assuming that the individual is familiar with these words or the corresponding words in his or her language). In Chapter 9 (p. 189) we mentioned the phenomenon

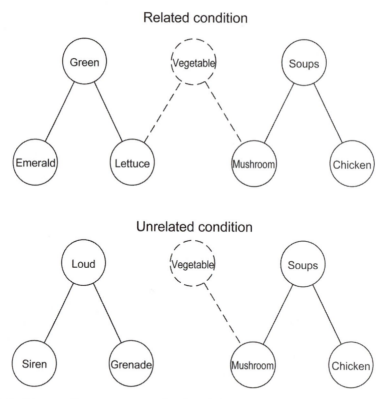

FIGURE 10.8. Diagram illustrating retrieval-induced forgetting across categories. In the Related Condition, the solid lines indicate the practiced stimulus response pair. The dotted lines indicate the relationship of two items through a category name ("vegetable") that was never presented in the experiment. As a result of this relationship, the response "mushroom" to the stimulus "soups" is suppressed as well as the response "lettuce" by the practice (i. e., retrieval) of the response "emerald" to the stimulus "green." The Unrelated Condition is a control condition. The response "grenade" is suppressed because of the practice of "siren," to the stimulus "loud," but the response "mushroom" to the stimulus "soups" is not suppressed because it is not related to "grenade." (From Anderson & Spellman, 1995)

termed transfer of function, whereby functions established for one member of an equivalence class transfer automatically to other members. In this section we have seen that apparently when one member of an equivalence class is inhibited through retrieval-induced forgetting, all members are inhibited. Thus, it appears that retrieval-induced forgetting is another example of a process that transfers across equivalence classes.

We may well wonder why, from an evolutionary point of view, retrieval-induced forgetting occurs—and especially why it occurs across equivalence classes. The reason it occurs may be that it tends to prevent us from following unproductive lines of thought in solving a problem. Moreover, inhibition may spread the way it does across equivalence classes because if one member of an equivalence class is irrelevant to solving a particular problem, other members are also likely to be irrelevant.

A free-recall procedure.   In the free-recall method of studying retrieval-induced forgetting, an individual is given a list of words to study and then asked to recall as many words that were on the list as he or she can. Not too surprisingly, words individuals emit first tend to be recalled better (e.g., more quickly) than words they recall later. More remarkably, if we prompt certain words to occur early in a recall test by presenting the first letters of those words, other words tend to be suppressed—that is, they have a lower probability of being emitted than would be the case if some words had not been prompted first. Thus, retrieval-induced forgetting occurs with the free-recall method as well as with the paired-associates method of learning and remembering.

Retrieval-induced forgetting appears not to be affected by whether the retrieved responses are strongly or weakly conditioned. The retrieval of a weakly conditioned response—for example, one that has been studied for a shorter period of time—will suppress a response it has much as the retrieval of a strongly conditioned response will (Bäuml, 1997). Moreover, responses that have been learned appear not to induce forgetting unless and until they are retrieved. For example, learning lists of words after learning an original list of words does not seem to interfere with free recall of the original list. If the individual practices recalling the subsequent lists, however, the amount of forgetting of the original list is a direct function of the number of new lists the individual learns after learning the original list (Bäuml, 1996).

FALSE MEMORIES

Although various recording and record keeping devices, including computers, provide popular analogies for memory, these analogies all have serious limitations. It is obvious to everyone who has struggled to memorize information for a test that if memory is a recording device it is clearly an imperfect one. Nowhere do analogies between recording devices and memory break down more dramatically, however, than in the fact that it is possible to have false memories; that is, strong memories for events and situations that they never actually experienced. That false memory is a real phenomenon is indicated by the fact that there are several confirmed methods for inducing false memories. These demonstrations underscore the care that should be taken when using memory (e.g., eyewitness reports) in the investigation of crimes, alleged childhood sexual abuse, and other serious social matters (Wells et al., 2000).

Intruding Associates

Perhaps the simplest method for creating a false memory is ask individuals to read over a list of words that have frequently occurred in close association with a word that is not present in the list. Many individuals will then report that the word whose associates were in the list was also in the list (Deese, 1959; Roediger & McDermott, 1995). For example if the list contained the words "thread," "pen," "eye," "thimble," and "sharp" many people will assert that they remember seeing the word "needle" on the list even though in reality it was not there. Clearly this follows from principles already discussed in this book. Although "needle" was not on this list, words that tend to evoke it were. Thus, the response "needle" was strongly evoked by words on the list and became conditioned to other stimuli paired with the list (e.g., the word "list" in the question "Recite the words you recall seeing on the list.").

Embedded False Information

False memories can be induced by questions that contain false information (Loftus, 1975). For example, after seeing a video clip of an accident in which a blue car goes into a ditch, individuals might be given a questionnaire containing the question, "Was the passenger injured when the red car went into the ditch?" On a later test these individuals will identify red as the color of the car significantly more often than individuals who did not receive this false information embedded in the questionnaire. The more the false information has been repeated in the questions, the stronger the effect is (Zaragoza & Mitchell, 1996). Surprisingly, informing individuals that they may receive misleading information on the questionnaire does not reduce the effect and may even enhance it (Winkelspecht & Mowrer, 1999; Zaragoza & Lane, 1994). These findings are also consistent with principles discussed earlier in this book. Images elicited by certain stimuli in the questions (the misleading information) become conditioned to images elicited by the original event (i.e., the memory of the original event).

Fabrication

Someone in a position to know an individual's history can often implant verbal behavior in that individual descriptive of a fictitious event that supposedly occurred to the individual (Loftus & Pickrell, 1995). For example, an experimenter might ask collaborators to tell siblings or other close relatives a fabricated story about "the time you got lost on a shopping trip with mom when you were about five." Up to 25% of individuals told such a story claim to remember the event and even provide additional details. Research indicates that the story must seem plausible to the individual in order for him or her to report it as a memory of a real event (Pezdek et al., 1997). This is because the method works by conditioning verbal behavior in an individual that is similar to verbal behavior that is already strong in the individual.

FLASHBULB MEMORIES

People often have clear memory of the specific context (e.g., where they were, who they were with, what they were doing) in which a surprising, consequential, and emotionally arousing event occurred (Brown & Kulik, 1977). This might be some momentous news event such as the sudden and tragic death of a famous person. It might also be some momentous personal news. These memories are called flashbulb memories because it is as though the event has caused a photograph to be taken of the situation in which the individual first learned of the event. That is, the memories are often vivid and long lasting. People have reported remembering in vivid detail many years after the event exactly where they were and what they were doing at the moment they heard, for example, that President Kennedy, John Lennon, or Princes Diana were seriously injured or dead.

The term flashbulb memory is somewhat unfortunate because it implies that, like a photograph, all of these memories are entirely accurate and unchanging. This is not the case (Neisser & Harsch, 1992). Even when extremely vivid, they can, like memories discussed in the previous section, be false. Their degree of inaccuracy ranges from slight to extreme (Brewer, 1992; McCloskey, 1992; Weaver, 1993).

Flashbulb memories are consistent with principles already discussed in this book. By definition, a surprising and consequential event is composed of many distinctive stimuli. The images that occur at the time of the surprising event become conditioned to those stimuli. Since these stimuli seldom reoccur (i.e., popular presidents, famous entertainers, and beloved princesses seldom die unexpectedly), few competing responses become conditioned to them. When images of these events are elicited, the contextual images that have been paired with them also occur. Occasionally a competing image may replace the original contextual image by one of the false-memory processes discussed in the preceding section. Even when false, a flashbulb memory may be very vivid and hence convincing. Its vividness may not, however, result from a strongly conditioned image (as we might expect of the images elicited by a real situation). Instead, it may be vivid because there are few competing images due to the distinctiveness of the stimuli corresponding to the momentous event (e.g., intense emotional outpourings). Telling and retelling of the event can also contribute to the vividness of a flashbulb memory and to its distortion due to social reinforcement for addition or omission of details.

MNEMONIC TECHNIQUES

Memory is not a static ability; it can be improved through mnemonic techniques, which are systemic methods based on effective ways of encoding materials to be remembered in a more permanent way than encoding (discussed on pp. 212–213).

Using Visual Imagery

An effective method to encode paired associates for later recall is to vividly imagining the objects they represent interacting with each other (Bellezza, 1986, 1987; Bower & Winzenz, 1970; Paivio, 1995). For example, to remember the first two items on the left-hand list on page 226 you might visualize a cake thrown against a door and a book sticking in a road. Then, when the word "cake" occurs it is likely to elicit the image of a cake thrown against a door, which will be an S^D for the verbal response "door." Likewise, when the word "book" occurs it will elicit the image of a book sticking in a road which will be an S^D for the verbal response "road," The method is more effective when the objects are imagined interacting with each other than when they are imagined together but not interacting (Begg, 1982; McKelvie, Sano, & Stout, 1994).

For the procedure to work, the words involved must elicit clear images. Hence, it is usually much easier to learn and recall concrete than abstract words (Paivio, 1971). However, abstract words can be recalled easily if they are encoded in a concrete way. An example of this would be encoding the word "happiness" paired with the word "justice" by imagining a broadly smiling happy person holding the scales of justice.

The procedure also works well for remembering peoples' names. For example, to remember Mr. Montaigne's name, for example, we might pair the image of his nose with the image of a mountain. The next time we see him, his nose will elicit the image of a mountain which will evoke the word "mountain," and we will recall his name because of the similarity to the word "mountain." Based on this simple principle, elaborate mnemonic techniques have been developed that involve first systematically learning associations (e.g., with numbers, cards) that can then be used to memorize numerous paired associates (e.g., birthdays of friends and relatives) or large sequences of items (e.g., shopping lists).

Chunking

The more items an individual has to learn, the more difficult it is to learn and recall them due to proactive and retroactive interference. Consider, for example, the task of remembering the following sequence of letters:

fbicbsibmirs

There are 12 letters in this string. Therefore, one might assume that it consists of a sequence of twelve responses. Looking at it another way, however, we can see that for anyone raised in the American culture there are actually only four responses in the sequence: FBI, CBS, IBM, and IRS. For most Americans these four responses comprise a much easier sequence to learn, even though it consists of the same letters as in the initial sequence. The process by which several responses become compressed, or bound together, into one response is called chunking (Miller, 1956). As can be seen from the above example, chunking can aid greatly in memory. To take another example, consider the task of attempting to memorize any sentence on this page as a sequence of letters versus remembering it as a sequence of words, or perhaps even better, as a sequence of phrases. Every word we know is a sequence of letters or, when spoken, phonemes. Thus, every word that we know is a chunk that is composed of smaller alphabetical or phonemic response elements. Likewise, any phrase we have learned is a chunk consisting of smaller verbal response units.

Hierarchical Organization

Similar to chunking, memory for items may be improved by organizing them according to categories, subcategories, and so on (Bower, Clark, Lesgold, & Winzenz, 1969). For example, given a list of animals to learn, one might encode them for later recall by grouping them according to whether they are fish, reptiles, birds, or mammals, and organizing them within each group by the type of fish, reptile, bird, or mammal that they are. Higher-order category names evoke lower-order ones, which then evoke the names of the animals that were on the list. Of course, this method would not work for recalling the order of the names on the list.

MEMORY AND EXECUTIVE FUNCTION

Because of the great importance memory has in human societies, humans learn various ways for remembering events that have occurred to them (episodic memory), things to do at specific times and places (time-place memory), and various types of factual information (semantic memory). These methods may have simply been shaped by the increased reinforcement they provide, without any verbal rule being involved. In most cases, however, they are under the control of a verbal rule that others say to us or that we say to ourselves. Often we use external memory aids, such as notes. In other cases we rely on covert processes. To remember where in the parking lot we parked our car, for example, we may give ourselves several respondent conditioning trials in which we pair our view of a given landmark with a view of our car. When we return to the parking lot later, that landmark will (if we have done the conditioning effectively) elicit the image of the car's location. In common everyday speech we call this technique learning (or remembering) "by association."

When we attempt to remember something, it may seem that our brain is acting like a computer searching its memory. Although this analogy can sometimes be useful, it might be more accurate to say that what we are doing is presenting private stimuli to elicit a weakly conditioned or suppressed response. In addition to that, we may also be engaging in behavior that is more akin to reconstructing than it is to searching. Somewhat like an archeologist reconstructing the plan of a city from a few stone blocks, pieces of pottery, and other artifacts, a paleontologist reconstructing the shape of an extinct animal from a few fossilized bones, or a detective reconstructing the way in which a crime occurred from various clues left at the scene, a person remembering may be reconstructing a complex sequence of events from a few private images elicited by stimuli similar to those present when the sequence of events occurred (Neisser, 1967, p. 285). The person remembering, like an archeologist, paleontologist, or detective, is using a reasoning or inferential process. Tom's memory that it was last Thursday that he had lunch with Sue, for example, might have been reconstructed from the fact that his classes for the other days of the week conflict with Sue's lunch hour. Of course he could be wrong. Perhaps, for example, his lab at noon on Tuesday had been canceled. What we refer to as "false memories" may actually, in at least some cases, be incorrect inferences.

In the theory of human memory illustrated in Figure 10.1, the Central Executive carries out the memory functions discussed above. To avoid the homunculus error we described earlier in this chapter, it is probably better to use the term "executive function" rather than "central executive." The executive function is a set of learned operations that we carry out when we are engaged in a memory task or problem. We, not a little person inside our head (as some theories seem to imply), are the central executive who carries out these operations (Edelman, 1992, p. 238; Searle, 1992, p. 214).

Because these operations are the product of learning and involve complex verbal behavior, it is incorrect to attribute them to members of other species as we are sometimes prone to do. Nonverbal animals cannot engage in these operations. Thus it is incorrect to say, for example, that a dog that learned to salivate to a bell in a respondent conditioning experiment associated the bell with food (in the sense that we used the term "associate" at the beginning of this section). To make such a statement is to commit the error known as anthropomorphism, which is defined as assuming that nonhuman animals engage in behavior that (so far, at least) is unique to humans. Although a nonhuman animal may superficially seem to perform behavior that would involve private verbal behavior if engaged in by a human, it is incorrect to assume that the animal engaged in verbal behavior. It is often difficult to detect the anthropomorphic error. One indication of its occurrence is any description of an animal's behavior that includes statements about what the animal may be thinking or saying covertly. It also occurs when someone imbues an animal with the ability to reminisce about the past or plan for the future. These activities require verbal behavior, and so cannot be done by nonverbal individuals. (We discuss verbal behavior more extensively in Chapter 17.)

SUMMARY AND CONCLUSIONS

"Memory" and related words, such as "forgetting," are words with numerous and varied meanings in common, everyday speech. In general, these words refer to situations in which a response might fail to occur despite having been conditioned and despite the occurrence of a relevant establishing operation and a stimulus that would be expected to evoke the response. Three types of situations that meet these criteria are when: (1) a comparison stimulus or stimuli occur when the sample stimulus is no longer present; (2) reinforcement becomes available a critical time following some stimulus that is no longer present; and (3) responses other than the target response (the response under consideration) interfere with the target response. The first type of situation requires either neurological encoding or encoding in a surrogate stimulus to account for the occurrence of the target response. When the retention interval—that is, the interval between the sample and comparison stimuli—is fairly short, mediating behavior—that is, behavior that occurs during the retention interval—generally provides the surrogate stimulus necessary for correct matching to occur. When the retention interval is quite long, however, and correct responding still occurs, other processes (such as conditioned covert responses, mnemonic techniques, and neurological encoding) are probably involved. Similarly, in the second type of situation, mediating behavior can provide the surrogate stimulus required for accurate timing of a relatively short interval. For the timing of long intervals, however, some sort of physiological clock seems to be operating. In the third type of situation, failure of the target response to occur is due to competing responses. In order for the target response to occur, the responses competing with it must become weak relative to the target.

In addition to failures to remember real occurrences, there are memories of events that never occurred. These false memories are conditioned responses that are as strong as those corresponding to real events, but their strengths derive from factors other than real events.

It is sometimes useful, both for descriptive and for theoretical purposes, to analogize between computer memory and the memory of humans and animals. When doing so, however, it is important to keep in mind that different processes are likely involved in these different types of memory. It is also important to keep in mind that human memory often involves the use of complex verbal behavior, which is not available to nonhuman animals.

11

Contingencies of
Conditioned Reinforcement

V ery little reinforcement in natural settings is primary; most is conditioned reinforcement. Therefore, we need to understand conditioned reinforcement in order to understand learning. Although it is a relatively simple concept, conditioned reinforcement can account for a great deal of the complexities of learning and behavior. This chapter
deals with the ways in which it does this, and some of the questions that are thereby raised. In
Chapter 3 we pointed out how conditioned reinforcement can establish new behavior or increase the amount of behavior that occurs during extinction. In this chapter the emphasis will
be on how conditioned reinforcement can function to maintain behavior that is already occurring under various contingencies.

BEHAVIORAL CHAINS

Up to this point in this book we have concentrated on fairly simple responses. As indicated in
Chapter 3, however, more complex behavior can be developed by chaining simple responses
together in a repetitive sequence called a behavioral chain.

Role of Conditioned Reinforcement in Chains

In Chapter 3 we mentioned that a neutral stimulus can become a reinforcer by being paired
with a stimulus that is already reinforcing. This newly created reinforcer is called a conditioned reinforcer, and can be used to condition and maintain new responses in the individual's
repertoire.

Conditioned reinforcement makes it possible to develop long chains of responses. A simple
two-response chain that is already familiar from previous chapters is as follows: (1) lever press
reinforced by sound of feeder operating; (2) when sound of feeder occurs approach to food
tray reinforced by food. In this chain the sound of the feeder is a conditioned reinforcer because it has been paired with food. Note, however, that it is also an S^D for approach to the food
tray because food is only in the tray after the feeder sound has occurred. We define a behavioral chain as a sequence of responses that are linked together in this fashion by stimuli that
are both conditioned reinforcers and discriminative stimuli.

The typical matching-to-sample procedure for pigeons (described in Chapter 9 and illustrated in Figure 9.1, p. 184) is an example of two three-response chains. One of these is as follows:

1. In the presence of a triangle on the center key a peck on that key is reinforced by the illumination of the two side keys.
2. In the presence of a triangle on the center key and a triangle on one of the side keys, the feeder light reinforces a peck on that side key.
3. In the presence of the feeder light, approach to the food tray is reinforced by food.

The other chain is similar, except that it begins with a square on the center key and involves pecking the square on one of the side keys. Note that in each of these chains, the correct comparison stimulus is both an S^D for pecking it and a reinforcer for pecking the sample. It acquires its reinforcing power from its association with the feeder light, which is both an S^D for approaching the food tray and a reinforcer for pecking the correct comparison stimulus. The feeder light, of course, acquires its reinforcing power from its association with food. Thus, although the chain is held together by a series of conditioned reinforcers, each of these reinforcers ultimately derives its reinforcing power from the primary reinforcer at the end of the chain. The most famous and probably longest behavioral chain ever established in a rat was a lab project conducted by some students at Brown University (Pierrel & Sherman, 1963). The chain was as follows:

1. climbing a spiral staircase;
2. crossing a narrow bridge;
3. climbing a ladder;
4. pulling in a chain attached to an open toy car;
5. getting in the car;
6. pedaling the car to a second staircase;
7. climbing the second staircase;
8. crawling through a tube;
9. entering an elevator and riding down to the starting platform;
10. pressing a lever which operated a feeder;
11. approaching and eating the food.

Everyday human behavior contains numerous examples of behavioral chains. For example, putting on a pair of pants is a behavioral chain: putting one leg into the pants is reinforced by the pants being in a position to put the other leg in; putting the other leg in is reinforced by the pants being in a position to be pulled up; pulling up the pants is reinforced by the pants being in a position to be buttoned at the top; buttoning the top of the pants is reinforced by the pants being easy to zip up. Similarly bed making is a behavioral chain. Many activities consist of a number of interrelated behavioral chains, such as a cashier counting out different amounts of change.

It seems reasonable to think that there must be a limit on how long a behavioral chain can be for any given individual or species, but it is not presently known what that limit is or how it differs among individuals and species. It is known, however, that the power of each conditioned reinforcer in a chain varies directly with the strength of the primary reinforcer at the end of the chain and indirectly with the distance of the conditioned reinforcer from the primary reinforcer (Kelleher & Gollub, 1962). Hence, the maximum length of a chain is directly related to the strength of the reinforcer on which the chain is based.

Chaining Procedures

Behavioral chaining—that is, conditioning or teaching a behavioral chain—involves (1) conditioning the stimulus-response links or units in the chain, and (2) linking the units together. Since the units may be conditioned in any order, and the linking together of the separate units can also be done in any order, the number of ways to teach a behavioral chain increases factorially as the number of links in the chain increases.

Three major chaining procedures.   Three major procedures have been studied fairly extensively: backward chaining, forward chaining, and total-task presentation.

Backward chaining.   In backward chaining the last stimulus-response unit is conditioned first, then the next-to-last stimulus-response unit is conditioned and linked to the last, and so on, with the S^D for each response being used to reinforce the response that precedes it in the chain. A simple example of backward chaining occurs in conditioning an animal to press a lever. First the feeder sound is established as an S^D for approaching the food tray, then the sound of the feeder operating is used to reinforce lever pressing (or approximations to lever pressing if shaping is being used). Backward conditioning can be continued as more links are added to the front of the chain. For example, if a lever press produces the feeder sound only when a light above the lever is on, so that the light becomes an S^D for pressing the lever, the light can then be used to reinforce another response; for example, stepping on a treadle. The chain would then be as follows: (1) stepping on treadle is reinforced by illumination of light above lever; (2) in the presence of the light above the lever, pressing the lever is reinforced by the sound of the feeder; (3) upon the occurrence of the feeder sound, approaching the food tray is reinforced by food.

The most important thing to note about backward chaining is that each step in the process automatically establishes the conditioned reinforcer needed for the next step. Thus, all the reinforcement needed to maintain the chain is "built into" the chain as it is being constructed, and no additional reinforcement is needed in constructing (i.e., establishing) the chain.

Forward chaining.   The above behavioral chain could also be taught with forward chaining, which would involve first reinforcing the animal for stepping on the treadle. Technically this would mean that food would have to be put directly into the animal's mouth since the animal would not yet have been conditioned to approach the food tray. When stepping on the treadle is occurring reliably, food is no longer given immediately after this response. Instead, stepping on the treadle turns on the light above the lever and food is contingent on a lever press. Note that some difficulties might be expected at this point because the light is not yet a conditioned reinforcer and, therefore, stepping on the treadle will be undergoing extinction. If the lever-press response is established before treadle stepping decreases to zero, however, the light will have become a conditioned reinforcer and will maintain stepping on the treadle. The third and final step is to have the feeder operate after a lever press so that, following a lever press, the animal must now approach the food tray to obtain food. Since the sound of the feeder will not be a conditioned reinforcer until it has become an S^D for approaching the food tray, however, lever pressing will be undergoing extinction until this occurs.

Thus, some amount of weakening of a previously conditioned response occurs each time a new response is added to a chain by the forward-chaining method. This does not occur with backward chaining because previously established responses are always being maintained with primary (in the case of the last response) or conditioned reinforcement as new responses are added to the chain.

Total-task presentation. In total-task presentation the stimulus-response units are taught and linked together at the same time in a forward order. This procedure generally produces more errors (i.e., responses either failing to occur or occurring out of sequence) than the other two procedures (Spooner & Spooner, 1984), and this would be particularly true with long behavioral chains. In applied learning science (e.g., behavior modification programs), total-task presentation is more commonly used with well-trained individuals—normal humans in educational/training settings—than the other two chaining procedures are.

Comparisons of the major chaining procedures. The main conclusion one can draw from research studies on chaining is that if the task to be taught has been broken down into easily taught links or stimulus-response units (a process called task analysis), and if effective shaping and prompting-fading procedures (see Chapter 8) are used in conjunction with the chaining procedure, then all chaining procedures are generally effective.

Because each of its steps automatically establishes a conditioned reinforcer for the next step, backward chaining might be expected to be more effective than forward chaining. Experimental studies do not bear this out, however. In one experiment first-year university students were taught several six-link response chains in which numbers or letters were projected on six response keys. Each chain involved pressing the keys in the correct sequence as indicated by the stimuli appearing on the keys. Reinforcement at the end of the chain consisted of points that could later be exchanged for money. The result was that the students made many more errors when being taught by backward chaining than when being taught by forward chaining (Weiss, 1978). In another experiment pigeons were taught two four-link response chains in which the responses were pecks on different keys and the discriminative stimuli were colors, lines, or geometrical shapes projected on the keys. Reinforcement was access to grain delivered by the standard feeder mechanism used in most pigeon experiments. Each bird was taught one chain by forward chaining and one by backward chaining. The result was that the birds tended to make fewer errors in whichever chaining procedure was used first (Pisacreta, 1982b). A possible explanation for the apparent lack of superiority or even inferiority of backward over forward chaining is that the use of a strong terminal reinforcer (e.g., food) for each new response as it is being added to the chain in forward chaining, rather than a weaker conditioned reinforcer as in backward chaining, compensates or even overcompensates for the weakening effect extinction has on previously established responses in the forward procedure (Weiss, 1978).

Numerous comparisons of chaining procedures with developmentally disabled individuals have produced in mixed results—none of the chaining procedures consistently shows superiority over any of the others (Spooner & Spooner, 1984). One reason for this may be that different studies have tended to focus on different measures of effectiveness—time to criterion, number of trials to criterion, number of correct responses during training, number of incorrect responses during training, rate of correct responses during training, and rate of incorrect responses during training. Another possible reason is that the specific tasks (e.g., vocational ones such as threading an industrial sewing machine, putting together a 15-piece bicycle brake, putting together a 7-piece drain assembly) differ markedly across different studies. In addition, most comparisons of the chaining procedures have used variations that are known to be effective. It may be that there is little or no difference between the major chaining procedures when optimal versions (e.g., those that incorporate shaping and prompting/fading in an effective manner) of those procedures are compared.

Simultaneous forward chaining. In a variation of forward chaining called simultaneous forward chaining, no stimulus change (and hence no apparent reinforcement) occurs until after the terminal response at each stage. Thus, in the example of a chaining stepping on a treadle, followed by pecking a key, followed by eating from the feeder, reinforcement would first follow stepping on the treadle, exactly as in standard forward chaining. In the next stage, reinforcement would no longer follow stepping on the treadle; instead, it would follow lever pressing—but only if a treadle step had occurred first. In order for reinforcement to occur, the animal must therefore step on the treadle and then press the lever. Neither the light nor any other distinctive stimulus occurs following the treadle step (except, of course, the proprioceptive feedback and other feedback that naturally follows the response).

For another example of simultaneous chaining, consider an experiment in which four keys are simultaneously available. A different stimulus is on each key, and these stimuli change position randomly after each reinforcement. The experiment consists of the following stages:

Stage 1: reinforcement occurs after each response on stimulus A.

Stage 2: reinforcement occurs after each series of responses on stimuli A and B, in that order.

Stage 3: reinforcement occurs after each series of responses on stimuli A, B, and C, in that order.

Stage 4: reinforcement occurs after each series of responses on stimuli A, B, C, and D, in that order.

Pigeons and rhesus monkeys readily learn this task, despite the fact that no distinctive stimulus occurs after each correct response except the last (Swartz, Chen, & Terrace, 1991; Terrace, 1983). More remarkably, if we test with any pair of stimuli that the animal was trained to respond to consecutively, we find that it responds to them in the correct order. For example, if we present the animal with only stimuli B and C, the animal will first respond to B and then C. Even more remarkably, if we present a pair of stimuli that the animal was not trained to respond to consecutively, it will nevertheless respond to them in the order in which it was trained to respond. For example, if we present only stimuli B and D, the animal will first respond to B and then D. In addition, it will take longer to respond to D after having responded to B than it did to respond to C after having responded to B in the previous test. It seems clear that when an individual learns a chain of responses (particularly with this method), each response is not simply under the control of the stimulus that immediately preceded it. It is also to some extent under the control of recently occurring stimuli, including the feedback from recently occurring responses.

It can be seen why the "backward simultaneous chaining" counterpart to forward simultaneous chaining is ineffective. This would involve first reinforcing a response only to stimulus D and then reinforcing the response to stimulus D only if it had been preceded by a response to stimulus C. Before this would happen, however, the response to stimulus D would likely have extinguished. It is also easy to see that "simultaneous total task presentation" is not a very effective chaining procedure. If the chain were longer than several responses, the probability of responding in the correct sequence by chance would be so low that likely no reinforcement would occur and responding would extinguish. Interestingly, however, with a chain four responses long, pigeons exposed to simultaneous total task presentation develop above chance responding on the correct sequence (Terrace, 1983).

Stereotyped Sequences as Chains

Suppose that reinforcement is contingent on a sequence of responses, but the order in which the responses are emitted is not specified by the reinforcement contingency. For example, suppose that a pigeon is presented with nine lighted keys in a 3 × 3 matrix (i.e., three rows and three columns of keys). A peck on each key turns off the light behind that key and reinforcement occurs when all the key lights have been turned off. Although there are 362,880 possible reinforced sequences of key pecks, the bird will come to emit one specific sequence on most trials and relatively few different sequences (e.g., less than 100) on the other trials (Pisacreta, 1982a; Schwartz, 1980, 1981, 1982; Vogel & Annau, 1973). Thus it appears that individuals exposed to contingencies that require a sequence of responses will develop response chains even though a chaining procedure is not used and no specific response chain is specified by the reinforcement contingency. Interestingly, this result will occur even if a contingency to reinforce variability is imposed on the behavior such as, if the contingency specifies that a particular sequence will not be reinforced if it is the same as the sequence that occurred on the previous trial (Schwartz, 1980). This tendency to emit only a few different sequences of responses when no specific sequence is specified by the reinforcement contingency is called response stereotypy.

Behavioral Units

A behavioral chain that is repeated many times eventually begins to function as a behavioral unit. That is to say, the members or elements of the chain are emitted in their correct sequence without feedback from one member being required to reinforce the preceding member or to be an S^D for the subsequent member. This is why a pianist, for example, can play a series of notes in a well-practiced piece in less time than it takes for him or her respond to any feedback (including proprioceptive feedback) from the individual notes (Lashley, 1951). Note that chunking, described in Chapter 10 (p. 234), makes use of the formation of behavioral units.

It appears that the elements of a behavioral unit may tend to occur in their ordinal positions even when they are put into another behavioral unit (Shaofu, Swarz, & Terrace, 1997).

CHAINED SCHEDULES

Chains such as the above in which there is a different response in each link are called heterogeneous chains. Chains in which the responses are the same from one link to the next are called homogeneous chains. A chained schedule is a homogeneous chain in which responding in the presence of a particular discriminative stimulus produces another discriminative stimulus according to some schedule of reinforcement; responding in the presence of this second discriminative stimulus produces primary reinforcement (in the case of a two-component chained schedule) or another discriminative stimulus according to some schedule of reinforcement; and so on until a final discriminative stimulus occurs in the presence of which responding produces primary reinforcement on some schedule of reinforcement. Typically the discriminative stimuli occur in the same order and the sequence is repeated after each occurrence of primary reinforcement. Consider, for example, the following two-component chained schedule: in the presence of a red key light, responding on the key will turn the key light green according to an FI 1-minute schedule; in the presence of the green key light, responding on the key will produce food on an FR 30 schedule after which the key will turn red and the sequence will be repeated. This is called a chained fixed-interval 1-minute fixed-ratio 30 schedule of reinforcement (abbreviated chain FI 1-minute FR 30).

Conditioned Reinforcement in Chained Schedules

The stimulus correlated with each component of a chained schedule serves two functions:

- It is a conditioned reinforcer for responding in the previous component. (Of course, this function does not apply to the first component.)
- It a discriminative stimulus for responding in the current component.

Thus, the stimulus correlated with each component of a chained schedule controls the pattern of responding that is typically produced by the schedule of reinforcement in that component (Ferster & Skinner, 1957). For example, in a chained FI 1-minute FR 30 schedule, the stimulus correlated with the first component will control the typical FI 1-minute pattern of responding even though conditioned, rather than primary, reinforcement occurs in the presence of that stimulus.

The conditioned-reinforcement function in a chained schedule can be seen clearly by inserting a short delay (e.g., 3 seconds) between the components of a two-component chained schedule, so that the stimulus correlated with the second component does not occur immediately after the response that produces it. Controlling to ensure that the time of occurrence of the primary reinforcer is not affected by this operation, this slight modification has a drastic effect on responding in the first component of the chained schedule. Specifically, response rate in that component drops by between 70 and 90% (Royalty, Williams, & Fantino, 1987), which is the same amount of disruption that occurs when primary reinforcement is delayed by a comparable amount on a single schedule of reinforcement such as a simple VI schedule (Catania & Keller, 1981; Sizemore & Lattal, 1978; Williams, 1976). Thus, conditioned reinforcement in a chained schedule is analogous to primary reinforcement in a single schedule.

The function of conditioned reinforcement in a chained schedule also can be seen by a comparison involving what is called a tandem schedule, which is identical to a chained schedule except that it has no stimuli that are correlated with its components. That is, in a tandem schedule the stimuli remain the same throughout all components. For example, in a tandem FI 1-minute FR 30 schedule, the first response after one minute produces an FR 30 schedule of primary reinforcement with no change in the stimulus when the FR 30 component starts.

The different effects produced by chained and tandem schedules can be substantial. For example, a chained VI 1-minute DRL 2-seconds schedule will produce a moderately high, steady rate of responding during the first component followed by a pause of about 2 seconds during the second component. A tandem VI 1-minute DRL 2-seconds schedule, however, will produce a low, steady rate throughout both components. The reason for these differences is that during the first component of the chained schedule, short IRTs, as well as medium length and long IRTs, could be reinforced by the stimulus correlated with the second component; however, during the tandem schedule, as during the second component of the chained schedule, no IRT less than 2 seconds could be reinforced. Note how the chained and tandem schedules in this example illustrate effects of IRT reinforcement. These schedules often are used in this manner to study processes occurring at the moment of reinforcement.

Effects of the S^Ds in Chained Schedules

The reinforcement function of the S^Ds (i.e., the discriminative stimuli) in a chained schedule gives rise to the question of whether these stimuli produce more responding in a chained schedule than would occur if they were absent. This question is easily answered by comparing chained and tandem schedules. If we compare chained schedule (chain) FR 40 FR 40 FR 40 with tandem schedule (tandem) FR 40 FR 40 FR 40 (note that the latter schedule is equivalent to FR 120), for example, two results will be noted:

- The pause after primary reinforcement will be longer in the chained schedule than in the tandem schedule.
- A pause will occur after the completion of each component of the chained schedule but not after the completion of each component of the tandem schedule (Ferster & Skinner, 1957; Jwaideh, 1973; Thomas, 1964).

Similar results will be obtained if, instead of comparing chained and tandem FR schedules, we compare chained and tandem FI schedules (Gollub, 1958; Kelleher & Fry, 1962). In addition, suppose that we increase the number of links in a chained FR schedule while leaving the overall response requirement the same. For example, suppose that we compare chain FR 30 FR 30 FR 30 FR 30 with chain FR 40 FR 40 FR 40. The result will be that the chained schedule with the greater number of components will exhibit a longer postreinforcement pause (Jwaideh, 1973).

The above results indicate that increasing the amount of conditioned reinforcement in a chained schedule decreases responding by increasing the postreinforcement pause and by producing a pause at the completion of each component. This seems anomalous, since one would think that increasing the amount of reinforcement should increase responding. It is probably not the reinforcing function, however, but the discriminative function of the stimuli correlated with the components of the chained schedule that is responsible for the decreased responding. This is because a stimulus correlated with an FR schedule produces pausing prior to the start of responding on the schedule. It is probably these pauses that cause response rate to be lower in chained than in tandem schedules containing FR components.

Effects of Primary Reinforcement in Chained Schedules

Chained schedules are useful for studying the effects of various aspects of primary reinforcement, such as reinforcement rate and reinforcement amount or duration. The first component of two-component chained schedules appears to be particularly sensitive to these variables. For example, the responding of rats in the first component of a chain VI 4-minute VI x schedule is strongly affected by the value of x in the second component. The lower x is, the higher the response rate in the first component. The effect of varying x on response rate appears to be much greater in the first component than in the second component (Findley, 1962, pp. 127–128). It may also be greater than the effect of varying reinforcement rate in a single (i.e., unchained) VI schedule.

Pigeons' responding in the first component of chain FI FI and chain VI VI schedules varies directly with reinforcement duration (ranging from 2 to 8 seconds) in the second component (Lendenmann, Myers, & Fantino, 1982). As with reinforcement rate, the effect of varying reinforcement duration is much greater on response rate in the first component than it is on response rate in the second component. In addition, the effect seems to be greater than the effect of varying reinforcement duration or amount in simple FI and VI schedules, which often appear to be quite insensitive to this variable (e.g., Catania, 1963; Keesey & Kling, 1961).

BRIEF-STIMULUS PROCEDURES

We have considered two general ways of experimentally observing the effects of conditioned reinforcement while maintaining behavior: heterogeneous behavioral chains and chained schedules. Another procedure is to pair a brief stimulus with reinforcement at certain points in time (i.e., on a particular schedule) and present that stimulus alone at other times (i.e., on a different schedule). Three ways of doing this will now be described.

Second-Order Schedules

In a second-order schedule, satisfying the requirement of a particular schedule (called the minor schedule) is treated as a unit which is reinforced on another schedule (called the major schedule). For example, consider a second-order schedule in which the minor schedule is FI 1-minute and the major schedule is FR 10. What this means is that ten FI 1-minute schedules must be completed in order for primary reinforcement to occur. To take another example, suppose that the minor schedule is FR 20 and the major schedule is FI 10. Then the unit consists of 20 responses and primary reinforcement is presented for each unit that is completed after 10 minutes following the previous primary reinforcement. In the preceding two examples of second-order schedules, the first one would be abbreviated FR 10 (FI 1 min) and the second one would be abbreviated FI 10 min (FR 20); thus, the major schedule is written in the usual way and the minor schedule is placed in parentheses beside it.

A type of second-order schedule that is used for studying conditioned reinforcement is known as a brief-stimulus second-order schedule. In this type of schedule, a brief stimulus (e.g., a change in the color of the response key) occurs after the completion of each unit of the minor schedule. For example, in an FR (FI 1 minute-color change) 20- (color change + food) schedule, the key-light color might change for 0.7 seconds at the completion of each unit of the FI schedule, with both the key-color change and primary reinforcement (food) occurring at the completion of every 20th FI unit.

The brief stimulus in a second-order schedule should become a conditioned reinforcer because it occurs just prior to primary reinforcement. The question therefore arises as to whether it has effects typical of those of other reinforcers. In particular, does it generate a pattern of responding typical of that generated by the minor schedule (e.g., a scalloped pattern if the minor schedule is an FI schedule), and does it increase the rate of responding above that which occurs if a brief stimulus occurs that has not been paired with primary reinforcement? The answer to the first question is clearly affirmative (e.g., Kelleher, 1966b); however, the situation is complicated by the fact that brief stimuli that are not paired with primary reinforcement also can produce patterning typical of the schedule on which they occur. This suggests that the discriminative control of the brief stimuli may be as important as their conditioned reinforcing property. The answer to the second question is sometimes affirmative and sometimes not. The reasons for these different findings are not well understood at present. (For reviews of the literature on second-order schedules, see Gollub, 1977, Fantino, 1977, and Marr, 1979.)

Collateral Pairing

In a collateral pairing procedure, a brief stimulus that is continually paired with primary reinforcement is contingent on the same response in a different situation or on a different response in the same situation. The typical result is that the brief stimulus maintains the behavior for a considerable amount of time (perhaps indefinitely), and that the behavior exhibits the pattern typical of that produced by the schedule on which the brief stimulus occurs. Thus, a brief stimulus (e.g., food-hopper light) that is paired with food in one component of a multiple schedule will maintain responding in another component in which food never occurs (Thomas, 1969). Similarly, a brief stimulus that is paired with food when a pigeon responds on one key can maintain responding on a different key on which responses are never reinforced with food (Zimmerman, 1963; Zimmerman & Hanford, 1967).

Oppositional Pairing

One of the most dramatic demonstrations of the power of conditioned reinforcement is a procedure that pits conditioned reinforcement against primary reinforcement. If on a VT (i.e., variable-time) 60-seconds schedule (i.e., reinforcement occurs an average of once every 60 seconds noncontingent on responding) a contingency is added whereby each response postpones the reinforcer for six seconds, then responding will be at or near zero. If, however, the stimulus paired with reinforcement is contingent on responding, then there will be an increase in responding provided that the animal emits enough responses to come into contact with the contingency. A stimulus that has not been paired with reinforcement will not have this effect. Responding will be a direct function of the rate of conditioned reinforcement, and as long as the conditioned reinforcer continues to occur will apparently persist indefinitely even though it results in a large reduction in the rate of primary reinforcement (Zimmerman, Hanford, & Brown, 1967).

SOME PHENOMENA EXPLAINED BY CONDITIONED REINFORCEMENT

There are several types of behavioral phenomena which on the surface appear to be puzzling, but that on deeper analysis can be explained quite easily by the concept of conditioned reinforcement. Some of these phenomena are discussed here.

Delayed Reinforcement

Suppose that we arrange for a particular response to produce reinforcement a fixed amount of time, t, after the response occurs. If t is greater than a few seconds, reinforcement will likely occur just after the individual has engaged in some other behavior and will therefore increase the probability of that behavior rather than the response that produced reinforcement.

There is no question that even a brief delay of reinforcement can have major disruptive effects on operant responding. A 3-second delay between a response and reinforcement can decrease responding on a schedule of reinforcement from between 70 to 90% (Catania & Keller, 1981; Sizemore & Lattal, 1978; Williams, 1976). Yet individuals do learn to respond to receive delayed reinforcement. The question therefore arises as to how this is possible.

The answer appears to be that immediate conditioned reinforcement makes it possible for an individual to respond for delayed reinforcement (Spence, 1947). Another way to state this is that, in order for an operant response to be conditioned and maintained, reinforcement must be immediate; however, if primary reinforcement is delayed, conditioned reinforcement can bridge the gap between the response and primary reinforcement so that conditioning occurs and the behavior is maintained. Although immediate conditioned reinforcement can establish and maintain behavior, the longer the delay in reinforcement the less effective it is even when reinforcement rate is held constant (Cronin, 1980; Winter & Perkins, 1982). This makes sense from an evolutionary point of view, since it is advantageous for an animal to respond when reinforcement is somewhat delayed, but the longer it is delayed the more advantageous it becomes for an animal to allocate its time and energy to more immediate reinforcers.

We may distinguish several types of conditioned reinforcers that bridge the gap between a response and reinforcement.

Intangible gap-bridging reinforcers. Suppose that a rat receives delayed primary reinforcement if it goes to the goal box on the right in a T-maze (see Figure 4.1, p. 58), but no reinforcement if it goes to the goal box on the left. In each case, the animal is kept in the goal box until the end of a lengthy delay interval. If both goal boxes are identical, the animal will not learn the discrimination; that is, the frequency with which it turns to the right in the T-maze will not increase above chance. If, however, the inside of one goal box is painted black and the inside of the other is painted white, the animal will learn the discrimination quite readily (Grice, 1948; Spence, 1947). The reason is that the brightness of the goal box in which delayed primary reinforcement occurs becomes a conditioned reinforcer which immediately reinforces emitting the correct response at the choice point of the T-maze.

We can conceptualize the above example as a behavioral chain. The first link in the chain is the correct response at the choice point of the T-maze. This response is reinforced by the brightness of the goal box in which primary reinforcement occurs. Although the analogy of a behavioral chain seems to break down because no specific response in the goal box is required for primary reinforcement to occur, it is possible that the primary reinforcer adventitiously strengthens some response that then comes under the discriminative control of the brightness of the goal box. If this is the case, then there is no fundamental difference between this type of delayed reinforcement paradigm and a behavioral chain.

The effect of conditioned reinforcement in maintaining responding for delayed reinforcement can be demonstrated effectively using chained and tandem schedules. For example, if responding first is established on a chained FI 1-minute FT 2-seconds schedule, and then the schedule is changed to a tandem FI 1-minute FT 2-seconds schedule, responding will decrease in the FI 1-minute component because it are no longer followed by immediate reinforcement.

In the above examples, the conditioned reinforcer is continuously present during the delay interval. This does not have to be the case, however, in order for immediate conditioned reinforcement to maintain responding for delayed reinforcement. Consider, for example, a simultaneous discrimination with a pigeon in an operant conditioning chamber in which a peck on the correct response key produces a delay interval of one minute followed by primary reinforcement. An incorrect response also produces a one-minute delay interval, but no reinforcement occurs at the end of that interval. If the stimuli during the two types of delay intervals are identical the animal will not learn the discrimination, or will not learn it very effectively. If a distinct stimulus occurs during at least some correct responses (but not after incorrect responses), the animal will learn the discrimination readily. Moreover, even if the distinct stimulus occurs only during the first and last few seconds of the delay interval following a correct response, the animal will still learn the discrimination readily (Cronin, 1980; Williams, 1994).

Note that this follows from the previous discussion of collateral pairing procedures in which a brief stimulus paired with primary reinforcement in one situation can maintain a different response in a different situation. That is, a stimulus that has been paired with reinforcement at the end of the delay interval (one situation) maintains behavior that occurs just before the delay interval (another situation). In fact, the conditioned reinforcer will be more effective if it is present only during the first and last small parts of the delay interval because it will occupy a smaller percentage of time in which the reinforcer is not present (Williams, 1994). This is important, because there are many instances in the natural environment in which conditioned reinforcement is not present throughout the full extent of a delay interval. For example, a parent might praise a child for some desirable response immediately after the response occurs and then repeat the praise at a later time when giving the child a treat. If the parent were to continually repeat the praise throughout the day until time for the treat, we can predict from the foregoing that the praise would be less effective than if it were simply given briefly at the time of the desired behavior and then again briefly at the time that the treat is given.

Tangible gap-bridging reinforcers.   The above discussion centers on rather intangible stimuli (e.g., brightness, color) as conditioned reinforcers. A more tangible type of conditioned reinforcer that serves to strengthen and maintain behavior when primary reinforcement is not immediately available is one that can be saved and exchanged for primary reinforcement when it becomes available. This type of conditioned reinforcer, which (as mentioned in Chapter 3) is called a reinforcement token, has been studied extensively with both animals and humans. It has been found, for example, that chimpanzees can be trained to press a lever to obtain poker chips that can be exchanged later for food (Cowles, 1937; Wolfe, 1936). Although the delay between token delivery and primary reinforcement can be as long as several hours, tokens maintain behavior effectively and produce the same schedule patterns as do primary reinforcers (Kelleher, 1957, 1958, 1966a, pp. 194–199).

In applied learning science tokens have been used extensively to reinforce desired behavior in a wide variety of situations, ranging from institutional to community and home settings (Ayllon & Azrin, 1968; Kazdin, 1977). In addition, tokens in the form of money have evolved naturally in human societies. As with intangible conditioned reinforcers, tangible conditioned reinforcers do not have to be present throughout a delay interval in order to bridge the gap between a response and primary reinforcement. Money, for example, can do this even when kept out of sight, such as in a bank (and should be a more effective conditioned reinforcer when it is out of sight during most of the time between when it is received and spent).

Invisible gap-bridging reinforcers.   Suppose, however, that there are no apparent conditioned reinforcers to bridge the gap between a response and its reinforcement. Suppose that after a response occurs absolutely nothing changes in the environment until, some time later, reinforcement occurs. Suppose, in addition, that should the response occur again before the reinforcer occurs, the response restarts the delay interval which prevents the response from being adventitiously reinforced. From what has been said above, it might seem that acquisition of the response would be impossible under these conditions. In fact, however, this is not the case. For example, with no shaping and reinforcement delayed in the above manner by as much as 25 or 30 seconds pigeons learn to peck a key for food (Lattal & Gleeson, 1990), rats learn to press a lever (van Haaren, 1992; Wilkenfield, Nickel, Blakely, & Poling, 1992) or move in a specified space for food (Critchfield & Lattal, 1993), and male Siamese fighting fish learn to swim through a hoop for a view of their own mirror image (Lattal & Metzger, 1994). If it is true that a reinforcer can only strengthen (i.e., increase the probability of) a response that it follows immediately, how is this possible? The answer may be that there are strong sequential dependencies between responses; responses tend to occur in chains rather than in isolation. Thus, if a given response occurs and then reinforcement occurs, that response is strengthened (i.e., its probability is increased); and, in addition, all of the responses leading up to it are also strengthened, although to a lesser extent, depending on how far removed they are from the response that was followed by reinforcement (because the sequential dependency between two responses varies inversely with the number of responses between them). Thus, strengthening by reinforcement a response in a series of sequentially dependent responses strengthens earlier responses in the series. If one of those earlier responses actually produced the reinforcer, it will tend to be maintained by the reinforcement of the later responses in the series even though it was not directly reinforced. In a sequential dependency the conditioned reinforcer for each response is either the small amount of feedback the response provides or perhaps simply the next response; hence the conditioned reinforcers in the series of responses are not apparent or are "invisible" to an external observer of the behavior.

What might a series of sequentially dependent responses look like? It is easy to give an example in the case of conditioning a Siamese fighting fish to swim through a hoop. Due to the contour of the aquarium, and so forth, having swum through the hoop puts the fish on a different swimming path than not swimming through the hoop does. When reinforcement occurs sometime after the fish has swum through the hoop, the animal will be in a specific position swimming in a specific direction. Any behavior that tends to put the animal in that position swimming in that direction will therefore tend to be strengthened—and one such behavior is that which actually produced the reinforcement, namely, swimming through the hoop.

Despite the above, it should be noted that delayed reinforcement is weaker than immediate reinforcement. Responses are less likely to be acquired with delayed reinforcement than with immediate reinforcement, and they also are maintained at a lower rate. At delays beyond a certain point, responses cannot be acquired and responses that have been acquired cannot be maintained (Lattal & Gleeson, 1990; Mazur, 1985; Sizemore & Lattal, 1978). The use of distinctive—that is, intangible or tangible, as described above—gap-bridging conditioned reinforcers increases the amount by which reinforcement can be delayed and still be effective in conditioning and maintaining behavior.

Information as Positive Reinforcement

Can information be positively reinforcing even when it is aversive? Clearly this is a contradiction. How, then, can we explain the fact that people respond to receiving bad news?

Suppose that an individual is placed in an experimental space containing two operanda. On one operandum is programed a two-component mixed schedule in which one component is a VI or VR schedule and the other is extinction. (Recall from Chapter 8 that a mixed schedule is one in which the component schedules alternate and no stimulus change occurs when a new component begins.) The other operandum is programed to change the mixed schedule to a multiple schedule for a brief period (e.g., 30 seconds). In other words, if the reinforcement component is in effect when the individual responds on the second operandum an S^D occurs; if the extinction component is in effect an S^Δ occurs.

Responses on the second operandum are called observing responses (Wyckoff, 1952, 1969) because they enable the individual to observe which component of the mixed schedule is in effect. More generally, an observing response is any response that results in exposure to a discriminative stimulus (either an S^D or an S^Δ). That is, observing responses provide information to the individual regarding the prevailing contingencies. The question arises as to whether such information is reinforcing.

Pigeons (Dinsmoor, Browne, & Lawrence, 1972; Wyckoff, 1969) and rhesus monkeys (Lieberman, 1972) will emit observing responses at a high rate when exposed to the experimental situation described above. Observing responses are maintained at a high rate when the contingency is changed such that they produce the S^D but not the S^Δ. However, they quickly drop to near zero levels when the contingency is changed so that they produce only the S^Δ (Dinsmoor et al., 1972; Mueller & Dinsmoor, 1984). Similarly, humans playing a computer game called "Star Trek," in which the objective is to destroy Klingon invaders (which presumably was reinforcing), responded more to produce a stimulus correlated with the availability of the invaders than to produce a stimulus correlated with their unavailability—despite the fact that each stimulus reduced uncertainty about Klingon availability (Case, Ploog, & Fantino, 1990). Moreover, animals will not emit observing responses for a stimulus associated with a smaller amount (Auge, 1973) or a lower rate of reinforcement (Auge, 1974), even when the amount or rate of reinforcement is greater than zero. It appears that observing responses in the above situations are maintained by the conditioned reinforcement power of stimuli associated with a higher amount or rate of reinforcement, and not by the information provided by a stimulus associated with a lower amount or rate of reinforcement. To put it another way, bad news is not positively reinforcing under the types of conditions described above. Individuals may appear to be responding for bad news in these situations if there also is a chance that they will receive good news. As the ratio of the probability of receiving good news to the probability of receiving bad news decreases, the probability of emitting observing responses also decreases.

There are, however, conditions under which individuals do appear to respond for bad news. In some studies, monkeys have responded more on an operandum that produced either an S^D or an S^Δ in preference to one that produced only an S^D (Lieberman, 1972; Schrier, Thompson, & Spector, 1980). In addition, a study with university students who received points that could be exchanged for money in a lottery-type situation responded more on a button that provided negative information (e.g., "A poor score—this one is not a winner") than on a key that simply provided the verbal statement that they may or may not have won a point (Lieberman, Cathro, Nichols, & Watson, 1997). The conditions under which bad news may be positively reinforcing need to be investigated further. In the meantime, however, the vast majority of studies on this topic have found that bad news is not a positive reinforcer—which suggests that very special conditions are required in order for it to be one.

Other Learning Phenomena

Conditioned reinforcement can help to clarify some learning phenomena that otherwise might have to be considered as independent types of learning. We consider some of these in this section. (See Williams, 1994, for additional discussion of this topic.)

Imprinting. In Chapter 2 we considered imprinting to be nonassociative learning. Yet we noted in Chapter 3 that the imprinted stimulus is a reinforcer, in that ducklings will learn to emit an operant response to obtain it. In addition, note from Figure 3.4 in Chapter 3 that the imprinted stimulus reduces distress calls in the duckling. It is quite possible that the imprinted stimulus is a conditioned reinforcer, deriving its capacity to reduce distress and thus to reinforce by being paired with a particular phylogenetic (i.e., primary) reinforcer. This primary reinforcer may be the rapidly changing light patterns in the duckling's retina such as would be caused by any moving object. Typically, in the natural environment, the source of these flickering light patterns (i.e., the moving object) would be the duckling's mother. The approach of the duckling to the imprinted object would be due to the fact that it has become a conditioned reinforcer, and the approach response brings it closer and thus makes it more visible—just as pecking the response key in Figure 3.3 in Chapter 3 makes the imprinted object more visible (Bolhuis, 1991; Bolhuis et al., 1990; Hoffman & Ratner, 1973).

Some studies have indicated that there is a critical period for imprinting to occur. The conditioned reinforcement interpretation of imprinting could explain why this might appear to be the case. Newly hatched ducklings are relatively fearless. Over time, however, a fear of novel objects develops. Thus, young birds do not imprint after a certain critical period because the imprinting stimulus is novel and the animal tends to escape from it before it can become a conditioned reinforcer. If the birds are forced to remain in the presence of the stimulus after the apparent critical period has ended, they will imprint on the stimulus (i.e., it will, according to this interpretation, become a conditioned reinforcer).

Imitation.   In Chapter 5 we considered most forms of imitation (the exception being what is termed "true imitation") to be derived, not basic, types of learning because they appear to be reducible to more fundamental types of learning. Conditioned reinforcement explains a good deal of what is classified as imitation. For example, when a baby babbles a sound that resembles a sound it has heard its parents say (e.g., "ma ma" or "da da") the baby will be likely to repeat that sound even if no one is present to reinforce the response and no one has ever reinforced the response. The reason the response is more likely to occur is that the feedback from it (i.e., hearing it) is a conditioned reinforcer because that same sound has been paired with reinforcement from the parent when the parent made the sound. This explanation also applies to the way in which many species of birds learn to imitate sounds (Mowrer, 1950, Chapter 24).

Sign tracking.   In Chapter 6 we considered autoshaping, and more generally sign tracking, to be a form of respondent conditioning. Sign tracking is an atypical conditioned respondent, however, because it involves skeletal muscles (e.g., approaching and pecking a key light or manipulating a lever). Other conditioned respondents typically involve glands or smooth or cardiac muscle. Rather than being an atypical result of respondent conditioning, however, autoshaping might be the very natural outcome of a conditioned reinforcement procedure. Autoshaping involves pairing a stimulus (generally an operandum) with a reinforcer, resulting in the individual approaching and interacting with (e.g., operating) the operandum. This causes the stimulus to become a conditioned reinforcer. The individual then approaches it, just as an imprinted duckling approaches the stimulus on which it has been imprinted, because this makes the stimulus more prominent and hence more reinforcing. In the case of sign tracking, proximity to the stimulus leads to pecking or manipulating it in some way.

In support of this interpretation, if for pigeons a diffuse colored light, S_1, is paired with food, and then (in the absence of food) that light is paired with a different colored key light, S_2, pigeons will come to approach and peck the key in the presence of S_2 (Nairne & Rescorla, 1981). This looks like higher-order conditioning (see Chapter 3), except for one thing: The conditioned response—pecking—does not occur to S_1 because it is a nonlocalized stimulus. The result seems more consistent with the view that S_1 becomes a conditioned reinforcer through pairing with food, S_2 becomes a conditioned reinforcer through pairing with S_1, and approach to and pecking of S_2 occurs because it is a conditioned reinforcer (not a higher-order conditioned stimulus for approach and pecking).

Note that this interpretation does not go against the view, discussed in Chapter 6, that a conditioned reinforcer is a respondently conditioned stimulus. The response it elicits is, however, not a skeletal response but, rather, a response that we termed "positive value" in Chapter 6. In addition, conditioned reinforcement may not account for all aspects of sign tracking, just as it may not account for all aspects of imprinting and imitation. Understanding these phenomena, however, requires understanding the involvement of conditioned reinforcement in them.

CONDITIONED REINFORCEMENT
AND NUMERICAL OPERATIONS

We saw in Chapter 9 that conditional discriminations are typically involved in numerosity behavior. Anther aspect of advanced numerosity behavior is chaining, and hence conditioned reinforcement.

Ordering Spatial Arrays

We saw in Chapter 9 that many species of animals can learn to discriminate stimulus arrays containing different numbers of elements, such an array containing three elements versus one containing four elements. At least one nonhuman species, the rhesus monkey (*Macaca mulatta*), can learn to order up to four different stimulus arrays on the basis of the number (from one to four) of elements that they contain (Brannon & Terrace, 2000). This may be demonstrated using the simultaneous forward chaining procedure described earlier in this chapter. The chain may be taught in either an ascending (i.e. 1, 2, 3, 4) or descending (i.e., 4, 3, 2, 1) order. In the ascending order, the monkey first learns a two component simultaneous forward chain consisting of arrays containing one and two elements, respectively; then a component consisting of an array containing three elements is added; and, finally, a component consisting of an array containing four elements is added. In the descending order the reverse sequence is taught. The sizes and shapes of the elements, and their arrangements with the respective arrays, are varied so that to receive reinforcement consistently the animals have to respond on the basis of number rather than the amount or pattern of the background covered by the elements. Interestingly, it is much more difficult to teach the animals a sequence in which the sizes of the arrays do not consistently increase or decrease (e.g., 3, 2, 1, 4) than it is to teach them either the ascending or descending sequence. This indicates that the number of elements in a stimulus array is a stimulus dimension for these animals.

In addition to being capable of learning to order the arrays, at least some rhesus monkeys can, to a limited extent, generalize the behavior to stimulus arrays of sizes that they have not been taught (i.e., to arrays containing from five to nine elements). It should be noted that although the monkeys generally learn to respond with well above 90% accuracy on arrays they are trained on, their accuracy on arrays they have not been trained on drops precipitously.

Counting

Although it is not clear how nonverbal animals are able to discriminate between and even order different size arrays with above chance accuracy, it is clear that they do not use formal counting procedures to do this. Recall from Chapter 9 that counting involves applying an ordered set of tags (e.g., the numerals 1, 2, 3 . . .) to a set of items. Each of the items to be counted is a stimulus for the emission of one and only one tag in the sequence, with the name of the last tag emitted being the name of the number of items counted. Stated in this way, it is fairly obvious that counting is a heterogeneous stimulus-response chain, in which the first item to be counted is the S^D for the response "1," the second item to be counted is the (conditioned) reinforcer for the response "1" and the S^D for the response "2," and so on until the last item is counted. Reinforcement for naming the number of the last item counted consists of the consequences of correct counting, including obtaining the same count when the process is repeated on the same items.

Counting in the above sense is a product of human cultural evolution. The development of one-to-one correspondence of numerical tags with objects requires training. Learning higher levels of counting typically occurs in a special setting (i.e., a school), with stimulus-response chaining procedures such as those described earlier in this chapter being applied more or less systematically. As a result of this training, most people in our culture are capable of counting an almost unlimited number of items. Our extensive counting ability is greatly enhanced, of course, by the invention of an iterative numbering system (i.e., digits that are repeated in a systematic manner to create a unique numeral corresponding to every possible number of items).

Although, as we have seen, animals can be taught to respond to number, they do not count in the above sense in the absence of chaining procedures. By means of a chaining procedure, however, chimpanzees have been taught to count up to four or five boxes on a computer screen (Rumbaugh & Washburn, 1993). At the completion of training, the screen displays the Arabic numeral for the number of boxes the animal is to count and a greater number of boxes than the number specified. By operating a joy stick, the animal either places the cursor on each box which then disappears, or uses the cursor to mark the boxes with back dots. When the animal has removed or marked the number of boxes corresponding to the numeral on the screen, it moves the cursor to the numeral and receives reinforcement. As the number of boxes to be counted increases from one to five on given trials, the proportion of trials on which the animal's count is correct drops precipitously. Although the chimpanzees perform well above chance when there are fewer than five boxes to be counted, it is impossible to say whether the animals are counting as defined above because they do not overtly assign a numeral to each box when they remove or mark it. In the initial stages of training, however, numerals appear sequentially in the position of the boxes when the animal touches them with the cursor, and these numerals are faded out over trials. It is therefore possible that the animals count covertly by visualizing the numerals as they perform the counting task.

Other Numerical Operations

Other numerical operations can also be viewed as chains, much in the same way that counting can. For example, humans clearly engage in heterogeneous S-R chains when they add, subtract, multiply, and divide. There is evidence, as we saw in Chapter 9, that some animals can engage in behavior whose result is similar to that of addition. However, at present there is no evidence that any nonhuman animal has learned to perform any formal numerical operation involving a chain of responses other than (possibly) counting.

SUMMARY AND CONCLUSIONS

A conditioned reinforcer is a reinforcer that depends on another reinforcer. In contrast, a primary reinforcer is reinforcing in its own right. A stimulus becomes a conditioned reinforcer by being paired with a primary reinforcer, or with a stimulus that has been paired with a stimulus that has been paired with a primary reinforcer (one pairing removed from primary reinforcement), and so forth. The strength of a conditioned reinforcer decreases the more removed it is from primary reinforcement. A conditioned reinforcer gradually ceases to be a reinforcer if it is not at least occasionally directly (i.e., by one remove) or indirectly (i.e., by more than one remove) paired with a primary reinforcer. Continuous or intermittent direct or indirect pairings with a primary reinforcer, however, can maintain a conditioned reinforcer indefinitely.

Because it is paired with reinforcement, an S^D is a conditioned reinforcer. Behavioral chains consisting of an S^D controlling a response that produces another S^D controlling a response that produces yet another S^D, and so on, can develop and persist if the last response in the chain produces primary reinforcement. (Most responses, in fact, consist of behavioral chains involving simpler responses.) Behavioral chains are studied in chained schedules, which are multi-component schedules in which the reinforcement that maintains responding on one component schedule is the S^D for responding on another component schedule. Primary reinforcement occurs in the final or terminal component, which maintains each S^D as a conditioned reinforcer.

Conditioned reinforcers are also involved in second-order schedules and token systems. In a second-order schedule, conditioned reinforcers are superimposed on responding on a single schedule, affecting both rate and patterning of responses. In a token system, conditioned reinforcers (called tokens) contingent on specific responses accumulate in one situation and are exchanged for back-up reinforcers (which can be either primary reinforcers or other conditioned reinforcers) in another situation.

Conditioned reinforcement can account for the fact that delayed reinforcement can sometimes be effective and for the fact that individuals will often respond to produce information even when it may not be favorable to them. Conditioned reinforcement also helps us see how complex skills, such as arithmetical operations, can develop.

12

Concurrent Schedules, Choice, and Preference

*U*p to this point we have concentrated extensively on situations involving single responses in order to keep the exposition relatively simple. In natural settings, however, it is extremely rare that there is only one response alternative. Generally several alternatives are available; for example, to go to a movie or stay home and watch television. Thus, learning scientists have developed experimental arrangements for studying several schedules of reinforcement operating together. Called concurrent schedules, these arrangements have been used to study interactions between responses under the simultaneous control of different schedules and to study choice or preference. Concurrent schedules are an important tool in our efforts to understand learning in the natural environment, where usually there are several contingencies impinging on an individual at any given time.

TYPES OF CONCURRENT SCHEDULES

There are single-response and multiple-response concurrent schedules. In single-response concurrent schedules, also called conjoint schedules, two or more schedules are programmed on the same operandum. Thus, for example, on single-response concurrent FR 25 FI 1 minute (or conjoint FR 25 FI 1 minute) schedules, reinforcement would occur after every 25th response and after every response occurring at least one minute following the previous response reinforced on the FI 1-minute schedule.

Single-response concurrent schedules permit one to determine the interactive effect of two or more different schedules on a single response. A major disadvantage of these schedules, however, is that it is difficult to determine the relative contribution of the component schedules in controlling the behavior. Consider, for example, the problem of determining for any particular response on a conjoint FR 25 FI 1-minute schedule the extent to which that response occurred at that particular time because of the FR 25 schedule and the extent to which it occurred because of the FI 1-minute schedule. Multiple-response concurrent schedules permit the relative effects of the component schedules to be analyzed more easily. In the rest of this book, unless otherwise specified, the term "concurrent schedules" will be used to indicate multiple-response concurrent schedules, and the term "conjoint schedule" will refer to single-response concurrent schedules.

There are two main types of multiple-response concurrent schedules: standard and Findley. Standard concurrent schedules are the most obvious type: Each of the component schedules is programmed on a separate operandum. For example, on standard concurrent FR 25 FI 1-minute schedules, responding on one operandum would be reinforced on an FR 25 schedule and responding on another would be reinforced on a FI 1-minute schedule. Thus, provided that a strong discrimination exists between the two operandums, one can infer that a response on the first operandum is under the control of the FR 25 schedule and a response on the second is under the control of the FI 1-minute schedule. (It is possible to be mistaken in this inference, however, as will be explained below.)

We can conceptualize a set of concurrent schedules as a multiple schedule (see Chapter 8) in which the alternating stimuli are the operandums and changeovers (i.e., alternations or switches) between these stimuli are controlled by the individual rather than externally. Findley concurrent schedules, named after their originator (Findley, 1958), are based on this similarity between multiple schedules and standard concurrent schedules. In Findley concurrent schedules, as in multiple schedules, two or more stimuli alternate and responses are reinforced on the same operandum according to the schedules coupled with the alternating stimuli. The alternation of the stimuli and their associated reinforcement schedules, however, is determined by responses emitted on another operandum. The operandum on which the concurrent schedules are in effect is called the main operandum; the one on which responding alternates with the stimuli and their associated reinforcement schedules is called the changeover operandum.

Findley concurrent schedules have several advantages over standard concurrent schedules. First, with Findley concurrent schedules the amount of time the individual allocates to each schedule can be easily determined by recording the amount of time the individual spends in the presence of the stimulus associated with each schedule. Second, the number of changeovers from one schedule to another can be determined directly by recording responses on the changeover operandum. Third, the use of a changeover operandum makes it possible to study the effect of imposing various contingencies on changeovers from one component schedule to another, for example, requiring that an FR 15 be completed on the changeover operandum in order for an alternation between component schedules to occur.

A factor that may or may not be an advantage of Findley concurrent schedules, depending on the problem under investigation, is that the procedure precludes responses being emitted simultaneously on more than one of the component schedules. This is not necessarily the case with standard concurrent schedules, since the operandums may be within reach of each other. For example, if the operandums are two levers close to each other, a rat, monkey, or human could press both simultaneously. If this is not desirable, the levers are placed far enough apart to prevent it. The problem does not occur, of course, if the concurrent responses are key pecks by pigeons, since a bird cannot peck two keys at exactly the same time. In addition, in the vast majority of studies regardless of species, the operandums are separated far enough apart that they cannot be operated simultaneously. Unless otherwise indicated, the concurrent schedules referred to in the remainder of this book are concurrent schedules in which responses can occur on only one component schedule at a time; that is, the procedures used render the alternative responses mutually exclusive.

Studies of concurrent schedules often use a procedure known as a changeover delay (COD). This is a contingency that prevents a response on either of the component schedules from being reinforced a short time (usually a few seconds) after a switch to that schedule has occurred, regardless of whether the schedule would otherwise have delivered a reinforcer during that time. Typically, if a reinforcer is scheduled during the COD period it is delivered just after the first response on that schedule after the delay has elapsed. Consider, for example, standard concurrent VI 1-minute VI 5-minute schedules in which a pigeon's peck on one key is reinforced on a VI 1-minute schedule and its peck on another key is reinforced on a VI 5-minute schedule, and a COD of 2 seconds is being used. Whenever a reinforcer is "set up" by the VI schedule for one key, the first peck on that key following a peck on the other key will not produce reinforcement. Only a peck that occurs at least 2 seconds later will produce the reinforcer.

The orginal purpose of a COD is to prevent reinforcers programmed by one of the schedules from adventitiously reinforcing responses on the other schedule. Without an effective COD an individual might respond on schedule 1, then respond on schedule 2 and receive a reinforcer which could conceivably reinforce not only the response on schedule 2 but also the immediately preceding response on schedule 1. This could result in responses on one operandum being adventitiously chained (see p. 42) to responses on the other (in the case of standard concurrent schedules), or in an adventitious chain consisting of responding on one schedule followed by responding on the changeover operandum followed by responding on the other schedule (in the case of Findley concurrent schedules), which would make it impossible to assess the separate effects of the component schedules on responding. In other words, rather than (multiple-response) concurrent schedules we would have something close to conjoint schedules, where the adventitious chain would be the response unit. There are, however, other interpretations of how a COD works (see de Villiers, 1977, pp. 242–244).

CONCURRENT SCHEDULES AND SIMULTANEOUS DISCRIMINATIONS COMPARED

Concurrent schedules are similar to simultaneous discriminations (discussed in Chapter 8, pp. 162–164). The major difference is that in simultaneous discriminations the emphasis is on the individual's capacity to discriminate between the discriminative stimuli correlated with the alternatives. In concurrent schedules, the emphasis is on the sensitivity of responding to the reinforcement contingencies correlated with the alternatives. Hence, experimenters usually ensure a strong discrimination between the alternatives in concurrent schedules, whereas establishing a strong discrimination at the outset typically defeats the purpose of studies on simultaneous discriminations. Two other differences are: In concurrent schedules reinforcement is typically available for each alternative, whereas in a simultaneous discrimination it is typically available for only one alternative; and in concurrent schedules responding usually occurs as free operant, whereas in a simultaneous discrimination it usually occurs in discrete trials.

SCHEDULE EFFECTS IN CONCURRENT SCHEDULES

While there are a number of different ways to program concurrent schedules (as seen in the previous section), characteristic responding on the component schedules occurs according to the typical cumulative record patterns produced by those schedules when they are studied in isolation. For example, the FR schedule in concurrent FR VI schedules produces essentially the same response pattern that is produced by a single FR schedule; likewise, the VI schedule produces essentially the same response pattern that is produced by a single VI schedule. It does not appear to matter whether different reinforcers are used in the component schedules. For example, in concurrent FR FI schedules, the typical FR break-run pattern and the typical FI scallop pattern occur when food is the reinforcer in one component schedule and water is the reinforcer in the other (Wood, Martinez, & Willis, 1975).

Although concurrent schedules are typically programmed so that the individual can respond on only one of the component schedules at a time, the component schedules have independent effects on response patterning even when simultaneous responding on them is possible. This is illustrated in Figure 12.1, which shows data from two concurrent schedules in which a chimpanzee operated two toggle switches, one with each hand. Responses with the right hand were reinforced on an FR 120 schedule, while responses with the left hand were reinforced on a VI 5 schedule. The FR performance is shown in the upper part of the figure, and the VI performance is shown in the lower part. Note that as with responding on single FR schedules, responding on the FR schedule occurred at a high, steady rate with pauses typically occurring after reinforcement on the FR schedule. At the same time, as with single VI schedules, responding on the VI schedule occurred at a moderate, steady rate throughout. In general, the two behavior patterns were remarkably independent.

Independent effects of component schedules also occur in single-response concurrent schedules. For example, suppose that a pigeon is placed on a conjoint VI 1-minute DRL 10-second schedule and the results are compared to those obtained with the same pigeon on a VI 1-minute schedule alone and a DRL 10-second schedule alone. If the VI 1-minute schedule produces a modal IRT of about 2 seconds and the DRL 10-second produces one of about 8 seconds, the conjoint VI 1-minute DRL 10-second schedule might be expected to produce a modal IRT of about 6 seconds (the average of the effects of the two component schedules in isolation). Instead, however, most of the bird's IRTs on the conjoint schedule are either approximately 2 seconds or 8 seconds. It therefore appears that the bird distributes its time between the two components of the conjoint schedule such that some of its time is spent on the VI 1-minute component and the rest is spent on the DRL 10-second component. Interest-

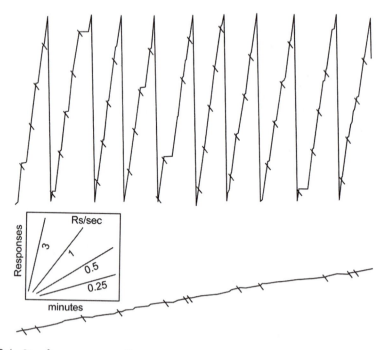

FIGURE 12.1. Simultaneous responding on concurrent FR VI. Cumulative records from a chimpanzee that simultaneously operated one toggle switch with its right hand on a FR schedule (upper curve) and another toggle switch with its left hand on a VI schedule (lower curve). Slash marks indicate reinforcements. (From Skinner, 1957b)

ingly, this occurs despite the fact that the bird would maximize its rate of reinforcement if it allocated all its time to the DRL 10-second component (Zeiler & Blakely, 1983).

VARIABLES AFFECTING PREFERENCE

The term "amount of behavior" in a component schedule of a set of concurrent schedules may used to designate either of the following:

- The response rate (i.e., number of responses divided by total session time) in the component schedule.
- The proportion of time allocated (i.e., time allocated over total session time) to the component schedule.

The amount of behavior on a component schedule relative to the amount of behavior on other component schedules can be taken as an indicator of the preference for that component schedule. The term "preference" is somewhat vague, however, so one should always indicate what measure of amount of behavior one is using to index it. In addition, where relative time allocated to and relative response rate on a component schedule differ, it is probably more consistent with the everyday meaning of "preference" to use time rather than response rate to indicate preference. One may work at a high rate at an unpleasant task, for example, but one would not spend much time at it if given the opportunity to do something more preferable. There is, however, a problem with accurately measuring time spent responding on each of the component schedules. Typical measures of this, such as the time spent in the presence of a stimulus in a Findley procedure, or time between changeovers in the standard procedure, include time spent in other activities (e.g., grooming and other bodily maintenance).

Regardless of the measure used, there are a number of variables that have fairly consistent effects on preference.

Reinforcement Rate

The matching law. When reinforcement rate is varied in concurrent schedules, a relation often emerges (e.g., Herrnstein, 1961; see Catania, 1966) that is so reliable that it has been formulated as a law. Called the matching law (not to be confused with matching-to-sample), this formulation states that the amount of behavior in each component schedule relative to the amount(s) of behavior in the other component schedule(s) matches (i.e., equals) the reinforcement rate on that component schedule relative to the reinforcement rate(s) on the other component schedule(s). The matching law can be written as

$$\frac{B_1}{B_1 + B_2} = \frac{r_1}{r_1 + r_2} \tag{12.1a}$$

or equivalently, as

$$\frac{B_1}{B_2} = \frac{R_1}{r_2} \tag{12.1b}$$

where B_1 and B_2 are the behavior (usually measured as response rate) on schedules 1 and 2, respectively, and r_1 and r_2 are the corresponding rates of reinforcements on the two schedules (provided that neither denominator is zero in equation 12.1b). (See Appendix B for a mathematical description of the matching law; Appendices C for a mathematical description relating to the matching law to Hernstein's formulation (equation 7.1, p. 139; and Appendix D for a mathematical alternative to the matching law.)

The generalized matching law (GML). The matching law does not always hold. Under a wide variety of conditions, there are two types of deviations from the matching law:

- behavior can be over- or undersensitive to relative reinforcement rate, so that the relative amount of behavior on component schedules with higher reinforcement rates exceeds or falls short, respectively, of matching.
- the relative amount of behavior shows a systematic deviation from matching that is unrelated to reinforcement rate.

If the first type of deviation occurs, the individual is said to overmatch or undermatch, depending on whether behavior is over- or undersensitive to relative reinforcement rate. If the second type of deviation occurs, the individual is said to show bias toward one of the component schedules. The presence of bias is readily seen when consistently more or consistently less than half the total amount of behavior occurs on one component schedule when half the overall reinforcements occur on that component schedule.

The above deviations from the matching law are taken into account in a formulation called the generalized matching law (GML), which states that in concurrent schedules the amount of behavior on each component schedule relative to the amount of behavior on the other component schedule(s) is a direct function—specifically, a function of a power that is usually slightly less than one—of the rate of reinforcement on that component schedule relative to the rate(s) of reinforcement on the other component schedule(s) (Baum, 1974). Another way of stating the GML is that the relative amount of some behavior is proportional to the relative rate of reinforcement for that behavior, raised to some power that is typically slightly less than one.

The equation for the generalized matching law is

$$\frac{B_1}{B_2} = c\left(\frac{r_1}{r_2}\right)^s$$

(12.2)

where c and s are constants, and the other symbols are defined as for equations 12.1a and 12.1b. The constant s represents sensitivity of behavior to the relative reinforcement rates in the two component schedules, and the constant c represents bias. Note that if both s and c are equal to one, equation 12.2 reduces to equation 12.1b. To the extent that c is greater than one, there is a corresponding amount of bias in favor of schedule 1; conversely, to the extent that c is less than one (but equal to or greater than zero), there is a corresponding amount of bias in favor of schedule 2. If s is greater than one, overmatching occurs, and if s is less than one, undermatching occurs. If s is zero there is no sensitivity to relative reinforcement rates. It usually is assumed that s cannot be less than zero, although (as well shall see later in this chapter when we talk about nonsubstitutability) there are situations in which this would may occur. Typically, as mentioned above, s is estimated to be slightly less than one. (See Appendix E for additional mathematical treatment of the GML and alternative versions of the matching law.)

Generality of the GML. The GML provides a fairly accurate description of behavior in a variety of situations (see Davison & McCarthy, 1988, for a review). It has been confirmed most often with pigeons pecking keys on concurrent VI VI schedules, however it also has been demonstrated for concurrent FR FI (Bacotti, 1977; Davison, 1982), concurrent FI FI (White & Davison, 1973), concurrent FI VI (Nevin, 1971; Trevitt, Davison, & Williams, 1972), concurrent VI VR (Herrnstein & Heyman, 1979), and concurrent FI FR (LaBounty & Reynolds, 1973; see Baum, 1974 and Davison & McCarthy, 1988). It occurs as well with concurrent second-order schedules—specifically concurrent VI (FR-brief stimulus) VI (FR-brief stimulus), where the behavioral unit was each completion of an FR schedule (Beautrais & Davison, 1977), and concurrent VI (DRL LH) (DRL LH), where the behavioral unit was a response satisfying the designated IRT categories (Shimp, 1968; see Davison & McCarthy, 1988, pp. 107–108).

For concurrent ratio schedules, the GML predicts a strong or exclusive preference for one of the component schedules. As a mathematical shortcoming of the GML, it does not necessarily predict which component schedule will be preferred (see Appendices B–E). However, as common sense would suggest, it is the alternative that provides the fewer number of responses per reinforcement (Herrnstein, 1958; Herrnstein & Loveland, 1975; Mace, McCurdge, & Quigley, 1990).

Besides being confirmed with pigeons pecking keys, the GML is seen in lever pressing by rats and humans, treadle pressing by pigeons (McSweeney, 1975), and eye movements by humans (Schroeder & Holland, 1969). It also appears with human behavior having social significance. For example, the GML describes the relationship between the proportion of time a speaker orients toward specific listeners and the relative rates of agreement statements by those listeners with the speaker (Conger & Killeen, 1974; Pierce, Epling, & Greer, 1981); the proportion of bets a gambler places on specific game options and the relative payoffs for those alternatives (Hamblin, Clairmont, & Chadwick, 1975); and the proportion of time adolescents with special education needs spend on specific sets of math problems and the relative rate of reinforcement for correctly solved problems in those sets (Mace et al., 1990; Mace, Neef, Shade, & Mauro, 1994). (For a modification of the GML that seems to often provide greater accuracy, see Appendix E.)

We saw in Chapter 4 that humans are less sensitive to schedules of reinforcement than other animals are, and that this may be due to the tendency of humans to verbalize and to respond to their own verbalizations. Compared to other animals, accordingly, humans are often extremely slow to change their relative rates of responding or time allocation to concurrent alternatives when the relative rates of reinforcement for those alternatives change. In fact, special procedures often seem to be required in order to cause humans to adjust their relative responding or time allocation to the relative rates of reinforcement in accordance with the GML. These special procedures include prior exposure to the schedules presented singly (rather than concurrently), correlating a unique stimulus with each schedule, providing instructions about the independence of the concurrent schedules, using a limited hold in which the opportunity for a response to produce a scheduled reinforcement is available only for a limited time (see Chapter 4), and making timers available and demonstrating their use (Horne & Lowe, 1993; Mace et al., 1994; Takahashi & Iwamoto, 1986). As in studies with other animals, CODs seem to help produce conformity to the GML, although they frequently are not sufficient to do so with humans. Providing humans with an attending response for observing stimuli correlated with concurrently programmed schedules, and a contingency to ensure emission of the attending response, also increases human sensitivity to concurrent schedules (Madden & Perone, 1999).

The GML holds when the number of component schedules is greater than two. For example, it occurs with pigeons pecking keys on three (Davison & Hunter, 1976; Pliskoff & Brown, 1976) and on five (Miller & Loveland, 1974) concurrent VI schedules, and with rats nose poking on eight concurrent FI or VI schedules at the ends of the arms of an eight-arm radial maze like the one shown in Figure 10.4 (Elsmore & McBride, 1994).

Factors influencing bias and sensitivity.

Both bias and sensitivity to reinforcement vary according to certain conditions. Most obvious among the wide variety of factors that can produce bias are those involving the responses required for reinforcement. For example, pigeons show a bias toward component schedules in which the response keys operate with a lighter force (Hunter & Davison, 1982) and toward component schedules in which key pecking as opposed to lever pressing is reinforced (Davison & Ferguson, 1978).

With regard to sensitivity to reinforcement, undermatching is far more common than overmatching (Baum, 1974, 1979). The reason for this is not known at present. It is known, however, that sensitivity to reinforcement can be increased so that undermatching is reduced and even replaced by overmatching. In particular, at least when there are only a few component schedules, sensitivity to reinforcement can be increased by any operation that decreases the number of changeovers (resulting in the individual allocating more time to component schedules with higher reinforcement rates). This can be accomplished by adding a COD if the concurrent schedule does not already have one (Scown, 1983; Shull & Pliskoff, 1967), by punishing changeovers with electric shock or timeout (Todorov, 1971), by putting changeovers on an FR schedule (Pliskoff, Cicerone, & Nelson, 1978), and by increasing the travel time (e.g., by means of partitions or hurdles) between the alternative operandums (Baum, 1982).

When a rat's nose-poking responses are reinforced on eight concurrent FI or VI schedules at the ends of the arms of an eight-arm radial maze, sensitivity to reinforcement shows somewhat different effects from those described for concurrent schedules with only a few component schedules. Although time allocation shows undermatching, response rate shows overmatching. In addition, adding a COD has no effect on the sensitivity to reinforcement of time allocation but causes response rate to become less sensitive to reinforcement rate, so that response rate then shows about the same degree of undermatching as time allocation does (Elsmore & McBride, 1994). Why the effects on sensitivity to reinforcement are different (i.e., overmatching of response rate when there is no COD, increased sensitivity of response rate with the addition of a COD) in this situation from those found in more commonly studied experimental arrangements is not known, but could have to do either with the type of apparatus (i.e., radial maze) or the large number of component concurrent schedules.

Matching versus maximizing formulations.

One of the most surprising aspects of the GML is that animals conform to it even at the expense of failing to maximize their overall reinforcement rates (e.g., Vaughan, 1981). It is difficult to see how animals that do not maximize their overall reinforcement rates could have evolved. For this and other reasons, many learning scientists have questioned whether the matching or GML describes a fundamental process, or whether the tendency to conform to them stems from some more basic tendency to maximize reinforcements, at least over some small time period (e.g., Shimp, 1969; Ziriax & Silberberg, 1984). Conforming to the GML often does result in the maximizing of reinforcements, and it is conceivable that—given the right conditions—this would have been sufficient for it to evolve as a fundamental behavioral mechanism. The circumstances in which conforming to the GML fails to maximize reinforcements may be largely peculiar to specially arranged laboratory conditions that would be rare or nonexistent in the natural environment, and thus have had no evolutionary effect.

Despite the successes of the matching law (equation 12.1a,b) and its generalized form (equation 12.2), however, some learning scientists hold that maximizing of reinforcement better characterizes choices of concurrently available reinforcement opportunities. There are two major arguments supporting this position: (1) Natural selection is a highly efficient process and animals that did not maximize their reinforcements would not be likely to survive to pass on their genes. (2) There are some noteworthy instances in which matching fails to occur and maximizing tends to be supported.

There are two major classes of maximizing theories: economic models (as discussed in Chapter 7, p. 142) and optimal foraging theories. Simplifying somewhat, economic models (Hursh, 1980, 1984; Kagel et al., 1995) assume that individuals attempt to minimize the discrepancies between ideal amounts of various commodities and the amounts that they actually have of those commodities. Since the ideal is never achieved, consumers balance the discrepancies in a manner that, given individual preferences, can be described mathematically (although the mathematics is too intricate to present here). Derivable from economic models, optimal foraging theories (Charnov, 1976a, b; Parker & Stuart, 1976; Pyke et al., 1977) are designed to account mainly for the choices animals make as they search for food in their natural environments. These theories assume that natural environments are divided into regions called patches and that animals maximize their net energy intake in their choices within and between patches. According to these theories, animals maximize their energy intake by selecting high-calorie over low-calorie food items within patches and switch from patches with less caloric value to those with more caloric value (taking into account calorie or energy loss due to time and effort involved in switching). Concurrent schedules in operant conditioning experiments provide instructive analogues to consumer behavior in an economy and foraging in natural environments.

We now review some of the major evidence relevant to maximizing versus matching of reinforcement in choice situations.

Non-substitutable reinforcers. Matching formulations work best when the concurrently available reinforcers are identical. They are poorest when the reinforcers are based on different establishing operations (see pp. 265–266 of this chapter). For example, responding for water on one schedule will not increase when food occurs less frequently on a concurrently available schedule. On the contrary, as food becomes more frequent on one schedule responding for water will increase (not decrease) on the other, and vice versa. One way for the generalized matching equation to handle this would be to allow the exponent s in equation 12.2 to be less than zero. Although this might work mathematically, however, it is unclear how it fits with the usual interpretation of s as an index of sensitivity to the differences between the schedules. In other words, the intuitive meaning of "negative sensitivity" in the context of complementary reinforcers is unclear.

Progressive-ratio schedules. A progressive ratio schedule is one in which the number of responses required for reinforcement increase by a fixed amount after each reinforcement. For example, at the beginning of the session the ratio may start at 10, and increase by 10 after each reinforcement. Thus, this progressive ratio schedule consists of the following sequence of FR schedules: FR 10, FR 20, FR 30, FR 40, FR 50, ... The number of responses required to obtain the first 5 reinforcements would be 150, or an average of 30 responses per reinforcement. Suppose that there is another operandum on which an FR 30 is programmed for a reinforcer identical to that available on the first lever. In addition, when ever reinforcement occurs on the second lever the schedule on the first lever resets to FR 10. In order for matching to hold, the individual should start responding on the first lever and continue responding on that lever until the fifth reinforcement occurs, at which point the individual should change to the second lever for one reinforcement. To maximize reinforcement, the individual should change over to the second lever after the second reinforcement on the first operandum. Experiments of this type that have been done with several species fail to support matching. In addition, they tend to support maximizing although further research needs to be done to establish the extent to which they support maximizing (Kagel et al., 1995, pp. 120–121).

Concurrent VI VR schedules. One of the strongest pieces of evidence for matching as opposed to maximizing is the fact that matching occurs on concurrent VI VR schedules. From a maximizing point of view, it seems that individuals should respond almost exclusively on the VR schedule and sample the VI schedule only occasionally (to check, as it were, whether reinforcement had been set up there while they were busy working for reinforcement on the VR schedule). That is, there should be far more responding per reinforcement on the VR than on the VI schedule, which would contradict matching. There are, however, several factors that could act against maximizing on concurrent VI VR schedules (Kagel, 1995, pp. 114–120). One is VI requires less energy expenditure (or, alternatively, provides more "leisure") than VR. Another is that responding at a higher response rate on a VI schedule results in more immediate reinforcement on VI schedules, and an immediately delivered commodity is generally assumed to be preferred over a delayed one in economic theory. A third factor may be a lack of discrimination between VI and VR schedules when they operate concurrently; that is, responding on concurrent VI VR schedules may be perceptually similar to responding to concurrent VI VI schedules. In other words, maximizing may fail to occur when individuals lack information regarding the contingencies they are operating under. Although these factors are plausible, it is unclear why they should come together to produce a result that conforms to matching.

We must conclude that the issue of matching versus maximizing awaits future research and theoretical development for its resolution. Matching formulations account for a considerable amount of data, but clearly need to be modified if they are to account for all data. Maximizing formulations appear to account for more data, but sometimes at the risk of excessive circularity. Rather than clearly defining optimality—that is, what constitutes maximizing—before applying the equations to predict an animal's behavior, maximizing theories sometimes define optimality as whatever an animal does (as in accounting for the matching behavior on concurrent VI VR schedules in the above example). All scientific theories have a certain amount of circularity built into them (Kuhn, 1970); however, excessive circularity leads to poor explanation and prediction. It remains to be seen whether the circularity in maximizing formulations will prove to be excessive.

Reinforcement Magnitude

The term magnitude of reinforcement refers to the amount, duration, or intensity of the reinforcer. For example, 2 food pellets, 2 seconds access to mixed grain, and 2 mg/ml concentration of sucrose in water are greater in magnitude than 1 food pellet, 1 second access to mixed grain, and 1 mg/ml concentration of sucrose in water, respectively. Relative amount of behavior varies with relative magnitude of reinforcement in a manner similar to that in which it varies with relative rate of reinforcement. This is true of food reinforcement (Brownstein, 1971; Catania, 1963; Davison & Hogsden, 1984; Fantino, Squires, Delbrück, & Peterson, 1972; Neuringer, 1967; Schneider, 1973; Todorov, 1973), reinforcing drugs such as cocaine (Iglauer & Woods, 1974; Johanson, 1975; Johanson & Schuster, 1975), and no doubt other reinforcers (although no studies have as yet reported on this).

Sensitivity to reinforcement magnitude, when measured in a manner analogous to that in which sensitivity to reinforcement rate is measured, is consistently lower than sensitivity to reinforcement rate (e.g., Todorov, 1973).

Attempts have been made to extend the GML to incorporate reinforcement magnitude, but they have thus far led to unresolved complications (see Davison & McCarthy, 1988, pp. 89–92).

Delay Between Token and Backup Reinforcer

If token reinforcement occurs on two component schedules, but the tokens received on one schedule can be exchanged immediately for backup reinforcers and the tokens earned on the other schedule can be exchanged for backup reinforcers only after a delay, the individual will show a preference for the first component schedule. This effect is quite important from a practical standpoint, and has been demonstrated in socially significant behavior such as adolescents who are emotionally disturbed and learning disabled solving math problems (Neef, Shade, & Miller, 1994).

Reinforcer Class and Quality

By different classes of reinforcers we refer to reinforcers that are based on different establishing operations. For example, food deprivation establishes food, but not water, as a reinforcer; water deprivation establishes water, but not food, as a reinforcer.

Different rates of reinforcement in different classes. The GML does not apply when the component schedules involve different reinforcer classes. In particular, when behavior on the component schedules is reinforced by different classes of reinforcement, increasing the relative rate of reinforcement in one component schedule does not decrease the amount of behavior in the other component schedule. For example, if food and water are the reinforcers on two concurrently programmed schedules, increasing the rate or magnitude of one of these reinforcers may cause the rate of responding for the other to increase rather than decrease (Hursh, 1978; cf. Nevin, 1984, p. 424). If daily intakes of food and water are held constant (i.e., by ending the session after a constant number of food or water reinforcements, and by providing additional food or water outside of the experimental session), rate of responding for water reinforcement shows little or no relationship to rate of food reinforcement (Hursh, 1978). Likewise, with rats that are maintained at a constant level of food and water deprivation and placed on concurrent FR FI schedules, rate of responding on the FI schedule varies inversely with the number of responses required for reinforcement on the FR schedule when food or water is the reinforcer on both schedules, but remains fairly constant when the reinforcer on the two schedules differ (Wood et al., 1975; Wood & Willis, 1974).

Reinforcer quality. Reinforcers in different classes necessarily differ in quality. Reinforcers in the same class also may be qualitatively different. For example, different types of food are in the same reinforcer class, but are qualitatively different. Some reinforcers in a given class will be consistently preferred over qualitatively different reinforcers in the same class.

Different conditioned reinforcers, as well as different primary reinforcers, may be qualitatively different from each other and differentially preferred. For example, a token that can be exchanged for certain items may be preferred over another token that can be used to buy different items (Neef et al., 1994).

Reinforcer substitutability. One issue regarding qualitatively different reinforcers is that of scaling the relative reinforcement value—also called hedonic value—of different reinforcers. Mathematical procedures derived from the GML can be used to construct such scales

(Davison & McCarthy, 1988, pp. 92–96; Hollard & Davison, 1978). These procedures have been used to scale the reinforcement value of, for example, three types of grain (buckwheat, hemp, and wheat) for pigeons (Miller, 1976) and two types of feed (hay and dairy meal) for cows (Matthews & Temple, 1979).

A related issue is that of the substitutability of reinforcers, which refers to the extent to which the tendency to respond for a given reinforcer in lieu of another reinforcer increases when the response requirement (or "cost") for a given magnitude of the latter reinforcer is increased. For example, consider visual and auditory reinforcers presented through a computer terminal contingent on pressing two keys on two concurrent FR schedules.

The left panel of Figure 12.2 shows data generated by this arrangement with a developmentally disabled person when the FR schedule providing auditory reinforcement was varied over sessions and the FR schedule providing visual reinforcement was held constant. Visual reinforcement consisted of colorful patterns and auditory reinforcement consisted of musical tones. Note that as the FR requirement for auditory reinforcement increased beyond that for visual reinforcement, there was a steep increase in visual reinforcements obtained and a correspondingly steep decrease in auditory reinforcements obtained. In contrast, the right panel of Figure 12.2 shows data produced when, instead of auditory reinforcement, social reinforcement—in the form of someone smiling at, nodding at, and praising the individual—occurred on the FR schedule that was varied. Note that as the FR requirement for the social reinforcer (attention) increased, there was a shallow increase in visual reinforcements obtained and a correspondingly shallow decrease in social reinforcements obtained. That the slopes of reinforcements (when one FR schedule was varied) were steeper when the concurrent FR schedules provided visual and auditory reinforcement than when they provided visual and social reinforcement indicates that—at least for this individual—visual and auditory reinforcers were more substitutable than visual and social reinforcers were.

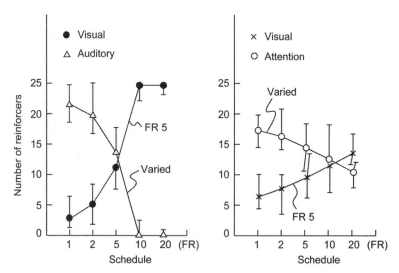

FIGURE 12.2. Reinforcer substitutability. The graph on the left shows number of reinforcers on each component schedule of concurrent FR 5 (visual reinforcement) FR x (auditory reinforcement) and the graph on the right shows number of reinforcers on each component schedule of concurrent FR 5 (visual reinforcement) FR x (attention reinforcement), where x varied from 1 to 20. The graphs are from a developmentally disabled individual. Note that the slopes for visual and auditory reinforcement as x varied are steeper than the slopes for visual and attention reinforcement, indicating that the former pair of reinforcers are more substitutable than the latter are for this individual. (From Tustin, 1994)

Substitutability of reinforcers has a special practical importance with regard to addictive drugs, because of the possibility of being able to treat an addiction by substituting a dangerous reinforcing drug with a relatively harmless substance. Along these lines it has been found, for example, that with monkeys on concurrent FR FR schedules where saccharin is the reinforcer in one schedule and phencyclidine (also known as "angel dust") is the reinforcer in the other schedule, increasing the concentration of saccharin will decrease the rate of responding for the drug. However, increasing the concentration of phencyclidine does not decrease responding for saccharin in all cases. Thus, for monkeys, it appears that the two substances are somewhat substitutable (Carroll, 1985). Even a powerful reinforcer such as food under severe food deprivation, however, has a very low or zero substitutability with cocaine for monkeys: When given a choice between cocaine and food, they respond almost exclusively for cocaine—and if permitted, would do so to the point of death from starvation (Aigner & Balster, 1978).

The substitutability of one drug for another also is of interest because it may provide information about whether two drugs have similar physiological effects. An example is the fact that *d,l*-cathinone and cocaine have been found to be substitutable in monkeys (Woolverton & Johanson, 1984). These two drugs may therefore be affecting overlapping parts of the nervous system.

Type of Reinforcement Schedule

Distributions of relative response rate and time allocation also are affected by the kinds of component schedules being used. For example, in concurrent FR FI schedules a strong bias occurs in favor of the FI schedule (LaBounty & Reynold, 1973). If one schedule is aperiodic (i.e., variable) and the other is fixed, there is a bias toward the aperiodic schedule. For example, in concurrent FI VI schedules, individuals respond more and spend more time on the VI schedule when both component schedules provide the same reinforcement rate (Lobb & Davison, 1975; Trevett et al., 1972). Likewise, strong biases exist toward the VR schedules in concurrent FI VR schedules (Rider, 1981) and in concurrent FR VR schedules (Bacotti, 1977).

Bias in favor of VR over FR can be demonstrated even with mixed-ratio (MR) schedules, which are VR schedules that contain only a few, usually randomly alternating, ratio requirements. For example, rats will respond more on an MR 50 schedule, consisting of equiprobable ratios of 1 and 99, than on an FR 50 schedule—even though both schedules require the same average number of responses per reinforcement. Equal responding on the two component schedules can be obtained only if the size of the FR schedule is decreased sufficiently. In some cases, a value as low as FR 35 might be required to obtain equal responding, although this value differs for different individuals (Rider, 1979, 1983b).

Response Properties

By response property, we refer to any way in which two given responses may differ from each other, such as in topography or force. For examples, if one component schedule consists of solving one type of math problem and another component schedule consists of solving another type, students may show a preference for one of the two types (Neef et al., 1994).

CONCURRENT CHAINS

Concurrent chains combine features of concurrent schedules and chained schedules. The initial links of two or more chained schedules are available concurrently. When one of these links is completed, the terminal link for that chained schedule occurs and no other alternatives are available. (See Figure 12.3.) Generally, the terminal link remains in effect until primary reinforcement occurs, after which the initial links are again present concurrently. In a common variation of this procedure, the terminal link remains in effect for a fixed period of time. Like simple concurrent schedules, concurrent chains provide (1) a way to study the mathematics of choice; and (2), a way to study preferences along various dimensions. We consider each of these in turn.

The Delay-Reduction Hypothesis

One of the most influential theories in the mathematics of choice is the delay-reduction hypothesis (Fantino, 1969, 1977, 1981; Fantino & Davison, 1983; Squires & Fantino, 1971). According to this hypothesis, the strength of a conditioned reinforcer is a function of the average amount in the delay to primary reinforcement that is correlated with that conditioned reinforcer. Both the green key light and the red key light in Figure 12.3 are conditioned reinforcers because they are paired with the primary reinforcement that occurs in their presence when the individual responds on each of their respective VI schedules. If the VI schedule paired with the green key light provides a higher rate of, or more immediate reinforcement than, the VI schedule paired with the red key light, the green key light should be a stronger

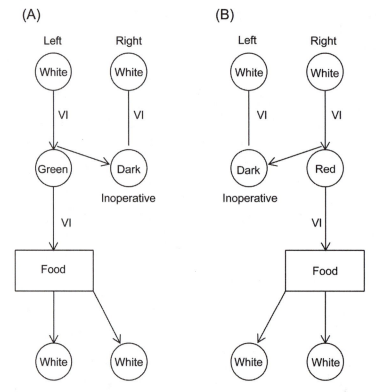

FIGURE 12.3. Sequences of events in a typical concurrent-chains procedure. A) the sequence of events if a response on the left key is reinforced in the first stage of the concurrent chains; B) the sequence of events if a response on the right key is reinforced in the first stage. Note that after reinforcement the key lights are white again and the cycle repeats. (From Fantino, 1969)

conditioned reinforcer than the red key light. But the question is how much stronger? The delay reduction hypothesis is designed to provide a quantitative answer to this question.

To see how the hypothesis works mathematically, we must consider three quantities: (1) T, the average time to reinforcement at the start of the initial links (i.e., the onset of the white key lights in Figure 12.3) to primary reinforcement (i.e., food in Figure 12.3); (2) t_{2L}, the average time to reinforcement during the second link of the chain on the left operandum (i.e., during the green light on the left key in Figure 12.3); and (3) t_{2R}, the average time to reinforcement during the second link of the chain on the right operandum (i.e., during the red light on the right key in Figure 12.3). Assume that two equal VI schedules, say VI 60 seconds, are operating in the initial links and that VI 10 seconds is operating in the terminal link on the left operandum and VI 20 seconds in the terminal link on the right key. Then T is equal to 30 seconds (the average amount of time it takes to get to either of the terminal links) plus one-half of 10 plus 20 seconds (because, since both initial-link VI schedules are equal, we assume that each terminal link will, on average, occur about one-half the time). That is, T is equal to 45 seconds. Similarly, in this example t_{2L} is equal to 5 seconds and t_{2R} to 10 seconds.

The average reduction in the delay to reinforcement correlated with the green key light is $T-t_{2L}$ (i.e., 45 seconds in the above example) and the average reduction in the delay to reinforcement correlated with the red key light is $T-t_{2R}$ (i.e., 30 seconds). Then the delay-reduction hypotheses states that

$$\frac{R_{1L}}{R_{1L} + R_{1R}} = \frac{T - t_{2L}}{(T - t_{2L}) + (T - t_{2R})} \qquad \text{for } t_{2L} \text{ and } t_{2R} < T$$

$$\frac{R_{1L}}{R_{1L} + R_{1R}} = 0 \qquad \text{for } t_{2L} > T, t_{2R} < T$$

$$\frac{R_{1L}}{R_{1L} + R_{1R}} = 1 \qquad \text{for } t_{2L} < T, t_{2R} > T, \qquad (12.3)$$

where R_{1L} is the rate of responding on the left operandum during the initial links and R_{1R} is the rate of responding on the right operandum during the initial links. (Applying equation 12.3 to the above example, relative response rate on the left key during the initial links is equal to 40/75 = 0.53).

There are several things to notice about equation 12.3. First, note that the equation specifies that relative response rate on either operandum during the initial links must be zero (and that on the other must be one) if the average delay reduction correlated with the conditioned reinforcer for responding on that operandum during the initial links is equal to or greater than T. (It can be shown that the delay reductions associated the terminal links cannot both be equal to or greater than zero.)

Second, note that the equation is similar to the matching law, equation 12.1a. If primary reinforcement occurred immediately in each terminal link—that is as soon as the green or red key light turned on—for example, equation 12.3 would give the same result (i.e., 0.50) as equation 12.1a for two concurrently programmed equal VI schedules. It is the presence of the second links, containing unequal VI schedules, that causes the result to be different from that given by equation 12.1a. (For further discussion of the relationship between the delay-reduction hypothesis and the matching law see Fantino & Davison, 1983.)

Third, note that if the VI schedules in the terminal links differ, preference between them, as measured by the relative rates of responding in the initial links, varies from indifference to exclusiveness. As T increases while t_{2L} and t_{2R} remain constant, relative response rate on each initial-link schedule approaches 0.50; as T decreases while t_{2L} and t_{2R} remain constant, relative response rate on the initial-link schedule leading to the conditioned reinforcer correlated with the more immediate primary reinforcer approaches 1.0. This, of course, means exclusive preference for the terminal link containing the more immediate primary reinforcer.

Exclusive preference characterizes the optimal-diet model (Charnov, 1976b), which is a variant of optimal-foraging theory (discussed on pp. 263–264 of this chapter). The optimal-diet model predicts animals will always reject food items that provide fewer calories (i.e., energy) in favor of those that provide more per unit of time spent searching for and handling those items. The delay-reduction hypothesis is similar to the optimal-diet model in that time in the initial links of current chains is analogous to time spent searching for food items while time spent in the terminal links is analogous to handling time (e.g., the time it takes to crack a nut or shell and extract the meat). Moreover, the delay-reduction hypothesis predicts that exclusive preference will occur under conditions that are analogous to conditions under which the optimal-diet model predicts exclusive preference (Fantino et al., 1987). Specifically, if the average handling time for one food item is larger than the average handling and search time for the alternative, the animal should show exclusive preference for the latter.

It is noteworthy that the optimal-diet model and the delay-reduction hypothesis converge in this manner. As we saw on pages 263–264 of this chapter, the optimal-diet model is a maximizing formulation, whereas—as we saw above—the delay-reduction hypothesis is compatible with the matching law. Choice situations in the natural environment may be more analogous to concurrent chains than to simple concurrent schedules. This may be because in the natural environment an individual is committed to a particular alternative for a certain period after embarking on it, whereas in simple concurrent schedules an individual can switch readily back-and-forth between alternatives. This difference may be why maximizing formulations seem to work better in the natural environment while matching formulations seem to work better in relatively simple operant conditioning situations. It is scientifically encouraging that a theory that unifies both matching and maximizing may be possible through the study of concurrent chains. This, however, is a matter to be resolved by future research and theoretical development.

Studies of Preference

We have seen that concurrent chains may be used to study the relative strengths of conditioned reinforcers. Alternatively, we may regard them as ways to study preference. When an individual more on the initial link leading to one terminal link than the initial link leading to the other terminal link, we may say that the individual "prefers" the conditions in former over those in the latter terminal link. Unlike the case with simple concurrent schedules, this way of studying preference is not confounded with the actual rate of responding in under the conditions being compared because the schedules in the initial links are identical. We may regard the type of experiment described in the previous section (on which equation 12.3 is based) as testing preference between two VI schedules. As we see from equation 12.3, the terminal-link VI schedule with a higher reinforcement rate is preferred to one with a lower reinforcement rate, in the sense that the individual will respond more on the initial link leading to that schedule. As equation 12.3 also shows, the schedules in the initial links can affect relative responding in the initial links of concurrent chains. For example, as the initial links are increased in length, relative responding in them approaches one even if the reinforcement rates in the terminal links are quite different (Fantino, 1969; Squires & Fantino, 1971). Provided that this property of concurrent chains is taken into account, we may say that concurrent chains demonstrate that individual preference VI schedules that provide more frequent reinforcement over those that provide less frequent reinforcement.

In addition to testing preferences between rates of primary reinforcement, concurrent chains have revealed preferences on other dimensions.

More versus less conditioned reinforcement.

As we have seen, conditioned reinforcement functions much like primary reinforcement. It therefore would seem that, other factors being equal, more would be preferred over less conditioned reinforcement. We may use concurrent chains to examine this issue in several ways.

Additional conditioned reinforcers. We saw in Chapter 11 when we discussed second-order schedules, that the addition of a brief conditioned reinforcer on its own schedule that is superimposed on a schedule of primary reinforcement can increase response rate. This is particularly true if the superimposed schedule is one that generates a high response rate (e.g., an FR schedule) and the schedule on which it is superimposed is one that generates a moderate response rate (e.g., a VI schedule). This effect holds true in the terminal links of concurrent chains. The question arises, therefore, as to whether the addition of conditioned reinforcement to one of the terminal links of a concurrent-chains procedure will result in a preference for that link; that is, will response rate be higher in the initial link leading to that terminal link than in the initial link leading to a terminal link in which there is no additional conditioned reinforcement? The answer is that animals will prefer the link in which there is no added conditioned reinforcement (Schuster, 1969).

This result is hard to explain if we assume that conditioned reinforcement functions like primary reinforcement because, as we saw above, there would be a preference for a terminal link in which additional primary reinforcers were scheduled. One possible explanation is that conditioned reinforcers presented without being followed by primary reinforcement are aversive, which subtracts from their reinforcing value (Williams, 1994, p. 459). (In Chapter 13 we discuss the aversive effects of omitting reinforcement following stimuli previously paired with reinforcement.)

Probabilistic conditioned reinforcement. The power of conditioned reinforcement is manifested, however, in a somewhat different concurrent-chains arrangement. Consider a concurrent-chains procedure with pigeons in which each of two terminal links consists of a stimulus that last for 30 seconds after which either a primary reinforcer or a short blackout (darkness and no reinforcement) occurs noncontingent on responding. In terminal-link A the primary reinforcer occurs 100% of the time; in terminal-link B the primary reinforcer occurs at random 50% of the time and the blackout occurs at random the other 50% of the time. As we would predict, given this choice, pigeons will choose terminal-link A much more often than terminal-link B.

Suppose, however, that the above situation is changed slightly: A distinctive stimulus (e.g., a distinctive key-light color) is present throughout terminal-link B when primary reinforcement occurs at the end of the link and a different distinctive stimulus is present throughout terminal-link B when the blackout occurs at the end of the link. Now the result is quite different. Pigeons choose the two terminal links about equally often, despite the fact that this causes them to receive about 25% less primary reinforcement than they would if they always choose terminal-link A (Belke & Spetch, 1994; Dunn & Spetch, 1990; McDevitt, Spetch, & Dunn, 1997; Spetch, Belker, Barnet, Dunn, & Pierce, 1990; Spetch, Mondloch, Belken, & Dunn, 1994).

The reason for this suboptimal preference appears to be that the probabilistic occurrence of the distinctive stimulus correlated with primary reinforcement in terminal-link B makes that distinctive stimulus into a powerful conditioned reinforcer. There are several facts that support this statement.

- The effect weakens as the terminal links are shortened below 30 seconds (Spetch et al., 1990). This is because with shorter terminal links, the primary reinforcer exerts more control over responding in the initial links.
- If a stimulus (keys darkened) lasting a brief time (e.g., 5 seconds) is inserted between the response in the initial link that produces the distinctive stimulus correlated with primary reinforcement in terminal-link B, the effect is greatly reduced (Belke & Spetch, 1994; McDevitt et al., 1997). This is because the conditioned reinforcer in terminal-link B no longer is directly contingent on initial-link responding.
- If a stimulus lasting a brief time is inserted between either the stimulus correlated with terminal-link A or the stimulus correlated with the blackout in terminal-link B, or both, but not between the stimulus correlated with primary reinforcement in terminal-link B, the effect persists (McDevitt et al., 1997). This is because responding for terminal-link B still receives conditioned reinforcement from the stimulus correlated with primary reinforcement in terminal-link B.
- If a brief stimulus is inserted between each terminal-link stimulus and the response that produces it, the effect is greatly weakened (McDevitt et al., 1997). The conditioned reinforcer in terminal-link B is no longer directly contingent on initial-link responding. Responding for terminal-link A no longer directly produces its conditioned reinforcer, but that conditioned reinforcer is relatively weak anyway because it occurred every time that an initial-link response produced terminal-link A.

If a stimulus lasting a brief time is inserted between the stimulus correlated with the blackout in terminal-link B and the initial-link producing terminal-link B, relative preference for the two terminal links is not affected (McDevitt, Spetch, & Dunn, 1997). Thus the stimulus correlated with a blackout in terminal-link B is not aversive enough for its aversiveness to be detected in this experimental arrangement. A more sensitive test of its aversiveness would be to provide a response that would immediately terminate the link, in which case the animal would probably emit that response because animals will respond to terminate a stimulus correlated with nonreinforcement.

Recall that the added conditioned reinforcers described previously were aversive enough to shift preference toward the terminal link that had fewer of them. This is quite different from the situation we are concerned with now, in which the distinctive stimulus correlated with the terminal link in which a blackout occurs is not aversive enough to offset the conditioned reinforcing power of the stimulus paired with positive reinforcement in that same terminal link. The stimuli in the situation described previously had been paired with reinforcement whereas the distinctive stimulus correlated with a blackout in terminal-link B in the experimental arrangement described in this section had never been paired with reinforcement. (As will be discussed in Chapter 13, stimuli previously paired with reinforcement are aversive when presented without being paired with reinforcement.)

Stimulus segmentation. If in a concurrent-chains procedure one terminal link is correlated with two sequential stimuli while the other is correlated with just one stimulus, then there will be a preference for the unsegmented terminal link. The reason seems to be that the stimulus at the beginning of the segmented terminal link is not paired with primary reinforcement, whereas the stimulus at the beginning of the unsegmented terminal link is. The effect is stronger for longer terminal links and weakest for segmentation that occurs at the middle rather than near the beginning or end of the segmented terminal link (Leung & Winton, 1988).

Signaled reinforcement. A terminal link in which reinforcement is signaled by being preceded by another stimulus is preferred over one in which reinforcement is not signaled. Consider a procedure that is slightly different from the usual concurrent-chains procedure, but still may be classified with them. On each side of a shuttle box—like the one shown in Figure 5.1—a rat receives food on a VT 60-seconds schedule (i.e., food occurs independent of responding at an average rate of once every 60 seconds), but on one side each food presentation is preceded by a 5-second tone. On some sessions the unsignaled reinforcement schedule is in effect at the beginning of the session, while on other sessions the signaled reinforcement schedule is in effect. The rat can change the schedule, and a stimulus light correlated with it, by moving from one side of the box to the other. The schedule change remains in effect for one minute, during which time further shuttle responses have no effect. At the end of the 1-minute period, the original schedule is reinstated and a shuttle response again will produce a change to the other schedule. Note that this is like a concurrent-chains procedure, except that rather than two responses being available in the initial link, there is just one response (the shuttle response). Making this response bring about the "terminal link"—signaled reinforcement on some sessions, unsignaled reinforcement on other sessions. The result of this procedure is that, regardless of the schedule in effect at the beginning of the session, the animal spends more time in the presence of the schedule in which reinforcement was signaled (Harsh, Badia, & Ryan, 1983).

Interestingly, the opposite result occurs on a simple concurrent schedule. For example, suppose that the above procedure is modified so that each shuttle response produces an alternation between the two schedules. In that case, the animal will allocate more time to the schedule of unsignaled reinforcement than to the schedule of signaled reinforcement. This may be understood by referring back to the section entitled "Information as Positive Reinforcement" in Chapter 11. Note that during signaled reinforcement, the absence of the signal is an S^Δ, and that therefore the animal would respond to terminate it—resulting in more time in the presence of the other schedule. If, however, the signal is lengthened say, to 5 seconds—so that the S^Δ period is shortened, and more conditioned reinforcement occurs, the animal may then allocate more time to the signaled condition (Harsh et al., 1983).

Aperiodic versus periodic reinforcement.

As with simple concurrent schedules (see p. 267), concurrent-chains procedures reveal a preference for aperiodic over periodic reinforcement. For example, VI terminal-link schedules are preferred over FI terminal-link schedules (Herrnstein, 1964b), and MR terminal-link schedules are preferred over FR terminal-link schedules (Fantino, 1967). For reasons not clearly understood at present, concurrent chains seem to magnify this preference over what is obtained with simple concurrent schedules. Thus, to obtain indifference between MR and FR schedules, the FR schedule must be lower in concurrent chains than in simple concurrent schedules (Rider, 1983b).

Interreinforcement interval versus response requirement.

Interreinforcement interval, rather than response requirement in the terminal link, appears to be the determining factor in preference between schedules. Thus, for example, individuals are indifferent between terminal links containing VI schedules and terminal links containing VT (variable-time; reinforcement noncontingent on responding) schedules (Autor, 1969; Herrnstein, 1964a; Killeen, 1968), and between terminal links containing FI schedules and terminal links containing FT schedules (Neuringer, 1969), given equal rates of reinforcement in the terminal links.

Long versus short terminal links.   Given equal rates of reinforcement, a terminal link in which more reinforcements occur will be preferred over one in which fewer reinforcements occur—that is, the longer lasting terminal link will be preferred (Fantino & Herrnstein, 1968; Poniewaz, 1984; Squires & Fantino, 1971; but see Moore, 1979).

Immediate verus less-immediate reinforcement.   A terminal link in which the first reinforcement occurs more quickly will be preferred over one in which it occurs less quickly (Davison, 1968; Moore, 1984; Rider, 1983a).

IMPULSE CONTROL

When an individual chooses a larger or more preferred delayed reinforcer over a smaller or less preferred immediate reinforcer, that individual is said to be showing impulse control. Everyday examples are numerous, ranging from saving one's money to buy a stereo rather than spending it immediately on junk food, to refusing fattening foods in order to have a more healthy and attractive body.

In one procedure used to study impulse control, a response on one operandum produces a small reinforcer immediately after a short delay period, while a response on another operandum produces a large reinforcer after a longer delay period. In a related procedure, large reinforcers occur on an FT schedule, and a specific response immediately produces a small reinforcer that cancels the large reinforcer.

Exposed to these procedures, animals and young children almost invariably choose a smaller or less preferred immediate reinforcer over a larger or more preferred delayed reinforcer (Grosch & Neuringer, 1981; Mischel, 1974). There are, however, several methods that promote choosing the larger or more preferred delayed reinforcer (and thus to exhibit impulse control):

- Begin with both reinforcers immediate or equally delayed, and then gradually increase the delay of the more preferred reinforcer or gradually decrease the delay of the less preferred reinforcer (Logue, Rodriguez, Peña, Correal, & Mauro, 1984; Mazur & Logue, 1978).
- In procedures in which a response during the delay interval produces the less preferred reinforcer and cancels the more preferred delayed reinforcer, provide an alternative response that the individual can emit during the delay interval. This has been done with pigeons by training them to peck a key at the rear of the chamber; the pigeon will then peck the key during the delay interval even if not reinforced for doing so (Grosch & Neuringer, 1981). Some pigeons peck an ineffective key during the delay interval, even if reinforcement has never been given for this behavior (Logue & Piña-Correal, 1984). An alternative response has been provided to children simply by giving them a toy to play with or having them think "fun" thoughts during the delay interval (Michel, Ebbesen, & Zeiss, 1972). Having the children think of the reinforcers during the delay interval, however, decreases the amount of time they will wait for the preferred reinforcer. Similarly, stimuli paired with food (e.g., the sight of food and illumination of the food-hopper light) decrease the amount of time pigeons will wait for the larger reinforcer (Grosch & Neuringer, 1981).
- Provide prior experience with reinforcers given after long delays; for example, tell children they will receive toys on the next day and present the toys as promised (Mahrer, 1956; Mischel & Staub, 1965).

- Use reinforcers that cannot be consumed immediately. For example, when tokens that can be exchanged for other reinforcers at the end of (or sometime after the session) are used, humans show a tendency to respond for a larger-but-delayed quantity of tokens (Logue, Peña, Correal, Rodriguez, & Kabela, 1986; Hyten, Madden, & Field, 1984).
- Use a commitment procedure, which is a procedure in which an individual can choose to remove a choice available at a later time. An individual choosing in a commitment procedure to forgo the later opportunity to choose a less preferred, immediate reinforcer over a more preferred, delayed reinforcer is, in a sense, removing the future possibility of being "tempted" by the less preferred, immediate reinforcer, and is thus committing to the larger, more preferred reinforcer. For example, a concurrent-chains procedure has been used in which:
  ⇒ one initial link leads to a terminal link containing a modified simple concurrent schedule consisting of a choice between a small immediate reinforcer and a large delayed reinforcer; and
  ⇒ another initial link leads to a terminal link containing only the large delayed reinforcer—there is no choice.
- If the initial links are fairly long, pigeons typically respond more on the second initial link, thus committing to a situation in which the small immediate reinforcer is unavailable (Rachlin & Green, 1972).

COMPLEX DECISION MAKING

People frequently find themselves confronted with a number of options with uncertain outcomes. Often the options are ordered in some fashion, with the outcome of any given option related in some way to its position in the ordering. Consider, for example, a prospective college student who has been accepted at several universities and must decide which one to attend. The student's verbal behavior and history of making similar decisions would probably combine with factors such as tuition at each university, average class size, and the university's reputation to determine the student's decision. Note that all such factors are ordered, and that the position of each university on each factor may vary with its position on the other factors. For example, the university with the lowest class size may have the highest tuition, while the university with the best reputation may rank in the middle with regard to class size and tuition. To resolve the conflict the student might weight the importance of these factors in some manner, thus arriving at a decision based on the combined weighted rankings. Exactly what goes into making these kinds of decisions and how these decisions are made important topics, but ones which we know little about at present.

We may treat situations like the above, in which options are ordered in some numerical manner that is related to the outcome, as ordered concurrent schedules. Note that in addition to being ordered, the concurrent schedules in the above example (i.e., the different educational options) differ from concurrent schedules discussed previously in this chapter in being nonrepeating (typically one chooses which educational institution to attend for a particular degree only once). For a repeating example, consider the stock market. An investor may choose repeatedly among different stocks in which to invest and among different amounts of money to invest in each stock chosen (depending of course, on the investor's financial resources). Another example of a repeating ordered concurrent schedule is a rating task in which a rater allots points to objects, persons, questionnaire items, and so forth, on the basis of some characteristic or characteristics. Reinforcement contingent on points allotted is not as obvious as it is with, say, investing a certain amount in a given stock. However, most people encounter many situations in which making the kinds of judgments required by rating scales is reinforced by accurate predictions, by social approval, or both—and the behavior thereby generated may generalize broadly to a variety of similar situations.

Ordered Concurrent Schedules and Schedule Effects

One type of experiment used to study complex decision making simulates investing in a financial market. Subjects, who are often students in business or related fields, are asked to imagine that they are working for an investment group whose goal is to make as much money as possible. The student sits at a computer terminal and on successive trials may invest an amount (simulated) ranging from $0 to $10,000 of a (simulated) client's money. After each trial, the student receives feedback on the outcome of the investment. Two types of outcomes are possible: The investment results either in a return of a certain percentage (which is generally constant throughout the experiment) of the amount invested or in a loss of a certain percentage (also constant throughout the experiment and less than the percentage of the return).

The above experimental arrangement produces effects on amount invested similar to effects produced on response rate by simple schedules of reinforcement. For example, amounts tend to be higher when returns occur on a continuous reinforcement schedule (i.e., every investment is successful) than when returns occur intermittently. A steady rate of investing tends to be generated by a VR 2 schedule of returns, where FR 2 generates large investments alternating with zero investments. These patterns of investing on VR and FR schedules of returns are similar to patterns of responding on VR and FR schedules of reinforcement. When the schedule of returns is changed to extinction (i.e., the outcome is always a loss), amount invested decreases more slowly after VR 2 than after either continuous reinforcement or FR 2. This is analogous to responding decreasing more slowly on extinction after partial reinforcement than after continuous reinforcement and after variable schedules of reinforcement than after fixed schedules of reinforcement (Goltz, 1992).

The indicated correspondences are far from exact, however, because each investment (regardless of size) in the above schedules of returns is a single response, and not a level of responding equivalent to the size of the investment. Thus, one way in which the analogy fails is that an investment of $0 advances the count in FR and VR schedules of returns, whereas zero responding does not do so in ratio schedules of reinforcement.

Ordered Concurrent Schedules and Behavioral Contrast

Effects similar to behavioral contrast have been found with the above experimental investing procedure. In an analogue to the first part of the standard procedure for producing behavioral contrast, two VI schedules of returns occur in two alternating conditions, called *markets*, that are correlated with distinctive stimuli. When investing in one of the markets is subsequently extinguished (i.e., no investment results in a return and every investment results in a loss), investing in that market decreases to zero. Concomitant with this decrease, in an effect analogous to behavioral contrast, amounts invested in the other market increases (Hantula & Crowell, 1994). Behavioral-contrast-like effects have also been found with rating scales (that, as mentioned at the beginning of this section, can also be viewed as ordered concurrent schedules). For example, a manager rating subordinates sequentially will tend to give higher ratings to subordinates who are preceded by subordinates with lower ratings (Wexley, Yukl, Kovacks, & Sanders 1972; Ivancevich, 1983).

Note that the contrast effects that occur in complex decision making appear to be irrational (not likely due to rational processes). The increase in amount invested in the market that contains a VI schedule of returns when investing in the other market is extinguished does not result in increased returns. On the contrary, it results in increased losses because, in this experimental situation, any investment that does not produce a return produces a loss. Likewise, a manager that rates a subordinate higher because his or her rating is preceded by that of a poorer subordinate is not acting rationally. Increased knowledge of the behavior principles involved in complex decision making will help us learn how to promote more rational decisions.

SUMMARY AND CONCLUSIONS

Concurrent schedules are two or more reinforcement schedules operating simultaneously. The schedules may be programmed on the same operandum, on different operandums that can be operated simultaneously, or on different operandums that cannot be operated simultaneously. The response patterns that each component schedule in all three cases produces are those that are characteristic of the schedules operating alone. The last is generally the most interesting, however, because it permits the separate effects of the schedules to be observed most clearly.

One of the strongest functional relations observed in concurrent schedules is the matching law, which is the tendency for relative response rate on each component schedule to match the relative reinforcement rate for responding on that schedule. Exceptions to the matching law appear to be due to bias that exists toward one response or the other independent of the reinforcement rate of that response and lack of sensitivity to the relative rate of reinforcement (which may be at least partly due to an imperfect discrimination between the responses reinforced by the component schedules). Mathematical formulations (e.g., the generalized matching law) that take these factors into account give good descriptions of relative rate of responding on concurrent schedules as a function of relative rate of reinforcement. Whether individuals match or maximize reinforcers to behavior is, however, still an unsettled issue.

Relative response rate on the component schedules provides an index of preference for those schedules. In addition to reinforcement rate, variables such as reinforcer magnitude, delay, class, and quality affect preference in concurrent schedules. Although these other variables can produce clear effects on preference, no strong mathematical formulation describing these effects has emerged.

In a combination of concurrent schedules and chained schedules called concurrent chains, the first components (or links) of two chained schedules are available simultaneously. Studies on concurrent chains verify and extend the major findings on preference obtained with simple concurrent schedules; for example, a high reinforcement rate is preferred over a low one; a large reinforcer is preferred over a small one; an immediate reinforcer is preferred over a delayed one; aperiodic reinforcement is preferred over periodic reinforcement; and, signaled reinforcement is preferred over unsignalled reinforcement.

Concurrent chains provide a means to study impulse control and commitment. When an individual produces the second link of one of two chained schedules whose first links are concurrently available, that individual has committed to that second link over its alternative because, once selected, the second link remains in effect until the condition for its termination (usually the passage of a certain amount of time) is met. Although there is a strong tendency to choose a small immediate reinforcer over a large delayed reinforcer, individuals may, under certain conditions, commit themselves to a second link that provides only a large delayed reinforcer over one that is itself a concurrent-chains procedure that provides a choice between a large delayed reinforcer and a small immediate reinforcer. This type of commitment seems to fit the definition of self-control. It is therefore somewhat surprising that it occurs in an animal as simple as the pigeon.

MOTIVATION AND EMOTION

*I*n addition to the contingencies that produce and maintain respondent and operant behavior, there are two other broad classes of variables that affect the conditioning and performance of behavior: motivational and emotional variables. Motivational variables influence behavior by affecting the potency of an unconditioned stimulus or a primary reinforcer. Emotional variables act directly on behavior itself (as opposed to acting through the unconditioned stimuli or primary reinforcers that maintain it), tending either to enhance or disrupt it. The distinction between these two classes of variables, however, is not completely sharp. There is some overlap between them as well as difficulty in some cases in determining whether a particular event is acting as a motivational variable, an emotional variable, or a combination of the two. What both classes of variables have in common is that they affect performance (i.e., ongoing behavior) in similar ways.

Chapter 13 consists of a general discussion of motivation, focusing on the two broad classes of appetitive and aversive motivation. Chapter 14 then deals with punishment, which may be considered to be an emotional variable because of its (generally) suppressive effect on ongoing behavior. Finally, Chapter 15 discusses how schedules of reinforcement, in addition to developing and maintaining operant behavior, generate a class of behavior (adjunctive behavior) that is not operant and that (at least in many cases) appears not to be respondent either. Chapter 15 is included in Part IV because of the disruptive and facilitative interactions adjunctive behavior may have with operant behavior.

13

Motivation

*T*he concept of motivation deals with the fact that, even for the same individual, a given reinforcer may be effective sometimes and ineffective at other times. The effectiveness of a given primary reinforcer in establishing and maintaining behavior, and in providing backup for a conditioned reinforcer, is a function of several variables. For example, food is sometimes an effective reinforcer and sometimes not. When it is an effective reinforcer for an individual, we say that the individual is "hungry" or "motivated for food." A variable that affects the effectiveness of a primary reinforcer is called a motivational variable.

Motivation is often thought of as something that is within an individual, but is more accurately seen as a relation between the individual's behavior and some prior event or occurrence. For example, we say that an individual is motivated for food when some occurrence—such as food deprivation, or a period of vigorous exercise—has made it likely that the individual will engage in food-reinforced behavior. We could say that such an event has caused food-motivation or hunger to be at a high value. A name we have used frequently in previous chapters for any event that produces a high value on a motivational variable is establishing operation (Michael, 1982, 1993).

There are two main classes of motivational variables. One consists of deprivation of a reinforcing stimulus—for example, food, water, sexual stimulation—over a period of time. The result is that the reinforcing effectiveness of the stimulus increases over the deprivation period. The other class of motivational variable is the presentation of an aversive stimulus; that is, a particular type of stimulus—for example, extreme heat, extreme cold, electric shock—that establishes the removal of the stimulus as reinforcing. These two classes of motivational variables correspond to the distinction between positive and negative primary reinforcement.

Various drugs constitute a third class of motivational variables. For example, amphetamines decrease the reinforcing effectiveness of food (i.e., hunger); morphine decreases the reinforcing effectiveness of aversive stimuli; aphrodisiacs increase the reinforcing effectiveness of sexual stimuli. For the most part, however, we shall be concerned with motivational variables that are located in the individual's external environment.

Although presentation of a negative reinforcer is clearly a motivational variable in that it makes removal of the stimulus reinforcing, negative reinforcers do not have to be present in order for them to strengthen behavior. A response that prevents or postpones the occurrence of a negative reinforcer will also be strengthened. This raises the problem of identifying the reinforcer that strengthens the behavior, since the failure of something to occur cannot be a stimulus and therefore cannot be a reinforcer.

A procedure in which a response prevents or postpones a negative reinforcer is called avoidance conditioning, in contrast to escape conditioning, a procedure in which a response removes or terminates a negative reinforcer. Escape and avoidance conditioning clearly seem to be related, but exactly how is not understood at present.

One prominent theory for relating escape and avoidance conditioning has been termed two-factor theory (Dinsmoor, 1954; Mowrer, 1960; Mowrer & Lamoreaux, 1942). This theory can best be illustrated by considering the following avoidance procedure. A rat in a chamber with a response lever is presented with a tone that lasts for a few seconds and is followed by a brief shock if no lever press occurs. However, a lever press immediately turns off the tone and prevents the shock from occurring. The result is that the probability of a lever press in the presence of the tone increases over trials. Essentially, two-factor theory explains this result by positing that the tone has become a conditioned aversive stimulus due to its having been paired with shock, and hence the termination of the tone is reinforcing.

Thus, the two factors in "two-factor" theory are:

1. a previously neutral stimulus becoming aversive due to pairing with an aversive stimulus;
2. negative reinforcement of a response that is followed by the removal of the conditioned aversive stimulus. (The fact that the response results in avoidance of the primary aversive event is incidental to the process.)

The first factor is typically assumed to be respondent conditioning in which, by being paired with a primary aversive stimulus, the previously neutral stimulus comes to elicit an aversive response or state (sometimes called "fear" or "anxiety") whose removal is reinforcing; the second factor is simply operant conditioning that occurs when the aversive response or state is terminated due to the removal of the conditioned aversive stimulus. To put it another way, two-factor theory proposes that avoidance conditioning is simply escape conditioning in which the individual escapes from an aversive stimulus that has been established through a respondent conditioning procedure. In this way, as with all good scientific theories, it seeks to reduce something that appears complex and confusing to a simpler, more understandable process.

There are avoidance situations, however, that are not so easily explained by two-factor theory. One of these is free-operant avoidance (also known as Sidman avoidance after Sidman, 1953), in which brief aversive stimuli (e.g., shocks) occur periodically (e.g., once every 20 seconds) unless a response occurs. Each response postpones the aversive stimulus for a fixed period of time following the response (e.g., 20 seconds). Thus, if the individual responds at some minimum steady rate throughout the session the aversive stimulus will never occur. Note that there is no explicit stimulus paired with aversive stimulus. Nevertheless, many animals learn to avoid it (i.e., respond to prevent it from occurring) on this schedule.

How does two-factor theory explain this? It does so by positing that feedback from the animal's own behavior constitutes a neutral stimulus that can become an aversive stimulus if it is paired with an aversive event. That is, not-emitting-the-avoidance-response provides a specific stimulus to the individual that differs from the stimulus provided by emitting-the-avoidance-response. In a free-operant avoidance paradigm the former stimulus is paired with the aversive stimulus, and so becomes a conditioned aversive stimulus. When the animal emits the avoidance response this conditioned aversive stimulus is removed, and thus the response is negatively reinforced in essentially the same way as a response in an avoidance paradigm involving an external conditioned aversive stimulus.

An experimental arrangement that is more difficult for two-factor theory to explain is the following. Rats are presented with shocks occurring at regular or irregular intervals. A lever press produces an alternative condition (with no correlated stimulus) for a fixed period of time, during which shocks still occur but at a reduced rate. Thus a response does not prevent shocks from occurring, but simply reduces their rate of occurrence. Despite the fact that there is no explicit stimulus paired with the reduced rate of shocks and apparently feedback from not-emitting-the-avoidance-response also is not paired with the reduced rate of shocks (since the reduced rate occurs whether or not the animal continues emitting the response after the first occurrence of the response), animals learn to emit the avoidance response (e.g., Gardner & Lewis, 1976; Herrnstein & Hineline, 1966; Hineline, 1970; Lewis, Gardner, & Hutton, 1976). In fact, the response can be learned even if it does not change the shock distribution until after the next shock has been delivered (Lewis et al., 1976). Because of these (and other) findings, a number of researchers have rejected the two-factor theory of avoidance in favor of a "shock-frequency reduction" hypothesis; that is, the hypothesis that avoidance behavior is reinforced directly by a reduction in the rate of the aversive event (e.g., Hineline, 1984). A problem with this view, however, is that a reduction in the rate of a stimulus is not an event that immediately follows a response, because a certain amount of time is required before a change in rate can be detected.

APPETITIVE MOTIVATION

The term appetitive motivation refers to variables that affect the strength of positive reinforcement. Under this general heading we shall consider categories of primary positive reinforcers and effects of varying deprivation, quantity, and quality of positive reinforcers.

Primary Positive Reinforcers

There are a number of different classes of primary positive reinforcers. In addition, the members of each class are often conglomerate reinforcers in that they are composed of other reinforcers.

Classes of primary positive reinforcers.   A complete list of primary positive reinforcers has never been composed for any species because of the difficulty in distinguishing primary from conditioned reinforcers. In order to demonstrate that stimulus X is a primary reinforcer for an individual, one must demonstrate that the individual has never been exposed to the stimulus in close temporal association with another reinforcer. This is often quite difficult to do. Imagine, for example, attempting to determine whether other members of an individual's species are primary reinforcers for that individual. Prior to testing whether presenting a conspecific contingent on a response would reinforce that response, one would have to ensure that the individual never ate or received any other type of reinforcement in the presence of other members of its species. Probably the only certain way to do this would be to raise the individual in isolation from other members of its species prior to conducting the test. However, social isolation may have deleterious effects on the individual's behavior that might interfere with the test. In addition, the novelty (or unfamiliarity) of the conspecific might cause it to be aversive to the individual.

Because of their strong biological significance, food, water, and sexual contact are undoubtedly primary reinforcers. Beyond these three, however, it is difficult to identify other primary reinforcers with a high degree of certainty. Various types of stimuli involved in social behavior appear to be primary reinforcers. For example, infant rhesus monkeys that have been separated from their mothers and raised with inanimate "surrogate mothers," one made of wire and another of terrycloth, will spend more time on the terrycloth mother, even if food is obtained only when the monkey is on the wire mother (Harlow, 1960). Apparently the physical softness of another individual (called "contact comfort") is an important factor in the reinforcement of social behavior in infant monkeys. It seems likely that a similar factor operates in humans, which would explain our fondness for soft, cuddly objects.

Social reinforcers that may be primary reinforcers have been demonstrated for other species as well. For example, a stimulus to which ducklings have been imprinted is a positive reinforcer (see Chapter 3). Such a stimulus is a primary reinforcer in the sense that it does not lose its reinforcing power over many presentations in which it is not paired with other reinforcers. Young male chaffinches will respond to hear the song of an adult chaffinch (Stevenson, 1967).

Seeing another male, toward which aggression may be displayed, is a primary reinforcer for the males of some species. For example, a rooster will respond for the opportunity to see another rooster or to seeing its own mirror image (T. J. Thompson, 1964). A male Siamese fighting fish will also respond to produce its own mirror image, which it will then attack as though it were another male invading its territory (Hogan, Kleist, & Hutchings, 1970).

Various types of manipulatory and sensory (e.g., auditory, visual) stimuli are primary reinforcers for some species. For example, running in a running wheel can maintain extremely persistent operant behavior (e.g., pressing a lever to unlock the wheel) in rats and other rodents, and thus is a primary reinforcer for them (Belke, 1996, 1997; Belke & Heyman, 1994; Collier & Hirsch, 1971; Iversen, 1993, 1998; Kagan & Berkun, 1954; Mazur, 1975; Premack, 1962; Premack, Schaeffer, & Hundt, 1964; Timberlake & Allison, 1974). Monkeys will take apart simple metal puzzles placed in their cages, and their speed at taking the puzzles apart increases with practice although no explicit external reinforcer follows the behavior. Moreover, the persistence of the behavior indicates that it is maintained by something other than conditioned reinforcement (Harlow, 1950; Harlow & McClearn, 1954). In addition, monkeys will press a lever to observe complex visual stimuli, such as a moving toy train, through a one-way window; and this behavior also is extremely persistent (Butler & Alexander, 1955; Butler & Harlow, 1954). Clearly, all sorts of social, manipulative, and sensory stimuli are extremely reinforcing to humans, and this is probably because they are primary reinforcers—although it also is possible that they are conditioned reinforcers as well, since a stimulus can be both. Novel stimuli also are often reinforcing to humans. Our capacity to be reinforced by a wide variety of complex and novel stimuli may be one of the factors that have given our species such a large degree of control over our environment. Indeed, there is some evidence that the more closely related genetically a species is to humans, the more reinforcing novel stimuli are to its members (Glickman, Sroges, & Hoff, 1961).

A question of considerable interest is whether all types of primary positive reinforcers generate the same behavior patterns as those that are generated by food and water reinforcers. This question does not yet have a clear answer. There are indications, however, that findings with food and water reinforcers generalize to some extent (but not completely) to other reinforcers. For example, rats responding on basic intermittent schedules for 4- to 6-seconds access to a running wheel show patterns of responding characteristic of those that schedules of food reinforcement generate (Iversen, 1993). Running wheel reinforcement also will develop and maintain simple and conditional stimulus discriminations in rats (Iversen, 1998). However, even when motivation appears high on the basis of the extent to which the running wheel reinforcement maintains correct responding, the time it takes animals to respond to the correct stimulus is longer than is typically the case with food and water reinforcement.

As we saw in Chapter 3, a stimulus that ducklings have been imprinted on is a primary reinforcer for them. However, although brief presentations of imprinted stimuli on intermittent schedules will maintain responding at high rates, they do not generate characteristic patterns on FR and FI schedules. In addition, responding reinforced by an imprinted stimulus does not seem to come under good stimulus control on multiple schedules (DePaulo & Hoffman, 1981).

Animals will respond at high rates to obtain direct electrical stimulation to certain brain regions (see Fifure 3.2, p. 32) when this reinforcer is given on a continuous reinforcement schedule. However, electrical brain stimulation will not maintain responding on high intermittent schedules unless it is preceded by a brief external stimulus (e.g., a light), in which case it will maintain patterns of responding characteristic of those maintained by food and water reinforcement (Cantor, 1971). This illustrates that failure to find similarities between the effects of food or water reinforcement and other types of reinforcement may be caused by subtle differences in procedures.

Conglomerate reinforcers.   Any given primary reinforcer may actually be a conglomerate of other reinforcers. We tend to treat food, for example, as a single reinforcer; however, it is actually composed of other reinforcers, including its taste and its caloric content. We may separate the components of a conglomerate reinforcer such as food. We may, for example, bypass taste by providing caloric content directly to the stomach or bloodstream. If a neutral odor or taste is paired with the direct injection of sugar or starch into the stomach (Azzara & Sclafani, 1998; Sclafani & Nissenbaum, 1988) or of glucose into the bloodstream (Tordoff & Friedman, 1986), that neutral stimulus will become a conditioned reinforcer. Likewise, we may stimulate the taste receptors without providing caloric content to the stomach. This could, of course, be done by surgically interfering with passage of food from the mouth to the stomach. Alternatively, we may give the individual a substance that has a reinforcing taste but no caloric content. One such substance is saccharin, which has a sweet taste but does not provide any nutrition. Saccharin is a reinforcer because animals will learn to press a lever, for example, to lick a saccharin solution. In addition, a neutral odor that is in the solution (and hence paired with saccharin) will become a conditioned reinforcer (as determined by a preference test) even if the animal is satiated with food (Fanselow & Birk, 1982; Holman, 1975). Thus a conditioned reinforcer can be based on a reinforcing taste alone. Likewise, a neutral odor dissolved in a sucrose (i.e., sugar) solution (and hence paired with sucrose) will become a conditioned reinforcer if the individual is satiated with food (Capaldi & Myers, 1982; Capaldi, Myers, Cambell, & Sheffer, 1983; Mehiel & Bolles, 1984, 1988a,b). Increasing food deprivation during conditioning increases the strength of a conditioned reinforcer based on sucrose, but not of a conditioned reinforcer based on saccharin (Capaldi, Owens, & Palmer, 1994; Fedorchak & Bolles, 1987). Thus, both the sweet taste and the caloric content of sugar are separate reinforcers, and each contributes to the establishment of a conditioned reinforcer based on sucrose.

This can also be shown through a blocking experiment (see Chapter 6). Suppose that a satiated rat drinks a saccharin solution unpaired with any specific odor on trials that precede or alternate with trials in which the rat drinks a sugar solution paired with an almond odor (which is a neutral stimulus) dissolved in the solution. The result will be that the almond odor will not become a conditioned reinforcer as shown by a preference test. The presentations of the saccharin solution will have blocked the conditioning of the almond odor to the sweet taste of the sugar solution (Harris et al., 2000). Although the almond odor also was paired with the caloric content of sugar, this is not reinforcing to a satiated animal. Hence the almond odor does not take on any reinforcement value, and thus does not become a conditioned reinforcer.

If the above procedure were done with a food deprived rat, however, the result would be different. The previously neutral almond odor will become a conditioned reinforcer (Harris et al., 2000). The reason is that it has been paired with the caloric content of sugar, which is reinforcing to a food deprived animal. This also shows that blocking of a potential conditioned reinforcer is specific to the primary reinforcer on which it is based; that is, exposure to one primary reinforcer will not block a conditioned reinforcer based on a different primary reinforcer, even when both primary reinforcers are components of the same overall reinforcer.

Deprivation

As pointed out in Chapter 3, deprivation of a positive reinforcer is necessary in order for that reinforcer to be effective. In this section we examine exactly what is meant by deprivation and why it establishes reinforcer effectiveness.

Behavioral equilibrium. From the matching law (and its variations, such as the GML), discussed in Chapter 12, we know that behavior allocation stabilizes in a constant environment. We refer to the stable state of behavior in a constant environment (i.e., one in which the contingencies of reinforcement are unvarying) as behavioral equilibrium, and to the stable-state amount of time allocated to performing each response as the equilibrium level of that response. We may think of deprivation as the restriction of some response to a level below its equilibrium level. For example, food deprivation is the restriction of eating to a level below that at which would occur if food were freely available. Although normally we speak of a reinforcer as a stimulus, it will be convenient in the following discussion to refer to it as a response (e.g., to speak of eating, rather than food, as a reinforcer). It is important to keep in mind, however, that this is just a manner of speaking: Reinforcers are actually stimuli.

Viewing deprivation as restricting a response below its equilibrium level has two important implications. The first is what is known as the probability-differential hypothesis (Premack, 1965, 1971)—also known as the Premack Principle—which states the following:

> If response B has a higher probability (i.e., if its equilibrium level is higher) than response A, then response B will reinforce response A if it is contingent on A. For example, if eating occurs with a higher probability than lever pressing, then eating will reinforce lever pressing if eating is contingent on lever pressing.

The second important implication, called the response-deprivation hypothesis (Allison & Timberlake, 1974; Timberlake & Allison, 1974), is a more general form of the first. It states that *any response that is below its equilibrium level will reinforce any other response if it is contingent on that response.*

It is easy to see why the probability-differential and response-deprivation hypotheses work. First, consider the probability-differential hypothesis. As soon as we make a high-probability response contingent on a low-probability response, a period of deprivation begins because the high-probability response is occurring less frequently than it normally would. To keep the high-probability response near its equilibrium level, the low-probability response must increase. It will not increase enough to completely restore the high-probability response to its equilibrium level, because this would require that the low-probability response increase above its equilibrium level. Since all behavior tends (by definition) to stabilize at its equilibrium level, this would be aversive (i.e., punishing; we discuss punishment in the next chapter). The two responses would interact to produce a new equilibrium level for each, involving some sort of averaging of the former equilibrium levels of the two responses.

Now consider the response-deprivation hypothesis. According to this hypothesis, we may use a low-probability response to reinforce a high-probability response. Before making the low-probability response contingent on the high-probability response, however, it is necessary to restrict the low-probability response below its equilibrium level. Otherwise the high-probability response would immediately begin to drive the low-probability response above its equilibrium level. This would be punishing rather than reinforcing (Heth & Warren, 1978). As long as the low-probability response remains below its equilibrium level, it will reinforce the high-probability response.

Eventually, if the process is allowed to run its course, the low-probability response will exceed its equilibrium level and will, at that point, punish the high-probability response.

Experiments on behavioral equilibrium. A number of experiments support the concept of behavioral equilibrium. For example, drinking or eating reduced below a rats equilibrium level will reinforce its running in an activity wheel; and, conversely, running below a rats equilibrium level will reinforce its drinking or eating (Marmaroff, 1971; Timberlake & Wozny, 1979). Similarly, human experimental participants will press a lever for the opportunity to crank a wheel if this response has been restricted below its baseline level (Eisenberger, Karpman, & Trattner, 1967).

Behavioral equilibrium appears to have practical value in applied learning science. For example, the opportunity to perform one academic task—for example, arithmetic or reading—that has been restricted below its equilibrium level can be used to reinforce another task—for example, reading or arithmetic—that is at its equilibrium level (Konarski, Crowell, & Dugan, 1985; Konarski, Crowell, Johnson, & Whitman, 1982; Konarski, Johnson, Crowell, & Whitman, 1980).

Homeostasis. The concept of behavioral equilibrium is similar to the physiological concept of homeostasis, which refers to the tendency of the body to keep its internal environment constant. If certain parameters of the internal environment, such as the levels of sugar and salt in the blood, body temperature, and so forth, deviate from a narrowly circumscribed range, metabolism can no longer occur and death ensues. Homeostasis can account for some aspects of behavioral equilibrium; for example, drinking water is reinforcing when the concentration of minerals in the blood is above the range that is optimal for metabolism and punishing when the blood is so diluted that the concentration of minerals is below the range that is optimal for metabolism. Homeostasis and behavioral equilibrium are not perfectly correlated, however. Individuals respond for many reinforcers that have no direct role in maintaining the constancy of the internal environment. (e.g., see earlier in this chapter).

It should also be noted that even with regard to basic physiological needs such as water and nutrition, drinking frequently starts before depletion of the critical substance in the body tissues occurs and ends before it is restored. Moreover, there are situations in which deviations from homeostasis are reinforcing; specifically, certain drugs are reinforcing even though they disrupt homeostasis. We saw in Chapter 6 that compensatory responses will occur that counteract the effects of toxins, thereby tending to restore the homeostatic balance that the toxins disrupt (Allan & Siegel, 1998). When the toxin is a drug such as morphine, heroin, caffeine, alcohol, or nicotine, however, these compensatory responses are responsible for the development of tolerance to the drug. In general, these drugs are reinforcing; hence, the drug-opponent response is aversive since it counteracts the reinforcing aspect of the drug. The occurrence of drug-opponent responses in the absence of the drug is what causes "withdrawal" symptoms.

In some cases a homeostatic response may have no apparent motivational effect. Staring at a particular color elicits a response that tends to oppose that color's physiological effects (its effects on color receptors in the eye and other parts of the visual system). The evolutionary reason for these color-opponent responses is unknown; perhaps they protect the parts of the eye and brain involved in color sensations, analogous to a screen saver in a computer monitor. These color-opponent responses are responsible for the tendency for the apparent saturation of a color to decrease as it is stared at, for afterimages that are complementary to a color that has been stared at, and for the McCollough effect (described in Chapter 6, pp. 109–110) in which a stimulus that has been paired with a color elicits an image of the complementary color (Allan & Siegel, 1998). None of these effects appear to have any strong positive or negative motivational properties.

Natural versus imposed deprivation. Thus far in this chapter we have tended to speak of deprivation as something that is imposed on the individual. Even in a situation of plenty, however, an individual will experience deprivation. Deprivation in a bountiful environment occurs naturally, simply as a result of not consuming the reinforcer for a while. No animal eats, drinks, or copulates continuously even in an environment in which food, water, and sex are continuously and freely available. Even if an individual were to engage in any of these activities for a prolonged period, deprivation would build up naturally in the others. At least for some reinforcers, the build up of deprivation that occurs naturally follows a circadian rhythm; that is, responding for the reinforcer tends to occur at about the same time (or times) each succeeding day as it did the previous day (although there may be gradual shifts in the times of the activity across days).

Natural versus imposed deprivation was alluded to in Chapter 7 when closed versus open economies were discussed. Recall that in a closed economy, the animal is in the experimental situation throughout the experiment and receives all its reinforcers in that situation. In a closed economy, deprivation builds up naturally and can be offset by responding for the reinforcer at any time. As was mentioned in Chapter 7, closed economies sustain more responding per reinforcement than open economies do (Zeiler, 1999). This is probably at least partly because, in order to prevent imposed deprivation, more of the reinforcer occurs per reinforcement in the closed economies typically studied in learning experiments. It should be noted that closed economies and natural deprivation are not synonymous. If the schedule of reinforcement is too high, or the amount of the reinforcer received at each reinforcement is too small, then a state of imposed deprivation will exist in a closed economy.

There is evidence that for at least some reinforcers natural deprivation may be more effective than imposed deprivation. With wheel-running reinforcement, for example, rats respond more when allowed to run freely in a wheel than when given as many as ten days deprivation of wheel-running (Looy & Eikelboom, 1989). Similarly, when rats can respond to initiate trials in a discrete-trials discrimination task for wheel-running reinforcement, their discrimination accuracy improves markedly over what it is when there is an imposed intertrial interval (and hence "local" or short-term imposed deprivation). In addition, responding and accuracy on a discrimination task for wheel-running reinforcement is very high when rats are given free access to the task in sessions lasting continuously over a number of days (Iversen, 1998). Reinforcers for which natural deprivation is more effective than imposed deprivation may be those (such as appears to be the case with wheel running) for which satiation occurs slowly enough that they do not require imposed deprivation to be effective.

For ethical reasons imposed deprivation usually is not appropriate in applied training situations with humans. Therefore, practitioners of learning science attempt to use natural reinforcers, which are reinforcers for which deprivation occurs naturally and that can be presented at about the time that they would occur naturally (Fisher et al., 1992; Pace, Irancic, Edwards, Iwata, & Page, 1985).

Effects of Varying Deprivation

Although we have concentrated thus far on the capacity of deprivation to increase the effectiveness of a primary positive reinforcer, it has other effects on behavior as well.

Effects on activity level.   Deprivation can increase general activity level. For example, rats placed in a cage that contains an exercise wheel will show increased running as a function of food deprivation (Baumeister, Hawkins, & Cromwell, 1964; Richter, 1922). Likewise, rats will show increased activity in a small rectangular cage as a function of food deprivation, provided that some external stimulus change such as one in general illumination or noise occurs (Campbell & Sheffield, 1953). However, food deprivation does not appear to have this effect on activity level for all species; for example, it does not increase activity level in rabbits (Campbell, Smith, Misanin, & Jaynes, 1966). In addition, not all types of deprivation have the same effect on activity level. For example, although water deprivation may increase running in an activity wheel by rats, it rarely or never increases activity in a small rectangular cage by rats (Campbell, 1964), chicks, guinea pigs, hamsters, or rabbits (Campbell et al., 1966).

Activity may also vary with biological states that are correlated with reinforcer effectiveness. For example, running in an exercise wheel occurs at a higher rate in female rats during estrus (Wang, 1923), which is a biological state clearly related to the reinforcing effectiveness of sexual stimulation.

In addition to sometimes increasing activity level, deprivation also may increase the frequency of phylogenetic (i.e., species-specific or innate) responses related to obtaining the reinforcer in the evolutionary history of the species. For example, food deprivation produces increases in sand digging by rats, even if the individual rats have never obtained food in this way (Wong, 1979). Another example is that the frequency of the vocal "awk" sound in the adult mynah increases with food deprivation (Hake & Mabry, 1979). This may be due to a relationship between this response and the phylogenetic food-begging response of juvenile mynahs.

Effects on response rate.   Response rate maintained by a particular reinforcer is a direct function of the amount of deprivation of that reinforcer. On FR schedules, the principal effect of deprivation is to decrease the postreinforcement pause; local response rates show little sensitivity to even large changes in deprivation (Ferster & Skinner, 1957, pp. 71–77; Sidman & Stebbins, 1954). On FI schedules, decreasing deprivation increases the postreinforcement pause and also seems to increase the curvature of the scallop (Ferster & Skinner, 1957, pp. 320–322). On VI schedules, it is not known to what extent increasing deprivation affects local response rate and to what extent it affects pausing; however, a low level of deprivation results in substantial pausing (Ferster & Skinner, 1957, pp. 364–373).

A consistent pause—especially a postreinforcement pause on a fixed schedule—reflects some sort of discrimination, in that the stimulus that produces the pause may be one that is consistently coupled with a period in which the probability of reinforcement is low. Thus, we might expect the effect of deprivation on discriminations to be similar to its effect on pausing. On multiple VI Ext, increasing deprivation increases response rate in both components; however, it increases response rate in the Ext component proportionately more than in the VI component, especially if the discrimination is weak (Powell, 1973). Thus, as we might expect from its effect on pausing, increased deprivation decreases stimulus control.

A variable that can have an effect on response rate similar to that of decreased deprivation is a stimulus correlated with an aversive event, which produces the conditioned suppression effect described in Chapter 6 (p. 121). Of course, the decreased responding that occurs in the presence of a conditioned aversive stimulus resembles the decreased responding that occurs when deprivation decreases, but this is not the only similarity. For example, the response rates of rats responding for a sucrose solution will increase very little with increased sucrose concentrations in the presence of a conditioned aversive stimulus, relative to the increase that occurs in the absence of the conditioned aversive stimulus when sucrose concentration increases. This is the same effect that making the animal less deprived has on responding for various concentrations of sucrose (Leslie, 1977). We may observe a similar effect in ourselves when we lose interest in (or motivation for) some appealing treat in the face of an impending calamity.

Effects on conditioned stimuli and conditioned reinforcers. Deprivation is necessary in order for respondent conditioning based on an appetitive unconditioned stimulus (e.g., food) to occur. It also is necessary in order for the conditioned stimulus to elicit the conditioned response after conditioning has occurred. Deprivation is not a necessary precondition, however, for a well-established higher-order conditioned stimulus to elicit its response and for a well-established conditioned reinforcer to be effective (Holland & Rescorla, 1975; Morgan, 1974; Rescorla, 1977, 1980). Even when satiation of the unconditioned stimulus has occurred, the strength of a higher-order conditioned stimulus or conditioned reinforcer based on that unconditioned stimulus (or primary positive reinforcer) will typically be little or not at all affected.

The above has an important implication for the treatment of addictions. A standard treatment for cigarette addiction, for example, is to first satiate the client on nicotine through the use of nicotine chewing gum or the nicotine patch. The next step is to gradually reduce the amount of nicotine administered until all craving for nicotine is eliminated. From the preceding paragraph, however, we see that the strength of the conditioned reinforcers, such as inhaled smoke, that are based on nicotine will likely not be reduced by nicotine satiation. To help ensure successful treatment, therefore, steps should be taken to weaken these conditioned reinforcers apart from the nicotine-satiation component of the treatment (Rose & Levin, 1991).

It should be noted that deprivation does not have to be direct in order to affect the development and effectiveness of a higher-order conditioned stimulus or a conditioned reinforcer. Depriving rats of water, for example, indirectly deprives them of food because water-deprived rats will not eat. Food deprivation brought about indirectly in this way may affect the development and effectiveness of a conditioned reinforcer based on food in the same way that direct food deprivation does (Harris et al., 2000).

Sensitization and Habituation to Reinforcers

With repeated exposure to a reinforcer, motivation for it tends first to increase and then to decrease (McSweeney & Swindell, 1999). The initial increase appears to be due to sensitization. The subsequent decrease may be partly due to habituation (see Chapter 2 for a discussion of sensitization and habituation.) The initial increase is known as the appetizer effect. (Yeomans, 1993). The subsequent decrease is due to satiation (such as seen in some of the curves in Figure 4.3 in Chapter 4), which may be partly a result of habituation but also is caused by factors such as (in the case of food motivation) increased blood glucose level and stomach distension (Bizo et al., 1998).

The appetizer effect is an experience that probably everyone can relate to. It does not occur just in restaurants with foods prepared specifically to sensitize us to the reinforcing effect of food. Many snack foods are particularly prone to sensitization, as implied by another name for the appetizer effect—the "salted-nut phenomenon." The phenomenon is especially well captured by the following advertisement slogan for a snack food: "We bet you can't eat just one!" Food habituation also is something everyone has experienced. We express our habituation to a particular food when we say that we are "bored" with it. This might occur when, for example, we have had the same food for several meals in a row. Some diet plans seem designed to induce food habituation by drastically restricting the variety of foods that a person eats.

Some motivational problems might be at least partly the result of problems with sensitization and habituation. Persons with obesity, for example, may habituate to food too slowly, whereas, persons with anorexia may habituate to food too quickly (McSweeney & Swindell, 1999).

Incentive Motivation

There is a class of motivational variables whose effect is based on the physical properties of a reinforcer, such as its magnitude and quality. For example, rats will run faster down a runway (see Figure 4.1, p. 58) after trials on which they experienced ten food pellets than after trials on which they experienced five pellets in the goal box. Similarly, they will enter fewer blind alleys in a complex maze if the goal box has consistently contained bran mash than if it has consistently contained sunflower seeds. The incentive motivation of a given individual for a given reinforcer, or alternatively the incentive value of a given reinforcer for a given individual, is that reinforcer's effectiveness for that individual as a function of the reinforcer's physical properties. Incentive motivation and incentive value are essentially identical, although we often speak as though incentive motivation is in an individual whereas incentive value is in a reinforcer. Of course, they are in neither, but are actually a relation between an individual's behavior and a reinforcer. Incentive motivation focuses on the individual's side of the relation, whereas incentive value focuses on the reinforcer's side.

Incentive devaluation.   We say that an incentive that has been paired with an aversive event (e.g., illness) has been devalued. As might be expected, a devalued incentive is less effective in reinforcing new behavior than it would be if it had not been devalued. The question arises, however, as to what effect devaluing an incentive has on behavior reinforced by it prior to its devaluation. Several studies have shown clearly that the behavior is reduced for a specific devalued incentive (but not for another, non-devalued incentive) even before the devalued incentive occurs following the behavior (Adams & Dickinson, 1981; Colwill & Rescorla, 1985; Holland & Straub, 1979). In the case of some devaluing stimuli, the reduction in responding may depend on the individual experiencing the negative effects (e.g., illness) elicited by the devalued incentive (Balleine & Dickinson, 1991).

Incentive contrast.   Incentive value is relativistic; that is, the incentive value of a reinforcer depends not only on its own properties but, at least to some extent, on the properties of prior reinforcers that the individual has experienced. Specifically, the incentive value of a reinforcer tends to vary inversely with the incentive values of previously experienced reinforcers. This phenomenon, which is called incentive contrast, can be readily appreciated by anyone who has ever been disappointed when a favorable outcome followed an effort that usually had an even better result. Incentive contrast is by no means unique to humans, however. To take an example from nonhuman primates, monkeys may discard or even vociferously reject a normally adequate reinforcer, such as lettuce, following a correct response that has usually produced a superior reinforcer such as banana (Tinklepaugh, 1928, p. 224).

There are two logical types of incentive contrast: negative and positive. Negative incentive contrast, the type illustrated by the above monkey example, is a decrease in a reinforcer's incentive value due to prior experience with a reinforcer having a higher incentive value. Positive incentive contrast is an increase in a reinforcer's incentive value due to prior experience with a reinforcer having a lower incentive value. Negative incentive contrast occurs reliably in data that statistically compares groups of individuals. Positive incentive contrast seems more difficult to demonstrate, but it does occur with a high degree of statistical reliability under the right experimental conditions (Flaherty, 1982).

Negative and positive incentive contrast have been demonstrated by two major types of procedures known as successive and simultaneous contrast procedures (although, as we shall see below, the latter term is somewhat misleading). To demonstrate successive negative incentive contrast, one group of animals receives conditioning trials with a high-valued incentive as the reinforcer while another group receives conditioning trials with a low-valued incentive as the reinforcer. After a number of trials the reinforcer for the first group is switched to the low-valued incentive, while the second group remains on the low incentive-value reinforcer. The typical effect of decreasing the value of the incentive for the first group of animals in this way is that their performance quickly drops below that of the second group. The effect then tends to dissipate over trials—performance of the first group gradually recovers to the level of that of the second group. The effect seems to be time dependent in other ways as well. For example, it varies inversely with the time between the last trial before the shift to the small incentive (Gleitman & Steinman, 1964) and with the intertrial interval (Capaldi, 1972).

Incentive contrast can be observed in consummatory responses as well as operant responses. Thus, if a reinforcer is degraded in some way (e.g., the sucrose concentration of a liquid is decreased, or a less preferred reinforcer is substituted for a more preferred one), the individual may reject or consume less of the reinforcer as well as respond less rapidly to obtain the reinforcer on subsequent trials.

Successive negative incentive contrast occurs in animals as diverse as rats (Crespi, 1942; Flaherty, Becker, & Checker, 1983; Zeaman, 1949) and opossums (Papini, Mustaca, & Bitterman, 1988), but not in turtles or goldfish (Bitterman, 1975; Couvillon & Bitterman, 1985; Flaherty, 1982, p. 422). Surprisingly, given its presence in newer vertebrate lines (mammals and marsupials) and its absence in some older ones (fish and reptiles), successive negative incentive contrast occurs in an invertebrate, namely, the honeybee (Couvillon & Bitterman, 1984). This implies that it evolved independently in more than one species.

Successive positive incentive contrast is demonstrated in the same way as its negative counterpart, except that for one group the incentive value is increased (rather than decreased) to the incentive value for a group for which the incentive value is held constant. The typical result is that the incentive value is greater for the former than for the latter group, even though the physical properties of the reinforcer after the shift in incentive are the same for both groups. In order to demonstrate successive positive incentive contrast, it is necessary to ensure that the animals are not already responding at their maximum levels. Any technique that decreases responding, such as increasing the amount of responding required for reinforcement or the delay of reinforcement, seems to effectively serve this purpose (Flaherty, 1982). Since this often has not been done, there are relatively few studies demonstrating successive positive incentive contrast and hence we know less about it than we do about its negative counterpart.

We set up the conditions for studying either simultaneous negative incentive contrast or simultaneous positive incentive contrast, or both simultaneously, by reinforcing responding with two differently valued incentives in two different situations that alternate. Simultaneous negative contrast occurs if responding for the smaller of the two incentives is less than responding by a control group that receives only the lower-valued incentive in the two situations. Similarly, simultaneous positive contrast occurs if responding for the larger of the two incentives is greater than responding by a control group that receives only the higher-valued incentive in the two situations.

The designation "simultaneous" to describe the above procedure is somewhat misleading because the two situations are not actually present simultaneously, as in simultaneous discriminations or concurrent schedules. Rather, the active ingredient of the procedure is a two-component multiple schedule in which the incentive values of the reinforcers in the two components differ. This is like the procedure for producing behavioral contrast (see Chapter 8), except that it is the incentive values instead of the reinforcement rates in the two components that differ. In fact, there is some question as to whether simultaneous incentive contrast is not more related to behavioral contrast than it is to successive incentive contrast (Gonzales & Champlin, 1974; Pert & Gonzales, 1974). In any case, simultaneous incentive contrast may be a different process from successive incentive contrast. One piece of evidence for this is that while successive negative incentive contrast tends to decrease over trials or time, simultaneous negative incentive contrast tends to be long lasting (Flaherty, 1982, p. 432). Another indication that they may be different processes is that while successive negative contrast does occur in goldfish and turtles, simultaneous incentive contrast does (Burns, Woodwards, Henderson, & Bitterman, 1974; Cochrane, Scobie, & Fallon, 1973; Gonzales & Powers, 1973; Pert & Gonzales, 1974).

Incentive effects on extinction.   Incentive value may interact with a number of reinforced trials to determine the number of responses that occur in extinction. There is some evidence that as the number of reinforced trials prior to extinction increases, the number of responses during extinction (or running speed in a runway situation) increases when incentive value is low and decreases when incentive value is high (Ison & Cook, 1964; Traupmann, 1972). If this result is reliable, it could be due to successive negative incentive contrast. When extinction begins, there is more of a decrease in incentive value when it was large than when it was small. Thus negative incentive contrast should be greater when extinction is introduced after a reinforcer with a large incentive value than after one with a small incentive value, and this effect should be enhanced by an increased number of training trials. However, it is unclear at present whether this interaction between number of reinforced trials and incentive value is a real phenomenon (Mackintosh, 1974, p. 425).

AVERSIVE MOTIVATION

The distinction between appetitive and aversive motivation corresponds to the distinction between positive and negative reinforcement. The standard distinction hinges on whether it is the presentation of the reinforcer (positive reinforcement) or the removal of the reinforcer (negative reinforcement) that increases the probability of the response it follows (Skinner, 1953). One may question the logical validity of this distinction on the grounds that the removal of one stimulus logically implies the presentation of another stimulus, and vice versa (Michael, 1975). For example, an empty plate is a different stimulus from a plate with food on it. Putting food on someone's plate, therefore, is logically equivalent to removing the empty plate and replacing it with an identical plate that has food on it. Thus, whether we view putting food on someone's plate contingent on a response as positive reinforcement (i.e., presenting the stimulus of a plate with food on it) or as negative reinforcement (i.e., removing the stimulus of a plate without food on it) is arbitrary. Since we can make this same argument regardless of what is being presented or removed in any event it follows that we cannot logically distinguish between positive and negative reinforcement—what one person claims is an instance of positive reinforcement another may, with equal validity, claim is an instance of negative reinforcement. From this argument, it follows that the distinction between appetitive and aversive motivation is also logically invalid.

We may preserve the distinction between a positive and negative reinforcer, however, if we make a slight addition to the standard definition of negative reinforcer. Suppose we define a negative reinforcer as a stimulus (a) whose removal following a response increases the probability of that response (i.e., reinforces the response), and (b) whose presentation is the only establishing operation required for this reinforcing function. For example, food (or the removal of the absence of food) requires an operation such as deprivation in order to effectively reinforce behavior. The removal of shock (or the presentation of nonshock), in contrast, requires nothing other than shock itself in order to effectively reinforce behavior. In addition to avoiding the logical difficulty of the standard distinction, this distinction seems to correspond well to all cases in which we usually wish to distinguish between positive and negative reinforcement and is consistent with the way in which positive and negative reinforcement are treated in this book.

Types of Primary Negative Reinforcers

There are difficulties in identifying primary negative reinforcers that are analogous to those in identifying primary positive reinforcers. Electric shock is by far the most commonly studied primary aversive stimulus. It is easy to administer automatically at precise times and intensities, it does not cause tissue damage (when administered at small enough intensities), and it is unlikely to be a conditioned negative reinforcer by association with other negative reinforcers. Other types of aversive events that seem to be primary negative reinforcers, however, also have been studied. For example, white rats will respond to turn off bright light (Keller, 1941), and mice and rats will respond to terminate intense noise (Barnes & Kish, 1957; Campbell & Bloom, 1965; Halpern & Lyon, 1966; Harrison & Abelson, 1959; however, see Knutson & Bailey, 1974, for report on difficulties establishing escape and avoidance behavior based on noise as an aversive stimulus). Monkeys addicted to morphine will, after receiving morphine, press a lever to escape or avoid injection of a drug (nalorphine or naloxone) that is antagonistic to morphine (Downs & Woods, 1975; Goldberg, Hoffmeister, Schlichting, & Wuttke, 1971).

The fine line between appetitive and aversive motivation is illustrated by the fact that removal of a primary or conditioned positive reinforcer is an aversive event, in that it can be used to establish and maintain avoidance behavior. For example, children watching cartoons will press a lever if lever presses prevent interruption of the cartoons (Baer, 1960). Similarly, under certain conditions, pigeons and rats will respond to avoid a timeout from positive reinforcement, a stimulus-correlated period of time during which positive reinforcement is withheld. Suppose that food occurs on a VT schedule except when a tone is present, during which no food is given. If the tone occurs periodically when no response on an operandum occurs, and responding on the operandum postpones the appearance of the tone, the animal will begin to emit responses on the operandum (D'Andrea, 1971; Thomas, 1965).

Thus, the removal of a stimulus paired with positive reinforcement (i.e., timeout) is usually aversive (although, as we shall see, this is not always true). Moreover, presenting a stimulus that has previously been paired with reinforcement but omitting the reinforcer or reducing its magnitude is also aversive. This effect has been given a special name, as indicated below.

The Frustration Effect

As we saw in Chapter 3, extinction following positive reinforcement sometimes produces emotional effects such as extinction bursting (i.e., very rapid responding at the start of extinction) and aggression toward animate and inanimate objects. Moreover, the omission or reduction of a reinforcer in the presence of a stimulus during which reinforcement previously occurred produces what is called the frustration effect, which collectively consists of three phenomena: (1) increased motivation for the reinforcer, which results in (2) increased activity level and (3) conditioned aversiveness of stimuli present during the omission of reinforcement. We consider each of these properties of the frustration effect in turn.

Motivating nature of the frustration effect. The classical method of demonstrating the frustration effect uses a double runway, consisting of two runways joined together so that the goal box of one is the start box of the other. When, after reinforcement has been present in both goal boxes on previous trials, omitting (Amsel & Roussel, 1952) or reducing (Bower, 1962; McHose & Ludvigson, 1965; Patten & Myers, 1970) it produces an increased speed of running toward the second goal box. The speed of running toward the second goal box for animals subjected to this procedure is greater on average than that of animals that never obtained reinforcement in the first goal box (Wagner, 1959); thus, the effect is not due to the absence of food per se in the first goal box.

The frustration effect occurs in other situations as well. Consider for example an FR or an FI schedule in which a stimulus paired with a primary reinforcer occurs along with the primary reinforcer at the completion of each ratio or interval. Now, if the primary reinforcer fails to occur or there is a smaller amount of it than usual at the completion of a given ratio or interval, the postreinforcement pause at the beginning of the next ratio or interval will tend to be shorter than usual (Perone & Courtney, 1992; Staddon & Innis, 1969).

Although studied mainly in vertebrates, the frustration effect may not be limited to them. For example, foraging honeybees alternating between two targets containing sucrose solutions will move more rapidly from one target to the other if the sucrose concentration in the first target is reduced below its usual level (Loo & Bitterman, 1992). This effect occurs only if there are distinctive stimuli—distinctive odors, for example—paired with the two targets (Couvillon, Nagrampa, & Bitterman, 1994), thus indicating that the effect is not due to the decreased sucrose concentration per se.

Activating nature of the frustration effect. In addition to producing more rapid responding for reinforcement, the motivational nature of the frustration effect may be manifested in increased activity. For example, rats cover more area per unit of time when placed on an enclosed large flat surface, called an open-field apparatus, just after they have missed a scheduled reinforcer than they do just after obtaining a scheduled reinforcer (Gallup & Altomari, 1969).

Aversiveness of the frustration effect. The aversiveness of the frustration effect is seen in the fact that animals will learn a response—such as jumping over a hurdle or pressing a lever to open a door—that enables them to escape from a situation in which a reinforcer that previously occurred has failed to occur (Adelman & Maatsch, 1955; Daly, 1969) or has been reduced (Daly & McCroskery, 1973).

The frustration effect explains why, although timeout from positive reinforcement is aversive under certain conditions (as we have seen), there are other conditions under which it reinforces responding. This might seem surprising for two reasons: (1) It seems contradictory because it seems to imply that a stimulus and the absence of that stimulus can both be reinforcing; and (2) the timeout provides nothing that the individual could not have obtained with less effort simply by ceasing to respond. Nevertheless, if a rat or pigeon, for example, has access to two operandums, one of which produces food on an FR schedule and the other produces a brief timeout (e.g., a 5-second period in which the chamber is dark and no reinforcement is available), the animal will respond frequently on the second operandum during the postreinforcement pause (Appel, 1963; Azrin, 1961; D. M. Thompson, 1964; Zimmerman

& Ferster, 1964). Similarly, monkeys emitting complex sequences of responses on several keys will tend to make errors early in the sequence if they produce timeout (Redd, Sidman, & Fletcher, 1974). The number of timeout responses emitted varies directly with the size of the response requirement and inversely with the level of deprivation. Timeout is also reinforcing on response-independent schedules such as VT and FT, where the proportion of session time allocated to it increases as mean interreinforcement interval increases (Lydersen, Perkins, Thomas, & Lowman, 1980). In these situations, it appears that timeout is reinforcing because it provides escape from stimuli paired with decreased reinforcement rate and perhaps also the individual's own tendency to begin responding for reinforcement that requires a large expenditure of behavior.

In addition to their removal being reinforcing, of aversive stimuli tend to elicit aggression. The aversiveness of the omission or reduction of reinforcement, therefore, is also seen in the resulting elicitation of attack on nearby individuals or inanimate objects (Azrin, Hutchinson, & Hake, 1966). This phenomenon is sometimes taken as support for the so-called frustration-aggression hypothesis, which is a theoretical postulate that an inner state called "frustration" leads to aggression (Dollard, Doob, Miller, Mowrer, & Sears, 1939). We consider aggression elicited by aversiveness (including frustration-elicited attack) in more detail in Chapter 15.

Frustration effect related to negative incentive contrast.   The procedure for producing the frustration effect is similar to the procedure for producing negative incentive contrast; both procedures involve degrading reinforcement (i.e., reducing it in amount or quality). Yet superficially the two procedures seem to produce opposite results. The frustration effect is an *increase* in motivation whereas negative incentive contrast is a *decrease* in motivation. To resolve this seeming contradiction, note that the increased motivation in the frustration effect is toward a reinforcer that is at a distance (either spatial or temporal) from the degraded reinforcer; the decreased motivation in negative incentive contrast is toward the degraded reinforcer. Both these effects can be understood by inferring that the degraded reinforcer has taken on some aversiveness that subtracts from its reinforcing capacity. This aversiveness results in decreased motivation toward it in negative incentive contrast and in motivation away from it and toward another reinforcer in the frustration effect. In short, negative incentive contrast and the frustration effect are two sides of the same basic phenomenon. These two sides correspond to punishment and negative reinforcement. Negative incentive contrast reflects the punishing aspect of the degraded reinforcer and the frustration effect reflects the negative reinforcing aspect.

Other aspects of the frustration effect.   In addition to the aspects of the frustration effect mentioned above, reduction or omission of reinforcement in the presence of stimuli paired with reinforcement has physiological effects such as pituitary-adrenal activation and changes in immune function. Reinforcement reduction or omission also causes odor emissions and distress vocalizations (see Figure 3.4, p. 49) (Papini & Dudley, 1997).

Evolutionary significance of the frustration effect.   Although society generally views frustration as an undesirable emotion because it is socially disruptive, the above aspects of the frustration effect have clear advantages from an evolutionary viewpoint. When a reinforcer becomes less plentiful in an animal's natural environment, it is to the animal's advantage to become active in searching for a richer source of reinforcement and (at least initially) to avoid the situation in which the reinforcer became less plentiful. In fact, the increased activity that occurs when reinforcement is decreased in experiments may represent the activation of a general search mode of responding rather than merely random activity (Pecoraro, Timberlake, & Tinsley, 1999; Timberlake & Lucas, 1989).

SIMILARITIES BETWEEN APPETITIVE AND AVERSIVE MOTIVATION

Aversive motivation has a number of parallels with appetitive motivation. Most of these parallels are so striking that one might question whether these two types of motivation are distinct processes or are basically the same process, especially in view of the fine line between the two types of motivation illustrated in some of preceding examples (cf. Michael, 1975).

Intensity of a Primary Aversive Stimulus

Intensity of a primary aversive stimulus could correspond to two things with regard to appetitive motivation: (1) level of deprivation, or (2) reinforcement magnitude. Studies of shock intensity on avoidance responding have suggested that higher shock intensities produce higher response rates than do lower shock intensities (Boren, Sidman, & Herrnstein, 1959; D'Amato, Fazzaro, & Etkin, 1967; Klein & Rilling, 1972; Leander, 1973; Powell, 1970; Riess, 1970). However, a more recent analysis of these data and some new data indicate that shock intensity has an "all-or-none" effect on avoidance response rate; that is, little or no avoidance responding occurs below a certain shock intensity (about 1.2 mA for rats) while responding is at or near it maximum level above that intensity (das Gracas de Souza, Alves de Moraes, & Todorov, 1984). Reinforcement magnitude also has an all-or-none effect on response rate (Catania, 1963, 1966), while, as we have seen, response rate varies directly with deprivation. Hence, intensity of an aversive stimulus appears to be more analogous to reinforcement magnitude than it is to deprivation level.

If the intensity of the aversive stimulus is analogous to magnitude of reinforcement, then one might expect that reductions in that intensity would not have to reduce to zero in order to be negatively reinforcing. In accordance with this expectation, studies have shown that animals will respond to reduce the intensity of shock even if the response does not result in escape or avoidance of the shock (e.g., Bersh & Alloy, 1978; Bower, Fowler, & Trapold, 1959; Campbell & Kraeling, 1953; Weiss & Laties, 1959, 1963). For example, rats will learn to respond on a modified free-operant avoidance schedule in which, instead of postponing shock for a fixed period of time following the response, each response simply reduces the intensity of any shock that occurs during a fixed period of time following that response (Powell & Peck, 1969). Similarly, animals will also respond to reduce the duration of an impending shock (Bersh & Alloy, 1980).

Schedule Effects

Another correspondence between appetitive and aversive motivation is that similar schedule effects are obtained with both positive and negative reinforcement. For example, suppose that shock occurs on a VT schedule in the presence of a particular stimulus, and no shock occurs in the absence of that stimulus. Then if responding on a key turns off the stimulus for a short period on an FI schedule, the animal will show the scalloped pattern of responding characteristic of performance on FI schedules (Hake & Campbell, 1972). Although all possible schedules have not been studied using this procedure, there is no reason to doubt that they too would produce their characteristic effects.

Schedule Preferences

Recall from Chapter 12 that studies with concurrent schedules show that animals prefer aperiodic over periodic reinforcement, and that they prefer signaled over unsignaled reinforcement. Similar procedures show that rats also prefer a VT over an FT schedule of shock—on concurrent FT VT shock schedules, they alternate more from FT to VT than from VT to FT (Badia, Harsh, & Coker, 1975). Moreover, rats allocate more time to schedules in which shock is signaled than to schedules in which it is unsignaled (Abbott & Badia, 1984). Preference for signaled shock emerges slowly or not at all if the signals are short (less than 1 second in length), but becomes strong with longer (i.e., 2 seconds) ones (Abbott & Badia, 1979).

Stimulus Generalization

Generalization gradients similar to those obtained using positive reinforcement have been obtained with negative reinforcement. For example, monkeys trained to press a lever to postpone shock on a free-operant avoidance schedule in the presence of a light of a specific intensity will, on subsequent testing at various light intensities, show a generalization gradient with a peak at the training intensity. However, the generalization gradient based on avoidance is generally broader than that obtained using food reinforcement on a VI schedule (Hearst, 1960, 1962, 1965). This may not be due to a fundamental difference between appetitive and aversive motivation. Rather, it may be for the same reason that DRL schedules produce broader generalization gradients than do VI schedules (see Chapter 8); namely, that responding on both DRL and free-operant avoidance schedules is controlled to a large extent by response-produced stimuli. To see this in the case of free-operant avoidance schedules, note that in this case any behavior that does not lead to a response can be paired with shock and therefore can become aversive. Thus, a period of not responding produces a stimulus that controls responding. This is similar to the DRL case in that a period in which no response has occurred produces a stimulus in the presence of which a response is likely to be reinforced. Since these response-produced stimuli are present at full strength regardless of how the external stimuli are varied during generalization testing, these response-produced stimuli will tend to make the generalization gradient broader than would be the case if they did not control responding.

The peak shift can also be obtained just as easily with negative reinforcement as with positive reinforcement. For example, if rats are exposed to a free-operant avoidance schedule in the presence of one click frequency and no shock is given in the presence of a different click frequency, subsequent generalization testing will reveal a shift in the peak of the gradient in the direction away from the frequency paired with no shock (Weiss & Schindler, 1981).

Warm-up

An animal exhibits warm-up if its performances early in sessions is consistently low relative to its performances late in previous sessions. Although we did not use the term, we discussed warm-up with regard to appetitive motivation when we talked about within-session changes in operant responding for positive reinforcement in Chapter 7 (pp. 146–147) and earlier in this chapter (p. 290) when we talked about sensitization to reinforcers. Warm-up is even more prevalent with responding under aversive motivation. It is especially characteristic of free-operant avoidance schedules. Figure 13.1 shows the cumulative records over several sessions of a rat's responding on a free-operant avoidance schedule. Shocks are indicated by downward deflections of the pen. Note that warm-up is evident in each of these sessions. It is particularly

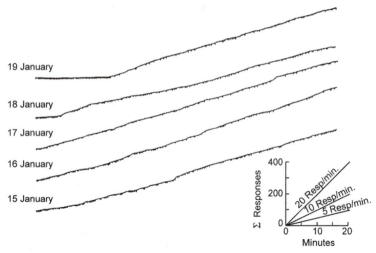

FIGURE 13.1. Warm-up in free-operant avoidance. The shock-shock and response-shock intervals were both 20 seconds. Downward deflections of the pen indicate shocks. Reading from the bottom up, note development of a low rate of responding at the beginnings of sessions. (From Hineline, 1978)

evident on the session labeled "19 January," where there is a complete absence of responding at the beginning which is then followed by an abrupt change to proficient performance.

Shock presentation appears to be the critical variable in warm-up on free-operant avoidance; that is, the effect occurs as a result of the shocks at the beginning of the session, and is not due merely to being in the chamber for a period of time or to exposure to the avoidance contingency. This is shown by the fact that warm-up is eliminated if shocks are given in the chamber with the lever removed prior to the regular session, but is not eliminated by mere confinement in the chamber prior to the session (Hoffman, Fleshler, & Chorny, 1961).

Although we cited sensitization to the reinforcer as a likely reason for warm-up in appetitive responding, this explanation may not seem to work for warm-up in free-operant avoidance because the duration of warm-up tends to increase as the shock-shock and response-shock intervals decrease (Hineline, 1978). As these intervals decrease, the number of shocks increases and therefore it might seem that sensitization should increase also. As the number of shocks increases, however, habituation should also increase, which might mask any increase in sensitization. Thus, sensitization may account for the warm-up effects that occur in responding under both appetitive and aversive motivation.

DIFFERENCES BETWEEN APPETITIVE AND AVERSIVE MOTIVATION

Despite the above similarities, there also appear to be some basic differences between behavior based on appetitive motivation and behavior based on aversive motivation.

Emotional Effects

Negative reinforcement appears to produce certain emotional effects that are produced either to a lesser extent or not at all by positive reinforcement. For example, some humans working in groups on a cooperative task (e.g., solving arithmetic problems) express (e.g., on a rating scale) more annoyance with other group members and the experimenter when completing a task criterion prevents a group monetary account from being decremented than when completing the criterion increments the group account (Emurian, Emurian, & Brady, 1985). The former contingency is, of course, an avoidance contingency whereas the latter is a positive reinforcement contingency. It is interesting that the contingencies have different emotional effects even though they result in the same amount of money for the same amount of work.

Response Specificity: Preparedness

Some responses are easy to condition using aversive motivation. These responses are said to be prepared to be learned to escape or avoid aversive stimulation (Seligman, 1970). Other responses, said to be contraprepared, are more difficult to condition with aversive motivation, although they may easily be conditioned with appetitive motivation. It is sometimes said that prepared responses are more readily learned using aversive motivation because they are highly similar to the animal's species-specific-defense-reactions (SSDRs), which include responses such as fleeing, freezing, and fighting (Bolles, 1970, 1971, 1972). Presumably, learning these responses readily under aversive motivation increased the likelihood of a species' survival, and thus the tendency to do so became part of the genetic makeup of the species through natural selection of those individuals possessing this tendency.

Thus, while rats readily learn to avoid shock by running or jumping from one compartment to another in a shuttle box (Brush, 1966)—like the one shown in Figure 5.1 (p. 92)—or jumping out of a box (Baum, 1965; Denny, 1971; Mackenzie, 1974), they often fail to learn to press a lever to avoid shock (D'Amato & Schiff, 1964; Meyer, Cho, & Weserman, 1960). Similarly, although pigeons readily learn to run from one compartment to another in a shuttle box (Macphail, 1968), they often fail to learn to peck a key to avoid shock. Thus, pressing a lever and pecking a key are contraprepared responses with respect to avoidance learning for rats and pigeons, respectively, although clearly they are prepared responses with respect to learning to respond for positive reinforcement.

Responses can be conditioned with motivation against which they are contraprepared, however, if special procedures are used. The reason that lever pressing is difficult to condition in rats with a shock-avoidance contingency seems to be that rats tend to freeze on the lever and hold it down. One way to improve lever-press avoidance learning in rats is to present shocks with a higher probability when the lever is being held down than when it is not being held down, thus in effect punishing lever holding (Feldman & Bremner, 1963). A related way is to have both pressing and releasing the lever postpone shock, with the latter postponing it for a longer period than the former (Keehn, 1967; Meltzer & Tiller, 1979). In discrete-trial avoidance, in which a conditioned aversive stimulus occurs prior to shock, rats will readily learn to press a lever to terminate the stimulus and avoid shock if the conditioned aversive stimulus is sufficiently long (Berger & Brush, 1975). It appears that rats freeze in the presence of the conditioned aversive stimulus if it is ten seconds or less.

Shaping has been used to train pigeons to peck a key to avoid shock. In this method shocks occur at frequent intervals and each successive criterion approximation (e.g., orienting toward the key, approaching it) produces a cessation of the shocks or a reduction in their intensity (Ferrari, Todorov, & Graeff, 1973; Todorov et al., 1974). Another method that is successful with both rats (Giulian & Schmaltz, 1973) and pigeons (Foree & LoLordo, 1974; Lewis, Lwein, Stoyak, & Muehleisen, 1974) is termed reinforcement switching. In this method the response is first shaped using positive reinforcement. An avoidance contingency is then superimposed on the positive reinforcement contingency, and finally the positive reinforcement contingency is removed.

Although certain responses may be difficult to condition using aversive motivation, once conditioned they are maintained as readily as any other response and seem to follow the same laws as any other response. Thus, there is no evidence at present that there are different laws of learning for prepared and unprepared (or contraprepared) responses (Seligman, 1970; Seligman & Hagar, 1972).

Conditioned Facilitation

Conditioned suppression was discussed in Chapter 6 (p. 121). This phenomenon is a suppression in operant responding when a conditioned aversive stimulus—a stimulus that has been paired with an aversive event such as shock—occurs. Conditioned suppression is reliably produced in responding that is being maintained by positive reinforcement; however, it is not reliably obtained when the conditioned aversive stimulus is superimposed on responding maintained on a free-operant avoidance schedule. In the latter case an effect opposite to conditioned suppression, called conditioned facilitation (or conditioned acceleration) often occurs—responding increases in the presence of the conditioned aversive stimulus.

Conditioned facilitation has been demonstrated with dogs (Waller & Waller, 1963), rhesus monkeys (Herrnstein & Sidman, 1958; Sidman, Herrnstein, & Conrad, 1957), squirrel monkeys (Kelleher, Riddle, & Cook, 1963), and chimpanzees (Belleville, Rohles, Crunzke, & Clark, 1963). The immediate effect of introducing the conditioned aversive stimulus paired with shock is an increase in responding in both the presence and absence of the conditioned aversive stimulus. This is followed by a decrease in responding in both the presence and absence of the conditioned aversive stimulus; however, the decrease occurs more rapidly in the absence of the stimulus so that responding is greater in its presence than in its absence. Responding then assumes a scalloped pattern (similar to that generated by an FI schedule) in the presence of the conditioned aversive stimulus; after the onset of the stimulus responding accelerates gradually until the primary aversive event is delivered at the termination of the conditioned aversive stimulus. Like conditioned suppression, conditioned facilitation gradually disappears if shock is discontinued following the conditioned aversive stimulus. Unlike conditioned suppression, however, the effect is transitory—at least for rhesus monkeys—even if shock is not discontinued. After responding no longer increases in the presence of the conditioned aversive stimulus, however, during extinction of avoidance responding by discontinuing the shock, responding decreases more slowly in the presence of the conditioned aversive stimulus than in its absence (Sidman et al., 1957).

In order for conditioned facilitation to occur, responding need not be maintained on an avoidance schedule. There must, however, have been a history of avoidance conditioning in the presence of the same or similar stimulus. Given such a history, conditioned facilitation may occur during food reinforcement or when baseline responding is at zero following extinction (through discontinuation of shock) of avoidance responding (Sidman et al., 1957).

There are certain cases in which conditioned suppression rather than conditioned facilitation of avoidance responding occurs. Although it is not clear exactly what conditions are responsible for these cases, one factor may be the species of animal involved. Specifically, rats show conditioned suppression rather than conditioned facilitation if the shock rate during the conditioned aversive stimulus is not greater than in its absence (Hurwitz & Roberts, 1969; Roberts & Hurwitz, 1970). As will be discussed in Chapter 15, shocks can elicit aggressive responding; if this aggressive responding is directed toward the operandum, it can result in bursts of responding following shock. If operant responding is suppressed during the conditioned aversive stimulus, there may be an increased shock rate during the stimulus that would cause an increase in the responses elicited by shock. This increase in shock-elicited responding may have been mistaken for conditioned facilitation in some studies with rats; however, examination of the data obtained with monkeys and dogs shows that the increased responding during the conditioned aversive stimulus is not due to an increased rate of shock during that stimulus for these species.

Persistence of Avoidance Behavior

Unlike the case with appetitive motivation, there are two ways to extinguish avoidance responses:

- the aversive stimulus no longer occurs, or
- the aversive stimulus continues to occur but the response no longer prevents it

Note that neither method is directly analogous to extinction of responding based on appetitive motivation. The first method is similar to discontinuing both the reinforcer and the establishing operation on which the reinforcer is based in appetitive motivation; the second is similar to removing the contingency between the response and the reinforcer and continuing to present the reinforcer. This lack of symmetry between responding based on appetitive and aversive motivation is due to the fact that the reinforcer and the establishing operation are distinct in the former and identical in the latter. Thus, direct comparisons between the two types of motivation with regard to extinction are difficult. Most research on the extinction of avoidance responding has used the first method.

Discontinuing the primary aversive stimulus.   One characteristic of avoidance behavior is that it can be extremely persistent even when the primary aversive stimulus on which it is based no longer occurs. Consider, for example, a shuttle-box (see Figure 5.1, p. 92) in which a dog has been conditioned to jump from one side to the other in the presence of a conditioned aversive stimulus (e.g., a light) based on shock; i.e., a shock occurs if the dog does not jump over the side a short time after the conditioned aversive stimulus occurs. The conditioned aversive stimulus might be, for example, the lights above the box. If the dog jumps to the other side shortly after the lights turn on, they go off, and no shock occurs. Suppose that the shocker is then disconnected so that no shock occurs whether or not the dog jumps in the presence of the conditioned aversive stimulus (the lights). The result in many cases is that the dog will continue to make the avoidance response in the presence of the stimulus for many hundreds of trials with no sign that the behavior is weakening (Annau & Kamin, 1961; Solomon, Kamin, & Wynne, 1953; Solomon & Wynne, 1954).

Perhaps because typical operant responses, such as lever presses, are contraprepared for escaping and avoiding aversive stimuli, responding on free-operant schedules often extinguish fairly rapidly when the primary aversive event no longer occurs (Shnidman, 1968). However, when responding on a free-operant avoidance schedule has occurred over a prolonged period, responding during extinction is highly persistent (Galizio, 1999).

Although it may not be possible to eliminate some avoidance responses simply by eliminating the primary aversive stimulus on which they are based, there are at least two ways in which the behavior can be reliably eliminated. One is straightforward extinction, that is the primary aversive stimulus occurs whether or not the avoidance response is emitted (Davenport & Olson, 1968). The other is termed flooding or response blocking. In this method the avoidance response is prevented from occurring in the presence of the S^D (e.g., by means of an obstruction in the shuttle box) and the S^D is not followed by the primary aversive stimulus (Baum, 1970). The speed with which the avoidance response is eliminated is directly related to the amount of time the animal remains in the presence of the S^D (Baum, 1996; Page & Hall, 1953; Schiff et al., 1972). Note that flooding is similar to latent extinction, as discussed in Chapter 5 (p. 91), in that in both cases the reinforced response does not occur in the presence of stimuli that have been paired with reinforcement. The primary difference between latent extinction and flooding is that the former involves positive reinforcement whereas the latter involves negative reinforcement.

Extinction of responding for timeout from avoidance.   One method for making extinction under aversive motivation more similar to extinction under appetitive motivation is to implement a timeout-from-avoidance response. In this procedure, a free-operant avoidance response is maintained by a primary aversive stimulus and another response, called a timeout response, briefly removes on some schedule a stimulus correlated with the avoidance schedule (Galizio & Allen, 1991; Galizio & Liborio, 1995). Extinction of the timeout response is done by making the response ineffective; that is, it no longer removes the stimulus correlated with the avoidance schedule. This is analogous to a response based on appetitive reinforcement, because it discontinues reinforcement (timeout from the avoidance schedule) while leaving the establishing operation (the avoidance schedule) for the timeout response intact. With this procedure, timeout responding quickly decreases after, in some cases, producing an initial response burst (Galizio, 1999). Similar to the response bursts that occur at the start of extinction following positive reinforcement (see Chapter 3). This demonstrates that extinction of responding based on aversive motivation can be directly analogous and similar to the extinction of responding based on appetitive motivation.

　　Suppose, however, that in the same arrangement (as above) the timeout response remains effective but the primary aversive stimulus no longer occurs on the avoidance schedule (i.e., extinction of avoidance responding is carried out in the usual manner). This removes the establishing operation for the timeout response and therefore is analogous to satiating the individual with the primary positive reinforcer in the case of responding based on appetitive motivation. However, although satiation decreases responding based on appetitive motivation, discontinuing the primary aversive stimulus in the above situation does not decrease timeout responding (Galizio, 1999). Even when avoidance responding has decreased to zero in this situation, timeout responding continues at a high level. Thus, by removing one asymmetry between appetitive and aversive motivation with regard to extinction, another one emerges. It is not clear why the stimulus correlated with an avoidance schedule continues to be aversive even when responding on the avoidance schedule has decreased to zero due to the nonoccurrence of the primary aversive stimulus. Further research on this question may help us to better understand and treat phobias and anxiety disorders in humans.

Session-Length Reduction as Reinforcement

It appears that reduction of the length of a session that contains primary aversive stimuli can be reinforcing. This has been demonstrated by providing rats with two levers during free-operant avoidance. Responses on both levers postpone shock by the same amount of time. However, each response on one of the levers also reduces the length of the session by one minute. The result is that some animals develop a strong preference for the latter lever (Mellitz,

Hineline, Whitehouse, & Laurence, 1983). This indicates that events that occur quite some time after a response can affect that response.

The analogous result with positive reinforcement would be that session-length increases would act as reinforcement (provided that the usual procedure of feeding animals immediately after experimental sessions was not followed). At the present time there is no evidence for or against this effect.

SUMMARY AND CONCLUSIONS

An unconditioned or a conditioned stimulus will not elicit its response, and a primary or a conditioned reinforcer will not reinforce responding, unless a specific establishing operation has occurred. Conditioning based on food (either as an unconditioned stimulus or a primary reinforcer) requires food deprivation, or something that functions like food deprivation (e.g., a hunger-inducing drug), in order to be effective. Establishing operations are also called motivational variables.

There are two types of motivational variables—appetitive and aversive—that correspond to positive and negative reinforcement. Deprivation of the reinforcer is an establishing operation for the former, while presentation of the reinforcer is the establishing operation for the latter.

Individuals will learn not only a response that removes a negative reinforcer, but also (if one is available) a response that prevents (or postpones) it. The latter type of response is called an avoidance response. Avoidance conditioning (i.e., conditioning of an avoidance response) proceeds most rapidly if there is an external stimulus, called a warning stimulus, a preaversive stimulus or conditioned aversive stimulus, whose removal (along with avoidance of the negative reinforcer) is contingent on the avoidance response. Avoidance conditioning will occur, however, even if there is no external conditioned aversive stimulus. An avoidance conditioning procedure in which there is no conditioned aversive stimulus and each response postpones the occurrence of the aversive stimulus by a fixed period of time following the response is called Sidman or free-operant avoidance. The two-factor theory of avoidance conditioning explains free-operant avoidance as being due to covert conditioned aversive stimuli generated by responses that do not prevent or postpone the aversive stimulus. There are problems with two-factor theory, however, so the issue is not settled.

There are a number of similarities between responding under appetitive motivation and responding under aversive motivation, suggesting that similar processes underlie both types of responding. For example, both types of responding show similar schedule effects. Both also show similarly shaped generalization gradients. There also are, however, differences between the two types of responding. For example, generalization gradients under aversive motivation tend to be broader than those under appetitive motivation. Aversive motivation tends to produce more emotional behavior (e.g., disruptions in learned responding) than appetitive motivation. Another difference is that a conditioned aversive stimulus occurring independently of responding tends to have a suppressive effect (called conditioned suppression) on responding under appetitive motivation but a facilitative effect (called conditioned facilitation) on responding under aversive motivation. Presenting a conditioned positive reinforcer independently of responding does not have comparable effects on responding under either appetitive or aversive motivation. A particularly strong difference between appetitive and aversive motivation is that the latter, in combination with an avoidance contingency produces responding that is much more persistent than responding under appetitive responding when the reinforcer no longer occurs (i.e., during extinction). This persistence during the extinction of avoidance by not presenting the reinforcer is probably partly due to the similarity between the stimulus conditions prevailing during well-conditioned avoidance responding (i.e., few occurrences of the aversive stimulus) and the absence of the aversive stimulus during extinction (but research indicates that other, as yet unknown, factors also are involved). In any case, it is noteworthy that well-conditioned avoidance responding persists a long time when there are few or no presentations of the reinforcer (i.e., the primary aversive stimulus).

14

Punishment

Thus far in this book we have focused on contingencies that develop and maintain new behavior; that is, contingencies that teach an individual what to do in a given situation. In this chapter we look at contingencies that, in effect, teach an individual what *not* to do in a given situation. In the science of learning there are two definitions of punishment (both of which, it should be noted, differ from the common use of the word in everyday English):

- Punishment is a contingency in which a stimulus following a response decreases the probability of that response (Azrin & Holz, 1966).
- Punishment is the presentation of a negative reinforcer or the removal of a positive reinforcer contingent on a response (Skinner, 1953).

In the second definition, it is important not to confuse "removal of" with "withholding" or "ceasing to present." To remove a positive reinforcer is to physically take it away; whereas withholding or ceasing to present a positive reinforcer is, of course, extinction.

Both definitions of punishment lead to similar ways of talking about the effects of aversive events, such as those discussed in the previous chapter, when contingent on behavior. A summary of the advantages and disadvantages of each of these definitions is provided in this section as a brief overview of the material to follow.

Two advantages of the first definition are that it is simple and that it makes good intuitive sense in that it accords with our view of what punishment usually does—suppress behavior. A disadvantage of the first definition is that it includes contingencies that we probably would not want to regard as punishing. For example, if after a pigeon has been trained to peck a key for food we cause the key light to change colors after each key peck, key pecking will decrease temporarily. Although changing the stimulus on the key after each key peck thus is punishment according to the first definition, it is probably more reasonable to attribute the resulting decrease in key pecking to decreased stimulus control (i.e., the failure to generalize to the changed stimulus situation). Alternately, another disadvantage of the first definition is that it excludes contingencies that we might wish to regard as punishment.

For example, consider the following two cases in which a response that is being reinforced is also being followed at least occasionally by electric shock.

Case 1: After the initial suppression of the response by electric shock contingent on it, the response recovers to its original level of occurrence even if shock continues to be contingent on it (Azrin, 1960b).

Case 2: The electric shock contingent on the response is too weak to suppress that response, even though the same intensity of shock would lead to escape if the animal had the opportunity to escape from it (Azrin, Hake, Holz, & Hutchinson, 1965).

In both cases, the first definition seems to imply that punishment is not occurring. This is somewhat awkward in Case 1 because according to the first definition we have to say that what was at first punishing stopped being punishing. In addition, if in both cases an alternative response is available that provides the same reinforcement (e.g., the same amount and frequency of food reinforcement) as the shocked response, that alternative response will increase and the shocked response will decrease (Azrin, Hake, Holz, et al., 1965). The first definition would then imply that making the shock contingent on responding is punishment because it suppresses the shocked behavior. This is a disadvantage of the first definition in that it seems awkward or strange to say that adding an alternative response converts a nonpunishment contingency into punishment.

A major advantage of the second definition is that, being derived from the concept of negative reinforcement, it does not require the introduction of a new elementary term ("punishment") into the behavioral scientific language. This is important because science strives to economize the number of elementary terms it uses. A major disadvantage of the second definition is that it implicitly requires that any stimulus used in a punishment contingency first be demonstrated to be a negative reinforcer. While stimuli used in punishment contingencies in specific experiments have often been demonstrated to be negative reinforcers in other experiments with other animals, it is often impossible to say for certain that those stimuli are negative reinforcers for the animals on which they are being used in a punishment contingency.

Although there thus are advantages and disadvantages to both definitions, this text book uses the second definition unless otherwise indicated. It also uses the term punisher to refer to a stimulus made contingent on a response in a punishment contingency.

THEORIES OF PUNISHMENT

Corresponding to the two definitions of punishment are two major theories of punishment. One theory holds that punishment is a primary process; that is, that punishment suppresses behavior it is contingent on in much the same way reinforcement increases the behavior it is contingent on (Azrin & Holz, 1966, pp. 381–382). In other words, punishment is the opposite of reinforcement.

The other theory of punishment holds that punishment is derived from negative reinforcement (Dinsmoor, 1954). According to this theory, punishment suppresses behavior it is contingent on because it negatively reinforces behavior that is incompatible with the punished behavior. (Note: Two responses are incompatible if both cannot occur at the same time.) For example, if an individual emitting a punished response begins to emit an alternative response that is incompatible with the punished response, the punished response will decrease simply because the individual cannot engage in both the punished and alternative response simultaneously. The decrease in the punished response results in the removal or avoidance of the punisher, which negatively reinforces the alternative response.

It is not clear which theory (if either) is correct. The remainder of this chapter considers a number of facts about punishment that bear on these two theories, although they do not decisively support either.

ESCAPE FROM AND AVOIDANCE OF PUNISHMENT

The close relationship between punishment and negative reinforcement is underscored by the fact that animals will respond to escape or avoid punishment in a wide variety of experimental arrangements. This tendency to escape or avoid punishment is one of the major disadvantages of using punishment in applied learning situations—individuals tend to escape or avoid the learning situation.

Availability of Escape/Avoidance Response

If two operanda are available, one of which produces both positive reinforcement and punishment and the other of which terminates the stimulus paired with punishment or provides avoidance of punishment, animals will learn to respond on the second operandum. For example, if a pigeon receives an equal amount and rate of food reinforcement on either of two concurrent schedules in which responding on one of the schedules produces electric shock while responding on the other schedule does not, the animal will show a preference for the schedule that does not produce shock (Azrin, Hake, Holz, et al., 1965). The degree to which animals show preference for the schedule in which shock does not occur is directly related to the intensity of the shock—the stronger the shock in one schedule the stronger the preference for the other schedule. In addition, it is inversely related to the amount of positive reinforcement the animal misses by abstaining from the schedule in which punishment occurs. Some animals may even respond on a second operandum to produce a timeout, in which a stimulus occurs for a short period during which both the positive reinforcement contingency and the punishment contingency are suspended. For example, rats that receive food on a VI schedule for pressing one lever may seldom or never press a second lever that produces a 10-minute timeout from positive reinforcement. If the positive-reinforcement lever also produces shock on an FR schedule, however, some rats will dramatically increase their presses on the timeout lever (Hearst & Sidman, 1961). Apparently the animals press the timeout lever because this provides escape from the punishment contingency, even though it also prevents them from obtaining positive reinforcement for a set period.

Recall that the second part of the second definition of punishment, above, states that punishment includes the response-contingent withdrawal of a positive reinforcer. As we have seen in earlier chapters, an S^D is a positive reinforcer; therefore, withdrawal of an S^D contingent on a response should constitute punishment. Withdrawal of an S^D (or, equivalently, presentation of an S^Δ) for a set period of time is, as we have seen, referred to as timeout. A question of considerable interest is whether timeout suppresses behavior on which it is contingent in the same manner that a stimulus such as electric shock does. If responses are punished by timeout, individuals will engage in an alternative response (if one is available) that will permit reinforcement to be obtained while avoiding punishment by the timeout. For example, mental patients pulling a plunger to obtain cigarettes on a VI schedule will switch to pressing a button on which the same reinforcement schedule is in effect if timeout is scheduled to occur after a fixed number of responses when the plunger is pulled but not when the button is pressed (Holz, Azrin, & Ayllon, 1963). Similarly, when responding by pigeons on one of the VI schedules in concurrent VI VI produces timeout on an FR schedule, responding on that VI schedule will decrease while responding on the other VI schedule will increase (Thomas, 1968).

Timeout delivered as punishment for incorrect matching-to-sample responses also has been found to be effective in increasing matching-to-sample accuracy in pigeons responding for food (Ferster & Appel, 1961; Zimmerman & Ferster, 1963) and humans responding for money (Zimmerman & Bayden, 1963). Correct responses when timeout is contingent on incorrect responses in matching-to-sample may be thought of as responses that are negatively reinforced because they avoid timeout in addition to being positively reinforced because they produce a reinforcer such as food or money.

Negative Reinforcement of Response Omission

The material in the above section shows clearly that punishment and negative reinforcement are closely related. However, in all the cases discussed above an alternative operandum was available for the escape or avoidance response. Situations can also be arranged in which escape or avoidance of punishment is produced by the omission of a response. For example, suppose that shock occurs after each response on an FR schedule of food reinforcement if the postreinforcement pause (PRP) is less than some specified time. The result is that most animals will increase their PRPs long enough to avoid most shocks while still responding to obtain food (Lattal & Cooper, 1969). Similarly, if food occurs on a VI 3-minute schedule and shock occurs on the same operandum on a VI 30-seconds schedule, animals will decrease their response rate if each IRT greater than a specified length results in the cancellation of any shock scheduled during that IRT (Arbuckle & Lattal, 1987). Likewise, if a pigeon's key pecks are reinforced with food on a VI 3-minutes schedule and each key peck increases shock intensity for key pecking while any pause of more than three seconds duration decreases shock intensity for key pecking, the pigeon will decrease its rate of key pecking below that which occurs when pauses do not decrease shock intensity (Rachlin, 1972, Exp. 1).

IRT Punishment and Negative Reinforcement

A number of studies have examined the effects of punishment and negative reinforcement at the level of the IRT. If IRTs greater than a certain length are punished while monkeys press a lever on a VI schedule for food, response rate will increase above that maintained by the VI schedule when punishment does not occur; conversely, if IRTs less than a certain length are punished, response rate will decrease below that maintained by the VI schedule when punishment is not given (Galbicka & Branch, 1981). A similar effect has been found when either long or short IRTs are punished on a free-operant avoidance schedule, even when the overall rate of punishment is held constant (Galbicka & Platt, 1984). These effects of punishing long or short IRTs can be interpreted in two ways: (1) the change in response rate that occurs when either long or short IRTs are differentially punished is due to suppression of the punished IRTs; or (2) the change in response rate is due to negative reinforcement of the unpunished IRTs. The first interpretation is in accord with the first definition of punishment given at the beginning of this chapter and the theory that punishment is a primary process; the second interpretation is more in accord with the second definition of punishment and the theory that punishment is derived from negative reinforcement.

Punishment of long IRTs on VI schedules does not necessarily increase response rate, however. For example, with rats, a low intensity of shock punishment of long IRTs increases response rate, but a high intensity of shock punishment of long IRTs decreases response rate (Sizemore & Maxwell, 1985). It appears that high shock intensities of IRT punishment act more to punish responding in general than to punish specific IRTs, because the same shock intensity that suppresses response rate in a long-IRT punishment contingency does not suppress responding when punishment is contingent on a pause that is equivalent to the length of the punished IRT (Sizemore & Maxwell, 1985). (In an IRT punishment contingency, punishment always occurs after a response, whereas it does not occur after a response in a pause-punishment contingency.)

PUNISHMENT AND BEHAVIORAL EQUILIBRIUM

As mentioned in the previous chapter, an increase in a response above its equilibrium level is punishing. For example, responding to produce an auditory stimuli may be reinforcing at a given rate, but aversive at a higher rate. Making the auditory stimulus contingent on another response that occurs at a higher rate than the equilibrium level of the response for the auditory stimulus would suppress that other response (Heth & Warren, 1978). This effect is called response satiation.

In applied settings response satiation may provide a form of punishment that does not involve the use of noxious stimuli. For example, in one applied study on a psychiatric ward, coffee drinking above its equilibrium level suppressed inappropriate vocalizations when it was made contingent on them (Dougher, 1983).

PARAMETERS OF PUNISHMENT

Two important parameters in determining the effectiveness of punishment are immediacy and intensity. In general, the more immediate and more intense a punisher is, the more it will suppress the behavior on which it is contingent.

Immediacy

Immediate punishment results in more suppression of behavior than delayed punishment does. For example, if every 50th lever press of a rat responding for food is followed by electric shock, responding will be suppressed more if the shock follows every 50th lever press by one second than if it follows every lever press by 15 seconds (Azrin, 1956). If the delay of punishment is too long (e.g., more than 30 seconds), responding may not be suppressed at all (or whatever suppression occurs may be due to general emotional effects rather than punishment per se).

There are some situations, however, in which punishment can be effective over extremely long delays. Specifically, these are what are called conditioned taste aversions. Consumption of flavored water by rats is suppressed when paired with illness (induced by X-irradiation or by a drug such as lithium-chloride or d-amphetamine) over delays as long as 90 minutes (Garcia, Ervin, & Koelling, 1966). Since there is an immediate stimulus that becomes a conditioned punisher—namely, the flavor of the water—due to its association with illness, this phenomenon is perhaps more accurately categorized under conditioned punishment rather than punishment per se. For rats, gustatory (i.e., taste) stimuli become conditioned punishers more readily over long delays than do other types of stimuli (lights, sounds) when paired with illness (Garcia & Koelling, 1966). However, for at least some birds (such as quail and pigeons), visual stimuli become conditioned punishers more readily than do gustatory stimuli when paired with illness (Wilcoxon et al., 1971). (For this reason, "conditioned taste aversion" when applied to birds is a misnomer.)

The evolutionary reason that taste becomes a conditioned punisher for mammals when paired with illness after a long delay, whereas color becomes a conditioned punisher for birds when paired with illness after a long delay, is that taste is a stronger stimulus for mammals (they are more sensitive to it) than birds are; birds are more sensitive to colors. Hence, for mammals there is a high correlation between certain tastes and naturally occurring poisons, whereas for birds there is a higher correlation between certain colors and naturally occurring poisons. Because colors paired with naturally occurring poisonous substances likely would be *on* the substances, it also follows from evolutionary principles that for birds colors on or near food would become more effective conditioned punishers based on illness than colors farther from food. This has been confirmed, in that a distinctive colored light in the feeder becomes a more effective conditioned punisher based on illness than a distinctive colored light projected through the response key does (Glowa & Barrett, 1983; Logue, 1980).

The above treatment of conditioned aversions based on illness under the category of punishment tends to be supported by studies involving drugs. Sedative, hypnotic compounds (e.g., pentobarbital, chlordiazepoxide) usually increase punished responding (Kelleher & Morse, 1968; McKearney & Barrett, 1978), and they also attenuate conditioned taste aversions (Cappell & Le Blanc, 1973; Concannon & Freda, 1980; Glowa & Barrett, 1983; Riley & Lovely, 1978).

Intensity

The principle of small increments which states that small cumulative changes have a less drastic affect than a large, sudden change applies to punishment intensity. Intense punishment is more effective if it is introduced suddenly than if it is built up to gradually. For example, strong electric shock occurring suddenly as punishment can completely suppress responding; however, the same intensity of shock introduced gradually may not completely suppress responding (Azrin, Holz, & Hake, 1963; Masserman, 1946; Miller, 1960). Conversely, prior exposure to an intense punisher increases the effectiveness of a weak punisher (Raymond, 1968). Note that some principles of sensitization and habituation mentioned in Chapter 2 thus apply to punishment.

The intensity of electric shock as a punisher is measured in milliamperes of current. When timeout is used as a punisher, intensity is assumed to be the duration of the timeout. Thus, if a rat receives a timeout every third lever press and food on the other lever presses, responding will be suppressed below that which occurs when no consequence follows every third lever press. The amount of suppression will increase as a direct function of the timeout duration; that is, more suppression will occur when the timeout is 120 seconds than when it is 10 seconds (Kaufman & Baron, 1968).

The amount of suppression that occurs as a result of punishment depends on the strength of the punished response and the availability of an alternative response that produces the same reinforcement. Suppression by punishment is markedly reduced if the strength of the punished response is increased by increasing the amount of the reinforcer or rate of reinforcement for the response (Church & Raymond, 1967) or by increasing the motivation (e.g., deprivation level) for the reinforcer (Kaufman & Baron, 1968). Relatively low intensities of punishment completely suppress responding when an alternative response that produces the same amount and rate of reinforcement is available (Azrin, Hake, Holz, et al., 1965).

SCHEDULES OF PUNISHMENT

Just as studies on schedules of reinforcement help us understand reinforcement, studies on schedules of punishment help us understand punishment. Schedules of punishment are analogous to schedules of reinforcement in some ways, but not in others.

Single Schedules

Analogous to a continuous reinforcement schedule, continuous punishment is the delivery of punishment following each response. Likewise, FR, FI, VI, and VR schedules of reinforcement have their corresponding schedules of punishment. Unlike the case when conducting basic research on reinforcement schedules, when conducting basic research on punishment schedules one has to be concerned with scheduling both reinforcement and punishment. If reinforcement is not scheduled the individual will not respond and the response will not be punished—in which case one cannot study the schedule of punishment selected for study. Often a VI schedule of reinforcement is used because it provides a uniform rate of responding against which to observe the effects of the punishment schedule, and because changes in response rate on VI schedules have little effect on reinforcement rate if they are not too large.

The typical result of any schedule of punishment is response suppression—rate of responding is decreased. Continuous punishment produces greater response suppression than intermittent schedules of punishment do (Filby & Appel, 1966). If punishment is not so intense that complete suppression of responding occurs, then there is at least a partial recovery of responding to its original level prior to the introduction of punishment (the prepunishment baseline) under all schedules of punishment (Azrin, 1960b). When any schedule of punishment is withdrawn (leaving the reinforcement schedule intact), recovery of the prepunishment baseline occurs if the behavior has not been suppressed completely by punishment. When continuous punishment is withdrawn, this recovery occurs immediately and there is an overshooting of—that is, an increase in responding above—the prepunishment baseline. This overshooting is temporary and responding returns to the prepunishment baseline quickly, usually within three or four daily sessions (Azrin, 1960a). When FR punishment is withdrawn overshooting the prepunishment baseline usually occurs three to four hours later—at least with rats (Azrin, Holz, & Hake, 1963). When VI punishment is removed, recovery may be gradual or abrupt and overshooting of the prepunishment baseline may not occur (Filby & Appel, 1966).

Moment-to-moment response rate patterns produced by various schedules of punishment typically are opposite to those produced by the corresponding schedules of reinforcement. For example, FI punishment (superimposed on a VI schedule of reinforcement) for key pecking by pigeons produces an inverse scallop—that is, each punishment is followed immediately by a high rate of pecking and that then gradually decreases as the time for the next punishment approaches (Azrin, 1956).

Multiple Schedules

When punishment occurs in one component of a multiple schedule, an effect similar to behavioral contrast may be obtained (see Chapter 8), especially if the stimuli correlated with the components are very distinct. That is, responding may increase in the component in which punishment does not occur. The more likely effect, however, is that responding will *decrease* in the component(s) in which punishment does not occur (although not as much as in the component in which punishment occurs) (Crosbie et al., 1997).

Concurrent Schedules

If punishment occurs in one component schedule of a pair of concurrent positive reinforcement schedules, responding decreases in that component schedule and increases in the other component schedule. Punished behavior is suppressed more quickly when reinforcement occurs for the alternative response (i.e., responding on the component schedule in which punishment does not occur) than when it does not (Holz et al., 1963). This is very important in applied settings in which it may be necessary to use punishment to suppress harmful behavior because the reinforcer maintaining it cannot be identified or extinction of it is not feasible for some other reason (Thompson, Iwata, Conners, & Roscoe, 1999). In these cases, applied learning scientists recommend that a desirable alternative response be positively reinforced to expedite the reduction of the undesirable response (Martin & Pear, 1999, p. 172).

PARADOXICAL REINFORCEMENT EFFECTS OF PUNISHMENT

Although the typical effect of presenting punishment intermittently is suppression of the punished behavior, under certain circumstances shock that is contingent on responding will mimic some of the effects of reinforcement. These paradoxical reinforcement effects of punishment have been documented with two species: cats (*Felis domestica*) and, more extensively, squirrel monkeys (*Saimiri sciureus*).

Specifically, if an operant response such as lever pressing is first established by either positive (at least with squirrel monkeys) or negative (both cats and squirrel monkeys) reinforcement and shock then occurs on either an FI schedule (cats and squirrel monkeys) or a VI schedule (squirrel monkeys), the animal will show the characteristic pattern of responding produced by the corresponding schedule of positive reinforcement. Thus, on FI-shock, the animal shows the type of scallops typically produced by FI schedules of reinforcement rather than the inverse scallops that typically occur on FI schedules of punishment. That is, after each shock the animal will first pause and then gradually increase its responding until it reaches a high terminal rate that continues until the next shock. The positive or negative reinforcement schedule under which responding was initially established need not be in effect in order for this phenomenon to occur—the pattern of responding will be developed and maintained provided that the response-contingent-shock schedule remains in effect. Moreover, this pattern of responding appears to be maintained indefinitely by the punishment schedule long after the positive or negative reinforcement schedule initially used to establish responding is withdrawn (Byrd, 1969; Kelleher & Morse, 1968; McKearney, 1969; Morse, & Kelleher, 1977; Morse, Mead, & Kelleher, 1967).

Responding maintained by contingent shock resembles responding maintained by positive reinforcement in other ways. For example, decreased responding due to extinction may be mimicked by no longer presenting shock following responding; reinstatement of responding due to reconditioning may be mimicked by again presenting shock contingent on responding (McKearney, 1969). Moreover, higher response rates are produced by higher rates of shock (McKearney, 1969), higher shock intensities (Morse & Kelleher, 1977), and more immediate (as opposed to delayed) shock (Byrd, 1972). In addition, with squirrel monkeys, a brief stimulus that is paired with shock on second-order schedules with FI components—for example, FR (FI 4 min-tone) 4-(tone + shock)—will produce a scalloped pattern (Byrd, 1972). If, however, the brief stimulus is not paired with shock in the second-order schedule—for example, FR (FI 4 min-tone) 4-(no tone + shock)—the brief stimulus will not produce a scalloped pattern; instead, a scallop will occur throughout the interval between shocks. Thus, response-contingent shock mimics positive reinforcement in that stimuli paired with it mimic conditioned reinforcers in their effect on response patterning when presented on FI schedules. With cats a brief stimulus in a second-order shock schedule with FI components also produces a scalloped response pattern, but only when the brief stimulus is not paired with shock. When the brief stimulus is paired with shock—for example, FR (FI 5 min-tone) 3-(tone + shock)—

responding is suppressed. It is not known whether this different result with cats and squirrel monkeys is due to a species difference or a procedural one (Byrd, 1969).

Despite the above similarities between positive reinforcement and shock presented on FI and VI schedules to cats and squirrel monkeys, there are a number of indications that shock is not a positive reinforcer for these animals:

- Response-contingent shock cannot be used to condition or shape new operant responses. The responding that it maintains must first be developed by either positive or negative reinforcement.
- At least with cats, a stimulus paired with shock in a second-order shock schedule suppresses responding. This indicates that pairing the brief stimulus with shock causes it to become a conditioned punisher, which implies that shock is a punisher rather than a positive reinforcer.
- At least in squirrel monkeys, ratio schedules (FR and VR) of shock either suppress responding or maintain it less readily than do FI schedules, even when rate of shock is held constant in the two types of schedules (McKearney, 1970; Morse & Kelleher, 1970). FR shock initially produces increases in responding and generates a response-rate pattern similar to that produced by FR reinforcement, except that the pattern generated by FR shock is a little more scalloped (Branch & Dworkin, 1981). FR shock then suppresses responding (Kelleher & Morse, 1968; McKearney, 1970) and the introduction of FI shock does not reestablish it (Branch & Dworkin, 1981). In addition, responding is even suppressed in the FR component while being maintained in the VI component of multiple FR-shock VI-shock (Morse & Kelleher, 1977).
- Given a response that switches them between high rate and low rate shock (e.g., between FI 2-minutes-shock and FI 6-minutes-shock schedules), squirrel monkeys will choose the latter much more often than the former (Pitts & Malagodi, 1991). Although it is unclear why they sometimes choose FI 2 minutes-shock over FI 6 minutes-shock, the fact that they usually choose the schedule that provides less frequent shock indicates that shock on FI schedules is not positively reinforcing for them even though it maintains the same pattern of responding that reinforcement on FI schedules generates and maintains.
- If DRL or DRH is added in tandem to an FI-shock schedule that is maintaining responding—that is, if the FI-shock schedule is replaced with a tandem FI DRL-shock or a tandem FI DRH-shock schedule—squirrel monkeys will increase responding in the first case and decrease responding (or cease responding altogether) in the second (Laurence, Hinelline, & Bersh, 1994). If shock is a positive reinforcer, response rate should have decreased in the first case and increased in the second (Ferster & Skinner, 1957).

It therefore seems clear that, although response-contingent shock can mimic some of the effects of positive reinforcement, it is not a positive reinforcer. On the contrary, it is a punisher according to the second definition of punishment given at the beginning of this chapter, even though making it contingent on responding may not suppress responding. It is, however, not at all clear why response-contingent shock maintains responding on certain schedules—specifically, interval schedules—of punishment. One suggestion is that response-contingent shock on interval schedules punishes long IRTs, so that short IRTs tend to predominate (Galbicka & Branch, 1981). But this explanation does not tell us why the short IRTs continue to occur in the absence of any clear reinforcement contingency for them. In addition, it does not tell us why short IRTs, which occur just before shock in the scalloped pattern during FI-shock, also are not eliminated due to punishment. Thus, an explanation based on IRT punishment does not seem adequate to account for the maintenance of responding by response-contingent shock.

Another suggested explanation is that shock is a discriminative stimulus for responding maintained by response-contingent shock (Laurence et al., 1994). This explanation applies when the initial responding is developed by a free-operant avoidance schedule, because on such a schedule the probability of shock increases over time following the previous shock if no response occurs during that time. This does not explain, however, why shock continues to be a discriminative stimulus long after the initial avoidance schedule has been removed. It also does not explain why responding that initially is developed by positive reinforcement can be maintained by response-contingent shock. Thus, at present, there appears to be no satisfactory explanation for responding maintained by response-contingent shock. We return to this topic in the next chapter.

Another puzzling aspect of behavior maintained by response-contingent shock is its apparent lack of survival value. Any animal that acted to produce a stimulus that ordinarily would be punishing likely would not survive long in its natural environment, and thus would be unlikely to pass on its genetic material. In understanding how this phenomenon can exist in any living species, however, it is important to consider the contrived nature of the experimental situation in which the phenomenon has been demonstrated. The cats were tested in small cages and the monkeys were confined in specially designed restraining chairs. These animals likely would never be in such a restricted situation in their natural environments; instead, they likely would escape or avoid any situation comparable to the one that generates responding maintained by response-contingent shock in the laboratory, since the evidence indicates that such situations are aversive to them.

SUMMARY AND CONCLUSIONS

There are two technical definitions of punishment: (1) the response-contingent presentation of a negative reinforcer or withdrawal of a positive reinforcer; and (2) the suppression of a response by a stimulus contingent on that response. Since a negative reinforcer or the withdrawal of a positive reinforcer tends to suppress any response it follows, which definition is preferred is primarily a theoretical matter with little practical importance. The theoretical issue concerns whether punishment suppresses responses directly or through the reinforcement of responses that are incompatible with the punished response (and hence suppress it through response competition).

Punishment suppresses a response more rapidly and completely if an alternative response that produces the same reinforcer at the same (or higher) rate is available. This is likely because emitting the alternative response results in avoidance of punishment while providing the same rate of reinforcement. The punishment of long IRTs on VI schedules of reinforcement provides a good illustration of the relationship between punishment and avoidance. This procedure results in an increase in response rate, even though some responses (the ones terminating long IRTs) are punished. The reason is that emitting short IRTs avoids the punishment while still permitting reinforcement to occur.

The more intense punishment is, the more suppressive it is. However, intense punishment will be less suppressive if introduced by small increments in intensity than if it occurs at full intensity when first introduced.

Like different schedules of reinforcement, different schedules of punishment have characteristic effects on behavior. Continuous punishment produces greater suppression than intermittent punishment does. When punishment is discontinued, rate of responding first exceeds the level it was at before the introduction of punishment and then returns to that level. Response-rate patterns produced by various schedules of punishment are typically opposite to those produced by the corresponding schedules of reinforcement.

Although the usual effect of punishment is response suppression, under certain conditions intermittent punishment mimics the effects of reinforcement in maintaining responding and in the response-rate patterns it produces. At present there is no clear explanation for this phenomenon. It may be a form of superstitious avoidance behavior, or adjunctive behavior (see next chapter), or a combination of these.

15
Adjunctive Behavior

Thus far in this book we have seen how reinforcement and punishment tend to strengthen and weaken the behavior that they follow. These effects belong to the category of operant behavior. We have also seen that reinforcers and punishers are stimuli that elicit behavior, such as when food elicits salivation or shock elicits flexion of a limb. These effects belong to the category of respondent behavior. In this chapter we consider what appears to be another category of behavior—behavior that is neither strengthened and maintained by reinforcement nor elicited by stimuli, but that nevertheless is generated by some schedules of reinforcement. This third category is termed adjunctive behavior. Because it is generated by schedules of reinforcement although not reinforced by the scheduled reinforcers, adjunctive behavior is a by-product of learning (and may be a type of learning). It also has motivational properties, as we shall see. Thus we consider it in this part of our overview of the science of learning.

SCHEDULES THAT GENERATE ADJUNCTIVE BEHAVIOR

Schedules of both positive and negative reinforcement can generate adjunctive behavior. We begin with positive reinforcement, concentrating on schedules involving food.

Schedules of Positive Reinforcement: Focus on Food

Consider a rat pressing a lever for food with water freely available. If food is programmed on a VI 1 schedule, the animal will drink after almost every reinforcement and, consequently, will consume a large quantity of water over the entire session (Falk, 1961). The amount of water the animal will drink over the session will be considerably more than it would have drunk had it received the same amount of food in a single feeding and had access to water for the same amount of time. Rats on VI food schedules with free access to water have drunk as much as 1/2 their body weights in approximately 3 hours, and three times as much as their daily average prior to being exposed to the schedule of reinforcement in an experimental session (Falk, 1961). This overdrinking, or polydipsia, usually takes a few days to develop (Reynierse & Spanier, 1968; Staddon & Ayres, 1975). Once it develops it is persistent in that it continues indefinitely as long as the food schedule that produced it remains in effect (Falk, 1969).

Polydipsia produced by certain food schedules is not caused by a physiological imbalance due to ingestion of food. For one thing, schedules of liquid food produce it as well as schedules of dry food do (Falk, 1967). For another, unlike drinking produced by water deprivation or salty food, it is not reduced by injecting water directly into the stomach prior to the experimental session (Falk, 1969). However, it is reduced by giving the animal a large quantity of water to drink just prior to an experimental session (Cope, Sanger, & Blackman, 1976; McFarland, 1970).

Polydipsia produced by certain food schedules also is not caused by adventitious food reinforcement of drinking. Modifying the food scheduled such that food never occurs less than 15 seconds after drinking will not reduce the amount of water drunk (Falk, 1964). Thus, polydipsia produced by certain food schedules is not reinforced by the food occurring on those schedules, and so does not appear to be operant behavior.

It also does not appear to be respondent behavior. First, as mentioned above, it takes a few days to develop, whereas respondent behavior occurs in full strength after, at most, only a few presentations of the eliciting stimulus. Second, drinking is only elicited consistently by food on certain schedules of reinforcement. Were it respondent it would be elicited consistently by food regardless of the schedule of food reinforcement.

Of course, many species of animals drink after consuming a quantity of food simply because water aids in the digestion of food. Subjectively described as due to "thirst" produced by eating or the "dry-mouth" effect and more technically called postprandial drinking, this effect is not usually observed after every bite of food unless the animal is exposed to certain reinforcement schedules. Instead, it typically occurs after a fairly large quantity of food—a "meal-size" amount—has been eaten. It is possible that in some way not yet understood, the animal treats the small amounts of food it receives on certain schedules of reinforcement as though they were regular-size meals. According to this view, polydipsia produced by certain schedules of food reinforcement is simply due to an increase in the number of opportunities available for postprandial drinking on these schedules relative to the number of opportunities available when there is free access to food. In support of this view, the distribution of a rat's drinking following a food delivery on a schedule that produces polydipsia strongly resembles the distribution of drinking following eating when the animal has free access to food (Lucas, Timberlake, & Gawley, 1988).

Since the polydipsia produced by certain schedules of food appears to be neither operant nor respondent, it is considered to be adjunctive. Adjunctive behavior is often characterized as "excessive." The amounts of water drunk by rats during adjunctive drinking clearly are much greater than needed physiologically, and hence are excessive. In general, however, "excessiveness" is difficult to define (Roper, 1982; Timberlake, 1982a; Wetherington & Brownstein, 1982). What constitutes excessive drinking, for example, may be clear enough in many instances; however, there probably would be considerable disagreement on what constitutes, for example, excessive running. Adjunctive behavior often does occur in extraordinarily large amounts, and this fact may be useful in helping to identify it; however, excessiveness is probably not a valid defining characteristic of adjunctive behavior.

Another adjunctive behavior commonly seen on schedules of positive reinforcement is aggressive behavior. A pigeon pecking a key on certain food schedules will repeatedly attack a semi-restrained pigeon shortly after each reinforcement (Azrin et al., 1966). (An apparatus for studying such attack is shown in Fig. 15.1.) Similarly, restrained squirrel monkeys will bite a bar or rubber tube in front of them after reinforcement. Aggressive adjunctive behavior induced by positive reinforcement schedules appears to be due to the unavailability of the reinforcer after it is consumed and the absence of subsequent reinforcers. Factors that decrease the availability of subsequent reinforcers increase the probability of attack. Thus, bar biting by

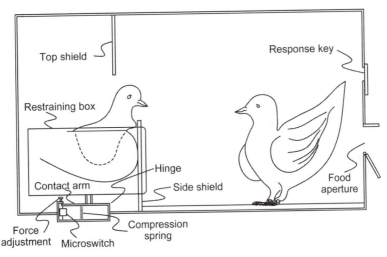

FIGURE 15.1. Apparatus for studying elicited aggression in pigeons. The switch in the bottom left of the figure detects attacks on the pigeon (or model of a pigeon) on the left by the pigeon the right. (From Azrin et al., 1966)

restrained squirrel monkeys (DeWeese, 1977; Hutchinson, Azrin, & Hunt, 1968) and pecking of another pigeon by an unrestrained pigeon (Gentry, 1968) are highly probable during the postreinforcement pause of high FR and long FI schedules. Similarly, the probability of attack is high when extinction is introduced after a period of positive reinforcement.

Aversive Schedules

As mentioned in Chapter 6, schedules of aversive stimuli generate biting attacks directed at animate or inanimate objects immediately following the presentation of the aversive stimulus (Azrin, Hutchinson, & Hake, 1963; Ulrich & Azrin, 1962). For example, rats pressing a lever on a free-operant avoidance schedule may bite and attack the lever after each shock (Pear, Hemmingway, & Keizer, 1978; Pear, Moody, & Persinger, 1972). These biting attacks are clearly elicited by stimuli (i.e., shock) that the schedule presents. Therefore, these attacks do not qualify as adjunctive behavior according to the definition of adjunctive behavior given at the beginning of this chapter. They perhaps do, however, give us some insight as to what may be causing at least some adjunctive behavior. There are striking similarities between attacks elicited by aversive stimuli and some adjunctive behavior. For example, as with schedule-induced polydipsia, aversive-stimulus-elicited behavior occurs reliably but is not reinforced by the schedule. Also as with schedule-induced polydipsia, aversive-stimulus-elicited attack is reinforcing: Animals will learn a response that gives them access to an object to attack immediately after receiving an aversive stimulus (Azrin, Hutchinson, & McLaughlin, 1965). For example, a food-deprived pigeon on an intermittent food schedule will peck a key on various schedules for access to a pigeon it can attack (Cherek, Thompson, & Heistad, 1973; Cole & Parker, 1971), where such attack is considered adjunctive. This suggests that schedule-induced polydipsia (and perhaps other adjunctive behavior on schedules of positive reinforcement) may be caused by a brief aversive period that follows the positive reinforcer (similar, perhaps, to the period of aversiveness that may produce the frustration effect, as described in Chapter 13). Aggression as adjunctive behavior is discussed later in this chapter.

As discussed in Chapter 14, some schedules of electric shock maintain patterns of responding in cats and squirrel monkeys similar to the corresponding schedule of reinforcement (Byrd, 1969; Morse & Kelleher, 1977). For example, an FI shock schedule for lever pressing maintains a scalloped pattern of lever pressing, while a VI shock schedule maintains a steady, moderate rate of responding. Likewise, response rates and patterns maintained by chain and second-order shock schedules are usually similar to those produced by comparable food schedules. The reason or reasons for this effect are not clear. It is not shock-elicited, however, because it does not occur immediately after shock.

As mentioned in Chapter 14, shock is not positively reinforcing for monkeys because when allowed to switch between FI shock 2-minute and FI shock 6-minute schedules, they choose the latter much more often than the former (Pitts & Malagodi, 1991). It is possible that the patterns of responding maintained by certain shock presentation schedules are adjunctive behavior (Hutchinson, 1977). This may be supported by the fact that squirrel monkeys on tandem FI DRH-shock schedules continue to respond, although at low enough rates that they miss almost all shocks; and, conversely, some squirrel monkeys on tandem FI DRL respond at a high enough rates that they miss many shocks (Laurence et al., 1994). This responding may be induced in some way by shock avoidance. However, it is important to keep in mind that this is simply labeling or classifying the behavior rather than explaining it.

SCHEDULE-INDUCED BEHAVIOR

A concept closely related to adjunctive behavior is that of schedule-induced behavior; however, there are important differences between these concepts. Schedule-induced behavior (at least as that term is used in this book) is any behavior that is produced by a schedule of reinforcement, regardless of the process by which the schedule produces the behavior (i.e., regardless of whether the behavior is operant, respondent, or adjunctive). Figure 15.2 illustrates the concept of schedule-induced behavior as elaborated by J. E. R. Staddon (1977). The figure depicts how three categories of behavior—interim, facultative, and terminal—tend to occupy an interreinforcement interval as a function of the size of the interval. Of these three categories, only interim and terminal are considered to be schedule induced. The apex of the triangle in the figure indicates the smallest interreinforcement interval, while the largest is indicated by the base. At all interreinforcement intervals, interim behavior immediately follows reinforcement and terminal behavior immediately precedes reinforcement. As the interreinforcement interval increases from zero, a point is reached at which facultative behavior emerges somewhere in the middle of the interval. As the interreinforcement interval size increases further, a larger proportion of the interval is taken up by facultative behavior.

Interim behavior tends to occur when the probability of reinforcement is low; terminal behavior occurs when it is high and may resemble the response of consuming the reinforcer (e.g., pecking). Facultative behavior is behavior that the animal would engage in from time to time if the reinforcement schedule was not in effect and is not considered to be produced by the schedule—hence, it is not considered schedule induced. Interim and terminal behavior typically are stereotyped and compete with facultative behavior, so that facultative behavior tends to occur when the probabilities of interim and terminal behavior are low. Thus facultative behavior tends to occur during the middle portions of interreinforcement intervals if there is time available for it. Interim and terminal behavior tend to vary together, except at very short interreinforcement intervals when terminal behavior competes with and suppresses interim behavior (Roper, 1980; Staddon, 1977). Variables such as rate or amount of reinforcement, deprivation level, and palatability of the reinforcer generally have the same effect on interim behavior that they have on terminal behavior (Bond, 1973; Cohen, 1975; Falk, 1971, 1977; Heyman & Bouzas, 1980; Wetherington, 1979). However, as would be expected if facultative behavior is not schedule induced, these same variables have either no effect or the opposite effect on facultative behavior (Penney & Schull, 1977).

To illustrate the relationship between interim, facultative, and terminal behavior, consider a rat on an FT 1-minute food schedule with water and a running wheel present. During the 10 seconds or so following reinforcement the animal drinks due to schedule induction. During the next 30 seconds or so, the animal runs in the running wheel. This running, which the animal would likely engage in to the same extent or more if the food schedule was not in effect, is facultative behavior. Its occurrence now is due not to schedule induction but to the fact that the probability of schedule-induced (i.e., interim and terminal) behavior is low at this particular time. During the remainder of the interval the animal engages in behavior around the feeder, such as sticking its head in the feeder opening. This feeder-directed behavior is terminal behavior. If we now decrease the FT schedule, so that food occurs more frequently, less wheel running occurs. If we continue to decrease the FT schedule, eventually less drinking also occurs (Penney & Schull, 1977). Thus, as the interreinforcement interval decreases, terminal behavior tends to occupy a larger portion of the interval leaving less time for interim and facultative behavior.

Interim behavior most likely is adjunctive because (by definition) it usually has ceased some time prior to reinforcement, and therefore is unlikely to be directly reinforced. In fact, one definition of interim behavior is schedule-induced behavior that "occurs at times when a

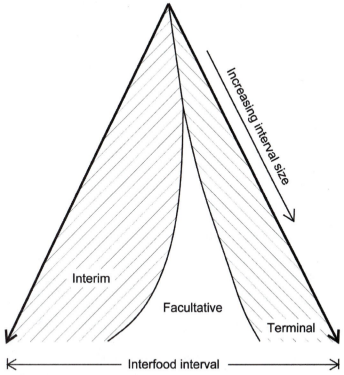

FIGURE 15.2. Schedule-induced behavior as a function of interfood interval. The drawing illustrates the relationship between the size of the interreinforcement interval and the proportion of the interval taken up by the two categories (interim and terminal) of schedule-induced behavior and by facultative behavior. (From Staddon, 1977)

reinforcer is unlikely to be delivered" (Staddon, 1977, p. 126). Facultative behavior is not adjunctive because it is not produced by the reinforcement schedule—it would occur if the reinforcement schedule were not in effect. Terminal behavior, defined as schedule-induced behavior that "emerges in the presence of, or is directed toward, stimuli that are highly predictive of food or some other positive reinforcer" (Staddon, 1977, p. 126), may be either adjunctive or operant. An example of operant terminal behavior would be lever pressing on an FI schedule reinforcing lever pressing. A clear example of adjunctive terminal behavior is much more difficult (if not impossible) to give. The feeder-directed behavior (e.g., sniffing around the feeder and poking its head into it) of a rat on an FT food schedule might be an example. Since such behavior typically occurs just before food on an FT schedule, however, it might also be reinforced by the food—and hence operant. The reinforcement may not be entirely adventitious, since such behavior brings the animal closer to the feeder so that it obtains food sooner than it would have if it was engaging in some other behavior when food arrives.

The above treatment of interim, facultative, and terminal behavior is not universally accepted by learning scientists. Alternative classification schemes for adjunctive behavior have been put forth by Cohen and colleagues (1985) and by Lucas and colleagues (1988). The latter scheme, which is based partly on the former, proposes several categories of interreinforcement behavior that correspond roughly to interim, facultative, and terminal behavior. These categories reflect phylogenetic foraging tendencies that would be manifested in the animal's natural environment. Immediately following reinforcement the animal first searches the area in which reinforcement occurred. This is followed by transitional behavior that is often identified as interim behavior. Search behavior then expands into what has been called facultative behavior, becoming less focused on the location of reinforcement. Finally, search behavior narrows into what has been called terminal behavior, becoming more directed at the location of reinforcement as the time for reinforcement approaches. Note that according to this scheme, unlike the above classification, facultative behavior (i.e., expanded search) is schedule induced. While recognizing that alternative classification schemes for treating schedule-induced behavior exist, in this book I shall use the one involving interim, facultative, and terminal behavior.

GENERALITY OF ADJUNCTIVE BEHAVIOR

Adjunctive behavior is so varied that it is difficult to make general statements about it. The following are some areas in which some general statements seem possible, although with some qualifications.

Generality Across Species and Behavior

One thing that makes adjunctive behavior hard to identify is that it is not the same under the same conditions for all species. Adjunctive polydipsia induced by food schedules occurs in a number of mammals, including laboratory rats (Falk, 1961), mice (Palfai, Kutscher, & Symons, 1971), and monkeys (Schuster & Woods, 1966). It does not, however, occur in birds such as pigeons, which tend to engage in attack instead. Behavior identified as or thought to be adjunctive in at least some animals includes polydipsia, consuming large amounts of food (called polyphagia), chewing inedible substances such as wood shavings (called pica) (Villarreal, 1967), shredding paper, aggression, grooming, licking at a continuous stream of air (Mendelson & Chillag, 1970), pecking at a bolt or spot on a wall (Miller & Gollub, 1974; Palya & Zacny, 1980), defecation (Rayfield, Segal, & Goldiamond, 1982), and attack on animate and inanimate objects (see reviews by Christian et al., 1978; Falk, 1971; Staddon, 1977). Running in a running wheel has been considered adjunctive (King, 1974; Levitsky & Collier, 1968), al-though—as seen above—it also may be facultative. In addition to polydipsia, food schedules can induce alcohol drinking (Falk, Samson, & Winger, 1972) and intravenous self-administration of drugs such as heroin, methadone, cannabis, and nicotine (Oei, Singer, & Jefferys, 1980; Smith & Lang, 1980; Takahashi & Singer, 1980). Other intermittent reinforcers can apparently induce cigarette smoking by nicotine-addicted humans (Cherek & Brauchi, 1981; Wallace & Singer, 1976). Thus some drug-taking may be adjunctive behavior.

Asymmetry Between Food and Water Schedules

Although certain food schedules induce polydipsia in many animals, water schedules do not consistently induce adjunctive eating and often even produce a slight decrease in eating (Carlisle, Shanab, & Simpson, 1972; King, 1974; Myerson & Christiansen, 1979; Rachlin & Krasnoff, 1983; Taylor & Lestor, 1969; Timberlake & Lucas, 1991; Wetherington & Brownstein, 1979; Wetherington & Riley, 1985). One reason that adjunctive eating is difficult to detect on water schedules (assuming that it does occur) may be that it is physiologically impossible to eat more than a certain amount of food in a given state of water deprivation. Another reason might be that drinking by water-deprived animals tends to suppress eating under some conditions. Although having consumed a certain amount of water may enable eating, however, it does not appear to induce it in the same way that eating induces drinking (Timberlake & Lucas, 1991). Thus, food and water schedules are not symmetrical in their effects on drinking and eating, respectively.

Food and water schedules also differ in their effects on gross motor movements (or general activity, which can be considered an index of certain adjunctive behavior). Both rats (Lucas et al., 1988; Timberlake & Lucas, 1991) and pigeons (Reberg, Mann, & Innis, 1977) show considerable activity between reinforcers on interval food schedules (e.g., FT) and much less activity between reinforcers on interval water schedules. For example, while rats on FT food schedules engage in drinking, rearing, and wheel-running, rats of FT water schedules spend much of their time waiting by the location of the reinforcer. Rats on FT food schedules move near the feeder but continue to be active as the time for reinforcement approaches, while rats on FT water schedules are often motionless or even lying down (except on very short—e.g., 8 seconds—FT schedules) as the time for reinforcement approaches (Timberlake & Lucas, 1991). This difference between the effects of food and water schedules makes sense from the perspective of evolution. In an animal's natural environment, food found in one place often indicates the presence of other food nearby but not in the exact same location. The locations in which water can be found, in contrast, generally remain fairly constant (Timberlake & Lucas, 1991).

Although adjunctive eating is not produced consistently by water schedules, it can be induced by schedules of reinforcing brain stimulation (Atrens, 1973; Wilson & Cantor, 1987). Lever pressing by rats on an intermittent brain-stimulation reinforcement schedule eat several times as much wet mash as they do when on continuous brain-stimulation reinforcement or after extinction of responding for brain-stimulation reinforcement. Conditions must be just right to produce this effect, however. For example, if dry food instead of wet mash is used or if the food is not distinctively illuminated, adjunctive eating may be less consistent and more transient (Cantor, 1981). Adjunctive drinking can also be induced by schedules of reinforcing brain stimulation (Cantor & Wilson, 1978).

Adjunctive Behavior in Humans

Because of our interest in our own species, we treat generality of adjunctive behavior to humans separately. Adjunctive behavior does appear to show generality from other species to humans.

Schedules of positive reinforcement. Studies with children have found a number of responses that appear to be adjunctive, such as drinking and vocalizing on fixed-interval food-reinforcement schedules (Porter, Brown, & Goldsmith, 1982), and grooming (Granger, Porter, & Christoph, 1984). Adults performing complex motor tasks, such as tracking an irregularly moving target with a stylus, typically eat snack foods, drink, and engage in facial grooming, during brief timeouts from the task. This behavior generally increases when the task is made more demanding, such as when the target being tracked moves at a higher speed, which suggests that this behavior is adjunctive (Cantor, 1981; Cantor, Smith, & Bryan, 1982; Fallon, Allen, & Butler, 1979; Wallace, Singer, & Wayner, 1975). Interestingly, people who are more skillful at the task tend to snack during a timeout whereas people who are less skillful tend to groom (Cantor et al., 1982). Two other examples of possible adjunctive behavior in adult humans are fidgeting in gambling situations (Clarke et al., 1977), and increased smoking when given brief periodic access to a maze problem (Wallace & Singer, 1976).

Normal humans on a variety of reinforcement schedules engage in a variety of activities that might be adjunctive, such as fidgeting, wriggling, pacing, grooming, doodling, and vocalizing (Muller, Crow, & Cheney, 1979; Wallace, Singer, Wagner, & Cook, 1978; Wallace & Oei, 1981). Which of these activities a given person engages in tends to change from one session to the next, which is different from what is found in animal studies. In addition, although obtained readily in rats, adjunctive drinking has tended to be difficult to demonstrate with normal adult humans. While some schizophrenic patients show considerable adjunctive drinking when placed on intermittent token-reinforcement schedules (Kachanoff, Leveille, McLelland, & Wayner, 1973), normal humans do not show this effect—even when the reinforcer is a salty snack (Wallace & Oei, 1981).

Many common human habits and quirks may be adjunctive behavior. For example, excessive snacking, excessive coffee and alcohol drinking, smoking, nail biting, pencil chewing, hair twirling, and beard stroking may often be adjunctive. Movie viewers who stuff popcorn into their mouths when the scene becomes tense, writers who make trips to the refrigerator during blocks, and people who light up a cigarette after eating or sex are possible examples of individuals engaging in adjunctive behavior.

Certain types of repetitive behavior of some retarded and autistic individuals—such as finger gazing, finger flicking, head weaving, heavy breathing, towel chewing, rumination (i.e., vomiting and reswallowing food), pulling at clothing, spitting, and vocalizing—could in some cases be adjunctive (e.g., Lerman, Iwata, Zarcone, & Ringdahl, 1994; Rast, Johnston, Allen, & Drum, 1985; Rast, Johnston, Drum, & Conrin, 1981; Scherer & Sanger, 1981). A type of repetitive behavior engaged in by some developmentally handicapped individuals that seems not to be adjunctive is self-injurious behavior, which is generally unintentionally shaped and maintained by social and other reinforcement from caregivers (Lerman et al., 1994).

Studies on adjunctive behavior in humans are often difficult to interpret because certain controls have not been in place. These controls include (1) sessions in which reinforcement is freely available to ensure that it is intermittency (i.e., the schedule of reinforcement) and not just the reinforcer that is inducing the possible adjunctive behavior; and, (2) sessions in which the reinforcer is unavailable to ensure that the increase in the potential adjunctive behavior is not the result of an increased opportunity to engage in the behavior due to a decrease in the behavior reinforced on the intermittent schedule (Roper, 1981). Given the differences that exist between the findings of animal and human studies on adjunctive behavior, these controls will be essential in clarifying the extent to which humans engage in adjunctive behavior.

Aversive schedules. Unlike many other animals, humans typically do not engage in biting attacks when presented with an aversive stimulus. They do, however, show jaw clenching when given an aversive stimulus such as a loud noise (Hutchinson, Pierce, Emley, Proni, & Saver, 1977). This may be a remnant of an evolutionary tendency to bite that we have inherited from our pre-human ancestors. The tendency to bite may have been modified by social reinforcement and punishment. Aggression as adjunctive behavior is discussed later in this chapter.

VARIABLES AFFECTING ADJUNCTIVE BEHAVIOR

Adjunctive behavior is a function of a number of variables. The study of the effects of these variables on adjunctive behavior provides valuable information about its nature and properties.

Species

As already mentioned, food-schedule-induced polydipsia occurs in laboratory rats, mice, and monkeys (see review by Falk, 1981). It occurs seldom or not at all with wild Norway rats (Hoppmann & Allen, 1979), pigeons (Dale, 1979; Miller & Gollub, 1974; Whalan & Wilkie, 1977), and humans (Wallace & Oei, 1981).

Food-schedule-induced attack tends not to occur with rats (Gentry & Schaefer, 1969; Hymowitz, 1971). Rats on FR food schedules with the opportunity to either drink water or attack another rat tend to do the former immediately after reinforcement (Knutson & Schrader, 1975). They do the latter, if at all, after drinking—and sometimes even after they have begun responding on the FR schedule. In contrast, pigeons on FR food schedules with the opportunity to either drink or attack another pigeon do the latter immediately after reinforcement and, as already mentioned, do not do the former (Yoburn & Cohen, 1979).

Although food on certain reinforcement schedules induces attack in a limited number of species, aversive stimuli on a wide variety of schedules induce biting or pecking attacks in a wide variety of species, including rats, pigeons, and monkeys (Azrin, 1964; Azrin, Hake, & Hutchinson, 1965; Azrin, Hutchinson, & Hake, 1963; Azrin, Hutchinson, & Sallery, 1964; Ulrich & Azrin, 1962; Ulrich et al., 1965; Ulrich et al., 1964). Aversive stimuli can also produce sexual attacks by male rats on female rats (Caggiula, 1972; Caggiula & Eibergen, 1969).

The aggressive tendencies elicited in humans (such as jaw clenching) by aversive stimuli may tend to find other forms of expression, however. For example, people in experimental situations who are exposed to foul odors, irritating cigarette smoke, disgusting scenes, frightening information, or unpleasantly high room temperatures tend to show hostility toward others as measured by ratings on questionnaires or the tendency to administer punishment (e.g., Baron & Bell, 1975; Griffitt & Veitch, 1971; Jones & Bogat, 1978; Riordan & Tedeschi, 1983; Rotton, Barry, Frey, & Soler, 1978; White, 1979; Zillmann, Bryant, Comisky, & Medoff, 1981). Moreover, other factors being equal, individuals who are present when aversive stimuli (e.g., the "frightening information" that one will soon be given electric shock) occur tend to be judged less attractive than individuals who are not present when such stimuli occur (Riordan & Tedeschi, 1983). Further, individuals required to punish a child whom they do not actually see for mistakes on an assigned task will tend to give more severe punishment if they are told that the child is both handicapped and unattractive than if they are told that the child is not handicapped and normal looking (Berkowitz & Frodi, 1979). This and the general hostility often directed toward the handicapped may be because they have been paired with aversive events such as newspaper stories of wars and horrible accidents (cf. Berkowitz, 1983).

Primary versus Conditioned Reinforcement or Punishment

As we have seen, stimuli that are paired with reinforcement or punishment become reinforcers or punishers, respectively, and are called conditioned reinforcers or conditioned punishers. Schedules of conditioned reinforcement and conditioned punishment produce adjunctive behavior, although not as strongly as schedules of primary reinforcement and punishment do. For example, adjunctive drinking occurs after the brief stimuli on second-order food schedules (Alferink, Bartness, & Harder, 1980; Allen & Porter, 1977; Corfield-Sumner, Blackman, & Stainer, 1977; Rosenblith, 1970). This drinking occurs less reliably, however, than drinking after food on the second-order schedule. An example of adjunctive behavior induced by conditioned punishment might be biting attacks elicited by a stimulus paired with shock (Vernon & Ulrich, 1966).

Different Reinforcement Classes

Different reinforcement classes can differentially affect quantity and type of adjunctive behavior. For example, periodic brief access to a maze problem (a "cognitive" reinforcer) produces more adjunctive behavior in humans (in the form of increased activity) than does periodic food, even when the individuals are on a food-restricted diet (Wallace & Oei, 1981). Both periodic food and periodic water induce attack in pigeons; however, whereas periodic food induces a postreinforcement burst of attacking in most pigeons, periodic water does not (Campagnoni, Cohen, & Yoburn, 1981; Yoburn, Cohen, & Campagnoni, 1981).

Qualitatively different reinforcers from the same class also can have differential effects on adjunctive behavior. For example, even a small amount of sucrose in food depresses adjunctive drinking in rats (Christian & Schaeffer, 1973).

Schedule Parameters

Various schedule parameters affect adjunctive behavior.

Programmed contingencies. In order for adjunctive behavior to occur, the reinforcer or punisher need not be contingent on a response. Thus, adjunctive drinking and adjunctive attack occur on FT food as well as FI food schedules (Falk, 1971; Flory, 1969a). A response contingency, however, can increase the amount of adjunctive behavior. For example, an FI shock schedule for lever pressing or key pushing produces a higher rate of this behavior in monkeys than an FT shock schedule does (Malagodi, Gardner, & Palermo, 1978; McKearney, 1974).

Type of schedule. Adjunctive behavior depends critically on the type of reinforcement or punishment schedule—in order for it to occur, the schedule must provide discriminable periods in which the reinforcer or punisher is not present. Thus, it is not produced by continuous reinforcement. In addition, the more nearly constant the probability of the reinforcer is over time (i.e., the more nearly random it is), the less likely adjunctive behavior is to occur (Lashley & Rosellini, 1980; Millenson, Allen, & Pinker, 1977). It follows that FI and FT are most effective in inducing adjunctive behavior. If reinforcement on a constant probability schedule is preceded by a distinctive stimulus, however, the probability of adjunctive behavior increases and it may occur as readily as it does on FI and FT schedules (Lashley & Rosellini, 1980; Plonsky, Driscoll, Warren, & Rosellini, 1984).

Interreinforcement interval.   There is often an inverted-U relation (also called a "bitonic" function) between adjunctive behavior and interreinforcement interval. Adjunctive behavior is at its maximum when the interreinforcement interval is between approximately 30 and 180 seconds, depending on the animal and species (Bond, 1973; Falk, 1966b; Flory, 1969a, 1971; Hawkins, Schrot, Githens, & Everett, 1972; Roper, 1980). Figure 15.3 shows data illustrating this bitonic function. The graph on the left side of the figure shows the amount of adjunctive drinking by rats and rhesus monkeys as a function of interfood interval. The graph on the right shows the amount of pecking attack on a stuffed target pigeon by a pigeon and amount of biting on a rubber hose by two squirrel monkeys as a function of interfood interval. Since the graphs are all very similar—which is the point being made—we do not distinguish between them. The bitonic function relating adjunctive behavior to interreinforcement interval apparently holds for humans as well as other animals. For example, humans pressing the space bar on a keyboard to obtain a gambling display engage in more adjunctive behavior on FI 60-seconds than on FI 5-seconds (Wallace et al., 1975). The bitonic function also holds for biting attacks by monkeys on shock schedules—that is, there is an inverted-U function between amount of biting and intershock interval (DeWeese, 1977).

In addition to determining the amount of adjunctive behavior, interreinforcement interval also can determine the type of adjunctive behavior that occurs—at least with regard to terminal behavior. For example, with pigeons on FT schedules, during short interfood intervals (e.g., FT 12-seconds) terminal behavior consists in activity directed toward the feeder. During long interfood intervals (e.g., FT 60-seconds), terminal behavior consists in pacing along a wall in the experimental chamber—usually the wall on which the feeder is situated or an adjacent wall (Innis, Simmelhag-Grant, & Straddon, 1983).

Reinforcement Magnitude

The relation between adjunctive behavior and reinforcement magnitude is unclear and appears to be fairly complex. Some studies have found that the amount of adjunctive behavior is

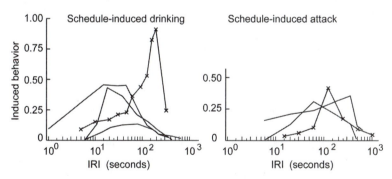

FIGURE 15.3. The bitonic function of schedule-induced behavior. In the graph on the left, the plots are from Falk's (1966b) experiment with rats; from one rat in Roper's (1980) experiment; and from Allen and Kenshalo's (1976) experiment with rhesus monkeys. The dependent variables are amount of water ingested per session in relative units, ml per minute, and licks per second, respectively. In the graph on the right, from Flory's (1969a) experiment with pigeons, and from DeWeese's (1977) experiment with squirrel monkeys. The dependent variables are attacks per minute (divided by three for scaling purposes) and hose bites per second, respectively. IRI = interreinforcement interval. (From Hineline, 1986)

a direct function of reinforcement magnitude provided that reinforcement magnitude is constant over at least one session (Couch, 1974; Flory, 1971; Jacquet, 1972; Rosellini & Burdette, 1980; Yoburn & Flory, 1977). Other studies, however, have found just the opposite (Allison & Mack, 1982; Falk, 1967; Freed & Hymowitz, 1972; Lotter, Woods, & Vasselli, 1973; Urbain, Poling, & Thompson, 1979). A variable that may at least partly account for these apparently inconsistent findings is session length. Consider, for example, the effect of a long session on adjunctive drinking when each reinforcement consists of a large amount of food. The animal may satiate on the food quickly, and thus show little adjunctive drinking over the entire session compared to a equally long session in which each reinforcement consists of a small amount of food. If the session is short, however, the animal would not become satiated on food before the end of the session and might therefore show considerably more adjunctive drinking relative to a session of equal length in which each reinforcement consists of a small amount of food (Reid & Staddon, 1987, p. 290). This possibility is supported by the fact that the relation between drinking and reinforcement magnitude is positive in short sessions and negative in long sessions (Reid & Staddon, 1982).

When amount of food per reinforcement varies within a session, there is an inverse relation between amount of adjunctive drinking and reinforcement magnitude (Reid & Dale, 1983; Reid & Staddon, 1982). In addition, there is an inverted-U relation between amount of adjunctive drinking and reinforcement magnitude (Reid & Staddon, 1987). Thus if a rat is exposed to a VT 50-seconds food schedule in which different amounts of food vary randomly from one interval to the next, the animal likely will drink the most following intermediate amounts of food and the least following small and large amounts of food. This seems to rule out the possibility that adjunctive drinking is simply postprandial (i.e., due to "thirst" produced by eating or the so-called "dry mouth" effect), because if it were there should be a direct relation between amount of drinking per reinforcement and amount of food. Another possibility, however, is that a large amount of food may produce more food-related activities that compete successfully with drinking. In support of this possibility, a larger amount of food produces more head-in-feeder activity than does a smaller amount of food (Reid & Dale, 1983). (Interestingly, a stimulus paired with the larger amount of food also produces more head-in-feeder activity than does a stimulus paired with the smaller amount of food.)

Discriminative Stimuli

Discriminative stimuli can have several effects on adjunctive behavior.

Effect on interim behavior. A stimulus paired with decreased reinforcement rate can produce interim behavior. For example, a rat exposed to a multiple VT 30-seconds Ext food schedule will drink large quantities of water during the extinction component, provided that stable adjunctive drinking was not already established prior to the introduction of the multiple schedule (Minor, 1987; Minor & Coulter, 1982). Development of adjunctive drinking during the extinction component of the multiple schedule occurs faster than during the extinction component of an equivalent mixed schedule, indicating the importance of discriminative stimuli on adjunctive behavior. If the animal continues on the multiple schedule long enough, adjunctive drinking eventually will begin occurring during the VI component as well as during the extinction component. At that point any increase in adjunctive drinking that might have been occurring during the extinction component will cease, suggesting some sort of competition between adjunctive drinking during the VI component and during the extinction component. Decreases in component duration increase the rate of adjunctive drinking during the extinction component and the number of sessions it occurs without adjunctive drinking developing during the VI component.

As indicated previously, pigeons do not engage in adjunctive drinking on food schedules. They do display adjunctive attack if an attack object is present, however, and this holds for multiple schedules as well as for simple schedules. Thus, pigeons will attack a target during the extinction component of a multiple schedule, usually with a burst of pecking at the start of the component (Rilling & Caplan, 1973).

In addition to stimuli paired with extinction, stimuli paired with a change to less (but greater than zero) reinforcement may induce adjunctive behavior. For example, a stimulus paired with a sudden shift from an FR 10 to an FR 90 food schedule can produce adjunctive drinking in rats (Alferink, 1980). Similarly, as indicated earlier, the brief stimuli in second-order food schedules can also produce adjunctive drinking (e.g., Corfield-Sumner et al., 1977). As with the S$^\Delta$ in a multiple VI Ext food schedule (Minor, 1987), in order for adjunctive drinking to be induced by these discriminative stimuli adjunctive drinking must not have been developed prior to their introduction.

Effect on terminal behavior.   While stimuli paired with decreased reinforcement induce interim behavior, stimuli paired with increased reinforcement induce terminal behavior. As seen in previous chapters, this clearly is true for operant terminal behavior. It is not clear whether it is true for adjunctive terminal behavior, however, because of the difficulty of distinguishing adjunctive terminal behavior from superstitious behavior. For example, a pigeon exposed to a multiple VT Ext food schedule will engage in more activity in the VT component than in the extinction component, although the activity level in the extinction component will be greater than it would if extinction occurred without being alternated with VT (Buzzard & Hake, 1984). This activity typically consists of stereotyped behavior such as head bobbing or pacing along the wall in the experimental chamber on which the feeder is located. This activity is terminal behavior since it occurs just before food occurs on the VT schedule.

The longer the extinction component, the larger the difference between the two components in amount of activity. When the extinction component is as long as seven minutes, activity level during the first part of the extinction component is high relative to the middle part—suggesting a "spill-over" effect from the reinforcement component. During the middle of the extinction component the pigeon engages in what might be either interim or facultative behavior: preening, roosting, and standing in place while looking around the experimental chamber. Then, as the time for the S^D to appear approaches, activity level during the S$^\Delta$ gradually increases.

Motivation

Adjunctive behavior is directly related to motivation for the reinforcer. Thus, there is a direct function between amount of adjunctive drinking by rats (Falk, 1969, 1971), licking at a continuous air stream by rats (Chillag & Mendelson, 1971), and attack of a target by pigeons (Dove, 1976) on food schedules and amount of food deprivation. When the amount of food deprivation is gradually decreased a point is reached at which adjunctive drinking begins to decrease (Falk, 1969). It still continues to occur, however, even when deprivation is minimal or absent (Petersen & Lyon, 1978).

Humans may be an exception to this direct relation between adjunctive behavior and food deprivation. For ethical reasons, however, studies of the effects of food deprivation on humans must rely on self-imposed food deprivation (e.g., Wallace & Oei, 1981) which may not be comparable to the externally imposed deprivation used in animal studies.

Target Stimuli

Some adjunctive behavior cannot occur unless certain target stimuli are present. For example, adjunctive drinking requires water and adjunctive attack requires an attack object. The target stimuli affect the individual's responding on the reinforcement schedule. Thus, in rats the presence of water produces longer postreinforcement pauses on an FR food schedule (Iversen, 1976) and lower response rates in the initial link of a food-based chain schedule (Segal & Bandt, 1966). Likewise, in pigeons, the presence of an attack object produces longer postreinforcement pauses even for those pigeons that do not attack the target. Pigeons on food schedules tend to attack live restrained pigeons (Gentry, 1968), stuffed pigeons (Flory, 1969a, b), their mirror images (Cohen & Looney, 1973), and pictures of pigeons (Looney & Cohen, 1976). Live targets generate the most attacks.

SIMILARITIES WITH AVERSIVE-STIMULUS-ELICITED BEHAVIOR

As mentioned earlier in this chapter, there are striking similarities between adjunctive behavior on schedules of positive reinforcement and behavior elicited by aversive stimuli. In this section we discuss the similarities more extensively.

Both positive reinforcement and aversive schedules can produce the same types of adjunctive behavior. For example, adjunctive drinking (Hutchinson & Emley, 1977) and eating (Antelman & Szechtman, 1975) can be induced by shock. These reactions occur less reliably than biting, however, and follow it. Painful noises (90 db) can also induce eating by rats, particularly those with low pain thresholds (Cantor, 1981; Cantor & Wilson, 1985; Wilson, 1982).

Conversely, positive reinforcement schedules can induce attack. A pigeon pecking a key on certain food schedules will repeatedly attack a semi-restrained pigeon shortly after each reinforcement (Azrin et al., 1966). Aggressive adjunctive behavior induced by positive reinforcement schedules appears to be due to the unavailability of the reinforcer after it is consumed and the absence of subsequent reinforcers. Factors that decrease the availability of subsequent reinforcers increase the probability of attack. Thus, bar biting by restrained squirrel monkeys (DeWeese, 1977; Hutchinson et al., 1968) and pecking of another pigeon by an unrestrained pigeon (Gentry, 1968) are highly probable during the postreinforcement pause of high FR and long FI schedules. Similarly, the probability of attack is high when extinction is introduced after a period of positive reinforcement. Although humans are less likely to attack due to social conditioning, smokers prohibited from smoking show increased jaw clenching and contractions. Similarly, human adults show increased jaw clenching when a response that produced points exchangeable for money no longer does so (Hutchinson, 1977). Human adults placed on extinction for pulling a knob to earn money will increase their rate of punching a cushion when engaging in that behavior to avoid an aversive noise (Kelly & Hake, 1970). (See Fig. 15.4.) Likewise, nursery school children working for pennies on continuous reinforcement engage in considerable aggression when extinction is introduced (Frederiksen & Peterson, 1974).

The fact that a period of nonreinforcement induces attack similar to the way in which aversive stimuli do suggests a commonality between the two types of events. Specifically, it suggests that a period of nonreinforcement possesses aversive characteristics. It further suggests that not only attack, but perhaps also other schedule-induced behavior on positive reinforcement schedules is a result of an aversive period following reinforcement on intermittent reinforcement schedules. This suggestion is supported by the fact that, as seen in Chapter 13, timeout is reinforcing during postreinforcement pauses and other periods of nonreinforcement.

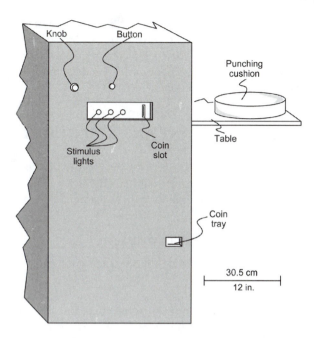

FIGURE 15.4. Apparatus for studying elicited aggression in humans. A switch under the punching cushion detects forceful responses on the cushion. Participants may avoid or escape an aversive tone by pushing the button or by hitting the cushion. When pulling the knob to receive coins in the tray is extinguished, hitting the cushion increases even though button pushing was the preferred escape/avoidance response prior to extinction. (From Kelly & Hake, 1970)

As also seen in Chapter 13, however, the proportion of session time allocated to self-imposed timeout increases as mean interreinforcement interval increases for both FT and FI schedules (Lydersen et al., 1980). This contrasts with adjunctive behavior, that, as was seen earlier in this chapter (see Fig. 15.3), often first increases and then decreases as interreinforcement interval increases.

In addition, the probabilities of self-imposed timeout on positive reinforcement schedules and adjunctive behavior are distributed differently across an interreinforcement interval. For example, with pigeons that have an attack object (e.g., a restrained or stuffed pigeon, as illustrated in Fig. 15.1) and a timeout key available during an FR food schedule, attacking generally occurs soon after reinforcement while timeout generally is initiated later in the postreinforcement pause or occasionally even after responding on the FR schedule has started (Ator, 1980). Having both an attack object and a timeout key available simultaneously does not alter the likelihood of either activity; both occur with probabilities similar to those obtained when the activities are available singly and each retains its characteristic temporal distribution across the interreinforcement interval.

In view of the motivational nature of adjunctive behavior, we might redefine it as behavior that becomes reinforcing as a result of exposure to a reinforcement schedule that does not directly reinforce that behavior (cf. Falk, 1971, p. 578). This definition seems appropriate because animals on one schedule will respond on a second schedule to obtain the opportunity to engage in behavior considered adjunctive to the first schedule. For example, a food-deprived rat that is not deprived of water will press a lever on various reinforcement schedules to obtain water when food occurs intermittently (Falk, 1966a). Behavior reinforced on various schedules by the opportunity to engage in adjunctive behavior shows characteristic schedule effects. Moreover, when access to adjunctive behavior is available on concurrent schedules, it tends to conform to the matching law (Cohen, 1975). (Recall from Chapter 12 that the matching law states that relative responding in concurrent schedules tends to equal relative reinforcement rates in those concurrent schedules.)

SIMILARITIES WITH OPERANT AND RESPONDENT BEHAVIOR

Despite apparent differences between adjunctive behavior and operant and respondent behavior, from the above it should not be surprising that adjunctive behavior has commonalties with these two other classes of behavior. Some of these commonalties are as follow.

Reinforcement and Punishment Contingencies

Although adjunctive behavior is not operant, it is affected by reinforcement and punishment contingencies.

Examples of reinforcement of adjunctive behavior.   For example, if a rat on a food schedule receives extra food for drinking, it may drink more; conversely, if it receives extra food for not drinking, it may drink less (Reberg, 1980). Attacking elicited by aversive stimuli also can be strengthened by reinforcement (Hutchinson & Renfrew, 1978; Konorski & Miller, 1937).

Examples of punishment of adjunctive behavior.   Adjunctive drinking can be decreased by punishing it with shock. The more intense the shock, the more drinking is suppressed (Bond, Blackman, & Scruton, 1973; Galantowicz & King, 1975). Adjunctive drinking also can be suppressed by a contingent delay in reinforcement. For example, if each lick on a drinking tube results in a stimulus that is paired with a 10-second delay in food, licking will be suppressed. If no stimulus is paired with the delay, some suppression of licking will still occur, but not as much (Pellon & Blackman, 1987).

Conditioned Suppression and Overall Suppression

Recall from Chapter 6 that a phenomenon called conditioned suppression is said to occur when operant behavior is suppressed in the presence of a stimulus (called a "conditioned aversive stimulus") that has been paired with an aversive stimulus. Conditioned suppression of adjunctive behavior also occurs. For example, both lever pressing for food and adjunctive drinking will be suppressed in the presence of a stimulus that has been paired with shock (Hymowitz, 1981a). In addition, both overall lever pressing and overall adjunctive drinking are suppressed more if shock is not preceded by a conditioned aversive stimulus (i.e., "unsignaled" shock). For both adjunctive and operant behavior, overall suppression is more sensitive than conditioned suppression is to such variables as body weight (i.e., deprivation level), shock intensity, and certain drugs such as diazepam (Hymowitz, 1981a, b).

Behavioral Contrast

Recall from Chapter 8 that a phenomenon called behavioral contrast is said to occur when responding in one component of a multiple schedule increases or decreases as a function of reinforcement rate decreasing or increasing, respectively, in another component. A phenomenon similar to behavioral contrast occurs in multiple schedules in which adjunctive drinking is occurring. This phenomenon can be demonstrated in two ways: (1) If a multiple VI VT food schedule is changed to multiple VI Ext, adjunctive drinking during the VI component increases (Jacquet, 1972). This is termed polydipsia contrast. As with behavioral contrast the amount of polydipsia contrast is inversely related to component duration (Minor, 1987). Unlike behavioral contrast whose reliable occurrence requires a distinct stimulus in each component (Gutman, Minor, & Sutterer, 1984), polydipsia contrast reliably occurs in mixed as well as multiple schedules. (2) If water is unavailable in one component of a multiple food schedule, drinking in the other component(s) will increase (Porter & Allen, 1977).

Stimulus Generalization

A phenomenon similar to stimulus generalization also occurs with adjunctive behavior, in that its tendency to occur in the presence of a given stimulus decreases the more that stimulus differs from the stimulus in the presence of which the adjunctive behavior was established. For example, rats tested for generalization of adjunctive drinking after being trained on a multiple RT 30-seconds Ext food schedule show a clear generalization gradient—that is, more drinking occurs during the S^Δ of the multiple schedule than during other stimuli (Hamm, Porter, & Kaempf, 1981). The food schedule must be in effect during testing in order for this generalization effect to occur, which is understandable since adjunctive drinking does not occur in the absence of the food schedule. It is interesting, however, that food occurring during testing does not mask or overshadow the test stimuli.

Within-Session Changes

In Chapter 7 we mentioned that both operant and respondent behavior show a distinct within-session pattern: an increase early in the session, followed by a decrease as the session progresses. The adjunctive drinking and adjunctive wheel running of rats on fixed-interval food reinforcement schedules also show this within-session pattern (McSweeney, Swindell, & Weatherly, 1996b). Interestingly, even though they resemble each other, the operant and adjunctive within-session patterns seem to be largely independent of each other. The operant pattern is not significantly affected by the presence or absence of either a water source or running wheel for the adjunctive behavior; correlations between the operant and adjunctive rates are inconsistent. It has been suggested that this within-session pattern reflects a sensitization-habituation effect; if so, however, it is unclear why sensitization and habituation interact in different ways with different categories of behavior.

SUMMARY AND CONCLUSIONS

Operant behavior is schedule-induced (or schedule-generated) behavior, but not all schedule-induced behavior is operant. For example, reinforcement schedules induce respondent as well as operant behavior. As an unconditioned stimulus, a reinforcer elicits unconditioned responses and causes stimuli that happen to be paired with it to become conditioned stimuli. In addition, there is a third class of behavior—a class that is neither operant nor respondent—that is schedule induced. This third class is called adjunctive behavior.

Very clear schedule-induced patterns of behavior occur when there are fixed time intervals between reinforcements—that is, during FI and FT schedules (where in the former reinforcement is contingent on the first response after a fixed interval of time following the previous reinforcement, whereas in the latter reinforcement occurs at regular time intervals independent of responding). There are three distinct parts to a schedule-induced pattern of behavior: (1) interim behavior, (2) facultative behavior, and (3) terminal behavior. Interim behavior occurs immediately after reinforcement, while terminal behavior occurs prior to reinforcement. If the interval between reinforcements is sufficiently long, facultative behavior will occur between interim and terminal behavior. Although facultative behavior may be part of a schedule-induced pattern, it is not itself schedule induced because it would have occurred even if the schedule had not been in effect. Interim behavior is likely not operant because it occurs immediately after reinforcement—that is, when the probability of reinforcement is low or zero. It is, however, somewhat more difficult to distinguish between interim behavior that is respondent and interim behavior that is adjunctive. It may be an unconditioned response elicited by the reinforcer.

Terminal behavior is likely not an unconditioned response elicited by the reinforcer because it occurs too long after the reinforcer. It is, however, somewhat more difficult to distinguish among terminal behavior that is respondent behavior conditioned to stimuli preceding the reinforcer, terminal behavior that is reinforced, and terminal behavior that is adjunctive.

Probably the clearest example of adjunctive behavior is schedule-induced polydipsia, which is the drinking of extremely large quantities of water (or other available liquids) immediately after food reinforcement on intermittent schedules of reinforcement. Common examples of adjunctive behavior in humans might include snacking, smoking, hair twirling, and nail biting when reinforcement rate is low on a particular task in which the person is engaged. Furthermore, the occurrence of adjunctive behavior might, at least partly, explain the tendency of certain intermittent schedules of punishment to generate response patterns similar to those generated by intermittent schedules of reinforcement, as described in the previous chapter.

Adjunctive behavior has a number of similarities with respondent and operant behavior. For example, it can be modified by its consequences—that is, reinforcement increases it (or at least topographically similar behavior) and punishment decreases it. It can be suppressed by the noncontingent presentation of a conditioned aversive stimulus (conditioned suppression), and it shows behavioral contrast and stimulus generalization. Moreover, it shows the same within-session pattern of increase followed by decrease that operant and respondent behavior show.

PART V

EXTENSIONS TO NATURAL SETTINGS

Thus far we have discussed learning in rather restricted experimental settings. These restrictions are necessary for proper experimental control and to enable us to see the principles and phenomena of learning in their simplest and clearest aspects. The question that naturally arises, however, is to what extent do these principles and phenomena apply in the real world? Part V highlights the wide generality that these principles and phenomena have outside of laboratory settings.

Chapter 16 points out that the learning principles described in this book are part of the biological heritage of all animals above a minimal level of complexity. Like all other aspects of an animal's biological heritage, learning principles came about through the evolutionary process of natural selection. Detailing numerous examples, the chapter shows how learning principles contribute to the survival of animals as they go about their normal activities in their natural environments.

Most of us are, quite naturally, most interested in our own species. In addition, more than any other species, humans have greatly modified their "natural" environments. In fact, perhaps the only thing natural about most current human environments is that they are social environments. Thus, Chapter 17 deals with how the learning principles described in this text apply to humans in social environments. The chapter endeavors to show that, although the complexity of our behavior distinguishes us from other species, we possess a clear continuity with other species in the learning principles we exhibit as well as in the other aspects of our biology.

16

Animals in Their Natural Environments

*P*henomena studied in the lab would be of little interest if they also did not occur outside the lab. Thus, we turn now to the question of how the learning principles and phenomena discussed in previous chapters apply to animals in their natural environments. Although much is known about the behavior of animals in their natural environments, little is known about how learning contributes to this behavior. This is because natural environments are so complex that many instances of learning go unobserved and unrecorded, even when scientists are observing the animal's behavior closely. It would be strange, however, if any phenomenon observed under controlled laboratory conditions did not manifest itself, in some way, in other situations. This is especially true of phenomena like those of learning, that evolved in environments that are more similar to current natural environments than they are to laboratory settings. This chapter has two goals: its main goal is to suggest through numerous examples how learning phenomena are manifested in the natural environment; the other goal is to suggest how these phenomena came about through evolution.

GENETICS AND LEARNING

In reading this chapter, there are four major points to keep in mind. The first is that some behavior appears in such a complex form when first engaged in by an animal, and is so consistent across members of that animal's species, that learning could play little, if any, role in its development. Such behavior is said to be genetically determined, because it is determined by an individual's genes just as, for example, eye color is. An example is web building by a spider, which is such a complex behavior the first time it occurs that it is inconceivable that it could be learned. The learning of a behavior of such complexity requires processes such as shaping and chaining, but these processes are so gradual that any spider would likely starve to death before they could produce a web that would catch enough food to sustain it. It should be noted that even if no learning is involved in the development of a particular trait or behavior, however, it is technically incorrect to say that that trait or behavior is completely genetically determined. The physical and chemical properties of the embryonic milieu interact with genetics during the embryonic development of an organism.

The second major point to keep in mind is that the involvement of genetics in some specific behavior does not preclude learning having an effect on that behavior; and conversely, the involvement of learning in some specific behavior does not preclude genetics having an effect on that behavior. Clearly, even when learning is involved in the development of any given behavior, genetics is necessarily also involved. For example, in order for a key-peck response to be conditioned in a pigeon, the bird must have the body structure and capacity to peck, which are genetically determined. In addition, unconditioned stimuli and primary reinforcers, on which respondent and operant conditioning are based, are genetically determined. Moreover, the capacity and tendency to learn are genetically determined. There also are different genetically determined propensities for learning different responses, and for different stimuli to enter into learned functional relations with behavior by becoming conditioned stimuli, discriminative stimuli, conditioned reinforcers, and conditioned aversive stimuli. To further complicate matters, these different propensities vary according to the type of unconditioned stimuli, primary reinforcers, or primary aversive stimuli on which the learned responses or functional relations are based. Thus, learning and genetics interact in complex ways, probably duplicating or complementing each other in many instances. We should not conclude that the involvement of one of these functions in a particular behavior means that the other does not also participate in that behavior.

The third major point to keep in mind is that an animal's genes (which determine its learning tendencies and capabilities, as well as its physical characteristics) are the product of evolutionary processes based on the survival and perpetuation of that animal's genetic material. This point is crucial because in order to clearly understand the behavior of an animal in its natural environment, we must understand how that animal tends (or, more accurately, how its ancestors tended) to perpetuate its genetic material. Note that the key factor in evolution is not the survival of a given animal, nor the survival of its species. Rather, it is the perpetuation of that animal's genetic material. This observation, which is a refinement of the view that evolution is based on the "survival of the fittest," is called the principle of inclusive fitness (Hamilton, 1964, 1967, 1970).

According to the principle of inclusive fitness, the fittest organisms (and, hence, those whose descendents are present today) were those that were best able to perpetuate their genetic material. Since that genetic material (or, more precisely, copies of it) is present to some degree in an animal's relatives, it follows from the principle of inclusive fitness that animals will tend to promote the survival (and hence reproduction) of their relatives as well as their own survival (and, in fact, sometimes over their own survival). More generally, since more of an animal's genetic material (i.e., more exact copies of it) is present in closer relatives, the more closely related animal A is to animal B, the stronger will be the tendency of animal A to promote the survival of animal B.

The fourth major point to keep in mind is that learning plays an important role in the principle of inclusive fitness, in that in many species the extent to which animals tend to promote each other's survival depends on particular experiences they have had with each other. Usually, these experiences will be those that only closely related animals would have had with each other because the experiences come from being reared together (Sherman & Holmes, 1985). Conditioned reinforcement is probably important in this learning, but other factors that may be involved are not well understood at present.

BEHAVIOR ESSENTIAL TO SURVIVAL AND GENE PERPETUATION

In selecting organisms that perpetuate their genetic material under a wide variety of environmental conditions, evolution has produced animals that engage in a rich variety of behavior in their natural environments. We shall review this behavior, with—as already mentioned—special attention to the participation of learning in it, under four broad categories essential to the survival and the perpetuation of genetic material: (1) food- and water-directed behavior; (2) defensive behavior; (3) sexual behavior; and, (4) caring for the young.

Food- and Water-Directed Behavior

In order to survive long enough to perpetuate their genetic material, animals must consume food. In addition, terrestrial animals must drink water. Therefore, evolution has rendered these substances primary reinforcers—that is, animals have a genetically determined tendency for these stimuli to strengthen and maintain responses that they follow.

Response shaping.   Response shaping of food-directed behavior is probably common in the natural environments of animals. In some cases the shaped behavior may be so similar across different members of a species that we might easily mistake it for behavior whose learned component is small relative to its genetic component. However, the similarity across animals is due to the fact that a similar shaping process is operating on them, and not to the similarity of their genetics (except insofar as anatomical and physiological similarities lead shaping to follow similar courses). We now consider some examples of this.

Guiding. The food-directed behavior from which the African greater honeyguide (*Indicator indicator*) derives its names is a possible example of this. In addition to feeding on insects, these birds eat beeswax, which they can digest (Friedmann & Kern, 1956). Honeyguides are unable to break open bee nests, so they must wait until another animal has done so before they can obtain the wax from the honeycombs. They typically do not simply wait passively for this to happen, however. As their name implies, honeyguides lead animals that eat honey to bee nests. Typically the animal they lead is the ratel (*Mellivora capensis*), also known as the "honey badger." However, they also lead human honey gatherers to bee nests. The bird leads by emitting a repetitive series of chirring notes and, as the honey eater moves toward it, flitting between a position near the honey eater and the general direction of the bee nest (Friedmann, 1955; Isack & Reyer, 1989; Short & Horne, 1985). When the honeyguide and follower reach the nest, the bird perches nearby while the follower breaks open the nest and takes the honey (see Fig. 16.1). After the follower leaves, the honeyguide eats the wax left behind.

What is particularly noteworthy about the guiding behavior is that the bird may initiate it as many as several miles away from a bee nest. In fact, people have reported being guided to bee nests as far as five miles away. Despite the remarkable nature of this behavior, it is easy to see how it could have been shaped (Skinner, 1966). If a honey eater encountered a nest and broke it open in the vicinity of a honeyguide, the honeyguide's behavior in the presence of the honey eater and the nest would be reinforced. The probability of approach toward that or a similar honey eater in the presence of a bee nest would then be increased. If subsequently a honey eater followed the honeyguide a short distance to the nest, the behavior that lead the honey eater that short distance to the nest would be reinforced by the beeswax.

Similarly, the honey eater's following of the honeyguide is reinforced by the honey. The fact that this sort of interaction would occur at different times between a number of different honeyguides and a number of different honey eaters in the same general area would tend to result in very similar guiding behavior among the honeyguides in that area. Gradually the honeyguide's tendency to attract the attention of a honey eater and lead that person or animal toward a bee nest at increasingly larger distances from the nest would be reinforced. Note that, in addition to shaping, stimulus discrimination on the part of both the honeyguide and the honey eater is involved in this example. Honeyguides learn to discriminate potential bee nest breakers and honey gatherers and eaters learn to discriminate honeyguides and the cues they generate.

FIGURE 16.1. Having led some honey gatherers to a bee nest, the bird waits for them to break it open and leave. (From Roots, 1988)

As with the majority of behavior discussed in this chapter, there is undoubtedly a strong genetic component involved in the honeyguide's guiding behavior. This does not, however, preclude a learning component as described above.

Singing. Another response that appears to be shaped in an animal's natural environment is the song of the male cowbird (*Molothrus ater*). During the time period during which male and female cowbirds are on prospective breeding grounds but prior to the time in which the females become sexually receptive, they emit a certain wing movement following some of the males' songs and not others. These wing movements appear to be reinforcing to the males in that songs wing movements follow tend to occur more frequently while the songs these movements do not follow tend not to be repeated. Presumably the females are reinforcing closer and closer approximations to (i.e., shaping) certain songs by the males. Later when the females are sexually receptive, the songs they had shaped by their wing movements were more effective than other songs in eliciting their copulation postures (King & West, 1989; West & King, 1988; West, King, & Freeberg, 1994).

Tool use. Shaping probably is also involved in tool use by animals. Chimpanzees in particular show considerable skill in this regard. For example, chimpanzees at the Gombe Stream Reserve (Tanzania) are adept at plunging sticks into termite mounds and pulling out masses of crawling, edible insects (Goodall, 1968, 1986). Chimpanzees also show considerable skill in using two tools in conjunction, as when they crack nuts by positioning them on one rock and hitting them with another in a hammer-and-anvil fashion. These skills take years for individual chimpanzees to perfect. For example, to be successful, termite probing must be done in an extremely delicate manner; and successful nut cracking depends on precise positioning and hitting of the nuts (Boesch & Boesch, 1983; Sugiyama, Fushimi, Sakura, & Matsuzawa, 1993). Although more than shaping is involved in the initial learning of these skills, it is clearly involved in the refinement of them.

Other examples of tool use by animals in their natural environments can be similarly explained. These include parrots scooping water with nutshells (Pepperberg, 1989) and monkeys hammering open oyster shells with stones (Falk, 1989). Likewise, shaping appears to be involved in the modification or manufacture of tools by animals. Examples of this behavior include crows (Hunt, 1996) and chimpanzees (Goodall, 1968) modifying leaves or twigs to make them more effective for extracting insects from holes; and chimpanzees chewing leaves to make them into sponges for picking up water to drink (Goodall, 1968). In addition to shaping, chaining seems to be involved when animals employ several tools in a specific sequence, such as a chimpanzee using a pointed branch to pierce the wax coating of a honey source and then extracting the dripping honey with a vine (Brewer & McGrew, 1990).

A commonly asked question is whether animals understand what they are doing when they use tools. Unfortunately, the question is not easy to answer because "understand" is not a well-defined scientific term. The answer thus depends on how one chooses to define the term. If, for example, we define "understand" as "being able to verbalize a cogent explanation," then clearly animals do not understand their use of tools. If, however, we mean simply "behaving in what appears to be a deliberate, goal-directed manner," then they do (but this is true of all operant behavior, not just that involving tool use). In any case, it is important to note an important difference between animal and human tool use: The latter is typically under the control of verbal stimuli (such as occur in planning and instruction), whereas the former is not. (We consider the role of verbal behavior in human activities in the next chapter.)

Basic schedules of reinforcement. Since food and water are the most commonly studied reinforcers in the laboratory, it should not be surprising that there is a wealth of examples of basic reinforcement schedules involving food and water in the natural environment. A bear going to a stream for water is an example of an animal on a continuous water-reinforcement schedule. This is continuous reinforcement because, unless it dries up, the stream is always there so the response of going to it for water is always reinforced. A bear fishing in a stream is an example of an animal on a variable-interval food-reinforcement schedule with a limited hold, assuming that fish swim past the bear's fishing spot at varying time intervals. A lion going to a water hole at dawn when potential prey come to drink and a fox going to a bush at a time when its berries are likely to be ripe are examples of animals responding on fixed-interval food-reinforcement schedules (with the position of the sun, amount of daylight, or other temporal cues constituting an external clock—see Chapter 10). The foraging pattern of the common vole (*Microtus arvalis*) on which kestrels (*Falco tinnunculus*) feed provides a fixed-interval schedule to kestrels. Voles living in a given area tend to come out of their holes at about the same time every two or three hours to forage on plants, and kestrels tend to hunt in a given area during the times when voles in that area are likely to be foraging (Rijnstrop, Daan, & Dijkstro, 1981). The tides generate a fixed-interval schedule for oystercatchers (*Haematopus ostralegus*) that forage on tidal mud flats for mussels. Even when the mud flats are not visible to the oystercatchers, they fly to them at about the time that the mussels become exposed by low tide (Daan & Koene, 1981). Human outdoor eating patterns provide fixed-interval schedules for scavenging birds, such as pigeons (*Columba liva*), starlings (*Sturnus vulgaris*), crows (*Corvus caurinus*), and sparrows (*Melospiza melodia*). These birds tend to arrive at outdoor eating places, such as markets and plazas, just before the time at which the number of people taking their lunch breaks peaks (Wilkie et al., 1996).

Animals that chase down their quarry are on variable-ratio schedules. For the tigers in Kanha National Park in India, for example, an average of about one hunt in twenty ends in success (Breeden & Wright, 1985). For the lions of the Serengeti Park in Tanzania, the variable-ratio schedule in effect depends on the hunting method (Schaller, 1972, p. 254). For example, on average, running after prey by single lions results in an 8% success, while ambushing results in a 19% success rate. Hunting by several lions together increases the success rate to 30% on average (which clearly provides a contingency favoring group hunting).

The honeyguide whose behavior was described above is on a variable-ratio schedule in several ways. First, it may have to flit and chirr a variable number of times before a potential bee nest breaker will begin to follow it. Second, the probability that a potential bee nest breaker will follow on any given occasion is less than one. All predators are on variable-ratio schedules for their prey, because the probability of catching any animal that they pursue is usually less than one. An interesting example of a predator on a variable-ratio schedule is that of a fox chasing a bird with one wing outstretched on the ground and the other fluttering. Occasionally such a bird has a broken wing and the fox will catch it. More often, however, the bird has no injury and flies away after the fox has been led some distance from the bird's young (Skutch, 1976). The fox's behavior of chasing after any fluttering bird with an outstretched wing on the ground has been reinforced with an easy prey when a bird really did have a broken wing.

For an example of a differential-reinforcement-of-low-rates (DRL) schedule for food in the natural environment, consider that many species of birds when feeding in a flock give an alarm call when they see a hawk. Sometimes, however, a bird will give an alarm call when no hawk is present and then grab food when the other birds fly away (Møller, 1988; Munn, 1986). To see that this false-alarm sounding is on a DRL schedule, note that if an animal sounds a false alarm frequently, other members of the flock will habituate to that animal's alarm calls—since responses to alarm calls when no predator is present will habituate (Cheney & Seyfarth, 1990, pp. 154–163). Thus, the bird's false-alarm calls will, through extinction, drop to a low rate. However, as its false alarm calls decrease, the habituation of the other members of the flock to them also will decrease, so that they will again be reinforced. In this manner, a low rate of sounding false alarms will be developed and maintained on a DRL schedule based on habituation of responding to false alarm calls by the members of a flock of birds.

Stimulus discrimination learning.   Stimulus discrimination learning is manifested in many ways in food- and water-directed behavior in the natural environment. Generally, both food and water are found in particular locations, and stimuli associated with those locations become discriminative stimuli for moving toward the food or water source. In addition, these discriminative stimuli are conditioned reinforcers, since they are paired with reinforcement. Thus, through stimulus discrimination and conditioned reinforcement, moving toward the location of food or water is guided by stimuli that both evoke and reinforce movements in the appropriate direction.

Because food generally is more varied than water is, there are more examples of how stimulus discrimination learning is involved in food-directed behavior. For many animal species food can come in many different forms, some of which may never have been encountered by the animal's ancestors. In times of food scarcity, animals that learned to eat new food types would have a better chance of surviving and reproducing than animals that did not. Thus, animals have a genetic tendency to sample potential foods, and any that satisfies genetically determined criteria that happen to be correlated with nutritional or caloric value—for example, certain tastes and textures—reinforce the behavior that led to eating it. Moreover, through stimulus generalization, animals will sample new foods that resemble those that are reinforcing, thus expanding the range of food resources available to them. Shaping is also involved in learning new food types, as when an animal learns to break open a shell efficiently.

Unlike water, potential food for animals is always other life forms—either plant or animal—that therefore have evolved characteristics that counter (or, in the case of certain plants, promote) feeding on them. Some potential food items have evolved cryptic characteristics, that is, characteristics that hinder discrimination learning by predators. Some examples are insects or fish that resemble twigs or leaves. Through stimulus discrimination learning, however, animals that feed on cryptic prey become more adept at detecting them (Gendron, 1986; Kamil, 1989). Some potential food items are dangerous or unpalatable, and animals learn to escape or avoid them, or engage in a combination of approach and avoidance behavior (i.e., "cautious" behavior) when procuring them. These potential food items often have evolved conspicuous characteristics, such as the rattle of a rattlesnake, that facilitate stimulus discrimination learning. Moreover, because animals learn to avoid toxic prey through stimulus discrimination learning, some nontoxic animals (the "nontoxic mimics") have evolved physical characteristics remarkably similar to those of toxic animals.

The behavior of animals that feed on fruits is brought under both positively reinforcing and aversive stimulus control by physical characteristics that fructiferous (i.e., fruit-bearing) plants have evolved. For example, ripe and nutritious fruit has conspicuous colors (e.g., bright red, orange, or yellow skin) that, through stimulus discrimination learning based on food reinforcement, evoke procurement by animals which then spread the seeds over a wide range. Other conspicuous characteristics (e.g., dark green skin) are correlated with noxious chemicals that are present when the fruit is unripe, so that stimulus discrimination learning based on punishment keeps animals away from the fruit before the seeds are fully formed. Simultaneous with the evolution of fruit colors, many species that feed on fruits during daylight evolved highly-sensitive color vision that enable the colors of fruits to become highly effective discriminative stimuli for them (Gautier-Hion et al., 1985; Mollon, 1989, pp. 32–33; Polyak, 1957, pp. 972–973). The process whereby interacting species evolve characteristics (e.g., plant colors and animal color receptors) that mutually promote their survival and gene population and gene perpetuation is called co-evolution.

Sometimes characteristics that have evolved for other reasons become discriminative stimuli for food-directed behavior. For example, the sexual advertisement calls of male Tungara frogs is a discriminative stimulus for the carnivorous bat (*Trachops cirrhosus*) in locating them (Ryan, Tuttle, & Rand, 1982).

Many potential food items (both plant and animal) contain strong poisons. Because these poisons can be debilitating or fatal, and their aversive effect (i.e., illness) does not occur until they are absorbed into the system, stimulus discrimination learning (or possibly respondent conditioning) based on food poisoning has evolved to occur rapidly in such cases. The stimuli that become conditioned to illness consistently accompany food—for example, taste stimuli in the case of mammals, certain visual stimuli in the case of birds—that helps make learning to avoid food poisoning extremely efficient. In fact, most poisonous plants and animals have evolved distinct coloration and other characteristics to aid the discrimination learning of their potential predators.

The above examples mainly illustrate successive stimulus discriminations. Simultaneous discriminations, where two or more discriminative stimuli are present simultaneously, are perhaps even more common. As an example, consider a pack of wolves stalking a herd of deer. Within that herd some animals will be easier to catch than others, and the wolves therefore obtain reinforcement with a higher probability when they go after one of these. These easier deer often have distinctive characteristics—for example, being very young, old, or ill—that facilitate discrimination learning by the wolves. In some animals, characteristics have evolved because they provide discriminative stimuli to predators. For example, Thompson's gazelles (*Gazella thomsoni*) engage in behavior called stotting, in which they jump off the ground with their legs stiff and straight, when confronted by African hunting dogs (*Lycaon pictus*). This behavior appears to be a discriminative stimulus correlated with a low probability of reinforcement for the dogs, because the dogs chase and are more likely to catch gazelles that stot at low rates or not at all (Fitzgibbon & Fanshawe, 1988).

Some instances of apostatic selection, which is a tendency for animals to select common over uncommon food types (Allen, 1988; Curio, 1976; Endler, 1986, 1988; Fullick & Greenwood, 1979; Murdoch, 1969), could be examples of simultaneous discriminations. Assuming that the food items are initially selected randomly, reinforcement for selecting the more numerous food item necessarily occurs at a higher rate, which should cause that item to be selected even more frequently.

Concurrent schedules. Concurrent food-reinforcement schedules are well represented in the natural environments of most animals. For example, foraging animals move within and between patches that are rich in food items relative to surrounding areas. Within patches, food-seeking behavior is reinforced on a particular schedule, so that several (i.e., as many as there are different patches) schedules are available simultaneously. Consider, for example, a pigeon turning over leaves in a patch under a tree. Since only some leaves have seeds under them, and which ones do is unpredictable, the pigeon is on a variable-ratio schedule. If two such patches were available, this would be an example of concurrent VR VR food-reinforcement schedules. (Actually, the constituent schedules are more accurately described as progressive VR schedules because, as more seeds are eaten within a patch, the probability of reinforcement in that patch decreases.)

Concurrent schedules with interval schedule components also are present in the natural environments of animals, in that patches that are depleted often are replenished over time. For example, a bush whose ripe berries have been eaten eventually produces new ripe berries. Multiple resources that renew at fairly constant rates generate contingencies that are similar to concurrent FI schedules. Nectar, for example, accumulates gradually in flowers. If a bee or a hummingbird depletes the nectar in a particular flower, returning to that flower will not result in any additional nectar until a given amount of time has elapsed. Similarly, floating dead insects that are washed up on a riverbank accumulate gradually along the bank. If a bird that feeds on dead insects depletes the insects on a given part of the river bank, returning to that location will not result in many (or any) additional insects until a given amount of time has elapsed. Such contingencies cause foraging animals to move from one location to another, arriving at each location at about the time that the resource at that location has been renewed (Davies & Houston, 1981; Gill, 1988; Janzen, 1971). Animals may visit resource locations in a fairly fixed sequence called a trapline because of its resemblance to the systematic sequences followed by human trappers checking their traps for caught animals. It should be noted, however, that the sequences that nonhuman traplining animals follow, being contingency shaped rather than rule governed, are not necessarily optimal in terms of distance traveled (Collett, Fry, & Wehner, 1993; Janzen, 1971). The traplining-behavior of animals can be accounted for on the basis of stimuli paired with recently visited locations becoming aversive (Wilkie et al., 1992; see Chapter 10, pp. 221–222).

The contingencies operating on some nonhuman traplining animals are complicated by the fact that if the animal does not return soon enough to a given resource another animal may deplete that resource. This added contingency acts as a limited hold causing the animal in the case of some species, such as long-tailed hermit hummingbirds (*Phaethornis superciliosus*) that feed on the nectar in flowers, to return to the resource frequently to deplete it before another animal does (Gill, 1988). Other species, such as a pied wagtail (*Motacilla alba*) feed on dead insects washed up on a river bank to chase off intruders on its trapline (Davies & Houston, 1981). Apparently, many animals display remarkable memory by returning to the places in their trapline they had left when preventing other animals from depleting resources in their territories.

There are many variables in addition to reinforcement rate that determine how animals on concurrent schedules allocate their behavior. One such variable is reinforcement magnitude. For example, if the worms in one patch are larger than those in another, a foraging robin likely will spend more time and peck the ground more in the former than in the latter patch. Qualitative differences between reinforcers in different patches—worms may predominate in one patch, spiders in another—also affect behavior allocation among the patches.

Another variable that determines time and response allocation to different patches is the presence of aversive stimuli. For example, gray squirrels (*Sciurus carolinesis*) allocate less time to patches far from trees than to patches close to trees (Newman & Caraco, 1987). Apparently, open spaces are aversive to squirrels either (1) because of previous close encounters with predators in open spaces, or (2) because squirrels for which they were not aversive in the past have no surviving descendents. Similarly, animals shift preferences toward poorer patches when predators are in or near richer ones (Abrahams & Dill, 1989; Dill, 1987; Gilliam & Fraser, 1987; Sih, 1987). Food deprivation, however, can counteract this shift. Thus, food-deprived animals are more likely than well-fed ones to forage in a patch in which the danger of predation is greater but in which the food-intake rate is also higher (Dill & Fraser, 1984; Krebs, 1980; Milinski & Heller, 1978; Werner, Gilliam, Hall, & Mittelbach, 1983).

There also are genetically determined biases toward certain patches relative to others equal to them in terms of food reinforcement and the presence of aversive stimuli. For example, pied wagtails will sometimes feed in their territories and sometimes with other members of their flock on the meadow (Davies & Houston, 1984). However, although the relative amount of time wagtails spend feeding in their territories and feeding with the flock varies as a direct function of the relative reinforcement rate in these locations, there is a bias toward feeding in their territories (Houston, 1986). Such a bias may have evolved because of the fitness value of defending one's territory from intruders (see next section), which requires spending time in it. Animals' territories appear to have fitness value for them, at least in part because of behavior that they have learned in the territories that enable them to find food and protect themselves from predators (Stamps, 1995).

Defensive Behavior

In order to survive to perpetuate their genetic material, animals must defend against predators and other dangers that may injure or kill them, members of their own species that compete with them for resources and mates, and parasites that sap their capacity to engage in survival and reproductive functions.

Although it may seem strange at first, stimuli correlated with a potential predator have evolved to be positively reinforcing (at least when initially encountered). For example, minnows will swim up to inspect a potential predator (Pitcher et al., 1986). There are at least three plausible reasons for this evolutionary development. First, in order to defend against a predator (or other dangerous species), animals must first detect it with some degree of accuracy. Animals that constantly flee from harmless animals, for example, would not be acting efficiently. Second, inspection of a potential predator may condition escape or avoidance of a given predator by pairing a view of the predator with stimuli (such as the "alarm substance" discussed below) correlated with predatory behavior (G. Brown, & Godin, 1999). Third, an animal that evokes pursuit by a predator that it inspects may thereby learn effective escape behavior (C. Brown & Warburton, 1999).

Technically, to defend against a dangerous animal is to remove or avoid stimuli that are paired with it. Animals do this either by fleeing from the predator (thus, removing aversive stimuli by removing themselves from the presence of those stimuli), threatening the predator (so that it is driven away), or attacking it (so that it is driven away or killed). Any of these may occur as an unconditioned response to the pain inflicted by a predator, because pain elicits running or aggressive behavior. Through respondent conditioning and stimulus generalization, running or aggressive behavior will tend to occur the next time that the animal encounters the predator that attacked it or an animal resembling that predator. In addition, if it successfully removes or avoids stimuli accompanying the predator, the defensive behavior will be reinforced and thus, increase in probability upon subsequent exposure to those stimuli. In short, the animal will become efficient in defending against predators. As another example, fish learn to respond to substances paired with a predator. For example, minnows learn to escape and avoid areas that have the smell of food that a predator has eaten regularly and hence, that is associated with the predator (Brown & Smith, 1996; Mathis & Smith, 1993).

The conditioning of escape behavior with stimuli paired with a predator is efficient only if the individual survives the first attack. Therefore, processes have evolved by which predator defense may occur prior to physical attack. For example, some species of birds have a genetically determined tendency to escape from any overhead-moving silhouette, regardless of its shape. If no attack comes from a particular shaped object moving overhead, the tendency to escape and other emotional responses eventually habituate (Schleidt, 1961). Escape behavior to shapes to which habituation has not occurred, or that have preceded an attack, remain strong. In this way, the animal refrains from squandering energy escaping from harmless stimuli, while still avoiding potential predators.

Three learning processes can be seen in the preceding example: habituation, respondent conditioning, and operant conditioning. For another example involving respondent conditioning, consider the fact that an animal engaging in defensive behavior—which includes the sounding of alarm calls—can be an unconditioned stimulus for other members of its species to engage in defensive behavior. Thus, a stimulus that is paired with an animal engaging in defensive behavior will become a conditioned stimulus for other members of the defending animal's species to engage in defensive behavior. Through this process, European blackbirds (*Turdus merula*) that have never been attacked by an owl, for example, learn to mob (i.e., attack in a group) and flee from owls (Curio, 1988; Curio et al., 1978). Similarly rhesus monkeys (*Macaca mulatta*) that have never been attacked or bitten by a snake learn to withdraw from snakes and to exhibit other defensive behavior in the presence of snakes (Cook, Mineka, Wolkenstein, & Laitsch, 1985; Mineka & Cook, 1988). Animals that have acquired defensive behavior against predators and other dangerous species through respondent conditioning may transmit this behavior, through the same respondent-conditioning process, to other members of their groups. In this manner, defensive behavior may be transmitted across a group of animals, and through generations of animals as a sort of "tradition," with few animals in the group having to experience and survive an attack by the dangerous species in order to pass on the tradition of defending against that species.

The tendency for animals to sound alarm calls in the presence of animals that have attacked them evolved because it tended to promote the survival of animals that responded to the calls and animals that were related to them. The calls themselves are likely genetically determined to a large extent. However, as we have seen above, responding appropriately to alarm calls can involve respondent conditioning. It can also involve operant conditioning. For example, adult vervet monkeys (*Cercopithecus aethiops*) give at least three distinct alarm calls: one for a leopard, one for a hawk, and one for a snake (Struhsaker, 1967). Infant vervet monkeys learn to respond appropriately to these calls by climbing a tree when hearing the leopard-alarm call, running into the bushes when hearing the hawk-alarm call, and standing bipedally and looking around when hearing the snake-alarm call (Cheney & Seyfarth, 1990, p. 135; Seyfarth & Cheney, 1986). These responses may be conditioned to the alarm calls because they occur in the presence of animals that already evoke the specific defensive responses corresponding to the specific calls. That avoidance conditioning is involved in learning to respond to alarm calls is supported by the fact that animals learn to respond to the alarm calls of other species; for example, vervet monkeys that inhabit areas inhabited by superb starlings (*Spreo supurbus*) learn to run toward trees when they hear the starling's ground-predator alarm call and to look upward when they hear its aerial-predator alarm call (Cheyenne & Seyfarth, 1988, pp. 258–259; Hauser, 1988).

This is not to say that all responding to alarm calls is learned. For example, infant squirrel monkeys (*Saimiri sciureus*) reared in isolation respond appropriately to the different alarm calls given by conspecifics (Herzog & Hopf, 1984).

In addition to learning to respond, through operant conditioning, to different alarm calls sounded by members of their groups, animals learn to respond differentially to the alarm calls of different members of their groups. An example of this that we have already mentioned is that of birds learning (through habituation or extinction) not to respond to the alarm calls of members of their species that give false alarms. Similarly, jackdaws tend to respond more reliably to alarm calls given by older members of their groups than to those given by younger members (Lorenz, 1963/1966, p. 36). This is probably because the alarm calls of younger members are less consistently correlated with predators, because they have not yet formed strong discriminations between stimuli correlated with predators and other stimuli.

Reinforcement by conspecifics can play a role in animals learning to emit alarm calls in the presence of specific stimuli. For example, infant vervet monkeys frequently give their species' alarm calls to harmless animals (e.g., a hawk-alarm call to a pigeon or a leopard-alarm call to a warthog). When this happens, adults look up or around and then return to what they were doing. If the alarm call is in response to a predator, however, adults are very likely to give the call themselves, which apparently reinforces the emission of the call by the infant in the presence of the appropriate stimulus (Cheney & Seyfarth, 1990, p. 133). That the behavior of other members of their species reinforces their alarm calls is indicated by the fact that, in an example of stimulus discrimination learning, adult vervet monkeys typically do not emit alarm calls when other vervet monkeys are not present (Dennett, 1988, p. 189).

Warning stimuli exist in other sensory modalities as well. An example is a chemical called alarm substance (also known by its German name, Schreckstoff) present in epidermal cells of European minnows (*Phoxinus phoxinus*) and released when the epidermis is ruptured (Pfeiffer, 1962, 1963a,b; von Frisch, 1938). Other minnows respond to this substance by escaping from it and hence, from the predator that caused its release. This example is puzzling, however, because its obvious explanation does not seem to hold up. The minnows in each shoal, or school, tend not to be closely related to each other (Naish et al., 1993). Thus the principle of inclusive fitness may not explain it. An alternative explanation is that its evolutionary function is to attract other predators that then distract the original predator, thus increasing the chance of successful escape by the injured minnow (Chivers et al., 1996; Mathis et al., 1995). The escape responses of other minnows to the substance are selected for genetically or learned as a result of the pairing of the substance with predators. Interestingly, alarm substance is effective in evoking escape responses only if (or to the extent that) other sense modalities such as vision are obstructed, as in hazy water (Hartman & Abrahams, 2000). Thus, alarm substance is effective only if it is part of a compound stimulus in which a vision-obstructing stimulus the other part of the compound.

Rather than warning other members of one's group, some alarms attract animals two levels higher on the food chain. An example of such a burglar alarm, as it called from the analogy with alarms that summon police, appears to be the bioluminescence response of some species of dinoflagellates. These are aquatic unicellular organisms that emit light when there is distortion of their cell membranes (as would happen when being fed upon by a predator, such as small marine crustaceans). Some species of dinoflagellates are toxic, so the light may serve to warn off the predator. However, it also attracts a predators of dinoflagellates' predators (such as sticklebacks) (Buckenroad, 1943; Abrahams & Townsend, 1993). In this example, we have three species interacting and learning occurring in at least two of them. The predator of dinoflagellates' predator learns bioluminescence as a discriminative stimulus to move toward, and dinoflagellates' predator learns to escape or avoid the bioluminescence of dinoflagellates because of the pairing of that stimulus with the predators' predator.

Some defensive behavior has been effective so consistently throughout the evolutionary history of a particular species that the behavior has become genetically determined for that species. Sometimes the behavior is quite distinctive, as in the case of stotting, which, as mentioned in the previous section, provides a negative discriminative stimulus (i.e., an S^Δ, or discriminative stimulus coupled with extinction) for predators by its correlation with the ability to outrun them. Often certain physical characteristics have evolved along with specific behavior, such as the conspicuous diamond-shaped skin pattern of a rattlesnake or the inconspicuous visage of a leaf-mimicking insect (Edmunds, 1974). Note that learning processes in predators have driven the evolution of both conspicuousness and crypsis, as in the preceding examples.

Defense against other groups of conspecifics. Members of the same social group typically defend their group from other conspecific groups that compete with their group for resources. Sometimes groups of the same species that inhabit adjacent areas are in a state that—in human terms—is somewhere between "war" and "uneasy peace." Fighting may break out any time that members of opposing groups encounter each other, especially if members of one group have infringed on the other group's territory. Through punishment, animals learn not to emit responses that are likely to evoke attack from other groups; and, through negative reinforcement, animals learn to respond in ways that minimize the chance of attack from other groups. For example, members of a group of chimpanzees (*Pan troglodytes*) patrolling peripheral parts of their ranges maintain silence for long stretches of time (up to three hours or more). They avoid stepping on dry leaves, males do not utter the pant hoots that normally are part of their dominance displays (see next subsection), and females do not give copulation calls (a high-pitched scream that occurs at the point of sexual climax). Infants or juveniles that make loud motion noise, vocalize, or hiccup may be given a reprimand, or hit or embraced until silent (Goodall, 1986, pp. 490–491). Noise when on patrol may become aversive for infants and juveniles instructed in this manner, so that in a kind of cultural transmission, the tradition of noise suppression when on patrol will tend to be perpetuated in the group independently of encounters with other groups.

During fights with other groups, animals learn through negative reinforcement behavior that aids in defense, or at least that reduces the danger of injury. For example, vervet monkeys sometimes give false alarm calls during intergroup encounters, causing members of the opposing group (as well as their own) to scurry away (Cheney & Seyfarth, 1990, p. 196).

Although fighting in groups to gain or defend territory (i.e., engaging in war) is commonly thought of as a human trait, it is by no means uniquely human. It is particularly well developed in chimpanzees, who significantly are the closest evolutionary relative of humans. Chimpanzees do not plan their battles as humans do—that, as discussed in the next chapter, requires language—but they do systematically attack members of other groups and sometimes kill them. This killing is generally carried out in a crude and inefficient manner, and appears to be reinforced by the immobilization of the opposing group members that have been killed (Goodall, 1986, pp. 525–530).

Within-group defense against conspecifics.   Animals usually do not kill or seriously injure members of their own groups because animals that had no genetically determined inhibition against this would have destroyed their own genetic material, and so have no surviving descendants. Animals do, however, compete with each other for resources and mates. For example, males of many bird species establish territories that they defend by attacking conspecific male intruders. In addition, a male owner of a territory sings a characteristic song that, because being attacked is aversive, becomes a conditioned aversive stimulus for conspecific males close to its territory. Although being attacked is aversive, detection of an intruder approaching one's territory is a primary positive reinforcer (T. I. Thompson, 1964; Hogan et al., 1970). The evolutionary reason for this is that it ensures that vigilantly patrolling one's territory when intruders are likely to encroach on it will be strengthened and maintained.

Learned defensive behavior against conspecifics plays an important role in dominance hierarchies (also called pecking or ranking orders; Lorenz, 1963/1966) which are rankings that social animals form within their groups. These relatively stable social structures often develop through real or ritualized fighting by pairs of group members. At some point in a hostile encounter, one animal engages in an action called submissive behavior. The animal engaging in submissive behavior is said to be subordinate, and the other animal is said to be dominant or superior.

In some species submissive behavior appears to be behavior that renders the animal vulnerable to its opponent. In many birds (e.g., the jackdaw, gulls, members of the Corvidae family, such as ravens and crows), for example, it consists of presenting the base of the skull or back of the head to the opponent (Lorenz, 1963/1966, pp. 113–115). In dogs and wolves, in contrast, it is the superior animal that exposes a vulnerable part of its body (Schenkel, 1967). As seen in Part A of Figure 16.2, the superior animal (on the right) exposes its head and throat, while the inferior animal grips the opponent's head with its teeth. The superior animal remains poised to counterattack forcefully if the inferior animal carries through and, as seen in

Part B of the figure, the latter's bite is suppressed. Other species engage in submissive behavior that superficially appears unrelated to fighting; for example, baboons present their posteriors to their opponents in a gesture that resembles female copulatory invitations (Lorenz, 1963/1966, p.116–117). Generally, the opponent ceases attacking immediately after the submissive behavior occurs.

In some species special markings correspond to an animal's dominance status. For example, male red-winged blackbirds (*Agelaius phoeniceus*) are less like to intrude into territories of males with large red "epaulettes" on their wings than into territories of those with smaller ones (Roskraft & Rohwer, 1987). Males that do intrude frequently cover their own epaulettes, and are attacked less often and less vigorously than males with exposed epaulettes (Hansen & Rohwer, 1986). Covering of the epaulettes therefore appears to be submissive behavior in this species and is also, in the terminology of this book, avoidance behavior.

There is a strong correlation between markings corresponding to dominance status and dominance behavior; that is, animals tend to behave in accordance with their markings. If the markings are artificially changed (as in an experiment), animals continue to behave in accordance with them. For example, although the extent of black feathering in the throats of Harris sparrows (*Zonotrichia querula*), dyeing subordinates blacker does not result in the becoming more dominant. On the contrast, they come under heavy attack—apparently because of the incongruence between their markings and their behavior. Administering testosterone, however, increases the status of both blackened and unblackened birds (Rohwer & Rohwer, 1978). Further, bleaching the feathers of dominant birds causes them to fight more to retain their status (Rohwer, 1977). Clearly there is a strong genetic component determining both dominance markings and the corresponding behavior in Harris sparrows. The extent to which learning plays a role in the behavior is not as clear.

Animals may avoid or escape punishment from superiors by deferring to them with respect to reinforcement. For an example, consider a fledgling male brown-headed cowbird (*Molothrus ater*) that has just joined a flock of cowbirds. Although this male would not have learned his song from other members of his species—cowbirds are not raised by their own species because the female lays her eggs in the nests of various other species—he will sing a species-specific song that excites females in the flock to copulate. The song will also tend to elicit aggression from the superior males, however. As a result of this punishment, the newly arrived male will alter his song so that it is less sexually exciting to females. If over time the male moves up the dominance hierarchy and is under less pressure from attackers, he will alter his song so that it is more sexually exciting to females and will attack other males with sexually exciting songs (West & King, 1988; West et al., 1981).

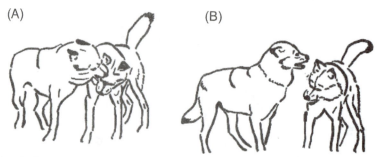

FIGURE 16.2. A) The wolf on the left grips the jaw of the other wolf, which maintains an ideal position for body checking his opponent and biting his throat. B) The maintained position of the wolf on the right inhibits the bite of his opponent, who backs off. (From Schenkel, 1967)

Dominance hierarchies are said to be context independent if, for each animal in the hierarchy, if animal A is dominant over animal B with respect to one reinforcer (e.g., food, grooming partner, mate, resting site) in *one* situation then A is dominant over B with respect to *all* reinforcers and in *all* situations. Dominance hierarchies are said to be transitive if A is dominant over B and B is dominant over C implies A is dominant over C. Among primates, at least, dominance hierarchies generally are not strictly context independent or transitive. For example, the dominance hierarchies of vervet monkeys are transitive within the sexes, while males typically dominate females across the sexes. The dominance of male over female vervet monkeys is context dependent, however, in that two allied females can easily drive away one male (Seyfarth, 1980). But even dominance hierarchies that are context dependent may be very consistent with regard to the submissive display that a given member will show to another (de Waal, 1986). A rhesus monkey may, for example, consistently bare her teeth in a character-istic submissive gesture toward a particular conspecific while at the same time slapping him (Maestripieri, 1996, p. 404).

Changes within dominance hierarchies can occur as a result of previously subordinate animals initiating and winning fights over superior animals (de Waal, 1982, 1996). In a number of species, kin relationships are important in the establishment and maintenance of domi-nance hierarchies, in that animals that are genetically related help each other in fights for dominance. Since superior animals tend to win fights, it follows that their close relatives also will tend to become dominant due to the support that they receive from their dominant rela-tives. For example, high-ranking rhesus monkeys (*Macaca mulatta*) tend to support their younger and smaller relatives in fights (Datta, 1983a, b; Sade, 1965, 1972). Similarly, in vervet monkeys, a close relative—usually a mother or sibling—will often come to the aid of another monkey in a fight (Cheney, 1983; Horrocks & Hunte, 1983). Thus, in species such as the above, rank in a dominance hierarchy tends to be "inherited." The learning mechanism by which this works apparently is that seeing a close relative lose a fight is aversive while seeing that relative win a fight is reinforcing.

Submissive behavior often is so uniform that it seems clear that a strong genetic compo-nent is involved. In some cases, however, learning seems to be implicated. For example, when attacked by a superior member of their group, a subordinate male baboon may consort with an infertile female or carry an unrelated infant (Packer, 1979, 1980). These activities may have occurred initially as a type of adjunctive behavior, but to the extent that they successfully inhibited the attack, they probably were learned through negative reinforcement.

Sometimes an animal's aggressive or defensive behavior toward another member of its species resembles human behavior that occurs as a result of planning. Planning, however, requires verbal behavior that, except in the case of special training, is absent in animals. In most cases where animals appear to show planning an alternative explanation based on prin-ciples of learning generally is not too difficult to find. For example, a chimpanzee that had been attacked by another chimpanzee enticed that chimpanzee with what appeared to be friendly behavior. When the former attacker came close, however, the enticing chimpanzee proceeded to attack him ferociously. On the surface, it looked as though the enticing chimpan-zee had deliberately plotted to lure the other chimpanzee into a trap in order to take revenge on him. Given that these chimpanzees did not have verbal behavior, however, a much more plausible explanation based on principles of learning is available. Consider from the vantagepoint of the enticing chimpanzee the fact that generalization gradients based on positive reinforce-ment are narrower but higher than those based on aversive stimuli. While he was a consider-able distance from the enticing chimpanzee, the other chimpanzee's positive reinforcing quali-ties—due to previous pairings of that chimpanzee with positive reinforcement—were stronger than his aversive qualities for the enticing chimpanzee. As he approached the enticing chimpanzee, there came a point at which his aversive qualities—that is, the stimuli paired with his recent attack on the enticing chimpanzee—became stronger than his positive reinforcing qualities. At that point, the stimuli paired with the recent attack elicited aggression by the enticing chimpanzee (Mackintosh, 1994, p. 47).

Respondent conditioning also plays a role in defense against members of one's own species. For example, male Siamese fighting fish (*Betta splendens*) defend their territories against other males of their species. When no other males are present, they engage in patrolling behavior in which they swim about in their territories. When another male encroaches on its territory, a male will engage in gill erection (a "threat" display) and move toward the intruder. This patrolling behavior becomes conditioned to the region where the encroacher appeared, since the intruder will patrol that site more often and engage in occasional gill erections while there (Bronstein, 1986).

Defense against parasites.   Members of some species (e.g., most primates) clean each other of parasites. This activity is reinforcing for the groomer as well as for the animal being groomed, which makes sense according to the principle of inclusive fitness. An animal that is free of parasites has a better chance of surviving and reproducing, so in grooming individuals which might be relatives one is potentially helping to perpetuate one's genetic material. In addition, among primates at least, grooming appears to serve a social function by making individuals within a group conditioned reinforcers for each other, as will be discussed later in this chapter.

Sometimes members of one species are groomed by members of another species as part of their feeding behavior. For example, a certain coral reef wrasse (*Labroides dimidiatus*) feeds on the parasites of various other fish species, and the host fish return regularly to be cleaned by the wrasses (Robertson & Hoffman, 1977). The return of the host fish is probably learned as a result of the reinforcement of being cleaned of parasites.

Sexual Behavior

Animals perpetuate their genetic material by helping relatives and by reproducing. Of these two methods, other factors being equal, the latter typically results in the perpetuation of more of the animal's genetic material (i.e., more of the genetic code is replicated). For mammals, birds, fish, and other multicellular animals, sexual behavior is prerequisite to reproduction. In sexually reproducing animals, there are two sexes with specialized functions (usually, but not necessarily, in different individuals) for combining genetic material, but the behavior leading up to this is extremely varied across species. It can range from brief encounters to elaborate courtship displays by one individual (usually the male).

In many species long-term mating occurs, in that the animals stay together for an extended period. A number of different mating arrangements exist both across different species and within the same species. Both monogamy, in which one male mates with one female, and polygamy, in which more than one male mates with one or more females, or more than one female mates with one or more males, occur in different species and sometimes within the same species. Polygamous mating systems that occur include all logical possibilities:

- polyandry, in which one female mates with multiple males;
- polygeny, in which one male mates with multiple females; and,
- polygenandry, in which multiple males mate with multiple females.

Polygeny is more common than polyandry because in most species more copies of the male's genes are perpetuated if the male devotes more time to siring offspring than caring for them.

Females are more limited in the number of offspring they can have, and thus, there is a tendency for them to devote more time into caring for offspring than for males. If males vary a lot genetically, however, having multiple mates may increase the probability that the female will mate with males having a high degree of genetic fitness. This could be particularly true in regard to animals for which multiple paternity within a clutch is possible.

Evolution of sex. The explanation for the evolution and pervasiveness of sexual reproduction when it is fully known will probably have manifold parts. One plausible reason is that sex increases the variability of an animal's offspring and this ensures that a least some of those offspring will survive in an environment in which conditions fluctuate between different states (Shields, 1988). To take an example illustrating how sexual reproduction can enhance inclusive fitness, consider that within certain bird species (e.g., some warblers, the European robin, the European blackbird) some birds migrate and some do not (Berthold, 1988). The tendency to stay at home and the tendency to migrate have strong genetic components; therefore, if sexual reproduction did not exist all of a given bird's progeny would have the same migratory tendency that it did. If the bird was genetically predisposed to stay at home, then all its progeny would tend not to migrate and might die off during years in which food resources at home were scarce. If the bird was genetically predisposed to migrate, then all its progeny would tend to migrate and might die off when migration was particularly dangerous due to poor weather conditions or numerous predators along the way. By combining its genetic material with another member of its species, however, the bird increases the probability above zero that it will have progeny that tend to stay at home and progeny that will tend to migrate. Indeed, the probability is raised to an extremely high level by the fact that its progeny will also reproduce sexually. Thus, sexual reproduction maximizes the chances that at least some of the bird's progeny will survive to perpetuate its genetic material, regardless of the vicissitudes at home and along the migratory route.

In addition to the advantages of sexual reproduction, there are also costs. Chief among these is the fact that one's genetic material is diluted by half. Other costs include increased risk of diseases and increased vulnerability to predators. From an evolutionary point of view, it appears that the advantages must outweigh the disadvantages.

Evolution of sexually attractive characteristics. Animals with which an animal may combine its genetic material—that is, members of the opposite sex—are primary reinforcers for that animal, ensuring that animals generally will learn to do whatever they must to combine their genetic material with another member of their species. This implies that within a given species each sex must have characteristics that are distinctive and sexually attractive to members of the opposite sex. These characteristics may range from physical features such as male facial hair, to odorous substances called pheromones, to species-specific behavior patterns such as those that occur in courtship. The evolutionary causes of many specific sexual characteristics are far from simple and not completely understood (Andersson, 1994). The primary reason for this complexity is that the evolution of sexually attractive characteristics must occur simultaneously in two types of individuals—one that produces large, nutritious eggs (females) and the other that produces small, mobile sperm (males). In order for these two sexes to combine their genetic material, each must evolve characteristics that attract the other and simultaneously must evolve the tendency to be attracted by the characteristics of the other sex. Further, to maximize the viability of their progeny, each sex must be preferentially attracted to characteristics in the other sex that are correlated to the greatest extent with viability and reproductive success. We turn now to the major variables that appear to be involved in this extremely complex sexually interactive evolutionary process.

Fisherian Runaway Processes. Often the sex-distinguishing characteristics of one sex—usually the male—are far more elaborate than would seem necessary to provide sex-distinguishing stimuli to members of the other sex. This can be the result what is often called a Fisherian runaway process (after Fisher, 1930) whereby individuals in succeeding generations selected sex partners with increasingly more exaggerated sex-distinguishing characteristics. Opposite-sex progeny with those characteristics were more likely to be selected as sex partners, and thus more likely to reproduce and perpetuate their genetic material (O'Donald, 1962, 1967, 1977; Lande, 1980, 1981; Kirkpatrick, 1982; Seger, 1985). Consider, for example, the possible evolutionary origin of the elaborate tail feathers and courting display of the peacock (i.e., the male peafowl, *Pavo critatus*). In the distant past, primitive peacocks evolved distinctive tail feathers along with a relatively modest courting display because these, originally occurring as a result of mutations, provided a basis for sexual selection by peahens (i.e., female peafowl). Once females began to select males with these sex-distinguishing characteristics, selecting for exaggerations of them helped ensure that they would be present in their male progeny. For these exaggerated characteristics to be primary reinforcers for females also required mutations, but those mutations were perpetuated because, through selection of males with reinforcing characteristics, females enhanced the potential sexual success of their male descendants. Thus, over many generations, females selected males with increasingly more elaborate tail feathers and courting displays, resulting finally in the flamboyant modern peacock.

Note that there are factors operating against Fisherian runaway processes. First, the characteristics that result from them consume energy, thus putting a strain on food resources. Second, they make an animal conspicuous to predators. Fisherian runaway processes are similar to the shaping of complex superstitions. Whereas the former results from selection of successively more elaborate characteristics by potential mates over successive generations, the latter result from the selection of successively more elaborate responses by chance reinforcement. In both cases, the greater the chance a particular characteristic or response has of being selected, the more likely it is to occur; and, the more likely it is to occur, the greater the chance it has of being selected. In both cases there are factors operating against the process. In the former, the factors are energy expenditure and predation; in the latter, they are response cost and the inefficiency of the response in procuring reinforcement.

Fitness Indicators. Characteristics developed through a Fisherian runaway process are correlated with fitness only in the sense that individuals of the opposite sex select them; that is, they are selected because they are selected. For example, peahens that select males with long tails will be more likely to have male offspring that have long tails and be selected by females. There are other characteristics that appear to be selected because they are correlated with increased likelihood that the offspring will survive to reproduce.

Handicapping principle. Fisherian runaway processes explain the evolution of characteristics that seemingly handicap individuals by increased energy costs or increased vulnerability to predators. An alternative theory called the handicapping principle provides a fitness explanation of such characteristics (Zahavi, 1975, 1977). The reasoning is that an animal that has survived despite an obvious handicap must have features that compensate for the handicap. The appearance of the handicapping characteristic might also be correlated with the health of the individual, such as its freedom from parasites. Thus, there would be a selection pressure on females to mate with males whose apparent handicap meets certain criteria. Note that Fisherian runaway processes and the handicapping principle are not mutually exclusive.

Correlates of fitness. There are also indicators of fitness that do not appear to be handicaps. These are characteristics that are correlated with fitness because they are produced by the same variables that produce fitness. For example, other factors being equal, healthy people generally (although not always) are more sexually attractive than those who are obviously ill. There is also evidence that bilateral symmetry is attractive to humans (Grammer & Thornhill, 1994; Mazur, 1986; Rhodes et al., 1999; Thornhill & Gangestad, 1993) and perhaps some other animals (Thornhill, 1992), presumably because it is correlated with fitness. One piece of supporting evidence for this is the fact that the scent of men with more bilateral symmetry is more attractive to ovulating women than is the scent of men with less bilateral symmetry (Thornhill & Gangestad, 1999). It appears that factors responsible for fitness in men jointly affects both their symmetry and their pheromones.

If an animal's sexual attractiveness is correlated with its fitness, then the attraction of members of the opposite sex to it is also correlated with its fitness. Thus, there is a tendency for animals to be attracted to conspecifics of the opposite sex that they observe attracting conspecifics of their own sex (Wade & Pruett-Jones, 1990). For example, female guppies (*Poecilia reticulata*) show a preference to mate with males they have seen another female with over males they have seen unaccompanied by a female, when all other variables associated with the two males are kept constant or randomized (Dugatkin, 1992; Dugatkin & Godin, 1992). This mate-choice imitation is a form of stimulus enhancement, as described in Chapter 5 (p. 96). There is a stronger tendency for younger female guppies to imitate the mate choices of older, and hence more experienced, females than for older females to imitate the mate choice of younger females (Dugatkin & Godin, 1993). This makes sense if mate-choice imitation evolved because it reduces the costs (e.g., time lost from foraging, increased risk of being preyed upon) of assessing potential mates (Real, 1991). As described in Chapter 5 similar stimulus enhancement occurs for food and other primary reinforcers, probably for a similar evolutionary reason.

Learning based on sexual reinforcement.   As with learning the location of food or water, stimulus discrimination learning and conditioned reinforcement are involved in animals going to locations where members of the opposite sex are likely to be. For example, receptive female natterjack toads (*Bufo calamita*) tend to be attracted to louder-calling males. Males with less loud calls tend to settle around the louder callers and intercept females going toward them (Arak, 1988). It appears that the louder call is a discriminative stimulus for less loud males, in that their behavior of lying in wait near the louder callers is reinforced by encounters with receptive females. (See Fig. 16.3.)

In some species, there are special locations called leks, at which males congregate and to which females are then attracted. Some leks attract more females than others, either because of something about the males that are in them or something about the locations themselves. In any case, males have a strong tendency to cluster on those leks or around those males to which females are attracted in greater numbers. Stimulus discrimination learning could be involved in this behavior, in that the more attractive males or leks are stimuli in the presence of which reinforcing encounters with females occur at a higher rate than they do in their absence.

Respondent conditioning appears to be important in the learning of sexual behavior. Stimuli present when the male Japanese quail (*Coturnix coturnix japonica*), for example, copulates with a female come to elicit sexual excitement and approach in the male (Domjan, Greene, & North, 1989; Domjan, Lyon, & North, 1986). This can result in the male becoming more responsive to certain plumage characteristics of females and more ready to mate in specific locations in which he has sexually encountered a female. As another example, stimuli present when male blue gourami fish (*Trichogaster trichopterus*) copulate with females come to inhibit aggressive behavior toward females and also result in males spending more time nest building and clasping females (Hollis et al., 1989; Hollis et al., 1997). Stimuli paired with copulation in the natural environment apparently enhance reproductivity in males (and probably females as well).

FIGURE 16.3. Potential interception of female frog. A female (right) enters the pond in response to a male (left) who calls from his territory. A smaller male waits close by to intercept the female. (From Krebs & Davies, 1993)

Sexual competition. To increase the chances of perpetuating one's genetic material it is necessary to compete for sexual partners. Competition is greatest for potential sex partners having physical and behavioral characteristics correlated with genetic viability. For example, animals prefer sexual partners with more symmetrical physical features, a preference that probably evolved because asymmetrical features are often the result of a disease process stemming from some genetic weakness (Møller, 1992; Swaddle & Innis, 1994).

Sexual competition can continue even after typically monogamous animals mate: Animals tend to hinder others from copulating with their mates. The evolutionary reason for this in the case of the male is that if another male copulates with his mate, that other male's genes rather than his own may be perpetuated. In the case of the female, if her mate copulates with another female, he may tend to neglect her offspring to provide care to the offspring of the other female. (This, of course, would be a factor only in those species in which the male provides care for the offspring.) Thus, it follows from the principle of inclusive fitness that an animal's mate copulating with an individual other than itself typically is a primary aversive stimulus for that animal. It also follows, however, that copulation with members of the opposite sex other than their mates is a primary reinforcer for both males and females. For the male it increases the number and variety of his progeny; for the female, it increases the potential viability of her progeny if the sex partner has more attractive physical and behavioral characteristics than her mate does.

The fact that copulating with an individual other than its mate may be positively reinforcing for an animal and aversive to its mate can lead to complex interactions between reinforcement from sexual activity and punishment from the mate. One outcome of this interaction can be "sneaked" or covert copulation between individuals that are not mated. Punishment also can result in sneaked copulation in species that have very loose or flexible mating arrangements, such as chimpanzees. For example, punishment by superior male chimpanzees can result in females learning not to emit copulation calls when copulating with subordinate males, although they still show the facial expressions and other behavioral components that accompany the call when copulating with subordinate males and still give the calls when copulating with superior males (de Waal, 1982, p. 49; Goodall, 1986, p. 579). Sometimes sexual conflicts are resolved through polygamous mating arrangements (e.g., Davies, 1985; Davies & Lundberg,

1984). This may be most likely to occur when the competing parties have nearly equal capacities to inflict punishment on each other.

Care of the Young

In many species the young must be fed, protected, and otherwise cared for if they are to survive and perpetuate their (and their parents') genetic material. Either or both parents may perform these functions. When only one parent performs them it usually is the mother. The evolutionary reason for this is that a male generally can fertilize many more ova than one female can produce, especially in those species in which the female reproductive system is highly specialized for egg or fetus development. Therefore, males can maximize the number of their offspring that survive by producing a large number of them while neglecting parental care; whereas, females can maximize the number of their surviving offspring only through parental care.

Many species of birds (Brown, 1987; Skutch, 1935) and mammals (Riedman, 1982) engage in cooperative breeding, in which individuals in addition to the parents aid in caring for the young. These supplementary caregivers usually are related to the young; thus, in helping care for them they help perpetuate their own genetic material. In addition, the helpers learn care-taking behavior. For example, during the period bell miners (*Manorina melanophrys*) spend as helpers, their alloparenting, or helping, skills improve in terms of such factors as nestling care activities, the items brought to the nestlings, and interactions with the parents (Poiani, 1993). Often helpers eventually leave the home territory and mate, and the behavior they learned in helping care for their younger siblings may generalize to the rearing of their own young.

Feeding.   Many aspects of feeding the young clearly are genetically determined, but many also are learned. Food that an animal procures for the young under its care reinforces its behavior in the same way that food it consumes does (in fact, in many bird species, the food is first eaten by the caregiver and then regurgitated to the young). Thus, the learning phenomena related to food-directed behavior that already have been discussed apply when the ultimate consumer of the food is an immature animal rather than the animal procuring the food.

Mammalian mothers provide milk secreted by their mammary glands to their young before they can eat solid food. This activity likely is positively reinforcing to the mother—and perhaps negatively reinforcing, too, when there is a large buildup of milk in the glands. Suckling may be one of the primary reinforcers involved in causing the mother to keep close to the young and keep them close to her, so that caring for them is facilitated. Other primary reinforcers probably also are involved in this. For example, physical contact with the young probably is a primary reinforcer for the mother, just as physical contact with the mother is a primary reinforcer for the young (Harlow, 1960).

Feeding the young is controlled by responses they make, such as crying, that are correlated with food deprivation. These responses are primary aversive stimuli for the caregivers. Proper feeding of the young is learned, at least in a "fine-tuning" sense, because it reduces the intensity of these aversive stimuli. The food provided by the caregivers in turn reinforces the young's hunger-related responses, so they are strengthened and maintained.

Protection.   The protective behavior of parents often appears to have a particularly strong genetic basis. A bird engaging in behavior resembling that resulting from a broken wing when a predator approaches its young (Skutch, 1976) has had no opportunity to learn this behavior. The behavior is too complex and appears too quickly in its final (or near final) form to have been shaped environmentally. It must therefore have been shaped through evolution—the progeny of those birds that were genetically predisposed to engage in increasingly closer approximations to that behavior in the presence of a predator survived to perpetuate their genetic material.

For a possible example of the role learning plays in parental protection, consider that some wild cat mothers, such as lions and tigers, move their cubs from one hiding place to another (Guggisberg, 1975, pp. 173, 213; Joubert & Joubert, 1992). The scent of a predator near her cubs is a primary aversive stimulus to the mother, and moving her cubs is an escape response. With each new hiding place, a certain amount of time is required for predators to pick up the scent of the cubs and close in on it. This fits the description of a free-operant avoidance schedule for the mother, and thus she eventually will learn to move her cubs in advance of predators picking up their scent.

Protecting the young from dangerous substances is much less common than protecting them from dangerous animals. Even primates other than great apes and humans do not prevent their young from eating harmful material. For example, a mother baboon will not interfere with her infant eating a toxic item that the mother has learned not to eat (King, 1994). There have been reports, however, of orangutan, chimpanzees, and gorillas removing nonfood items from infants (Byrne, 1995, p. 142).

Training.   The young of many species must learn behavior they need to survive and reproduce. Parenting in these species generally includes behavior that conditions responses in the young that enable them to survive.

Learning initial feeding.   Newborn mammals must learn the location of the mother's nipple. An odor that the mother secretes, called the nipple-search pheromone, guides the newborn rabbit (*Oryctolagus cuniculus*) to the nipple. This odor may be learned by exposure to it in the uterus (Coureaud et al., 1997) just as later food preferences may be learned in that way (see below). In addition, further learning to the nipple-search pheromone occurs as a result of exposure to it after birth (Hudson, 1985; Hudson & Distel, 1986, 1987; Kinderman, Hudson, & Distel, 1994).

Learning what to eat.   For mammals, the initial learning of what foods to eat may come from exposure to the odors of foods the mother has eaten. This exposure may occur in the uterus prior to birth (Bilkó, Altbäcker, & Hudson, 1994; Hepper, 1988; Schaal & Orgeur, 1992; Schaal, Orgeur, & Arnould, 1995) and from the mother's milk after birth (Altbäcker, Hudson, & Bilkó, 1995; Galef & Sherry, 1973; Nolte & Provenza, 1992). African elephant calves (*Loxodonta africana*) learn what to eat by taking food from mouths of their mothers and other adults, and also by eating the fresh dung of other elephants (Lee & Moss, 1999, pp. 110, 120). Odors of foods in the feces of adult rats cause weanling rats to eat foods with similar odors (Laland & Plotkin, 1991, 1993). Animals such as kittens (Wyrwicka, 1978) and lambs (Lobato, Pearce, & Beilharz, 1980) when alone will eat foods their mothers have previously eaten in their presence, even when these foods are not normally in these animals' diets.

Parents and other adults in nonhuman primate species do not provide specific training of the young. Learning by the young generally occurs through passive tolerance by adults rather than direct teaching. For example, infant tufted capuchin monkeys (*Cebus apella*) and infant savanna baboons (*Papio cynocephalus*) learn which foods are eatable by taking small bits of food from adults who are tolerant of this (Fragaszy & Visalberghi, 1996, p. 75; King, 1994). Interestingly, the infant capuchins develop a stimulus discrimination between adults that are competent openers of nuts and those that are not (Fragaszy, Feuerstein, & Mitra, 1997).

Adult cotton-top tamarins (*Saguinus oedipus*) when eating give special infant-directed calls that seem to be highly correlated with giving up the food to infants. The infants learn to respond to these calls (Roush, 1996).

Learning where to eat. Weanling rats tend to go to feeding sites that are marked with adult rats' feces and urine (Galef & Heiber, 1976; Laland & Plotkin, 1991). These sites then likely become conditioned reinforcers for the weanlings, which as adults in turn establish these sites as conditioned reinforcers for new generations of weanlings (Laland, 1999, pp. 180–181).

Some animals learn where to feed by following their mothers to feeding places. Later they go to those feeding places by following the same routes that their mothers took (Higgenbottom & Croft, 1999, pp. 89–92; Klein, 1999, p. 134; 1999; Lent, 1971).

Learning self-feeding. Birds and mammals are initially totally dependent on adults (usually one or both parents) for food. Later, however, the young animal must obtain food on its own, and this may require some form of training. Fading is often involved in such training, as when parents gradually reject the begging behavior of their offspring, thus forcing the offspring to gradually begin feeding themselves. For example, the parents of ring dove (*Streptopelia risoria*) chicks initially provide them with "crop milk," which consists of sloughed off cells of the esophagus, mixed with regurgitated seeds. The pairing of the seeds with crop milk increases, by respondent conditioning, the reinforcing effect of seeds, and the gradual rejection of begging causes the chicks to increasingly peck for seeds that are not regurgitated by the parents (Balsam, Graf, & Silver, 1992).

Learning to hunt and kill prey is important for carnivores. For many members of the cat family (*Felidae*), early training to kill prey occurs through a fading procedure carried out by the mother (Caro, 1980a,b, 1981; Caro & Hauser, 1992; Ewer, 1969; Kitchener, 1999, p. 240). First the mother brings dead prey to the young. Next she brings live prey which she may kill in front of the young and allow them to eat. Then she brings live prey that the young catch and kill with perhaps some assistance from the mother. Eventually, the main assistance provided by the mother is that of preventing the prey from escaping. As the young become more adept at killing prey brought by the mother, less and less assistance is provided. It is important to note that this fading procedure occurs naturally rather than as a result of direct planning, and may not be quite so systematic as described here.

For big cats (e.g., lions) the prey is too large to be brought to the young. In these cases the mother may emit a call that brings the cubs to the prey. Again in a fading-type procedure the mother may kill the prey or incapacitate it just enough to allow the young to kill it (Estes, 1991; Schaller, 1967, 1972).

Many carnivores, such as cats (Kitchener, 1999, pp. 240, 246) and dolphins (Boran & Heimlich, 1999, p. 285; Herzing, 1996) also learn hunting by accompanying their mothers on hunting trips. For example, on hunting trips the young of the spotted dolphin (*Stenella frontalis*) swim behind and beneath their mother who drives out bottom-dwelling fish for the young calves to chase and attempt to capture.

Some bottlenose dolphins (*Tursiops truncatus*) and killer whales (*Orcinus orca*) use an interesting hunting technique called stranding, which is herding fish into shore where they may be caught more easily (Guinet,1991; Guinet & Bouvier, 1995; Hoese, 1971; Lopez & Lopez, 1985; Silber & Fertl, 1995). This technique is especially dangerous for larger animals, which may become stuck on land. Animals that strand can usually disengage themselves, but this requires skill. There is some evidence that these mammals teach their offspring to strand successfully, such as by pushing the young toward the beach and helping them extract themselves when they become stuck (Boran & Heimlich, 1999, pp. 285, 292–294).

Learning what to fear. Alarm calls appear to be very important in teaching infants what to fear. Infant hare wallabies (*Lagorchestes hirsutus*), for example, learn to hide from potential predators in the presence of which hare wallaby alarm calls occur (McLean, Lindie-Jenkins, & Jarman, 1995). The potential predator is a conditioned stimulus for the fear response elicited by the unconditioned stimulus, the alarm call.

Learning social calls. In Chapter 2 we discussed how many species of birds learn songs through exposure to the songs of their groups. Similarly, lesser spear-nosed bat (*Phyllostomus discolor*) infants (Esser, 1994) and killer whale (*Orcinus orca*) calves (Bowles, Young, & Asper, 1988) learn communication calls similar to the calls of their mothers. These calls enable infant and mother to locate each other.

Learning locomotion. There is great variability in the extent to which different species of parent birds teach their young to fly (Attenborough, 1998, p. 276). In some species the parents simply stop feeding the young, thereby forcing them to leave the nest to find food. In one species (*Falco peregrinus*) one parent (usually the mother) carries out a shaping procedure that begins with coaching the young from the nest by holding food in its talons in a nearby tree and calling to the young. Over trials, the young bird must fly farther and farther to obtain food from the parent. Later, the food is contingent on the young bird taking it from the parent in midair. Eventually, the parent drops the food before the young bird reaches it, forcing the young to swoop to grab it. In this way the young learn to catch prey in midair. Because the use of this shaping technique is so elaborate and so consistent across the members of this species, it appears unlikely to have been learned. It therefore provides an interesting example of the genetic determination of a teaching method.

Other teaching of locomotion appears not to be genetically determined. Consider a mother chimpanzee helping her infant to learn to cling to her, to crawl, and to walk by providing support for these activities and then gradually withdrawing it (King, 1999, p. 26; Ritj-Plooij & van de Plooij, 1987; Savage, 1975; Yerkes & Tomilin, 1935). Although it is natural for us to think in this case that the mother is deliberately teaching her infant, we should keep in mind that the mother does not have language and therefore has no concept of future in the sense that we do. We may explain the mother's actions by noting that for the infant to cling to her and to move on its own are reinforcing to her. Guiding or pushing the infant through these actions is therefore reinforced when the infant starts doing them on its own.

Learning tool use. As described earlier in this chapter, chimpanzees are adept at using tools. Cracking nuts with two stones in a hammer-and-anvil arrangement is perhaps the most complex tool-using skill that chimpanzees exhibit in their natural environments, and it may take almost ten years for chimpanzees to learn it to the highest level of proficiency (Boesch, 1993, p. 174; Matsuzawa, 1996, p. 199). Many factors contribute to learning tool use by chimpanzees. Shaping by the physical nature of the task, as indicated earlier in this chapter, is clearly involved. Imitation of the mother performing the task (see Chapter 5) also may be involved. In addition, maternal prompting may be a factor (Boesch, 1991). For example, when a juvenile is applying the hammer-and-anvil method of cracking nuts, a mother may effectively position the nut on the anvil or the hammer in the juvenile's hand. Reports of such teaching behavior are rare, however. In addition, it should be noted that they are explainable by conditioned reinforcement rather than as deliberate attempts to teach. Having been paired with effective cracking of nuts, the appropriate positions of the nut and the hammer are conditioned reinforcers for the mother. In addition, the effective cracking of nuts by juveniles could be a conditioned reinforcer for the mother. Over a period of years an experienced mother might receive many trials in which some behavior leads to this and other behavior does not. To the human observer the behavior that leads to this may incorrectly appear to be deliberate teaching. A human adult may also guide or correct a child because this produces immediate reinforcement for the adult rather than as a direct attempt to teach, even though it may indirectly do so.

Because humans have language, however, they can plan to teach. There is evidence of deliberate teaching of tool use in human societies as far back as the last part of the stone age. The pattern of debris found around some prehistoric hearths indicate that 11,000 or more years ago novices sat around experts who demonstrated the technique of chipping blades and hand axes from chunks of flint (Fisher, 1990; Pigeot, 1990). We discuss human language and its role in teaching in the next chapter.

AUXILIARY BEHAVIOR

The categories of behavior that we considered in the previous sections must exist in order for animals to survive and perpetuate their genetic material. In this section we consider two classes of behavior that are not essential to survival and gene perpetuation, although they may tend to promote them.

Social Bonding

Certain behavior of members of social species must be reinforcing to other members. At least some of this reinforcement is genetically determined. This primary social reinforcement, along with conditioned reinforcement developed from it, affects the learning of much of the behavior necessary for social animals to function effectively within their groups.

Bonding behavior.   There are several types of reinforcing behavior that animals in social groups emit that act as "social glue"—that is, that tend to bind the group members together.

Social-contact touching. Members of the biological family Felidae—which includes lions, tigers, jaguars, and wild and domestic cats—touch members of their social group with their heads or rub up against them as reinforcing social acts (Joubert & Joubert, 1992; Schaller, 1972, pp. 85–88). Primates groom each other, which is an activity that seems to be more important for establishing and maintaining social bonds than for getting rid of parasites (Carpenter, 1942; Marler, 1965; Hinde, 1976a, b). That grooming serves a social function in primates is indicated by the fact that, especially among Old World monkeys and apes, there is a positive correlation between the amount of time spent in social grooming and group size (Dunbar, 1991).

Although less well studied in non-mammalian species, social-contact touching also occurs in some birds. Fledgling budgerigars (*Melopsitticus undulatus*), for example, engage in social contact by mutual preening and beak tussling (Stamps et al., 1990).

Social-contact vocalizing. Another type of behavior that seems to act as social glue is social-contact vocalizing—that is, vocalizing that maintains social contact between members of a group. For example, vervet monkeys engage in vocal interchanges in which one individual emits a grunt and another individual emits a similar grunt (Cheney & Seyfarth, 1990, pp. 126–127). Pygmy marmosets emit "trills" while foraging for insects, and these vocalizations alternate among animals in a manner that resembles the way humans take turns speaking when engaged in conversation (Snowden & Cleveland, 1984). Likewise, gelda monkeys exchange vocalizations in a way that resembles the rhythmic and melodic patterns of human speech (Richman, 1978, 1987). Unlike alarm calls, these social-contact vocalizations appear to be meaningless, at least with regard to anything that can be described as "communication of information." It is thus possible that they have no referential function and merely serve to maintain social bonds that keep the group together.

Vocalizing as social-bonding behavior has at least three advantages over grooming. First, whereas social grooming requires animals to be in close proximity, social vocalizing does not. Thus, vocalizing can keep individuals in social contact and maintain social bonds even when the animals are far apart or separated by obstacles that block their view of each other. Second, while an animal generally can groom only one other animal at time, vocalizations can be heard by many animals at once. Third, while animals that are grooming cannot be engaged in other manipulative activities, vocalizing imposes no such restriction.

The above advantages may have been particularly important in the evolution of human language. By relying more on vocalizations than grooming to develop and maintain social bonds, animals leading up to humans could have larger social groups (Dunbar, 1993), could keep in social contact through obstacles and at a distance, and could maintain social contact while using their hands for other activities. We will consider this further in the next chapter.

Selective bonding. In large groups it may be difficult for an animal to spend a great deal of time interacting with more than one other specific individual. This may make it difficult for strong mutually reinforcing bonds to form between more than two individuals. This may explain the fact that social mammals (Bekoff, 1981; Colvin, 1983; Stevenson & Poole, 1982) and birds (Rogers & McCulloch, 1981; Stamps et al., 1990) in large groups tend to form social attachments with only one partner. This is also true of human children. In small groups children tend to interact with all group members (Hartup & Rubin, 1986).

Exploration and Play

Although exploration and play have been defined in various ways, we use these terms here to refer to behavior that is reinforced by stimulus change (Baldwin & Baldwin, 1977). Exploration tends to be reinforced more by novel stimulus change and is generally less vigorous than play. In addition, play often has components of behavior that belong to other categories but are out of sequence or exaggerated (Burghardt, 1998). An example of exploration is an infant monkey looking at and manipulating ("inspecting" or "exploring") a leaf. An example of play is a kitten clawing a ball similar to the way in which cats attack prey. As suggested by these examples, exploration and play appear to be more prevalent in younger than in older animals (Chalmers, 1980), but do occur in the latter as well (Hall & Bradshaw, 1998). The play of older animals often tends to be slower and less vigorous than the play of younger animals (Symons, 1973).

It is important not to confuse "exploration" and "play" as we use these terms here with their use in everyday, nonscientific speech. In everyday speech these words tend to imply highly symbolic activity characteristic of language. For example, "exploration" in everyday speech commonly refers to obtaining information that one puts in a symbolic or verbal form (e.g., a map) about some aspect of the environment. "Play" in everyday speech commonly refers to engaging in certain activities that are governed by verbally expressed rules. Generating or conveying information or rules, however, is verbal behavior that animals (with the possible exception of specially trained ones such as discussed in Chapter 9) do not possess. We therefore should avoid the anthropomorphic error of identifying animal exploration and play with their highly verbal human counterparts. We also should be careful not to confuse exploration and play, as defined here, with behavior whose ultimate reinforcement depends on something other than stimulus change. For example, an animal may learn to search because this behavior has been reinforced with finding food or some other reinforcer, but this is not exploration as we define it here. Similarly, an animal may be taught with food reinforcement to engage in behavior resembling a human game (e.g., tic-tac-toe or Ping-Pong), but this does not count as play as we use that term here.

Probably all animals at a certain minimal level of complexity explore. A snake sampling substances in the air near it by flicking out its tongue, for example, is exploring its chemical environment (Chiszar et al., 1976). Newly hatched iguanas (*Iguana iguana*) explore by walking up to and touching objects (particularly novel ones) with their tongues (Burghardt, 1984, p. 10; Burghardt, Green, & Rand, 1977; Drummond & Burghardt, 1982). Animals that play, however, are much less common. Some octopuses may play by directing streams of water through their funnels at small objects (Mather & Anderson, 1999), and some turtles may play by manipulating novel objects (Burghardt, Ward, & Rosscoe, 1996). Play has been convincingly reported, however, in only some species of birds and mammals (Burghardt, 1998). In birds play is perhaps most common among species in the genus *Corvus* (Ficken, 1977), which includes ravens and crows. In mammals it is most common among carnivores and primates (Glickman & Sroges, 1966; Welker, 1971). It should be emphasized, however, that play is subject to interpretation and, therefore, very difficult to distinguish from other categories of behavior.

Following we distinguish two broad types of play: nonsocial and social.

Nonsocial play. Nonsocial play includes interacting with objects (manipulating them, climbing on them) and making movements that have no apparent function but appear to be reinforcing in themselves.

Birds. Some examples of nonsocial play in birds are:

- A common raven, carrion crow (*Corvus corone*), or rook (*Corvus frugilegus*) hangs upside down on an electric wire, falls forward, and lets go first with one foot and then the other (Gwinner, 1966).
- A raven hangs upside down on an electric wire and switches a piece of food from the beak to the foot and back again repeatedly (Gwinner, 1966).
- A young garden warbler (*Sylvia borin*) picks up and drops small stones, and listens for the sound of each stone as it strikes something on the ground (Sauer, 1956).
- Some common eiders (*Somateria mollissima*) ride down rapids and return to the starting point to repeat the activity (Roberts, 1934).
- An Anna's hummingbird (*Calypte anna*) repeatedly floats down a stream of water from a hose (Stoner, 1947).
- Some Adélie penguins (*Pygoscelis adeliae*) ride on small ice floes and return to the starting point to repeat the activity (A. L. Thompson, 1964, p. 636).
- A frigate bird picks up and drops leaves and other objects floating in the sea (A. L. Thompson, 1964, p. 636).
- A hawk or eagle carries a piece of wood with its feet and repeatedly drops and catches it (Chisholm, 1958).
- A young song sparrow makes short flights with sudden turns, frequently dodging around trees, as though being chased although nothing is pursuing it (Nice, 1943).

Some singing by birds may also be a type of play (Ficken, 1977, p. 579). We saw in Chapter 2 that bird songs delineate the territories of different members of a species, attract sexual partners, and enable members of a flock and mates within a flock to locate each other. However, some birds—especially young ones—sometimes engage in rambling, unstructured vocalizations (called subsongs) that have no clear immediate function and therefore may fit the definition of play.

Mammals. Mammals appear to show less nonsocial play than birds do. Some possible examples of nonsocial play in mammals are:

- A rat (*Rattus norvegicus*) runs, jumps, and shakes its head (Wilson & Kleiman, 1974).
- A house mouse (*Mus musculus*) runs as though being chased even though it is not (Wilson & Kleiman, 1974).
- A brown bear (*Ursus arctos*) cub chases birds (Bennett, 1982). However, this might also be an unsuccessful attack.

At least several troops of Japanese macaque monkeys (*Macaca fuscata*) engage in an interesting type of play: They manipulate stones (Huffman, 1984, 1996). In a troop at the Iwatayama Natural Park in Arashiyama, Kyoto, stone handling apparently began when one member of the troop initiated it sometime around 1979. Later, other members of the troop also began handling stones. Frequently a member of the troop will snatch a stone from a member who was handling it, or pick up a stone that another member has discarded, even though similar stones are readily available.

Unlike the case with birds, there is little or no evidence that mammals engage in acoustic play such as dropping objects to hear the sound when they hit the ground or emitting vocalizations that have no clear function. Humans are an exception to this statement, in that they clearly make a variety of sounds that appear to be reinforcing by themselves (i.e., primary reinforcers). Making music, for example, may be a form of auditory play.

Social play. Social play involves two or more individuals (usually but not necessarily of the same species) playing together in a reciprocal manner. The fact that the behavior is reciprocal is an important distinction. For example, a major way in which play chasing and attacking differs from real chasing and attacking is that the role of the chaser or attacker alternates fairly rapidly between participants (Hole & Einon, 1984, p. 105).

Birds. Birds show much less social play than mammals do. There are, however, some examples of social play in birds, such as:

- Two young African white-necked ravens (*Corvus albicollis*) alternate wresting a small object (such as a twig or lump of dung) from each other. Occasionally the bird with the object throws it to the other (Moreau & Moreau, 1944).
- A common raven (*Corvus corax*) and a dog alternate chasing each other around a tree (Thorpe, 1966).
- A white-winged chough (*Corcorax melanorhamphos*) picks up a small stone and resists others attempting to take it away from him (Chisholm, 1958).

Mammals. With mammals there are generally specific visual, auditory, tactile, or olfactory responses signaling that the behavior occurring is play. For example, many mammals when playing hold their mouths open in an expression called play face (Fagen, 1981, p. 164).

Almost everyone has witnessed, and probably even participated in, many examples of social play with carnivore pets such as cats and dogs. Some other examples of social play in mammals are:

- Two young rats wrestle with exaggerated movements and inhibited biting (Small, 1899).
- Two caribou calves run together over rugged terrain (Müller-Schwarze, 1984, p. 149).
- Two chimpanzees interact in a behavior sequence that includes tickling, wrestling, biting, hitting, pushing, chasing, making certain facial expressions (called "play-face") characteristic of play, and laughing (Merrick, 1977).

Evolutionary basis of exploration and play. Exploration appears to have two functions:

- It brings individuals into contact with biologically significant stimuli. Through exploration an individual may encounter aversive stimuli that it can then escape prior to some impending harmful event.
- It develops behavior that later may be conditioned by a more powerful primary reinforcer. A response that has been reinforced by stimulus change will condition more quickly when the reinforcer is food, water, or sex than a response that has never been reinforced.

Exploration also has disadvantages: "Curiosity killed the cat" is not an idle saying. Through exploration an animal may expose itself to attack by a predator or an increased risk of accidental injury. However, over the long span of evolution, the advantages apparently outweighed the disadvantages.

Play also has its disadvantages; for example, young vervet monkeys playing in groups away from adults are susceptible to being killed and eaten by baboons (Campbell, 1996, pp. 1184–1185). The advantages of play are less clear. Three possibilities are that it provides exercise, it provides practice and reinforcement of behavior that does have immediate survival value, and social play might contribute to social bonding. It has been surprisingly difficult to demonstrate any benefits of play. For example, movements that occur in play show very little further improvement after their first few occurrences (Campbell, 1996, p. 1185). Neither object play nor social play by kittens and by young coyotes (*Canis latrans*) appear to strongly affect these animals' later predatory behavior (Caro, 1979, 1980b, 1981; Vincent & Bekoff, 1978). Populations of mountain sheep (*Ovis canadensis*) that are not playful have the same locomotor and social skills as more playful populations (Berger, 1979). Moreover, squirrel monkeys (*Saimiri sciureus*) and vervet monkeys (*Cercopithecus aethiops*) that have no opportunity to engage in social play when young develop social behavior that differs little from, and seems just as effective as, the social behavior of conspecifics that did play when young (Baldwin & Baldwin, 1973, 1974; Lee, 1981). In general, animals that have not played much as infants and juveniles show no obvious impairments relative to conspecifics that have played a great deal. In addition, there is at least one striking example of a species for which early social play occurs without later social benefit. Polecats engage in a great deal of social play as infants and juveniles even though they are solitary and hence nonsocial as adults (Poole, 1966).

Moreover, if play is practice it should closely resemble effective behavior in later situations, but this does not seem to be the case. For example, play fighting is so different from real fighting that it is difficult to see how it could provide much practice for real fighting (Bekoff, 1977; Eibl-Eibesfeldt, 1975).

The fact that play is not very widespread indicates that it may not be very important for survival. While some species exhibit a lot of play, most appear to engage in little or none. The amount of their total time budget that most mammals spend playing has been estimated to range between 1% and 10% with more species being closer to the former than the latter (Fagen, 1981, p. 273). Even closely related species differ greatly in the degree to which they play. Chimpanzees, for example, tend to be very playful (Merrick, 1977) whereas gorillas are not (Schaller, 1963). As another example, two species of lemurs have quite different play patterns. While their troop rests from foraging, *Lemur catta* infants regularly form playgroups in which they mainly chase and wrestle. Juveniles soon join in the play, and adults also sometimes join in for brief periods. In *Lemur fuvus*, however, playgroups do not form regularly (Sussman, 1977). Other primates that show little or no social play are squirrel monkeys, orangutans (*Pongo*), tamarins (*Sauinus*), night monkeys (*Aotus*), aye-ayes (*Daubentonia*), Nilgiri langurs (*Presbytis*), and howling monkeys (*Alouatta palliata*) (MacKinnon, 1971; Moynihan, 1964, 1970; Petter & Petter, 1967; Poirier, 1972; Richard, 1970). Thus, despite their close relatedness to humans, many primates show little or no play. Even within species that do play there is considerable individual variation in the amount of play engaged in (Clark, 1977, p. 253).

Another indication that play may not have much survival value is that it appears to be weak relative to other reinforcers. Animals for which food is in short supply, for example, do not spend much time playing (Baldwin & Baldwin, 1973, 1974, 1976; Fagen, 1981, p. 370).

It may be that play does not have a single function; it may in fact have different functions for different species and different types of play. Back-and-forth running play, for example, may facilitate an animal's learning to traverse its territory (Stamps, 1995). In some cases play may have no survival value at all, but rather be a by-product of behavior that does have survival value. For example, the fact that batting an inanimate moveable object such as a ball is reinforcing to a cat may simply be a by-product of the fact that attacking prey is reinforcing.

Some forms of play may also be by-products of processes discussed earlier in this book. For example, the spread of stone handling by a troop of Japanese macaque monkeys mentioned above may be a case of stimulus enhancement, as described in Chapter 5. That is, through stimulus enhancement, observing others interacting with stones enhanced them as reinforcers. Although stone handling does not have survival value among these monkeys, stimulus enhancement does. Of course, at a later stage in evolution stone handling could lead to tool use, which clearly has survival value, but this cannot explain its origin (Huffman & Quiatt, 1986).

SUMMARY AND CONCLUSIONS

The principles of learning described in this book evolved because the genetic material of animals whose behavior was modifiable according to those principles tended to be propagated. Moreover, the tendency for certain kinds of events to be stimuli for a given organism, and for certain of those stimuli to be unconditioned stimuli and primary reinforcers, evolved to serve a number of behavioral functions analogous to the way in which organ systems evolved to serve physiological functions.

Some of these behavioral functions are essential to the survival of an organism at least long enough to perpetuate its genetic material, and to the perpetuation of that genetic material. The social functions, although not essential in the above sense, evolved because other members of an animal's species potentially aid that animal in carrying out its essential functions. It has evolved to be reinforcing for them to do so because of the principle of inclusive fitness, that states that an animal will tend to perpetuate the genetic material of its close relatives due to the similarity between its genetic material and theirs. Exploration has evolved because conditioning that occurs during exploration may frequently turn out to be useful to survival (although too much exploration may have the opposite effect). The evolutionary reasons for play are more difficult to understand. Most instances of behavior that we label as "play" may be by-products of processes that have survival value.

The essential functions include obtaining food and water, defending against predators and competitors, producing vigorous progeny, and providing for the care of that progeny. Social functions include activities that keep members of a group in close contact, such as social grooming and vocalizing. In humans these functions evolved into the capacity for language to develop through operant conditioning.

17

Humans in Social Environments

Many of the points made in the previous chapter apply to humans as well as to other animals. In this chapter, however, we focus on how the learning principles and phenomena discussed in this book apply to behavior that is uniquely human—if not in type, at least in the extent to which humans exhibit it.

- Humans engage in complex social interactions in which verbal behavior plays a critical role. Moreover, verbal behavior is highly varied. The form it takes differs considerably from one region to another (e.g., Chinese is quite different from English). In addition, the medium in which it occurs differs within and across cultures. While the larynx and respiratory tract are usually involved, verbal behavior can occur by means of other physical movements (e.g., gestures, sign language) and manipulations of the physical environment (e.g., smoke signals, beating on drums, writing). In fact, any operant response that humans can make, or any effect they can have on their environment, can be verbal. (We shall see why this is the case when a definition of verbal behavior is presented later in this chapter.)
- Humans make and use wide variety of tools and other functional objects. They have made functional objects for getting food (e.g., spears, sickles, plows), for carrying water (e.g., jugs, buckets), for defending against predators and enemies (e.g., spears, swords, guns), for protection from the physical environment (e.g., clothing, houses), for facilitating child care (e.g., cribs, baby carriages), for transportation (e.g., boats, carriages, cars), for entertainment (e.g., musical instruments, board games, movies), for measurement (e.g., rulers, clocks, thermometers), and even for making other functional objects (e.g., axes, hammers, needles). No other animal begins to approach the inventiveness of humans in this regard.
- Humans devote a great deal of time to activities that appear not to be directly related to survival and reproduction. They spend much time, for example, observing animate and inanimate aspects of their environment, playing games, conversing, telling stories, creating art, and performing and listening to music.
- Humans adapt readily to a wide variety of situations and environments. Thriving human societies can be found in almost all regions and climates, from tropical rain forests to arid deserts and frozen tundra. Humans learn a variety of different tasks and jobs

within their respective cultures. In addition, humans from any culture can—and often do—learn the language and customs of another.

GENETIC FACTORS ACCOUNTING FOR DISTINCTIVE HUMAN BEHAVIOR

The behavioral characteristics that distinguish humans are so striking that it is tempting to assume that there must be vast genetic differences between humans and other species. This, however, is not the case. As mentioned in Chapter 1, there is about 2% difference between the genetic code of humans and that of chimpanzees (Caccone & Powell, 1989; Goodman et al., 1990; Kim & Takenaka, 1996; Sibley et al., 1990), which is small relative to that which exists between many other closely related species. This not only shows how closely related humans and chimpanzees are, but—more to our present purpose—it indicates that the portion of genetically determined human characteristics that are uniquely human is not large. Some of this genetic difference must include unique primary reinforcers that are necessary to human survival and reproduction, such as specific types of food that are especially nutritious to humans and specific types of individuals (i.e., humans of the opposite sex) with whom reproduction is possible. Much of it also includes distinctive physical characteristics.

One of these distinctive physical characteristics is a pelvic structure in humans that facilitates upright walking (Jablonski & Chaplin, 1993), as illustrated in Figure 17.1. This upright stance allowed the hands to be free, permitted humans to evolve a morphological feature (e.g., an opposable thumb) suited for the precise grips employed in human tool use (Marzke, 1997).

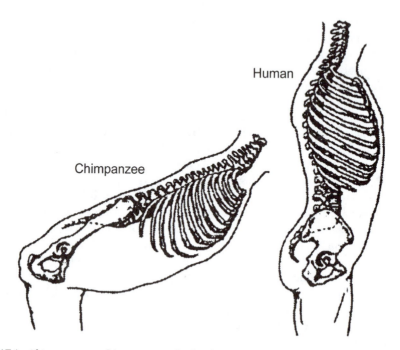

FIGURE 17.1. Chimpanzee and human vertebral column and pelvis. Note that the human vertebral column and pelvis support upright walking, freeing the hands for other tasks (e.g., carrying, tool use). (From Schultz, 1968)

Another important distinctive human physical characteristic is a vocal apparatus capable of producing all the sounds of every language (Lieberman, Laitman, Reidenberg, & Gaunon, 1992). A critical difference between the chimpanzee and human vocal apparatus is illustrated in Figure 17.2. Note from this figure that the chimpanzee epiglottis (a trap-door-like structure) closes securely over the opening of the trachea (by making contact with the velum) whenever the animal swallows. This serves a very important evolutionary function: it prevents the animal from choking on its food or drink. It also makes it impossible for the animal to inhale or exhale through its mouth, thus restricting its vocalizing primarily to nasal vowel sounds. The human larynx (voice box) has descended, however, so that the epiglottis permits air to pass between the lungs and mouth, thereby increasing the risk of food or drink entering the trachea but permitting exhaled air to vibrate the vocal cords and exit through the mouth. This, along with other modifications, such as increased muscular control over the vocal cords and changes in the tongue, teeth, lips, and so forth, enables humans to make a huge variety of vocal sounds. Evidently the evolutionary benefits that these modifications provided in the form of enhanced communication within a social group offset the increased danger of choking.

Along with the evolution of the above distinctive human physical characteristics was a huge enlargement of certain brain areas. There is no known neural structure in the brains of humans that does not also exist in the brains of monkeys and apes (Gibson, 1996; Holloway, 1996). However, the sizes of the structures, relative to each other and relative to overall body size differ. Figure 17.3 compares the gross structure of the brains of several mammals relative to body size, including the chimpanzee and human. Note that the chimpanzee brain is quite large in comparison to those of the other nonhuman mammals (including another primate) and that the human brain is quite large in comparison to the chimpanzee brain. The region known as the prefrontal cortex is especially large in humans and may be largely responsible for the development of language (Deacon, 1997), although very little is yet known about what brain areas are involved in language (Pulvermüller, 1999).

Looking at the preceding list of uniquely human behavioral characteristics, two major themes seem to run through them: language, and a large capacity for learning. It is unlikely that what is uniquely human could involve any new learning principles, however, since it represents such a small percentage of the genetic difference between humans and the species most closely related to humans. This indicates that the uniquely human behavioral characteristics listed at the beginning of this chapter are largely (if not entirely) due to factors such as

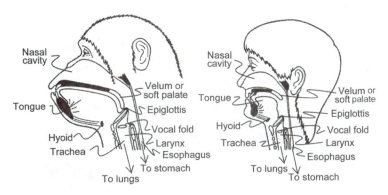

FIGURE 17.2. Chimpanzee and human vocal apparatus. The chimpanzee's epiglottis completely closes off any connection between the mouth and lungs, whereas the human's permits such a connection. This greatly increases the human's range of vocalizations. (From Bradshaw & Rogers, 1993)

changes in the human vocal tract that make speech possible and, perhaps, some quantitative increase in learning capacity (e.g., with regard to the number of different responses to different stimuli and the length of stimulus-response chains that humans can learn). It follows that only learning principles that apply to other animals need to be posited to account for uniquely human behavior. The burden of this chapter is to suggest how this can be possible.

LINGUAL BEHAVIOR

Perhaps the most obvious behavioral characteristic of humans is an enormous propensity to learn and use language, for language is involved in all other uniquely human behavior and may be what makes other uniquely human behavior possible. In this section we consider how the principles of learning discussed in earlier chapters apply to learning to speak and respond to a human language. To do this, however, we need a few definitions. Verbal behavior is defined as behavior that is reinforced through the mediation of other persons and that has no other appreciable effect on the environment (Skinner, 1957a, p. 14).

For example, the utterance "a glass of water please" (as typically emitted by a water-deprived English speaker) is verbal behavior because it has been reinforced by someone giving the individual water, and has no appreciable effect on the environment other than causing someone to get the individual a glass of water. The stimulus "Thank you" said by the person receiving the water reinforces the behavior of getting water for someone. However, although reinforced through the mediation of another person, getting someone a glass of water is not verbal behavior because it has an appreciable effect on the environment (Skinner, 1972). Note that according to the above definition, verbal behavior does not have to be vocal. For example, signaling a bid at an auction meets the definition.

We define a speaker as a person emitting verbal behavior, and a listener as a person reinforcing verbal behavior. Thus, someone saying "I'm hungry" is a speaker and someone

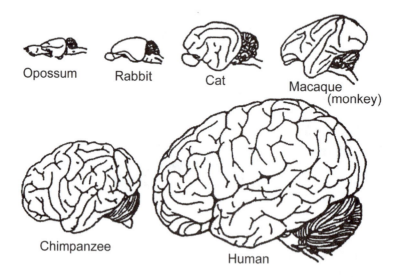

FIGURE 17.3. Brains of several different mammals drawn on the same scale. Note the differences in the cerebrum (the large creased area) and, to a lesser extent, the cerebellum (the smaller structure in back of or just below the cerebrum). (From Eccles, 1989)

responding by giving the speaker food (primary reinforcement) or simply with other verbal behavior such as "we'll eat soon" (conditioned reinforcement) is a listener.

Finally, we will use the term lingual behavior to refer to the behavior of either a speaker or a listener. Thus, for example, someone asking for a glass of water is engaging in verbal behavior and is a speaker. The person who responds to the stimulus "May I have a glass of water, please" by getting a glass of water is a listener but not a speaker and is not engaging in verbal behavior (unless he or she says something such as, "Here's your water"). Both of these individuals would, however, be engaging in lingual behavior.

Origins of Lingual Behavior

Many animals communicate vocally. Nonhuman primates even make distinct sounds that correspond to significant aspects of their environments. For example, as mentioned in the previous chapter, vervet monkeys emit different grunts corresponding to a leopard, an eagle, and a snake. Animals also emit sounds that indicate dominance or submissiveness, and their emotional state—that is, whether they are likely to attack or not. It appears likely, however, that the human capacity for lingual behavior evolved more from social-contact vocalizations than from other types of vocalizations (although these could have contributed to some extent to its evolution). The reason is that social-contact vocalizations, as mentioned in the previous chapter, appear simply to have the function of establishing and maintaining social bonds within a group by making and keeping members of the group conditioned reinforcers for each other. Not already controlling specific behavior in a listener, these vocalizations could be readily modified by operant conditioning—a necessary property of language, as we shall see later in this chapter—without compromising the function that originally resulted in their evolution. For an intuitive understanding of social-contact vocalizations, note that they correspond roughly to standard human expressions that have more of a reinforcing function than an informational one—for example, "I like you," "I love you," "You're my friend," "Hello," "How are you?," "Nice weather," "Have a nice day." Anyone who stopped uttering these expressions would rather quickly lose most (if not all) of his or her conditioned reinforcing value for those close to him or her.

It is not possible to say exactly how social-contact vocalizations gave rise to language capacity. Perhaps as primitive hominids began to walk upright and use their hands more, social-contact vocalizations came to facilitate cooperative tasks. For example, we can imagine scenarios such as the following: A hominid dragging a carcass into camp might emit a particular social vocalization grunt that was, perhaps, modulated by the heaviness of the burden. Helping behavior by other hominids in the presence of those grunts, who perhaps came on the scene by chance or by way of greeting the returning hominid, would be reinforced when the carcass was brought into camp. The grunts of the hominid who discovered the carcass would be reinforced by the assistance of the others in bringing the carcass into camp. The next time that hominid was in a situation in which help would be reinforcing, it likely would grunt in a similar way, and those whose helping behavior had been reinforced in the presence of those grunts likely would go toward them and help with the task at hand. Loosely translated, a particular type of grunt had come to mean, "I need some help." Soon others in the group would learn to emit that grunt when they needed help as well, because there would be a number of individuals in the group who had learned to come running when they heard it.

Suppose now that a hominid that had learned the grunt meaning "I need some help" emitted it while chasing a rabbit into camp. Those hominids who ran in the direction of the grunt likely would have missed the rabbit as it ran past them, which could have led to some extinction of the grunt in this type of situation. The next time that hominid was chasing an animal into camp, therefore, it might emit a variation of the grunt. Those hominids who came running upon hearing this new grunt likely would have missed the animal, whereas some of those who looked up alertly would have had a better chance of catching it. The former behavior in the presence of the new grunt therefore would extinguish whereas the latter would be strengthened and maintained by the group members. The members would then, through their behavior of looking up alertly, reinforce the new grunt in any of their members who was chasing a small animal into camp. At the same time, through their behavior of assisting with a heavy load, they would continue to reinforce the old grunt in any of the members who had found a carcass outside the camp.

In a manner such as the above, early hominids began emitting more and more different sounds corresponding to different situations and aspects of their environments. This process had survival value for these early hominids—since it enabled them to respond more effectively to their environments. Hence there was a selection pressure on the structure of the hominid vocal apparatus to increase the varieties of sounds it could produce despite the negative selection pressure of an increased risk of choking (see Fig. 17.2). Natural selection thus interacted with the increasing variety of hominid vocalizations to produce further increases in the variety of sounds humans could make. A corresponding increase in brain size (see Fig. 17.3) occurred to facilitate the use of these sounds in communication, as well as to facilitate complex manipulations made possible by upright walking (see Fig. 17.1) and the development of the hands.

The mechanisms by which humans acquire verbal behavior also were refined and developed by natural selection. Infant babbling and the shaping of it into speech through reinforcement by adults are important parts of this process. Another important part of the process is automatic reinforcement of certain vocalizations. Certain vocal sounds are reinforcing to an infant because they have been paired with adults and the reinforcers adults provide. Reinforcement of vocal behavior that generates these speech sounds (or approximations to them) therefore occurs automatically; that is, it does not require the immediate presence of an adult (Smith et al., 1995; Sundberg et al., 1995). (See the discussion of copying in Chapter 5, pp. 97 and 99.)

It was once believed that human infants spontaneously babble all the sounds in every human language (Jakobson, 1968), but this is not the case. Human infants babble only a few repetitive sounds such as "bababa" and "mamama" (Davis & MacNeilage, 1995; MacNeilage, 1998, pp. 227–228). Moreover, it appears that the speech sounds that children hear have an effect on their babbling. This is indicated by the fact that, while infants normally begin babbling on at about seven months of age, hearing-impaired children begin babbling on average several months later and their babbling clearly is abnormal (Eilers & Oller, 1994). Although babbling does not consist of the variety of sounds it was once thought to do, it is important in providing responses that can be shaped into speech sounds. Some of this shaping occurs when an infant receives conditioned reinforcement from sounds that approximate vocalizations the infant has heard adults make. Other vocal shaping occurs when adults reinforce successively closer approximations to speech sounds (e.g., "ma ma," "mommy," "mother").

As the variety of vocal sounds hominids made increased and the reinforcement mechanisms for shaping those sounds into speech developed, the complexity of hominid lingual behavior correspondingly increased. Finally, modern humans emerged along with their propensity to produce highly complex languages that have characterized all cultures throughout history.

A Classification Scheme for Verbal Behavior

The idea that humans learn verbal behavior in the same way that they learn other behavior is not universally accepted. Instead, some popular theories suggest that merely hearing speech is all that is necessary for children to learn to speak (Chomsky, 1986; Pinker, 1994a). There is some evidence, however, that humans must emit vocal responses and have them reinforced in order to learn to speak. Specifically, it appears that infants who (due to a surgical procedure done for medical reasons) are temporarily prevented from vocalizing during the period that babbling and early speech occur may require at least several months to develop normal speech after they are physically able to speak (Locke & Pearson, 1990; Simon, Fowler, & Handler, 1983).

The complexity of verbal behavior, however, makes it difficult to understand how it is developed and maintained through operant conditioning. The following covers the highlights of a classification scheme Skinner (1957a) developed that aids in elucidating this.

Mand: a verbal response that is under the control of a specific type of reinforcement. For example, responses such as "wa wa" and "Please give me some water" emitted when water deprived typically are under the control of water reinforcement, and thus are mands.

Echoic: a verbal response under the control of an auditory stimulus to which it bears a point-to-point physical similarity. Echoics are reinforced by stimuli, called generalized conditioned reinforcers, that have been paired with a variety of primary reinforcers. An example of an echoic would be a child saying "ma ma" in response to a parent saying "Say 'ma ma,'" who then reinforced the child's response with "Good!," "That's right!," or "Yes!" As this example suggests, echoics are shaped from the initial babbling of infants. Once some echoics have been established in a person's verbal repertoire, they can facilitate teaching mands and other verbal responses. It should be noted that the production of verbal responses is not automatic; it requires a history of emitting vocalizations some of which are reinforced and others are not.

Tact: a verbal response under the control of a nonverbal environmental stimulus and reinforced by a generalized conditioned reinforcer. An example would be "doggie" said by a child in the presence of a dog and reinforced by an adult saying "Yes, that's right!" Echoics are generally used in teaching tacts. For example, when teaching the tact "doggie," a parent may say "That's a doggie, say 'doggie' and reinforce the response "doggie" with "Good!" Often parents add some echoic training when reinforcing the response, such as by saying "That's right, doggie!" The child is said to have learned "doggie" as a tact if, in the absence of the verbal stimulus "doggie," the child emits the response consistently when a dog or a picture of one is present.

Autoclitic: a verbal response under the control of the speaker's other verbal behavior, and that is reinforced by modifications one makes to the listener's responses to that other verbal behavior. Autoclitics are escape or avoidance responses, in that they are reinforced by the termination or prevention of stimuli produced by the listener responding in a nonreinforcing or punishing manner to the speaker's verbal behavior. An example of an autoclitic emitted by a young child might be "red one" in the utterance "Give truck, red one." The first part of this utterance is a mand that had been reinforced in the past by the specified item (a toy truck in this example), but now there is more than one toy truck present and the child prefers the red one. Hence "red one" was emitted after the initial mand ("Give truck") because it modified the response of the listener, who might otherwise have given the child the less preferred truck (and may even have started to do so just before the autoclitic was emitted).

Intraverbal: a verbal response that is analogous to a tact, except that the S^D controlling it is verbal. For example, when one person asks another to repeat an utterance ("What did you say?"), the subsequent verbal behavior is under the control of the prior utterance. It is an intraverbal. Within-utterance intraverbals also occur. To see a quick example, complete the following: "Fit as a _____." Many people will respond with "fiddle" because of its frequent occurrence following the first part of the phrase in their verbal community. The "f" sound in the response "fiddle" could also be an echoic because it is the same as that in "fit," but the "iddle" is an intraverbal.

378 EXTENSIONS TO NATURAL SETTINGS

The form of a verbal response does not tell us what type it is, because several different types of verbal responses can have exactly the same form. To see this, note that "wa wa" is: (1) a mand if emitted by a water-deprived child as a result of that response having been reinforced with water when the child was water-deprived in the past; (2) an echoic if emitted by a water-satiated child in the presence of the verbal stimulus "Say 'wa wa'" as a result of that response of the child having been reinforced with "Good!" when someone said "Say 'wa wa'" in the past; and (3) a tact if emitted by a water-satiated child in the presence of some water as a result of that response having been reinforced with "Good!" when water was present in the past. That mands and tacts are distinct verbal classes is indicated by the fact that young developmentally delayed children taught to emit certain responses as mands (e.g., "I want a whole crayon please") do not emit them as tacts (e.g., "That is a whole crayon"), and vice versa, until trained to do so. Moreover, training a word in one function does not seem to facilitate learning it in the other (Twyman, 1995).

Manding and tacting are essentially the same as requesting and labeling, as discussed in Chapter 9; however, the terms mand and tact focus on the functional relation of the response to discriminative and reinforcing stimuli rather than on the form of the response (e.g., a response that has the usual form of a tact—such as "I'm hungry"—may be a mand). Note also that, as indicated in Chapter 9, manding and tacting (or requesting and labeling) as responses that are learned separately, even when their form is the same.

Advanced speakers weave autoclitics seamlessly into the fabric of their utterances, but the process is essentially the same as defined above. Examples of autoclitics in a fairly smooth-sounding utterance might be the words "me," "the," "red," and "please" in the utterance "Give me the red truck, please." Like the child in the previous example illustrating the definition, the speaker's initial tendency might have been to say "Give truck," but this blunt utterance is unlikely to be reinforced—and may be punished with puzzled looks, requests for clarification, or worse—if there is more than one person to give the truck to, if there are trucks of other colors present, if there is only one red truck present and there are other red trucks that the listener might get for the speaker, and if the listener only reinforces mands that the culture defines as "polite" or "respectful." Thus, the importance of autoclitics lies in the many ways in which an utterance that does not contain them may go unreinforced or even punished. Autoclitics are added to an utterance, and in the proper order (in fact, order itself is an autoclitic), very soon after the verbal responses that they accompany are instigated; and, in the case of advanced speakers, generally before those other verbal responses are emitted overtly.

Responses such as "no" and "not" that negate verbal behavior are frequently autoclitics. When negation occurs there generally is some prior tendency to affirm what is being negated. For example, one usually says "It is not raining" only if there is an initial tendency to say "It is raining"—perhaps, for example, because of having just seen a dark cloud in the sky. Responses that negate verbal behavior differ from other autoclitics in the extent to which the listener's response is modified (i.e., in the case of negation, it is modified to the greatest degree—i.e., close to the opposite of what it would have been without the autoclitic). This is why, as research has shown, utterances containing negation generally take more processing time (i.e., more time for a listener or reader to respond) than corresponding affirmative utterances (Clark & Chase, 1972).

Note that autoclitics give language its hierarchical structure. Consider, for example, a sentence such as "The woman in the blue dress got into the car." Clearly, such a sentence cannot be considered to be a stimulus-response chain (as discussed in Chapter 11) in which each word is the stimulus for the next word and the reinforcer for the previous word (unless, of course, the sentence is learned in that way as it might be in a song or a poem in another language). Instead, the sentence is probably produced in something like the following manner: first the fragment "woman got into car" comes into strength under appropriate stimulus conditions, followed by the modifier "the" in front of "woman" and "car," followed by "in blue dress," and finally the modifier "the" in front of "blue dress." The sentence may be emitted overtly only when it reaches its completed form, or some of the fragments may be emitted overtly before the completed form is in full strength (e.g., when the speaker is not very experienced in the language, or is in a rushed or excited state). Of course, it must be recognized that this is only one plausible path out of many others to the production of the complete sentence. (More on how syntax forms in utterances is given later in this chapter.)

Intraverbals are important in the formation of verbal units, which are segments of verbal behavior that can be regarded as single responses in that they are under the control of single environmental variables. Intraverbals may become so strongly bound together that they function as a verbal unit in this sense. For example, a given physician may never emit the word "fit" as a tact after examining a healthy patient without adding "as a fiddle," in which case "fit as a fiddle" probably is a verbal unit for this particular physician.

The parts of a verbal unit may have the same form as other types of verbal responses, but it would be incorrect to classify them in the same verbal category. For example, in the first emission of the expression "fit as a fiddle," "as a" and "fiddle" may have been autoclitics—with "fiddle" also being partly an "echoic" because of the similarity of its "f" sound with that of "fit," and also partly a tact that generalized from the similarity between a healthy patient and a well-playing fiddle—but these categories no longer apply to these words after the phrase "fit as a fiddle" has become a verbal unit. Instead, they then are simply elements in a tact for a healthy person.

Skinner's classification system is especially useful for relating verbal behavior to operant conditioning. There are also other classification systems. For example, one system (Talmy, 1985, 1988) divides language into two categories. One category includes members belonging to parts of speech (e.g., nouns and verbs) that correspond directly to objects and events. It is called "open class" because it readily admits new members. The other category is called "closed class" because it does not readily admit new members. It consists of items (e.g., "a," "the," the past tense ending "-ed," the plural ending "s," prepositions) that provide structure to language. Note that the latter category overlaps with the autoclitic in Skinner's system.

Lingual Processes

Verbal behavior that is emitted immediately as it is generated often is rambling, disjointed, bizarre, and difficult to understand. Because of this, verbal behavior usually is processed further after it is generated and before it is emitted overtly. After it is emitted overtly, it may then enter into further processes. The processes verbal behavior undergoes from the time it is generated, including processes produced in the listener, are considered below (for detailed theoretical treatments of the following topics, see Skinner, 1953, 1957a).

Composition.   As it is being generated or shortly thereafter, verbal behavior is organized in a way that is likely, on the basis of previous reinforcements, to be effective for the listener. During this organizational process, which is termed composition, verbal behavior takes on syntax—which, as explained in Chapter 9, is a structure that usually resembles, but is not to be confused with, the structure dictated by the formal grammatical rules of the language being spoken. (For example, the sentence "It is surprising how many different rules of grammar there are" has a syntactical structure that is very common in English although it is not grammatically correct according to the technical rules of English grammar.)

Although the syntaxes of different languages differ, a popular linguistic theory maintains that the human brain is programmed with a universal grammar that underlies the syntaxes of all languages (Chomsky, 1980, 1986). There are three major problems with this theory of a universal grammar. First, it is not apparent how it could have come about through a series of small evolutionary steps (Newmeyer, 1998). Second, it is not clear how connections or linkages are made between the hypothesized universal grammar and the syntax of a given language (Pinker, 1991, 1994b). Third, the existence of a universal grammar within each individual that automatically links up with the syntax of his or her native language suggests that each syntactical structure in a language should be learned rapidly with few or no intermediate steps. The evidence seems to suggest that this is not the case. Children learn syntax gradually, proceeding from simple structures to more complex ones. Early in development, a child may learn simple two word structures. One simple structure, for example, develops from instances such as the following: "See Maria," "See Daddy," "See this." Eventually, "See _____" becomes a syntactical frame (also called an autoclitic frame; Skinner, 1957, p. 336) into which the child inserts any tact for something or someone seen. Another type of structure may develop from instances such as the following: "Daddy's bread," "Daddy's ball," "Daddy's salad." Eventually, "Daddy's _____" becomes a frame into which the child inserts any tact for any object that belongs to her father. In addition, the child is able to build more complex utterances by combining basic frames. For example, as a result of learning the above two frames, upon seeing her father's car the child says "See Daddy's car" (Tomasello, 2000, pp. 243–244).

In addition to combining smaller frames into larger one, children learn components of larger utterances through imitation of adults. Examples of this can be seen from errors children make in their progress toward adult syntax. For example, a child may say "Her open it," or "She eat grapes." Such structures are probably learned initially from echoing components of adult utterances such as "Let her open it," "Help her open it," "Does she eat grapes?" (Tomasello, 2000, p. 240). When children emit these nonstandard speech forms, adults typically model and reinforce imitations of the acceptable forms.

It seems likely that processes discussed in previous chapters—for example, stimulus generalization, response generalization, equivalence class learning—are operating in the development of syntax. A great deal of research will be required to work out the details of exactly how these processes are involved, and what other processes may also be involved. It seems clear, however, that syntactical structures exist because listeners reinforce them by responding more effectively when they are present than when they are absent or malformed; syntax is the product of a social-interactive process (Skinner, 1957; Tomasello, 2000, p. 247).

Self-editing.   Experienced writers usually produce several drafts of a manuscript before writing the final version. Typically, no one but themselves sees the drafts before the final one. In a similar manner, a speaker may emit some verbal behavior covertly or privately, and then amend it prior to emitting it overtly or publicly. This process of self-editing often can be inferred when there is a lengthy pause during or just before the start of a speech episode. Self-editing typically is under aversive control, in that unedited verbal behavior tends to be punished for a variety of reasons—such as, it is unclear, it is incorrect, it is unflattering to someone hearing it, and it provides information that is detrimental to the speaker. Self-editing is common among adults in our culture, but it takes a long time to learn, which is why children are said to be open and frank.

Listener functions.   Since speakers are of no use to a society without listeners, societies condition and maintain listening behavior as well as verbal behavior. The distinction between speaker and listener functions is the same as that made in Chapter 9 between productive and receptive language, except that in using the terms speaker and listener we are focusing on the interactive nature of these two functions in a social context. We saw in Chapter 9 in teaching language to animals that productive and receptive language (i.e., speaker and listener functions) must be taught independently, and it likewise appears that speaker and listener functions develop independently in humans. An indication of this is the fact that children in the early stages of language learning are more likely to respond to commands uttered in syntactical structures that are well formed than to ones that are not, even when the well-formed structures are not ones that they themselves yet emit (Shipley, Smith, & Gleitman, 1969). Similarly, we saw in Chapter 9 that Kanzi, a language-trained chimpanzee, was able to respond to syntactical structures far more complex than ones he could emit.

The sophisticated discriminations listeners make can be illustrated by the problem, which has puzzled linguists, of how a sentence having exactly the same words in the same order can have two different meanings, and how a listener can learn to respond appropriately to the intended meaning. Consider, for example, the sentence, "They are eating apples." This sentence could mean that some individuals are eating apples; or, it could mean that some particular apples are good for eating. We can see how listeners can learn to respond appropriately to such sentences if we consider them as comparison stimuli in a conditional discrimination. Under one sample or setting condition (e.g., having been told that one's friends are hungry and having just asked if some apples a vendor is selling are good to eat) an appropriate response would be to buy some of the apples to take back to one's friends. Under another sample or setting condition)e.g., someone answering the question, "Should we take these apples back to our friends") the sentence would be an S^Δ for buying the apples to take back.

Self-talk.   All linguistically competent individuals within a given verbal community are both speakers and listeners. They can therefore alternate these functions within themselves, which means that each individual can talk to himself or herself. Typically done privately or covertly, this self-talk is at least part of what we mean by "thinking. Another important part of what we call "thinking" is visualization or imagery, as described in Chapter 1 and Chapter 6.

The fact that a speaker can be his or her own listener may seem to contradict the definition of verbal behavior given above. It should be noted, however, that the listeners who developed the individual's verbal behavior were necessarily external to the individual. Thus, the verbal behavior that the individual emits to him/herself was initially reinforced through the mediation of other people, even though such mediation may no longer be necessary to maintain the behavior. Thus, a linguistically competent individual stranded alone on a desert island might continue to engage in verbal behavior indefinitely. Even though no one else was present to reinforce the behavior, reinforcement would likely come from the aid that verbal behavior provides in solving problems and coping with the environment.

Self-talk and imagery may enable us to engage in highly complex behavior. They may be particularly useful in the invention of tools and other functional objects, since such inventions often appear in conjunction with long sequences of overt and covert self-talk. They may also give rise to the subjective feeling of self-awareness or consciousness.

Rule-governed behavior.   An extremely powerful aspect of verbal behavior is that it enables listeners to come under the control of contingencies to which they have not been directly exposed. This aspect of verbal behavior is captured by the distinction between contingency-shaped behavior and rule-governed behavior. The former is behavior that has developed under the control of a reinforcement contingency without the involvement of verbal stimuli whereas the later is behavior under the control of a verbal S^D which is called a rule. All instances described in this book of reinforcing behavior in animals—with the possible exception of some cases in which lingual behavior was taught to animals—are examples of contingency-shaped behavior. Pure examples of contingency-shaped behavior in humans are difficult to find because of the prevalence of verbal behavior in humans. One reasonably good example, however, would be learning to perform some skill with a ball (e.g., catching a baseball, hitting a golf or tennis ball) simply from the feedback received from the ball. The corresponding example of rule-governed behavior would be learning to perform the skill by following an instruction given by an expert.

While rule-governed behavior is clearly defined, several different ways to define a rule have been proposed. These definitions differ only in the source of the reinforcement contingent on following the rule. According to one definition (Baum, 1994), the reinforcement initially comes from the person stating the rule but ultimately comes from other sources in the environment. For example, a parent may give a child the rule "Eat your vegetables," and reinforce that behavior with praise; eventually, however, the natural consequences (e.g., better health) reinforce the behavior. Another definition (Zettle & Hayes, 1982) distinguishes between two types of rules:

- Ply: a rule for which the reinforcement mediated primarily by the person stating the rule (e.g., "Your money or your life," said by a mugger).
- Track: a rule for which the reinforcement comes from sources other than the person stating the rule (e.g., directions from a stranger on how to get to a particular location where reinforcement will occur).

All definitions agree, however, that a rule is a verbal S^D that specifies some behavior and that there is reinforcement (which also may be specified by the rule) contingent on engaging in the specified behavior.

It is important to note that rules are functionally defined. Just as the same mand may occur in many different forms, the same rule may occur in many different forms ("Eat your vegetables," "Vegetables are good for you"). It also is important to note that reinforcement for rule-following need not come from the rule giver and that rule-following need not necessarily come under control of ultimate contingencies. One follows the directions of strangers because people generally give valid directions and the behavior of following directions has generally been reinforced in the past. This is an example of long-term consequences reinforcing rule following. However, one may follow the rule to eat one's vegetables simply because that is reinforced by other people; the ultimate reinforcement (health or other advantages) may never come into play. The reasons for rule giving, however, are often traceable to the long-term consequences.

Rule-governed behavior often can be established much more quickly and efficiently than contingency-shaped behavior (which is one of the reasons that verbal behavior evolved). For example, through the shaping that occurred from gradual increments in heat output, some early humans learned that rapidly rubbing two dry sticks together produces fire. But it must have taken a long time for this natural contingency to take effect, and even then probably for only a few select humans with just the right kind of conditioning history. Upon hearing the rule, "Rapidly rubbing two dry sticks together produces fire," however, anyone who understands the language spoken does not have to undergo the same shaping process as the discoverer in order to make a fire by rubbing two dry sticks together.

Speakers supply rules to themselves as well as to other listeners. We repeat to ourselves maxims that we have heard (e.g., "The early bird catches the worm") and these self-statements may control our own behavior. We also repeat complex instructions, to ourselves, such as when practicing a complex skill that someone has taught us. We also say rules to ourselves that we ourselves have discovered (e.g., "I have to get up by seven-fifteen to catch the eight-thirty bus") and these self-statements may strengthen the control of certain contingencies over our behavior.

Although rule-governed behavior makes learning complex tasks more efficient, the rules become less important and the natural contingencies take over as one becomes more skilled at a task. An experienced driver, for example, is controlled more by the moment-to-moment feedback from the vehicle and the road than by the instructions that governed early driving.

Talking About Private Events

Several times in this book we assumed that people are able to describe their images, feelings, and other private events with some degree of accuracy. There should be no problem with conceptualizing these inner events as having the capacity to control verbal responses. These inner events are either internal stimuli or responses that produce internal stimuli, and should be able to control verbal behavior in the same way that external stimuli do. How we learn to describe private stimuli with a fair amount of agreement among speakers, however, requires explanation. We have seen that all verbal behavior is learned by reinforcement of appropriate responses from other members of one's verbal community. If other people have no access to a person's private events—which, by the definition of privacy, is the case—how can they consistently reinforce appropriate verbal responses to them? There appear to be four basic ways in which they do so (Skinner, 1945, 1957a).

- Publicly observable stimuli may accompany the private stimuli. For example, an adult sees a child fall and says, "Oh, that hurt!" When the child repeats "hurt," the adult reinforces the response. Later the child may say "hurt" in the presence of a private stimulus like the one that was present when the child's response "hurt" was reinforced.
- There may be publicly observable responses that accompany the private stimuli. For example, an adult sees a child smiling and says, "You look happy." When the child repeats "happy," the adult reinforces the response. Later the child may say "happy" in the presence of a private stimulus like the one that was present when the child's response "happy" was reinforced.
- A response that was originally public may have receded to the private level. For example, an adult hearing a child talking out loud to herself (as children often do) while solving a problem may say, "My but you are thinking hard!" When the child repeats "thinking," the adult reinforces the response. Later the child may talk silently (i.e., covertly or privately) and, in the presence of these self-generated verbal stimuli, say "thinking."
- A private stimulus may evoke a verbal response through stimulus generalization from a public stimulus in the presence of which the response was originally reinforced. Giving a child a heavily carbonated beverage, an adult may say, "This drink is tingly." When the child says "tingly," the adult reinforces the response. Later, in the presence of an internal stimulus similar to the one produced by the carbonated drink (e.g., the child's leg goes to sleep), the child may say "tingly."

Note that although only one instance of a reinforced response is given in each of the above examples, the number of similar instances throughout a person's life—beginning from early childhood—are many and varied. Moreover, much refinement occurs whereby, through reinforcement and punishment from other members of the verbal community, the individual learns to emit appropriate tacts and autoclitics when responding to private as opposed to public stimuli. Thus we see how it is that people can learn to talk about their private events with a fair amount of agreement and accuracy. We also see that talking about private events is necessarily less precise than talking about publicly observable events. Speech about private events, by the very nature of such events, can never receive the highly discriminated reinforcement from others that is necessary to make it as precise as speech about publicly observable events.

CULTURES

Humans live in social groups or societies. Every society has a distinctive culture—that is, a set of practices relating to the functioning of all aspects of the society. Following these practices tends to be reinforced within a society, whereas not following or opposing them tends to be punished. These practices are often codified in rules that may be transmitted through word of mouth or, if the society has developed it, writing. Some reinforced or punished practices are not specified verbally, and members learn them through imitation of other members of the society or direct exposure to the contingencies. Sometimes the practices codified in the rules of a culture differ from the practices actually reinforced in the culture, such as in the case of a culture that professes strict monogamy as a rule but has many members who practice various forms of polygamy.

Cultural Practices

Cultural practices differ widely across societies. Every society has its traditional foods, food-preparation methods, and customs for serving and consuming food; its customary clothes and rules for wearing them; its techniques for defending itself from outside invaders and from internal disruptions. Every society reinforces certain mating practices and punishes others (e.g., some cultures are mainly monogamous, others explicitly reinforce polygamy or polygyny). Every culture has its own approach to child rearing. Also within every culture there are practices, such as those relating to art, storytelling, music, and religion, that provide social and other reinforcers that tend to bind the members together as a group.

For individuals raised in, or extensively exposed to, more than one culture, discriminative stimuli that differentiate each of his or her particular cultures control the corresponding cultural practices. This is clearly seen when a bicultural individual switches between languages and other behavior as a function of the presence of certain cultural discriminative stimuli (e.g., an audience consisting of members of one of the cultures). Sensitive experimental designs and statistical tests, however, can detect more subtle effects. For example, Chinese-Americans asked to interpret a given sample of behavior (e.g., a fish swimming in front of a number of fish) tend to give an "internal" interpretation of the behavior (e.g., the fish in front is leading the other fish) if they have recently seen symbols of American culture. Conversely, these same individuals are more likely to give an "external" interpretation (e.g., the fish in front is being chased by the other fish) if they have been recently shown a picture of the Great Wall of China and other Chinese symbols (Hong, Chiu, & Kung, 1997; Hong, Morris, Chui, & Benet-Martínez, 2000). Presumably in America, internal interpretations of behavior are more strongly reinforced than they are in Chinese culture, whereas as external interpretations are more strongly reinforced in Chinese culture than they are in American culture. Internal interpretations are those for which external controlling variables are less obvious than they are for external interpretations.

There are two major types of contingencies involved in the development and maintenance of the practices of a culture: interlocking contingencies and metacontingencies.

Interlocking contingencies.   Most cultural practices involve interlocking contingencies. An interlocking contingency is one in which two (or more) individuals provide discriminative and reinforcing stimuli for each other. To take a simple example, consider a dinner table scene in which one person, A, asks another, B, to pass the pepper. A's mand "Please pass the pepper" is an S^D for B to pass the pepper to A, thereby reinforcing A's mand. A then says "Thank you" which reinforces B's response of passing the pepper. Polite table conversation reinforces further culturally prescribed interactions between the people at the table.

Metacontingencies.   A metacontingency is a contingency that applies to a group as a whole, rather than to any specific individual within the group (Glenn, 1988). Thus, a metacontingency specifies that some action of a group will result in some consequence for the group.

Metacontingencies may be either technological or ceremonial. In the former, the metacontingency brings about some effect on the environment external to the members; in the latter, it applies to the organizational structure of the group. An invasion by another society provides a technological metacontingency in which resistance (e.g., warfare) is a group behavior that may stop the invasion. Animals that may be hunted and crops that may be planted to supply food for the society provide other examples of technological metacontingencies. Political rallies, elections, coronations, holiday festivities, weddings, and birthday parties are examples of ceremonial metacontingencies.

Although metacontingencies are described at the level of the group, their effects necessarily are exerted through individual group members. In particular, metacontingencies act by increasing or strengthening interlocking contingencies within a group. In order for a metacontingency to be effective, the behavior of the group's members with respect to it must be discriminative stimuli for other group members so that they can reinforce behavior that is in the direction of satisfying the metacontingency.

If the behavior of the members with respect to the metcontingency is not clearly detectable and clearly specified interlocking contingencies are not in place, a problem called a social dilemma will develop (Dawes, 1980; Dawes & Messick, 2000). This is a situation in which each member of a group may increase his or her reinforcement by behaving in ways that decrease the total reinforcement available to the group (and hence, ultimately, decrease the individual's reinforcement). Social dilemmas result in a phenomenon called social loafing, in which some members contribute little or nothing to meeting the specifications of the metacontingency (Harkins & Szaymanski, 1989; Kunkel, 1991; Latané, Williams, & Harkins, 1979). Social dilemma problems are often referred to as the tragedy of the commons (Hardin, 1968) and the collective action problem (Ostrom, 1998).

The problem of social dilemmas has been addressed in many disciplines. Most solutions that have been proposed involve invoking rule-governed behavior relating to an individual's group membership (e.g., Messick, 1999; Dawes & Messick, 2000). This can be somewhat effective for some individuals, depending on how strongly rule-governed behavior has been conditioned in them. Research may show how it can be made more effective for more individuals, thereby helping to solve many serious social problems, including those involving international conflict and the environment. The principles of learning covered in this book, however, suggest that a general solution will involve the development of more effective interlocking contingencies.

Evolution of Cultures

Cultures evolve in a manner somewhat similar to that in which organisms evolve. What is passed on from one generation to the next, however, is not genes but cultural practices. Some cultures have practices that lead to their demise. For example, an extremely warlike culture may be overpowered and destroyed by its neighbors. A culture that does not enforce rules against murder, theft, and other aversive acts by its members against each other may break apart. A culture in which aversive control predominates may suffer defections that cause it to break down. Conversely, those cultures whose practices promote good relations with their neighbors, that maintain order with the society, and that positively reinforce rather than punish their members, tend to survive.

In an analogy to gene mutation, random changes in a culture's practices occasionally can have effects that tend to promote its survival. Moreover, in an analogy with sexual reproduction, cultures that adopt practices from other cultures often are strengthened by the increased variability this produces in the culture. It can be seen from these analogies that planning is not a prerequisite for the evolution of cultures, any more than it is for the evolution of a species. With the increasing sophistication of verbal behavior, however, it became possible for cultural changes to be planned. Constitutions, bills of rights, the increasing codification of the legal systems of modern societies, and the publication of utopian novels (e.g., Skinner, 1948b), indicate that many people are not content to let cultural change occur entirely by chance.

CULTURAL INSTITUTIONS

Within a society there are broad sets of interlocking contingencies, often referred to as cultural institutions, that tend to perpetuate the society's cultural practices (Skinner, 1953). The following constitutes merely a brief overview of these institutions. To receive full justice each requires, at the very least, an entire university department devoted to its study. The important points to take from the following discussion, however, is that these institutions are the product of cultural evolution, as described above, and that the learning principles discussed in this book are integral to the activities carried out within these institutions.

Government

Government controls the strongest punishers and reinforcers society can mete out. Government can inflict punishment not only on violators of order within the community, but also—through control of the army—societies that pose a threat or that stand in the way of certain positive reinforcers for the society or its leaders. In addition, through its control of the economy, government can economically punish (e.g., with fines, taxes) or positively reinforce (e.g., with tax exemptions, tax refunds, political appointments, money) behavior that supports its policies.

Religion

Government and religion were almost indistinguishable in early societies, but many modern societies have evolved some degree of separation between church and state. Religion provides strong generalized conditioned reinforcers, in the form of social reinforcement, to individuals who follow its prescribed practices. By virtue of rule-governed behavior, it is also able to invoke strong reinforcement and punishment contingencies that have never been experienced (e.g., Heaven, Hell). The delay to the presumed consequence is so long, however, that it often has little effect on behavior. Frequently, however, rules of the form "If you do X you will go to Hell" function equivalently to "Members of the community punish doing X."

Education

It is the young of a culture who carry it into the future. Therefore, any culture that does not educate its young in its practices and the metacontingencies relating to its survival would appear to be destined for extinction. In early cultures, education was carried out by all adults in the society. In modern industrial and technological societies, however, education has become a specialized function of certain individuals (teachers) in specific locations (schools). Although this specialization seems necessary for teaching the complex behavior individuals require in modern societies, it has removed responsibility for education from the majority of adults in the societies. One result is that some adults object to paying taxes for education, so that the metacontingency that has maintained education in the past tends to break down.

Therapy

In early cultures, therapy—or healing—and religion were tied closely together. A shaman derived healing powers from gods or spirits, and the behavior of consulting the shaman was reinforced (probably superstitiously, to a large extent) by the fact that the patient often recovered. Modern medical, psychological, and other scientifically-based therapists have replaced the shaman because they provide more consistent reinforcement. This has strengthened the culture by helping to keep its members physically and psychologically healthy.

Technology

Humans are virtuoso tool makers and users. Tools clearly enable humans to obtain reinforcers that otherwise would be unobtainable. Tool use has reached its highest point with the rise of modern technological societies, greatly increasing short-term reinforcement for members of those societies. But the long-term consequences are not known, and could result in the extinction of all the cultures we call civilization.

Science

At least partly because rule-governed behavior is so effective in producing reinforcement, humans have a strong tendency to seek explanations—rules, rules about rules, and so on—for the phenomena around them. Initially, religion provided these explanations. Over time, however, it was discovered that the experimental method produced explanations that proved more reinforcing than others because of the control they provided over the environment. In addition to being reinforcing because of their consistency with observation, the rules derived from science have given rise to the enormous expansion of modern technology.

Science has now evolved to the point that we have begun to apply it to our own behavior. This book has summarized many of the rules that have been discovered about an important aspect of behavior—learning. Although still a very young science, learningology has given rise to a technology that—under names such as behavior analysis, behavior modification, and learning-based interventions—is being applied with much success to behavior in several of the areas mentioned above; specifically, education and therapy. There is reason to believe (e.g., Skinner, 1971) that it can be applied successfully to all cultural institutions, and that this may be the best hope for the survival of civilization and our species.

SUMMARY AND CONCLUSIONS

Humans are distinguished from other animals by language and a large capacity for learning. Neither of these, however, necessitates any additional learning principles. It appears that the human propensity for language and culture can be accounted for by the learning principles described in the earlier chapters of this book. Lingual behavior consists in behavioral interactions between a speaker and a listener (interpreted broadly to include writing and sign language). In these interactions the speaker's behavior is reinforced by the listener and the listener's behavior is reinforced by the speaker or by aspects of the environment that control the speaker's behavior. Once a person has learned (i.e., been conditioned) to be a listener as well as a speaker, that person will then respond effectively to his or her own verbal behavior. A speaker and listener "within the same skin" results in hierarchies of verbal behavior occurring covertly and rapidly in one individual—a phenomenon known as cognitive processing due to its resemblance to information processing by computers.

Human societies or cultures arise from interlocking contingencies in which people mediate reinforcements and punishments for others. Metacontingencies, which are contingencies applied to a group of individuals bound together by interlocking contingencies, have effects on the group similar to the effects the same contingencies would have on single individuals. Metacontingencies generate practices (behavior patterns reinforced by a group of individuals, such as a society or culture) that are analogous to the behavior a contingency generates in a single individual. Cultural practices also are analogous to genes: Practices that promote the survival of the culture in which they occur tend to be perpetuated along with their culture, and those practices that do not promote a culture's survival are eliminated when that culture becomes extinct. Because our verbal behavior enables us to describe and respond effectively to metacontingencies, we can modify cultural practices that would lead to the extinction of our culture.

APPENDICES

Mathematics is a highly compact language that is ideal for scientific description. For this reason mathematics is sometimes called the language of science. It should therefore come as no surprise that learning scientists have developed powerful mathematical formulations of many of the functional relationships described in this book. These appendices outline several mathematical theories or models that show extraordinary promise in describing learning processes. One of these models—the Rescorla-Wagner (1972) model—deals mainly with the acquisition of behavior while the others focus on behavior in the stable state (although, as several of the appendices make clear, there is no clear dividing line separating these two states).

The models described here are by no means flawless; on the contrary, there are instances in which they are *not* consistent with data. In addition, although quantitative in form, the models mainly describe the general forms of functions rather than the exact values they take on. The focus of these appendices, however, is to explain rather than critique the models. While far from perfect, the models are accurate enough often enough to suggest that, with appropriate modifications, they may reach a higher level of accuracy (perhaps ultimately, for example, the level of Newton's or even Einstein's theories in physics). Failing that, they at least have considerable heuristic value by providing a glimpse of what more accurate mathematical learning models might look like and perhaps indicating how such models might be constructed and evaluated (see Church, 1997).

Readers whose mathematical background is weak should note that no mathematics beyond high school algebra is needed to follow the mathematics in these appendices. Moreover, all steps (or at least as many as feasible) are included in all derivations so that readers do not have to supply missing steps in order to follow any derivation. Finally, aside from occasional cross-referencing to show the logical connections between the models, each appendix is self-contained so that it can be read independently of the others without seriously sacrificing comprehension.

Several things that some readers might expect to find in these appendices are absent. First, there is no systematic attempt to evaluate the models. This is because a comprehensive evaluation of the models is outside the scope of these appendices, and anything less than a comprehensive evaluation would serve little purpose here. Second, there are no illustrations of experimental findings described or predicted by the models. The reader can, however, find numerous qualitative illustrations in the main body of the book; in fact, the models may serve as a review of many of the experimental findings and learning principles described in the text. Third, there are no concrete computational examples of the equations presented here. This is simply to conserve space. Readers who wish to see concrete computational examples may easily construct them by plugging arbitrary numbers into the equations. In fact, readers of these appendices are strongly encouraged to do this, as it is an excellent way to develop a clear understanding of the models.

APPENDIX A
The Rescorla-Wagner Model

The Rescorla-Wagner model (Rescorla & Wagner, 1972) describes the acquisition of Pavlovian conditioned responses (or respondents), operant responses, and stimulus control over respondent and operant behavior. In order to include all of these phenomena in the treatment below, we will slightly modify the terminology from that used in the main part of this book. The term "conditioned stimulus" will refer to either a conditioned stimulus (in respondent conditioning) or a discriminative stimulus (in operant conditioning). The expression "to reinforce" and its variations will refer either to presenting a reinforcer contingent on a response (operant conditioning) or to presenting an unconditioned stimulus contingent on a conditioned stimulus (respondent conditioning). The term "conditioning trial" will refer to either a respondent conditioning trial, a discrete-trials operant conditioning trial, or a single emission of a free-operant response. As in the main body of the text, "conditioning" will refer to either respondent or operant conditioning.

In the Rescorla-Wagner model[1], a quantity called *associative value* (or *associative strength*) becomes assigned to either a conditioned stimulus, a stimulus element of a compound conditioned stimulus, or an operant response. The greater the associative value (V) of a stimulus is, the more likely it is to elicit or evoke a response conditioned to it. Likewise, the greater the associative value of an operant response is, the more likely it is to occur on a given occasion.

To see how associative value is assigned to a conditioned stimulus, let $X = \{x_1, x_2, \ldots, x_i, \ldots, x_m\}$ be the set of conditioned stimuli that are simultaneously present on a given conditioning trial, and let y be the unconditioned stimulus or reinforcer on that conditioning trial. It is important to note that these m conditioned stimuli may be separate stimuli or stimulus elements in a compound stimulus—all that matters is that they are simultaneously present on a conditioning trial. Then the Rescorla-Wagner model may be expressed in the following three interconnected equations:

$$V_{j,n+1} = V_{j,n} + \Delta V_{j,n+1}, \tag{A1}$$

$$\Delta V_{j,n+1} = \alpha_j \beta_y d_n, \tag{A1.1}$$

and

$$d_n = \lambda_y - \sum_{i=1}^{m} V_{i,n}, \tag{A1.2}$$

where $V_{j,n+1}$ is the associative value of stimulus x_j as a result of conditioning trial $n + 1$ with unconditioned stimulus y, $\Delta V_{j,n+1}$ is the change in associative value of x_j as a result of conditioning trial $n + 1$ (note that the symbol "Δ" in front of a variable indicates a change in that variable), $\alpha_j (0 \leq \alpha_j \leq 1)$ is the salience or conditionability of x_j, $\beta_y (0 \leq \beta_y \leq 1)$ is

---

1. The Rescorla-Wagner model is based on an earlier influential learning model by Bush and Mosteller (1951), and in its simplest form (namely, when we are dealing with a single conditioned stimulus rather than a compound conditioned stimulus) reduces to that model.

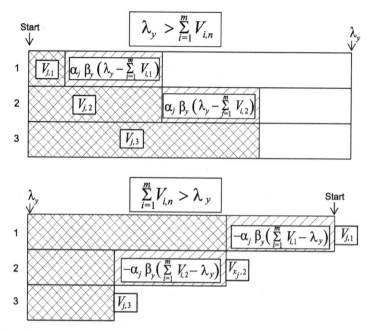

FIGURE A.1. Effects of two consecutive trials (labeled 1 and 2) in which associative value is incremented (top) or decremented (bottom). In the former case, the change in associative value is positive and a small piece is added to the total after each trial. In the latter case, the change is negative and a small piece is subtracted. Single cross-hatched portions represent the amounts to be added or subtracted at the end of trials 1 and 2 to yield the total amounts (indicated by double cross hatching) at the start of trials 2 and 3.

the effectiveness of y as an unconditioned stimulus, d_n is the amount of associative value remaining to be conditioned (i.e., attached to stimuli) at the end of trial n, $\sum_{i=1}^{m} V_{i,n}$ is the sum of associative values (from $i = 1$ to m) on trial n of all m conditioned stimuli present on that trial, and λ_y is a constant whose value is a direct function of the intensity or magnitude of y (i.e., the unconditioned stimulus).

One way to think of λ_y is as the total amount of associative value present, and for which all the stimuli present ($X = \{x_1, x_2, \ldots, x_i, \ldots, x_m\}$) on a conditioning trial are competing. This view is illustrated in the top portion of Figure A.1. In that part of the figure, the total amount of the associative value ($\sum_{i=1}^{m} V_{i,n}$) already collected by the stimuli present is less than λ_y.; therefore, there is still some "free" associative value (represented by $d_n = \lambda_y - \sum_{i=1}^{m} V_{i,n}$ in Equation A1.2) available to be distributed among the stimuli. The top portion of the figure illustrates one of those stimuli (x_j) "taking its share" ($\Delta V_{j,n+1} = \alpha_j \beta_y d_n$ in Equation A1.1) of the remaining associative value. This analogy breaks down, however, if the sum of the associative values of all stimuli present is greater than λ_y, as illustrated in the bottom portion of Figure A1.1. In that case, d_n is negative (and hence $\Delta V_{j,n+1}$ is negative) and all of the stimuli present begin to lose associative value on successive trials. Instead of a competition among stimuli to gain "free" associative value, then, the analogy is that of a competition to shed "excess" associative value. (There are several situations that are not represented in the figure. Specifically, it is possible for the associative value of a particular stimulus to be greater than λ_y when the sum of the associative values of all the stimuli is less than λ_y; and, conversely, it is possible for the associative value of a particular stimulus to be less than λ_y when the total associative values is greater than λ_y. These situations do not, however, affect the behavior of the model as illustrated in the figure.)

To apply the model to an operant response, let m be equal to 1 (because we are assuming that only one response occurs at a time), and let $V_{j,n+1}$ be the associative value of operant response x_j as a result of conditioning trial $n + 1$ with reinforcer y. Then α_j is the conditionability of operant response x_j, β_y is the effectiveness of y as a reinforcer, $\sum_{x=1}^{m=1} V_{i,n} = V_{1,n}$ is the associative value on trial n of operant response x_j, and λ_y is the limit or asymptote that the associative value of operant response x_j tends to approach over trials when that response is followed by reinforcer y.

Although the Rescorla-Wagner model appears complicated because of all the subscripts needed to formulate it, the model simplifies greatly when applied to situations that involve just a single stimulus or response.

CONDITIONING

Consider conditioning involving a simple conditioned stimulus or an operant response. Equation A1, in combination with Equations A1.1 and A1.2, then becomes

$$
\begin{aligned}
V_{1,n+1} &= V_{1,n} + \Delta V_{1,n+1}, \\
&= V_{1,n} + \alpha_1 \beta_y d_n, \\
&= V_{1,n} + \alpha_1 \beta_y (\lambda_y - V_{1,n}).
\end{aligned}
\tag{A2}
$$

Equation A2 describes how $V_{1,n}$ (the associative value on trial n of x_1) changes as a function of n (the number of conditioning trials). For simplicity, we assume that before conditioning, that is, when n is equal to zero, $V_{1,n}$ is equal to zero. Equation A2 says that as n grows larger and larger, $V_{1,n}$ also grows larger and larger, but at a decreasing (i.e., negatively accelerating) rate, and asymptotes at λ_y. To see that it grows larger at a decreasing rate, note that on each succeeding trial a smaller and smaller number ($\Delta V_{1,n+1} = \alpha_1 \beta_y [\lambda_y - V_{1,n}]$) is added to it. (This is also illustrated in the top part of Figure A1.1.) To see that it asymptotes at λ_y, note that as $V_{1,n}$ grows increasingly larger the quantity $d_n = \lambda_y - V_{1,n}$ grows smaller and smaller. Eventually it reaches zero, or at least arbitrarily close to it. Therefore, setting it equal to zero, we obtain $0 = \lambda_y - V_{1,\infty}$, or in other words, $V_{1,\infty} = \lambda_y$, where $V_{1,\infty}$ is $V_{1,n}$ at asymptote.

Note also from Equation A2 that the rate at which $V_{1,n}$ approaches λ_y as a limit depends on the parameters α_1 and β_y. To see how an equation works, it is often helpful to plug extreme values into it. Note that if $\alpha_1 \beta_y = 0$, which is the lowest value that this product can take on (since neither α_1 nor β_y can be less than zero), then $V_{1,n+1}$ will be equal to $V_{1,0}$ (which by assumption will be equal to zero) for all values of n. In other words, no conditioning will occur—either because the salience or conditionability of x_1 is zero or the effectiveness of y as an unconditioned stimulus or reinforcer is zero. Conversely, if $\alpha_1 \beta_y = 1$ (that is, if both the salience, or conditionability of x_1 and the effectiveness of y as an unconditioned stimulus or reinforcer are at their maximum values of one), then $V_{1,n}$ will go immediately from zero to its maximum of λ_y on the first conditioning trial and remain there on all subsequent trials. In other words, maximum conditioning would occur on a single trial (this is known as "one-trial learning"). Normally, α_1 and β_y will each be greater than zero and less than one so that conditioning occurs gradually over trials.

Finally, note that Equation A2 represents the effects of increasing the strength of the unconditioned stimulus or reinforcer on conditioning in two ways: (1) β_y is increased to represent the fact that increasing the strength or magnitude of the unconditioned stimulus/reinforcer increases the rate with which conditioning occurs, and (2) λ_y is increased to represent the fact that it also increases the level of associative value that conditioning can produce.

EXTINCTION

In extinction there is a radical change in the unconditioned stimulus or reinforcer—namely, there is none. We will indicate this by setting y to y', and letting $\lambda_{y'} = 0$. The effect of this is apparent in the bottom portion of Figure A1.1: on each trial an amount is subtracted from $V_{1,n}$ (because $\sum_{x=1}^{m=1} V_{i,n} = V_{1,n}$ and $\lambda_{y'} < V_{1,n}$). Although a smaller and smaller amount is subtracted on each trial, $V_{1,n}$ steadily approaches $\lambda_{y'} = 0$. We may also see this algebraically by plugging $\lambda_y = \lambda_{y'} = 0$ into Equation A2 as follows:

$$V_{1,n+1} = V_{1,n} + \alpha_1 \beta_{y'}(\lambda_{y'} - V_{1,n}),$$
$$= V_{1,n} + \alpha_1 \beta_{y'}(0 - V_{1,n})$$

(by substitution),

$$= V_{1,n} - \alpha_1 \beta_{y'} V_{1,n}$$

(by multiplying through by the minus sign), and finally

$$= V_{1,n}(1 - \alpha_1 \beta_{y'}). \tag{A3}$$

(by factoring out $V_{1,n}$). Now call the trial just before extinction "trial 0" so that extinction trials are numbered beginning at one. Then on extinction trial 1 ($n = 1$)

$$V_{1,1} = V_{1,0}(1 - \alpha_1 \beta_{y'}),$$

and on extinction trial 2 ($n = 2$)

$$V_{1,2} = V_{1,1}(1 - \alpha_1 \beta_{y'}),$$
$$= V_{1,0}(1 - \alpha_1 \beta_{y'})(1 - \alpha_1 \beta_{y'}),$$
$$= V_{1,0}(1 - \alpha_1 \beta_{y'})^2.$$

Following the above process through, we see that we can write

$$V_{1,n} = V_{1,0}(1 - \alpha_1 \beta_{y'})^n \tag{A4}$$

for all extinction trials, beginning with extinction trial 1, where $V_{1,0}$ (for this equation) is the associative value (i.e., the level of conditioning) just before the first extinction trial. Note that because the quantity in parentheses is always between one and zero, the associative value on trial n ($V_{1,n}$) will decrease toward zero as n increases—which is the actual effect of extinction. Since extinction typically takes longer (requires more trials) than conditioning, we assume that $\beta_{y'}$ is greater than β_y.

Note that α_1 also affects the rate of extinction—the lower the salience or conditionability of the conditioned stimulus or operant response, the longer extinction will take (i.e., the slower it will be). To take an extreme example, suppose we let α_1 be equal to zero. In that case, Equation A4 says that no extinction at all will occur for conditioned stimulus or operant response x_1. This makes sense, because letting $\alpha_1 = 0$ is the same as not presenting the conditioned stimulus or not providing an opportunity for the operant response to occur—and extinction will not occur if the conditioned stimulus or operant response does not occur. Conversely, suppose that we set α_1 at a higher level (e.g., increase the intensity of the conditioned stimulus) than it was during conditioning. Equation A4 says that this will result in faster extinction than would be the case if the level of the conditioned stimulus during extinction had been the same as its level during conditioning. This makes sense because increasing the intensity, for example, of the conditioned stimulus during extinction speeds up extinction to the conditioned stimulus (at, of course, the same intensity it was at during conditioning).

STIMULUS AND RESPONSE GENERALIZATION

To use the Rescorla-Wagner model to describe stimulus generalization, we first note that the model treats a compound stimulus in exactly the same manner that it treats a simple stimulus—the distinction between simple and compound stimuli is simply a relative matter and has no other importance or even meaning to the model. To see this, consider a compound stimulus consisting of the set of elements that we will label $X = \{x_1, x_2, \ldots, x_i, \ldots, x_m\}$. In what we will refer to as the Summation Assumption, the Rescorla-Wagner model assumes that the associative value of a compound is equal to the sum of the associative values of the elements of the compound. Thus, if we let $V_{X,n}$ be the associative value of the compound stimulus consisting of the elements $X = \{x_1, x_2, \ldots, x_i, \ldots, x_m\}$, we may write

$$V_{X,n+1} = \sum_{i=1}^{m} V_{i,n+1}, \qquad \text{(Summation Assumption)}$$

where $V_{i,n+1}$ is the associative value of element x_i at the end of trial $n + 1$. Then from Equation A1, in combination with Equations A1.1 and A1.2, we may write

$$V_{X,n+1} = \sum_{i=1}^{m} \left[V_{i,n} + \alpha_i \beta_y \left(\lambda_y - \sum_{i=1}^{m} V_{i,n} \right) \right]$$

(by definition),

$$= \sum_{i=1}^{m} [V_{i,n} + \alpha_i \beta_y (\lambda_y - V_{X,n})]$$

(by substitution),

$$= \sum_{i=1}^{m} V_{i,n} + \sum_{i=1}^{m} \alpha_i \beta_y (\lambda_y - V_{X,n})$$

(by the distributive property of summation),

$$= \sum_{i=1}^{m} V_{i,n} + \left(\sum_{i=1}^{m} \alpha_i \right) \beta_y (\lambda_y - V_{X,n})$$

(by factoring out the constants in the summation), and finally

$$V_{X,n+1} = V_{X,n} + \alpha_X \beta_y (\lambda_y - V_{X,n}) \tag{A5}$$

where $\alpha_X = \sum_{i=1}^{m} \alpha_i$.

Note that Equation A5 has exactly the same form as Equation A2. In effect we have mathematically transformed a compound stimulus into a simple stimulus. If we can view a compound stimulus as a simple stimulus, it stands to reason that we might regard a simple stimulus to be a compound stimulus. We use this idea to apply the Rescorla-Wagner model to stimulus generalization (cf. Blough, 1975; Rescorla, 1976). Assume the following:

1. A stimulus consists of a number of stimulus elements that conform to Equations A1, A1.1 and A1.2.
2. Two stimuli are similar to the extent that they share stimulus elements— the amount of generalization that will occur between two stimuli is a direct function of the number of stimulus elements they have in common.

Then, applying Equation A1.2 to the m stimulus elements of any given stimulus, we obtain

$$\sum_{i=1}^{m} V_{i,n} = \lambda_y - d_n \tag{A6}$$

(by adding $\sum_{i=1}^{m} V_{i,n} - d_n$ to both sides of the equation). If, for simplicity, we assume that the associative values of all the stimulus elements are equal (i.e., $V_1 = \cdots = V_i = \cdots = V_m$), Equation A6 becomes

$$m V_{i,n} = \lambda_y - d_n,$$

from which, by dividing both sides by m, we may write

$$V_{i,n} = \frac{\lambda_y - d_n}{m}, \tag{A7}$$

which is the associative value for each stimulus element at the end of the nth conditioning trial. Thus, the more elements of the original conditioned stimulus that are present in a second stimulus that occurs during (for example) a generalization test, the stronger will be the generalization to that second (e.g., test) stimulus (because the associative value of that stimulus will be larger). Note that Equation A7 also says that the amount of stimulus generalization will vary directly with the amount of training, because d_n decreases as n increases.

We may extend the model to account for operant response generalization by regarding operant responses to be composed of response elements in the same way that stimuli are composed of stimulus elements, and defining two responses to be similar to the extent that they have elements in common. Reinforcement of a given response would increase the probability of all responses that contain the elements in the reinforced response, in proportion to the extent that they share elements with the reinforced response. The probability of a given response would, in this view, be a direct function of the associative value of that response (which, of course, would be the sum of the associative values of its elements).

STIMULUS AND RESPONSE DISCRIMINATION

Suppose we want to condition a discrimination between two compound stimuli: stimulus A and stimulus B. The fact that we are considering establishing a discrimination between these stimuli implies that there is currently some generalization between them; which, from the previous section, implies that they have some stimulus elements in common. Let "1" be the collective label of all of the stimulus elements of A that are not in B, let "2" be the collective label of all the stimulus elements in B that are not in A, and, let "3" be the collective label for all the stimulus elements that are common to A and B. From the Summation Assumption introduced earlier, we may write

$$V_{A,n+1} = V_{1,n+1} + V_{3,n+1} \tag{A8}$$

and

$$V_{B,n+1} = V_{2,n+1} + V_{3,n+1}, \tag{A9}$$

where $V_{1,n+1}$, $V_{2,n+1}$, and $V_{3,n+1}$ are the sums of the associative values of the stimulus elements labeled "1," "2," and "3," respectively, after trial $n+1$. Suppose that trials on which A occurs alternate in some random or quasi-random manner with trials on which B occurs, and that reinforcement occurs on the former trials but not on the latter (i.e., we conduct discrimination training between A and B). After trials on which A (and reinforcement) occurred, we may write the following:

$$V_{1,n+1} = V_{1,n} + \alpha_1 \beta_y (\lambda_y - V_{1,n} - V_{3,n}) \tag{A10}$$

which follows from Equation A1 (in combination with Equations A1.1 and A1.2) and the fact that A contains the elements labeled "1" and "3";

$$V_{3,n+1} = V_{3,n} + \alpha_3 \beta_y (\lambda_y - V_{1,n} - V_{3,n}) \tag{A11}$$

which also follows from Equation A1 (in combination with Equations A1.1 and A1.2) and the fact that A contains the elements labeled "1" and "3"; and

$$V_{2,n+1} = V_{2,n}$$

which follows from the fact that the elements labeled "2" are not present on trials on which A is reinforced.

After trials on which B (and *no* reinforcement) occurred, we may write:

$$V_{2,n+1} = V_{2,n} + \alpha_2 \beta_0 (0 - V_{2,n} - V_{3,n})$$

which follows from Equation A1 (in combination with Equations A1.1 and A1.2) and the fact that B contains the elements labeled "2" and "3"; then, factoring -1 out of the parentheses, we obtain

$$V_{2,n+1} = V_{2,n} - \alpha_2 \beta_0 (V_{2,n} + V_{3,n}). \tag{A12}$$

Similarly, we may write

$$V_{3,n+1} = V_{3,n} - \alpha_3 \beta_0 (V_{2,n} + V_{3,n}) \tag{A13}$$

and

$$V_{1,n+1} = V_{1,n},$$

because B contains the elements labeled "2" and "3" but not "1."

What the above equations do will depend on:

$$\Delta V_{1,n+1} = \alpha_1 \beta_y (\lambda_y - V_{1,n} - V_{3,n}) \tag{A14}$$

and

$$\Delta V_{2,n+1} = -\alpha_2 \beta_0 (V_{2,n} + V_{3,n}), \tag{A15}$$

and on

$$\Delta V_{3,n+1} = \alpha_3 \beta_y (\lambda_y - V_{1,n} - V_{3,n}) \tag{A16}$$

on reinforced trials, and

$$\Delta V_{3,n+1} = -\alpha_3 \beta_0 (V_{2,n} + V_{3,n}) \tag{A17}$$

on unreinforced trials.

To see what will happen to the above quantities, recall that $V_{1,n}$ is the sum of the associative values on trial n of the elements present only on reinforced trial (i.e., the elements unique to stimulus A), $V_{2,n}$ is the sum of the associative values on trial n of the elements present only on unreinforced trials (i.e., the elements unique to stimulus B), and $V_{3,n}$ is the sum of the associative values on trial n of the elements present on both reinforced and unreinforced trials (i.e., the elements shared by stimuli A and B). Now, if A and B are very dissimilar—that is, if they have very few elements in common—those elements collectively will pick up very little associative value during reinforced trials and will tend to lose it during unreinforced trials. Therefore, $V_{3,n}$ will tend to stay close to zero. But if $V_{3,n}$ is essentially zero, Equations A10 and A12 are, in effect, essentially the same as Equations A2 and A4, respectively. This means that $V_{3,n}$ will go quickly to λ_y and $V_{2,n}$ will go quickly to zero as n increases. That is, the discrimination will tend to be learned quickly. Plugging these values into Equations A14–A17 shows that all of these equations will eventually be approximately zero for the case in which there are few common elements between the two stimuli. If we increase the number of shared elements, we correspondingly increase the number of trials required for the discrimination to develop—because $V_{3,n}$ becomes more significant and it is being increased on reinforced trials and decreased on unreinforced trials. That is, by increasing the similarity between the two stimuli, we make the discrimination more difficult to learn. If we make the number of shared elements very large, we may even make the discrimination impossible to learn, just as happens when two stimuli are highly similar in a real discrimination problem. Setting this possibility aside, we may assume that given enough trials the discrimination will be learned, which is represented by Equations A14–A17 being zero (i.e., no further significant change occurs in the associative values of the stimulus elements represented in the above equations). Thus, at some point, Equations A14–A17 will all be zero (or arbitrarily close to it). Setting Equation A14 to zero, we obtain

$$0 = \alpha_1 \beta_y (\lambda_y - V_{1,n} - V_{3,n}).$$

Dividing both sides of the equation by $\alpha_1 \beta_y$ and adding $V_{1,n} + V_{3,n}$ to both sides, we obtain

$$V_{1,n} + V_{3,n} = \lambda_y. \tag{A18}$$

Similarly, from Equation A15,

$$V_{2,n} + V_{3,n} = 0. \tag{A19}$$

Finally, to obtain the associative values for stimuli A and B at the end of discrimination training, we write

$$V_{A,n+1} = V_{1,n+1} + V_{3,n+1},$$

(from Equation A8)

$$= \lambda_y.$$

(from Equation A18); and

$$V_{B,n+1} = V_{2,n+1} + V_{3,n+1},$$

(from Equation A9)

$$= 0$$

(from Equation A19).

Similar to the way in which we extended the model to account for response generalization, we may extend the model to account for response discrimination by simply considering operant responses to be composed of response elements in the same way that stimuli are composed of stimulus elements, and defining two responses to be similar to the extent that they have elements in common.

CONDITIONED INHIBITION

Suppose stimulus A is always reinforced when it occurs alone but never when it occurs in combination with stimulus B. For simplicity, we assume that these two stimuli are so distinct that they have no elements in common. After trials on which A occurs alone (and is reinforced) we may write

$$\Delta V_{A,n+1} = \alpha_A \beta_y (\lambda_y - V_{A,n}), \tag{A20}$$

and after trial on which A occurs with B (and is not reinforced) we may write

$$\Delta V_{A,n+1} = \alpha_A \beta_0 (0 - V_{A,n} - V_{B,n}),$$

$$= -\alpha_A \beta_0 (V_{A,n} + V_{B,n}); \tag{A21}$$

and

$$\Delta V_{B,n+1} = -\alpha_B \beta_0 (V_{A,n} + V_{B,n}). \tag{A22}$$

Note from the above equations that $V_{B,n}$ must start out by decreasing, and at some point it must decrease below zero. At this point, if not sooner, we can see from Equations A20 and A21 that $V_{A,n}$ must start increasing faster than it is decreasing. At some point it will be large enough that changes in it after reinforced trials will be essentially zero because it will be at or near its asymptote of λ_y. In addition, from Equation A22, the absolute value of $V_{B,n}$ cannot go much above that of $V_{A,n}$, because then $\Delta V_{B,n+1}$ would become positive and that would decrease the absolute value of $V_{B,n}$. The upshot of all this is that Equations A20, A21, and A22 must all approach zero. Setting them at zero, we obtain

$$V_{A,\infty} = \lambda_y,$$

and

$$V_{B,\infty} = -V_{A,\infty},$$

$$= -\lambda_y,$$

where $V_{A,\infty}$ and $V_{B,\infty}$ are $V_{A,n}$ and $V_{B,n}$, respectively, at asymptote. Hence, from the Summation Assumption we may write

$$V_{AB,n} = V_{A,n} + V_{B,n},$$

where $V_{AB,n}$ is the associative value of the compound stimulus consisting of A and B on trial n. Hence at asymptote, the associative value of the compound stimulus consisting of stimuli A and B is

$$V_{AB,\infty} = \lambda_y - \lambda_y,$$

$$= 0.$$

Note that stimulus B has acquired negative associative value, which is how inhibition is represented in the Rescorla-Wagner model. Hence, stimulus B has become a conditioned inhibitor.

OVERSHADOWING

Let A and B be two stimuli in a compound stimulus. Suppose that the salience of A is greater than that of B; that is, $\alpha_A > \alpha_B$. It follows from Equation A1.1 that

$$\frac{\Delta V_{A,n+1}}{\Delta V_{B,n+1}} = \frac{\alpha_A \beta_y d_n}{\alpha_B \beta_y d_n},$$

$$= \frac{\alpha_A}{\alpha_B};$$

and thus

$$\Delta V_{A,n+1} = \frac{\alpha_A}{\alpha_B}(\Delta V_{B,n+1}).$$

In other words, every time an amount of associative value of $\Delta V_{B,n+1}$ is added to the associative value of stimulus B after each trial, a factor of $\frac{\alpha_A}{\alpha_B} > 1$ times that amount is added to the associative value of stimulus A. From Equation A1, the associative value of stimulus B on any trial, n, is

$$V_{B,n} = V_{B,0} + \Delta V_{B,1} + \Delta V_{B,2} + \cdots + \Delta V_{B,n},$$
$$= \Delta V_{B,1} + \Delta V_{B,2} + \cdots + \Delta V_{B,n}$$

(because of our assumption that the associative value of any stimulus before trial 1 is zero). It follows that

$$V_{A,n} = V_{A,0} + \frac{\alpha_A}{\alpha_B}\Delta V_{B,1} + \frac{\alpha_A}{\alpha_B}\Delta V_{B,2} + \cdots + \frac{\alpha_A}{\alpha_B}\Delta V_{B,n},$$
$$= \frac{\alpha_A}{\alpha_B}\Delta V_{B,1} + \frac{\alpha_A}{\alpha_B}\Delta V_{B,2} + \cdots + \frac{\alpha_A}{\alpha_B}\Delta V_{B,n},$$
$$= \frac{\alpha_A}{\alpha_B}(\Delta V_{B,1} + \Delta V_{B,2} + \cdots + \Delta V_{B,n}),$$
$$= \frac{\alpha_A}{\alpha_B}V_{B,n}. \qquad (A23)$$

Thus the extent to which stimulus A will overshadow stimulus B will be proportional to the ratio of α_A, to α_B for all n.

To see what the overshadowing of A over B looks like when the associative value of the compound stimulus reaches asymptote, note first from Equations A1.1 and A1.2 that

$$\Delta V_{A,n+1} = \alpha_A \beta_y (\lambda_y - V_{A,n} - V_{B,n})$$

and

$$\Delta V_{B,n+1} = \alpha_B \beta_y (\lambda_y - V_{A,n} - V_{B,n}).$$

At asymptote there will be, by definition, no further change in the associative values of A and B; therefore, at asymptote $\Delta V_{A,n+1}$ and $\Delta V_{B,n+1}$ will each be equal to zero. Setting either one of them, let's say $\Delta V_{A,n+1}$, equal to zero we obtain

$$0 = \alpha_A \beta_y (\lambda_y - V_{A,\infty} - V_{B,\infty}),$$

where $V_{A,\infty}$ and $V_{B,\infty}$ are the associative values of A and B, respectively, at asymptote. Dividing both sides of the above equation by $\alpha_A \beta_y$ and then adding $V_{A,\infty} + V_{B,\infty}$ we obtain

$$V_{A,\infty} + V_{B,\infty} = \lambda_y.$$

Then, substituting $\frac{\alpha_A}{\alpha_B}V_{B,\infty}$ for $V_{A,\infty}$ (Equation A23) and carrying out some algebraic manipulations we obtain

$$\frac{\alpha_A}{\alpha_B}V_{B,\infty} + V_{B,\infty} = \lambda_y,$$

$$V_{B,\infty}\left(\frac{\alpha_A}{\alpha_B} + 1\right) = \lambda_y,$$

$$V_{B,\infty} = \frac{\lambda_y}{\left(\dfrac{\alpha_A}{\alpha_B} + 1\right)}, \tag{A24}$$

and by symmetry

$$V_{A,\infty} = \frac{\lambda_y}{\left(\dfrac{\alpha_B}{\alpha_A} + 1\right)}. \tag{A25}$$

Taken together, Equations 24 and 25 show that the larger α_A is relative to α_B, the smaller $V_{B,\infty}$ will be and the larger $V_{A,\infty}$ will be. As a limit, the former will approach zero and the latter will approach λ_y.

BLOCKING AND UNBLOCKING

Suppose that stimulus A, through conditioning alone, has acquired the maximum possible amount of associative value. In other words, through the conditioning of stimulus A by itself, we have

$$V_{A,n} = \lambda_y.$$

If we now condition a compound stimulus consisting of A and B, we obtain (from Equations A1.1 and A1.2) the following increase in the associative value for B on the next trial:

$$\Delta V_{B,n+1} = \alpha_B\beta_y(\lambda_y - [V_{A,n} + V_{B,n}]),$$

$$\Delta V_{B,n+1} = \alpha_B\beta_y(\lambda_y - [\lambda_y + 0]),$$

$$\Delta V_{B,n+1} = \alpha_B\beta_y(\lambda_y - \lambda_y),$$

$$\Delta V_{B,n+1} = 0.$$

In other words, nothing will be added to the associative value of B on any trial with the A-B compound. All of the available associative value (i.e., λ_y) will already have gone to A, and so the associative value of B relative to that of A will stay at zero over successive trials. In this situation we would say that B has been totally blocked by A.

Suppose, however, that while continuing trials with the compound we increase the intensity or magnitude of the unconditioned stimulus or reinforcer to $\lambda_{y^*} = \lambda_y + c$. On the next trial after we do this, the result will be that

$$\Delta V_{B,n+1} = \alpha_B \beta_{y^*}(\lambda_{y^*} - [V_{A,n} + V_{B,n}]),$$

$$\Delta V_{B,n+1} = \alpha_B \beta_{y^*}(\lambda_y + c - [V_{A,n} + V_{B,n}]),$$

$$\Delta V_{B,n+1} = \alpha_B \beta_{y^*}(\lambda_y + c - \lambda_y + 0),$$

$$\Delta V_{B,n+1} = \alpha_B \beta_{y^*}(\lambda_y - \lambda_y + c),$$

$$\Delta V_{B,n+1} = \alpha_B \beta_{y^*} c.$$

Now some amount of associative value greater than zero (the amount depending on how much the intensity or magnitude of the unconditioned stimulus or reinforcer has been increased by) will be added to the associative value of B on succeeding trials; that is, B will be unblocked. Note that as a bonus, so to speak, the unblocking effect is enhanced by the increase in the effectiveness of the unconditioned stimulus or reinforcer from β_y to β_{y^*}.

THE OVEREXPECTATION EFFECT

Suppose that stimuli A and B are each conditioned separately to asymptote, so that we may write

$$V_{A,\infty} = V_{B,\infty} = \lambda_y.$$

Now suppose that we institute conditioning trials with the two stimuli compounded together. After the first trial of this, from Equations A1.1 and A2.2, we will find that

$$\Delta V_{A,1} = \alpha_A \beta_y(\lambda_y - [V_{A,0} + V_{B,0}])$$

(where the subscript "1" indicates the first conditioning trial with the compound stimulus, and the subscript "0" indicates the last trial of each component stimulus by itself, after its associative value had reached asymptote),

$$\Delta V_{A,1} = \alpha_A \beta_y(\lambda_y - [\lambda_y + \lambda_y]),$$
$$= \alpha_A \beta_y(\lambda_y - 2\lambda_y);$$

and thus

$$\Delta V_{A,1} = -\alpha_A \beta_y \lambda_y.$$

By similar reasoning,

$$\Delta V_{B,1} = -\alpha_B \beta_y \lambda_y.$$

In other words, both stimuli will lose associative value as a result of being compounded together on a conditioning trial. This has been called the "overexpectation" effect because it is as though compounding the stimuli on a conditioning trial causes the individual to "expect" that the unconditioned stimulus or reinforcer will be greater than it was when the stimuli were presented separately, and it is the "disappointment" of this "overexpectation" that causes the decrease in responding to the individual stimuli. The mathematics in the Rescorla-Wagner model, however, describe the effect more succinctly and unambiguously.

After the initial decrease in the associative value of each stimulus, a straightforward application of Equations A1, A1.1, and A1.2 shows that further conditioning with the compound stimulus will result in a gradual increase in the associative values of each stimulus Conditioning them as elements of a compound, however, can never restore the asymptotic value to each stimulus that it attained when conditioned separately because, as we have seen repeatedly, the sum of the associative values of the elements of a compound stimulus can never be greater than λ_y.

LATENT INHIBITION

Suppose that stimulus A has never been reinforced (i.e., has never been paired with an unconditioned stimulus and no response has ever been reinforced in its presence) and occurs a number of times without reinforcement. If we now compute its associative value after the $(n + 1)$th trial of this, we find (from Equations A1, A1.1. and A1.2) that

$$V_{A,n+1} = V_{A,n} + \alpha_A \beta_y (\lambda_y - V_{A,n}),$$
$$= 0 + \alpha_A \beta_y (0 - 0),$$
$$= 0.$$

In other words, the associative value of stimulus A should remain at zero as a result of this procedure. It should definitely not become negative. Yet the procedure strongly retards subsequent conditioning of stimulus A (see Chapter 3, p. 47).

It appears that the only way for the model to account for this effect of stimulus preexposure is to assume the preexposure to a stimulus decreases its salience (α_A), perhaps (for example) by decreasing the tendency to attend to it. Although this assumption may work, some see the need for it as a weakness of the model.

PUNISHMENT

The Rescorla-Wagner model can account for punishment by assuming a negative λ_y when conditioning is based on aversive stimuli. The model is symmetrical around zero in that if associative value starts at zero, reversing the sign of λ_y simply reverses the direction of the function relating associative value to the number of trials (see Fig. A.1). Thus, according to the model, an operant response that is paired with an aversive stimulus is suppressed because the stimulus imbues the response with negative associative value. At the same time, we also must assume (on the basis of experimental data) that a stimulus with negative associative value (e.g., a stimulus that has been paired with shock) can elicit a conditioned response. We have also seen however, that a stimulus with negative associative value can inhibit a conditioned response. It appears, then, that the model may require us to assume that stimuli with negative associative value may have both inhibitory and excitatory properties. A way to avoid this assumption is to assume that λ_y differs in respondent and operant conditioning. This possibility is explored further below.

NEGATIVE REINFORCEMENT

In negative reinforcement (which encompasses both escape and avoidance conditioning) an operant response terminates a primary or conditioned aversive stimulus, and, as a result, the rate of that response increases. This creates a problem for the Rescorla-Wagner model because if a response produces neither a positive reinforcer nor an aversive stimulus, λ_y should be zero and so no conditioning should occur. Vaughan (1997) has suggested that a resolution is to let y for operant conditioning be, not a stimulus, but a transition from a less reinforcing (or more aversive) to a more reinforcing (or less aversive) situation, or from a more reinforcing (or less aversive) to a less reinforcing (or more aversive) situation. In the former case, λ_y would be positive and in the latter it would be negative. The former case would account for both positive and negative reinforcement, while the latter would account for punishment. In this view, we would not need to assume that a stimulus can be both inhibitory and excitatory to account for the same stimulus (e.g., shock) serving as both the unconditioned stimulus for respondent conditioning and the punisher of an operant response. Rather, the same stimulus gives rise to two different λ_ys: one for respondent conditioning, in which the stimulus has an eliciting function, and the other for punishment of the operant response, in which the stimulus is the endponit of a transition from a less aversive to a more aversive situation. Thus, the same stimulus may give rise to a positive λ_y in respondent conditioning and a negative λ_y in operant conditioning, and vice versa. This implies that respondent and operant conditioning are different learning processes (as stated in Chapter 3 of this book; also see Pear & Eldridge, 1984). Appendix D, contains further discussion of the application of the Rescorla-Wagner model to reinforcement in operant conditioning.

CONTINGENCY

One of the most remarkable achievements of the Rescorla-Wagner model is its treatment of contingency. Consider the following 2×2 contingency table:

	A occurs	A does not occur
Reinforcement occurs	Event #1 (p_1)	Event #2 (p_2)
No Reinforcement occurs	Event #3 (p_3)	Event #4 (p_4)

$$\pi_1 = \frac{p_1}{p_1 + p_3} \qquad \pi_2 = \frac{p_2}{p_2 + p_4}$$

In the above table, A represents either a conditioned stimulus or an operant response. "Reinforcement" is either the unconditioned stimulus or reinforcement of an operant response. Inside the table we have four possible events represented, along with their probabilities: A occurs followed by reinforcement (Event #1, with probability of p_1); A does not occur but, following an opportunity for A to occur, reinforcement occurs (Event #2, with probability of p_2); A occurs followed by no reinforcement (Event #3, with probability of p_3); and A does not occur and, following an opportunity for it to occur, neither does reinforcement (Event #4, with probability of p_4). At the bottom of the table are two conditional probabilities: π_1 and π_2. The former is the probability that reinforcement will occur *given* that A *has* occurred; the latter is the probability that reinforcement will occur *given* that A *has not* occurred during an opportunity for it to occur. Our interest here is to determine what effect these conditional probabilities have on the associative value of A.

Present during each of the four events in the table are stimuli that we will call *background stimuli*. Although these stimuli are often of little interest in a learning experiment, because they are not manipulated in the experiment and are not correlated with any experimental manipulations, it turns out that they are crucial in accounting for the effects of contingency in the Rescorla-Wagner model. Under certain conditions the background stimuli, which we will designate collectively as B, "drain" associative value from A. To see how this can happen, we look first at how the associative value of A (the conditioned stimulus or operant response of interest) and of B (the background stimuli, collectively) are changed by each of the events in the above table.

From Equations A.1 and A.2, we see that after Event #1

$$\Delta V_{A,n+1} = \alpha_A \beta_y (\lambda_y - [V_{A,n} + V_{B,n}])$$

and

$$\Delta V_{B,n+1} = \alpha_B \beta_y (\lambda_y - [V_{A,n} + V_{B,n}]).$$

After Event #2

$$\Delta V_{A,n+1} = 0$$

and

$$\Delta V_{B,n+1} = \alpha_B \beta_y (\lambda_y - V_{B,n})$$

(because A didn't occur).

After Event #3

$$\Delta V_{A,n+1} = \alpha_A \beta_{y'} (0 - [V_{A,n} + V_{B,n}])$$

and

$$\Delta V_{B,n+1} = \alpha_B \beta_{y'} (0 - [V_{A,n} + V_{B,n}])$$

(because reinforcement didn't occur).

After Event #4

$$\Delta V_{A,n+1} = 0$$

and

$$\Delta V_{B,n+1} = \alpha_B \beta_{y'} (0 - V_{B,n})$$

(because neither A nor reinforcement occurred).

Now assume a large number of trials, and let N be the number of trials in the last large block of trials. If N is large enough, we may expect to have (approximately) $p_1 N$ instances of Event #1, $p_2 N$ instances of Event #2, $p_3 N$ instances of Event #3, and $p_4 N$ instances of Event #4. To obtain the expected sum over those N trials of $\Delta V_{A,n+1}$ and $\Delta V_{B,n+1}$, we sum these quantities multiplied by their respective probabilities over the block of N trials. Thus the expected sum of the $\Delta V_{A,n+1}$ quantities over the N trials is

$$\sum_{k=1}^{N} \Delta V_{A,k} = p_1 \sum_{k=1}^{N} \alpha_A \beta_y \{\lambda_y - (V_{A,k-1} + V_{B,k-1})\}$$

$$- p_3 \sum_{k=1}^{N} \alpha_A \beta_{y'} (V_{A,k-1} + V_{B,k-1}) \qquad (A26)$$

and the expected sum of the $\Delta V_{B,n+1}$ quantities over the block of N trials is

$$\sum_{k=1}^{N} \Delta V_{B,k} = p_1 \sum_{k=1}^{N} \alpha_B \beta_y (\lambda_y - [V_{A,k-1} + V_{B,k-1}])$$

$$+ p_2 \sum_{k=1}^{N} \alpha_B \beta_y (\lambda_y - V_{B,k-1}) - p_3 \sum_{k=1}^{N} \alpha_B \beta_{y'} (V_{A,n} + V_{B,n})$$

$$- p_4 \sum_{k=1}^{N} \alpha_B \beta_{y'} V_{B,k-1}, \qquad (A27)$$

assuming that the four types of events are random so that they are fairly evenly distributed over the N trials.

Let $\overline{\Delta V}_A$, $\overline{\Delta V}_B$, $\overline{V}_A$, and $\overline{V}_B$ be the means of $\Delta V_{A,k}$, $\Delta V_{B,k}$, $V_{A,k}$, and $V_{B,k}$, respectively, over the block of N trials (e.g., $\overline{\Delta V}_A = \frac{\sum_{k=1}^{N} \Delta V_{A,k}}{N}$). Factoring the constants from the summations on the right side of Equations A26 and A27, using the distributive property of summation to apply the summation sign ($\sum$) to each term on the right side of the equations, and then dividing both sides of each equation by N, we obtain from Equation A26

$$\overline{\Delta V}_A = p_1 \alpha_A \beta_y \lambda_y - p_1 \alpha_A \beta_y \overline{V}_A - p_1 \alpha_A \beta_y \overline{V}_B - p_3 \alpha_A \beta_{y'} \overline{V}_A$$

$$- p_3 \alpha_A \beta_{y'} \overline{V}_B \qquad (A28)$$

and from Equation A27

$$\overline{\Delta V}_B = p_1 \alpha_B \beta_y \lambda_y - p_1 \alpha_B \beta_y \overline{V}_A - p_1 \alpha_B \beta_y \overline{V}_B$$

$$+ p_2 \alpha_B \beta_y \lambda_y - p_2 \alpha_B \beta_y \overline{V}_B - p_3 \alpha_B \beta_{y'} \overline{V}_A - p_3 \alpha_B \beta_{y'} \overline{V}_B$$

$$- p_4 \alpha_B \beta_{y'} \overline{V}_B. \qquad (A29)$$

We now consider what $\overline{\Delta V}_A$ and $\overline{\Delta V}_B$ will do as the number of trials increases. After Event #1, $\overline{V}_A$ and $\overline{V}_B$ will each move toward λ_y; after Event #2 $\overline{V}_B$ will move toward λ_y while $\overline{V}_A$ will remain unchanged; after Event #3 $\overline{V}_A$ and $\overline{V}_B$ will each move toward 0; and, after Event #4 $\overline{V}_B$ will move toward 0 while $\overline{V}_A$ will remain unchanged. Thus, $\overline{\Delta V}_A$ will increase after some trials, decrease after others, and stay the same after yet others; likewise, $\overline{\Delta V}_B$ will increase after some trials and decrease after others. It is extremely unlikely, however, that the increases and decreases in each of these quantities will exactly balance each other out. A much more likely scenario is that, depending on the probabilities of the four events and the parameters β_y and $\beta_{y'}$, $\overline{V}_A$ and $\overline{V}_B$ will each eventually begin to move steadily in one direction or the other (i.e., either toward 0 or λ_y), and thus that both $\overline{\Delta V}_A$ and $\overline{\Delta V}_B$ will each eventually approach closer and closer to zero. We may therefore set each to zero and solve for $\overline{V}_A$ and $\overline{V}_B$.

Setting $\overline{\Delta V}_A$ equal to zero in Equation A28 and performing standard algebraic manipulations, we obtain

$$\overline{V}_A = \frac{p_1 \beta_y \lambda_y - \overline{V}_B(p_1 \beta_y + p_3 \beta_{y'})}{p_1 \beta_y + p_3 \beta_{y'}}. \tag{A30}$$

Setting $\overline{\Delta V}_B$ equal to zero in Equation A29, dividing both sides by α_B, collecting all terms containing $\overline{V}_B$ on the left side of the equation, collecting terms containing λ_y together and terms containing $\overline{V}_A$ together on the right side, and then factoring out $\overline{V}_A$ we first obtain

$$p_1 \beta_y \overline{V}_B + p_2 \beta_y \overline{V}_B + p_3 \beta_{y'} \overline{V}_B + p_4 \beta_{y'} \overline{V}_B = p_1 \beta_y \lambda_y + p_2 \beta_y \lambda_y - \overline{V}_A(p_1 \beta_y + p_3 \beta_{y'}).$$

Next, we substitute the quantity on the right side of Equation A30 for $\overline{V}_A$ in the above equation. Note that the quantity in parentheses in the above equation is identical to the quantity in the denominator of the right side of Equation A30. This quantity therefore nicely cancels out when we make the substitution. Then, performing algebraic manipulations to remove the parentheses, collecting terms containing $\overline{V}_B$ on the left side of the equation, and canceling out terms whose absolute values are equal but that have opposite signs, we obtain

$$p_2 \beta_y \overline{V}_B + p_4 \beta_{y'} \overline{V}_B = p_2 \beta_y \lambda_y.$$

Finally, solving for $\overline{V}_B$ yields

$$\overline{V}_B = \frac{p_2 \beta_y \lambda_y}{p_2 \beta_y + p_4 \beta_{y'}}. \tag{A31}$$

Now return to Equation A30 and note that if we divide through by the denominator of that equation we obtain

$$\overline{V}_A = \frac{p_1 \beta_y \lambda_y}{p_1 \beta_y + p_3 \beta_{y'}} - \overline{V}_B. \tag{A32}$$

Recall that at the beginning of this section we defined two conditional probabilities: $\pi_1 = \frac{p_1}{p_1 + p_3}$, the probability that reinforcement will occur *given that A has occurred*; and $\pi_2 = \frac{p_2}{p_2 + p_4}$, the probability that reinforcement will occur *given that A has not occurred* during an opportunity for it to occur. Note that $\frac{p_3}{p_1 + p_3} = 1 - \pi_1$ and that $\frac{p_4}{p_2 + p_4} = 1 - \pi_2$. Thus, if we divide both numerator and denominator of the right side of Equation A32 by $p_1 + p_3$ we obtain

$$\overline{V}_A = \frac{\pi_1 \beta_y \lambda_y}{\pi_1 \beta_y + (1 - \pi_1)\beta_{y'}} - \overline{V}_B; \tag{A33}$$

and if we divide both numerator and denominator of the right side of Equation A31 by $p_2 + p_4$ we obtain

$$\overline{V}_B = \frac{\pi_2 \beta_y \lambda_y}{\pi_2 \beta_y + (1 - \pi_2)\beta_{y'}}. \tag{A34}$$

(Readers wishing to compare Equations A33 and A34 with the corresponding equations in the original Rescorla-Wagner [1972] article should be aware that there is an error in the denominators on the right side of both equations on page 89 of that article: the left "$-$" sign in each denominator should be a "$+$" sign.)

Note that because we have assumed that there is no further change in the associative value of either A or B, Equations A33 and A34 describe the stable-state results of various contingencies—that is, conditional probabilities—of reinforcement. We may summarize the most important functional relations emerging from the equations as follows:

- The equations describe the stable-state result of conditioning. If π_1 is greater than zero and π_2 is zero, the result will be $\overline{V}_A$ greater than zero and $\overline{V}_B$ equal to zero. In other words, when the conditional probability of reinforcement after the occurrence of A is greater than zero and the conditional probability of reinforcement after the nonoccurrence of A is zero, conditioning of A will occur.
- The equations describe the stable-state result of extinction. If both π_1 and π_2 are zero, the result will be that both $\overline{V}_A$ and $\overline{V}_B$ will be zero; the conditioned response will not occur.
- The equations describe the stable-state result of increasing or reducing the probability of reinforcement given the occurrence of A. If π_1 is one and π_2 is zero, $\overline{V}_A$ will be at its maximum of λ_y. Decreasing π_1 causes $\overline{V}_A$ to decrease.
- The equations describe the stable-state result of increasing or reducing the effectiveness of the reinforcer. Note that if β_y is zero, for example, the conditioned response will not occur.
- The equations describe the effect on the stable-state of the salience or conditionability of the conditioned stimulus or operant response and the salience of the background stimuli. Note that both α_A and α_B have dropped out of the equations. They affect the rate of conditioning, but not its final state.
- The equations describe the stable-state result of noncontingent reinforcement. If π_1 and π_2 are equal, $\overline{V}_A$ will be zero (because Equation A33, in combination with Equation A34, will reduce to $\overline{V}_A = \overline{V}_B - \overline{V}_B$). In other words, noncontingent reinforcement of A results in A having no associative value. In addition, reducing the contingency by providing some reinforcement in the absence of A will correspondingly reduce the associative value of A, even if the reinforcement probability of A is unchanged. (This seems to rule out superstitious behavior as described on page 42; however, see Appendix D.)
- The equations describe conditioned inhibition. If π_1 is less than π_2, $\overline{V}_A$ will be negative (because the left term on the right side of Equation 33 will be less than $\overline{V}_B$). That is, the equations say that reinforcing less frequently (i.e., with lower conditional probability) in the presence than in the absence of A causes it to become inhibitory. The greater this disparity between reinforcement in the presence and absence of A, the more strongly inhibitory A will become.

It is noteworthy that equations derived from the Rescorla-Wagner model describe stable-state behavior as well as the transition states of acquisition and extinction. This is consistent with the definition of learning given in Chapter 1 (p. 12). In discussing that definition, we pointed out that just as through interaction with a changed environment an individual learns that the environment has changed, through interaction with an unchanged environment an individual learns that the environment has stayed the same (also see Appendix D).

There is an interesting, and perhaps somewhat puzzling, asymmetry between $\overline{V}_A$ and $\overline{V}_B$ in Equations A33 and A34. While A can have negative associative value, the associative value of B—the background stimuli—can never be less than zero. In addition, while the associative value of A can be zero or less even when there is reinforcement in the presence of A, the associative value of B will always be greater than zero when there is reinforcement in the absence of A—even during noncontingent reinforcement, which, as we have seen, causes the associative value of A to be zero. Adding to this asymmetry is the fact that associative value of A in the model ($\overline{V}_A$) is readily translated into the empirical fact of conditioning, it is not entirely clear how we should translate the associative value of the background stimuli ($\overline{V}_B$). Its only function seems to be that of "draining" associative value from A (Equation 33) so that we see less conditioning of A when there is more frequent reinforcement of the background stimuli. Whether, and if so in what way, $\overline{V}_B$ translates into behavior in the presence of the background stimuli may be elucidated by future experiments and further theoretical developments.

CRITIQUES OF THE RESCORLA-WAGNER MODEL

For detailed critiques of the Rescorla-Wagner model see Gallistel (1990, pp. 408–417), Miller, Barnet, and Grahame (1995), and Siegel and Allan (1996). Gallistel concluded that the large number of parameters in the model that are free to vary from one set of experimental data to another makes it difficult to assess the validity of the model. Although also finding serious flaws in the model, Miller et al. concluded:

> [T]he Rescorla-Wagner model has distinct merits. . . . Investigators continue to use it for lack of a better model, which is neither inappropriate nor unusual in the history of science. . . . The Rescorla-Wagner model has stimulated much important research, the results of which will probably be central to the models of associative learning that will ultimately displace the Rescorla-Wagner model. (p. 382)

Siegel and Allan noted that the model not only has been enormously influential in the field of animal learning, but has also found application in a variety of other areas such as verbal learning, human category learning, human judgments of correlational relationships, reasoning, social psychology, perception, and physiological regulation. Siegel and Allan point out that there now exist alternatives that address some data better than the Rescorla-Wagner model does, and that one of these newer models may eventually displace the Rescorla-Wagner model.

Whereas the Rescorla-Wagner model describes the acquisition of behavior, the matching law applies to behavior in the stable-state (i.e., when responding has stabilized after the end of the acquisition process). Suppose that there are N independent concurrently available operant responses that we will enumerate 1 to N. Let $B_i (i = 1$ to N) be a behavioral measure—specifically, either response rate or time spent responding—of the ith concurrently available operant response. Then we may write the matching law as

$$\frac{B_j}{\sum_{i=1}^{N} B_i} = \frac{r_j}{\sum_{i=1}^{N} r_i}, \tag{B1}$$

where j is any arbitrary number between 1 and N (i.e., j is some specific i), r_i is the reinforcement rate for the ith concurrently available operant response, $\sum_{i=1}^{N} B_i$ is the sum from 1 to N of the B_is, and $\sum_{i=1}^{N} r_i$ is the sum from 1 to N of the r_is. Equation B1 is called the "matching law" because it states that the relative response rate and relative time allocation on concurrently available responses tend to "match" (i.e., be equal to) the relative reinforcement rates for those responses.

For any two concurrently available responses, which we will arbitrarily label "1" and "2," we may also write the matching law as

$$\frac{B_1}{B_1 + B_2} = \frac{r_1}{r_1 + r_2}, \tag{B1.1}$$

or as

$$\frac{B_1}{B_2} = \frac{r_1}{r_2}. \tag{B1.2}$$

Since division by zero is undefined in mathematics, Equations B1, B1.1, and B1.2 are equivalent only if none of their denominators is zero. Any fraction whose denominator is zero is undefined and hence impermissible. The numerators, however, may be zero. Note that if the numerators are zero, the equations say that there will be no responding on an alternative if there is no reinforcement for that alternative. This is the case of extinction of an alternative. Thus, extinction conforms to the matching law, although it is a rather uninteresting special case of it and is therefore sometimes called "matching in a trivial sense."

To see that Equations B1, B1.1, and B1.2 are indeed equivalent (assuming nonzero denominators), first note that from Equation B1.2 we may write

$$\frac{B_2}{B_1} = \frac{r_2}{r_1},$$

$$1 + \frac{B_2}{B_1} = 1 + \frac{r_2}{r_1},$$

$$\frac{B_1 + B_2}{B_1} = \frac{r_1 + r_2}{r_1},$$

and, by inverting the fractions on both sides of the above equation, we obtain Equation B1.1. Since the derivation works in both directions, we have proven that Equations B1.1 and B1.2 are equivalent.

Similarly, note that from Equation B1.2 we may write

$$\frac{B_1}{B_1} + \frac{B_2}{B_1} + \cdots + \frac{B_N}{B_1} = \frac{r_1}{r_1} + \frac{r_2}{r_1} + \cdots + \frac{r_N}{r_1},$$

or, by putting each side over its common denominator and using standard summation notation,

$$\frac{\sum_{i=1}^{N} B_i}{B_1} = \frac{\sum_{i=1}^{N} r_i}{r_1},$$

from which, by inverting the fractions on both sides of the equation, Equation B1 follows. (Note that we could have written "j" instead of "1" in the above derivation, since which response we label "1" is arbitrary.) Since the derivation works in both directions, we may conclude that B1.2 is equivalent to B1, and hence that equations B1, B1.1, and B1.2 are simply different but equivalent ways of writing the matching law.

As mentioned, the B_i s in the matching law are either response rate on or time allocation to concurrently available responses. Both measures generally conform well, but not precisely, to the matching law. For reasons that are not clear at present, time allocation typically conforms more closely to the matching law than response rate does. When both measures conform reasonably well to the matching law we can write

$$\frac{R_1}{R_2} = \frac{r_1}{r_2}$$

and

$$\frac{T_1}{T_2} = \frac{r_1}{r_2},$$

where R_1 and R_2 are the response rates on alternative 1 and 2, T_1 and T_2 are the amounts of time spent responding on alternatives 1 and 2, and r_1 and r_2 are the reinforcement rates for responding on alternatives 1 and 2. From the preceding two equations we may write

$$\frac{R_1}{R_2} = \frac{T_1}{T_2}.$$

Multiplying both sides by $\frac{R_2}{T_1}$ (or "cross multiplying"), we obtain

$$\frac{R_1}{T_1} = \frac{R_2}{T_2}. \tag{B2}$$

Now it useful to make the following definitions:

$$R_i = \frac{n_i}{T_{\text{total}}}.$$

and

$$L_i = \frac{n_i}{T_i},$$

where the subscript i indicates either alternative 1 or 2, and T_{total} is an amount of time (e.g., total session time) during which responding can occur on any of the concurrent alternatives. R_i, which is the response rate on the ith alternative, is sometimes called "overall response rate" on alternative i, to distinguish it from L_i, the "local response rate" on alternative i.

Using the above definitions in conjunction with Equation B2 we obtain

$$\frac{n_1/T_{\text{total}}}{T_1} = \frac{n_2/T_{\text{total}}}{T_2},$$

$$\frac{n_1}{T_1} = \frac{n_2}{T_2}$$

(which follows from multiplying both sides of the above equation by T_{total}), and hence

$$L_1 = L_2$$

(which follows from the above definition of local response rate). Thus, that the matching law is true for both response rate and time allocation implies equality of local response rates.

The matching law leads to some interesting predictions regarding responding on different concurrently available reinforcement schedules.

CONCURRENT RATIO-RATIO SCHEDULES

On a ratio schedule of reinforcement (either FR or VR), the rate of reinforcement is directly proportional to rate of responding. Thus, for response alternative i reinforced on a ratio schedule we may write

$$r_i = \frac{R_i}{c_i}, \tag{B3}$$

where c_i is the mean number of responses required for reinforcement on response alternative i.

Now from Equations B1.2 and B3 we have

$$\frac{R_1}{R_2} = \frac{R_1/c_1}{R_2/c_2}.$$

In writing the above equation, we assume, of course, that R_2 is not zero. Note that if R_1 is zero, however, we have matching (although in the trivial sense that $0 = 0$) regardless of the values of c_1 and c_2. Assuming that R_1 is *not* zero and multiplying numerator and denominator of the right side of the above equation by c_2 and both sides of the equation by $\frac{c_1 R_2}{R_1}$, we obtain $c_1 = c_2$. In other words, if neither R_1 nor R_2 is zero, then matching can occur only if the mean number of responses required for reinforcement is the same on both schedules. Thus, if different mean numbers of responses are required on the two schedules, then matching can occur only if no responding occurs on one of the schedules, or to put it another way, only if the individual shows exclusive preference for one of the alternatives. The matching law does not say, however, which alternative that will be (although, perhaps not surprisingly, empirically it turns out to be the one with the lower ratio of responses to reinforcement; Herrnstein & Loveland, 1975). The equation is also silent regarding how responding will be distributed across the alternatives when the mean number of responses required for reinforcement is the same for both alternatives, because if $c_1 = c_2$ relative response rates match relative reinforcement rates no matter how responding is distributed across the alternatives. (We return to these points later when we discuss melioration in Appendix D.)

CONCURRENT INTERVAL-RATIO SCHEDULES

On an interval reinforcement schedule (either FI or VI), reinforcement rate is largely independent of response rate and time spent responding as long as some minimal amount of responding is occurring. Let T_1 be the amount of time spent responding on an interval schedule, T_2 be the amount of time spent responding on a concurrently available ratio schedule, and $T_{\text{total}} = T_1 + T_2$ be the total amount of time spent responding on both schedules. Then the total number of reinforcements on the interval schedule during the period of time represented by T_{total}, the total time spent responding on both schedules, is

$$T_{\text{total}} \times r_1 = (T_1 + T_2) \times r_1$$

and the total number of reinforcements on the ratio schedule during the period of time corresponding to T_{total} is

$$T_{\text{total}} \times r_2 = \frac{T_2 L_2}{c},$$

where r_1 and r_2 are the reinforcement rates during the time period T_{total} on the interval and ratio schedules, respectively, L_2 is the local response rate on the ratio schedule (i.e., the response rate on the ratio schedule during the time spent responding on it), and c is the mean number of responses per reinforcement on the ratio schedule. (This can be seen simply by multiplying through each side of the above two equations, using the definitions of r_1, r_2, and L_2.) It follows that the reinforcement rates on each schedule during the time period corresponding to T_{total} is

$$r_1 = \frac{(T_1 + T_2) \times r_1}{T_{\text{total}}} \tag{B4}$$

and

$$r_2 = \frac{T_2 L_2 / c}{T_{\text{total}}} \tag{B5}$$

From Equation B1.2 we may write

$$\frac{T_1}{T_2} = \frac{r_1}{r_2},$$

and thus from Equations B4 and B5,

$$\frac{T_1}{T_2} = \frac{(T_1 + T_2) \times r_1}{T_{\text{total}}} \bigg/ \frac{T_2 L_2/c}{T_{\text{total}}}.$$

Multiplying numerator and denominator of the complex fraction on the right side of the above equation by T and multiplying both sides of the equation by $\frac{T_2}{T_1 + T_2}$ we obtain

$$\frac{T_1}{T_1 + T_2} = \frac{r_1}{L_2/c}. \tag{B6}$$

Note from the above equation that $r_1 = L_2/c$ implies $\frac{T_1}{T_1+T_2} = 1$ and hence $T_2 = 0$. As the rate of reinforcement for responding on the interval schedule increases, assuming that L_2/c is constant, responding on the ratio schedule decreases steadily (specifically, in a linear manner) until, eventually, it ceases altogether. The converse does not hold; as long as r_1 is greater than zero, T_1 will be greater than zero.

CONCURRENT INTERVAL-INTERVAL SCHEDULES

We have seen that (according to the matching law) a high reinforcement rate on either a ratio or an interval schedule can eliminate responding on a concurrently available ratio schedule, whereas a high rate of reinforcement on a ratio schedule will reduce but not eliminate responding on a concurrently available interval schedule. In addition, a high rate of responding on an interval schedule will reduce but not eliminate responding on a concurrently available interval schedule. To see this, rewrite Equation B1.1 as

$$\frac{B_1}{B_1 + B_2} = \frac{1}{1 + \frac{r_2}{r_1}}$$

by dividing the numerator and denominator of the right side of Equation B1.1 by r_1. If we assume that alternatives 1 and 2 are each reinforced on an interval schedule, we may assign any arbitrary value we wish to the ratio $\frac{r_2}{r_1}$; specifically, we may hold r_2 constant while increasing r_1. Note that as r_1 grows larger, $\frac{r_2}{r_1}$ approaches zero, hence $\frac{B_1}{B_1+B_2}$ approaches one, and thus B_2 approaches zero. It never actually equals zero, however, as long as r_2 is greater than zero.

PRACTICAL IMPLICATIONS OF THE MATCHING LAW

The preceding derivations suggest that reinforcing desirable behavior on interval schedules in practical situations may cause it to compete more effectively with undesirable behavior than reinforcing it on ratio schedules (Myerson & Hale, 1984). The rationale for this is as follows. One typically does not know what schedule undesirable behavior is being reinforced on. The two major possibilities, however, are that it is being reinforced on a ratio schedule or on an interval schedule (or some complex schedule involving either or both of these possibilities). If it is being reinforced on a ratio schedule, then reinforcing the desirable alternative on a ratio schedule will have no effect on the undesirable behavior unless (possibly) the amount of desirable behavior required for reinforcement is less than the amount of undesirable behavior required for reinforcement. In contrast, any amount of reinforcement of the desirable behavior on an interval schedule will reduce the undesirable behavior; and, if the reinforcement rate for the desirable behavior is high enough, the undesirable behavior will decrease to zero.

If the undesirable behavior is being reinforced on an interval schedule, then reinforcing the desirable behavior on a ratio schedule may have no effect because the interval schedule may prevent responding on the ratio schedule. In order for desirable behavior reinforced on a ratio schedule to compete effectively with undesirable behavior reinforced on an interval schedule, the amount of responding required for reinforcement on the ratio schedule would have to be quite small. Thus, the reinforcement rate on the ratio schedule would have to be quite large. In contrast, any rate of reinforcement of desirable behavior on an interval schedule will cause a proportionate decrease in undesirable behavior reinforced on an interval schedule.

For further discussion of the advantages of interval over ratio schedules in practical situations, see Myerson and Hale (1984).

Herrnstein's Formulation of the Matching Law

A ssume that the totality of an individual's behavior in a given situation can be broken down into $N + 1$ independent concurrently available operant responses that we will enumerate 0 to N, where Responses 1 to N are under experimental control and Response 0 represents collectively all operant responses that are not under experimental control (and that, therefore, are generally unknown). Let B_i $(i = 0 \text{ to } N)$ be a behavioral measure—specifically, either response rate or time spent responding—of the ith concurrently available operant response. Then we may write the matching law—the tendency for either relative response rate or relative time allocation to match relative reinforcement rate (Appendix B, Equation B1)—as

$$\frac{B_j}{\sum\limits_{i=0}^{N} B_i} = \frac{r_j}{\sum\limits_{i=0}^{N} r_i}, \tag{C1}$$

where j is any arbitrary number between 0 and N (i.e., j is some specific i), r_i is the reinforcement rate (scaled equivalently across all responses, including Response 0) for the ith concurrently available operant response, $\sum_{i=0}^{N} B_i$ is the sum from 0 to N of the B_is, and $\sum_{i=0}^{N} r_i$ is the sum from 0 to N of the r_is.

Herrnstein's (1970) formulation of the matching law assumes that the behavioral measure for all the independent operant responses in which an individual can engage in a given situation always sums to a constant. Note that this assumption is necessarily true if the B_is are time allocations. We may write the assumption as

$$\sum_{i=0}^{N} B_i = k,$$

where k is a constant. Substituting the above in Equation C1 we obtain

$$\frac{B_j}{k} = \frac{r_j}{\sum\limits_{i=0}^{N} r_i},$$

$$B_j = \frac{k r_j}{\sum\limits_{i=0}^{N} r_i}, \tag{C2}$$

or as Herrnstein's formulation of the matching law is often written,

$$B_j = \frac{k r_j}{\sum\limits_{i=1}^{N} r_i + r_0}, \tag{C2.1}$$

Equation C2 is used to describe behavior in single schedules as well as in concurrent schedules, as we shall see.

CONCURRENT SCHEDULES

Because Equation C2 is essentially the matching law, we can use it to derive any of the equations in Appendix B. For example, to use it to derive the matching law for the case of two concurrent operant responses simply write

$$\frac{B_1}{B_1 + B_2} = \frac{\dfrac{kr_1}{\sum\limits_{i=0}^{N} r_i}}{\dfrac{kr_1}{\sum\limits_{i=0}^{N} r_i} + \dfrac{kr_2}{\sum\limits_{i=0}^{N} r_i}},$$

and then multiply numerator and denominator of the right side of the equation by

$$\frac{\sum\limits_{i=0}^{N} r_i}{k}$$

to obtain

$$\frac{B_1}{B_1 + B_2} = \frac{r_1}{r_1 + r_2}.$$

Equation C2 permits a very straightforward derivation of the tendency (seen in Appendix B) for reinforcement on an interval (either FI or VI) schedule to abolish responding on a concurrently available ratio (either FR or VR) schedule. Let R_1 be the response rate on an interval schedule, and R_2 be the response rate on a concurrently available ratio schedule. The rate of reinforcement on the ratio schedule will be

$$r_2 = \frac{R_2}{c}, \tag{C3}$$

where c is the mean number of responses required for reinforcement on the ratio schedule. From Equation C2.1 we may write

$$R_2 = \frac{kr_2}{\sum\limits_{i=1}^{2} r_i + r_0} = \frac{kr_2}{r_1 + r_2 + r_0},$$

(because there are only two experimentally programmed alternatives), and substituting for r_2 as indicated in Equation C3 to obtain

$$R_2 = \frac{k\dfrac{R_2}{c}}{r_1 + \dfrac{R_2}{c} + r_0},$$

dividing both sides of the right side of the equation by R_2 to obtain

$$1 = \frac{\dfrac{k}{c}}{r_1 + \dfrac{R_2}{c} + r_0},$$

multiplying both sides of the equation by $r_1 + \frac{R_2}{c} + r_0$, and solving for R_2 we obtain

$$R_2 = k - c(r_1 + r_0). \tag{C4}$$

Note that as r_1 increases, R_2 decreases steadily (specifically as a straight-line, or linear, function) until it reaches zero. Since R_2 can never be negative, we assume that it remains at zero with further increases in r_1 (cf. Appendix B, Equation B6).

SINGLE SCHEDULES

For response rate on single schedules Equation C2 becomes

$$R_1 = \frac{kr_1}{r_1 + r_0}. \tag{C5}$$

Note that R_1 is zero when r_1 is zero. As r_1 increases, R_1 increases, at a negatively accelerating rate, to an asymptote (or limit) of k. To see that k is the limiting value that R_1 can attain, divide the numerator and denominator of Equation C5 by r_1 to obtain

$$R_1 = \frac{k}{1 + \dfrac{r_0}{r_1}}. \tag{C6}$$

Note from Equation C6 that as r_1 grows indefinitely large (and assuming that r_0 is a constant), the ratio $\frac{r_0}{r_1}$ approaches zero, so that R_1 approaches, but can never reach, k (because $\frac{r_0}{r_1}$ can never reach zero).

The same reasoning that permitted us to derive Equation C4 leads to an interesting prediction about single ratio schedules. If c is the mean number of responses required for reinforcement on a ratio schedule, from Equations C3 and C5 we may write

$$R_1 = \frac{k\dfrac{R_1}{c}}{\dfrac{R_1}{c} + r_0},$$

$$1 = \frac{\dfrac{k}{c}}{\dfrac{R_1}{c} + r_0},$$

$$\frac{R_1}{c} + r_0 = \frac{k}{c},$$

$$\frac{R_1}{c} = \frac{k}{c} - r_0,$$

and hence

$$R_1 = k - cr_0. \tag{C7}$$

Equation C7 says that as the mean number of responses required for reinforcement on a ratio schedule increases, response rate decreases linearly (since the equation for a straight line is $y = ax + b$, where a and b are constants). In addition, the equation says that a response requirement increased beyond a certain point (namely, $c \geq \frac{k}{r_0}$) cannot sustain behavior. In other words, there is a limit to schedule shaping on ratio schedule (see pp. 73–74).

For further discussion about the implications of Herrnstein's formulation of the matching law for ratio responding see Pear (1975); for a critical evaluation of these implication see Timberlake (1977, 1982b).

A ssume that a number of alternative operant responses are simultaneously available to an individual. For any arbitrary pair of these alternative response, i and j, let T_i and T_j be the amounts of time spent engaging in Responses i and j during some time period T_{total}, N_i and N_j be the number of occurrences of Responses i and j, and n_i and n_j be the number of reinforcements received by Responses i and j, during T_i and T_j time periods, respectively. Define $L_i = \frac{N_i}{T_i}$ and $L_j = \frac{N_j}{T_j}$ as the local response rates and $l_i = \frac{n_i}{T_i}$ and $l_j = \frac{n_j}{T_j}$ as the local reinforcement rates of Responses i and j during the T_i and T_j time periods, respectively. The theory of melioration states that individuals will tend to allocate time between any two response alternatives so as to maximize local reinforcement rate (Herrnstein, 1982; Herrnstein & Vaughan, 1980). Using terms just defined, we may say that

$$l_i < l_i \Rightarrow T_i < T_j \text{ and } l_i > l_i \Rightarrow T_i > T_{j_i}.$$

What this says is that local reinforcement rate of Response i less than local reinforcement rate of Response j implies that the individual will subsequently spend less time emitting Response i than Response j; and local reinforcement rate of Response i greater than local reinforcement rate of Response j implies that the individual will subsequently spend more time emitting Response i than Response j. Thus, another way of stating this is that individuals will tend to respond in such a way as to maximize local reinforcement rate.

All of the results derived from the matching law (Appendix B) and Herrnstein's formulation (Appendix C) follow from melioration. This will be seen in the following sections.

CONCURRENT SCHEDULES

Melioration may be the basic process underlying the matching of relative response rates to relative reinforcement rates on concurrent schedules. To see this we look separately at combinations of specific types of concurrently programmed schedules.

Concurrent Interval-Interval Schedules

Increasing or decreasing the amount of time spent responding on an interval (either FI or VI) schedule has little effect on the number of reinforcements that occur on that schedule in a given time period. Therefore, from the definition of local reinforcement rate given above, it can be seen that (within limits) the less time spent responding on an interval schedule the greater will be the local reinforcement rate on that schedule. Suppose that on two concurrently programmed interval schedules for Responses i and j, respectively, the local reinforcement rate for the former is greater than that for the latter (i.e., $l_i > l_j$). Due to melioration, the individual will shift time allocation from Response j to Response i. But this will drive the local reinforcement rate for Response i lower and that for Response j higher. Eventually the latter will be higher than the former (i.e., $l_j > l_i$), and thus response allocation will shift toward Response j and away from Response i. This will drive the local reinforcement rate for Response j lower and that for Response i higher. This result of this constant shifting of time allocation back and forth between Responses i and j is that, over a long period of time, their local rates will tend, on average, to be equal. Thus we may write

$$l_i = l_j,$$

which by definition is the same as

$$\frac{n_i}{T_i} = \frac{n_j}{T_j}.$$

Multiplying both sides by $\frac{T_i}{n_j}$ ("cross multiplying") and changing sides we obtain

$$\frac{T_i}{T_j} = \frac{n_i}{n_j},$$

from which, by dividing both numerator and denominator of the right side by total time, T_{total}, we obtain

$$\frac{T_i}{T_j} = \frac{r_i}{r_j} \tag{D1}$$

where r_i and r_j are the overall (as opposed to local) reinforcement rates. Equation D1 is the matching law for time allocation; that is, the matching of relative time allocation to relative reinforcement rate (Appendix B; see Equation B1.2). To obtain the matching law for relative response rate (i.e., the matching of relative response rate to relative reinforcement rate), we assume equality of local response rates. Thus, making this assumption, we may write

$$L_i = L_j,$$

which by definition is the same as

$$\frac{N_i}{T_i} = \frac{N_j}{T_j}.$$

Multiplying both sides by $\frac{T_i}{N_j}$ ("cross multiplying") we obtain

$$\frac{N_i}{N_j} = \frac{T_i}{T_j},$$

from which, by dividing numerator and denominator of the left side by T_{total} and substituting as indicated by Equation D1, we obtain

$$\frac{R_i}{R_j} = \frac{r_i}{r_j}. \tag{D2}$$

Concurrent Ratio-Ratio Schedules

On a ratio (either FR or VR) schedule, the number of reinforcements of a response is directly proportional to the number of occurrences of that response. Thus, for Response i we may write

$$\frac{N_i}{c_i} = n_i,$$

$$= \frac{n_i}{T_i} T_i,$$

$$= l_i T_i,$$

where c_i is the mean number of occurrences of Response i required for reinforcement and the other terms are as already defined. Dividing both sides of the above equation by T_i and exchanging sides, we obtain

$$l_i = \frac{N_i}{T_i c_i},$$

$$= \frac{L_i}{c_i}. \tag{D3}$$

Similarly, if Response j, is a concurrently available response that is also reinforced on a ratio schedule, we have

$$l_j = \frac{L_j}{c_j} \tag{D4}$$

where the terms in the above equation are defined for Response j in the same way that the corresponding terms are defined for Response i. Equations D3 and D4 say that the local reinforcement rates of Responses i and j are equal to their respective local response rates divided by their respective mean number of occurrences required for reinforcement.

Since we assume that the local response rates (L_i and L_j) are equal, we see that the local reinforcement rates (l_i and l_j) depend solely on the response requirement (c_i and c_j): the fewer responses required for reinforcement, the higher the local reinforcement rate. Therefore, more and more responding will occur on the ratio schedule with the smaller response requirement until eventually responding is occurring exclusively on that schedule. This is consistent with the matching law, which predicts exclusive responding on one or the other of two concurrently programmed ratio schedules when the response requirements of the two schedules differ. The matching law does not say, however, which schedule will be the beneficiary of this exclusive responding (see Appendix B). In correctly predicting that it will be the one with the smaller response requirement, melioration scores an advantage over the matching law in this regard.

What about when the response requirements on the two concurrently programmed ratio schedules are equal? In this case, neither the matching law nor melioration makes a specific prediction. Melioration makes no specific prediction because when the response requirements are equal the local reinforcement rates will also be equal regardless of how responding is allocated between the two alternatives (see Equations D3 and D4, keeping in mind that we are assuming equality of local response rates). Exact equality of local reinforcement rates, however, is probably something that can never occur in practice. No matter how conscientiously an experimenter tries to achieve equality of local reinforcement rates, slight and unavoidable response biases will probably result in some inequality and thus "push" responding toward one alternative or the other. (Appendix E looks more closely at response bias.)

Concurrent Interval-Ratio Schedules

Suppose that Response i is reinforced on an interval schedule and Response j is concurrently reinforced on a ratio schedule. We may derive the local response rate of Response i as follows:

$$l_i = \frac{n_i}{T_i}$$

by definition,

$$= \frac{n_i}{T_i} \times \frac{T_{total}}{T_{total}}$$

by multiplying the right side by the total time (i.e., the time spent responding on both schedules) divided by total time, which is equal to one,

$$= \frac{n_i}{T_{total}} \times \frac{T_{total}}{T_i}$$

by exchanging denominators in the two fractions multiplied together on the right side of the equation, and thus

$$= r_i \times \frac{T_{total}}{T_i} \tag{D5}$$

by substituting r_i, overall response rate, for its definition (number of occurrences of Response i divided by the total amount of time available for it to have occurred). (For a somewhat different equation see Herrnstein, 1982, Equation 19.10, p. 439.) Note that $\frac{T_{total}}{T_i} \geq 1$.

As for the local reinforcement rate for Response j, which is reinforced on a ratio schedule, we may simply refer to Equation D4: $l_j = \frac{L_j}{c_j}$, where (as already defined) L_j is the local response rate of Response j and c_j is the mean number of occurrences of Response j required for reinforcement.

From Equation D5 we see that on the interval schedule local reinforcement rate varies directly with overall reinforcement rate and inversely with time spent responding on the schedule. On the ratio schedule, however, local reinforcement rate varies only with local response rate which we are assuming is a constant. If overall reinforcement rate on the interval schedule is higher than local reinforcement rate on the ratio schedule, local reinforcement rate on the interval schedule will always be above the local reinforcement rate on the ratio schedule, and responding will occur exclusively on the interval schedule. (The matching law [Appendix B, Equation B6] and Herrnstein's formulation of the matching law [Appendix C, Equation C4] also predict this result.) If the overall response rate on the interval schedule is less than the local response rate on the ratio schedule, however, whether more time is allocated to the interval schedule or to the ratio schedule will vary with the local reinforcement rate on the interval schedule. The more time allocated to the interval schedule, the lower its local reinforcement rate will be. As the local reinforcement rate on the interval schedule falls below that on the ratio schedule, responding will shift to the ratio schedule. But this will cause local response rate on the interval schedule to increase. As it moves above that on the ratio schedule, responding will shift back to the interval schedule. As long as the overall reinforcement rate on the interval schedule is below the local response rate on the ratio schedule, responding will shift back and forth between the two schedules—because increases in time spent on the interval schedule will result eventually in a decrease in local response rate below that on the ratio schedule; and conversely, decreases in time spent on the interval schedule will result eventually in an increase in local response rate above that on the ratio schedule. This shifting time allocation from one schedule to the other whenever the former schedule's local reinforcement rate is less than that of the other will result in the local reinforcement rates of the two schedules averaging out to be about equal.

Now consider the following derivation:

$$\frac{T_i l_i}{T_j l_j} = \frac{T_i \dfrac{n_i}{T_i}}{T_j \dfrac{n_j}{T_j}},$$

$$= \frac{n_i}{n_j},$$

$$= \frac{n_i / T_{\text{total}}}{n_j / T_{\text{total}}},$$

$$= \frac{r_i}{r_j}.$$

But if the local reinforcement rates of the two schedules are equal (as we have seen will be the case if the overall reinforcement rate of the interval schedule is less than the local reinforcement rate of the ratio schedule), l_i and l_j in the above equation cancel out and we may write $\frac{T_i}{T_j} = \frac{r_i}{r_j}$, which is the matching law for time allocation. If we assume equality of local response rates, then the matching law for response rate follows (see the introduction of Appendix B). In actuality, local response rates on ratio schedules tend to be higher than local response rates on interval (or, at least, VI) schedules, apparently because of topographical differences in the responding on the two types of schedules (Herrnstein, 1982, p. 443).

RELATION OF MELIORATION TO HERRNSTEIN'S FORMULATION

Melioration is consistent with Herrnstein's formulation of the matching law (Appendix C). Note that, in all the above derivations from melioration, whenever neither time allocation for two concurrently available responses was zero, we found the matching law to hold (at least for time allocation; and, if we can assume equality of local response rates, for response rate also). Consulting Appendix B, we may say that melioration implies Equation B1.2 for all pairs of nonzero concurrently available responses. If the time allocation for a given response is zero, it may be disregarded for our present purpose (although, in a trivial sense, it still conforms to the matching law—since zero responses lead to zero reinforcement). Appendix B shows how Equation B1 can be derived from Equation B1.2. But Equation C1 in Appendix C is simply Equation B1 expanded to include all behavior (with responses not under experimental observation being designated as B_0). Thus, melioration gives rise to Equation C1 if we assume that is applies to the totality of all concurrently available behavior. To make it completely consistent with Herrnstein's formulation, we need simply add the assumption that the sum of all concurrently available behavior, $\sum_{i=0}^{N} B_i$, is a constant (note that this is necessarily true if the B_is are time allocation).

RELATION OF MELIORATION TO THE RESCORLA-WAGNER MODEL

Consider two operant response alternatives, A and B. When emitting Response A, an individual has the option of continuing to emit Response A or switching over to (perhaps among other response alternatives) Response B. Likewise, when emitting Response B the individual has the option of continuing to emit Response B or switching over to (perhaps among other response alternatives) Response A. In order to derive melioration from the Rescorla-Wagner model, we assume that—in addition to Responses A and B—there are specific responses of switching between these two responses. Let's designate the response of switching from Response A to Response B as Response $A \rightarrow B$, and the response of switching from Response B to Response A as Response $B \rightarrow A$. Let λ_{B-A} be the associative value limit of Response $A \rightarrow B$ and λ_{A-B} be the associative value limit of Response $B \rightarrow A$. Assume that λ_{B-A} and λ_{A-B} are functions of the difference between the local reinforcement rates, l_A and l_B, of Responses A and B, respectively, such that

$$l_A - l_B < 0 \Rightarrow \lambda_{B-A} < 0 \text{ and } \lambda_{A-B} > 0,$$

$$l_A - l_B > 0 \Rightarrow \lambda_{B-A} > 0 \text{ and } \lambda_{A-B} < 0,$$

$$l_A - l_B = 0 \Rightarrow \lambda_{B-A} = 0 \text{ and } \lambda_{A-B} = 0.$$

In other words, the associative value limit of switching from one response alternative to another will be positive if the change results in an increase in local reinforcement, negative if it results in a decrease in local reinforcement rate, and zero if it results in no change in local reinforcement rate. We will also assume that $\lambda_{A-B} = -\lambda_{B-A}$.

Applying the Rescorla-Wagner model (Equations A1, A1.1, and A1.2) to the preceding assumptions, we obtain

$$V_{A \rightarrow B, n+1} = V_{A \rightarrow B, n} + K(\lambda_{B-A} - V_{A \rightarrow B, n})$$

and

$$V_{B \rightarrow A, n+1} = V_{B \rightarrow A, n} + K(\lambda_{A-B} - V_{B \rightarrow A, n}),$$

where $V_{A \rightarrow B, n}$ and $V_{B \rightarrow A, n}$ are the current associative values and $V_{A \rightarrow B, n+1}$ and $V_{B \rightarrow A, n+1}$ the succeeding associative values of Responses $A \rightarrow B$, and $B \rightarrow A$, respectively, and K is a constant from 0 to 1, representing the conditionability of Responses $A \rightarrow B$ and $B \rightarrow A$ and the effectiveness of the reinforcer (we are assuming that K is the same for both Responses $A \rightarrow B$, and $B \rightarrow A$).

We assume that the probability of emitting a specific switching response (Response $A \rightarrow B$ or $B \rightarrow A$) is a direct function of the current associative value of that response ($V_{A \rightarrow B, n}$ or $V_{B \rightarrow A, n}$). If the local reinforcement rate of Response B is greater than that of Response A, λ_{B-A} will be positive while λ_{A-B} will be negative; thus, it can be seen from the above equations that Response $A \rightarrow B$ will gain associative value while Response $B \rightarrow A$ will lose it. Conversely, if the local reinforcement rate of Response A is greater than that of Response B, Response $B \rightarrow A$ will gain associative value while Response $A \rightarrow B$ will lose it. Figure A.1 illustrates the process involved. Note that the current associative value moves in the positive direction when it is less than λ_y, and in the negative direction when it is greater than λ_y. If λ_y is constantly changing, associative value may never "catch up" to it.

The above provides an alternative way of describing the predictions of the theory of melioration regarding responding on various concurrent schedules. On concurrent interval-interval schedules and, within a certain range, on concurrent interval-ratio schedules associative value never continues steadily in one direction because as time spent responding on an alternative increases local reinforcement rate for that alternative decreases; and, conversely, as time spent responding on an alternative increases local reinforcement rate for that alternative decreases. For concurrent ratio-ratio schedules and, at some parameters, concurrent interval-ratio schedules, local reinforcement rate does not vary inversely with time spent on an alternative and so responding gradually decreases to zero on one or the other alternative. Thus, it appears that melioration is derivable from the Rescorla-Wagner model. Since the matching law is derivable from melioration, it follows that the matching law is derivable from the Rescorla-Wagner model. It is interesting to note the close relationship between these formulations, considering that the Rescorla-Wagner model was developed to describe the acquisition of behavior whereas the matching law and melioration were developed to describe behavior in the stable state. This indicates the arbitrariness of distinguishing between acquisition and stable-state behavior. Thus, if we ask when does learning stop, the answer would seem to be—never. Note that this is consistent with the definition of learning given in Chapter 1 (p. 12). (For further details on the relationship between melioration and the Rescorla-Wagner model, see Vaughan, 1982, 1997.)

RESPONSE ACQUISITION, SHAPING, AND STEREOTYPY

In addition to describing stable-state behavior, melioration also describes response acquisition, as indicated in the previous section. When a response first begins to be reinforced, the local reinforcement rate for that response is greater than that for all other available behavior. The newly reinforced response then increases until its local reinforcement rate is at least equal to that of all other available behavior. Response shaping speeds up this move toward equilibrium by providing a gradient in which local reinforcement densities (i.e., reinforcement rates) increase with increasingly closer approximations to a target response. Melioration can also describe shaping with reference to the Rescorla-Wagner model because, as indicated earlier, it is derivable from that model. The Rescorla-Wagner model's description of shaping would be based on it descriptions of response generalization and response discrimination (see Appendix A).

When it has just begun to be reinforced, a response will vary in its topography. With successive reinforcements, the topography of the response will become more stereotyped— that is, less varied. We may view each topographical variation of a response as a different response with its own local reinforcement rate. Less efficient topographies will tend to be eliminated because they (by definition) have lower local reinforcement rates. Even when the local reinforcement rates of two topographical variations of a response are equal, a slight bias toward one or the other variation could lead to that one becoming exclusively preferred (see Appendix E for discussion of response bias).

The above can also describe the development of superstitious behavior. During response independent reinforcement, every response (by definition) has the same local rate of reinforcement. Slight biases, however, will result in some responses being favored over others. Eventually, one response will tend to predominate even though it does not produce reinforcement (see Pear, 1988).

Extensions of the Matching Law

eviations from the matching law (Appendix B) may occur for a number of reasons; for example, because of topographical differences in response alternatives, biases toward or away from some response alternatives, lack of discrimination between the alternatives or their reinforcement rates, and differences in reinforcement variables other than reinforcement rate; or because the matching law may simply not be the most accurate way to describe the way in which relative response and time allocation relate to relative reinforcement rate. In this appendix we look at extensions of the matching law that attempt to encompass these deviations.

OVERVIEW OF EXPONENTS AND LOGARITHMS

Some extensions of the matching law require familiarity with exponents and logarithms. This section provides a brief review of these concepts.

Exponents

We define $a^1 = a, a^2 = a \times a, a^3 = a \times a \times a$, and so on, where a is any number and the exponents (represented by superscripts) are integers greater than zero (1, 2, 3, etc.). Note that $a^x \times a^y = a^{x+y}$; for example, $a^2 \times a^3 = (aa)(aaa) = aaaaa = a^{2+3} = a^5$. This is the addition rule of exponents. We now generalize the addition rule, so that an exponent may be any number—not just an integer greater than zero. When we do this, $a^0 = 1$. This can be proved as follows:

$$a^0 \times a^x = a^{0+x},$$
$$= a^x;$$
$$a^0 = \frac{a^x}{a^x},$$
$$= 1.$$

Moreover, we can show that $a^{-x} = \frac{1}{a^x}$ as follows:

$$a^{-x} \times a^x = a^{-x+x},$$
$$= a^0,$$
$$= 1;$$
$$a^{-x} = \frac{1}{a^x}.$$

Similarly, it is easy to see that $a^{\frac{1}{x}} = \sqrt[x]{a}$. For example,

$$a^{\frac{1}{2}} \times a^{\frac{1}{2}} = a^{\frac{1}{2}+\frac{1}{2}},$$
$$= a^1;$$
$$(a^{\frac{1}{2}})^2 = a,$$
$$a^{\frac{1}{2}} = \sqrt{a}.$$

Thus, a zero exponent and negative and fractional exponents are all meaningful, and follow from the addition rule of exponents.

Logarithms

We define $\log_a x$ ("log of x to the base a") to be that exponent (or power) that will raise a to x. Thus, $y = \log_a x$ is simply an alternative way of writing $a^y = x$. We use the addition rule of exponents to derive two important rules about logarithms: (1) $\log_a xy = \log_a x + \log_a y$ and (2) $\log_a x^y = y\log_a x$. Note from the addition rule that

if $\qquad\qquad\qquad\qquad\qquad\qquad a^u = x \qquad\qquad\qquad\qquad\qquad\qquad$ (E1)

and $\qquad\qquad\qquad\qquad\qquad\qquad a^v = y, \qquad\qquad\qquad\qquad\qquad\qquad$ (E2)

then $\qquad\qquad\qquad\qquad\qquad\qquad a^u a^v = xy,$

and hence $\qquad\qquad\qquad\qquad\qquad a^{u+v} = xy. \qquad\qquad\qquad\qquad\qquad$ (E3)

To derive the first rule, from Equation E3 we write

$$\log_a xy = u + v,$$

from Equation E1 we write $\qquad\qquad\qquad\qquad u = \log_a x,$

and from Equation E2 we write $\qquad\qquad\qquad v = \log_a y,$

and hence by substitution $\qquad\qquad\qquad \log_a xy = \log_a x + \log_a y.$

To derive the second rule, note from the above that

$$\log_a x^y = \log_a x + \cdots + \log_a x$$
$$= y\log_a x.$$

This, of course, only proves the rule for the case in which y is a positive integer. However, the proof may be extended to the general case in which y can be any number.

In most simple applications of logarithms, such as those discussed below, the base is ten because of the nice mathematics that result. Note, for example, that $\log_{10} 1 = 0$, $\log_{10} 100 = 2$, $\log_{10} 1000 = 3$, and so forth. When the value of the base is specified or clear from context, it generally is not written: for example, we usually write $\log_{10} x$ simply as $\log x$ when the base is clearly understood to be ten.

THE GENERALIZED MATCHING LAW

The generalized matching law can be written

$$\frac{B_i}{B_j} = c\left(\frac{r_i}{r_j}\right)^s, \tag{E1}$$

where B_i and B_j are the values on some behavioral measure—either response rate or time allocation—of Responses i and j, respectively, r_i and r_j are the corresponding reinforcement rates, and c and s are constants that are equal to or greater than zero. Note that if both c and s are equal to one, Equation E1 is the simply matching law described in Appendix B (see Equation B1.2). If c is greater than one we say that there is a bias toward Response i, whereas if c is less than one (but still greater than zero) we say that there is a bias toward Response j. Bias toward one response over another is due to an inequality between the responses that leads to a preference (i.e., a higher response rate or greater time allocation) for one even when the reinforcement rate is the same for both.

The value of s for a given individual indicates the sensitivity of that individual to relative reinforcement rates. For example if $s = 0$, then $\frac{B_i}{B_j} = c$ regardless of $\frac{r_i}{r_j}$; thus $s = 0$ implies that the individual is totally insensitive to relative reinforcement rates. Note that if $c = 1$ and $s > 1$, $\frac{B_i}{B_j}$ will be greater than $\frac{r_i}{r_j}$ if $r_i > r_j$ (but less than $\frac{r_i}{r_j}$ if $r_i < r_j$); and, if $c = 1$ and $s < 1$ (but greater than zero), $\frac{B_i}{B_j}$ will be less than $\frac{r_i}{r_j}$ if $r_i > r_j$ (but greater than $\frac{r_i}{r_j}$ if $r_i < r_j$). For these reasons, we say that $s > 1$ produces "overmatching" and that $s < 1$ produces "undermatching." In most experiments s turns out to be slightly less than one (Baum, 1979); thus it appears that slight undermatching is typically the case.

Taking the logarithm (using any base) of both sides of Equation E1, and applying the rules of logarithms discussed in the previous section, we obtain

$$\log\frac{B_i}{B_j} = \log c\left(\frac{r_i}{r_j}\right)^s,$$

$$= \log c + \log\left(\frac{r_i}{r_j}\right)^s,$$

$$= s\log\left(\frac{r_i}{r_j}\right) + \log c.$$

The above equation describes a straight line (the formula for a straight line being $y = ax + b$). Thus it is generally preferred over Equation E4 because the linear form makes it easier to determine the extent to which a given data set fits the equation and to estimate the values of s and b for the data set.

Herrnstein's formulation of the matching law (Appendix C) and melioration (Appendix D) are easily modifiable to make them compatible with the generalized matching law. For example, we can make Equation C1 of Appendix C compatible with the generalized matching law by writing it as

$$\frac{B_j}{\sum\limits_{i=0}^{N} B_i} = \frac{w_j r_j^s}{\sum\limits_{i=0}^{N} w_i r_i^s},$$

where the w_i^s are weights for determining bias, s is sensitivity to relative reinforcement, and the other terms are as defined in Appendix C. Melioration can be made compatible with the generalized matching law by a similar modification of the quantity that individuals tend to maximize; that is, rather than local reinforcement rates, it would be local reinforcement rate raised to a power indicating sensitivity and multiplied by a factor representing response bias.

THE CONCATENATED GENERALIZED MATCHING LAW

We may extend the generalized matching law to include other reinforcement parameters as factors in the equation as follows (Baum, 1974; Logue, Rodriguez, & Peña-Correal, 1984):

$$\frac{B_i}{B_j} = c \left(\frac{r_i}{r_j} \right)^{s_r} \times \left(\frac{a_i}{a_j} \right)^{s_a} \times \left(\frac{1/d_i}{1/d_j} \right)^{s_d},$$

where a_i and a_j are the magnitudes (i.e., intensities or amounts) of the reinforcer and d_i and d_j are the delays in the reinforcer (i.e., the time between a reinforced response and the presentation of the reinforcer) during each reinforcement for Responses i and j, respectively; s_r, s_a and s_d are the sensitivities to relative reinforcement rate, amount, and delay, respectively; and the other terms in the equation are as defined above.

   Note that the above equation states that the longer the delay between a response and reinforcement on a particular response alternative, the less responding or time will be allocated to that alternative. Even if the reinforcement rate and magnitude are larger on the alternative with the longer delay of reinforcement, the delay may outweigh these factors if the sensitivity to delay is large. If we define self-control as showing a low sensitivity to delay relative to sensitivity to reinforcement rate and magnitude, we might conceptualize the problem of self-control as being that of altering one's sensitivity to delay of reinforcement (e.g., Logue, 1988).

THE CONTINGENCY-DISCRIMINABILITY MODEL

According to the generalized matching law, the tendency for undermatching to occur is due to sensitivity to relative reinforcement rate being less than one. The contingency-discriminability model (Davison, 1996; Davison & Jenkins, 1985; Davison & Jones, 1995) attributes undermatching to lack of discrimination (or "confusion") between the reinforcement contingencies, and thus does not posit an exponent in the equation. For two responses alternatives, Responses i and j, the model is

$$\frac{B_i}{B_j} = c \left(\frac{r_i - pr_i + pr_j}{r_j - pr_j + pr_i} \right),$$

where p is a measure of "confusion" (lack of discrimination) between the response alternatives, and the other terms are as previously defined. The value of p can range from 0.5 (complete confusion, or no discrimination) between the alternatives to zero (no confusion, or perfect discrimination). Note the model essentially assumes matching, but with response bias represented by c (as in the generalized matching law) and some portion (p) of each reinforcement rate being subtracted from one response alternative and added to the other to represent lack of discrimination between the alternatives. The contingency-discriminability model appears to provide a better fit to the data from concurrent schedules than the generalized matching law does. In addition, it predicts (correctly) that when the reinforcement rate for one alternative is zero, responding on that alternative will not decrease to zero as long as the other alternative continues to be reinforced.

In comparison with the generalized matching law, the contingency-discrimination model has several disadvantages: (1) it can predict overmatching only when one can assume that responding produces some, perhaps mild, punishment; (2) the model becomes increasingly cumbersome when applied to more than two response alternatives; and (3) there is no concatenated version of the model.

References

Abbott, B., & Badia, P. (1979). Choice for signaled over unsignaled shock as a function of signal length. *Journal of the Experimental Analysis of Behavior, 32,* 409–417.

Abbott, B. B., & Badia, P. (1984). Preference for signaled over unsignaled shock schedules: Ruling out asymmetry and response fixation as factors. *Journal of the Experimental Analysis of Behavior, 41,* 45–52.

Abrahams, M., & Dill, L. M. (1989). A determination of the energetic equivalence of the risk of predation. *Ecology, 70,* 999–1007.

Abrahams, M. V., & Townsend, L. D. (1993). Bioluminescence in dinoflagellates: A test of the burglar alarm hypothesis. *Ecology, 74,* 258–260.

Abramson, C. I., & Bitterman, M. E. (1986). Latent inhibition in honeybees. *Animal Learning & Behavior, 14,* 184–189.

Adams, C. D., & Dickinson, A. (1981). Instrumental responding following reinforcer devaluation. *Quarterly Journal of Experimental Psychology, 33B,* 109–121.

Adelman, H. M., & Maatsch, J. L. (1955). Resistance to extinction as a function of the type of response elicited by frustration. *Journal of Experimental Psychology, 50,* 61–65.

Ader, R. (1985). Conditioned immunopharmacologic effects in animals: Implications for a conditioning model of pharmacoltherapy. In L. White, B. Tursky, & G. E. Schwartz (Eds.), *Placebo: theory, research, and mechanisms* (pp. 306-323). Westport, CT: Guilford Press.

Ader, R., & Cohen, N. (1975). Behavioral conditioned immunosuppression. *Psychosomatic Medicine, 37,* 333–340.

Ader, R., & Cohen, N. (1982). Behaviorally conditioned immunosuppression and murine systemic lupus erythematosus. *Science, 215,* 1534–1536.

Ader, R., & Cohen, N. (1993). Psychoneuroimmunology. *Annual Review of Psychology, 44,* 53–85.

Aigner, T. G., & Balster, R. L. (1978). Choice behavior in rhesus monkeys: Cocaine versus food. *Science, 201,* 534–535.

Airapetyantz, E., & Bykov, K. (1966). Physiological experiments and the psychology of the subconscious. In T. Verhave (Ed.), *The experimental analysis of behavior* (pp. 140–157). New York: Appleton-Century-Crofts.

"Air Miles plan flying high just four years after takeoff." (1996). *Winnipeg Free Press,* October 11, p. B4.

Alberts, J. R. (1984). Sensory-perceptual development in the Norway rat: A view toward comparative studies. In R. Kail & N. E. Spear (Eds.), *Comparative perspectives on the development of memory* (pp. 65-102). Hillsdale, NJ: Erlbaum.

Alferink, L. A., Bartness, T. J., & Harder, S. R. (1980). Control of the temporal location of polydipsic licking in the rat. *Journal of the Experimental Analysis of Behavior, 33,* 119–129.

Allan, L. G., & Siegel, S. (1997a). Assessing a new analysis of the McCollough effect. *Cognition, 64,* 207–222.

Allan, L. G., & Siegel, S. (1997b). Contingent color aftereffects: Reassessing old conclusions. *Perception & Psychophysics, 59,* 129–141.

Allan, L. G., & Siegel, S. (1998). Learning and homeostasis: Drug addiction and the McCollough effect. *Psychological-Bulletin, 124,* 230–239

Allen, J. A. (1988). Frequency-dependent selection by predators. *Philosophical Transactions of the Royal Society of London. Series B: Biological Sciences, 319,* 485–503.

Allen, J. D., & Kenshalo, D. R. (1976). Schedule-induced drinking as a function of interreinforcement interval in the Rhesus monkey. *Journal of the Experimental Analysis of Behavior, 26,* 257–267.

Allen, J. D., & Porter, J. H. (1977). Sources of control over schedule-induced drinking produced by secondary schedules of reinforcement. *Physiology & Behavior, 18,* 853–863.

Allison, J., & Mack, R. (1982). Polydipsia and autoshaping: Drinking and leverpressing as substitutes for eating. *Animal Learning & Behavior, 10,* 465–475.

Allison, J., & Timberlake, W. (1974). Instrumental and contingent saccharin licking in rats: Response deprivation and reinforcement. *Learning and Motivation, 5,* 231–247.

Alloway, T. M. (1973). Learning in insects except

435

Apoidea. In W. C., Corning, J. A. Dyal, & A. O. D. Willows (Eds.), *Invertebrate learning* (vol. 2, pp. 131–171). New York: Plenum.

Allport, F. H. (1924). *Social psychology*. Boston: Houghton Mifflin Company.

Altbäcker, V., Hudson, R., & Bilkó, A, (1995). Rabbit mothers' diet influences pups' later food choice. *Ethology, 99*, 107–116.

Amsel, A. (1992). *Frustration theory: An analysis of dispositional learning and memory*. Cambridge: Cambridge University Press.

Amsel, A., & Roussel, J. (1952). Motivational properties of frustration: I. Effect on a running response of the addition of frustration to the motivational complex. *Journal of Experimental Psychology, 43*, 363–368.

Anderson, J. R., Awazu, S., & Fujita, K. (2000). Can squirrel monkeys (*Saimiri sciureus*) learn self-control? A study using food array selection tests and reverse-reward contingency. *Journal of Experimental Psychology: Animal Behavior Processes, 26*, 87–97.

Anderson, M. C., Bjork, R. A., & Bjork, E. L. (1994). Remembering can cause forgetting: Retrieval dynamics in long-term memory. *Journal of Experimental Psychology: Learning, Memory, & Cognition, 20*, 1063–1087.

Anderson, M. C., & Spellman, B. A. (1995). On the status of inhibitory mechanisms in cognition: Memory retrieval as a model case. *Psychological Review, 102*, 68–100.

Andersson, M. (1994). *Sexual selection*. Princeton, NJ: Princeton University Press.

Andresen, G. V., Birch, L. L., & Johnson, P. A. (1990). The scapegoat effect on food aversions after chemotherapy. *Cancer, 66*, 1649–1653.

Anisman, H., DeCatanzaro, D., & Remington, G. (1978). Escape performance following exposure to inescapable shock: Deficits in motor response maintenance. *Journal of Experimental Psychology: Animal Behavior Processes, 4*, 197–218.

Annau, Z., & Kamin, L. J. (1961). The conditioned emotional response as a function of the intensity of the US. *Journal of Comparative and Physiological Psychology, 54*, 428–432.

Antelman, S. M., & Szechtman, H. (1975). Tail pinch induces eating in sated rats which appears to depend on nigrostriatal dopamine. *Science, 189*, 731–733.

Antonitis, J. J. (1951). Response variability in the white rat during conditioning, extinction, and reconditioning. *Journal of Experimental Psychology, 42*, 273–281.

Appel, J. B. (1963). Aversive aspects of a schedule of positive reinforcement. *Journal of the Experimental Analysis of Behavior, 8*, 423–428.

Arabian, J. M. (1982). Imagery and Pavlovian heart rate conditioning. *Psychophysiology, 19*, 286–293.

Arak, A. (1988). Callers and satellites in the natterjack toad: Evolutionary stable decision rules. *Animal Behaviour, 36*, 416–432.

Arbuckle, J. L., & Lattal, K. A. (1987). A role for negative reinforcement of response omission in punishment? *Journal of the Experimental Analysis of Behavior, 48*, 407–416.

Arendt, D., & Nübler-Jung, K (1994). Inversion of the dorsoventral axis? *Nature, 371*, 26.

Aschoff, J. (1981). *Biological rhythms*. New York: Plenum.

Ator, N. A. (1980). Mirror pecking and timeout under a multiple fixed-ratio schedule of food delivery. *Journal of the Experimental Analysis of Behavior, 34*, 319–328.

Atrens, D. M. (1973). Schedule-induced polydipsia and polyphagia in nondeprived rats reinforced by intracranial stimulation. *Learning and Motivation, 4*, 320–326.

Attenborough, D. (1998). *The life of birds*. Princeton, NJ: Princeton University Press.

Auge, R. J. (1973). Effects of stimulus duration on observing behavior maintained by differential reinforcement magnitude. *Journal of the Experimental Analysis of Behavior, 20*, 429–438.

Auge, R. J. (1974). Context, observing behavior, and conditioned reinforcement. *Journal of the Experimental Analysis of Behavior, 22*, 525–533.

Autor, S. M. (1969). The strength of conditioned reinforcers as a function of frequency and probability of reinforcement. In D. P. Hendry (Ed.), *Conditioned reinforcement* (pp. 127–162). Homewood, IL: Dorsey Press.

Ayllon, T., & Azrin, N. H. (1968). *The token economy: A motivational system for therapy and rehabilitation*. New York: Appleton-Century-Crofts.

Ayres, J. J. B., Albert, M., & Bombace, J. C. (1987). Extending conditioned stimuli before versus after unconditioned stimuli: Implications for real-time models of conditioning. *Journal of Experimental Psychology: Animal Behavior Processes, 13*, 168–181.

Ayres, J. J., & Quinsey, V. L. (1970). Between-groups incentive effects on conditioned suppression. *Psychonomic Science, 21*, 294–296.

Azrin, N. H. (1956). Effects of two intermittent schedules of immediate and non-immediate punishment. *Journal of Psychology, 42*, 3–21.

Azrin, N. H. (1958). Some effects of noise on human behavior. *Journal of the Experimental Analysis of Behavior, 1*, 183–200.

Azrin, N. H. (1960 a). Sequential effects of punishment. *Science, 131*, 605–606.

Azrin, N. H. (1960 b). Effects of punishment intensity during variable-interval reinforcement. *Journal of the Experimental Analysis of Behavior, 3*, 123–142.

Azrin, N. H. (1961). Time-out from positive reinforcement. *Science, 133*, 382–383.

Azrin, N. H. (1964). *Aggressive responses of paired animals*. Paper presented at the Symposium on Medical Aspects of Stress. Walter Reed Institute of Research, Washington, April.

Azrin, N. H., Hake, D. F., Holz, W. C., & Hutchinson, R. R. (1965). Motivational aspects of escape from punishment. *Journal of the Experimental Analysis of Behavior, 8,* 31–44.

Azrin, N. H., Hake, D. F., & Hutchinson, R. R. (1965). Elicitation of aggression by a physical blow. *Journal of the Experimental Analysis of Behavior, 8,* 55–57.

Azrin, N. H., & Holz, W. C. (1966). Punishment. In W. K. Honig (Ed.), *Operant behavior: Areas of research and application* (pp. 380–447). New York: Appleton-Century-Crofts.

Azrin, N. H., Holz, W. C., & Hake, D. F. (1963). Fixed-ratio punishment. *Journal of the Experimental Analysis of Behavior, 6,* 141–148.

Azrin, N. H., Hutchinson, R. R., & Hake, D. F. (1963). Pain-induced fighting in the squirrel monkey. *Journal of the Experimental Analysis of Behavior, 6,* 620–621.

Azrin, N. H., Hutchinson, R. R., & Hake, D. F. (1966). Extinction-induced aggression. *Journal of the Experimental Analysis of Behavior, 9,* 191–204.

Azrin, N. H., Hutchinson, R. R., & McLaughlin, R. (1965). The opportunity for aggression as an operant reinforcer during aversive stimulation. *Journal of the Experimental Analysis of Behavior, 8,* 171–180.

Azrin, N. H., Hutchinson, R. R., & Sallery, R. D. (1964). Pain-aggression toward inanimate objects. *Journal of the Experimental Analysis of Behavior, 7,* 223–228.

Azrin, N. H., & Nunn, R. G. (1973). Habit reversal: A method of eliminating nervous habits and tics. *Behaviour Research and Therapy, 11,* 619–628.

Azrin, N. H., & Nunn, R. G. (1977). *Habit control in a day.* New York: Simon & Schuster.Azrin, N. H., Nunn, R. G., & Frantz, S. E. (1980). Habit reversal vs. negative practice treatment of nervous tics. *Behavior Therapy, 11,* 169–178.

Azzara. A. V., & Sclafani, A. (1998). Flavor preferences conditioned by intragastric sugar infusion in rats: Maltose is more reinforcing than sucrose. *Physiology & Behavior, 64,* 535–541.

Bacotti, A. V. (1977). Matching under concurrent fixed-ratio variable-interval schedules of food presentation. *Journal of the Experimental Analysis of Behavior, 27,* 171–182.

Baddeley, A. D. (1986). *Working memory.* New York: Oxford University Press.

Baddeley, A. D. (1991). *Human memory: Theory and practice.* London: Allyn & Bacon.

Baddeley, A. D. (1992). Working memory. *Science, 255,* 556–559.

Baddeley, A. D., & Hitch, G. J. (1977). Recency re-examined. In S. Durnic (Ed.), *Attention and performance* (vol. 6, pp. 647–667). Hillsdale, NJ: Erlbaum.

Badia, P., Harsh, J., & Coker, C. C. (1975). Choosing between fixed time and variable time shock. *Learning and Motivation, 6,* 264–278.

Badia, P., Suter, S., & Lewis P. (1966). Rat vocalization to shock with and without a CS. *Psychonomic Science, 4,* 117–118.

Baer, D. M. (1960). Escape and avoidance response of pre- school children to two schedules of reinforcement withdrawal. *Journal of the Experimental Analysis of Behavior, 3,* 155–159.

Baer, D. M., Peterson, R. F., & Sherman, J. A. (1967). The development of imitation by reinforcing behavioral similarity to a model. *Journal of the Experimental Analysis of Behavior, 10,* 405–416.

Baer, D. M., & Sherman, J. A. (1964). Reinforcement control of generalized imitation in young children. *Journal of Experimental Child Psychology, 1,* 37–49.

Baeyens, F., Crombez G., De Houwer, J., & Eelen, P. (1996). No evidence for modulation of evaluative flavor-flavor associations in humans. *Learning and Motivation, 27,* 200–241.

Baeyens, F., Crombez, G., Hendrickx, H., & Eelen, P. (1995). Parameters of human flavor-flavor conditioning. *Learning and Motivation, 26,* 141–160.

Baeyens, F., Eelen, P., Van den Bergh, O., & Crombez, G. (1990). Flavor-flavor and color-flavor conditioning in humans. *Learning and Motivation, 21,* 434–455.

Baldwin, J. D., & Baldwin, J. I. (1973). The role of play in social organization: Comparative observations on squirrel monkeys (*Saimiri*). *Primates, 14,* 369–381.

Baldwin, J. D., & Baldwin, J. I. (1974). Exploration and social play in squirrel monkeys. (*Saimiri oerstedi*). *American Zoologist, 14,* 303–314.

Baldwin, J. D., & Baldwin, J. I. (1976). Effects of food ecology on social play: A laboratory simulation. *Zeitschrift für Tierpsychologie, 40,* 1–14.

Baldwin, J. D., & Baldwin, J. I. (1977). The role of learning phenomena in the ontogeny of exploration and play. In S. Chevalier-Skolnikoff & F. E. Poirier (Eds.), *Primate bio-social development: Biological, social, and ecological determinants* (pp. 343–406). New York: Garland Publishing.

Ball, J. (1938). A case of apparent imitation in a monkey. *Journal of Genetic Psychology, 52,* 439–442.

Balleine, B. W., & Dickenson, A. (1991). Instrumental performance following reinforcer devaluation depends upon incentive learning. *Quarterly Journal of Experimental Psychology, 43B,* 279–296.

Balsam, P. D., Deich, J. D., Ohyama, T., & Stokes, P. D. (1998). Origins of new behavior. In W. T. O'Donohue (Ed.), *Learning & behavior therapy* (pp. 403–420). Needham Heights, MA: Allyn & Bacon.

Balsam, P. D., Graf, J. S., & Silver, R. (1992). Operant and Pavlovian contributions to the ontogeny of pecking in ring doves. *Developmental Psychobiology, 25,* 389–410.

Bandura, A. (1982). The psychology of chance encounters and life paths. *American Psychologist, 37,* 747–755.

Baptista, L. F. (1977). Geographic variation in song and dialects of the Puget Sound white-crowned sparrow. *Condor, 79,* 356–370.

Baptista, L. F., & Morton, M. L. (1982). Song dialects and mate selection in montane white-crowned sparrows. *The Auk, 99,* 537–547.

Baptista, L. F., & Petrinovich, L. (1986). Song development in the white-crowned sparrow: Social factors and sex differences. *Animal Behaviour, 34,* 1359–1371.

Barnes, G. W. (1956). Conditioned stimulus intensity and temporal factors in spaced trial classical conditioning. *Journal of Experimental Psychology, 51,* 192–198.

Barnes, G. W., & Kish, G. B. (1957). Reinforcing properties of termination of intense auditory stimulation. *Journal of Comparative and Physiological Psychology, 50,* 40–43.

Barnet, R. C., & Miller, R. R. (1996). Second-order excitation mediated by a backward conditioned inhibitor. *Journal of Experimental Psychology: Animal Behavior Processes, 22,* 279–296.

Barnett, J. E. (1998). *Time's pendulum: From sundials to atomic clocks, the fascinating history of time keeping and how our discoveries changed the world.* San Diego: Harcourt Brace.

Barnett, S. A. (1968). The "instinct to teach." *Nature, 220,* 747–749.

Barofsky, I., & Hurwitz, D. (1968). Within ratio responding during fixed ratio performance. *Psychonomic Science, 11,* 263–264.

Baron, A., Kaufman, A., & Stauber, K. A. (1969). Effects of instructions and reinforcement feedback on human operant behavior maintained by fixed-interval reinforcement. *Journal of the Experimental Analysis of Behavior, 12,* 701–712.

Baron, R. A., & Bell, P. A. (1975). Aggression and heat: Mediating effects of prior provocation and exposure to an aggressive model. *Journal of Personality and Social Psychology, 31,* 825–832.

Baron, A. & Galizio, M. (1983). Instructional control of human operant behavior. *The Psychological Record, 33,* 495–520.

Bateson, P. P. G. (1979). How do sensitive periods arise and what are they for? *Animal Behaviour, 27,* 470–486.

Batson, J. D., Hoban, J. S., & Bitterman, M. E. (1992). Simultaneous conditioning in honeybees (*Apis mellifera*). *Journal of Comparative Psychology, 106,* 114–119.

Baum, M. (1965). An automated apparatus for the avoidance training of rats. *Psychological Reports, 16,* 1205–1211.

Baum, M. (1966). Rapid extinction of an avoidance response following a period of response prevention in the avoidance apparatus. *Psychological Reports, 18,* 59–64.

Baum, M. (1969). Extinction of an avoidance response following response prevention: Some parametric investigations. *Canadian Journal of Psychology, 23,* 1–10.

Baum, M. (1970). Extinction of avoidance responding through response prevention (flooding). *Psychological Bulletin, 74,* 276–284.

Baum, W. M. (1974). On two types of deviation from the matching law: Bias and undermatching. *Journal of the Experimental Analysis of Behavior, 22,* 231–242.

Baum, W. M. (1979). Matching, undermatching, and overmatching in studies of choice. *Journal of the Experimental Analysis of Behavior, 32,* 269–281.

Baum, W. M. (1981). Optimization and the matching law as accounts of instrumental behavior. *Journal of the Experimental Analysis of Behavior, 36,* 387–403.

Baum, W. M. (1982). Choice, changeover, and travel. *Journal of the Experimental Analysis of Behavior, 38,* 35–49.

Baum, W. M. (1989). Quantitative prediction and molar description of the environment. *The Behavior Analyst, 12,* 167–176.

Baum, W. M. (1994). Rules, culture, and fitness. *The Behavior Analyst, 18,* 1–21.

Baum, W. M., & Rachlin, H. C. (1969). Choice as time allocation. *Journal of the Experimental Analysis of Behavior, 12,* 861–874.

Baumeister, A., Hawkins, W., & Cromwell, R. (1964). Need states and activity level. *Psychological Bulletin, 61,* 438–453.

Bäuml, K.-H. (1996). Revisiting an old issue: Retroactive interference as a function of the degree of original and interpolated learning. *Psychonomic Bulletin & Review, 3,* 380–384.

Bäuml, K.-H. (1997). The list-strength effect: Strength-dependent competition or suppression? *Psychonomic Bulletin & Review, 4,* 260–264.

Beard, K. C., Tong, Y., Dawson, M. R., Wang, J., & Huang, X. (1996). Earliest complete dentition of an anthropoid primate from the late Middle Eocene of Shanzi Province, China. *Science, 272,* 82–85.

Beautrais, P. G., & Davison, M. C. (1977). Response and time allocation in concurrent second-order schedules. *Journal of the Experimental Analysis of Behavior, 25,* 61–69.

Beecroft, R. S. (1966). *Classical conditioning.* Goleta, CA: Psychonomic Press.

Begg, I. (1982). Imagery, organization, and discriminative processes. *Canadian Journal of Psychology, 36,* 273–290.

Bekoff, M. (1977). Mammalian dispersal and ontogeny of individual behavioral phenotypes. *American Naturalist, 111,* 715–732.

Bekoff, M. (1981). Mammalian sibling interactions: Genes, facilitative environments, and the coefficient of familiarity. In D. J. Gubernick & P. H. Klopfer (Eds.), *Parental care in mammals* (pp. 307–345). New York: Plenum.

Belke, T. W. (1996). The effect of a change in body weight on running and responding reinforced by the opportunity to run. *The Psychological Record, 46,* 421–433.

Belke, T. W. (1997). Running and responding reinforced by the opportunity to run: Effect of reinforcer duration. *Journal of the Experimental Analysis of Behavior, 67,* 337–351.

Belke, T. W., & Heyman, G. M. (1994). A matching law analysis of the reinforcing efficacy of wheel running in rats. *Animal Learning & Behavior, 22,* 267–274.

Belke, T. W., & Spetch, M. L. (1994). Choice between reliable and unreliable reinforcement revisited. *Journal of the Experimental Analysis of Behavior, 62,* 353–366.

Belleville, R. E., Rohles, F. H., Grunzke, M. E., & Clark, F. C. (1963). Development of a complex multiple schedule in the chimpanzee. *Journal of the Experimental Analysis of Behavior, 6,* 549–556.

Bellezza, F. S.(1986). Mental cues and verbal reports in learning. In G. H. Bower (Ed.), *The psychology of learning and motivation* (vol. 20, pp. 237–273). New York: Academic Press.

Bellezza, F. S.(1987). Mnemonic devices and memory schemas. In M. A. McDaniel & M. Pressley (Eds.), *Imagery and related mnemonic processes: Theories, individual differences, and applications* (pp. 34–55). New York: Springer-Verlag.

Bennett, J. (1982). Islands of the bears (16 mm sound film). London: Survival Anglia.

Berger, D. F., & Brush, F. R. (1975). Rapid acquisition of discrete-trial lever-press avoidance: Effects of signal-shock interval. *Journal of the Experimental Analysis of Behavior, 24,* 227–239.

Berger, J. (1979). Social ontogeny of and behavioural diversity: Consequences for bighorn sheep Ovis canadensis inhabiting desert and mountain environments. *Journal of Zoology (London), 188,* 251–266.

Berkowitz, L. (1983). Aversively stimulated aggression: Some parallels and differences in research with animals and humans. *American Psychologist, 38,* 1135–1144.

Berkowitz, L., & Frodi, A. (1979). Reactions to a child's mistakes as affected by her/his looks and speech. *Social Psychology Quarterly, 42,* 420–425.

Bernheim, J. W., & Williams, D. R. (1967). Time-dependent contrast effects in a multiple schedule of food reinforcement. *Journal of the Experimental Analysis of Behavior, 10,* 243–249.

Bernstein, I. L. (1978). Learned taste aversions in children receiving chemotherapy. *Science, 200,* 1302–1303.

Bernstein, I. L., & Webster, M. M. (1985). Learned food aversions: A consequence of cancer chemotherapy. In T. G. Burish, S. M. Levy, & B. E. Meyerowitz (Eds.), *Cancer, nutrition and behavior: A biobehavioral perspective* (pp. 103–116). Hillsdale, NJ: Erlbaum.

Bernstein, I. L. (1978). Learned taste aversions in children receiving chemotherapy. *Science, 200,* 1302–1303.

Bersh, P. J., & Alloy, L. B. (1978). Avoidance based on shock intensity *Journal of the Experimental Analysis of Behavior, 30,* 293–300.

Bersh, P. J., & Alloy, L. B. (1980). Reduction of shock duration as negative reinforcement in free-operant avoidance. *Journal of the Experimental Analysis of Behavior, 33,* 265–273.

Berthold, P. (1988). The control of migration in European warblers. In H. Ouellet (Ed.), *Acta XIX Congressus Internationalis Ornithologi* (vol.1, pp. 215–249). Ottawa, ON: University of Ottawa Press.

Bertram, B. (1970). The vocal behavior of the Indian hill mynah, Gracula religiosa. *Animal Behavior Monographs, 3,* 81–192.

Betts, S. L., Brandon, S. E., & Wagner, A. R. (1996). Dissociation of conditioned eyeblink and conditioned fear following a shift in unconditioned stimulus locus. *Animal Learning & Behavior, 24,* 459–470.

Biegler, R., & Morris, R. G. M. (1999). Blocking in the spatialdomain with arrays of discrete landmarks. *Journal of Experimental Psychology: Animal Behavior Processes, 25,* 334–351.

Bilbrey, J., & Winokur, S. (1973). Controls for and constraints on auto-shaping. *Journal of the Experimental Analysis of Behavior, 20,* 323–332.

Bilkó, A., Altbäcker, V., & Hudson, R. (1994). Transmission of food preference in the rabbit: The means of information transfer. *Physiology & Behavior, 56,* 907–912.

Bitterman, M. E. (1975), The comparative analysis of learning. *Science, 188,* 699–709.

Bitterman, M. E. (1996). Comparative analysis of learning in honeybees. *Animal Learning & Behavior, 24,* 123–141.

Bizo, L. A., Bogdanov, S. V., & Killeen, P. R. (1998).Satiation causes within-session decreases in instrumental responding. *Journal of Experimental Psychology: Animal Behavior Processes, 24,* 439–452.

Bjork, R. A. (1972). Theoretical implications of directed forgetting. In A. W. Melton & E. Martin (Eds.), *Coding processes in human memory* (pp. 217–235). New York: Winston & Wiley.

Black, A. H., Carlson, N. J., & Solomon, R. L. (1962). Exploratory studies of the conditioning of autonomic responses in curarized dogs. *Psychological Monographs, 76*(29, Whole No. 548).

Blackman, D. (1977). Conditioned suppression and the effects of classical conditioning on operant behavior. In W. K. Honig & J. E. R. Staddon (Eds.), *Handbook of Operant Behavior* (pp. 340–363). Englewood Cliffs, NJ: Prentice-Hall.

Blair, M. E., & Shimp, T. A. (1992). Consequences of an unpleasant experience with music: A second-order negative conditioning perspective. *Journal of Advertising, 21*(1), 35–43.

Blaisdell, A. P., Denniston, J. C., Savastano, H. I., & Miller, R. R. (2000). Counterconditioning of an overshadowed cue attenuates overshadowing. *Journal of Experimental Psychology: Animal Behavior Processes, 26,* 74–86.

Blair, M. E., & Shimp, T. A. (1992). Consequences of an unpleasant experience with music: A second-order negative conditioning perspective. *Journal of Advertising, 21*(1), 35–43.

Blaxton, T. A., & Neely, J. H. (1983). Inhibition from semantically related primes: Evidence of a category-specific inhibition. *Memory & Cognition, 11,* 500–510.

Bloomfield, T. M. (1966). Two types of behavioral contrast in discrimination learning. *Journal of the Experimental Analysis of Behavior, 9*, 155–161.

Blough, D. S. (1958). A method for obtaining psychophysical thresholds from the pigeon. *Journal of the Experimental Analysis of Behavior, 1*, 31–43.

Blough, D. S. (1959). Delayed matching in the pigeon. *Journal of the Experimental Analysis of Behavior, 2*, 151–160.

Blough, D. S. (1961). The shape of some wavelength generalization gradients. *Journal of the Experimental Analysis of Behavior, 4*, 31–40.

Blough, D. S. (1969). Generalization gradient shape and summation in steady-state tests. *Journal of the Experimental Analysis of Behavior, 12*, 91–104.

Blough, D. S. (1972). Recognition by the pigeon of stimuli varying in two dimensions. *Journal of the Experimental Analysis of Behavior, 18*, 345–367.

Blough, D. S. (1975). Steady state data and a quantitative model of operant generalization and discrimination. *Journal of Experimental Psychology: Animal Behavior Processes, 1*, 3–21.

Blough, P. M. (1972). Wavelength generalization and discrimination in the pigeon. *Perception and Psychophysics, 12*, 342–348.

Blough, P. M. (1983). Local contrast in multiple schedules: The effect of stimulus discriminability. *Journal of the Experimental Analysis of Behavior, 39*, 427–435.

Boakes, R. A. (1977). Performance on learning to associate a stimulus with positive reinforcement. In H. Davis & H. M. B. Hurwitz (Eds.), *Operant-Pavlovian interactions* (pp. 67–101). Hillsdale, NJ: Erlbaum.

Boesch, C. (1991). Teaching among chimpanzees. *Animal Behaviour, 41*, 530–532.

Boesch, C. (1993). Aspects of transmission of tool-use in wild chimpanzees. In K. R. Gibson & T. Ingold (Eds.), *Tools, language and cognition in human evolution* (pp. 171–183). Cambridge: Cambridge University Press.

Boesch, C., & Boesch, H. (1983). Optimization of nutcracking with natural hammers by wild chimpanzees. *Behaviour, 26*, 265–286.

Bolhuis, J. J. (1991). Mechanisms of avian imprinting: A review. *Biological Reviews of the Cambridge Philosophical Society, 66*, 303–345.

Bolhuis, J. J., de Vos, G. J., & Kruijt, J. P. (1990). Filial imprinting and associative learning. *Quarterly Journal of Experimental Psychology, 42B*, 313–329.

Bolles, R. C. (1970). Species-specific defense reactions and avoidance learning. *Psychological Review, 77*, 32–48.

Bolles, R. C. (1971). Species-specific defense reactions. In F. R. Brush (Ed.), *Aversive conditioning and learning* (pp. 183–233). New York: Academic Press.

Bolles, R. C. (1972). Reinforcement, expectancy, and learning. *Psychological Review, 79*, 394–409.

Bond, N. W. (1973). Schedule-induced polydipsia as a function of the consummatory rate. *The Psychological Record, 23*, 377–382.

Bond, N. W., Blackman, D. E., & Scruton, P. (1973). Suppression of operant behavior and schedule-induced licking in rats. *Journal of the Experimental Analysis of Behavior, 20*, 375–383.

Boran, J. R., & Heimlich, S. L. (1999). Social learning in cetaceans: Hunting, hearing and hierarchies. In H. O. Box & K. R. Gibson (Eds.), *Mammalian social learning: Comparative and ecological perspectives* (pp. 282–307). Cambridge, UK: Cambridge University Press.

Boren, J. J., Moerschbaecher, J. M., & Whyte, A. A. (1978). Variability of response location on fixed-ratio and fixed-interval schedules of reinforcement. *Journal of the Experimental Analysis of Behavior, 30*, 63–67.

Boren, J. J., Sidman, M., & Herrnstein, R. J. (1959). Avoidance, escape, and extinction as functions of shock intensity. *Journal of Comparative and Physiological Psychology, 52*, 420–425.

Bottjer, S. W. (1982). Conditioned approach and withdrawal behavior in pigeons: Effects of a novel extraneous stimulus during acquisition and extinction. *Learning and Motivation, 13*, 44–67.

Boughman, J. W. (1998). Vocal learning by greater spear-nosed bats. *Philosophical Transactions of the Royal Society of London. Series B: Biological Sciences, 265*, 227–233.

Boughman, J. W., & Wilkinson, G. S. (1998). Greater spear-nosed bats discriminate group mates by vocalizations. *Animal Behaviour, 55*, 1717–1732.

Bouton, M. E., & Bolles, R. C. (1980). Conditioned fear assessed by freezing and by the suppression of three different baselines. *Animal Learning & Behavior, 8*, 429–434.

Bower, G. H. (1962). The influence of graded reductions in reward and prior frustrating events upon the magnitude of the frustration effect. *Journal of Comparative and Physiological Psychology, 55*, 582–587.

Bower, G. H., Clark, M. C., Lesgold, A. M., & Winzenz, D. (1969). Hierarchical retrieval schemes in recall of categorized word lists. *Journal of Verbal Learning and Verbal Behavior, 8*, 323–343.

Bower, G. H., Fowler, H., & Trapold, M. A. (1959). Escape learning as a function of amount of shock reduction. *Journal of Experimental Psychology, 58*, 482–484.

Bower, G. H., & Winzenz, D. (1970). Comparison of associative learning strategies. *Psychonomic Science, 20*, 119–120.

Bowles, A. E., Young, W. G., & Asper, E. D. (1988). Ontogeny of stereotyped calling of a killer whale calf, *Orcinus orca*, during her first year. *Rit Fiskideildar, 11*, 251–275.

Boysen, S. T. (1992). Counting as the chimpanzee views it. In G. Fetterman & W. K. Honig (Eds.), *Cognitive aspects of stimulus control* (pp. 367–383). Hillsdale, NJ: Erlbaum.

Boysen, S. T. (1993). Counting in chimpanzees: Nonhuman principles and emergent properties of number. In S. T. Boysen & E. J. Capaldi (Eds.), *The de-*

velopment of numerical competence: Animal and human models (pp. 39–59). Hillsdale, NJ: Erlbaum.

Boysen, S. T., & Berntson, G. G. (1989). The development of numerical competence in the chimpanzee (*Pan troglodytes*). *Journal of Comparative Psychology, 103,* 23–31.

Boysen, S. T., Mukobi, K. L., & Berntson, G. C. (1999). Overcoming response bias using symbolic representations of number by chimpanzees (*Pan troglodytes*). *Animal Learning & Behavior, 27,* 229–235.

Bradshaw, J., & Rogers, L. (1993). *The evolution of lateral asymmetries, language, tool use, and intellect.* New York: Academic Press.

Branch, M. N., & Dworkin, S. I. (1981). Effects of ratio contingencies on responding maintained by schedules of electric-shock presentation (response-produced shock). *Journal of the Experimental Analysis of Behavior, 36,* 191–205.

Brannon, E. M., & Terrace, H. S. (2000). Representation of the numerosities 1–9 by rhesus macaques (*Macaca mulatta*). *Journal of Experimental Psychology: Animal Behavior Processes, 26,* 31–49.

Breeden, S. (writer, producer), & Wright, B. (producer). (1985). *Land of the tiger.* National Geographic Society. (Video)

Breland, K., & Breland, M. (1961). The misbehavior of organisms. *American Psychologist, 16,* 681–684.

Breland, K., & Breland, M. (1966). *Animal behavior.* San Diego, CA: Academic Press.

Brelsford, J., Jr., & Theios, J. (1965). Single session conditioning of the nictitating membrane in the rabbit: Effect of intertrial interval. *Psychonomic Science, 2,* 81–82.

Breuggeman, J. A. (1973). Parental care in a group of free-ranging rhesus monkeys. *Folia Primatologica, 20,* 178–210.

Brethower, D. M., & Reynolds, G. S. (1962). A facilitative effect of punishment on unpunished behavior. *Journal of the Experimental Analysis of Behavior, 5,* 191–199.

Brewer, S. M., & McGrew, W. C. (1990). Chimpanzee use of a tool set to get honey. *Folia Primatologica, 54,* 100–104.

Brewer, W. F. (1992). The theoretical and empirical status of the flashbulb memory hypothesis. In E. Winograd & U. Neisser (Eds.), *Affect and accuracy in recall: Studies of "flashbulb" memories* (pp. 274–305). New York: Cambridge University Press.

Brimer, C. J. (1970). Disinhibition of an operant response. *Learning and Motivation, 1,* 346–371.

Brimer, C. J. (1972). Disinhibition of an operant response. In R. A. Boakes & M. S. Halliday (Eds.), *Inhibition and learning* (pp. 205–227). New York: Academic Press.

Broberg, D. J., & Bernstein, I. L. (1987). Candy as a scapegoat in the prevention of food aversions in children receiving chemotherapy. *Cancer, 60,* 2344–2347.

Brogden, W. J. (1939). Sensory preconditioning. *Journal of Experimental Psychology, 25,* 323–332.

Bronstein, P. D. (1986). Socially mediated learning in male *Betta splendens. Journal of Comparative Psychology, 100,* 279–284.

Bronstein, P. M. (1994). On the predictability, sensitization, and habituation of aggression in male bettas (*Betta splendens*). *Journal of Comparative Psychology, 108,* 45–57.

Bronstein, P. M., Neiman, H., Wolkoff, F. D., & Levine, M. J. (1974). The development of habituation in the rat. *Animal Learning & Behavior, 2,* 92–96.

Brown, B. L., Hemmes, N. S., Cabeza de Vaca, S., & Pagano, C. (1993). Sign and goal tracking during delay and trace autoshaping in pigeons. *Animal Learning & Behavior, 21,* 360–368.

Brown, C., & Warburton, K. (1999) Differences in timidity and escape responses between predator-naive and predator-sympatric rainbowfish populations. *Ethology, 105,* 491–502

Brown, G. E., & Godin, J. G. J. (1999).Who dares, learns: Chemical inspection behaviour and acquired predator recognition in a characin fish. *Animal Behaviour, 57,* 475–481

Brown, G. E., & Smith, R. J. F. (1996). Foraging tradeoffs in fathead minnows (*Pimephales promelas,* Osteichthyes, Cyprinidae): Acquired predator recognition in the absence of an alarm response. *Ethology, 102,* 776–785.

Brown, G. E., Chivers, D. P., & Smith, R. J. F. (1995). Fathead minnows avoid conspecific and heterospecific alarm pheromones in the faeces of northern pike. *Journal of Fish Biology, 47,* 387–393.

Brown, H. M. (1967). Effects of ultraviolet and photorestorative light on the phototaxic behavior of planaria. In W. C. Corning & S. C. Ratner (Eds.), *Chemistry of learning: Invertebrate research* (pp. 295–309). New York: Plenum.

Brown, J. L. (1987). *Helping and communal breeding in birds.* Princeton, NJ: Princeton University Press.

Brown, P. L., & Jenkins, H. M. (1968). Auto-shaping of the pigeon's key-peck. *Journal of the Experimental Analysis of Behavior, 11,* 1–8.

Brown, R., & Kulik, J. (1977). Flashbulb memories. *Cognition, 5,* 73–99.

Brownstein, A. J. (1971). Concurrent schedules of response- independent reinforcement: Duration of a reinforcing stimulus. *Journal of the Experimental Analysis of Behavior, 15,* 211–214.

Brownstein, A. J., & Hughes, R. G. (1970). The role of response suppression in behavioral contrast: Signaled reinforcement. *Psychonomic Science, 18,* 50–52.

Brownstein, A. J., & Newsome, C. (1970). Behavioral contrast in multiple schedules with equal reinforcement rates. *Psychonomic Science, 18,* 25–26.

Brunjes, P. C., & Alberts, J. R. (1979). Olfactory stimulation induces filial huddling preferences in rat pups. *Journal of Comparative and Physiological Psychology, 93,* 548–555.

Brush, F. R. (1966). On the differences between animals that learn and do not learn to avoid electric shock. *Psychonomic Science, 5,* 123–124.

Buchanan, J. P., Gill, T. V., & Braggio, J. T. (1981). Serial position and clustering effects in chimpanzee's "free recall." *Memory and Cognition, 9,* 651–660.

Buck, S. L., Rothstein, B., & Williams, B. A. (1975). A reexamination of local contrast in multiple schedules. *Journal of the Experimental Analysis of Behavior, 24,* 291–301.

Buckle, G. R., & Greenberg, L. (1981). Nestmate recognition in sweat bees (*Lasioglossum zephyrun*): Does an individual recognize its own odour or only odours of its nestmates? *Animal Behaviour, 29,* 802–809.

Bull, J. A., & Overmier, J. B. (1968). Additive and subtractive properties of excitation and inhibition. *Journal of Comparative and Physiological Psychology, 66,* 511–514.

Burdick, C. K., & James, J. P. (1970). Spontaneous recovery of conditioned suppression of licking by rats. *Journal of Comparative and Physiological Psychology, 72,* 467–470.

Burghardt, G. M. (1984). On the origins of play. In P. K. Smith (Ed.), *Play in animals and humans* (pp. 5–41). Oxford: Basil Blackwell.

Burghardt, G. M. (1998). Play. In G. Greenberg & M. H. Haraway (Eds.), *Comparative psychology: A handbook* (pp. 725–735). New York: Garland.

Burghardt, G. M., Greene, H. W., & Rand, A. S. (1977). Social behavior in hatchling green iguanas: Life at a reptile rookery. *Science, 195,* 689–691.

Burghardt, G. M., Ward, B., & Rosscoe, R. (1996). Problem of reptile play: Environment enrichment and play behavior in a captive Nile soft-shelled turtle, *Trionyx triunguis. Zoo Biology, 15,* 223–238.

Burkenroad, M. D. (1943). A possible function of bioluminescence. *Journal of Marine Research, 5,* 161–164.

Burkhardt, P. E. (1980). One trial backward fear conditioned as a function of US intensity. *Bulletin of the Psychonomic Society, 15,* 9–11.

Burns, M., & Domjan, M. (1996). Sign tracking versus goal tracking in the male Japanese quail *Coturnix japonica. Journal of Experimental Psychology: Animal Behavior Processes, 22,* 297–306.

Burns, M., & Domjan, M. (2000). Sign tracking in domesticated quail with one trail a day: Generality across CS and US parameters. *Animal Behavior Learning & Behavior, 28,* 109–119.

Burns, R. A., Woodward, W. T., Henderson, T. B., & Bitterman, M. E. (1974). Simultaneous contrast in the goldfish. *Animal Learning & Behavior, 2,* 97–100.

Bush, R. R., & Mosteller, F. (1951). A mathematical model for simple learning. *Psychological Review, 58,* 313–323.

Buskist, W. F., & Miller, H. L., Jr., (1986). Interaction between rules and contingencies in the control of human fixed-interval performance. *The Psychological Record, 36,* 109–116.

Butler, R. A., & Alexander, H. M. (1955). Daily patterns of visual exploratory behavior in monkeys. *Journal of Comparative and Physiological Psychology, 48,* 247–249.

Butler, R. A., & Harlow, H. F. (1954). Persistence of visual exploration in monkeys. *Journal of Comparative and Physiological Psychology, 47,* 258–263.

Butter, C. M. (1963). Stimulus generalization along one and two dimensions in pigeons. *Journal of Experimental Psychology, 65,* 339–346.

Buzzard, J. H., & Hake, D. F. (1984). Stimulus control of schedule-induced activity in pigeons during multiple schedules. *Journal of the Experimental Analysis of Behavior, 42,* 191–209.

Byrd, L. D. (1969). Responding in the cat maintained under response-independent electric shock and response-produced electric shock. *Journal of the Experimental Analysis of Behavior, 12,* 1–10.

Byrd, L. D. (1972). Responding in the squirrel monkey under second-order schedules of shock delivery. *Journal of the Experimental Analysis of Behavior, 18,* 155–167.

Byrne, R. (1995). *The thinking ape: Evolutionary origins of intelligence.* Oxford: Oxford University Press.

Caccone, A., & Powell, J. R. (1989). DNA divergence among hominoids. *Evolution, 43,* 925–942.

Caggiula, A. R. (1972). Shock-elicited copulation and aggression in male rats. *Journal of Comparative and Physiological Psychology, 80,* 393–397.

Caggiula, A. R., & Eibergen, R. (1969). Copulation of virgin male rats evoked by painful peripheral stimulation. *Journal of Comparative and Physiological Psychology, 69,* 414–419.

Campagnoni,-F.-R., Cohen,-P.-S., & Yoburn,-B.-C. (1981). Organization of attack and other behaviors of White King pigeons exposed to intermittent water presentations. *Animal Learning & Behavior, 9,* 491–500

Campbell, B. A. (1964). Theory and research on the effects of water deprivation on random activity in the rat. In M. Wayner (Ed.), *Thirst—proceedings of the first international symposium on thirst in the regulation of body water* (pp. 317–334). New York: MacMillan.

Campbell, B. A., & Bloom, J. M. (1965). Relative aversiveness of noise and shock. *Journal of Comparative and Physiological Psychology, 60,* 440–442.

Campbell, B. A., & Kraeling, D. (1953). Response strength as a function of drive level and amount of drive reduction. *Journal of Experimental Psychology, 45,* 97–101.

Campbell, B. A., & Sheffield, F. D. (1953). Relation of random activity to food deprivation. *Journal of Comparative and Physiological Psychology, 46,* 320–322.

Campbell, B. A., Smith, N. F., Misanin, J. R., & Jaynes, J. (1966). *Journal of Comparative and Physiological Psychology, 61,* 123–127.

Campbell, N. A. (1996). *Biology* (Fourth edition). Menlo Park, CA: The Benjamin/Cummings.

Cantor, M. B. (1971). Signaled reinforcing brain stimulation facilitates operant behavior under schedules of intermittent reinforcement. *Science, 174,* 610–613.

Cantor, M. B. (1981). Bad habits: Models of induced ingestion in satiated rats and people. In S. Miller (Ed.), *Behavior and nutrition* (pp. 31–49). Philadelphia: Franklin Institute Press.

Cantor, M. B., Smith, S. E., & Bryan, B. R. (1982). Induced bad habits: Adjunctive ingestion and grooming in human subjects. *Appetite, 3,* 1–12.

Cantor, M. B., & Wilson, J. F. (1978). Polydipsia induced by a schedule of brain stimulation reinforcement. *Learning and Motivation, 9,* 428–445.

Cantor, M. B., & Wilson, J. F. (1985). Feeding the face: New directions in adjunctive behavior research. In F. R. Brush & J. B. Overmier (Eds.), *Affect, conditioning, and cognition: Essays on the determinants of behavior* (pp. 299–312). Hillsdale, NJ: Erlbaum.

Capaldi, E. D., & Myers, D. E. (1982). Taste preferences as a function of food deprivation during original taste exposure. *Animal Learning & Behavior, 10,* 211–219.

Capaldi, E. D., Myers, D. E., Campbell, D. H., & Sheffer, J. D. (1983). Conditioned flavor preferences based on hunger level during original flavor exposure. *Animal Learning & Behavior, 11,* 107–115.

Capaldi, E. D., Owens, J., & Palmer, K. A. (1994). Effects of food deprivation on learning and expression of flavor preferences conditioned by saccharin or sucrose. *Animal Learning & Behavior, 22,* 173–180.

Capaldi, E. J. (1972). Successive negative contrast effect: Intertrial interval, type of shift, and four sources of generalization decrement. *Journal of Experimental Psychology, 96,* 433–438.

Capaldi, E. J. (1985). Anticipation and remote associations: A configural approach. *Journal of Experimental Psychology: Learning, Memory, and Cognition, 11,* 444–449.

Capaldi, E. J. (1992). Levels of organized behavior in rats. In W. K. Honig & J. T. Spence (Eds.), *Cognitive aspects of stimulus control* (pp. 385–404). Hillsdale, NJ: Erlbaum.

Capaldi, E. J. (1993). Animal number abilities: Implications for a hierarchical approach to instrumental learning. In S. T. Boysen & E. J. Capaldi (Eds.), *The development of numerical competence: Animal and human models* (pp. 191–209). Hillsdale, NJ: Erlbaum.

Capaldi, E. J., & Lynch, D. (1966). Patterning at a 24-hour ITI: resolution of a discrepancy more apparent than real. *Psychonomic Science, 6,* 229–230.

Capaldi, E. J., & Miller, D. J. (1988). Counting in rats: Its functional significance and the independent cognitive processes that constitute it. *Journal of Experimental Psychology: Animal Behavior Processes, 14,* 3–17.

Capaldi, E. J., Miller, D. J., Alprekin, S., & Barry, K. (1990). Organized responding in instrumental learning: Chunks and superchunks. *Learning and Motivation, 21,* 415–433.

Capaldi, E. J., & Verry, D. R. (1981). Serial order anticipation learning in rats: Memory for multiple hedonic events and their order. *Animal Learning & Behavior, 9,* 441–453.

Capehart, G. W., Eckerman, D. A., Guilkey, M., & Shull, R. L. (1980). A comparison of ratio and interval reinforcement schedules with comparable interreinforcement times. *Journal of the Experimental Analysis of Behavior, 34,* 61–76.

Cappell, H., & LeBlanc, A. E. (1973). Punishment of saccharin drinking by amphetamine in rats and its reversal by chlordiazepoxide. *Journal of Comparative and Physiological Psychology, 85,* 97–104.

Caraco, T. (1981). Energy budgets, risk and foraging preferences in dark-eyed juncos (*Junco hyemalis*). *Behavioral Ecology and Sociobiology, 8,* 213–217.

Caraco, T. (1982). Aspects of risk-aversion in foraging white-crowned sparrows. *Animal Behaviour, 20,* 210–217.

Caraco, T. (1983). White-crowned sparrows: (*Zonotrichia leucophrys*): Foraging preferences in a risky environment. *Behavioral Ecology and Sociobiology, 12,* 63–69.

Carey, M. P., & Burish, T. G. (1988). Etiology and treatment of the psychological side effects associated with cancer chemotherapy: A critical review and discussion. *Psychological Bulletin, 104,* 307–323.

Carew, T., Castellucci, V. F., & Kandel, E. R. (1979). Sensitization in Aplysia: Restoration of transmission in synapses inactivated by long-term habituation. *Science, 205,* 417–419.

Carlisle, H. J., Shanab, M. E., & Simpson, C. W. (1972). Schedule-induced behaviors: Effect of intermittent water reinforcement on food intake and body temperature. *Psychonomic Science, 26,* 35–36.

Caro, T. M. (1979). Relations between kitten behavior and adult predation. *Zeitschrift für Tierpsychologie, 51,* 158–168.

Caro, T. M. (1980a). Predatory behavior in domestic cat mothers. *Behaviour, 74,* 128–148.

Caro, T. M. (1980b). Effects of the mother, object play, and adult experience on predation in cats. *Behavioral and Neural Biology, 29,* 29–51.

Caro, T. M. (1981). Predatory behavior and social play in kittens. *Behaviour, 76,* 1–24.

Caro, T. M., & Hauser, M. D. (1992). Is there teaching in nonhuman animals? *Quarterly Review of Biology, 67,* 151–174.

Carpenter, C. P. (1942). Sexual behavior of free-ranging rhesus monkeys, *Macaca mulatta*. I. Specimens, procedures, and behavioral characteristics of estrus. *Journal of Comparative Psychology, 33,* 113–142.

Carr, J. A. R., & Wilkie, D. M. (1997). Ordinal, phase, and interval timing. In C. M. Bradshaw & E. Szabai (Eds.), *Time and behaviour: Psychological and neurobiological analyses* (pp. 265–327). Amsterdam: Elsevier Science.

Carroll, M. E. (1985). Concurrent phencyclidine and saccharin access: Presentation of an alternative reinforcer reduces drug intake. *Journal of the Experimental Analysis of Behavior, 43,* 131–144.

Carter, D. E., & Eckerman, D. A. (1975). Symbolic matching by pigeons: Rate of learning complex discriminations predicted from simple discriminations. *Science, 187,* 662–664.

Carter, D. E., & Werner, T. J. (1978). Complex learning and information processing by pigeons: A critical analysis. *Journal of the Experimental Analysis of Behavior, 29,* 565–601.

Casey, L., & Kerr, N. (1977). Auditory-visual and language production (Monograph). *Rehabilitation Psychology, 24,* 137–155.

Case, D. A., Ploog, B. O., & Fantino, E. (1990). Observing behavior in a computer game. *Journal of the Experimental Analysis of Behavior, 54,* 185–199.

Catania, A. C. (1963). Concurrent performances: A baseline for the study of reinforcement magnitude. *Journal of the Experimental Analysis of Behavior, 6,* 299–300.

Catania, A. C. (1966). Concurrent operants. In W. K. Honig (Ed.), *Operant behavior: Areas of research and application* (pp. 213–270). New York: Appleton-Century-Crofts.

Catania, A. C., & Keller, K. J. (1981). Contingency, contiguity, correlation, and the concept of causation. In P. Harzem & M. D. Zeiler (Eds.), *Advances in the analysis of behavior* (vol. 2): *Predictability, correlation, and contiguity* (pp. 125–167). Chichester, UK: Wiley.

Catania, A. C., Matthews, B. A., & Shimoff, E. (1982). Instructed versus shaped human verbal behavior: Interactions with nonverbal responding. *Journal of the Experimental Analysis of Behavior, 38,* 233–248.

Catania, A. C., & Reynolds, G. S. (1968). A quantitative analysis of the responding maintained by interval schedules of reinforcement. *Journal of the Experimental Analysis of Behavior, 11,* 327–383.

Caza, P. A., & Spear, N. E. (1984). Short-term exposure to an odor increases its subsequent preference in preweaning rats: A descriptive profile of the phenomenon. *Developmental Psychobiology, 17,* 407–422.

Cerutti, D. T. (1991). Discriminative versus reinforcing properties of schedules as determinants of schedule insensitivity in humans. *The Psychological Record, 41,* 51–67.

Chalmers, N. R. (1980). The ontogeny of play in feral olive baboons (*Papio anubis*). *Animal Behaviour, 28,* 570–585.

Charnov, E. L. (1976a). Optimal foraging: The marginal value theorem. *Theoretical Population Biology, 9,* 129–136.

Charnov, E. L. (1976b). Optimal foraging: Attack strategy of a mantid. *The American Naturalist, 110,* 141–151.

Cheney, D. L. (1983). Extra-familial alliances among vervet monkeys. In R. A. Hinde (Ed.), *Primate social relationships: An integrated approach* (pp. 278–286). Oxford: Blackwell Scientific.

Cheney, D. L., & Seyferth, R. M. (1988). Social and non- social knowledge in vervet monkeys. In R. W. Byrne & A. Whiten (Eds.), *Machiavellian intelligence: Social expertise and the evolution of intellect in monkeys, apes, and humans* (pp. 255–270). Oxford: Clarendon.

Cheney, D. L., & Seyfarth, R. M. (1990). *How monkeys see the world: Inside the mind of another species.* Chicago: University of Chicago Press.

Cheng, K. (1988). Some psychophysics of pigeons' use of landmarks. *Journal of Comparative Physiology: A Sensory, Neural, and Behavioral Physiology, 162,* 815–826.

Cheng, K. (1989). The vector sum model of pigeon landmark use. *Journal of Experimental Psychology: Animal Behavior Processes, 15,* 366–375.

Cherek, D. R., & Brauchi, J. T. (1981). Schedule-induced cigarette smoking behavior during fixed-interval monetary reinforced responding. In C. M. Bradshaw, E. Szabadi, & C. F. Lowe (Eds.), *Quantification of steady-state operant behavior* (pp. 389–392) Amsterdam: Elsevier/North-Holland Biomedical.

Cherek, D. R., Thompson, T., & Heistad, G. T. (1973). Responding maintained by the opportunity to attack during an interval food reinforcement schedule. *Journal of the Experimental Analysis of Behavior, 19,* 113–123.

Cherot, C., Jones, A., & Neuringer, A. (1996). Reinforced variability decreases with approach to reinforcers. *Journal of Experimental Psychology: Animal Behavior Processes, 22,* 497–508.

Chillag, D., & Mendelson, J. (1971). Schedule-induced airlicking as a function of body-weight deficit in rats. *Physiology & Behavior, 6,* 603–605.

Chisholm, A. H. (1958). *Bird wonders of Australia.* Lansing: Michigan State University Press.

Chiszar, D., Carter, T., Knight, L., Simonsen, L., & Taylor, S. (1976). Investigatory behavior in the plains garter snake (*Thamnophis sirtalis*) and several additional species. *Animal Learning & Behavior, 4,* 273–278.

Chivers, D. P., Brown, G. E., & Smith, R. J. F. (1996). The evolution of chemical alarm signals: Attracting predators benefits alarm signal senders. *American Naturalist, 148,* 649–659.

Chomsky, N. (1980). Rules and representations. *Behavioral and brain sciences, 3,* 1–61.

Chomsky, N. (1986). *Knowledge of language: Its nature, origin, and use.* New York: Praeger.

Christian, W. P., & Schaeffer, R. W. (1973). The effects of sucrose concentrations upon schedule-induced polydipsia on a FFI-60-sec dry food reinforcement schedule. *Psychological Reports, 32,* 1067–1073.

Christian, W. P., Schaeffer, R. W., & King, G. D. (1978). *Schedule-induced behavior.* Montreal: Eden Press.

Church, R. M. (1957).Two procedures for the establishment of imitative behavior. *Journal of Comparative and Physiological Psychology, 50,* 315–318.

Church, R. M. (1997). Quantitative models of animal

learning and cognition. *Journal of Experimental Psychology: Animal Behavior Processes, 23,* 379–389.

Church, R. M., & Meck, W. H. (1984). The numerical attribute of stimuli. In H. L. Roitblat, T. G. Bever, & H. S. Terrace (Eds.), *Animal cognition: Proceedings of the Harry Frank Guggenheim Conference, June 2–4, 1982* (pp. 445–464). Hillsdale, NJ: Erlbaum.

Church, R. M., & Raymond, G. A. (1967). Influence of the schedule of positive reinforcement on punished behavior. *Journal of Comparative and Physiological Psychology, 63,* 329–332.

Churchland, P. (1991). Folk psychology and the explanation of human behavior. In J. D. Greenwood (Ed.), *The future of folk psychology: Intentionality and cognitive science* (pp. 51–69). Cambridge: Cambridge University Press.

Clark, C. B. (1977). A preliminary report on weaning among chimpanzees of the Gombe National Park, Tanzania. In S. Chevalier-Skolnikoff & F. E. Poirier (Eds.), *Primate bio-social development: Biological, social, and ecological determinants* (pp. 235–260). New York: Garland Publishing.

Clark, H. H., & Chase, W. G. (1972). On the process of comparing sentences against pictures. *Cognitive Psychology, 3,* 472–517.

Clarke, J., Gannon, M., Hughes, I., Keogh, C., Singer, G., & Wallace, M. (1977). Adjunctive behavior in humans in a group gambling situation. *Physiology & Behavior, 18,* 159–161.

Clayton, M. C., & Hayes, L. J. (1999). Conceptual differences in the analysis of stimulus equivalence. *The Psychological Record, 49,* 145–161.

Cleland, G. G., & Davey, G. C. L. (1983). Autoshaping in the rat: The effects of localizable visual and auditory signals for food. *Journal of the Experimental Analysis of Behavior, 40,* 47–56.

Clifford, T. (1964). Extinction following continuous reward and latent extinction. *Journal of Experimental Psychology, 68,* 456–465.

Cochrane, T. L., Scobie, S. R., & Fallon, D. (1973). Negative contrast in goldfish (*Carassius auratus*). *Bulletin of the Psychonomic Society, 1,* 411–413.

Cohen, I. L. (1975). The reinforcement value of schedule-induced drinking. *Journal of the Experimental Analysis of Behavior, 23,* 37–44.

Cohen, L. R., Brady, J., & Lowry, M. (1981). The role of differential responding in matching-to-sample and delayed matching performance. In M. L. Commons & J. A. Nevin (Eds.), *Quantitative analyses of behavior* (vol. 1): *Discriminative properties of reinforcement schedules* (pp. 345–364). Cambridge, MA: Ballinger.

Cohen, L. R., Looney, T. A., Brady, J. H., & Aucella, A. F. (1976). Differential sample response schedules in the acquisition of conditional discriminations by pigeons. *Journal of the Experimental Analysis of Behavior, 26,* 301–314.

Cohen, P. S., & Looney, T. A. (1973). Schedule-induced mirror responding in the pigeon. *Journal of the Experimental Analysis of Behavior, 19,* 395–408.

Cohen, P. S., Looney, T. A., Campagnoni, F. R., & Lawler, C. P. (1985). A two-state model of reinforcer-induced motivation. In F. R. Brush & J. B. Overmier (Eds.), *Affect, conditioning, and cognition: Essays on the determinants of behavior* (pp. 281–297). New York: Erlbaum.

Cole, J. M., & Parker, B. K. (1971). Schedule-induced aggression: Access to an attackable target bird as a positive reinforcer. *Psychonomic Science, 22,* 33–35.

Cole, L. E. (1939). A comparison of the factors of practice and knowledge of experimental procedures. *Journal of General Psychology, 20,* 349–373.

Collett, T. S., Fry, S. N., & Wehner, R. (1993). Sequence learning by honeybees. *Journal of Comparative Physiology, 172,* 693–706.

Collier, G., & Hirsch, E. (1971). Reinforcing properties of spontaneous activity in the rat. *Journal of Comparative and Physiological Psychology, 7,* 155–160.

Collier, G., Hirsch, E., & Hamlin, P. H. (1972). The ecological determinants of reinforcement in the rat. *Physiology & Behavior, 9,* 705–716.

Colvin, J. (1983). Description of sibling and peer relationships among immature male rhesus monkeys. In R. A. Hinde (ed), *Primate social relationships: An integrated approach* (pp. 20–27). Oxford: Blackwell Scientific Publications.

Colwill, R. M., & Rescorla, R. A. (1985). Post-conditioning devaluation of a reinforcer affects instrumental responding. *Journal of Experimental Psychology Animal Behavior Processes, 11,* 120–132.

Commentary on Horne and Lowe's 1996 article (1997). *Journal of the Experimental Analysis of Behavior, 68,* 233–300.

Concannon, J. T., & Freda, J. (1980). Modulation of conditioned taste aversion by sodium pentobarbital. *Pharmacology, Biochemistry & Behavior, 13,* 762–764.

Conger, R., & Killeen, P. (1974). Use of concurrent operants in small group research: A demonstration. *Pacific Sociological Review, 17,* 399–416.

Cook, M., & Mineka, S. (1990). Selective associations in the observational conditioning of fear in rhesus monkeys. *Journal of Experimental Psychology: Animal Behavior Processes, 16,* 372–389.

Cook, M., Mineka, S., Wolkenstein, B., & Laitsch, K. (1985). Observational conditioning of snake fear in unrelated rhesus monkeys. *Journal of Abnormal Psychology, 94,* 591–610.

Cook, R. G., Brown, M. F., & Riley, D. A. (1985). Flexible memory processing by rats: Use of prospective and retrospective information in the radial maze. *Journal of Experimental Psychology: Animal Behavior Processes, 11,* 453–469.

Cook, R. G., & Katz, J. S. (1999). Dynamic object perception by pigeons. *Journal of Experimental Psychology: Animal Behavior Processes, 25,* 194–210.

Cook, R. G., Katz, J. S., & Cavoto, B. R. (1997). Pigeon same-different concept learning with multiple stimulus classes. *Journal of Experimental Psychology: Animal Behavior Processes, 23,* 417–433.

Cope, C. L., Sanger, D. J., & Blackman, D. E. (1976). Intragastric water and the acquisition of schedule-induced drinking. *Behavioral Biology, 17,* 267–270.

Corfield-Sumner, P. K., Blackman, D. E., & Stainer, G. (1977). Polydipsia induced in rats by second-order schedules of reinforcement. *Journal of the Experimental Analysis of Behavior, 27,* 265-273.

Corning, W. C., & Kelly, S. (1973). Platyhelminthes: The turbellarians. In W. A. Corning, J. A. Dyal, & A. O. D. Willows (Eds.), *Invertebrate learning* (vol. 1, pp. 171–224). New York: Plenum.

Corning, W. C., & Von Burg, R. (1973). Protozoa. In W C.. Corning, J. A. Dyal, & A. O. D. Willows (Eds.), *Invertebrate learning* (vol. 1, pp. 49–122). New York: Plenum.

Couch, J. V. (1974). Reinforcement magnitude and schedule- induced polydipsia: A reexamination. *The Psychological Record, 24,* 559–562.

Coureaud, G., Schaal, B., Orgeur, P., Hudson, R., Lebas, F., & Coudert, P. (1997). Perinatal odour disruption impairs neonatal milk intake in the rabbit. *Advances in Ethology, 32,* 134.

Couvillon, P. A., & Bitterman, M. E. (1980). Some phenomena of associative learning in honeybees. *Journal of Comparative and Physiological Psychology, 94,* 878–885.

Couvillon, P. A., & Bitterman, M. E. (1984). The overlearning-extinction effect and successive negative contrast in honeybees. *Journal of Comparative and Physiological Psychology, 98,* 100–109.

Couvillon, P. A., & Bitterman, M. E. (1985). Effect of experience with a preferred food on consummatory responding for a less preferred food in goldfish. *Animal Learning & Behavior, 14,* 225–231.

Couvillon, P. A., & Bitterman, M. E. (1988). Compound-component and conditional discrimination of colors and odors by honeybees: Further tests of a continuity model. *Animal Learning & Behavior, 16,* 67–74.

Couvillon, P. A., & Bitterman, M. E. (1992). A conventional conditioning analysis of "transitive inference" in pigeons. *Journal of Experimental Psychology: Animal Behavior Processes, 18,* 308–310.

Couvillon, P. A., Nagrampa, J. A., & Bitterman, M. E. (1994). Learning in honeybees (*Apis mellifera*) as a function of sucrose concentration: Analysis of the retrospective effect. *Journal of Comparative Psychology, 108,* 274–281.

Cowan, P. E. (1977). Neophobia and neophilia: New-object and new-place reactions of three Rattus species. *Journal of Comparative and Physiological Psychology, 91,* 63–71.

Cowan, P. E. (1983). Exploration in small mammals: Ethology and ecology. In J. Archer & L. I. A. Birke (Eds.), *Exploration in animals and humans* (pp. 147–175). Cambridge: Van Nostrand Reinhold.

Cowill, R. M., & Rescorla, R. A. (1985). Post-conditioning devaluation of a reinforcer affects instrumental responding. *Journal of Experimental Psychology: Animal Behavior Processes, 11,* 120–132.

Cowles, J. T. (1937). Food-tokens as incentives for learning by chimpanzees. *Comparative Psychology Monographs, 14*(5), 1–96.

Craig, C. L. (1994). Limits to learning: Effects of predator pattern and colour on perception and avoidance-learning by prey. *Animal Behaviour, 47,* 1087–1099.

Crawford, F. T., & Skeen, C. L. (1967). Operant responding in the planarian: A replication study. *Psychological Reports, 20,* 1023–1027.

Crawford, M. P. (1939). The social psychology of the vertebrates. *Psychological Bulletin, 36,* 407–466.

Crelin, E. S. (1987). The human vocal tract: Anatomy, function, development, and evolution. New York: Vantage Press.

Crespi, L. P. (1942). Quantitative variation in incentive and performance in the white rat. *American Journal of Psychology, 55,* 467–517.

Critchfield, T. S., & Lattal, K. A. (1993). Acquisition of a spatially defined operant with delayed reinforcement. *Journal of the Experimental Analysis of Behavior, 59,* 373–387.

Cronin, P. B. (1980). Reinstatement of postresponse stimuli prior to reward in delayed-reward discrimination learning by pigeons. *Animal Learning & Behavior, 8,* 352–358.

Crosbie, J., Williams, A. M., Lattal, K. A., Anderson, M. M., & Brown, S. M. (1997). Schedule interactions involving punishment with pigeons and humans. *Journal of the Experimental Analysis of Behavior, 68,* 161–175.

Crowell, C. R., & Anderson, D. C. (1981). Influence of duration and number of inescapable shocks on intrashock activity and subsequent interference effects. *Animal Learning & Behavior, 9,* 28–37.

Curio, E. (1976). *The ethology of predation.* Berlin: Springer-Verlag.

Curio, E. (1988). Cultural transmission of enemy recognition by birds. In T. R. Zentall & B. G. Galef, Jr. (Eds.), *Social learning: Psychological and biological perspectives* (pp. 75–97). Hillsdale, NJ: Erlbaum.

Curio, E., Ernst, U., & Vieth, W. (1978). The adaptive significance of avian mobbing. II. Cultural transmission of enemy recognition in blackbirds: Effectiveness and some constraints. *Zeitschrift für Tierpsychologie, 48,* 184–202.

Custance, D., & Bard, K. (1994). The comparative and developmental study of self-recognition and imitation: The importance of social factors. In S. T. Parker, R. W. Mitchell, & M. L. Boccia, (Eds.), *Self-awareness in animals and humans: Developmental perspectives* (pp. 207–226). Cambridge: Cambridge University Press.

Daan, S., & Koene, P. (1981). On the timing of foraging flights by oystercatchers, Haematopus ostralegus, on tidal mudflats. *Netherlands Journal of Sea Research, 15,* 1–22.

Dadds, M. R., Bovbjerg, D. H., & Redd, W. H. (1997). Imagery in human classical conditioning. *Psychological Bulletin, 122,* 89–103.

Dallery, J., McDowell, J. J., & Lancaster, J. S. (2000).

Falsification of matching theory's account of single-alternative responding: Herrnstein's k varies with sucrose concentration. *Journal of the Experimental Analysis of Behavior, 73,* 23–43.

Davis, B. L., & MacNeilage, P. F. (1995). The articulatory basis of babbling. *Journal of Speech & Hearing Research, 38,* 1199–1211.

Delamater, A. R. (1998). Associative mediational processes in the acquired equivalence and distinctiveness of cues. *Journal of Experimental Psychology: Animal Behavior Processes, 24,* 467–482.

Dale, R. H. (1979). Concurrent drinking by pigeons on fixed-interval reinforcement schedule. *Physiology & Behavior, 23,* 977–980.

Daly, H. B. (1969). Learning of a hurdle-jump response to escape cues paired with reduced reward or frustrative nonreward. *Journal of Experimental Psychology, 79,* 146–157.

Daly, H. B., & McCroskery, J. H. (1973). Acquisition of a bar-press response to escape frustrative nonreward and reduced reward. *Journal of Experimental Psychology, 98,* 109–112.

D'Amato, M. R. (1973). Delayed matching and short-term memory in monkeys. In G. H. Bower (Ed.), *The psychology of learning and motivation* (vol. 7): *Advances in research and theory.* New York: Academic Press.

D'Amato, M. R., Fazzaro, J., & Etkin, M. (1967). Discriminated bar-press avoidance maintenance and extinction in rats as a function of shock intensity. *Journal of Comparative and Physiological Psychology, 63,* 351–354.

D'Amato, M. R., & O'Neill, W. (1971). Effect of delay-interval illumination on matching behavior in the capuchin monkey. *Journal of the Experimental Analysis of Behavior, 15,* 327–333.

D'Amato, M. R., & Schiff, D. (1964). Long-term discriminated avoidance performance in the rat. *Journal of Comparative and Physiological Psychology, 58,* 344–349.

D'Amato, M. R., & Worsham, R. W. (1972). Delayed matching in the capuchin monkey with brief sample durations. *Learning and Motivation, 3,* 304–312.

D'Andrea, T. (1971). Avoidance of timeout from response- independent reinforcement. *Journal of the Experimental Analysis of Behavior, 15,* 319–325.

Danson, C., & Creed, T. (1970). Rate of response as a visual social stimulus. *Journal of the Experimental Analysis of Behavior, 13,* 233–242.

Darczewska, M, & Shapiro, L. J. (1997). *What do mallard ducklings find more attractive, the hen or the brood?* Poster presented at the Brain, Behaviour and Cognition Conference, Winnipeg, June.

Darwin, C. J., Turvey, M. T., & Crowder, R. G. (1972). The auditory analogue of the Sperling partial report procedure: Evidence for brief auditory storage. *Cognitive Psychology, 3,* 255–267.

das Gracas de Souza, D., Alves de Moraes, A. B., & Todorov, J. C. (1984). Shock intensity and signaled

avoidance responding. *Journal of the Experimental Analysis of Behavior, 42,* 67–74.

Dashevskii, B. A., Karás A. Y., & Udalova, G. P. (1990). Behavioral plasticity of Myrmica rubra ants during learning in a multi-alternative symmetrical labyrinth. *Neuroscience and Behavioral Physiology, 20,* 18–26.

Datta, S. B. (1983 a). Patterns of agonistic interference. In R. A. Hinde (Ed.), *Primate social relationships: An integrated approach* (pp. 289–297). Oxford: Blackwell Scientific.

Datta, S. B. (1983 b). Relative power and the maintenance of dominance. In R. A. Hinde (Ed.), *Primate social relationships: An integrated approach* (pp. 93–103). Oxford: Blackwell Scientific.

Davenport, D. G., & Olson, R. D. (1968). A reinterpretation of extinction in discriminated avoidance. *Psychonomic Science, 13,* 5–6.

Davey, G. C. L., & Cleland, G. G. (1982). The effect of partial reinforcement on the acquisition and extinction of sign-tracking and goal-tracking in the rat. *Bulletin of the Psychonomic Society, 19,* 115–118.

Davey, G. C. L., Oakley, D., & Cleland, G. G. (1981). Autoshaping in the rat: Effects of omission on the form of the response. *Journal of the Experimental Analysis of Behavior, 36,* 75–91.

Davies, N. B. (1985). Cooperation and conflicts among dunnocks, *Prunella modularis* in a variable mating system. *Animal Behaviour, 33,* 628–648.

Davies, N. B., & Houston, A. L. (1981). Owners and satellites: The economics of territory defense in the pied wagtail, *Motacilla alba. Journal of Animal Ecology, 50,* 157–180.

Davies, N. B., & Houston, A. I. (1984). Territory economics. In J. R. Krebs & N. B. Davies (Eds.), *Behavioral ecology: An evolutionary approach* (2nd ed.) (pp. 148–169). Oxford: Blackwell Scientific.

Davies, N. B., & Lundberg, A. (1984). Food distribution and a variable mating system in the dunnock *Prunella modularis. Journal of Animal Ecology, 53,* 895–912.

Davis, B. L., & MacNeilage, P. F. (1995). The articulatory basis of babbling. *Journal of Speech & Hearing Research, 38,* 1199–1211.

Davis, C. A., Brady, M. P., Hamilton, R., McEvoy, M. A., & Williams, R. E. (1994). Effects of high-probability requests on the social interactions of young children with severe disabilities. *Journal of Applied Behavior Analysis, 27,* 619–637.

Davis, H., & McIntire, R. W. (1969). Conditioned suppression under positive, negative, and no contingency between conditioned and unconditioned stimuli. *Journal of the Experimental Analysis of Behavior, 12,* 633–640.

Davis, M., & Wagner, A. R. (1969). Habituation of startle response under incremental sequence of stimulus intensities. *Journal of Comparative and Physiological Psychology, 67,* 486–492.

Davison, M. C. (1968). Reinforcement rate and immediacy of reinforcement as factors in choice. *Psychonomic Science, 10,* 181–182.

Davison, M. (1982). Performance in concurrent variable- interval fixed-ratio schedules. *Journal of the Experimental Analysis of Behavior, 37,* 81–96.

Davison, M. (1996). Stimulus effects on behavior allocation in three-alternative choice. *Journal of the Experimental Analysis of Behavior, 66,* 149–168.

Davison, M., & Ferguson, A. (1978). The effects of different component response requirements in multiple and concurrent schedules. *Journal of the Experimental Analysis of Behavior, 29,* 283–295.

Davison, M., & Hogsden. I. (1984). Concurrent variable- interval schedule performance: Fixed versus mixed reinforcer durations. *Journal of the Experimental Analysis of Behavior, 41,* 169–182.

Davison, M. C., & Hunter, I. W. (1976). Performance on variable-interval schedules arranged singly and concurrently. *Journal of the Experimental Analysis of Behavior, 25,* 335–345.

Davison, M., & Jenkins, P. E. (1985). Stimulus discriminability, contingency discriminability, and schedule performance. *Animal Learning & Behavior, 13,* 77–84.

Davison, M., & Jones, M. (1995). A quantitative analysis of extreme choice. *Journal of the Experimental Analysis of Behavior, 64,* 147–162.

Davison, M., & McCarthy, D. (1988). *The matching law: A research review*. Hillsdale, NJ: Erlbaum.

Dawes, R. M. (1980). Social dilemmas. *Annual Review of Psychology, 31,* 169–193.

Dawes, R. M., & Messick, D. M. (2000). Social dilemmas. *International Journal of Psychology, 35,* 111–116.

Dawson, B. V., & Foss, (1965). Observational learning in budgerigars. *Animal Behaviour, 13,* 470–474.

Deacon, T. W. (1997). *The symbolic species*. New York: Norton.

Dearing, M. F., & Dickinson, A. (1979). Counterconditioning of shock by a water reinforcer in rabbits. *Animal Learning & Behavior, 7,* 360–366.

DeCarlo, L. T. (1985). Matching and maximizing with variable-time schedules. *Journal of the Experimental Analysis of Behavior, 43,* 75–81.

de Castro, J., & Brewer, E. M. (1992). The amount eaten in meals by humans is a power function of the number of people present. *Physiology & Behaviour, 51,* 121–125.

Deeke, L., Grötzinger, B., & Kornhuber, H. H. (1976). Voluntary finger movements in man: Cerebral potentials and theory. *Biological Cybernetics, 23,* 99.

Deese, J. (1959). On the prediction of occurrence of particular verbal intrusions in immediate recall. *Journal of Experimental Psychology, 58,* 17–22.

Delgado, J. (1963). Cerebral heterostimulation in a monkey colony. *Science, 141,* 161–163.

Dennett, D. C. (1988). The intentional stance in theory and practice. In R. Byrne & A. Whiten (Eds.), *Machiavellian intelligence* (pp. 180–202). Oxford: Clarendon Press.

Denney, J., & Neuringer, A. (1998). Behavioral variability is controlled by discriminative stimuli. *Animal Learning & Behavior, 26,* 154–162.

Denny, M. R. (1971). Relaxation theory and experiments. In F. R. Brush (Ed.), *Avoidance conditioning and learning* (pp. 235–295). New York: Academic Press.

DePaulo, P., & Hoffman, H. S. (1981). Reinforcement by an imprinting stimulus versus water on simple schedules in ducklings. *Journal of the Experimental Analysis of Behavior, 36,* 151–169.

Devany, J. M., Hayes, S., & Nelson, R. (1986). Equivalence class formation in language-able and language-disabled children. *Journal of the Experimental Analysis of Behavior, 46,* 243–257.

de Villiers, P. (1977). Choice in concurrent schedules and a quantitative formulation of the law of effect. In W. K. Honig & J. E. R. Staddon (Eds.), *Handbook of Operant Behavior* (pp. 233–287). Englewood Cliffs, NJ; Prenice-Hall.

de Waal, F. B. M. (1982). *Chimpanzee politics*. New York: Harper & Row.

de Waal, F. B. M. (1986). The integration of dominance and social bonding in primates. *Quarterly Review of Biology, 61,* 459–479.

de Waal, F. B. M. (1996). Ranks and order. In F. B. M. de Waal (Ed.), *Good natured* (pp. 89–132, 234–242). Cambridge, MA: Harvard University Press.

DeWeese, J. (1977). Schedule-induced biting under fixed- interval schedules of food or electric-shock presentation. *Journal of the Experimental Analysis of Behavior, 27,* 419–431.

Dielenberg, R. A., & McGregor, I. S. (1999). Habituation of the hiding response to cat odor in rats. *Journal of Comparative Psychology, 113,* 376–387.

Dill, L. M. (1987). Animal decision making and its ecological consequences: The future of aquatic ecology and behavior. *Canadian Journal of Zoology, 65,* 803–811.

Dill, L. M., & Fraser, A. H. G. (1984). Risk of predation and feeding behaviour of juvenile coho salmon (*Onchorynchus kisutch*). *Behavioral Ecology and Sociobiology, 16,* 65–71.

Dilly, P. N. (1963). Delayed responses in Octopus. *Journal of Experimental Biology, 40,* 393–401.

Dinsmoor, J. A. (1954). Punishment: I. The avoidance hypothesis. *Psychological Review, 61,* 34–46.

Dinsmoor, J. A. (1995). Stimulus control: Part 2. *The Behavior Analyst, 18,* 253–269.

Dinsmoor, J. A., Browne, M. P., & Lawrence, C. E. (1972). A test of the negative discriminative stimulus as a reinforcer for observing. *Journal of the Experimental Analysis of Behavior, 18,* 79–85.

Dixon, M. H. (1978). Teaching conceptual classes with receptive label training. *Acta Symbolica, 30,* 205–212.

Dixon, M. H., & Dixon, L. S. (1978). The nature of standard control in children's matching-to-sample. *Journal of the Experimental Analysis of Behavior, 30,* 205–212.

Dixon, M., & Spradlin, J. (1976). Establishing stimulus equivalence among retarded adolescents. *Journal of Experimental Child Psychology, 21,* 144–164.

Dollard, J., Doob, L. W., Miller, N. E., Mowrer, O. H., & Sears, R. R. (1939). *Frustration and aggression.* New Haven, CT: Yale University Press.

Domjan, M. (1980). Ingestional aversion learning: Unique and general processes. In J. S. Rosenblatt, R. A. Hinde, C. Beer, & M.-C. Busnel (Eds.), *Advances in the study of behavior* (vol. 11, pp. 275–336). New York: Academic Press.

Domjan, M. (1983). Biological constraints on instrumental and classical conditioning 10 years later: Implications for general process theory. In G. H. Bower (Ed.), *The psychology of learning and motivation* (vol. 17). New York: Academic Press.

Domjan, M., Greene, P., & North, N. C. (1989). Contextual conditioning and the control of copulatory behavior by species-specific sign stimuli in male Japanese quail. *Journal of Experimental Psychology: Animal Behavior Processes, 15,* 147–153.

Domjan, M., Lyons, R., North, N. C., & Bruell, J. (1986). Sexual Pavlovian conditioned approach behavior in male Japanese quail (*Coturnix coturnix japonica*). *Journal of Comparative Psychology, 100,* 413–421.

Donahoe, J. W., & Palmer, D. C. (1994). *Learning and complex behavior.* Boston: Allyn & Bacon.

Donahoe, J. W., Palmer, D. C., & Burgos, J. E. (1997). The S-R issue: Its status in behavior analysis and in Donahoe and Palmer's Learning and Complex Behavior. *Journal of the Experimental Analysis of Behavior, 67,* 193–211.

Donegan, N. H. (1981). Priming-produced facilitation or diminution of responding to a Pavlovian unconditioned stimulus. *Journal of Experimental Psychology: Animal Behavior Processes, 7,* 295–312.

Dougan, J. D., & McSweeney, F. K. (1985). Variations in Herrnstein's r_0 as a function of alternative reinforcement rate. *Journal of the Experimental Analysis of Behavior, 43,* 215–223.

Dougher, M. J. (1983). Clinical effects of response deprivation and response satiation procedures. *Behavior Therapy, 14,* 286–289.

Dougher, M. J., Augustson, E., Markham, M. R., Greenway, D. E., & Wulfert, E. (1994). The transfer of respondent eliciting functions through stimulus equivalence classes. *Journal of the Experimental Analysis of Behavior, 62,* 331–351.

Dove, L. D. (1976). Relation between level of food deprivation and rate of schedule-induced attack. *Journal of the Experimental Analysis of Behavior, 25,* 63–68.

Downs, D. A., & Woods, J. H. (1975). Fixed-ratio escape and avoidance-escape from naloxone in morphine-dependent monkeys: Effects of naloxone dose and morphine pretreatment. *Journal of the Experimental Analysis of Behavior, 23,* 415–427.

Drummond, H., & Burghardt, G. M. (1982). Orientation in dispersing hatchling green iguanas, *Iguana iguana.* In G. M. Burghardt & A. S. Rand (Eds.), *Igua-*

nas of the world: Their behavior, ecology and conservation (pp. 271–291). Park Ridge, NJ: Noyes.

Drummond, P., White, K., & Ashton, R. (1978). Imagery vividness affects habituation rate. *Psychophysiology, 15,* 193–203.

Ducharme, J. M., & Worling, D. E. (1994). Behavioral momentum and stimulus fading in the acquisition and maintenance of child compliance in the home. *Journal of Applied Behavior Analysis, 27,* 639–647.

Dugatkin, L. A. (1992). Sexual selection and imitation: Females copy the mate choice of others. *American Naturalist, 139,* 1384–1389.

Dugatkin, L. A., & Godin, J.-G. L. (1992). Reversal of female mate choice by copying in the guppy (*Poecilia reticulata*). *Proceedings of the Royal Society of London B, 249,* 179–184.

Dugatkin, L. A., & Godin, J.-G. L. (1993). Female mate copying in the guppy (*Poecilia reticulata*): Age-dependent effects. *Behavioral Ecology, 4,* 289–292.

Dugdale, N., & Lowe, C. F. (2000). Testing for symmetry in the conditional discriminations of language-trained chimpanzees. *Journal of the Experimental Analysis of Behavior, 73,* 5–22.

Dukas, R., & Visscher, P. K. (1994). Lifetime learning by foraging honey bees. *Animal Behaviour, 48,* 1007–1012.

Dunbar, R. I. M. (1991). Functional significance of social grooming in primates. *Folia Primatologica, 57,* 121–131.

Dunbar, R. I. M. (1993). Coevolution of neocortical size, group size and language in humans. *Behavioral and Brain Sciences, 16,* 681–735.

Dunn, R., & Spetch, M. (1990). Conditioned reinforcement on schedules with uncertain outcomes. *Journal of the Experimental Analysis of Behavior, 53,* 201–218.

Durlach, P. J., & Rescorla, R. A. (1980). Potentiation rather than overshadowing in flavor-aversion learning: An analysis in terms of within-compound associations. *Journal of Experimental Psychology: Animal Behavior Processes, 6,* 175–187.

Eales, L. A. (1985). Song-learning in zebra finches: Some effects of song model availability on what is learnt and when. *Animal Behaviour, 33,* 1293–1300.

Ebbinghaus, H. E. (1902). *Grundzüge der psychologie* [*Basic psychology*]. Leipzig: Von Veit.

Ebenholtz, S. M. (1972). Serial learning and dimensional organization. In G. H. Bower (Ed.), *The psychology of learning and motivation* (vol. 5, (pp. 267–314). New York: Academic Press.

Eccles, J. C. (1989). *Evolution of the brain: Creation of the self.* New York: Routledge.

Eckerman, D. A. (1970). Generalization and response mediation of a conditional discrimination. *Journal of the Experimental Analysis of Behavior, 13,* 301–316.

Eckerman, D. A., Hienz, R. D., Stern, S., & Kowlowitz, V. (1980). Shaping the location of a pigeon's peck: Effect of rate and size of shaping steps. *Journal of the Experimental Analysis of Behavior, 33,* 299–310.

Eckerman, D. A., & Lanson, R. N. (1969). Variability of response location for pigeons responding under continuous reinforcement, intermittent reinforcement, and extinction. *Journal of the Experimental Analysis of Behavior, 12,* 73–80.

Eckerman, D. A., Lanson, R. N., & Cumming, W. W. (1968). Acquisition and maintenance of matching without a required observing response. *Journal of the Experimental Analysis of Behavior, 11,* 435–441.

Edelman, G. M. (1992). *Bright air, brilliant fire: On the matter of the mind.* New York: Basic Books.

Edmunds, M. (1974). *Defense in animals: A survey of anti- predator defenses.* London: Longmans.

Edwards, C. A., & Honig, W. K. (1987). Memorization and "feature-selection" in the acquisition of natural concepts in pigeons. *Learning and Motivation, 18,* 235–260.

Eibl-Eibesfeldt, I. (1975). *Ethology: The biology of behaviour* (Second edition). New York: Holt.

Eilers, R. E., & Oller, D. K. (1994). Infant vocalizations and the early diagnosis of severe hearing impairment. *Journal of Pediatrics, 124,* 199–203.

Eisenberger, K., Karpman, M., & Trattner, J. (1967). What is the necessary and sufficient condition for reinforcement in the contingency situation? *Journal of Experimental Psychology, 74,* 342–350.

Ellson, D. G. (1939). Spontaneous recovery of the galvanic skin response as a function of the recovery interval. *Journal of Experimental Psychology, 25,* 586–600.

Elsmore, T. F., & McBride, S. A. (1994). An eight- alternative concurrent schedule: Foraging in a radial maze. *Journal of the Experimental Analysis of Behavior, 61,* 331–348.

Emmerton, J. (1998).Numerosity differences and effects of stimulus density on pigeons' discrimination performance. *Animal Learning & Behavior, 26,* 243–256.

Emurian, H. H., Emurian, C. S., & Brady, J. V. (1985). Positive and negative reinforcing effects on behavior in a three-person microsociety. *Journal of the Experimental Analysis of Behavior, 44,* 157–174.

Endler, J. A. (1986). Natural selection in the wild. Princeton, NJ: Princeton University Press.Endler, J. A. (1988). Frequency-dependent predation, crypsis and aposematic coloration. *Philosophical Transactions of the Royal Society of London. Series B: Biological Sciences, 319,* 505–523.

Epstein, R. (1983). Resurgence of previously reinforced behavior during extinction. *Behavior Analysis Letters, 3,* 391–397.

Epstein, R. (1984). Spontaneous and deferred imitation in the pigeon. *Behavioural Processes, 9,* 347–354.

Epstein, R. (1985) Extinction induced resurgence: Preliminary investigations and possible applications. *The Psychological Record, 35,* 143–153.

Epstein, R., Kirshnit, C., Lanza, R., & Rubin, L. (1984). "Insight" in the pigeon: Antecedents and determinants of an intelligent performance. *Nature, 308,* 61–62.

Epstein, R., Lanza, R. P., & Skinner, B. F. (1980). Symbolic communication between two pigeons (*Columba livia domestica*). *Science, 207,* 543–545.

Epstein, W. (1972). Mechanisms of directed forgetting. In G. H. Bower (Ed.), *The psychology of learning and motivation* (vol. 6, pp. 147–191). New York: Academic Press.

Esser, K.-H. (1994). Audio-visual learning in a non-human mammal: The lesser spear-nosed bat *Phyllostomus discolor. Neuroreports, 5,* 1718–1720.

Estes, R. D. (1991). *The behavior guide to African mammals.* Berkley: University of California Press.

Estes, W. K., & Skinner, B. F. (1941). Some quantitative properties of anxiety. *Journal of Experimental Psychology, 29,* 390–400.

Etscorn, F., & Stephens, R. (1973). Establishment of conditioned taste aversions with a 24-hour CS-US interval. *Physiological Psychology, 1,* 251–253.

Ewer, R. F. (1969). The "instinct to teach." *Nature, 222,* 698.

Fagen, R. (1981). *Animal play behavior.* New York: Oxford University Press.

Falk, D. (1989). Primate tool use: But what about their brains? *Behavioral and Brain Sciences, 12,* 595–596.

Falk, J. L. (1961). Production of polydipsia in normal rats by an intermittent food schedule. *Science, 133,* 195–196.

Falk, J. L. (1964). Studies on schedule-induced polydipsia. In M. J. Wayner (Ed.), *Thirst: First international symposium on thirst in the regulation of body water* (pp. 95–116). New York: Pergamon Press.

Falk, J. L. (1966 a). The motivational properties of schedule-induced polydipsia. *Journal of the Experimental Analysis of Behavior, 9,* 19–25.

Falk, J. L. (1966 b). Schedule-induced polydipsia as a function of fixed interval length. *Journal of the Experimental Analysis of Behavior, 9,* 37–39.

Falk, J. L. (1967). Control of schedule-induced polydipsia: Type, size, and spacing of meals. *Journal of the Experimental Analysis of Behavior, 10,* 199–206.

Falk, J. L. (1969). Conditions producing psychogenic polydipsia in animals. *Annals of the New York Academy of Sciences, 157,* 569–593.

Falk, J. L. (1971). The nature and determinants of adjunctive behavior. *Physiology & Behavior, 6,* 577–588.

Falk, J. L. (1977). The origin and functions of adjunctive behavior. *Animal Learning & Behavior, 5,* 325–335.

Falk, J. L. (1981). The environmental generation of excessive behavior. In S. J. Mulé (Ed.), *Behavior in excess: An examination of the volitional disorders.* New York: Free Press.

Falk, J. L., Samson, H. H., & Winger, G. (1972). Behavioral maintenance of high concentrations of blood ethanol and physical dependence in the rat. *Science, 177,* 811–813.

Fallon, J. J., Jr., Allen, J. D., & Butler, J. A. (1979). Assessment of adjunctive behavior in humans using a stringent control procedure. *Physiology & Behavior, 22,* 1089–1092.

Fanselow, M. S., & Birk, J. (1982). Flavor-flavor associations induce hedonic shifts in taste preference. *Animal Learning & Behavior, 10,* 223–228.

Fantino, E. (1967). Preference for mixed versus fixed-ratio schedules. *Journal of the Experimental Analysis of Behavior, 10,* 35–43.

Fantino, E. (1969). Choice and rate of reinforcement. *Journal of the Experimental Analysis of Behavior, 12,* 723–730.

Fantino, E. (1977). Conditioned reinforcement: Choice and information. In W. K. Honig & J. E. R. Staddon (Eds.), *Handbook of Operant Behavior* (pp. 313–339). Englewood Cliffs, NJ: Prentice-Hall.

Fantino, E. (1981). Continuity, response strength, and the delay-reduction hypothesis. In P. Harzem & M. D. Zeiler (Eds.), *Advances in the Analysis of Behaviour (vol 2): Predictability, correlation and contiguity* (pp. 169–201). Chichester, UK: Wiley.

Fantino, E., Abarca, N., & Ito, M. (19817). Choice and optimal foraging: Tests of the delay-reduction hypothesis and the optimal-diet model. In M. L. Commons, A. Kacelnik, & S. J. Shettleworth (Eds.), *Quantitative Analyses of Behavior (vol 6): Foraging* (pp. 181–207). Hillsdale, NJ: Erlbaum.

Fantino, E., & Davison, M. (1983). Choice: Some quantitative relations. *Journal of the Experimental Analysis of Behavior, 40,* 1–13.

Fantino, E., & Herrnstein, R. J. (1968). Secondary reinforcement and number of primary reinforcements. *Journal of the Experimental Analysis of Behavior, 11,* 9–14.

Fantino, E., Squires, N., Delbrück, N., & Peterson, C. (1972). Choice behavior and the accessibility of the reinforcer. *Journal of the Experimental Analysis of Behavior, 18,* 35–43.

Farah, M. J. (1988). Is visual imagery really visual? Overlooked evidence from neuropsychology. *Psychological Review, 95,* 307–317.

Farris, H. F. (1967). Classical conditioning of courting behavior in the Japanese quail, Coturnix coturnix japonica. *Journal of the Experimental Analysis of Behavior, 10,* 213–217.

Farthing, G. W. (1972). Overshadowing in the discrimination of successive compound stimuli. *Psychonomic Science, 28,* 29–32.

Fath, S. J., Fields, L., Malott, M. K., & Grossett, D. (1983). Response rate, latency, and resistance to change. *Journal of the Experimental Analysis of Behavior, 39,* 267–274.

Fedorchak, P. M., & Bolles, R. C. (1987). Hunger enhances the expression of caloric- but not taste-mediated conditioned flavor preferences. *Journal of Experimental Psychology: Animal Behavior Processes, 13,* 73–79.

Feigley, D. A., Parsons, P. J., Hamilton, L. W., & Spear, N. E. (1972). Development of habituation to novel environments in the rat. *Journal of Comparative and Physiological Psychology, 79,* 443–452.

Feldman, R. S., & Bremner, F. J. (1963). A method for rapid conditioning of stable avoidance bar pressing behavior. *Journal of the Experimental Analysis of Behavior, 6,* 393–394.

Fernandes, D. M., & Church, R. M. (1982). Discrimination of the number of sequential events by rats. *Animal Learning & Behavior, 10,* 171–176.

Ferrari, E. A., Todorov, J. C., & Graeff, F. G. (1973). Nondiscriminated avoidance of shock by pigeons pecking a key. *Journal of the Experimental Analysis of Behavior, 19,* 211–218.

Ferster, C. B. (1960). Intermittent reinforcement of matching to sample in the pigeon. *Journal of the Experimental Analysis of Behavior, 3,* 259–272.

Ferster, C. B. (1964). Arithmetic behavior in chimpanzees. *Scientific American, 210,* 98-100.

Ferster, C. B., & Appel, J. B. (1961). Punishment of S) responding in matching-to-sample by time-out from positive reinforcement. *Journal of the Experimental Analysis of Behavior, 4,* 45–56.

Ferster, C. B., & Skinner, B. F. (1957). *Schedules of reinforcement.* Englewood Cliffs, NJ: Prentice-Hall.

Ficken, M. S. (1977). Avian play. *The Auk, 94,* 573–582.

Field, A. P., & Davey, G. C. (1999). Reevaluating evaluative conditioning: A nonassociative explanation of conditioning effects in the visual evaluative conditioning paradigm. *Journal of Experimental Psychology: Animal Behavior Processes, 25,* 211–224.

Fields, L., & Verhave, T. (1987). The structure of equivalence classes. *Journal of the Experimental Analysis of Behavior, 48,* 317–332.

Filby, Y., & Appel, J. B. (1966). Variable-interval punishment during variable-interval reinforcement. *Journal of the Experimental Analysis of Behavior, 9,* 521–527.

Fiorito, G., von Planta, C., & Scotto, P. (1990). Problem solving ability of Octopus vulgaris Lamarck (*Mollusca, Cephalopoda*). *Behavioral and Neural Biology, 53,* 217–230.

Findley, J. D. (1958). Preference and switching under concurrent scheduling. *Journal of the Experimental Analysis of Behavior, 1,* 123–144.

Findley, J. D. (1962). An experimental outline for building and exploring multi-operant behavior repertoires. *Journal of the Experimental Analysis of Behavior, 5,* 113–166.

Fisher, A. (1990). On being a pupil of a flint knapper 11 000 years ago. A preliminary analysis of settlement organization and flint technology based on conjoined flint artefacts from the Trollesgave site. In E. Cziesala, S. Eickhoff, N. Arts, & D. Winter (Eds.), *The big puzzle: International symposium on refitting stone artefacts* (pp. 447–464). Bonn: Holos.

Fisher, R. A. (1930). *The genetical theory of natural selection.* Oxford: Clarendon Press.

Fisher, W., Piazza, C. C., Bowman, L. G., Hagopian, L. P., Owens, J. C., & Slevin, I. (1992). A comparison of two approaches for identifying reinforcers for persons with severe and profound disabilities. *Journal of Applied Behavior Analysis, 25,* 491–498.

FitzGerald, R. E., Isler, R., Rosenberg, E., Oettinger, R., & Bättig, K. (1985). Maze patrolling by rats with and without food reward. *Animal Learning & Behavior, 13,* 451–462.

Fitzgibbon, C. D., & Fanshawe, J. H. (1988). Stotting in Thompson's gazelles: An honest signal of condition. *Behavioral Ecology and Sociobiology, 23,* 69–74.

Flaherty, C. F. (1982). Incentive contrast: A review of behavioral changes following shifts in reward. *Animal Learning & Behavior, 10,* 409–440.

Flaherty, C. F., Becker, H. C., & Checke, S. (1983). Repeated successive contrast in consummatory behavior with repeated shifts in sucrose concentration. *Animal Learning & Behavior, 11,* 407–414.

Flannery, R. B., & Harvey, M. R. (1991). Psychological trauma and learned helplessness: Seligman's paradigm reconsidered. *Psychotherapy, 28,* 374–378.

Flory, R. (1969-a). Attack behavior as a function of minimum inter-food interval. *Journal of the Experimental Analysis of Behavior, 12,* 825–828.

Flory, R. K. (1969-b). Attack behavior in a multiple fixed-ratio schedule of reinforcement. *Psychonomic Science, 16,* 156–157.

Flory, R. K. (1971). The control of schedule-induced polydipsia: Frequency and magnitude of reinforcement. *Learning and Motivation, 2,* 215–227.

Flory, R. K., Smith, E. L. P., & Ellis, B. B. (1977). The effects of two response-elimination procedures on reinforced and induced aggression. *Journal of the Experimental Analysis of Behavior, 25,* 5–15.

Fois, C., Medioni, J., & le Bourg, E. (1991). Habituation of the proboscis extension response as a function of age in Drosophila melanogaster. *Gerontology, 37,* 187–192.

Ford, J. K. B. (1989). Acoustic behaviour of resident killer whales (*Orcinus orca*) off Vancouver Island, British Columbia. *Canadian Journal of Zoology, 67,* 727–745.

Ford, J. K. B. (1991). Vocal traditions among resident killer whales (*Orcinus orca*) in coastal waters of British Columbia. *Canadian Journal of Zoology, 69,* 1454–1483.

Ford, J. K. B., & Fisher, H. D. (1983). Group-specific dialects of killer whales (*Orcinus orca*) in British Columbia. In R. Payne (Ed.), *Communication and behavior of whales* (pp. 129–161). Boulder, CO: Westview Press.

Foree, D. D., & LoLordo, V. M. (1974). Attention in the pigeon: Differential effect of food-getting vs. shock-avoidance procedures. *Journal of Comparative and Physiological Psychology, 85,* 551–558.

Forey, P., & Janvier, P. (1994). Evolution of the early vertebrates. *American Scientist, 82,* 554–565.

Fragaszy, D. M., Feuerstein, J. M., & Mitra, D. (1997). Transfers of food from adults to infants in tufted capuchins (*Cebus apella*). *Journal of Comparative Psychology, 111,* 194–200.

Fragaszy, D. M., & Visalberghi, E. (1996). Social learning in monkeys: Primate "primacy" reconsidered. In C. M. Heyes & B. G. Galef, Jr. (Eds.) *Social learning in animals: The roots of culture* (pp. 65–84). San Diego: Academic Press.

Frederiksen, L. W., & Peterson, G. L. (1974). Schedule-induced aggression in nursery school children. *The Psychological Record, 24,* 343–351.

Freed, E. X., & Hymowitz, N. (1972). Effects of schedule, percent body weight, and magnitude of reinforcer on acquisition of schedule-induced polydipsia. *Psychological Reports, 31,* 95–101.

Freeman, B. J. (1971). The role of response-independent reinforcement in producing behavioral contrast effects in the rat. *Learning and Motivation, 2,* 138–147.

Freeman, W. J. (1990). Searching for signal and noise in the chaos of brain waves. In S. Krasner (Ed.), *The ubiquity of chaos* (pp. 47–55). Washington, DC: American Association for the Advancement of Science.

Friedmann, H. (1955). The honey-guides. *U.S. Natural Museum Bulletin, 208,* 1–292.

Friedmann, H., & Kern, J. (1956). The problem of cerophagy or wax-eating in the honey-guides. *Quarterly Review of Biology, 31,* 19–30.

Fujita, K. (1983). Formation of the sameness-difference concept by Japanese monkeys from a small number of color stimuli. *Journal of the Experimental Analysis of Behavior, 40,* 289–300.

Fullick, T. G., & Greenwood, J. J. D. (1979). Frequency dependent food selection in relation to two models. *American Naturalist, 113,* 762–765.

Galantowicz, E. P., & King, G. D. (1975). The effects of three levels of lick-contingent footshock on schedule-induced polydipsia. *Bulletin of the Psychonomic Society, 5,* 113–116.

Galbicka, G. (1994). Shaping in the 21st century: Moving percentile schedules into applied settings. *Journal of Applied Behavior Analysis, 27,* 739–760.

Galbicka, G., & Branch, M. N. (1981). Selective punishment of interresponse times. *Journal of the Experimental Analysis of Behavior, 35,* 311–322.

Galbicka, G., & Platt, J. R. (1984). Interresponse-time punishment: A basis for shock-maintained behavior. *Journal of the Experimental Analysis of Behavior, 41,* 291–308.

Galef, B. G., Jr. (1988). Imitation in animals: History, definition, and interpretation of data from the psychological laboratory. In T. R. Zentall & B. G. Galef, Jr. (Eds.), *Social learning: Psychological and biological perspectives* (pp. 3–28). Hillsdale, NJ: Erlbaum.

Galef, B. G., Jr., & Heiber, L. (1976). Role of residual olfactory cues in the determination of feeding site selection and exploration patterns of domestic rats. *Journal of Comparative and Physiological Psychology, 90,* 727–739.

Galef B. G., Jr., & Kennett, D. J., & Wigmore, S. W. (1984). Transfer of information concerning distant food in rats: A robust phenomenon. *Animal Learning & Behavior, 12,* 292–296.

Galef, B. G., Jr., & Sherry, D. F. (1973). Mother's milk: A medium for transmission of cues reflecting the flavor of mother's diet. *Journal of Comparative and Physiological Psychology, 4,* 432–439.

Galef B. G., Jr., & Wigmore, S. W. (1983). Transfer of information concerning distant foods: A laboratory investigation of the "information-centre" hypothesis. *Animal Behaviour, 31,* 748–758.

Galizio, M. (1999). Extinction of responding maintained by timeout from avoidance. *Journal of the Experimental Analysis of Behavior, 71,* 1–11.

Galizio, M., & Allen, A. R. (1991). Variable-ratio schedules of timeout from avoidance: Effects of *d*-amphetamine and morphine. *Journal of the Experimental Analysis of Behavior, 56,* 193–203.

Galizio, M., & Liborio, M. O. (1995). The effects of cocaine on behavior maintained by timeout from avoidance. *Journal of the Experimental Analysis of Behavior, 63,* 19–32.

Gallistel, C. R. (1990). *The organization of learning.* Cambridge, MA: MIT Press.

Gallup, G. G., & Altomari, T. S. (1969). Activity as a postsituation measure of frustrative nonreward in a straight alley. *Psychonomic Science, 3,* 99–100.

Gamzu, E., & Schwam, E. (1974). Autoshaping and automaintenance of a key-press response in squirrel monkeys. *Journal of the Experimental Analysis of Behavior, 21,* 361–371.

Gamzu, E., & Schwartz, B. (1973). The maintenance of key pecking by stimulus-contingent and response-independent food presentation. *Journal of the Experimental Analysis of Behavior, 19,* 65–72.

Garcia, E., Baer, D. M., & Firestone, I. (1971). The development of generalized imitation within topographically determined boundaries. *Journal of Applied Behavior Analysis, 4,* 101–112.

Garcia, J., Clark, J. C., & Hankins, W. G. (1973). Natural responses to scheduled rewards. In P. P. G. Bateson & P. H. Klopfer (Eds.), *Perspectives in ethology* (vol. 1, pp. 1–41). New York: Plenum.

Garcia, J., Ervin, F. R., & Koelling, R. A. (1966). Learning with prolonged delay of reinforcement. *Psychonomic Science, 5,* 121–122.

Garcia, J., & Koelling, R. (1966). Relation of cue to consequence in avoidance learning. *Psychonomic Science, 4,* 123–124.

Gardner, E. T., & Lewis, P. (1976). Negative reinforcement with shock-frequency increase. *Journal of the Experimental Analysis of Behavior, 25,* 3–14.

Gardner, R. A., & Gardner, B. T. (1969). Teaching sign language to a chimpanzee. *Science, 165,* 664–672.

Gardner, R. A., & Gardner, B. T. (1988). Feedforward versus feedbackward: An ethological alternative to the law of effect. *Behavioral and Brain Sciences, 111,* 429–446.

Gautier-Hion, A., Duplantier, J.-M., Quris, R., Feer, F., Sourd, C., Decoux, J.-P., Dubost, G., Emmons, L., Erard, C., Hecketsweiler, P., Moungazi, A., Roussilhon, C., & Thiollay, J.-M. (1985). Fruit characteristics as a basis of fruit choice and seed dispersal in a tropical forest vertebrate community. *Oecologia, 65,* 324–337.

Gelperin, A. (1975). Rapid food-aversion learning by a terrestrial mollusk. *Science, 189,* 567–570.

Gendron, R. P. (1986). Searching for cryptic prey: Evidence for optimal search rates and the formation of search images in quail. *Animal Behaviour, 34,* 898–912.

Gentry, G. D., Weiss, B., & Laties, V. G. (1983). The microanalysis of fixed-interval responding. *Journal of the Experimental Analysis of Behavior, 39,* 327–343.

Gentry, W. D. (1968). Fixed-ratio schedule-induced aggression. *Journal of the Experimental Analysis of Behavior, 11,* 813–817.

Gentry, W. D., & Schaeffer, R. W. (1969). The effect of FR response requirement on aggressive behavior in rats. *Psychonomic Science, 14,* 236–238.

Gibbons, A. (1995). The mystery of humanity's missing mutations. *Science, 267,* 35–36.

Gibson, K. R. (1996). The ontogeny and evolution of the brain, cognition and language. In A. Lock & C. Peters (Eds.), *Handbook of symbolic evolution* (pp. 407–432). Oxford: Oxford University Press.

Gill, F. B. (1988). Trapline foraging by hermit hummingbirds: Competition for an undefended renewable resource. *Ecology, 69,* 1933–1942.

Gillan, D. J. (1981). Reasoning in the chimpanzee: II. Transitive inference. *Journal of Experimental Psychology: Animal Behavior Processes, 7,* 150–164.

Gilliam, J. F., & Fraser, D. F. (1987). Habitat selection when foraging under predation hazard: A model and a test with stream-dwelling minnows. *Ecology, 68,* 1227–1253.

Giulian, D., & Schmaltz, L. W. (1973). Enhanced discriminated bar-press avoidance in the rat through appetitive preconditioning. *Journal of Comparative and Physiological Psychology, 83,* 106–112.

Glazer, H. I., & Weiss, J. M. (1976 a). Long-term and transitory interference effects. *Journal of Experimental Psychology: Animal Behavior Processes, 2,* 191–201.

Glazer, H. I., & Weiss, J. M. (1976 b). Long-term interference effect: An alternative to "learned helplessness." *Journal of Experimental Psychology: Animal Behavior Processes, 2,* 202–213.

Gleitman, H., & Steinman, F. (1964). Depression effect as a function of retention interval before and after shift in reward magnitude. *Journal of Comparative and Physiological Psychology, 57,* 158–160.

Glenn, S. S. (1988). Contingencies and metacontingencies: Toward a synthesis of behavior analysis and cultural materialism. *The Behavior Analyst, 11,* 161–179.

Glickman, S. E., & Sroges, R. W. (1966). Curiosity in zoo animals. *Behaviour, 26,* 151–188.

Glickman, S. E., Sroges, R., & Hoff, W. (1961). The evolution of response to novel objects. *American Psychologist, 16,* 445.

Glowa, J. R., & Barrett, J. E. (1983). Response suppression by visual stimuli paired with post-session-amphetamine injections in the pigeon. *Journal of the Experimental Analysis of Behavior, 39,* 165–173.

Gogan, P. (1970). The startle and orienting reactions in man: A study of their characteristics and habituation. *Brain Research, 18,* 117–135.

Goldberg, S. R., Hoffmeister, F., Schlichting, U., & Wuttke, W. (1971). Aversive properties of nalorphine and naloxone in morphine-dependent rhesus monkeys. *Journal of Pharmacology and Experimental Therapeutics, 179,* 268–276.

Gollub, L. R. (1958). *The chaining of fixed-interval schedules.* Unpublished doctoral dissertation, Harvard University, Cambridge, MA.

Gollub, L. R. (1977). Conditioned reinforcement: Schedule effects. In W. K. Honig & J. E. R. Staddon (Eds.), *Operant behavior: Areas of research and application* (pp. 288–312). Englewood Cliffs, NJ: Prentice-Hall.

Goltz, S. M. (1992). A sequential learning analysis of decisions in organizations to escalate investments despite continuing costs or losses. *Journal of Applied Behavior Analysis, 25,* 561–574.

Gonzalez, R. C., & Champlin, G. (1974). Positive behavioral contrast, negative simultaneous contrast and their relation to frustration in pigeons. *Journal of Comparative and Physiological Psychology, 87,* 173–187.

Gonzalez, R. C., & Powers, A. S. (1973). Simultaneous contrast in goldfish. *Animal Learning & Behavior, 1,* 96–98.

Goodall, J. (1968). The behaviour of free living chimpanzees in the Gombe Stream Reserve (Tanzania). *Animal Behaviour Monographs, 1,* 161–311.

Goodall, J. (1986). *The chimpanzees of Gombe: Patterns of behavior.* Cambridge, MA: Harvard University Press.

Goodman, M., Tagle, D. A, Fitch, D. H. A., Bailey, W., Czelusniuk, J., Koop, B. F., Benson, P., & Slightom, J. L. (1990). Primate evolution at the DNA level and a classification of hominoids. *Journal of Molecular Evolution, 30,* 260–266.

Gormezano, I., & Tait, R. W. (1976). The Pavlovian analysis of instrumental conditioning. *Pavlovian Journal of Biological Science, 11,* 37–55.

Gould, S. J. (1977). *Ever since Darwin: Reflections in natural history.* New York: Norton.

Gould, S. J. (1994). The evolution of life on earth. *Scientific American, 271,* 84–91.

Gould, S. J. (1995). Of it, not above it. *Nature, 377,* 681–682.

Gourevitch, G., & Hack, M. H. (1966). Audibility in the rat. *Journal of Comparative and Physiological Psychology, 62,* 289–291.

Graham, J. M., & Desjardins, C. (1980). Classical conditioning: Induction of luteinizing hormone and testosterone secretion in anticipation of sexual activity. *Science, 210,* 1039–1041.

Grammer, K., & Thornhill, R. (1994). Human (*Homo sapiens*) facial attractiveness and sexual selection: The role of symmetry and averageness. *Journal of Comparative Psychology, 108,* 233–242.

Granger, R. G., Porter, J. H., & Christoph, N. L. (1984). Schedule-induced behavior in children as a function of interreinforcement interval length. *Physiology & Behavior, 33,* 153–157.

Grant, D. S. (1981). Stimulus control of information processing in pigeon short-term memory. *Learning and Motivation, 12,* 19–39.

Grant, D. S. (1982). Stimulus control of information processing in rat short-term memory. *Journal of Experimental Psychology: Animal Behavior Processes, 8,* 154–164.

Grant, D. S., & Roberts, W. A. (1976). Sources of retroactive inhibition in pigeon short-term memory. *Journal of Experimental Psychology: Animal Behavior Processes, 2,* 1–16.

Grastyan, E., & Vereczkei, L. (1974). Effects of spatial separation of the conditioned signal from the reinforcement: A demonstration of the conditioned character of the orienting response or the orientational character of conditioning. *Behavioral Biology, 10,* 121–146.

Greenway, D. E., Dougher, M. J., & Wulfert, E. (1992). *Transfer of consequential functions via stimulus equivalence: The role of generalization.* Paper presented at the 18th Annual Convention of the Association for Behavior Analysis, San Francisco, May.

Greenwood, M. R. C., Quartermain, D., Johnson, P. R., Cruce, J. A. F., & Hirsch, J. (1974). Food-motivated behavior in genetically obese and hypothalamic-hyperphagic rats and mice. *Physiology & Behavior, 13,* 687–692.

Grice, G. R. (1948). The relevance of secondary reinforcement to delayed reward in visual discrimination learning. *Journal of Experimental Psychology, 38,* 1–16.

Griffitt, W., & Veitch, R. (1971). Hot and crowded: Influence of population density and temperature on interpersonal affective behavior: Ambient effective temperature and attraction. *Journal of Personality and Social Psychology, 17,* 92–98.

Grosch, J., & Neuringer, A. (1981). Self-control in pigeons under the Mischel paradigm. *Journal of the Experimental Analysis of Behavior, 35,* 3–21.

Grossman, K. E. (1973). Continuous, fixed-ratio, and fixed-interval reinforcement in honey bees. *Journal of the Experimental Analysis of Behavior, 20,* 105–109.

Grossman, R. P., & Till, B. D. (1998). The persistence of classically conditioned brand attitudes. *Journal of Advertising, 27*(1), 23–31.

Groves, P. M., Lee, D., & Thompson, R. F. (1969). Effects of stimulus frequency and intensity on habituation and sensitization in acute spinal cat. *Physiology & Behavior, 4,* 383–388.

Groves, P. M., & Thompson, R. F. (1970). Habituation: A dual-process theory. *Psychological Review, 77,* 419–450.

Guggisberg, C. A. W. (1975). *Wild cats of the world.* New York: Taplinger Publishing Company.

Guinee, L., Chu, K., & Dorsey, E. M. (1983). Change over time in the songs of known individual humpback whales (*Megaptera novaeangliae*). In R. Payne (Ed.), *Communication and behavior of whales* (pp. 59–80). Boulder, CO: Westview Press.

Guinet, C. (1991). Intentional stranding apprenticeship and social play in killer whales (*Orcinus orca*). *Canadian Journal of Zoology, 69,* 2712–2716.

Guinet, C., & Bouvier, J. (1995). Development of intentional stranding hunting techniques in killer whale (*Orcinus orca*) calves at Crozet Archipelago. *Canadian Journal of Zoology, 73,* 27–33.

Gutiérrez, G., & Domjan, M. (1997). Differences in the sexual conditioned behavior of male and female Japanese quail (*Coturnix japonica*). *Journal of Comparative Psychology, 111,* 135–142.

Gutman, A. (1977). Positive contrast, negative induction, and inhibitory stimulus control in the rat. *Journal of the Experimental Analysis of Behavior, 27,* 219–233.

Gutman, A., Minor, T. R., & Sutterer, J. R. (1984). Discrimination training in semimixed and multiple schedules. *The Psychological Record, 34,* 427–435.

Guttman, N. (1965). Effects of discrimination formation on generalization measured from the positive-rate baseline. In D. I. Mostofsky (Ed.), *Stimulus generalization* (pp. 210–217). Stanford: Stanford University Press.

Guttman, N., & Kalish, H. I. (1956). Discriminability and stimulus generalization. *Journal of Experimental Psychology, 51,* 79–88.

Gwinner, E. (1966). Über einige Bewegungsspiele des Kolkraben. *Zeitschrift für Tierpsychologie, 23,* 28–36.

Haggbloom, S. J., Birmingham, K. M., & Scanton, D. L. (1992). Hierarchical organization of series information by rats: Series chunks and list chunks. *Learning and Motivation, 23,* 183–199.

Hake, D. F., & Campbell, R. L. (1972). Characteristics and response-displacement effects of shock-generated responding during negative reinforcement procedures: Pre-shock responding and post-shock aggressive responding. *Journal of the Experimental Analysis of Behavior, 17,* 303–323.

Hake, D. F., Donaldson, T., & Hyten, C. (1983). Analysis of discriminative control by social behavioral stimuli. *Journal of the Experimental Analysis of Behavior, 39,* 7–23.

Hake, D. F., & Mabry, J. (1979). Operant and nonoperant vocal responding in the mynah: Complex schedule control and deprivation-induced responding. *Journal of the Experimental Analysis of Behavior, 32,* 305–321.

Hall, G. A., & Lattal, K. A. (1990). Variable-interval schedule performance in open and closed economies. *Journal of the Experimental Analysis of Behavior, 54,* 13–22.

Hall, J. F. (1984). Backward conditioning in Pavlovian type studies: Reevaluation and present status. *Pavlovian Journal of Biological Science, 19,* 163–169.

Hall, S. L., & Bradshaw, J. W. S. (1998). The influence of hunger on object play by adult domestic cats. *Applied Animal Behaviour Science, 58,* 143–150.

Hamblin, R. L., Clairmont, D. L., & Chadwick, B. A. (1975). Utility and gambling decisions: Experiments and equations. *Social Science Research, 4,* 1–15.

Hamilton, W. D. (1964). The genetical evolution of social behavior. *Journal of Theoretical Biology, 7,* 1–52.

Hamilton, W. D. (1967). Extraordinary sex ratios. *Science, 156,* 477–488.

Hamilton, W. D. (1970). Selfish and spiteful behavior in an evolutionary model. *Nature, 228,* 1218–1220.

Halpern, M., & Lyon, M. (1966). The stability and control of conditioned noise aversion in the tilt cage. *Journal of the Experimental Analysis of Behavior, 9,* 357–367.

Hamm, R. J., Porter, J. H., & Kaempf, G. L. (1981). Stimulus generalization of schedule-induced polydipsia. *Journal of the Experimental Analysis of Behavior, 36,* 93–99.

Hansen, A. J., & Rohwer, S. (1986). Coverable badges and resource defence in birds. *Animal Behaviour, 34,* 69–76.

Hantula, D. A., & Crowell, C. R. (1994). Behavioral contrast in a two-option analogue task of financial decision making. *Journal of Applied Behavior Analysis, 27,* 607–617.

Harchik, A. E., & Putzier, V. S. (1990). The use of high-probability requests to increase compliance with instructions to take medication. *Journal of the Association for Persons with Severe Handicaps, 15,* 40–43.

Hardin, G. (1968). The tragedy of the commons. *Science, 162,* 1243–1248.

Harkins, S. G., & Szymanski, K. (1989). Social loafing and group evaluation. *Journal of Personality and Social Psychology, 56,* 934–941.

Harlow, H. F. (1932). Social facilitation of feeding in the albino rat. *Journal of Genetic Psychology, 41,* 211–221.

Harlow, H. F. (1949). The formation of learning sets. *Psychological Review, 56,* 51–65.

Harlow, H. F. (1950). Learning and satiation of response in intrinsically motivated complex puzzle performance by monkeys. *Journal of Comparative and Physiological Psychology, 43,* 289–294.

Harlow, H. F. (1960). Of love in infants. *Natural History, 69,* 18–23.

Harlow, H. F., & McClearn, G. E. (1954). Object discrimination by monkeys on the basis of manipulation motives. *Journal of Comparative and Physiological Psychology, 47,* 73–76.

Harlow, H. F., & Yudin, H. C. (1933). Social behavior of primates. I. Social facilitation of feeding in the monkey and its relation to attitudes of ascendance and submission.. *Journal of Comparative Psychology, 16,* 171–185.

Harper, D. N., & McLean, A. P. (1992). Resistance to change and the law of effect. *Journal of the Experimental Analysis of Behavior, 57,* 317–337.

Harris, J. A., Gorissen, M. C., Bailey, G. K., & Westbrook, R. F. (2000). Motivational state regulates the content of learned flavor preferences. *Journal of Experimental Psychology: Animal Behavior Processes, 26,* 15–30.

Harris, J. D. (1943). Studies in nonassociative factors inherent in conditioning. *Comparative Psychology Monographs, 18,* (Serial No. 93).

Harrison, J. M., & Abelson, R. M. (1959). The maintenance of behavior by the termination and onset of intense noise. *Journal of the Experimental Analysis of Behavior, 2,* 23–42.

Harsh, J., Badia, P., & Ryan, K. (1983). Factors affecting choice of signaled over unsignaled food schedules. *Journal of the Experimental Analysis of Behavior, 40,* 265–273.

Hartman, E. J., & Abrahams, M. V. (2000). Sensory compensation and the detection of predators: The interaction between chemical and visual information. *Proceedings of the Royal Society of London B, 267,* 571–575.

Hartup, W. W., & Rubin, Z. (Eds.), *Relationships and development.* Hillsdale, NJ: Lawrence Erlbaum.

Harzem, P., Lowe, C. F., & Bagshaw, M. (1978). Verbal control in human operant behavior. *The Psychological Record, 28,* 405–423.

Hasler, A. D., Scholz, A. T., & Horrall, R. M. (1978). Olfactory imprinting and homing in salmon. *American Scientist, 66,* 347–355.

Hauser, M. D. (1988). How infant vervet monkeys learn to recognize starling alarm calls: The roll of experience. *Behaviour, 105,* 187–201.

Hawkins, R. D., Greene, W., & Kandel, E. R. (1998). Classical conditioning, differential conditioning, and second-order conditioning of the *Aplysia* gill-withdrawal reflex in a simplified mantle organ prepatration. *Behavioral Neuroscience, 112,* 636–645.

Hawkins, T. D., Schrot, J. F., Githens, S. H., & Everett, P. B. (1972). An analysis of water and alcohol ingestion. In R. M. Gilbert & J. D. Keehn (Eds.), *Schedule effects: Drugs, drinking, and aggression* (pp. 95–128). Toronto: University of Toronto Press.

Hayes, S. C., Brownstein, A. J., Zettle, R. D., Rosenfarb, I., & Korn, Z. (1986). Rule-governed behavior and sensitivity to changing consequences of responding. *Journal of the Experimental Analysis of Behavior, 45,* 237–256.

Hayes, K. J., & Hayes, C. (1952). Imitation in a home-reared chimpanzee. *Journal of Comparative and Physiological Psychology, 45,* 450–459.

Hayes, S. C., Kohlenberg, B. S., & Hayes, L. J. (1991). The transfer of specific and general consequential functions through simple and conditional equivalence relations. *Journal of the Experimental Analysis of Behavior, 56,* 119–137.

Hearst, E. (1960). Simultaneous generalization gradi-ents for appetitive and aversive behavior. *Science, 132,* 1769–1770.

Hearst, E. (1962). Concurrent generalization gradients for food-controlled and shock-controlled behavior. *Journal of the Experimental Analysis of Behavior, 5,* 19–31.

Hearst, E. (1965). Approach, avoidance, and stimulus generalization. In D. I. Mostofsky (Ed.), *Stimulus generalization* (pp. 331–355). Stanford: Stanford University Press.

Hearst, E. (1984). Absence as information: Some implications for learning, performance, and representational processes. In H. L. Roitblat, T. G. Bever, & H. S. Terrace (Eds.), *Animal cognition: Proceedings of the Harry Frank Guggenheim Conference. June 2-4, 1982* (pp. 311–332). Hillsdale, NJ: Erlbaum.

Hearst, E., Franklin, S. R., & Mueller, C. G. (1974). The "disinhibition" of extinguished operant behavior in pigeons: Trial-tempo shifts and novel stimulus effects. *Animal Learning & Behavior, 2,* 229–237.

Hearst, E., & Jenkins, H. M. (1974). *Sign-tracking: The stimulus-reinforcer relation and directed action.* Austin, TX: The Psychonomic Society.

Hearst, E., Koresko, M., & Poppen, R. (1964). Stimulus generalization and the response-reinforcement contingency. *Journal of the Experimental Analysis of Behavior, 7,* 369–380.

Hearst, E., & Sidman, M. (1961). Some behavioral effects of a concurrently positive and negative stimulus. *Journal of the Experimental Analysis of Behavior, 4,* 251–256.

Hepper, P. G. (1988). Adaptive fetal learning: Prenatal exposure to garlic affects postnatal preferences. *Animal Behaviour, 36,* 935–936.

Herman, L. M. (1986). Cognition and language competencies of bottlenosed dolphins. In R. J. Schusterman, J. A. Thomas, & F. G. Wood (Ed.), *Dolphin cognition and behavior: A comparative approach* (pp. 221–252). Hillsdale, NJ: Erlbaum.

Herman, L. M., & Gordon, J. A. (1974). Auditory delayed matching in the bottlenose dolphin. *Journal of the Experimental Analysis of Behavior, 21,* 19–26.

Herrnstein, R. J. (1958). Some factors influencing behavior in a two-response situation. *Transactions of the New York Academy of Sciences, 21,* 35–45.

Herrnstein, R. J. (1961). Relative and absolute strength of response as a function of frequency of reinforcement. *Journal of the Experimental Analysis of Behavior, 4,* 267–272.

Herrnstein, R. J. (1964 a). Secondary reinforcement and rate of primary reinforcement. *Journal of the Experimental Analysis of Behavior, 7,* 27–36.

Herrnstein, R. J. (1964 b). Aperiodicity as a factor in choice. *Journal of the Experimental Analysis of Behavior, 7,* 179–182.

Herrnstein, R. J. (1970). On the law of effect. *Journal of the Experimental Analysis of Behavior, 13,* 243–266.

Herrnstein, R. J. (1979). Acquisition, generalization, and

discrimination reversal of a natural concept. *Journal of Experimental Psychology: Animal Behavior Processes, 5,* 116–129.

Herrnstein, R. J. (1982). Melioration as behavioral dynamism. In M. L. Commons, R. J. Herrnstein, & H. Rachlin (Eds.), *Quantitative analyses of behavior* (vol. 2): *Matching and maximizing accounts* (pp. 433–458). Cambridge, MA: Ballinger.

Herrnstein, R. J., & deVilliers, P. A. (1980). Fish as a natural category for people and pigeons. In G. H. Bower (Ed.), *The psychology of learning and motivation* (vol. 14) (pp.). New York: Academic Press.

Herrnstein, R. J., & Heyman, G. M. (1979). Is matching compatible with reinforcement maximization on concurrent variable interval, variable ratio? *Journal of the Experimental Analysis of Behavior, 31,* 209–223.

Herrnstein, R. J., & Hineline, P. N. (1966). Negative reinforcement as shock-frequency reduction. *Journal of the Experimental Analysis of Behavior, 9,* 421–430.

Herrnstein, R. J., & Loveland, D. H. (1964). Complex visual concept in the pigeon. *Science, 146,* 549–551.

Herrnstein, R. J., & Loveland, D. H. (1975). Maximizing and matching on concurrent ratio schedules. *Journal of the Experimental Analysis of Behavior, 24,* 107–116.

Herrnstein, R. J., Loveland, D. H., & Cable, C. (1976). Natural concepts in pigeons. *Journal of Experimental Psychology: Animal Behavior Processes, 2,* 285–302.

Herrnstein, R. J., & Sidman, M. (1958). Avoidance conditioning as a factor in the effects of unavoidable shocks on food-reinforced behavior. *Journal of Comparative and Physiological Psychology, 51,* 380–385.

Herrnstein, R. J., & Vaughan, W., Jr. (1980). Melioration and behavioral allocation. In J. E. R. Staddon (Ed.), *Limits to action: The allocation of individual behavior* (pp. 143–176). New York: Academic Press.

Herzing, D. (1996). Vocalizations and associated underwater behaviour of free-ranging Atlantic spotted dolphins, *Stenella frontalis*, and bottlenose dolphins, *Tursiops truncatus. Aquatic Mammalogy, 22,* 61–79.

Herzog, M., & Hopf, S. (1984). Behavioral responses to species-specific warning calls in infant squirrel monkeys reared in isolation. *American Journal of Primatology, 7,* 99–106.

Hess, E. H. (1959). Imprinting. *Science, 130,* 133–141.

Heth, C. D. (1976). Simultaneous and backward fear conditioning as a function of number of CS-UCS pairings. *Journal of Experimental Psychology: Animal Behavior Processes, 2,* 117–129.

Heth, C. D., & Warren, A. G. (1978). Response deprivation and response satiation as determinants of instrumental performance. *Animal Learning & Behavior, 6,* 294–300.

Heyes, C. M., & Dawson, G. R. (1990). A demonstration of observational learning in rats using a bidirectional control. *Quarterly Journal of Experimental Psychology, 42B,* 59–71.

Heyes, C. M., Dawson, G. R., & Nokes, T. (1992). Imitation in rats: Initial responding and transfer evidence. *Quarterly Journal of Experimental Psychology, 45B,* 81–92.

Heyman, G. M., & Bouzas, A. (1980). Context dependent changes in the reinforcing strength of schedule-induced drinking. *Journal of the Experimental Analysis of Behavior, 33,* 327–335.

Higgenbottom, K., & Croft, D. B., (1999). Social learning in marsupials. In H. O. Box & K. R. Gibson (Eds.), *Mammalian social learning: Comparative and ecological perspectives* (pp. 80–101). Cambridge, UK: Cambridge University Press.

Hilgard, E. R., & Marquis, D. G. (1935). Acquisition, extinction, and retention of conditioned lid responses to light in dogs. *Journal of Comparative Psychology, 19,* 29–58.

Hill, A., Ward, S., Deino, A., Curtis, G., & Drake, R. (1992). Earliest *Homo. Nature, 355,* 719–722.

Hinde, R. A. (1976 a). Interactions, relationships and social structure. *Man, 11,* 1–17.

Hinde, R. A. (1976 b). On describing relationships. *Journal of Child Psychology and Psychiatry, 17,* 1–19.

Hineline, P. N. (1970). Negative reinforcement without shock reduction. *Journal of the Experimental Analysis of Behavior, 14,* 259–268.

Hineline, P. N. (1978). Warmup in free-operant avoidance as a function of the response-shock = shock-shock interval. *Journal of the Experimental Analysis of Behavior, 30,* 281–291.

Hineline, P. N. (1984). Aversive control: A separate domain? *Journal of the Experimental Analysis of Behavior, 42,* 495–509.

Hineline, P. N. (1986). Re-tuning the operant-respondent distinction. In T. Thompson & M. D. Zeiler (Eds.), *Analysis and integration of behavioral units* (pp. 55–79). Hillsdale, NJ: Erlbaum.

Hinson, J. M., & Malone, J. C., Jr. (1980). Local contrast and maintained generalization. *Journal of the Experimental Analysis of Behavior, 34,* 263–272.

Hinson, R. E., & Siegel, S. (1980). Trace conditioning as an inhibitory procedure. *Animal Learning & Behavior, 8,* 60–66.

Hoban, J. S., Couvillon, P. A., & Bitterman, M. E. (1996). Odor-preference in honeybees as a function of amount of reward: Tests of two hypotheses. *Journal of Insect Behavior, 9,* 121–132.

Hodos, W., Ross, G. S., & Brady, J. V. (1962). Complex response patterns during temporally spaced responding. *Journal of the Experimental Analysis of Behavior, 5,* 473–479.

Hoese, A. D. (1971). Dolphin feeding out of water in a salt marsh. *Journal of Mammalogy, 52,* 222–223.

Hoffman, H. S. (1996). *Amorous turkeys and addicted ducklings: A search for the causes of social attachment.* Boston: Authors Cooperative.

Hoffman, H. S., Fleshler, M., & Chorny, H. (1961). Discriminated bar-press avoidance. *Journal of the Experimental Analysis of Behavior, 4,* 309–316.

Hoffman, H. S., & Kozma, F. Jr. (1967). Behavioral control by an imprinted stimulus: Long-term effects. *Journal of the Experimental Analysis of Behavior, 10,* 495–501.

Hoffman, H. S., & Ratner, A. M. (1973). A reinforcement model of imprinting: Implications for socialization in monkeys and man. *Psychological Review, 80,* 527–546.

Hoffman, H. S., Searle, J. L., Toffey, S., & Kozma, F. Jr. (1966). Behavioral control by an imprinted stimulus. *Journal of the Experimental Analysis of Behavior, 9,* 177–189.

Hogan, D. E., & Zentall, T. R. (1977). Backward associations in the pigeon. *American Journal of Psychology, 90,* 3–15.

Hogan, J. A., Kleist, S., & Hutchings, C. S. L. (1970). Display and food as reinforcers in the Siamese fighting fish (*Betta splendens*). *Journal of Comparative and Physiological Psychology, 70,* 351–357.

Hole, G. J., & Einon, D. F. (1984). Play in rodents. In P.K. Smith (Ed.), *Play in animals and humans* (pp. 95–117). Oxford: Basil Blackwell.

Holder, M. D. (1991). Conditioned preferences for the taste and odor components of flavors: Blocking but not overshadowing. *Appetite, 17,* 29–45.

Holland, J. G. (1958). Human vigilance. *Science, 128,* 61–66.

Holland, P. C. (1979). Differential effects of omission contingencies on various components of Pavlovian appetitive conditioned behavior in rats. *Journal of Experimental Psychology: Animal Behavior Processes, 5,* 178–193.

Holland, P. C. (1980). Influence of visual conditioned stimulus characteristics on the form of Pavlovian appetitive conditioned responding in rats. *Journal of Experimental Psychology: Animal Behavior Processes, 6,* 81–97.

Holland, P. C. (1990). Event representation in Pavlovian conditioning: Image and action. *Cognition, 37,* 105–131.

Holland, P. C., & Rescorla, R. A. (1975). The effect of two ways of devaluing the unconditioned stimulus after first- and second-order appetitive conditioning. *Journal of Experimental Psychology: Animal Behavior Processes, 1,* 355–363.

Holland, P. C., & Straub, J. J. (1979). Differential effect of two ways of devaluing the unconditioned stimulus after Pavlovian appetitive conditioning. *Journal of Experimental Psychology: Animal Behavior Processes, 5,* 67–68.

Hollard, V., & Davison, M. C. (1971). Preference for qualitatively different reinforcers. *Journal of the Experimental Analysis of Behavior, 16,* 375–380.

Hollard, V., & Davison, M. C. (1978). Histological data: Hollard and Davison (1971). *Journal of the Experimental Analysis of Behavior, 29,* 149.

Hollis, K. L., Cadieux, E. L., & Colbert, M. M. (1989). The biological function of Pavlovian conditioning: A mechanism for mating success in the blue gourami (*Trichogaster trichopterus*). *Journal of Comparative Psychology, 103,* 115–121.

Hollis, K. L., Pharr, V. L., Dumas, M. J., Britton, G. B., & Field, J. (1997). Classical conditioning provides paternity advantage for territorial male blue gouramis (*Trichogaster trichopterus*). *Journal of Comparative Psychology, 111,* 219–225.

Holloway, R. (1996). Evolution of the human brain. In A. Lock & C. Peters (Eds.), *Handbook of symbolic evolution* (pp. 74–116). Oxford: Oxford University Press.

Holman, E. W. (1975). Immediate and delayed reinforcers for flavor preferences in rats. *Learning and Motivation, 6,* 91–100.

Holman, J., Goetz, E., & Baer, D. (1977). The training of creativity as an operant and an examination of its generalization characteristics. In B. Etzel, J. Le Blanc, & D. Baer (Eds.), *New developments in behavioral research: Theory, method, and application* (pp. 441–471). Hillsdale, NJ: Erlbaum.

Holmes, P. W. (1979). Transfer of matching performance in pigeons. *Journal of the Experimental Analysis of Behavior, 31,* 103–114.

Holz, W. C., Azrin, N. H., & Ayllon, T. (1963). Elimination of behavior of mental patients by response-produced extinction. *Journal of the Experimental Analysis of Behavior, 6,* 407–412.

Holzman, A. D., & Levis, D. J. (1991). Differential aversive conditioning of an external (visual) and internal (imaginal) CS: Effects of transfer between and within CS modalities. *Journal of Mental Imagery, 15,* 77–90.

Honey, R. C., & Good, M. (2000). Associative modulation of the orienting response: Distinct effects revealed by hippocampal lesions. *Journal of Experimental Psychology: Animal Behavior Processes, 26,* 3–14.

Honey, R. C., Good, M., & Manser, K. L. (1998). Negative priming in associative learning: Evidence from a serial habituation procedure. *Journal of Experimental Psychology: Animal Behavior Processes, 24,* 229–237.

Honig, W. K. (1993). Numerosity as a dimension of stimulus control. In S. T. Boysen & E. J. Capaldi (Eds.), *The development of numerical competence: Animal and human models* (pp. 61–86). Hillsdale, NJ: Erlbaum.

Honig, W. K., Boneau, C. A., Burstein, K. R., & Pennypacker, H. S. (1963). Positive and negative generalization gradients obtained after equivalent training conditions. *Journal of Comparative and Physiological Psychology, 56,* 111–116.

Honig, W. K., & Stewart, K. (1988). Pigeons can discriminate locations presented in pictures. *Journal of the Experimental Analysis of Behavior, 50,* 541–551.

Honig, W. K., & Stewart, K. E. (1989). Discrimination of relative numerosity by pigeons. *Animal Learning & Behavior, 17,* 134–146.

Hong, Y.-Y., Chiu, C.-Y., & Kung, T. M. (1997). Bringing culture out in front: Effects of cultural meaning system activation on social cognition. In K. Leung, Y. Kashima, U. Kim, & S. Yamaguchi (Eds.), *Progress in Asian social psychology* (vol. 1) (pp. 135–146). Singapore: Wiley.

Hong, Y.-Y., Morris, M. W., Chiu, C.-Y., & Benet-Martínez, V. (2000). Multicultural minds: A dynamic constructivist approach to culture and cognition. *American Psychologist, 55,* 709–720.

Hoppman, R. A., & Allen, J. D. (1979). A test of the generality of schedule-induced polydipsia to wild-caught Norway rats. *Physiology & Behavior, 22,* 195–198.

Horne, P. J., & Lowe, C. F. (1993). Determinants of human performance on concurrent schedules. *Journal of the Experimental Analysis of Behavior, 59,* 29–60.

Horai, S., Hayasaka, K., Kondo, R., Tsugane, K., & Takahata, N. (1995). Recent African origin of modern humans revealed by complete sequences of hominid mitochondrial DNAs. *Proceedings of the National Academy of Sciences, 92,* 532–536.

Horne, P. J., & Lowe, C. F. (1996). On the origins of naming and other symbolic behavior. *Journal of the Experimental Analysis of Behavior, 65,* 185–241.

Horne, P. J., & Lowe, C. F. (1997). Toward a theory of verbal behavior. *Journal of the Experimental Analysis of Behavior, 68,* 271–296.

Horner, R. H., Day, H. M., Sprague, J., O'Brien, M., & Heathfield, L. T. (1991). Interspersed requests: A nonaversive procedure for reducing aggression and self- injury during instruction. *Journal of Applied Behavior Analysis, 24,* 265–278.

Horrocks, J., & Hunte, W. (1983). Maternal rank and offspring rank in vervet monkeys: An appraisal of the mechanisms of rank acquisition. *Animal Behaviour, 31,* 772–782.

Houston, A. (1986). The matching law applied to wagtails' foraging in the wild. *Journal of the Experimental Analysis of Behavior, 45,* 15–18.

Huber, B, Couvillon, P. A., & Bitterman, M. E. (1994). Place and position learning in honeybees (*Apis mellifera*). *Journal of Comparative Psychology, 108,* 213–219.

Hublin, J.-J. (1999). The quest for Adam. *Archaeology, 52,* 26–35.

Hudson, R. (1985). Do newborn rabbits learn the odor stimuli releasing nipple-search behavior? *Developmental Psychobiology, 18,* 575–585.

Hudson, R. & Distel, H. (1986). Pheromonal release of suckling in rabbits does not depend on the vomeronasal organ. *Physiology & Behavior, 37,* 123–129.

Hudson, R. & Distel, H. (1987). Regional autonomy in the peripheral processing of odor signals in newborn rabbits. *Brain Research, 421,* 85–94.

Huffman, M. A. (1984). Stone-play of *Macaca fuscata* in Arashiyama B troop: Transmission of a non-adaptive behavior. *Journal of Human Evolution, 13,* 725–735.

Huffman, M. A. (1996). Acquisition of innovative cultural behaviors in nonhuman primates: A case study of stone handling, a socially transmitted behavior in Japanese macaques. In C. M. Heyes & B. G. Galef, Jr. (Eds.), *Social learning in animals: The roots of culture* (pp. 267–289). New York: Academic Press.

Huffman, M. A., & Quiatt, D. (1986). Stone handling by Japanese macaques (*Macaca fuscata*): Implications for tool use of stone. *Primates, 27,* 427–437.

Hugdahl, K., & Kärker, A.-C. (1981). Biological vs. experiential factors in phobic conditioning. *Behaviour Research and Therapy, 19,* 109–115.

Hughes, R. G. (1971). Probability of signaled reinforcement in multiple variable-interval schedules. *Psychonomic Science, 22,* 57–59.

Humphrey, G. (1930). Extinction and negative adaptation. *Psychological Review, 37,* 361–363.

Humphrey, G. K. (1998). The McCollough effect: Misperception and reality. In V. Walsh & J. Kulikowski (Eds.), *Visual constancies: Why things look as they do* (pp. 31–68). Cambridge, England: Cambridge University Press.

Hunt, G. R. (1996). Manufacture and use of hook-tools by New Caledonian crows. *Nature, 379,* 249–251.

Hunter, I., & Davison, M. (1982). Independence of response force and reinforcement rate on concurrent variable-interval schedule performance. *Journal of the Experimental Analysis of Behavior, 37,* 183–197.

Hursh, S. R. (1978). The economics of daily consumption controlling food- and water-reinforced responding. *Journal of the Experimental Analysis of Behavior, 29,* 475–491.

Hursh, S. R. (1980). Economic concepts for the analysis of behavior. *Journal of the Experimental Analysis of Behavior, 34,* 219–238.

Hursh, S. R. (1984). Behavioral economics. *Journal of the Experimental Analysis of Behavior, 42,* 435–452.

Hurwitz, H. M. B., & Roberts, A. E. (1969). Suppressing an avoidance response by a pre-aversive stimulus. *Psychonomic Science, 17,* 305–306.

Hutchinson, R. R. (1977). By-products of aversive control. In W. K. Honig & J. E. R. Staddon (Eds.), *Handbook of Operant Behavior* (pp. 415–431). Englewood Cliffs, NJ: Prentice- Hall.

Hutchinson, R. R., Azrin, N. H., & Hunt, G. M. (1968). Attack produced by intermittent reinforcement of a concurrent operant response. *Journal of the Experimental Analysis of Behavior, 11,* 489–495.

Hutchinson, R. R., & Emley, G. S. (1977). Electric shock produced drinking in the squirrel monkey. *Journal of the Experimental Analysis of Behavior, 28,* 1–12.

Hutchinson, R. R., Pierce, G. E., Emley, G. S., Proni, T. J., & Sauer, R. A. (1977). The laboratory measurement of human anger. *Biobehavioral Reviews, 1,* 241–259.

Hutchinson, R. R., & Refrew, J. W. (1978). Functional parallels between the neural and environmental antecedents of aggression. *Neuroscience and Biobehavioral Reviews, 2,* 33–58.

Hutchinson, R. R., Renfrew, J. W., & Young, G. A.

(1971). Effects of long-term shock and associated stimuli on aggressive and manual responses. *Journal of the Experimental Analysis of Behavior, 15,* 141–166.

Hutton, L, Gardner, E. T., & Lewis, P. (1978). Matching with a key-peck response in concurrent negative reinforcement schedules. *Journal of the Experimental Analysis of Behavior, 30,* 225–230.

Hymowitz, N. (1971). Schedule-induced polydipsia and aggression in rats. *Psychonomic Science, 23,* 226–228.

Hymowitz, N. (1981 a). Effects of signaled and unsignaled shock on schedule-controlled lever pressing and schedule-induced licking: Shock intensity and body weight. *Journal of the Experimental Analysis of Behavior, 35,* 197–207.

Hymowitz, N. (1981 b). Effects of diazepam on schedule-controlled and schedule-induced behavior under signaled and unsignaled shock. *Journal of the Experimental Analysis of Behavior, 36,* 119–132.

Hyten, C., Madden, G. J., & Field, D. P. (1994). Exchange delays and impulsive choice in adult humans. *Journal of the Experimental Analysis of Behavior, 62,* 225–233.

Iglauer, C., & Woods, J. H. (1974). Concurrent performances: Reinforcement by different doses of intravenous cocaine in rhesus monkeys. *Journal of the Experimental Analysis of Behavior, 22,* 179–196.

Innis, N. K., Simmelhag-Grant, V. L., & Staddon, J. E. R. (1983). Behavior induced by periodic food delivery: The effects of interfood interval. *Journal of the Experimental Analysis of Behavior, 39,* 309–322.

Isaacs, W., Thomas, J., & Goldiamond, I. (1960). Application of operant conditioning to reinstate verbal behavior in psychotics. *Journal of Speech and Hearing Disorders, 25,* 8–12.

Isack, H. A., & Reyer, H.-U. (1989). Honeyguides and honey gatherers: Interspecific communication in a symbiotic relationship. *Science, 243,* 1343–1346.

Ison, J. R., & Cook, P. E. (1964). Extinction performance as a function of incentive magnitude and number of acquisition trials. *Psychonomic Science, 1,* 245–246.

Ivancevich, J. M. (1983). Contrast effects in performance evaluation and reward practices. *Academy of Management Journal, 26,* 465–476.

Iversen, I. H. (1976). Interactions between reinforced responses and collateral responses. *The Psychological Record, 26,* 399–413.

Iversen, I. H. (1993). Techniques for establishing schedules with wheel running as reinforcement in rats. *Journal of the Experimental Analysis of Behavior, 60,* 219–238.

Iversen, I. H. (1998). Simple and conditional visual discrimination with wheel running as reinforcement in rats. *Journal of the Experimental Analysis of Behavior, 70,* 103–121.

Jablonski, N. G., & Chaplin, G. (1993). Origin of habitual terrestrial bipedalism in the ancestor of the Hominidae. *Journal of Human Evolution, 24,* 259–280.

Jacobsen, P. B., Bovbjerg, D. H., Schwartz, M. D., Andrykowski, M. A., Futterman, A. D., Gilewski, T., Norton, L., & Redd, W. H. (1993). Formation of food aversions in cancer patients receiving repeated infusions of chemotherapy. *Behaviour Research and Therapy, 31,* 739–748.

Jacobson, A. L., Horowitz, S. D., & Fried, C. (1967). Classical conditioning, pseudoconditioning, or sensitization in the planarian. *Journal of Comparative and Physiological Psychology, 64,* 73–79.

Jacobson, E. (1932). The electrophysiology of mental activities. *American Journal of Psychology, 44,* 677–694.

Jacquet, Y. F. (1972). Schedule-induced licking during multiple schedules. *Journal of the Experimental Analysis of Behavior, 17,* 413–423.

Jaffe, K., Zabala, N. A., de Bellard, M. E., Granier, M., Aragort, W., & Tablante, A. (1990). Amino acids and memory consolidation in the cricket: II. Effect of injected amino acids and opioids on memory. *Pharmacology, Biochemistry & Behavior, 35,* 133–136.

Jakobson, R. (1968). *Child language, aphasia, and phonological universals.* (trans: A.R. Keiler; original work published in 1941). The Hague, Netherlands: Mouton.

James, W. T. (1960). The development of social facilitation of eating in puppies. *Journal of Genetic Psychology, 96,* 123–127.

James, W. T., & Gilbert, T. F. (1955). The effect of social faeilkitation on food intake of puppies fed separately and together for the first 90 days of life. *British Journal of Animal Behaviour, 3,* 131–133.

Janik, V. M., & Slater, P. J. B. (1997). Vocal learning in mammals. *Advanced Studies in Behavior, 26,* 59–99.

Janzen, D. H. (1971). Euglossine bees as long-distance pollinators of tropical plants. *Science, 171,* 203–205.

Jenkins, H. M., & Harrison, R. H. (1960). Effect of discrimination training on auditory generalization. *Journal of Experimental Psychology, 59,* 246–253.

Jenkins, H. M., & Harrison, R. H. (1962). Generalization gradients of inhibition following auditory discrimination learning. *Journal of the Experimental Analysis of Behavior, 5,* 435–441.

Jenkins, H. M., & Moore, B. R. (1973). The form of the auto-shaped response with food or water reinforcers. *Journal of the Experimental Analysis of Behavior, 20,* 163–181.

Jenkins, H. M., & Sainsbury, R. S. (1969). The development of stimulus control through differentiated reinforcement. In N. J. Mackintosh & W. K. Honig (Eds.), *Fundamental issues in associative learning* (pp. 123–161) Halifax: Dalhousie University Press.

Jensen, A. R. (1962). Spelling errors and the serial-position effect. *Journal of Educational Psychology, 53,* 105–109.

Jitsumori, M., & Sugimoto, S. (1982). Memory for two stimulus-response items in pigeons. *Journal of the Experimental Analysis of Behavior, 38,* 63–70.

Johanson, C. E. (1975). Pharmacological and environmental variables affecting drug preference in rhesus monkeys. *Pharmacological Reviews, 27,* 343–355.

Johanson, C. E., & Schuster, C. R. (1975). A choice procedure for drug reinforcers: Cocaine and methylphenidate in the rhesus monkey. *Journal of Pharmacology and Experimental Therapeutics, 193,* 676–688.

Johnson, D. F. (1970). Determiners of selective stimulus control in the pigeon. *Journal of Comparative and Physiological Psychology, 70,* 298–307.

Johnson, D. F., & Cumming, W. W. (1968). Some determiners of attention. *Journal of the Experimental Analysis of Behavior, 11,* 157–166.

Johnson, E. W., Briggs, D. E. G., Suthren, R. J., Wright, J. L., & Tunnicliff, S. P. (1994). Nonmarine arthropod traces from the subaerial Ordovician Borrowdale Volcanic Group, English Lake District. *Geological Magazine, 131,* 395–406.

Johnson, H. M. (1994). Processes of successful intentional forgetting. *Psychological Bulletin, 116,* 274–292.

Jones, J. W., & Bogat, G. (1978). Air pollution and human aggression. *Psychological Reports, 43,* 721–722.

Joubert, D. (writer, producer), & Joubert, B. (producer). (1992). *Eternal enemies: Lions and hyenas.* National Geographic Society. (Video)

Jwaideh, A. R. (1973). Responding under chained and tandem fixed-ratio schedules. *Journal of the Experimental Analysis of Behavior, 19,* 259–267.

Kachanoff, R., Leveille, R., McLelland, J. P., & Wayner, M. J. (1973). Schedule-induced behavior in humans. *Physiology & Behavior, 11,* 395–398.

Kagan, J., & Berkun, M. (1954). The reward value of running activity. *Journal of Comparative and Physiological Psycology, 47,* 108–110.

Kagel, J. H., Battalio, R. C., & Green, L. (1995). *Economic choice theory: An experimental analysis of animal behavior.* Cambridge: Cambridge University Press.

Kamil, A. C. (1989). Studies of learning and memory in natural contexts: Integrating functional and mechanistic approaches to behavior. In R. J. Blanchard, P. Brain, D. C. Blanchard, & S. Parmigiani (Eds.), *Ethoexperimental approaches to the study of behavior* (pp. 30–50). Dordrecht: Kluwer Academic.

Kamil, A. C., & Sargent, T. D. (1981). *Foraging behavior: Ecological, ethological, and psychological approaches.* New York: Garland.

Kamin, L. J. (1968). "Attention-like" processes in classical conditioning. In M. R. Jones (Ed.), *Miami symposium on the prediction of behavior: Aversive stimulation* (pp. 9–31). Miami, FL: University of Miami Press.

Kamin, L. J. (1969). Predictability, surprise, attention, and conditioning. In B. A. Campbell & R. M. Church (Eds.), *Punishment and aversive behavior* (pp. 279–296). New York: Appleton-Century-Crofts.

Kanarek, R. B. (1975). Availability and caloric density of the diet as determinants of meal patterns in cats. *Physiology & Behavior, 15,* 611–618.

Kandel, E. R. (1979). Small systems of neurons. *Scientific American, 241*(3), 66–76.

Kaplan, P. S., & Werner, J. S. (1986). Habituation, response to novelty, and dishabituation in human infants: Tests of a dual process theory of visual attention. *Journal of Experimental Child Psychology, 42,* 199–217.

Kato, E. (1999a). Elements of syntax in the systems of three language-trained animals. *Animal Learning & Behavior, 27,* 26–27.

Kato, E. (1999b). Response to Pepperberg, Herman, and Savage-Rumbaugh. *Animal Learning & Behavior, 27,* 1–14.

Kaufman, A., & Baron, A. (1968). Suppression of behavior by time out punishment when suppression results in loss of positive reinforcement. *Journal of the Experimental Analysis of Behavior, 11,* 595–607.

Kaufman, A., Baron, A., & Kopp, R. E. (1966). Some effects of instructions on human operant behavior. *Psychonomic Monograph Supplements, 1,* 243–250.

Kaufman, M. A., & Bolles, R. C. (1981). A nonassociative aspect of overshadowing. *Bulletin of the Psychonomic Society, 18,* 318–320.

Kazdin, A. E. (1977). *The token economy: A review and evaluation.* New York: Plenum Press.

Keehn, J. D. (1967). Double discrimination bar press and bar release avoidance. *Psychonomic Science, 8,* 189–190.

Keesey, R. E., & Kling, J. W. (1961). Amount of reinforcement and free-operant responding. *Journal of the Experimental Analysis of Behavior, 4,* 125–132.

Kelleher, R. T. (1957). Conditioned reinforcement in chimpanzees. *Journal of Comparative and Physiological Psychology, 49,* 571–575.

Kelleher, R. T. (1958). Fixed-ratio schedules of conditioned reinforcement with chimpanzees. *Journal of the Experimental Analysis of Behavior, 1,* 281–289.

Kelleher, R. T. (1966 a). Chaining and conditioned reinforcement. In W. K. Honig (Ed.), *Operant behavior: Areas of research and application* (pp. 160–212). New York: Appleton-Century-Crofts.

Kelleher, R. T. (1966 b). Conditioned reinforcement in second-order schedules. *Journal of the Experimental Analysis of Behavior, 9,* 475–485.

Kelleher, R. T., & Fry, W. T. (1962). Stimulus functions in chained fixed-interval schedules. *Journal of the Experimental Analysis of Behavior, 5,* 167–173.

Kelleher, R. T., & Gollub, L. R. (1962). A review of positive conditioned reinforcement. *Journal of the Experimental Analysis of Behavior, 5,* 543–597.

Kelleher, R. T., & Morse, W. H. (1968). Schedules using noxious stimuli. III. Responding maintained with response-produced electric shocks. *Journal of the Experimental Analysis of Behavior, 11,* 819–838.

Kelleher, R. T., Riddle, W. C., & Cook, L. (1963). Persistent behavior maintained by unavoidable shocks. *Journal of the Experimental Analysis of Behavior, 6,* 507–517.

Keller, F. S. (1941). Light aversion in the white rat. *The Psychological Record, 4,* 235–250.

Kelly, J. F., & Hake, D. F. (1970). An extinction-induced

increase in an aggressive response with humans. *Journal of the Experimental Analysis of Behavior, 14,* 153–164.

Kelsey, J. E., & Allison, J. (1976). Fixed-ratio lever pressing by VMH rats: Work vs. accessibility of sucrose reward. *Physiology & Behavior, 17,* 749–754.

Kendrick, D. F. (1992). Pigeon's concept of experienced and non-experienced real-world locations: Discrimination and generalization across seasonal variation. In W. K. Honig & J. G. Fetterman (Eds.), *Cognitive aspects of stimulus control* (pp. 113–134). Hillsdale, NJ: Erlbaum.

Kendrick, D. F., Rilling, M. E., & Stonebraker, T. B. (1981). Stimulus control of delayed matching in pigeons: Directed forgetting. *Journal of the Experimental Analysis of Behavior, 36,* 241–251.

Kerr, N., & Meyerson, L. (1977). Further evidence on ordering from the AVC scale: AVC skills in deaf-retarded adults (Monograph). *Rehabilitation Psychology, 24,* 129–131.

Kerr, N., Meyerson, L., & Flora, J. A. (1977). The measurement of motor, visual, and auditory discrimination skills (Monograph). *Rehabilitation Psychology, 24,* 95–112.

Kerr, R. A. (1993). Evolution's big bang gets even more explosive. *Science, 261,* 1274–1275.

Kesner, R. P., & Novak, J. M. (1982). Serial position curve in rats: Role of the dorsal hippocampus. *Science, 218,* 173–175.

Killeen, P. (1968). Response rate as a factor in choice. *Psychonomic Science, 12,* 34.

Killeen, P. R. (1994). Mathematical principles of reinforcement. *Behavioral and Brain Sciences, 17,* 105–172.

Kim, H.-S., & Takenaka, O. (1996). A comparison of TSPY genes from Y-chromosomal DNA of the great apes and humans: Sequence, evolution and phylogeny. *American Journal of Physical Anthropology, 100,* 301–309.

Kinderman, U., Hudson, R., & Distel, H. (1994). Learning of suckling odors by newborn rabbits declines with age and suckling experience. *Developmental Psychobiology, 27,* 111–122.

King, A. P., & West, M. J. (1989). Presence of female cowbirds (*Molothrus ater ater*) affects vocal improvisation in males. *Journal of Comparative Psychology, 103,* 39–44.

King, B. J. (1994). *The information continuum.* Sante Fe, NM: SAR Press.

King, B. J. (1999). The dominant approach to social learning. In H. O. Box & K. R. Gibson (Eds.), *Mammalian social learning: Comparative and ecological perspectives* (pp. 17–32). Cambridge, UK: Cambridge University Press.

King, G. D. (1974). Wheel running in the rat induced by a fixed-time presentation of water. *Animal Learning & Behavior, 2,* 325–328.

King, J. E. (1973). Learning and generalization of a two-dimensional sameness-difference concept by chimpanzees and orangutans. *Journal of Comparative and Physiological Psychology, 84,* 140–148.

Kirkpatrick, M. (1982). Sexual selection and the evolution of female choice. *Evolution, 36,* 1–12.

Kish, G. B. (1966). Studies of sensory reinforcement. In W. K. Honig, *Operant behavior: Areas of research and application* (pp. 109–159). New York: Appleton-Century-Crofts.

Kitchener, A. C. (1999). Watch with mother: A review of social learning in the Felidae. In H. O. Box & K. R. Gibson (Eds.), *Mammalian social learning: Comparative and ecological perspectives* (pp. 236–258). Cambridge, UK: Cambridge University Press.

Klahr, D. (1973). Quantification processes. In W. G. Chase (Ed.), *Visual information processing* (pp. 3–34). New York: Academic Press.

Klein, D. R. (1999). Comparative social learning among arctic herbivores: The caribou, muskox and arctic hare. In H. O. Box & K. R. Gibson (Eds.), *Mammalian social learning: Comparative and ecological perspectives* (pp. 126–140). Cambridge, UK: Cambridge University Press.

Klein, M., & Rilling, M. (1972). Effects of response-shock interval and shock intensity on free-operant avoidance responding in the pigeon. *Journal of the Experimental Analysis of Behavior, 18,* 295–303.

Klugh, H. E. (1961). Speed of running in extinction as a function of differential goal box retention time. *Journal of Experimental Psychology, 61,* 172–177.

Knoll, A. H. (1994). Proterozoic and early Cambrian protists: Evidence for accelerating evolutionary tempo. *Proceedings of the National Academy of Sciences, 91,* 6743–6750.

Knutson, J. F., & Bailey, M. I. (1974). Free-operant escape-avoidance of noise by rats. *Journal of the Experimental Analysis of Behavior, 22,* 219–229.

Knutson, J. F., & Schrader, S. P. (1975). A concurrent assessment of schedule-induced aggression and schedule-induced polydipsia in the rat. *Animal Learning & Behavior, 3,* 16–20.

Kodera, T. L., & Rilling, M. (1976). Procedural antecedents of behavioral contrast: A re-examination of errorless learning. *Journal of the Experimental Analysis of Behavior, 25,* 27–42.

Koegel, R. L., Egel, A. L., & Williams, J. A. (1980). Behavioral contrast and generalization across settings in the treatment of autistic children. *Journal of Experimental Child Psychology, 30,* 422–437.

Kohler, W. (1927). *The mentality of apes* (Second edition; trans: E. Winter). London: Routledge, & Kegan Paul.

Koltermann, R. (1974). Periodicity in the activity and learning performance of the honeybee. In L. B. Browne (Ed.), *Experimental analysis of insect behaviour.* New York: Springer-Verlag.

Konarski, E. A., Jr., Crowell, C. R., & Duggan, L. M. (1985). The use of response deprivation to increase the academic performance of EMR students. *Applied Research in Mental Retardation, 6,* 15–31.

Konarski, E. A., Jr., Crowell, C. R., Johnson, M. R., & Whitman, T. L. (1982). Response deprivation, reinforcement, and instrumental academic performance in an EMR classroom. *Behavior Therapy, 13,* 94–102.

Konarski, E. A., Jr., Johnson, M. R., Crowell, C. R., & Whitman, T. L. (1980). Response deprivation and reinforcement in applied settings: A preliminary analysis. *Journal of Applied Behavior Analysis, 13,* 595–609.

Konishi, M. (1965). The role of auditory feedback in the control of vocalizations in the white-crowned sparrow. *Zeitschrift für Tierpsychologie, 22,* 770–783.

Konorski, J., & Miller, S. (1937). On two types of conditional reflex. *Journal of General Psychology, 16,* 264–272.

Kramer, S. P. (1982). Memory for recent behavior in the pigeon. *Journal of the Experimental Analysis of Behavior, 38,* 71–85.

Krebs, J. R. (1980). Optimal foraging, predation risk and territory defense. *Ardea, 68,* 83–90.

Krebs, J. R., & Davies, N. B. (1993). *An introduction to behavioural ecology* (Third edition). London: Blackwell Scientific Publications.

Kuhn, T. S. (1970). *The structure of scientific revolutions.* Chicago: University of Chicago Press.

Kunkel, J. H. (1991). Apathy and irresponsibility in social systems. In P, A. Lamal (Ed.), *Behavioral analysis of societies and cultural practices* (pp. 219–240). New York: Hemisphere.

LaBounty, C. E., & Reynold, G. S. (1973). An analysis of response and time matching to reinforcement in concurrent ratio-interval schedules. *Journal of the Experimental Analysis of Behavior, 19,* 155–166.

Lachter, G. D., & Corey, J. R. (1982). Variability of the duration of an operant. *Behavior Analysis Letters, 2,* 97–102.

Laland, K. N. (1999). Exploring the dynamics of social transmission with rats. In H. O. Box & K. R. Gibson (Eds.), *Mammalian social learning: Comparative and ecological perspectives* (pp. 174–187). Cambridge, UK: Cambridge University Press.

Laland, K. N., & Plotkin, H. C. (1991). Excretory deposits surrounding food sites facilitate social learning of food preferences. *Animal Behaviour, 41,* 997–1005.

Laland, K. N., & Plotkin, H. C. (1993). Social transmission in Norway rats via excretory marking of food sites. *Animal Learning & Behavior, 21,* 35–41.

Lande, R. (1980). Sexual dimorphism, sexual selection and adaption in polygenic characters. *Evolution, 34,* 292–305.

Lande, R. (1981). Models of speciation by sexual selection on polygenic characters. *Proceedings of the National Academy of Sciences of the United States of America, 78,* 3721–3725.

Lang, P. J. (1979). A bio-informational theory of emotional imagery. *Psychophysiology, 16,* 495–512.

Lang, P. J., Kozak, M. J., Miller, G. A., Levin, D. N., & McLean, A. (1980). Emotional imagery: Conceptual structure and pattern of somato-visceral response. *Psychophysiology, 17,* 179–192.

Lanza, R. P., Starr, J., & Skinner, B. F. (1982). "Lying" in the pigeon. *Journal of the Experimental Analysis of Behavior, 38,* 201–203.

Lashley, K. S. (1951). The problem of serial order in behavior. In L. A. Jeffries (Ed.), *Cerebral mechanisms in behavior* (pp. 112–136). New York: Wiley.

Lashley, R. L., & Rosellini, R. A. (1980). Modulation of schedule-induced polydipsia by Pavlovian conditioned states. *Physiology & Behavior, 24,* 411–414.

Latané, B., Williams, K., & Harkins, S. G. (1979). Many hands make light the work: The causes and consequences of social loafing. *Journal of Personality and Social Psychology, 37,* 822–832.

Laties, V. G., & Weiss, B. (1963). Effects of a concurrent task on fixed-interval responding in humans. *Journal of the Experimental Analysis of Behavior, 6,* 431–436.

Laties, V. G., Weiss, B., Clark, R. L., & Reynolds, M. D. (1965). Overt "mediating" behavior during temporally spaced responding. *Journal of the Experimental Analysis of Behavior, 8,* 107–116.

Lattal, K. A., & Cooper, A. M. (1969). Escape from punishment by omission of responding. *Psychonomic Science, 15,* 263–264.

Lattal, K. A., & Gleeson, S. (1990). Response acquisition with delayed reinforcement. *Journal of Experimental Psychology: Animal Behavior Processes, 16,* 27–39.

Lattal, K. A., & Metzger, B. (1994). Response acquisition by Siamese fighting fish (*Betta splendens*) with delayed visual reinforcement. *Journal of the Experimental Analysis of Behavior, 61,* 35–44.

Laurence, M. T., Hineline, P. N., & Bersh, P. J. (1994). The puzzle of responding maintained by response-contingent shock. *Journal of the Experimental Analysis of Behavior, 61,* 135–153.

Laverty, T. M. (1994). Bumble bee learning and flower morphology. *Animal Behaviour, 47,* 531–545.

Lawson, R., Mattis, P. R., & Pear, J. J. (1968). Summation of response rates to discriminative stimuli associated with qualitatively different reinforcers. *Journal of the Experimental Analysis of Behavior, 11,* 561–568.

Lazar, R. M. (1977). Extending sequence class membership with matching to sample. *Journal of the Experimental Analysis of Behavior, 27,* 381–392.

Lazar, R. M., & Kotlarchyk, B. J. (1986). Second-order control of sequence-class equivalences in children. *Behavioural Processes, 13,* 381–392.

Leander, J. D. (1973). Shock intensity and duration interactions on free-operant avoidance behavior. *Journal of the Experimental Analysis of Behavior, 19,* 481–490.

Lee, P. (1981). Ecological and social influences on development of vervet monkeys. Unpublished doctoral dissertation, Cambridge University.

Lee, P. C., & Moss, C. J. (1999). The social context for learning and behavioural development among wild

African elephants. In H. O. Box & K. R. Gibson (Eds.), *Mammalian social learning: Comparative and ecological perspectives* (pp. 102–125). Cambridge, UK: Cambridge University Press.

Lee, R. M. (1963). Conditioning of a free operant response in planaria. *Science, 139,* 1048–1049.

Lee, R. M. (1969). Aplysia behavior: Effects of contingent water level variation. *Communications in Behavioral Biology, 3,* 157–164.

LeFrancois, J. R., Chase, P. N., & Joyce, J. H. (1988). The effects of a variety of instructions on human fixed-interval performance. *Journal of the Experimental Analysis of Behavior, 49,* 383–393.

Lendenmann, K. W., Myers, D. L., & Fantino, E. (1982). Effects of reinforcer duration on responding in two-linked chained interval schedules. *Journal of the Experimental Analysis of Behavior, 37,* 217–222.

Lent, P. C. (1971). Mother-infant relationships in ungulates. In V. Geist & F. Walther (Eds.), *The behaviour of ungulates and its relation to management* (pp. 14–55). Morges, Switzerland: IUCN.

Leon, M., Galef, B. G., & Behse, J. H. (1977). Establishment of pheromonal bonds in diet choice in young rats by odor preexposure. *Physiology & Behavior, 18,* 387–391.

Leonard, J. L., Edstrom, J., & Lukowiak, K. (1989). Reexamination of the gill withdrawal reflex of Aplysia californica cooper (*Gastropoda Opisthobranchia*). *Behavioral Neuroscience, 103,* 585–604.

Lerman, D. C., & Iwata, B. A. (1995). Prevalence of the extinction burst and its attenuation during treatment. *Journal of Applied Behavior Analysis, 28,* 93–94.

Lerman, D. C., Iwata, B. A., & Wallace, M. D. (1999). Side effects of extinction: Prevalence of bursting and aggression during the treatment of self-injurious behavior. *Journal of Applied Behavior Analysis, 32,* 1–8.

Lerman, D. C., Iwata, B. A., Zarcone, J. R., & Ringdahl, J. (1994). Assessment of stereotypic and self-injurious behavior as adjunctive responses. *Journal of Applied Behavior Analysis, 27,* 715–728.

Leslie, J. C. (1977). Effects of food deprivation and reinforcement magnitude on conditioned suppression. *Journal of the Experimental Analysis of Behavior, 28,* 107–115.

Leung, J.-P., & Winton, A. S. W. (1988). Preference for simple interval schedules of reinforcement in concurrent chains: Effects of segmentation ratio. *Journal of the Experimental Analysis of Behavior, 49,* 9–20.

Levey, A. B., & Martin, I. (1975). Classical conditioning of human "evaluative" responses. *Behaviour Research and Therapy, 13,* 221–226.

Levin, G. R., & Maurer, D. M. (1969). The solution process in children's matching-to-sample. *Developmental Psychology, 1,* 679–690.

Levine, M., & Harlow, H. F. (1959). Learning-sets with one- and twenty-trial oddity-problems. *American Journal of Psychology, 72,* 253–257.

Levitsky, D., & Collier, G. (1968). Schedule-induced wheel running. *Physiology & Behavior, 3,* 571–573.

Levy, M., Weller, A., & Susswein, A. J. (1994). Learned changes in the rate of respiratory pumping in Aplysia fasciata in response to increases and decreases in seawater concentration. *Behavioral Neuroscience, 108,* 161–170.

Lewis, D. J. (1956). Acquisition, extinction, and spontaneous recovery as a function of percentage of reinforcement and intertrial intervals. *Journal of Experimental Psychology, 51,* 45–53.

Lewis, P., Gardner, E. T., & Hutton, L. (1976). Integrated delays to shock as negative reinforcement. *Journal of the Experimental Analysis of Behavior, 26,* 379–386.

Lewis, P., Lewin, L., Stoyak, M., & Muehleisen, P. (1974). Negatively reinforced key pecking. *Journal of the Experimental Analysis of Behavior, 18,* 517–523.

Lewis, W. J., & Takasu, K. (1990). Use of learned odours by a parasitic wasp in accordance with host and food needs. *Nature, 348,* 635–636.

Libet, B. (1985). Unconscious cerebral initiative and the role of conscious will in voluntary action. *Behavioral and Brain Sciences, 8,* 529–566.

Libet, B., Curtis, A. G., Wright, E. W., & Pearl, D. K. (1983). Time of conscious intention to act in relation to onset of cerebral activity (readiness potential). The unconscious initiation of a freely voluntary act. *Brain, 106,* 640.

Lieberman, D. A. (1972). Secondary reinforcement and information as determinants of observing behavior in monkeys. *Learning and Motivation, 3,* 341–358.

Lieberman, D. A., Cathro, J. S., Nichol, K., & Watson, E. (1997). The role of S- in human observing behavior: Bad news is sometimes better than no news. *Learning and Motivation, 28,* 20–42.

Lieberman, D. E. (1995). Testing hypotheses about recent human evolution from skulls. *Current Anthropology, 36,* 159–197.

Lieberman, P., Laitman, J. T., Reidenberg, J. S., & Gannon, P. J. (1992). The anatomy, physiology, acoustics and perception of speech: Essential elements in analysis of the evolution of human speech. *Journal of Human Evolution, 23,* 447–467.

Lobato, J. F. P., Pearce, G. R., & Beilharz, R. G. (1980). Effect of early familiarization with dietary supplements on the subsequent ingestion of molasses-urea blocks by sheep. *Applied Animal Ethology, 6,* 149–161.

Lobb, B., & Davison, M. C. (1975). Performance in concurrent interval schedules: A systematic replication. *Journal of the Experimental Analysis of Behavior, 24,* 191–197.

Locke, J. L., & Pearson, D. M. (1990). Linguistic significance of babbling: Evidence from a tracheostomized infant. *Journal of Child Language, 17,* 1–16.

Loftus, E. F. (1975). Leading questions and the eyewitness report. *Cognitive Psychology, 7,* 560–572.

Loftus, E. F., & Pickrell, J. E. (1995). The formation of false memories. *Psychiatric Annals, 25,* 720–725.

Logan, C. A. (1975). Topographic changes in responding during habituation to waterstream stimulation in sea anemones (*Anthopleura elegantissima*). *Journal of Comparative and Physiological Psychology, 89,* 105–117.

Logan, C. A., & Beck, H. P. (1978). Long term retention of habituation in the sea anemone (*Anthopleura elegantissima*). *Journal of Comparative and Physiological Psychology, 92,* 928–936.

Logue, A. W. (1979). Taste aversion and the generality of the laws of learning. *Psychological Bulletin, 86,* 276–296.

Logue, A. W. (1980). Visual cues for illness-induced aversions in the pigeon. *Behavioral and Neural Biology, 28,* 372–373.

Logue, A. W. (1988). Research on self-control: An integrating framework. *Behavioral and Brain Sciences, 11,* 665–709.

Logue, A. W., & de Villiers, P. A. (1978). Matching in concurrent variable-interval avoidance schedules. *Journal of the Experimental Analysis of Behavior, 29,* 61–66.

Logue, A. W., & Peña-Correal, T. E. (1984). Responding during reinforcement delay in a self-control paradigm. *Journal of the Experimental Analysis of Behavior, 41,* 267–277.

Logue, A. W., Peña-Correal, T. E., Rodriguez, M. L., & Kabela, E. (1986). Self-control in adult humans: Variation in positive reinforcer amount and delay. *Journal of the Experimental Analysis of Behavior, 46,* 159–173

Logue, A. W., Rodriguez, M. L., Peña-Correal, T. E., & Mauro, B. E. (1984). Choice in a self-control paradigm: Quantification of experience-based differences. *Journal of the Experimental Analysis of Behavior, 41,* 53–67.

LoLordo, V. M., Jacobs, W. J., & Foree, D. D. (1982). Failure to block control by a relevant stimulus. *Animal Learning & Behavior, 10,* 183–192.

Loo, S. K., & Bitterman, M. E. (1992). Learning in honeybees (*Apis mellifera*) as a function of sucrose concentration. *Journal of Comparative Psychology, 106,* 29–36.

Looy, H., & Eikelboom, R. (1989). Wheel running, food intake, and body weight in male rats. *Physiology & Behavior, 45,* 403–405.

Looney, T. A., & Cohen, P. S. (1976). Pictorial target control affecting establishment of schedule-induced attack on pictorial targets in White King pigeons. *Journal of the Experimental Analysis of Behavior, 26,* 349–360.

Lopez, J. C., & Lopez, D. (1985). Killer whales (*Orcinus orca*) of Patagonia and their behavior of intentional stranding while hunting nearshore. *Journal of Mammalogy, 66,* 181–183.

Lorenz, K. (1935/1970). Der Kumpan in der Umwelt des Vogels. *Journal für Ornithologie, 83,* 137–213. [Translated in: K. Lorenz, *Studies in animal and human behaviour* (vol. 1) (pp. 101–258). Cambridge: Harvard University Press.]

Lorenz, K. (1937/1970). Uber dis Bildung des Instinkbegreffes. *Die Naturwissenschaften, 25,* 289–300, 324–331. [Translated in: K. Lorenz, *Studies in animal and human behaviour* (vol. 1) (pp. 259–315). Cambridge: Harvard University Press.]

Lorenz, K. (1963/1966). *Das Sogenannte Böse, zur Naturgeschichte der Aggression.* Vienna: Dr. G. Borotha- Schoeler Verlag. [Translated as: *On aggression* (trans: M. Latzke). London: Methuen.]

Lotter, E. C., Woods, S. C., & Vasselli, J. R. (1973). Schedule-induced polydipsia: An artifact. *Journal of Comparative and Physiological Psychology, 83,* 478–484.

Lowe, C. F. (1979). Determinants of human operant behavior. In M. D. Zeiler & P. Harzem (Eds.), *Advances in the analysis of behavior* (vol. 1): *Reinforcement and the organization of behavior* (pp. 159–192). Chichester: Wiley.

Lowe, C. F., Beasty, A., & Bentall, R. P. (1983). The role of verbal behavior in human learning: Infant performances on fixed-interval schedules. *Journal of the Experimental Analysis of Behavior, 39,* 157–164.

Lowe, C. F., & Horne, P. J. (1996). Reflections on naming and other symbolic behavior. *Journal of the Experimental Analysis of Behavior, 65,* 315–340.

Lubow, R. E. (1973). Latent inhibition. *Psychological Bulletin, 79,* 398–407.

Lubow, R. E. (1974). High-order concept formation in pigeons. *Journal of the Experimental Analysis of Behavior, 21,* 475–483.

Lubow, R. E. (1989). *Latent inhibition and attention theory.* New York: Cambridge University Press.

Lubow, R. E., & Moore, A. U. (1959). Latent inhibition: The effect of nonreinforced pre-exposure to the conditioned stimulus. *Journal of Comparative and Physiological Psychology, 52,* 415–419.

Lucas, G. A., Timberlake, W., & Gawley, D. J. (1988). Adjunctive behavior of the rat under periodic food delivery in a 24-hour environment. *Animal Learning & Behavior, 16,* 19–30.

Lydersen, T., & Perkins, D. (1974). Effects of response-produced stimuli upon conditional discrimination performance. *Journal of the Experimental Analysis of Behavior, 21,* 307–314.

Lydersen, T., Perkins, D., & Chairez, H. (1977). Effects of fixed-ratio sample and choice response requirements upon oddity matching. *Journal of the Experimental Analysis of Behavior, 27,* 97–101.

Lydersen, T., Perkins, D., Thome, S., & Lowman, E. (1980). Choice of timeout during response-independent food schedules. *Journal of the Experimental Analysis of Behavior, 33,* 59–76.

Mace, F. C., & Belfiore, P. (1990). Behavioral momentum in the treatment of escape-motivated stereotypy. *Journal of Applied Behavior Analysis, 23,* 507–514.

Mace, F. C., Hock, M. L., Lalli, J. S., West, B. J., Belfiore,

P., Pinter, E., & Brown, D. K. (1988). Behavioral momentum in the treatment of noncompliance. *Journal of Applied Behavior Analysis, 21,* 123–141.

Mace, F. C., Lalli, J. S., Shea, M. C., Lalli, E. P., West, B. J., Roberts, M., & Nevin, J. A. (1990). The momentum of human behavior in a natural setting. *Journal of the Experimental Analysis of Behavior, 54,* 163–172.

Mace, F. C., McCurdy, B., & Quigley, E. A. (1990). A collateral effect of reward predicted by matching theory. *Journal of Applied Behavior Analysis, 23,* 197–205.

Mace, F. C., Neef, N. A., Shade, D., & Mauro, B. C. (1994). Limited matching on concurrent-schedule reinforcement of academic behavior. *Journal of Applied Behavior Analysis, 27,* 585–596.

Machado, A. (1989). Operant conditioning of behavioral variability using a percentile reinforcement schedule. *Journal of the Experimental Analysis of Behavior, 52,* 155–166.

Machado, A. (1994). Polymorphic response patterns under frequency-dependent selection. *Animal Learning & Behavior, 22,* 53–71.

Machado, A., & Keen, R. (1999). The learning of response patterns in choice situations. *Animal Learning & Behavior, 27,* 51–271.

Macht, J. (1971).Operant measurement of subjective visual acuity in non-verbal children. *Journal of Applied Behavior Analysis, 4,* 23–36.

Mackenzie, D. L. (1974). *Aversively motivated two-choice discrimination learning.* Unpublished doctoral dissertation, Syracuse University.

MacKinnon, J. (1971). The orang-utan in Sabah today. *Oryx, 11,* 141–191.

Mackintosh, N. J. (1974). *The psychology of animal learning.* London: Academic Press.

Mackintosh, N. (1994). Intelligence in evolution. In J. Khalfa (Ed.), *What is intelligence?* (pp. 27–48). Cambridge: Cambridge University Press.

MacNeilage, P. F. (1998). Evolution of the mechanism of language output: Comparative neurobiology of vocal and manual communication. In J. R. Hurford, M. Studdert-Kennedy, & C. Knight (Eds.), *Approaches to the evolution of language: Social and cognitive bases* (pp. 222–241). Cambridge: Cambridge University Press.

Macphail, E. M. (1968). Avoidance responding in pigeons with negative reinforcement. *Journal of the Experimental Analysis of Behavior, 11,* 629–632.

Madden, G. J., & Perone, M. (1999). Human sensitivity to concurrent schedules of reinforcement: Effects of observing schedule-correlated stimuli. *Journal of the Experimental Analysis of Behavior, 71,* 303–318.

Maestripieri, D. (1996). Primate cognition and the bared-teeth display: A reevaluation of the concept of formal dominance. *Journal of Comparative Psychology, 110,* 402–405.

Mahoney, W. J., & Ayres, J. J. B. (1976). One-trial simultaneous and backward fear conditioning as reflected in conditioned suppression of licking in rats. *Animal Learning & Behavior, 4,* 357–362.

Mahrer, A. R. (1956). The role of expectancy in delayed reinforcement. *Journal of Experimental Psychology, 52,* 101–106.

Maier, S. F. (1993). Learned helplessness, fear, and anxiety. In C. Stanford & P. Salmon (Eds.), *Stress: An integrated approach.* San Diego, CA: Academic Press.

Maier, S. F., & Seligman, M. E. P. (1976). Learned helplessness: Theory and evidence. *Journal of Experimental Psychology: General, 105,* 3–46.

Maki, W. S. (1979). Discrimination learning without short- term memory: Dissociation of memory processes in pigeons. *Science, 204,* 83–85.

Maki, W. S., & Hegvik, D. K. (1980). Directed forgetting in pigeons. *Animal Learning & Behavior, 8,* 567–574.

Maki, W. S., Olson, D., & Rego, S. (1981). Directed forgetting in pigeons: Analysis of cue functions. *Animal Learning & Behavior, 9,* 189–195.

Malagodi, E. F., Gardner, M. L., & Palermo, G. (1978). Responding maintained under fixed-interval and fixed- time schedules of electric shock presentation. *Journal of the Experimental Analysis of Behavior, 30,* 271–279.

Malone, J. C., Jr. (1976). Local contrast and Pavlovian induction. *Journal of the Experimental Analysis of Behavior, 26,* 425–440.

Marcus, E. A., Nolen, T. G., Rankin, C. H., & Carew, T. J. (1988). Behavioral dissociation of dishabituation, sensitization, and inhibition in Aplysia. *Science, 241,* 210–213.

Margulies, S. (1961). Response duration in operant level, regular reinforcement, and extinction. *Journal of the Experimental Analysis of Behavior, 4,* 317–321.

Marler, P. (1970). A comparative approach to vocal learning: Song development in white-crowned sparrows. *Journal of Comparative and Physiological Psychology, 71,* 1–25.

Marler, P., & Nelson, D. A. (1993). Action-based learning: A new form of developmental plasticity in bird song. *Netherlands Journal of Zoology, 43,* 91–103.

Marler, P., & Peters, S. (1981). Sparrows learn adult song and more from memory. *Science, 213,* 780–782.

Marmaroff, S. (1971). *Reinforcement: A test of Premack's differential probability rules.* Unpublished master's thesis, Dalhousie University, Halifax, Nova Scotia.

Marr, J. (1993). Macht's nicht? A commentary on Staddon's "The conventional wisdom of behavior analysis." *Journal of the Experimental Analysis of Behavior, 60,* 473–476.

Marr, J. (1999). The whirligig of time: Some thoughts on Staddon and Higa. *Journal of the Experimental Analysis of Behavior, 71,* 281–284.

Marr, M. J. (1979). Second-order schedules and the generation of unitary response sequences. In M. D. Zeiler & P. Harzem (Eds.), *Advances in the analysis of behaviour* (vol. 1): *Reinforcement and the organization of behavior* (pp. 223–260). Chichester: Wiley.

Martens, B. K., Lochner, D. G., & Kelly, S. Q. (1992).

The effects of variable-interval reinforcement on academic engagement: A demonstration of matching theory. *Journal of Applied Behavior Analysis, 25,* 143–151.

Martin, G. L., England, G., Kaprowy, E., Kilgour, K., & Pilek, V. (1968). Operant conditioning of kindergarten- class behavior in autistic children. *Behaviour Research and Therapy, 6,* 281–294.

Martin, G., & Pear, J. (1999). *Behavior modification: What it is and how to do it* (Sixth edition). Englewood Cliffs, NJ: Prentice-Hall.

Martin, G., Yu D., Quinn, G., & Patterson, S. (1983). Measurement and training of AVC discrimination skills: Independent confirmation and extension. *Rehabilitation Psychology, 28,* 231–237.

Martin, I., & Levey, A. B. (1978). Evaluative conditioning. *Advances in Behaviour Research and Therapy, 23,* 57–101.

Marzke, M. W. (1997). Precision grips, hand morphology, and tools. *American Journal of Physical Anthropology, 102,* 91–110.

Maser, J. D., & Gallup, G. G., Jr. (1976). Tonic immobility in the chicken: Catalepsy potentiation by uncontrollable shock and alleviation by imipramine. *Psychosomatic Medicine, 36,* 199–205.

Masserman, J. H. (1946). *Principles of dynamic psychiatry*. Philadelphia: Saunders.

Mather, J. A., & Anderson, R. C. (1999). Exploration, play, and habituation in octopuses (*Octopus dofleini*). *Journal of Comparative Psychology, 113,* 333–338.

Mathews, B. A., Shimoff, E., Catania, A. C., & Sagvolden, T. (1977). Uninstructed human responding: Sensitivity to ratio and interval contingencies. *Journal of the Experimental Analysis of Behavior, 27,* 453–467.

Mathis, A., Chivers, D. P., & Smith, R. J. F. (1995). Chemical alarm signals: Predator deterrents or predator attractants?. *American Naturalist, 145,* 994–1005.

Mathis, A., & Smith, R. J. F. (1993). Fathead minnows, *Pimephales promelas*, learn to recognize northern pike, *Esox lucius*, as predators on the basis of chemical stimuli from minnows in the pike's diet. *Animal Behaviour, 46,* 645–656.

Matsuzawa, T. (1985). Use of numbers by a chimpanzee. *Nature, 315,* 57–59.

Matsuzawa, T. (1996). Chimpanzee intelligence in nature and in captivity: Isomorphism of symbol use and tool use. In W. C. McGrew, L. F. Marchant, & T. Nishida (Eds.), *Great ape societies*. Cambridge: Cambridge University Presss.

Matthews, L. R., & Temple, W. (1979). Concurrent-schedule assessment of food preferences in cows. *Journal of the Experimental Analysis of Behavior, 32,* 245–254.

Matzel, L. D., Schachtman, T. S., & Miller, R. R. (1985). Recovery of an overshadowed association achieved by extinction of the overshadowing stimulus. *Learning and Motivation, 16,* 398–412.

Mauro, B. C., & Mace, F. C. (1996). Differences in the effect of Pavlovian contingencies upon behavioral momentum using auditory versus visual stimuli. *Journal of the Experimental Analysis of Behavior, 65,* 389–399.

Mazur, A. (1986). U.S. trends in feminine beauty and overadaptation. *Journal of Sex Research, 22,* 281–303.

Mazur, J. E. (1975). The matching law and quantifications related to Premack's principle. *Journal of Experimental Psychology: Animal Behavior Processes, 1,* 374–386.

Mazur, J. E. (1982). A molecular approach to ratio schedule performance. In M. L. Commons, R. J. Herrnstein, & H. Rachlin (Eds.), *Quantitative analyses of behavior* (vol. 2): *Matching and maximizing accounts* (pp. 79–110). Cambridge, MA: Ballinger.

Mazur, J. E. (1985). Probability and delay of reinforcement as factors in discrete-trial choice. *Journal of the Experimental Analysis of Behavior, 43,* 341–351.

Mazur, J. E., & Logue, A. W. (1978). Choice in a "self-control" paradigm: Effects of a fading procedure. *Journal of the Experimental Analysis of Behavior, 30,* 11–17.

McCloskey, M. (1992). Special versus ordinary memory mechanisms in the genesis of flashbulb memories. In E. Winograd & U. Neisser (Eds.), *Affect and accuracy in recall: Studies of "flashbulb" memories* (pp. 227–235). New York: Cambridge University Press.

McCollough, C. (1965). Color adaptation of edge detectors in the human visual system. *Science, 149,* 1115–1116.

McDevitt, M. A., Spetch, M. L., & Dunn, R. (1997). Contiguity and conditioned reinforcement in probabilistic choice. *Journal of the Experimental Analysis of Behavior, 68,* 317–327.

McDowell, J. J. (1981). On the validity and utility of Herrnstein's hyperbola in applied behavior analysis. In C. M. Bradshaw, E. Szabadi, & C. F. Lowe (Eds.), *Quantification of steady-state operant behaviour* (pp. 311–324). Amsterdam: Elsevier/North-Holland Biomedical Press.

McFarland, D. J. (1970). Adjunctive behaviour in feeding and drinking situations. *Revue du Comportement Animal, 4,* 64–73.

McHose, J. H., & Ludvigson, H. W. (1965). Role of reward magnitude and incomplete reduction of reward magnitude in the frustration effect. *Journal of Experimental Psychology, 70,* 490–495.

McKearney, J. W. (1969). Fixed-interval schedules of electric shock presentation: Extinction and recovery of performance under different shock intensities and fixed- interval durations. *Journal of the Experimental Analysis of Behavior, 12,* 301–313.

McKearney, J. W. (1970). Responding under fixed-ratio and multiple fixed-interval fixed-ratio schedules of electric shock presentation. *Journal of the Experimental Analysis of Behavior, 14,* 1–6.

McKearney, J. W. (1974). Differences in responding under fixed-time and fixed-interval schedules of electric shock presentation. *Psychological Reports, 34,* 904–917.

McKearney, J. W., & Barrett, J. E. (1978). Schedule-controlled behavior and the effects of drugs. In D. E. Blackman & J. D. Sanger (Eds.), *Contemporary research in behavioral pharmacology*. New York: Plenum Press.

McKelvie, S. J., Sano, E. K., & Stout, D. (1994). Effects of colored separate and interactive pictures on cued recall. *Journal of General Psychology, 12,* 241–251.

McLean, A. P., & Blampied, N. M. (1995). Resistance to reinforcement change in multiple and concurrent schedules assessed in transition and at steady state. *Journal of the Experimental Analysis of Behavior, 63,* 1–17.

McLean, A. P., & White, K. G. (1981). Undermatching and contrast within components of multiple schedules. *Journal of the Experimental Analysis of Behavior, 35,* 283–291.

McLean, I. G., Lundie-Jenkins, G., & Jarman, P. J. (1995). Training captive rufous hare-wallabies to recognize predators. In M. Serena (Ed.), *Reintroduction biology of Australian and New Zealand fauna* (pp. 177–182). Chipping Norton, NSW, Australia: Surrey Beatty and Sons.

McNish, K. A., Betts, S. L., Brandon, S. E., & Wagner, A. R. (1997). Divergence of conditioned eyeblink and conditioned fear in backward Pavlovian training. *Animal Learning & Behavior, 25,* 43–42.

McSweeney, F. K. (1975). Matching and contrast on several concurrent treadle-press schedules. *Journal of the Experimental Analysis of Behavior, 23,* 193–198.

McSweeney, F. K. (1982). Prediction of concurrent treadle-pressing from simple schedule performance. *Behavior Analysis Letters, 2,* 11–20.

McSweeney, F. K. (1983). Positive behavioral contrast when pigeons press treadles during multiple schedules. *Journal of the Experimental Analysis of Behavior, 39,* 149–156.

McSweeney, F. K. (1992). Rate of reinforcement and session duration as determinants of within-session patterns of responding. *Animal Learning & Behavior, 20,* 160–169.

McSweeney, F. K., & Hinson, J. M. (1992). Patterns of responding within sessions. *Journal of the Experimental Analysis of Behavior, 58,* 19–36.

McSweeney, F. K., Hinson, J. M., & Cannon, C. B. (1996). Sensitization-habituation may occur during operant conditioning. *Psychological Bulletin, 120,* 193–198.

McSweeney, F. K., & Johnson, K. S. (1994). The effect of time between sessions on within-session patterns of responding. *Behavioural Processes, 31,* 207-218.

McSweeney, F. K., & Melville, C. L. (1991). Behavioral contrast as a function of component duration for leverpressing using a within-session procedure. *Animal Learning & Behavior, 19,* 71-80.

McSweeney, F. K. & Roll, J. M. (1993). Responding changes systematically within sessions during conditioning procedures. *Journal of the Experimental Analysis of Behavior, 60,* 621–640.

McSweeney, F. K., Roll, J. M., & Cannon, C. B. (1994). The generality of within-sessions patterning of responding: Rate of reinforcement and session length. *Animal Learning & Behavior, 22,* 252–266.

McSweeney, F. K., & Swindell, S. (1999). General-process theories of motivation revisited: The role of habituation.. *Psychological Bulletin, 125,* 437–457.

McSweeney, F. K., Swindell, S., & Weatherly, J. N. (1996 a). Within-session changes in responding during autoshaping and automaintenance procedures. *Journal of the Experimental Analysis of Behavior, 66,* 51–61.

McSweeney, F. K., Swindell, S., & Weatherly, J. N. (1996 b). Within-session changes in adjunctive and instrumental responding. *Learning and Motivation, 27,* 408–427.

McSweeney, F. K., Swindell, S., & Weatherly, J. N. (1999). Within-session response patterns during variable interval, random reinforcement, and extinction procedures. *Learning and Motivation, 30,* 221–240.

McSweeney, F. K., & Weatherly, J. N. (1998). Habituation to the reinforcer may contribute to multiple-schedule behavioral contrast. *Journal of the Experimental Analysis of Behavior, 69,* 199–221.

McSweeney, F. K., Weatherly, J. N., & Roll, J. M. (1995). Within-session changes in responding during concurrent schedules that employ two different operanda. *Animal Learning & Behavior, 23,* 237–244.

McSweeney, F. K., Weatherly, J. N., Roll, J. M., & Swindell, S. (1995). Within-session patterns of responding when the operandum changes during the session. *Learning and Motivation, 26,* 403–420.

McSweeney, F. K., Weatherly, J. N., & Swindell, S. (1995). Prospective factors contribute little to within-session changes in responding. *Psychonomic Bulletin & Review, 2,* 234–238.

Mechner, F. (1958). Probability relations within response sequences under ratio reinforcement. *Journal of the Experimental Analysis of Behavior, 1,* 109–122.

Mechner, F., & Guevrekian, L. (1962). Effects of deprivation upon counting and timing in rats. *Journal of the Experimental Analysis of Behavior, 5,* 463–466.

Meck, W. H., & Church, R. M. (1983). A mode control model of counting and timing processes. *Journal of Experimental Psychology: Animal Behavior Processes, 9,* 320–334.

Medin, D. L., Reynolds, T. J., & Parkinson, J. K. (1980). Stimulus similarity and retroactive interference and facilitation in monkey short-term memory. *Journal of Experimental Psychology: Animal Behavior Processes, 6,* 112–125.

Mehiel, R., & Bolles, R. C. (1984). Learned flavor preferences based on caloric outcome. *Animal Learning & Behavior, 12,* 421–427.

Mehiel, R., & Bolles, R. C. (1988a). Hedonic shift learning based on calories. *Bulletin of the Psychonomic Society, 26,* 459–462.

Mehiel, R., & Bolles, R. C. (1988b). Learned flavor preferences based on calories are independent of initial hedonic value. *Animal Learning & Behavior, 16,* 383–387.

Melchior, C. L. (1990). Conditioned tolerance provides protection against ethanol lethality. *Pharmacology, Biochemistry & Behavior, 37,* 205–206.

Mellgren, R. L., & Elsmore, T. F. (1991). Extinction of operant behavior: An analysis based on foraging considerations. *Animal Learning & Behavior, 19,* 317–325.

Mellitz, M., Hineline, P. N., Whitehouse, W. G., & Laurence, M. T. (1983). Duration-reduction of avoidance sessions as negative reinforcement. *Journal of the Experimental Analysis of Behavior, 40,* 57–67.

Meltzer, D. (1983). Conditional discrimination with ambiguous stimuli. *Journal of the Experimental Analysis of Behavior, 39,* 241–249.

Meltzer, D., & Tiller, J. E. (1979). Bar press and bar release as avoidance responses. *Journal of the Experimental Analysis of Behavior, 31,* 373–381.

Mendelson, J., & Chillag, D. (1970). Schedule-induced air licking in rats. *Physiology & Behavior, 5,* 535–537.

Menzel, R., Erber, J., & Mashur, T., (1974). Learning and memory in the honeybee. In L.B. Browne (Ed.), *Experimental analysis of insect behaviour* (pp. 195–217). New York: Springer-Verlag.

Merrick, N. J. (1977). Social grooming and play behavior of a captive group of chimpanzees. *Primates, 18,* 215–224.

Messenger, J. B., & Sanders, G. (1972). Visual preference and two cue discrimination learning in Octopus. *Animal Behaviour, 20,* 580–585.

Messick, D. M. (1999). Alternative logics for decision making in social situations. *Journal of Economic Behavior and Organization, 39,* 11–28.

Metz, J. R. (1965). Conditioning generalized imitation in autistic children. *Journal of Experimental Child Psychology, 3,* 389–399.

Meyer, D. R., Cho, C., & Weseman, A. F. (1960). On problems of conditioned discriminated lever-press avoidance responses. *Psychological Review, 67,* 224–228.

Meyerson, L., & Michael, J. (1964). Assessment of hearing by operant conditioning. In *Report of the proceedings of the International Congress on Education of the Deaf* (pp. 237–242). Washington, DC: U.S. Govt. Printing Office.

Michael, J. (1975). Positive and negative reinforcement, a distinction that is no longer useful; or, a better way to talk about bad things. *Behaviorism, 3,* 33–44.

Michael, J. (1982). Distinguishing between the discriminative and motivational functions of stimuli. *Journal of the Experimental Analysis of Behavior, 37,* 149–155.

Michael, J. (1993). Establishing operations. *Behavior Analyst, 16,* 191–206.

Midgely, M., Lea, S. E., & Kirby, R. M. (1989). Algorithmic shaping and misbehavior in the acquisition of token deposit of rats. *Journal of the Experimental Analysis of Behavior, 52,* 27–40.

Miles, H. L. (1983). Apes and language: The search for communicative competence. In J. de Luce & H. T. Wilder (Eds.), *Language in primates: Implications for linguistics, anthropology, psychology and philosophy* (pp. 592–597). New York: Springer-Verlag.

Miles, L., Mitchell, R., & Mitchell, R., & Harper, S. (1992). *Imitation and self-awareness in a signing orangutan.* Paper presented at the XIV Congress of the International Primatological Society, Strasbourg, August.

Milinski, M., & Heller, R. (1978). Influence of a predator on the optimal foraging behaviour of sticklebacks (*Gasterosteus aculeatus*). *Nature, 275,* 642–644.

Millard, W. J. (1979). Stimulus properties of conspecific behavior. *Journal of the Experimental Analysis of Behavior, 32,* 283–296.

Millenson, J. R., Allen, R. B., & Pinker, S. (1977). Adjunctive drinking during variable and random-interval food reinforcement schedules. *Animal Learning & Behavior, 5,* 285–290.

Millenson, J. R., & Hurwitz, H. M. B. (1961). Some temporal and sequential properties of behavior during conditioning and extinction. *Journal of the Experimental Analysis of Behavior, 4,* 97–106.

Miller, G.A. (1956). The magical number seven, plus or minus two: Some limits on our capacity for processing information. *Psychological Review, 63,* 81–97.

Miller, H. L., Jr. (1976). Matching-based hedonic scaling in the pigeon. *Journal of the Experimental Analysis of Behavior, 26,* 335–347.

Miller, H. L., & Loveland, D. H. (1974). Matching when the number of response alternatives is large. *Animal Learning & Behavior, 2,* 106–110.

Miller, J. S., & Gollub, L. R. (1974). Adjunctive and operant bolt pecking in the pigeon. *The Psychological Record, 24,* 203–208.

Miller, L., & Ackley, R. (1970). Summation of responding maintained by fixed-interval schedules. *Journal of the Experimental Analysis of Behavior, 13,* 199–203.

Miller, N., & Neuringer, A. (2000). Reinforcing variability in adolescents with autism. *Journal of Applied Behavior Analysis, 33.*

Miller, N. E. (1960). Learning resistance to pain and fear effects over learning, exposure, and rewarded exposure in context. *Journal of Experimental Psychology, 60,* 137–145.

Miller, N. E., & Dollard, J. (1941). *Social learning and imitation.* New Haven: Yale University Press.

Miller, R. R., Barnet, R. C., & Grahame, N. J. (1995). Assessment of the Rescorla-Wagner model. *Psychological Bulletin, 117,* 363–386.

Miller, R. R., & Matzel, L. D. (1988). The comparator hypothesis: A response rule for the expression of associations. In G. H. Bower (Ed.), *The psychology of learning and motivation* (vol. 22) (pp. 51–92). New York: Academic Press.

Mineka, S., & Cook, M. (1988). Social learning and the acquisition of snake fear in monkeys. In T. R. Zentall & B. G. Galef, Jr. (Eds.), *Social learning: Psychologi-*

cal and biological perspectives (pp. 51–73). Hillsdale, NJ: Erlbaum.

Minor, T. R. (1987). Stimulus- and pellet-induced drinking during a successive discrimination. *Journal of the Experimental Analysis of Behavior, 48,* 61–80.

Minor, T. R., & Coulter, X. (1982). Associative and post-prandial control of schedule-induced drinking: Implications for the study of interim behavior. *Animal Learning & Behavior, 10,* 455–464.

Minor, T. R., Dess, N. K., & Overmier, J. B. (1991). Inverting the traditional view of "learned helplessness." In M. R. Denny (Ed.), *Fear, avoidance, and phobias* (pp. 87–134). Hillsdale, NJ: Erlbaum.

Minor, T. R., Jackson, R. L., & Maier, S. F. (1984). Effects of task-irrelevant cues and reinforcement delay on choice-escape learning following inescapable shock: Evidence for a deficit in selective attention. *Journal of Experimental Psychology: Animal Behavior Processes, 10,* 543–556.

Mischel, W. (1974). Processes in delay of gratification. In L. Berkowitz (Ed.), *Advances in Experimental Social Psychology* (vol. 7, pp. 249–292). New York: Academic Press.

Mischel, W., Ebbesen, E. B., & Zeiss, A. (1972). Cognitive and attentional mechanisms in delay of gratification. *Journal of Personality and Social Psychology, 21,* 204–218.

Mischel, W., & Staub, E. (1965). Effects on expectancy on working and waiting for larger rewards. *Journal of Personality and Social Psychology, 2,* 625–633.

Mishkin, M., Prockop, E. S., & Rosvold, H. E. (1962). One-trial object-discrimination learning in monkeys with frontal lesions. *Journal of Comparative and Physiological Psychology, 55,* 178–181.

Moise, S. L. (1970). Short term retention in *Macaca speciosa* following interpolated activity during delayed matching from sample. *Journal of Comparative and Physiological Psychology, 73,* 506–514.

Møller, A. P. (1988). False alarm calls as a means of resource usurption in the great tit *Parus major. Ethology, 79,* 25–30.

Møller, A. P. (1992). Female swallow preference for symmetrical male sexual ornaments. *Nature, 357,* 238–240.

Mollon, J. D. (1989). "Tho' she kneel'd in that place where they grew . . . " The uses and origins of primate color vision. *Journal of Experimental Biology, 146,* 21–38.

Moltz, H. (1955). Latent extinction and the reduction of secondary reward value. *Journal of Experimental Psychology, 49,* 395–400.

Montgomery, K. C. (1953). The effect of activity deprivation upon exploratory behavior. *Journal of Comparative and Physiological Psychology, 46,* 438–441.

Moore, B. R. (1973). The role of directed Pavlovian reactions in simple instrumental learning in the pigeon. In R. A. Hinde, & J. Stevenson-Hinde (Eds.), *Constraints on learning* (pp. 159–188). New York: Academic Press.

Moore, B. R. (1992). Avian movement imitation and a new form of mimicry: Tracing the evolution of a complex form of learning. *Behaviour, 122,* 231–263.

Moore, J. (1979). Choice and number of reinforcers. *Journal of the Experimental Analysis of Behavior, 32,* 51–63.

Moore, J. (1984). Choice and transformed inter-reinforcement intervals. *Journal of the Experimental Analysis of Behavior, 42,* 321–335.

Moreau, R., & Moreau, W. (1944). Do young birds play? *Ibis, 86,* 93–94.

Morgan, D. L., & Lee, K. (1996). Extinction-induced response variability in humans. *The Psychological Record, 46,* 145–159.

Morgan, M. J. (1974). Resistance to satiation. *Animal Behaviour, 22,* 449–466.

Morse, W. H. (1966). Intermittent reinforcement. In W. K. Honig (Ed.), *Operant behavior: Areas of research and application* (pp. 52–108). New York: Appleton-Century-Crofts.

Morse, W. H., & Kelleher, R. T. (1970). Schedules as fundamental determinants of behavior. In W. N. Schoenfeld (Ed.), *Theory of reinforcement schedules* (pp. 139–185). Englewood Cliffs, NJ: Prentice-Hall.

Morse, W. H., & Kelleher, R. T. (1977). Determinants of reinforcement and punishment. In W. K. Honig & J. E. R. Staddon (Eds.), *Handbook of Operant Behavior* (pp. 174–200). Englewood Cliffs, NJ: Prentice-Hall.

Morse, W. H., Mead, R. N., & Kelleher, R. T. (1967). Modulation of elicited behavior by a fixed-interval schedule of electric shock presentation. *Science, 157,* 215–217.

Morse, W. H., & Skinner, B. F. (1957). A second type of superstition in the pigeon. *American Journal of Psychology, 70,* 308–311.

Mowrer, O. H. (1938). Preparatory set expectancy—A determinant in motivation and learning. *Psychological Review, 45,* 62–91.

Mowrer, O. H. (1950). *Learning theory and personality dynamics.* New York: The Ronald Press.

Mowrer, O. H. (1960). *Learning theory and the symbolic process.* New York: Wiley.

Mowrer, O. H., & Aiken, E. G. (1954). Contiguity vs. drive reduction in conditioned fear: Temporal variations in conditioned and unconditioned stimulus. *American Journal of Psychology, 67,* 26–38.

Mowrer, O. H., & Lamoreaux, R. R. (1942). Avoidance conditioning and signal duration—a study of secondary motivation and reward. *Psychological Monographs, 54,*(5, 247).

Moynihan, M. (1964). Some behavior patterns of platyrrhine monkeys. I. The night monkey (*Aotus trivirgatus*). *Smithsonian Miscellaneous Collection, 146,* 1–84.

Moynihan, M. (1970). Some behavior patterns of platyrrhine monkeys. II. *Saguinus geoffroyi* and some other tamarins. *Smithsonian Contributions to Zoology, 28,* 1–77.

Mpitsos, G. J, & Collins, S. D. (1975). Learning: Rapid aversion conditioning in the gastropod mollusc Pleurobranchaea. *Science, 188,* 954–957.

Mueller, K. L., & Dinsmoor, J. A. (1984). Testing the reinforcing properties of S-: A replication of Lieberman's procedure. *Journal of the Experimental Analysis of Behavior, 41,* 17–25.

Muller, P. G., Crow, R. E., & Cheney, C. D. (1979). Schedule-induced locomotor activity in humans. *Journal of the Experimental Analysis of Behavior, 31,* 83–90.

Müller-Schwarze, D. (1984). Analysis of play behavior: What do we measure and when? In P.K. Smith (Ed.), *Play in animals and humans* (pp. 147–158). Oxford: Basil Blackwell.

Munn, C. A. (1986). Birds that 'cry wolf'. *Nature, 319,* 143–145.

Murch, G. M. (1976). Classical conditioning of the McCollough effect: Temporal parameters. *Vision Research, 16,* 615–619.

Murdoch, W. W. (1969). Switching in general predators: Experiments on predator specificity and stability of prey populations. *Ecological Monographs, 39,* 335–354.

Murdock, B. B. (1960). The distinctiveness of stimuli. *Psychological Review, 67,* 16–31.

Myerson, J., & Christiansen, B. (1979). Temporal control of eating on periodic water schedules. *Physiology & Behavior, 23,* 279–282.

Myerson, J., & Hale, S. (1984). Practical implications of the matching law. *Journal of Applied Behavior Analysis, 17,* 367–380.

Nairne, J. S., & Rescorla, R. A. (1981). Second-order conditioning with diffuse auditory reinforcers in the pigeon. *Learning and Motivation, 12,* 65–91.

Naish, K.-A., Carvalho G. R., & Pitcher, T. J. (1993). The genetic structure and microdistribution of shoals of *Phoxinus phoxinus,* the European minnow. *Journal of Fish Biology (Suppl. A), 43,* 75–89.

Neef, N. A., Shade, D., & Miller, M. S. (1994). Assessing influential dimensions of reinforcers on choice in students with severe emotional disturbance. *Journal of Applied Behavior Analysis, 27,* 575–583.

Neisser, U. (1967). *Cognitive psychology.* New York: Appleton-Century-Crofts.

Neisser, U., & Harsch, N. (1992). Phantom flashbulbs: False recollections of hearing the news about *Challenger.* In E. Winograd & U. Neisser (Eds.), *Affect and accuracy in recall: Studies of "flashbulb" memories* (pp. 9–31). New York: Cambridge University Press.

Nelson, M. C. (1971). Classical conditioning in the blowfly (*Phormia regina*): Associative and excitatory factors. *Journal of Comparative and Physiological Psychology, 77,* 353–368.

Neuringer, A. J. (1967). Effects of reinforcement magnitude on choice and rate of responding. *Journal of the Experimental Analysis of Behavior, 10,* 417–424.

Neuringer, A. J. (1969). Delayed reinforcement versus reinforcement after a fixed interval. *Journal of the Experimental Analysis of Behavior, 12,* 375–383.

Neuringer, A. J. (1970). Superstitious key pecking after three peck-produced reinforcements. *Journal of the Experimental Analysis of Behavior, 13,* 127–134.

Neuringer, A. (1992). Choosing to vary and repeat. *Psychological Science, 3,* 246–250.

Neuringer, A., Deiss, C., & Olson, G. (2000). Reinforced variability and operant learning. *Journal of Experimental Psychology: Animal Behavior Processes, 26,* 98–111.

Nevin, J. A. (1967). Effects of reinforcement scheduling on simultaneous discrimination performance. *Journal of the Experimental Analysis of Behavior, 10,* 251–260.

Nevin, J. A. (1971). Rates and patterns of responding with concurrent fixed-interval and variable-interval reinforcement. *Journal of the Experimental Analysis of Behavior, 16,* 241–247.

Nevin, J. A. (1974). Response strength in multiple schedules. *Journal of the Experimental Analysis of Behavior, 21,* 389–408.

Nevin, J. A. (1984). Quantitative analysis. *Journal of the Experimental Analysis of Behavior, 42,* 421–434.

Nevin, J. A. (1988). Behavioral momentum and the partial reinforcement effect. *Psychological Bulletin, 103,* 44–56.

Nevin, J. A. (1992). An integrative model for the study of behavioral momentum. *Journal of the Experimental Analysis of Behavior, 57,* 301–316.

Nevin, J. A., Cumming, W. W., & Berryman, R. (1963). Ratio reinforcement of matching behavior. *Journal of the Experimental Analysis of Behavior, 6,* 149–154.

Nevin, J. A., Mandell, C., & Atak, J. R. (1983). The analysis of behavioral momentum. *Journal of the Experimental Analysis of Behavior, 39,* 49–59.

Nevin, J. A., & Shettleworth, S. J. (1966). An analysis of contrast effects in multiple schedules. *Journal of the Experimental Analysis of Behavior, 9,* 305–315.

Nevin, J. A., Tota, M. E., Torquato, R. D., & Shull, R. L. (1990). Alternative reinforcement increases resistance to change: Pavlovian or operant contingencies? *Journal of the Experimental Analysis of Behavior, 53,* 359–379.

Newman, J. A., & Caraco, T. (1987). Foraging, predation hazard, and patch use in grey squirrels. *Animal Behaviour, 35,* 1804–1813.

Newmeyer, F. J. (1998). On the supposed "counter-functionality" of Universal Grammer: Some evolutionary implications. In J. R. Hurford, M. Studdert-Kennedy, & C. Knight (Eds.), *Approaches to the evolution of language: Social and cognitive bases* (pp. 305–319). Cambridge: Cambridge University Press.

Nice, M. M. (1943). Studies in the life history of the song sparrow: The behavior of the song sparrow and other passerines (vol. 2). *Transactions of the Linnaean Society of New York,* No. 6. New York: Dover.

Nissen, H. W., Blum, J. S., & Blum, R. A. (1948). Analysis of matching behavior in chimpanzee. *Journal of Comparative and Physiological Psychology, 41,* 62–74.

Nolte, D. L., & Provenza, F. D. (1992). Food preferences in lambs after exposure to flavors in milk. *Applied Animal Behavioral Science, 32*, 381–389.

Notterman, J. M., Schoenfeld, W. N., & Bersh, P. J. (1952). Conditioned heart rate responses in humans during experimental anxiety. *Journal of Comparative and Physiological Psychology, 45*, 1–8.

Oden, D. L., Thompson, R. K. R., & Premack, D. (1990). Infant chimpanzees (*Pan troglodytes*) spontaneously perceive both concrete and abstract same/different relations. *Child Development, 61*, 621–631.

O'Donald, P. (1962). The theory of sexual selection. *Heredity, 17*, 541–552.

O'Donald, P. (1967). A general model of sexual and natural selection. *Heredity, 22*, 499–518.

O'Donald, P. (1977). Theoretical aspects of sexual selection. *Theoretical Population Biology, 12*, 298–334.

O'Donohue, W. T., Callaghan, G. M., & Ruckstuhl, L. E. (1998). Epistemological barriers to radical behaviorism. *The Behavior Analyst, 21*, 307–320.

Oei, T. P. S., Singer, G., & Jefferys, D. (1980). The interaction of a fixed time food delivery schedule and body weight on self-administration of narcotic analgesics. *Psychopharmacology, 67*, 171–176.

Öhman, A., Eriksson, A., & Olofsson, C. (1975). One-trial learning and superior resistance to extinction of autonomic responses conditioned to potentially phobic stimuli. *Journal of Comparative and Physiological Psychology, 88*, 619–627.

Öhman, A., Fredrikson, M., Hugdahl, K., & Rimmo, P.-A. (1976). The premise of equipotentiality in human classical conditioning: Conditioned electrodermal responses to potentially phobic stimuli. *Journal of Experimental Psychology: General, 105*, 313–337.

Olton, D. S. (1977). Spatial memory. *Scientific American, 236*(6), 82–98.

Olton, D. S. (1978). Characteristics of spatial memory. In S. H. Hulse, H. Fowler & W. K. Honig (Eds.), *Cognitive processes in animal behavior.* Hillsdale, NJ: Erlbaum.

Olton, D. S., & Collison, C. (1979). Intramaze cues and "odor trails" fail to direct choice behavior on an elevated maze. *Animal Learning & Behavior, 7*, 221–223.

Olton, D. S., Handelman, G. E., & Walker, J. A. (1981). Spatial memory and food-searching strategies. In A. C. Kamil & T. D. Sargent (Eds.), *Foraging Behavior: Ecological, ethological, and psychological approaches* (pp. 333–354). New York: Garland.

Olton, D. S., & Samuelson, R. J. (1976). Remembrance of places past: Spatial memory in rats. *Journal of Experimental Psychology: Animal Behavior Processes, 2*, 97–116.

Ornitz, E. M., & Guthrie, D. (1989). Long-term habituation and sensitization of the acoustic startle response in the normal adult human. *Psychophysiology, 26*, 166–173.

Osgood, C. E. (1946). Meaningful similarity and interference in learning. *Journal of Experimental Psychology, 36*, 277–301.

Osgood, C. E. (1949). The similarity paradox in human learning: A resolution. *Psychological Review, 56*, 132–143.

Ostrom, E. (1998). A behavioural approach to the rational choice theory of collective action: Presidential address. *The American Political Science Review, 92*, 1–22.

Overmier, J. B., & Seligman, M. E. P. (1967). Effects of inescapable shock upon subsequent escape and avoidance learning. *Journal of Comparative and Physiological Psychology, 63*, 23–33.

Owren, M. J., & Scheuneman, D. L. (1993). An inexpensive habituation and sensitization learning laboratory exercise using planarians. *Teaching of Psychology, 20*, 226–228.

Pace, G. M., Ivancic, M. T., Edwards, G. L., Iwata, B. A., & Page, T. J. (1985). Assessment of stimulus preference and reinforcer value with profoundly retarded individuals. *Journal of Applied Behavior Analysis, 18*, 249–255.

Packer, C. (1979). Male dominance and reproductive activity in Papio anubis. *Animal Behaviour, 27*, 37–45.

Packer, C. (1980). Male care and exploitation in Papio anubis. *Animal Behaviour, 28*, 512–520.

Page, H. A., & Hall, G. F. (1953). Experimental extinction as a function of the prevention of a response. *Journal of Comparative and Physiological Psychology, 46*, 33–34.

Page, S., & Neuringer, A. (1985). Variability is an operant. *Journal of Experimental Psychology: Animal Behavior Processes, 11*, 429–452.

Palfai, T., Kutscher, C. L., & Symons, J. P. (1971). Schedule-induced polydipsia in the mouse. *Physiology & Behavior, 6*, 461–462.

Palya, W. L., & Zacny, J. P. (1980). Stereotyped adjunctive pecking by caged pigeons. *Animal Learning & Behavior, 8*, 293–303.

Panlilio, L. V., Weiss, S. J., & Schindler, C. W. (1998). Motivational effects of compounding discriminative stimuli associated with food and cocaine. *Psychopharmacology, 136*, 70–74.

Papini, M. R., & Dudley, R. T. (1997). Consequences of surprising reward omissions. *Review of General Psychology, 1*, 175–197.

Papini, M. R., Mustaca, A. E., & Bitterman, M. E. (1988). Successive negative contrast in the consummatory responding of didelphid marsupials. *Animal Learning & Behavior, 16*, 53–57.

Parker, G. A., & Stuart, R. A. (1976). Animal behaviour as a strategy optimizer: Evolution of resource assessment strategies and optimal emigration thresholds. *American Naturalist, 110*, 1055–1076.

Parsons, J. A., & Ferraro, D. P. (1977). Complex interactions: A functional approach. In B. C. Etzel, J. M. LeBlanc, & D. M. Baer (Eds.), *New developments in behavioral research: Theory, method, and application. In honor of Sidney W. Bijou* (pp. 237–245). Hillsdale, NJ: Erlbaum.

Parsons, J. A., Taylor, D. C., & Joyce, T. M. (1981). Precurrent self-prompting operants in children: Remembering. *Journal of the Experimental Analysis of Behavior, 36,* 253–266.

Patten, R. L., & Myers, D. B. (1970). Number of training trials and frustration effects of nonzero reward reductions in the double alley. *Psychonomic Science, 18,* 291–292.

Patterson, F. G. (1978). Linguistic capabilities of a lowland gorilla. In F. C. C. Peng (Ed.), *Sign language and language acquisition in man and ape: New dimensions in comparative pedolinguistics* (pp. 161–201). Boulder, CO: Westview Press.

Paul, C. (1983). Sample-specific ratio effects in matching to sample. *Journal of the Experimental Analysis of Behavior, 39,* 77–85.

Paivio, A. (1971). *Imagery and verbal processes.* New York: Holt, Rinehart and Winston.

Paivio, A. (1995). Imagery and memory. In M. S. Gazzaniga (Ed.), *The cognitive neurosciences* (pp. 977–986). Cambridge, MA: MIT Press.

Pavlov, I. P. (1927). *Conditioned reflexes: An investigation of the physiological activity of the cerebral cortex* (trans: G. V. Anrep). London: Oxford University Press.

Pavlov, I. P. (1955). *Selected works* (trans: S. Belsky). Moscow: Foreign Languages Printing House.

Payne, R., & Guinee, L. (1983). Humpback whale (*Megaptera novaeangliae*) songs as an indication of "stocks." In R. Payne (Ed.), *Communication and behavior of whales* (pp. 333–358). Boulder, CO: Westview Press.

Pear, J. J. (1975). Implications of the matching law for ratio responding. *Journal of the Experimental Analysis of Behavior, 23,* 139–140.

Pear, J. J. (1983). Relative reinforcements for cognitive and behavioral terminologies. *The Psychological Record, 33,* 20–25.

Pear, J. J. (1985). Spatiotemporal patterns of behavior produced by variable-interval schedules of reinforcement. *Journal of the Experimental Analysis of Behavior, 44,* 217–231.

Pear, J. J. (1988). Behavioral stereotypy and the generalized matching equation. *Journal of the Experimental Analysis of Behavior, 50,* 87–95.

Pear, J. J., & Eldridge, G. D. (1984). The operant-respondent distinction: Future directions. *Journal of the Experimental Analysis of Behavior, 42,* 453–467.

Pear, J. J., Hemingway, M. J., & Keizer, P. (1978). Lever attacking and pressing as a function of conditioning and extinguishing a lever-press avoidance response in rats. *Journal of the Experimental Analysis of Behavior, 29,* 273–282.

Pear, J. J., & Legris, J. A. (1987). Shaping by automated tracking of an arbitrary operant response. *Journal of the Experimental Analysis of Behavior, 47,* 241–247.

Pear, J. J., Moody, J. E., & Persinger, M.A. (1972). Lever attacking by rats during free-operant avoidance. *Journal of the Experimental Analysis of Behavior, 18,* 517–523.

Pear, J. J., & Wilkie, D. M. (1971). Contrast and induc-

tion in rats on multiple schedules. *Journal of the Experimental Analysis of Behavior, 15,* 289–296.

Pecoraro, N. C., Timberlake, W. D., & Tinsley, M. (1999). Incentive downshifts evoke search repertoires in rats. *Journal of Experimental Psychology: Animal Behavior Processes, 25,* 153–167.

Peden, B. F., Browne, M. P., & Hearst, E. (1977). Persistent approaches to a signal for food despite food omission for approaching. *Journal of Experimental Psychology: Animal Behavior Processes, 3,* 377–399.

Peeke, H. V., & Dark, K. A. (1990). The effects of isolation on the sensitization and habituation of aggression on the threespine stickleback (*Gasterosteus aculeatus*). *Ethology, 85,* 35–42.

Pellon, R., & Blackman, D. E. (1987). Punishment of schedule-induced drinking in rats by signaled and unsignaled delays in food presentation. *Journal of the Experimental Analysis of Behavior, 48,* 417–434.

Penney, J., & Schull, J. (1977). Functional differentiation of adjunctive drinking and wheel running in rats. *Animal Learning & Behavior, 5,* 272–280.

Pepperberg, I. M. (1981). Functional vocalizations by an African Grey parrot (*Psittacus erithacus*). *Zeitschrift für Tierpsychologie, 55,* 139–160.

Pepperberg, I. M. (1983). Cognition in the African grey parrot: Preliminary evidence for auditory/vocal comprehension of the class concept. *Animal Learning & Behavior, 11,* 179–185.

Pepperberg, I. M. (1987 a). Evidence for conceptual quantitative abilities in the African grey parrot: Labeling of cardinal sets. *Ethology, 75,* 37–61.

Pepperberg, I. M. (1987 b). Interspecies communication: A tool for assessing conceptual abilities in the African Grey parrot (*Psittacus erithacus*). In G. Greenberg & E. Tobach (Eds.), *Language, cognition, consciousness: Integrative levels* (pp. 31–61). Hillsdale, NJ: Erlbaum.

Pepperberg, I. M. (1988). An interactive modeling technique for acquisition of communication skills: Separation of "labelling" and "requesting" in a psittacine subject. *Applied Psycholinguistics, 9,* 59–76.

Pepperberg, I. M. (1989). Tool use in birds: An avian monkey wrench? *Behavioral and Brain Sciences, 12,* 604–605.

Perone, M., & Courtney, K. (1992). Fixed-ratio pausing: Joint effects of past reinforcer magnitude and stimuli correlated with upcoming magnitude. *Journal of the Experimental Analysis of Behavior, 57,* 33–46.

Pert, A., & Gonzalez, R. C. (1974). Behavior of the turtle (*Chrysemys picta picta*) in simultaneous, successive, and behavioral contrast situations. *Journal of Comparative and Physiological Psychology, 87,* 526–538.

Petersen, M. R., & Lyon, D. O. (1978). Schedule-induced polydipsia in rats living in an operant environment. *Journal of the Experimental Analysis of Behavior, 29,* 493–503.

Peterson, G. B., Ackil, J. E., Frommer, G. P., & Hearst, E. S. (1972). Conditioned approach and contact behavior toward signals for food or brain-stimulation reinforcement. *Science, 177,* 1009–1011.

Peterson, N. (1960). Control of behavior by presentation of an imprinted stimulus. *Science, 132,* 1395–1396.

Peterzell, D. H. (1993). Individual differences in the visual attention of human infants: Further evidence for separate sensitization and habituation processes. *Developmental Psychobiology, 26,* 207–218.

Petrinovich, L. (1988). The role of social factors in white- crowned sparrow song development. In T. R. Zentall & B. G. Galef, Jr. (Eds.), *Social learning: Psychological and biological perspectives* (pp. 255–278). Hillsdale, NJ: Erlbaum.

Petrinovich, L., & Baptista, L. F. (1984). Song dialects, mate selection, and breeding success in white-crowned sparrows. *Animal Behaviour, 32,* 1078–1088.

Petrinovich, L., & Baptista, L. F. (1987). Song development in the white-crowned sparrow: Modification of learned song. *Animal Behaviour, 35,* 961–974.

Petrinovich, L., & Peeke, H. V. (1973). Habituation to territorial song in the white-crowned sparrow (*Zonotrichia levcophyrs*). *Behavioral Biology, 8,* 743–748.

Petter, J.-J., & Petter, A. (1967). The aye-aye of Madagascar. In S. A. Altman (Ed.), *Social communication among primates* (pp. 195–205). Chicago: University of Chicago Press.

Pezdek, K., Finger, K., & Hodge, D. (1997). Planting false childhood memories: The role of event plausibility. *Psychological Science, 8,* 437–441.

Pfeiffer, W. (1962). The fright reaction of fish. *Biology Review, 37,* 495–511.

Pfeiffer, W. (1963a). Alarm substances. *Experentia, 19,* 113–123.

Pfeiffer, W. (1963b). The fright reaction in North American fish.. *Canadian Journal of Zoology, 41,* 69–77.

Pfennig, D. W., et al. (1983). The mechanism of nestmate discrimination in social wasps (*Polistes,* Hymenoptera: Vespidae). *Behavioral Ecology and Sociobiology, 13,* 299–305.

Piaget, J. (1945/1951). *Play, dreams and imitation in childhood.* (Trans: C. Gategno & F. M. Hodgson). London: Heinemann.

Pierce, W. D., Epling, W. F., & Greer, S. M. (1981). Human communication and the matching law. In C. M. Bradshaw, E. Szabadi, & C. F. Lowe (Eds.), *Quantification of steady-state operant behavior* (pp. 345–352). Amsterdam: Elsevier/North Holland Biomedical Press.

Pierrel, R. A. (1958). Generalization gradient for auditory intensity in the rat. *Journal of the Experimental Analysis of Behavior, 1,* 303–313.

Pierrel, R., & Sherman, J. G. (1963). Barnabus, the rat with college training. *Brown Alumni Monthly,* February, 8–14.

Pigeot, N. (1990). Technical and social actors: Flint knapping specialists and apprentices at Magdalenian Etiolles. *Archaeological Review Cambridge, 9,* 126–141.

Pinel, J. P. J., & Mana, M. J. (1989). Adaptive interactions of rats with dangerous inanimate objects: Support for a cognitive theory of defensive behavior. In R. J. Blanchard, P. F. Brain, D. C. Blanchard, & S. Parmigiani (Eds.), *Ethoexperimental approaches to the study of behavior* (NATO ASI Series D, vol. 48) (pp. 137–150). Boston: Kluwer Academic.

Pinel, J. P. J., & Treit, D. (1978). Burying as a defensive response in rats. *Journal of Comparative and Physiological Psychology, 92,* 708–712.

Pinker, S. (1991). Rules of language. *Science, 253,* 530–535.

Pinker, S. (1994a). *The language instinct.* New York: Morrow.

Pinker, S. (1994b). How could a child use verb syntax to learn verb semantics? *Lingua, 92,* 337–410.

Pinsker, H. M., Hening, W. A, Carew, T. J, & Kandel, E. R. (1973). Long-term sensitization of a defensive withdrawal reflex in Aplysia. *Science, 182,* 1039–1042.

Pisacreta, R. (1982 a). Some factors that influence the acquisition of complex, stereotyped, response sequences in pigeons. *Journal of the Experimental Analysis of Behavior, 37,* 359–369.

Pisacreta, R. (1982 b). A comparison of forward and backward procedures for the acquisition of response chains in pigeons. *Bulletin of the Psychonomic Society, 20,* 233–236.

Pitcher, T. J., Green, D. A., & Magurran, A. E. (1986). Dicing with death: Predator inspection behavior in minnow shoals. *Journal of Fish Biology, 28,* 439–448.

Pittenger, D. J., & Pavlik, W. B. (1989). Resistance to extinction in humans: Analysis of the generalized partial reinforcement effect. *Learning & Motivation, 20,* 60–72.

Pitts, R. C., & Malagodi, E. F. (1991). Preference for less frequent shock under fixed-interval schedules of electric-shock presentation. *Journal of the Experimental Analysis of Behavior, 56,* 21–32.

Platt, J. J., & James, W. T. Social facilitation of eating behavior in young oppossums: I. Group vs. solitary feeding. *Psychonomic Science, 6,* 421–422.

Platt, J. R. (1973). Percentile reinforcement: Paradigms for experimental analysis of response shaping. In G. H. Bower (Ed.), *The psychology of learning and motivation* (vol. 7): *Advances in theory and research* (pp. 200–210). New York: Academic Press.

Platt, J. R. (1979). Interresponse-time shaping by variable- interval-like interresponse-time reinforcement contingencies. *Journal of the Experimental Analysis of Behavior, 31,* 3–14.

Platt, J. R., & Johnson, D. M. (1971). Localization of position within a homogeneous behavior chain: Effects of error contingencies. *Learning and Motivation, 2,* 386–414.

Plaud, J. J., & Gaither, G. A. (1996). Behavioral momentum: Implications and development from reinforcement theories. *Behavior Modification, 20,* 183–201.

Plaud, J. J., & Martini, J. R. (1999). The respondent

conditioning of male sexual arousal. *Behavior Modification, 23,* 254–268.

Pliskoff, S. S., & Brown, T. G. (1976). Matching with a trio of concurrent variable-interval schedules of reinforcement. *Journal of the Experimental Analysis of Behavior, 25,* 69–73.

Pliskoff, S. S., Cicerone, R., & Nelson, T. D. (1978). Local response-rate constancy on concurrent variable-interval schedules of reinforcement. *Journal of the Experimental Analysis of Behavior, 29,* 431–446.

Plonsky, M., Driscoll, C. D., Warren, D. A., & Rosellini, R. A. (1984). Do random time schedules induce polydipsia in the rat? *Animal Learning & Behavior, 12,* 355–362.

Plotkin, H. C., & Oakley, D. A. (1975). Backward conditioning in the rabbit (*Oryctolagus cuniculus*). *Journal of Comparative and Physiological Psychology, 88,* 586–590.

Poiani, A. (1993). Social structure and the development of helping behavior in the bell miner (*Manorina melanophrys, Meliphagidae*). *Ethology, 93,* 62–80.

Poirier, F. E. (1972). Introduction. In F. E. Poirier (Ed.), *Primate socialization* (pp. 3–28). New York: Random House.

Poniewaz, W. R. (1984). Effects on preference of reinforcement delay, number of reinforcers, and terminal-link duration. *Journal of the Experimental Analysis of Behavior, 42,* 255–266.

Poole, T. B. (1966) Aggressive play in polecats. *Symposium of the Zoological Society of London, 18,* 23–44.

Porter, J. H., & Allen, J. D. (1977). Schedule-induced polydipsia contrast in the rat. *Animal Learning & Behavior, 5,* 184–192.

Porter, J. H., Brown, R. T., & Goldsmith, P. A. (1982). Adjunctive behavior in children on fixed interval food reinforcement schedules. *Physiology & Behavior, 28,* 609–612.

Posadas-Andrews, A., & Roper, T. J. (1983). Social transmission of food preferences in adult rats. *Animal Behaviour, 31,* 265–271.

Powell, R. W. (1968). The effect of small sequential changes in fixed-ratio size upon the post-reinforcement pause. *Journal of the Experimental Analysis of Behavior, 11,* 589–593.

Powell, R. W. (1970). The effect of shock intensity upon responding under a multiple-avoidance schedule. *Journal of the Experimental Analysis of Behavior, 14,* 321–329.

Powell, R. W. (1973). Effects of stimulus control and deprivation upon discriminative responding. *Journal of the Experimental Analysis of Behavior, 19,* 351–360.

Powell, R. W., & Peck, S. (1969). Persistent shock-elicited responding engendered by a negative reinforcement procedure. *Journal of the Experimental Analysis of Behavior, 12,* 1049–1062.

Polyak, S. (1957). *The vertebrate visual system: Its origin, structure, and function and its manifestations in disease with an analysis of its role in the life of animals and in the origin of man.* Chicago: Chicago University Press.

Premack, D. (1962). Reversibility of the reinforcement relation. *Science, 136,* 255–257.

Premack, D. (1965). Reinforcement theory. In D. Levine (Ed.), *Nebraska symposium on motivation* (vol. 13, pp. 123–180). Lincoln: University of Nebraska Press.

Premack, D. (1971). Catching up with common sense or two sides of a generalization: Reinforcement and punishment. In R. Glaser (Ed.), *The nature of reinforcement* (pp. 121–150). San Diego, CA: Academic Press.

Premack, D., Schaeffer, R. W., & Hundt, A. (1964). Reinforcement of drinking by running: Effect of fixed ratio and reinforcement time. *Journal of the Experimental Analysis of Behavior, 7,* 91–96.

Pritchatt, D. (1968). Avoidance of electric shock by the cockroach Periplaneta americana. *Animal Behaviour, 16,* 178–185.

Pryor, K. W., Haag, R., & O'Reilly, J. (1969). The creative porpoise: Training for novel behavior. *Journal of the Experimental Analysis of Behavior, 12,* 653–661.

Pulvermüller, F. (1999). Words in the brain's language. *Behavioral and brain sciences, 22,* 253–336.

Pyke, G. H., Pulliam, H. R., & Charnov, E. L. (1977). Optimal foraging: A selective review of theory and tests. *The Quarterly Review of Biology, 52,* 137–154.

Rachlin, H. (1969). Autoshaping of key pecking in pigeons with negative reinforcement. *Journal of the Experimental Analysis of Behavior, 12,* 521–531.

Rachlin, H. (1972). Response control with titration of punishment. *Journal of the Experimental Analysis of Behavior, 17,* 147–157.

Rachlin, H. (1973). Contrast and matching. *Psychological Review, 80,* 217–234.

Rachlin, H., & Green, L. (1972). Commitment, choice, and self-control. *Journal of the Experimental Analysis of Behavior, 17,* 15–22.

Rachlin, H., & Krasnoff, J. (1983). Eating and drinking: An economic analysis. *Journal of the Experimental Analysis of Behavior, 39,* 385–404.

Rackham, D. (1971). *Conditioning of the pigeon's courtship and aggressive behavior.* Unpublished master's thesis, Dalhousie University. Halifax, Nova Scotia.

Randich, A., & LoLordo, V. M. (1979). Associative and non-associative theories of the UCS preexposure phenomenon: Implications for Pavlovian conditioning. *Psychological Bulletin, 86,* 523–548.

Rashotte, M. E., & Amsel, A. (1968). Transfer of slow-response rituals to extinction of a continuously rewarded response. *Journal of Comparative and Physiological Psychology, 66,* 432–443.

Rast, J., Johnston, J. M., Allen, J. E., & Drum, C. (1985). Effects of nutritional and mechanical properties of food on ruminative behavior. *Journal of the Experimental Analysis of Behavior, 44,* 195–206.

Rast, J., Johnston, J. M., Drum, C., & Conrin, J. (1981).

The relation of food quantity to rumination behavior. *Journal of Applied Behavior Analysis, 14,* 121–130.

Ratner, S. C. (1967). Comparative aspects of hypnosis. In J. E. Gordon (Ed.), *Handbook of clinical and experimental hypnosis* (pp. 550–587). New York: MacMillan.

Ratner, S. C., & Miller, K. R. (1959). Classical conditioning in earthworms, Lumbricus terrestris. *Journal of Comparative and Physiological Psychology, 52,* 102–105.

Raubenheimer, D., & Blackshaw, J. (1994). Locusts learn to associate visual stimuli with drinking. *Journal of Insect Behavior, 7,* 569–575.

Rayfield, F., Segal, M., & Goldiamond, I. (1982). Schedule- induced defecation. *Journal of the Experimental Analysis of Behavior, 38,* 19–34.

Raymond, G. A. (1968). *Accentuation and attenuation of punishment by prior exposure to aversive stimulation.* Unpublished doctoral dissertation, Brown University.

Razran, G. H. S. (1939). Decremental and incremental effects of distracting stimuli upon the salivary CRs of 24 adult human subjects (inhibition and disinhibition?) *Journal of Experimental Psychology, 24,* 647–652.

Real, L. (1991). Search theory and mate choice. I. Models of single-sex discrimination. *American Naturalist, 136,* 376–404.

Reberg, D. (1980). Reinforcing the occurrence or nonoccurrence of interim drinking. *Animal Learning & Behavior, 8,* 120–128.

Reberg, D., & Black, A. H. (1969). Compound testing of individually conditioned stimuli as an index of excitatory and inhibitory properties. *Psychonomic Science, 17,* 30–31.

Reberg, D., Mann, B., & Innis, W. K. (1977). Superstitious behavior for food and water in the rat. *Physiology & Behavior, 19,* 803–806.

Redd, W. H. (1989). Management of anticipatory nausea and vomiting. In J. C. Holland & J. H. Rowland (Eds.), *Handbook of psychological oncology: Psychiatric care of the patient with cancer* (pp. 423–433). New York: Oxford University Press.

Redd, W. H., & Andrykowski, M. A. (1982). Behavioral intervention in cancer treatment: Controlling aversive reactions to chemotherapy. *Journal of Consulting and Clinical Psychology, 50,* 1018–1029.

Redd, W. H., Dadds, M. R., Futterman, A. D., Taylor, K., & Bovbjerg, D. (1993). Nausea induced by mental images of chemotherapy. *Cancer, 72,* 629–636.

Redd, W. H., Sidman, M., & Fletcher, F. G. (1974). Timeout as a reinforcer for errors in a serial position task. *Journal of the Experimental Analysis of Behavior, 21,* 3–17.

Reese, E. P., Howard, J. S., & Rosenberger, P. B. (1977). Behavioral procedures for assessing visual capacities in nonverbal subjects. In B. C. Etzel, J. M. LeBlanc, & D. M. Baer (eds), *New developments in behaviorl research: Theory, methods, and applications. In honor*

of Sidney W. Bijou (pp. 279–301). Hillsdale, NJ: Lawrence Erlbaum.

Reid, A. K., & Dale, R. H. I. (1983). Dynamic effects of food magnitude on interim-terminal interaction. *Journal of the Experimental Analysis of Behavior, 39,* 135–148.

Reid, A. K., & Staddon, J. E. R. (1982). Schedule-induced drinking: Elicitation, anticipation, or behavioral interaction? *Journal of the Experimental Analysis of Behavior, 38,* 1–18.

Reid, A. K., & Staddon, J. E. R. (1987). Within-session meal-size effects on induced drinking. *Journal of the Experimental Analysis of Behavior, 48,* 289–301.

Reid, R. L. (1957). The role of the reinforcer as a stimulus *British Journal of Psychology, 49,* 292–309.

Reidman, M. L. (1982). The evolution of alloparental care and adoption in mammals and birds. *Quarterly Review of Biology, 57,* 405–435.

Relethford, J. H. (1995). Genetics and modern human origins. *Evolutionary Anthropology, 4,* 53–63.

Rescorla, R. A. (1968). Probability of shock in the presence and absence of CS in fear conditioning. *Journal of Comparative and Physiological Psychology, 66,* 1–5.

Rescorla, R. A. (1972). "Configural" conditioning in discrete-trial bar pressing. *Journal of Comparative and Physiological Psychology, 79,* 307–317.

Rescorla, R. A. (1976). Stimulus generalization: Some predictions from a model of Pavlovian conditioning. *Journal of Experimental Psychology: Animal Behavior Processes, 2,* 88–96.

Rescorla, R. A. (1977). Pavlovian second-order conditioning: Some implications for instrumental behavior. In H. Davis & H. M. B. Hurwitz (Eds.), *Operant-Pavlovian interactions* (pp. 133–164). Hillsdale, NJ: Erlbaum.

Rescorla, R. A. (1980). *Pavlovian second-order conditioning: Studies in associative learning.* Hillsdale, NJ: Erlbaum.

Rescorla, R. A. (1981). Within-signal learning in autoshaping. *Animal Learning & Behavior, 9,* 245–252.

Rescorla, R. A., & Cunningham, C. L. (1978). Recovery of the US representation over time during extinction. *Learning and Motivation, 9,* 373–391.

Rescorla, R. A., & Wagner, A. R. (1972). A theory of Pavlovian conditioning: Variations in the effectiveness of reinforcement and nonreinforcement. In A. H. Black & W. F. Prokasy (Eds.), *Classical conditioning II: Current research and theory* (pp. 64–99). New York: Appleton-Century-Crofts.

Reynierse, J. H., & Spanier, D. (1968). Excessive drinking in rats' adaptation to the schedule of feeding. *Psychonomic Science, 10,* 95–96.

Reynolds, G. S. (1961a). Behavioral contrast. *Journal of the Experimental Analysis of Behavior, 4,* 57–71.

Reynolds, G. S. (1961b). Attention in the pigeon. *Journal of the Experimental Analysis of Behavior, 4,* 203–208.

Reynolds, G. S., & Limpo, A. J. (1968). On some causes

of behavioral contrast. *Journal of the Experimental Analysis of Behavior, 11,* 543–547.

Rhodes, G., Sumich, A., & Byatt, G. (1999). Are average facial configurations attractive only because of their symmetry? *Psychological Science, 10,* 52–58.

Richard, A. (1970). A comparative study of the activity patterns and behavior of *Alouatta villosa* and *Ateles geoffroyi*. *Folia Primatologica, 12,* 241–263.

Richard, M. M., Grover, C. A., & Davis, S. F. (1987). Galef's transfer of information effect occurs in a free-foraging situation. *The Psychological Record, 37,* 79–87.

Richman, B. (1978). The synchronisation of voices by gelada monkeys. *Primates, 19,* 569–581.

Richman, B. (1987). Rhythm and melody in gelada vocal exchanges. *Primates, 28,* 199–223.

Richter, C. P. (1922). A behavioristic study of the activity of the rat. *Comparative Psychological Monograph, 1*(2, No. 55).

Rider, D. P. (1979). Concurrent ratio schedules: Fixed vs. variable response magnitudes. *Journal of the Experimental Analysis of Behavior, 31,* 225–237.

Rider, D. P. (1981). Concurrent fixed-interval variable-ratio schedules and the matching relation. *Journal of the Experimental Analysis of Behavior, 36,* 317–328.

Rider, D. P. (1983 a). Preference for mixed versus constant delays of reinforcement: Effect of probability of the short, mixed delay. *Journal of the Experimental Analysis of Behavior, 39,* 257–266.

Rider, D. P. (1983 b). Choice for aperiodic versus periodic ratio schedules: A comparison of concurrent and concurrent-chains procedures. *Journal of the Experimental Analysis of Behavior, 40,* 225–237.

Riess, D. (1970). Sidman avoidance in rats as a function of shock intensity and duration. *Journal of Comparative and Physiological Psychology, 73,* 481–485.

Rightmire, G. P. (1995). Geography, time and speciation in Pleistocene Homo. *South African Journal of Science, 91,* 450–454.

Rijnstrop, A., Daan, S., & Dijkstra, C. (1981). Hunting in the kestrel, *Falco tinnunculus*, and the adaptive significance of daily habits. *Oecologia, 50,* 391–406.

Riley, A. L., & Lovely, R. H. (1978). Chlordiazepoxide-induced reversal of an amphetamine-established aversion: Dipsogenic effects. *Physiological Psychology, 6,* 488–492.

Rilling, M. (1977). Stimulus control and inhibitory processes. In W. K. Honig & J. E. R. Staddon (Eds.), *Handbook of operant behavior* (pp. 432–480). Englewood Cliffs, NJ: Prentice-Hall.

Rilling, M., & Caplan,-H. J. (1973). Extinction-induced aggression during errorless discrimination learning. *Journal of the Experimental Analysis of Behavior, 20,* 85–92

Rilling, M., Caplan, H., Howard, R., & Brown, C. H. (1975). Inhibitory stimulus control following errorless discrimination learning. *Journal of the Experimental Analysis of Behavior, 24,* 121–133.

Rilling, M., & McDiarmid, C. (1965). Signal detection in fixed ratio schedules. *Science, 148,* 526–527.

Riordan, C. A., & Tedeschi, J. T. (1983). Attraction in aversive environments: Some evidence for classical conditioning and negative reinforcement. *Journal of Personality and Social Psychology, 44,* 683–692.

Risley, T., & Wolf, M. M. (1964/1966). *Experimental manipulation of autistic behaviors and generalization into the home.* Paper presented at the 72nd Annual Convention of the American Psychological Association. Reprinted in: Ulrich, R., Stachnik, T., & Mabry, J. *Control of human behavior* (vol. 1, pp. 193–198). Glenview, IL: Scott, Foresman, and Company.

Ritj-Plooij, H. H. C., & van de Plooij, F. X. (1987). Growing independence, conflict, and learning in mother-infant relations in free-ranging chimpanzees. *Behaviour, 101,* 1–86.

Robbins, D. (1971). Partial reinforcement: A selective review of the alleyway literature since 1960. *Psychological Bulletin, 76,* 415–431.

Robbins, S. J. (1990). Mechanisms underlying spontaneous recovery in autoshaping. *Journal of Experimental Psychology: Animal Behavior Processes, 16,* 235–249.

Robbinson, D. E., & Capaldi, E. J. (1958). Spontaneous recovery following nonresponse extinction. *Journal of Comparative and Physiological Psychology, 51,* 644–646.

Roberts, A. E., & Hurwitz, H. M. B. (1970). The effect of a pre-shock signal on a free-operant avoidance response. *Journal of the Experimental Analysis of Behavior, 14,* 331–340.

Roberts, B. (1934). Notes on the birds of central and south-east Iceland with special reference to food habits. *Ibis, 13,* 239–264.

Roberts, W. A. (1972). Short-term memory in the pigeon: Effects of repetition and spacing. *Journal of Experimental Psychology, 94,* 74–83.

Roberts, W. A., & Grant, D. S. (1976). Studies of short-term memory in the pigeon using the delayed matching-to-sample procedure. In R. T. Davis, D. L. Medin, & W. A. Roberts (Eds.), *Processes of animal memory* (pp. 79–112). Hillsdale, NJ: Erlbaum.

Roberts, W. A., & Grant, D. S. (1978). An analysis of light-induced retroactive inhibition in pigeon short-term memory. *Journal of Experimental Psychology: Animal Behavior Processes, 4,* 219–236.

Roberts, W. A., Mazmanian, D. S., & Kraemer, P. J. (1984). Directed forgetting in monkeys. *Animal Learning & Behavior, 12,* 29–40.

Robertson, D. R., & Hoffman, S. G. (1977). The roles of female mate choice and predation in the mating systems of some tropical labroid fishes. *Zeitschrift für Tierpsychologie, 45,* 298–320.

Robinson, A. W., & Capaldi, E. J. (1958). Spontaneous recovery following non-response extinction. *Journal of Comparative and Physiological Psychology, 51,* 644–646.

Robinson, J. S. (1955). The sameness-difference discrimination problem in chimpanzee. *Journal of Comparative and Physiological Psychology, 48,* 195–197.

Robinson, J. S. (1960). The conceptual basis of the

chimpanzee's performance on the sameness-difference discrimination problem. *Journal of Comparative and Physiological Psychology, 53,* 368–370.

Roche, B., & Barnes, D. (1997). A transformation of respondently conditioned stimulus function in accordance with arbitrarily applicable relations. *Journal of the Experimental Analysis of Behavior, 67,* 275–301.

Rodd, Z. A., Rosellini, R. A., Stock, H. S., & Gallup, G. G., Jr. (1997). Learned helplessness in chickens (*Gallus gallus*): Evidence for attentional bias. *Learning and Motivation, 28,* 43–55.

Rodewald, H. K. (1974). Symbolic matching-to-sample by pigeons. *Psychological Reports, 34,* 987–990.

Roediger, H. L., III, & Crowder, R. G. (1976). A serial position effect in recall of United States presidents. *Bulletin of the Psychonomic Society, 8,* 275–278.

Roediger, H. L., III, & McDermott, K. B. (1995). Creating false memories: Remembering words not presented in lists. *Journal of Experimental Psychology: Learning, Memory, and Cognition, 21,* 803–814.

Rogers, L. J., & McCulloch, H. (1981). Pair bonding in the galah, *Cacatua roseicapilla. Bird Behavior, 3,* 80–92.

Rohles, F. H., Jr. (1961). The development of an instrumental skill sequence in the chimpanzee. *Journal of the Experimental Analysis of Behavior, 4,* 323–325.

Rohwer, S. (1977). Status signalling in Harris sparrows: Some experiments in deception. *Behaviour, 61*(1-sup-2), 107–129.

Rohwer, S., & Rohwer, F. C. (1978). Status signalling in Harris sparrows: Experimental deceptions achieved. *Animal Behaviour, 26,* 1012–1022.

Roll, J. M., McSweeney, F. K., Johnson, K. S., & Weatherly, J. N. (1995). Satiety contributes little to within-session decreases in responding. *Learning and Motivation, 26,* 323–341.

Roots, C. (1988). *Tropical birds of the world.* Winnipeg: Hyperion.

Roper, K. L., Kaiser, D. H., & Zentall, T. R. (1995). True directed forgetting in pigeons may occur only when alternative working memory is required on forget-cue trials. *Animal Learning & Behavior, 23,* 280–285.

Roper, K. L., & Zentall, T. R. (1993). Directed forgetting in animals. *Psychological Bulletin, 113,* 513–532.

Roper, T. J. (1980). Changes in rate of schedule-induced behaviour in rats as a function of fixed-interval schedule. *Quarterly Journal of Experimental Psychology, 32,* 159–170.

Roper, T. J. (1981). What is meant by the term "schedule-induced" and how general is schedule induction? *Animal Learning & Behavior, 9,* 433–440.

Roper, T. J. (1982). Schedule induction: A reply to Timberlake and to Wetherington and Brownstein. *Animal Learning & Behavior, 10,* 540

Rose, J. E., & Levin, E. (1991). Inter-relationships between conditioned and primary reinforcement in the maintenance of cigarette smoking. *British Journal of Addiction, 86,* 605–609.

Rosellini, R. A., & Burdette, D. R. (1980). Meal size

and intermeal interval both regulate schedule-induced water intake in rats. *Animal Learning & Behavior, 8,* 647–652.

Rosenberger, P. B. (1974). Discriminative aspects of visual hemi-inattention. *Neurology,* January, 17–23.

Rosenblith, J. Z. (1970). Polydipsia induced in the rat by a second-order schedule. *Journal of the Experimental Analysis of Behavior, 14,* 139–144.

Roskaft, E., & Rohwer, S. (1987). An experimental study of the function of the red epaulettes and the black body colour of male red-winged blackbirds. *Animal Behaviour, 35,* 1070–1077.

Rotton, J., Barry, T., Frey, J., & Soler, E. (1978). Air pollution and interpersonal attraction. *Journal of Applied Social Psychology, 8,* 57–71.

Roush, R. (1996). Food-associated calling behavior in cotton-top tamarins (*Saguinus oedipus*): Environmental and developmental factors. Unpublished Ph.D. dissertation, University of Wisconsin, Madison.

Routtenberg, A. (1978). The reward system of the brain. *Scientific American, 239*(5), 154–164.

Royalty, P., Williams, B. A., & Fantino, E. (1987). Effects of delayed conditioned reinforcement in chain schedules. *Journal of the Experimental Analysis of Behavior, 47,* 41–56.

Ruddle, H. V., Bradshaw, C. M., Szabadi, E., & Foster, T. M. (1982). Performance of humans in concurrent avoidance/positive-reinforcement schedules. *Journal of the Experimental Analysis of Behavior, 38,* 51–61.

Rumbaugh, D. M., Savage-Rumbaugh, E. S., & Hegel, M. (1987). Summation in the chimpanzee (*Pan troglodytes*). *Journal of Experimental Psychology: Animal Behavior Processes, 13,* 107–115.

Rumbaugh, D. M., & Washburn, D. A. (1993). Counting by chimpanzees and ordinality judgments by macaques in video-formatted tasks. In S. T. Boysen & E. J. Capaldi (Eds.), *The development of numerical competence: Animal and human models* (pp. 87–106). Hillsdale, NJ: Erlbaum.

Rushforth, N. B. (1973). Behavioral modifications in coelenterates. In W. Corning, J. Dyal, & A. O. D. Willows (Eds.), *Invertebrate learning* (vol. 1). New York: Plenum.

Rushforth, N. B., Burnett, A. L., & Maynard, R. (1963). Behavior in Hydra. Contraction responses of Hydra pirardi to mechanical and light stimuli. *Science, 139,* 760–761.

Russell, M., Dark, K. A., Cummins, R. W., Ellman, G., Callaway, E., & Peeke, H. V. S. (1984). Learned histamine release. *Science, 225,* 733–734.

Ruvolo, M., Disotell, T. R., Allard, M. W., Brown, W. M., & Honeycutt, R. L. (1991). Resolution of the African hominoid trichotomy by use of a mitochondrial gene sequence. *Proceedings of the National Academy of Sciences, 88,* 1570–1574.

Ryan, M. J., Tuttle, M. D., & Rand, A. S. (1982). Bat predation and sexual advertisement in a neotropical anuran. *American Naturalist, 119,* 136–139.

Sacks, R. A., Kamil, A. C., & Mack, R. (1972). The effects of fixed-ratio sample requirements on matching to sample in the pigeon. *Psychonomic Science, 26,* 291–293.

Sade, D. S. (1965). Some aspects of parent-offspring and sibling relations in a group of rhesus monkeys, with a discussion of grooming. *American Journal of Physical Anthropology, 23,* 1–18.

Sade, D. S. (1972). A longitudinal study of social behavior of rhesus monkeys. In R. H. Tuttle (Ed.), *The functional and evolutionary biology of primates* (pp. 378–398). Chicago: Aldine.

Sadowsky, S. (1973). Behavioral contrast with timeout, blackout, or extinction as the negative condition. *Journal of the Experimental Analysis of Behavior, 19,* 499–507.

Sahley, C. L., Boulis, N. M., & Schurman, B. (1994). Associative learning modifies the shortening reflex in the semi-intact leech Hirudo medicinalis: Effects of pairing, predictability, and CS preexposure. *Behavioral Neuroscience, 108,* 340–346.

Saltzman, I. J. (1950). Generalization of secondary reinforcement. *Journal of Experimental Psychology, 40,* 189–193.

Sands, S. F., Lincoln, C. E., & Wright, A. A. (1982). Pictorial similarity judgments and the organization of visual memory in the rhesus monkey. *Journal of Experimental Psychology: General, 3,* 369–389.

Sands, S. F., & Wright, A. A. (1980). Primate memory: Retention of serial list items by a rhesus monkey and a human with 10- and 20-item lists. *Journal of Experimental Psychology: Animal Behavior Processes, 6,* 386–396.

Santi, A., & Savich, J. (1985). Directed forgetting effects in pigeons: Remember cues initiate rehearsal. *Animal Learning & Behavior, 13,* 365–369.

Sauer, F. (1956). Über das Verhalten junger Grassmüken (*Sylvia borin*). *Journal of Ornithology, 97,* 156–189.

Saunders, K. J., & Spradlin, J. E. (1993). Conditional discrimination in mentally retarded subjects: Programming acquisition and learning set. *Journal of the Experimental Analysis of Behavior, 60,* 571–585.

Saunders, R. R., & Green, G. (1999). A discrimination analysis of training-structure effects on stimulus equivalence outcomes. *Journal of the Experimental Analysis of Behavior, 72,* 117–137.

Savage, E. S. (1975). Mother-infant behavior among captive group-living chimpanzees (*Pan troglodytes*). Unpublished doctoral dissertation, University of Oklahoma at Norman.

Savage-Rumbaugh, S., & Lewin, R. (1994). *Kanzi: the ape at the brink of the human mind.* New York: Wiley.

Savage-Rumbaugh, E. S., Murphy, J., Sevcik, R. A., Brakke, K. E., Williams, S. L., & Rumbaugh, D. M. (1993). Language comprehension in ape and child. *Monographs of the Society for Research in Child Development, 58*(3–4, Serial No. 233).

Scavio, M. J. (1974). Classical-classical transfer: Effects of prior aversive conditioning on appetitive conditioning in rabbits. *Journal of Comparative and Physiological Psychology, 86,* 107–115.

Scavio, M. J. (1975). Classical-classical transfer: CR interactions involving appetitive and aversive CSs and USs. *Bulletin of the Psychonomic Society, 6,* 475–477.

Schaal, B., & Orgeur, P. (1992). Olfaction in utero: Can the rodent model be generalized? *Quarterly Journal of Experimental Psychology, 44,* 245–278.

Schaal, B., Orgeur, P., & Arnould, C. (1995). Olfactory preferences in newborn lambs: Possible influence of prenatal experience. *Behaviour, 132,* 351–365.

Schafe, G. B., & Bernstein, I. L. (1996). Taste aversion learning. In E. D. Capaldi (Ed.), *Why we eat what we eat: The psychology of eating* (pp. 31–51). Washington, DC: American Psychological Association.

Schaller, G. B. (1963). *The mountain gorilla.* Chicago: University of Chicago Press.

Schaller, G. B. (1967). *The deer and the tiger.* Chicago: Chicago University Press.

Schaller, G. B. (1972). *The Serengeti lion: A study of predator-prey relations.* Chicago: Chicago University Press.

Schatz, B., Beugnon, G., & Lachaud, J. P. (1994). Time-place learning by an invertebrate, the ant Ectatomma ruidum Roger. *Animal Behaviour, 48,* 236–238.

Schenkel, R. (1967). Submission: Its features and function in the wolf and dog. *American Zoologist, 7,* 319–329.

Scherer, M. B., & Sanger, D. J. (1981). Laboratory and applied analyses of adjunctive behavior. In C. M. Bradshaw, E. Szabadi, & C. F. Lowe (Eds.), *Quantification of steady-state operant behavior* (pp. 401–404). Amsterdam: Elsevier/North-Holland Biomedical.

Schiff, R., Smith, N., & Prochaska, J. (1972). Extinction of avoidance in rats as a function of duration and number of blocked trials. *Journal of Comparative and Physiological Psychology, 81,* 356–359.

Schindler, C. W., & Weiss, S. J. (1985). Modification of a stimulus-interaction by blocking. *Behavioural Processes, 11,* 123–130.

Schleidt, W. M. (1961). Reaktionen von Truthühnern auf fliegende Raubvögel und Versuche zur Analyse ihrer AAM's. *Zeitschrift für Tierpsychologie, 18,* 534–560.

Schneider, J. W. (1973). Reinforcer effectiveness as a function of reinforcer rate and magnitude: A comparison of concurrent performances. *Journal of the Experimental Analysis of Behavior, 20,* 461–471.

Schneiderman, N. (1966). Interstimulus interval function of the nictitating membrane response of the rabbit under delay versus trace conditioning. *Journal of Comparative and Physiological Psychology, 62,* 397–402.

Schneirla, T. C. (1943). The nature of ant learning: II. The intermediate stage of segmental maze adjustment. *Journal of Comparative Psychology, 34,* 149–176.

Schneirla, T. C. (1946). Ant learning as a problem in comparative psychology. In P. L. Harriman (Ed.),

Twentieth-century psychology (pp. 276–305). Freeport, NY: Philosophical Library.

Schoenfeld, W. N., Antonitis, J. J., & Bersh, P. J. (1950). Unconditioned response rate of the white rat in a barpressing apparatus. *Journal of Comparative and Physiological Psychology, 43,* 41–48.

Schopf, J. W. (1993). Microfossils of the Early Archean Apex Chart: New evidence of the antiquity of life. *Science, 260,* 640–646.

Schreurs, B. G. (1993). Long-term memory and extinction of the classically conditioned rabbit nictitating membrane response. *Learning and Motivation, 24,* 293–302.

Schreurs, B. G. (1998). Long-term memory and extinction of the rabbit nictitating membrane trace conditioning. *Learning and Motivation, 29,* 68–82.

Schrier, A. M., Thompson, C. R., & Spector, N. R. (1980). Observing behavior in monkeys (*Macaca arctoides*): Support for the information hypothesis. *Learning and Motivation, 11,* 355–365.

Schroeder, S. R., & Holland, J. G. (1969). Reinforcement of eye movement with concurrent schedules. *Journal of the Experimental Analysis of Behavior, 12,* 897–903.

Schultz, A. H. (1968). The recent hominoid primates. In S. L. Washburn & P. C. Jay. (Eds.), *Perspectives on human evolution* (vol. 1, pp. 122–195). New York: Holt, Rinehart and Winston.

Schuster, C. R., & Woods, J. H. (1966). Schedule induced polydipsia in the Rhesus monkey. *Psychological Reports, 19,* 832–828.

Schuster, R. H. (1969). A functional analysis of conditioned reinforcement. In D. Hendry (Ed.), *Conditioned reinforcement* (pp. 192–234). Homewood, IL: Dorsey.

Schusterman, R. J., & Kastak, D. (1993). A California sea lion (*Zalophus californianus*) is capable of forming equivalence relations. *The Psychological Record, 43,* 823–839.

Schusterman, R. J., & Kastak, D. (1998). Functional equivalence in a California sea lion: Relevance to animal social and communicative interactions. *Animal Behaviour, 55,* 1087–1095.

Schutz, F. (1965). Sexuelle Pragung bei Anatiden. *Zeitschrift für Tierpsychologie, 22,* 50–103.

Schutz, F. (1971). Pragung des Sexualverhaltens von Enten und Gansen durch Sozialeindrucke wahrend der Jugendphase. *Journal of Neurovisceral Relations, Supplementum, 10,* 339–357.

Schwartz, B. (1980). Development of complex stereotyped behavior in pigeons. *Journal of the Experimental Analysis of Behavior, 33,* 153–166.

Schwartz, B. (1981). Control of complex, sequential operants by systematic visual information in pigeons. *Journal of Experimental Psychology: Animal Behavior Processes, 7,* 31–44.

Schwartz, B. (1982). Interval and ratio reinforcement of a complex sequential operant in pigeons. *Journal of the Experimental Analysis of Behavior, 37,* 349–357.

Sclafani, A., & Nissenbaum, J. W. (1988). Robust conditioned flavor preference produced by intragastric starch infusions in rats. *American Journal of Physiology, 255,* R672–R675.

Scott, K. G. (1964). A comparison of similarity and oddity. *Journal of Experimental Child Psychology, 1,* 123–134.

Scott, T. R., & Powell, D. A. (1963). Measurement of a visual motion aftereffect in the rhesus monkey. *Science, 140,* 57–59.

Scown, J. M. (1983). *Changeover delay and concurrent schedules.* Unpublished doctoral dissertation, Waikato University, New Zealand.

Searle, J. R. (1992). *The rediscovery of the mind.* Boston: MIT Press.

Segal, E. F., & Bandt, W. M. (1966). Influence of collateral water drinking on bar pressing under complex reinforcement contingencies. *Psychonomic Science, 4,* 377–378.

Seger, J. (1985). Unifying genetic models for the evolution of female choice. *Evolution, 39,* 1185–1193.

Selekman, W. (1973). Behavioral contrast and inhibitory stimulus control as related to extended training. *Journal of the Experimental Analysis of Behavior, 20,* 245–252.

Seligman, M. E. P. (1970). On the generality of the laws of learning. *Psychological Review, 77,* 406–418.

Seligman, M. E. P. (1975). *Helplessness: On depression, development, and death.* San Francisco: Freeman.

Seligman, M. E. P., & Hager, J. L. (1972). *Biological boundaries of learning.* Englewood Cliffs, NJ: Prentice Hall.

Seligman, M. E. P., & Maier, S. F. (1967). Failure to escape traumatic shock. *Journal of Experimental Psychology, 74,* 1–9.

Sevenster, P. (1973). Incompatibility of response and reward. In R. A. Hinde & J. Stevenson-Hinde (Eds.), *Constraints on learning: Limitations and predispositions* (pp. 265–283). San Diego, CA: Academic Press.

Seward, J. P., & Levy, N. (1949). Sign learning as a factor in extinction. *Journal of Experimental Psychology, 39,* 660–668.

Seyfarth, R. M. (1980). The distribution of grooming and related behaviours among adult female vervet monkeys. *Animal Behaviour, 28,* 798–813.

Seyfarth, R. M., & Cheney, D. L. (1986). Vocal development in vervet monkeys. *Animal Behaviour, 34,* 1640–1658.

Shaffer, O. (1967). Role of object-discrimination responses in oddity. *Journal of Comparative and Physiological Psychology, 63,* 361–365.

Shaofu, C., Swartz, K. B., & Terrace, H. S. (1997). Knowledge of the ordinal position of list items in rhesus monkeys. *Psychological Science, 8,* 80–86.

Shapiro, M. M., Sadler, E. W., & Mugg, G. J. (1971). Compound stimulus effects during higher order salivary conditioning in dogs. *Journal of Comparative and Physiological Psychology, 74,* 222–226.

Shepp, B. E., & Eimas, P. D. (1964). *Journal of Comparative and Physiological Psychology*, 57, 357–361.

Sherman, J. A., Saunder, R. R., & Brigham, T. A. (1970). Transfer of matching and mismatching behavior in preschool children. *Journal of Experimental Child Psychology, 9,* 489–498.

Sherman, P. W., & Holmes, W. G. (1985). Kin recognition: Evidence and issues. In B. Holldobler & M. Lindauer (Eds.), *Experimental behavioral ecology and sociobiology* (pp. 437–460). New York: G. Fischer Varlag.

Sherrington, C. S. (1906/1961). *The integrative action of the nervous system.* New Haven, CT: Yale University Press.

Sherry, D. F. (1987). Foraging for stored food. In M. L. Commons, A. Kacelnik, & S. J. Shettleworth (Eds.), *Quantitative Analyses of Behavior* (vol. 6): *Foraging* (pp. 209–227). Hillsdale, NJ: Erlbaum.

Sherry, D. F., Krebs, J. R., & Cowie, R. J. (1981). Memory for the location of stored food in marsh tits. *Animal Behaviour, 29,* 1260–1266.

Shettleworth, S. J. (1994). Biological approaches to the study of learning. In N. J. Mackintosh (Ed.), *Animal learning and cognition* (pp. 185–219). New York: Academic Press.

Shettleworth, S. J., & Krebs, J. R. (1986). Stored and encountered seeds: A comparison of two spatial memory tasks in marsh tits and chickadees. *Journal of Experimental Psychology: Animal Behavior Processes, 12,* 248–257.

Shields, W. M. (1988). Sex and adaptation. In R. E. Michod & B. R. Levin (Eds.), *The evolution of sex* (pp. 253–269). Sunderland, MA: Sinauer Associates.

Shimoff, E., Catania, A. C., & Matthews, B. A. (1981). Uninstructed human responding: Sensitivity of low-rate performance to schedule contingencies. *Journal of the Experimental Analysis of Behavior, 36,* 207–220.

Shimp, C. P. (1968). Magnitude and frequency of reinforcement and frequencies of interresponse times. *Journal of the Experimental Analysis of Behavior, 11,* 525–535.

Shimp, C. P. (1969). Optimal behavior in free-operant experiments. *Psychological Review, 76,* 97–112.

Shimp, C. P. (1981). The local organization of behavior: Discrimination of and memory for simple behavioral patterns. *Journal of the Experimental Analysis of Behavior, 36,* 303–315.

Shimp, C. P. (1983). The local organization of behavior: Dissociations between a pigeon's behavior and self-reports of that behavior. *Journal of the Experimental Analysis of Behavior, 39,* 61–68.

Shimp, C. P., & Moffitt, M. (1974). Short-term memory in the pigeon: Stimulus-response associations. *Journal of the Experimental Analysis of Behavior, 22,* 507–512.

Shimp, T. A., Stuart, E. W., & Engle, R. W. (1991). A program of classical conditioning experiments testing variations in the conditioned stimulus and context. *Journal of Consumer Research, 18,* 1–12.

Shipley, E. F., Smith, C. S., & Gleitman, L. R. (1969). A study in the acquisition of language: Free responses to commands. *Language, 45,* 322–342.

Shnidman, S. R. (1968). Extinction of Sidman avoidance behavior. *Journal of the Experimental Analysis of Behavior, 11,* 153–156.

Short, L. L., & Horne, J. F. M. (1985). Behavioral notes on the nest-parasitic Afrotropical honeyguides (*Aves: Indicatoidae*). *American Museum Novitates, 25,* 1–46

Shull, R. L., & Pliskoff, S. S. (1967). Changeover delay and concurrent schedules: Some effects on relative performance measures. *Journal of the Experimental Analysis of Behavior, 10,* 517–527.

Shurtleff, D., & Ayres, J. J. B. (1981). One-trial backward excitatory fear conditioning in rats: Acquisition, retention, extinction, and spontaneous recovery. *Animal Learning & Behavior, 9,* 65–74.

Sibley, C. G., Ahlquist, J. E., & Monroe, B. L. (1988). A classification of the living birds of the world based on DNA-DNA hybridization studies. *The Auk, 105,* 409–423.

Sibley, C. G., Comstock, J. A., & Ahlquist, J. E. (1990). DNA hybridization evidence of hominoid phylogeny: A reanalysis of the data. *Journal of Molecular Evolution, 30,* 202–236.

Sidman, M. (1953). Avoidance conditioning with brief shock and no exteroceptive warning stimulus. *Science, 118,* 157–158.

Sidman, M. (1960). *Tactics of scientific research: Evaluating experimental data in psychology.* New York: Basic Books.

Sidman, M. (1971). Reading and auditory-visual equivalence. *Journal of Speech and Hearing Research, 14,* 5–13.

Sidman, M. (1990). Equivalence relations: Where do they come from? In D. E. Blackman & H. Lejeune (Eds.), *Behaviour analysis in theory and practice: Contributions and controversies* (pp. 93–114). Hillsdale, NJ: Erlbaum.

Sidman, M. (1994). *Equivalence relations and behavior: A research story.* Boston: Authors Cooperative.

Sidman, M. (1997). Equivalence: A theoretical or a descriptive model? *Mexican Journal of Behavior Analysis, 23,* 125–145.

Sidman, M. (2000). Equivalence relations and the reinforcement contingency. *Journal of the Experimental Analysis of Behavior.*

Sidman, M., & Cresson, O., Jr. (1973). Reading and cross- modal transfer of stimulus equivalences in severe retardation. *American Journal of Mental Deficiency, 77,* 515–523.

Sidman, M., Cresson, O., Jr., & Willson-Morris, M. (1974). Acquisition of matching to sample via mediated transfer. *Journal of the Experimental Analysis of Behavior, 22,* 261–273.

Sidman, M., & Fletcher, F. G. (1968). A demonstration of auto-shaping with monkeys. *Journal of the Experimental Analysis of Behavior, 11,* 307–309.

Sidman, M., Herrnstein, R. J., & Conrad, D. G. (1957). Maintenance of avoidance behavior by unavoidable shocks. *Journal of Comparative and Physiological Psychology, 50,* 553–557.

Sidman, M., Rauzin, R., Lazar, R., Cunningham, S., Tailby, W., & Carrigan, P. (1982). A search for symmetry in the conditional discriminations of rhesus monkeys, baboons, and children. *Journal of the Experimental Analysis of Behavior, 37,* 23–44.

Sidman, M., & Stebbins, W. C. (1954). Satiation effects under fixed-ratio schedules of reinforcement. *Journal of Comparative and Physiological Psychology, 47,* 114–116.

Sidman, M., & Stoddard, L. T. (1966). Programming perception and learning for retarded children. In N. R. Ellis (Ed.), *International review of research in mental retardation* (vol. 2, pp. 151–208). New York: Academic Press.

Sidman, M., & Stoddard, L. T. (1967). The effectiveness of fading in programming a simultaneous form discrimination for retarded children. *Journal of the Experimental Analysis of Behavior, 10,* 3–15.

Sidman, M., & Tailby, W. (1982). Conditional discrimination vs. matching to sample: An expansion of the testing paradigm. *Journal of the Experimental Analysis of Behavior, 37,* 5–22.

Siegel, R. H., & Honig, W. K. (1970). Pigeon concept formation: Successive and simultaneous acquisition. *Journal of the Experimental Analysis of Behavior, 13,* 385–390.

Siegel, S. (1977). Morphine tolerance acquisition as an associative process. *Journal of Experimental Psychology: Animal Behavior Processes, 3,* 1–3.

Siegel, S. (1978). Tolerance to the hyperthermic effect of morphine in the rat is a learned response. *Journal of Comparative and Physiological Psychology, 92,* 1137–1149.

Siegel, S. (1979). The role of conditioning in drug tolerance and addiction. In J. D. Keehn (Ed.), *Psychopathology in animals: Research and clinical implications* (pp. 143–168). New York: Academic Press.

Siegel, S. (1984). Pavlovian conditioning and heroin overdose: Reports by overdose victims. *Bulletin of the Psychonomic Society, 22,* 428–430.

Siegel, S. (1991). Feedforward processes in drug tolerance. In R. G. Lister & H. J. Weingartner (Eds.), *Perspectives in cognitive neuroscience* (pp. 405–416). New York: Oxford University Press.

Siegel, S., & Allan, L. G. (1992). Pairings in learning and perception: Pavlovian conditioning and contingent aftereffects. In D. Medin (Ed.), *The psychology of learning and motivation* (vol. 28): *Advances in research and theory* (pp. 127–160). San Diego: Academic Press.

Siegel, S., & Allan, L. G. (1996). The widespread influence of the Rescorla-Wagner model. *Psychonomic Bulletin & Review, 3,* 314–321.

Siegel, S., & Allan, L. G. (1998). Learning and homeostasis: Drug addiction and the McCollough effect. *Psychological Bulletin, 124,* 230–239.

Siegel, S., & Domjan, M. (1971). Backward conditioning as an inhibitory procedure. *Learning and Motivation, 2,* 1–11.

Siegel, S., & Domjan, M. (1974). The inhibitory effect of backward conditioning as a function of the number of backward pairings. *Bulletin of the Psychonomic Society, 4,* 122–124.

Siegel, S., & Ellsworth, D. W. (1986). Pavlovian conditioning and death from apparent overdose of medically prescribed morphine: A case report. *Bulletin of the Psychonomic Society, 24,* 278–280.

Siegel, S., Hinson, R. E., Krank, M. D., & McCully, J. (1982). Heroin "overdose" death: Contribution of drug- associated environment cues. *Science, 216,* 436–437.

Siegel, S., & Larson, S. J. (1996). Disruption of tolerance to the ataxic effect of ethanol by a novel stimulus. *Pharmacology, Biochemistry & Behavior, 55,* 125–130.

Sih, A. (1987). Predators and prey lifestyles: An evolutionary and ecological overview. In W. C. Kerfoot & A. Sih (Eds.), *Predation: Direct and indirect impacts on aquatic communities* (pp. 203––224). Hanover, NH: University of New England Press.

Silber, G. K., & Fertl, D. (1995). Intentional beaching by bottlenose dolphins (*Tursiops truncatus*) in the Colorado River Delta.. *Aquatic Mammalology, 21,* 183–186.

Silva, F. J., Silva, K. M., & Pear, J. J. (1992). Sign- versus goal-tracking: Effects of conditioned-stimulus-to-unconditioned-stimulus distance. *Journal of the Experimental Analysis of Behavior, 57,* 17–31.

Silva, F. J., Timberlake, W., & Cevik, M. O. (1998). A behavior systems approach to the expression of backward associations. *Learning and Motivation, 29,* 1–22.

Silva, F. J., Timberlake, W., & Koehler, T. L. (1996). A behavior systems approach to bidirectional excitatory conditioning. *Learning and Motivation, 27,* 130–150.

Silva, K. M., & Timberlake, W. (1997). A behavior systems view of conditioned states during long and short CS-US intervals. *Learning and motivation, 28,* 465–490.

Simon, B. M, Fowler, S. M., & Handler, S. D. (1983). Communication development in young children with long-term tracheostomies: Preliminary report. *International Journal of Pediatric Otorhinolaryngology, 6,* 37–50.

Simon, S. J., Ayllon, T., & Milan, M. A. (1982). Behavioral compensation: Contrastlike effects in the classroom. *Behavior Modification, 6,* 407–420.

Singer, G. H., Singer, J. S., & Horner, R. H., (1987). Using pretask requests to increase the probability of compliance for students with severe disabilities. *Journal of the Association for Persons with Severe Handicaps, 12,* 287–291.

Singh, S. D. (1959). Conditioned emotional response

in the rat: I. Constitutional and situational determinants. *Journal of Comparative and Physiological Psychology, 52,* 574–578.

Sizemore, O. J., & Lattal, K. A. (1978). Unsignalled delay of reinforcement in variable-interval schedules. *Journal of the Experimental Analysis of Behavior, 30,* 169–175.

Sizemore, O. J., & Maxwell, F. R. (1985). Selective punishment of interresponse times: The roles of shock intensity and scheduling. *Journal of the Experimental Analysis of Behavior, 44,* 355–366.

Skinner, B. F. (1933). On the rate of extinction of a conditioned reflex. *Journal of General Psychology, 8,* 114–129.

Skinner, B. F. (1938). *The behavior of organisms: An experimental analysis.* New York: Appleton-Century-Crofts.

Skinner, B. F. (1945). The operational analysis of psychological terms. *Psychological Review, 42,* 270–277.

Skinner, B. F. (1948 a). "Superstition" in the pigeon. *Journal of Experimental Psychology, 38,* 168–172.

Skinner, B. F. (1948 b). *Walden Two.* New York: MacMillan.

Skinner, B. F. (1950). Are theories of learning necessary? *Psychological Review, 57,* 193–216.

Skinner, B. F. (1953). *Science and human behavior.* New York: Macmillan.

Skinner, B. F. (1957a). *Verbal behavior.* New York: Appleton-Century-Crofts.

Skinner, B. F. (1957b). The experimental analysis of behavior. *American Scientist, 45,* 343–371.

Skinner, B. F. (1963). Behaviorism at fifty. *Science, 140,* 951–958.

Skinner, B. F. (1966). The phylogeny and ontogeny of behavior. *Science, 153,* 1204–1213.

Skinner, B. F. (1968). *The technology of teaching.* Englewood Cliffs, NJ: Prentice-Hall.

Skinner, B. F. (1971). *Beyond freedom and dignity.* New York: Knopf.

Skinner, B. F. (1972). Personal communication. April 10.

Skinner, B. F. (1974). *About behaviorism.* New York: Random House.

Skutch, A. F. (1935). Helpers at the nest. *The Auk, 52,* 257–273.

Skutch, A. F. (1976). *Parent birds and their young.* Austin: University of Texas Press.

Smith, B. H., Abramson, C. I., & Tobin, T. R. (1991). Conditional withholding of proboscis extension in honeybees (*Apis mellifera*) during discriminative punishment. *Journal of Comparative Psychology, 105,* 345–356.

Small, W. (1899).Notes on the psychic development of the young white rat. *American Journal of Psychology, 11,* 80–100.

Smith, J. P., Attwood, J. C., & Niedorowski, L. (1982). Delayed choice by pigeons when the correct response is not predictable from the sample stimulus. *Journal of the Experimental Analysis of Behavior, 37,* 57–63.

Smith, L. A., & Lang, W. J. (1980). Changes occurring in self-administration of nicotine by rats over a 28-day period. *Pharmacology, Biochemistry, & Behavior, 13,* 215–220.

Smith, R., Michael, J., & Sundberg, M. L. (1995). Automatic reinforcement and automatic punishment in infant vocal behavior. *Analysis of Verbal Behavior, 13,* 39–48.

Smith, S. M., Brown, H. O., Toman, J. E. P., & Goodman, L. S. (1947). The lack of cerebral effects of *d*-tubocurarine. *Anesthesiology, 8,* 1–14.

Snoddy, G. S. (1926). Learning and stability. *Journal of Applied Psychology, 10,* 1–36.

Snowden, C. T., & Cleveland, J. (1984). "Conversations" among pigmy marmosets. *American Journal of Primatology, 7,* 15–20.

Solomon, R. L., Kamin, L. J., & Wynne, L. C. (1953). Traumatic avoidance learning: The outcomes of several extinction procedures with dogs. *Journal of Abnormal and Social Psychology, 48,* 291–302.

Solomon, R. L., & Wynne, L. C. (1953). Traumatic avoidance learning: Acquisition in normal dogs. *Psychological Monographs, 67* (Whole No. 354).

Solomon, R. L., & Wynne, L. C. (1954). Traumatic avoidance learning: The principles of anxiety conservation and partial irreversibility. *Psychological Review, 61,* 353–385.

Spector, N. H. (1987). Old and new strategies in the conditioning of immune responses. In B. D. Janovic, B. M. Markovic, & N. H. Spector (Eds.), *Neuroimmune interactions: Proceedings of the Second International Workshop on Neuroimmunomodulation* (pp. 522–531). New York: New York Academy of Sciences.

Speers, M. J., Gillan, D. J., & Rescorla, R. A. (1980). Within-compound associations in a variety of compound conditioning procedures. *Learning and Motivation, 11,* 135–149.

Spence, K. W. (1937). Experimental studies of learning and higher mental processes in infra-human primates. *Psychological Bulletin, 34,* 806–-850.

Spence, K. W. (1947). The role of secondary reinforcement in delayed reward learning. *Psychological Review, 54,* 1–8.

Sperling, G. A. (1960). The information available in brief visual presentation. *Psychological Monographs, 74* (Whole No. 498).

Spetch, M. L., Belke, T. W., Barnet, R. C., Dunn, R., & Pierce, W. D. (1990). Suboptimal choice in a percentage-reinforcement procedure: Effects of signal condition and terminal-link length. *Journal of the Experimental Analysis of Behavior, 53,* 219–234.

Spetch, M. L., Cheng, K., & Mondloch, M. V. (1992). Landmark use by pigeons in a touch-screen spatial search task. *Animal Learning & Behavior, 20,* 281–292.

Spetch, M. L., & Mondloch, M. V. (1993). Control of pigeons' spatial search by graphic landmarks in a touch-screen task. *Journal of Experimental Psychology: Animal Behavior Processes, 19,* 353–372.

Spetch, M. L., Mondloch, M. V., Belke, T. W., & Dunn,

R. (1994). Determinants of pigeon's choice between certain and probabilistic outcomes. *Animal Learning & Behavior, 22,* 239–251.

Spetch, M. L., & Wilkie, D. M. (1981). Duration discrimination is better with food access as the signal than with light as the signal. *Learning and Motivation, 12,* 40–64.

Spetch, M. L., & Wilkie, D. M. (1994). Pigeons' use of landmarks presented in digitized images. *Learning and Motivation, 25,* 245–275.

Spiker, C. C. (1956). Stimulus pretraining and subsequent performance in the delayed reaction experiment. *Journal of Experimental Psychology, 52,* 107–111.

Spiker, V. (1977). Taste aversion: A procedural analysis and an alternative paradigmatic classification. *The Psychological Record, 27,* 753–769.

Spooner, F., & Spooner, D. (1984). A review of chaining techniques: Implications for future research and practice. *Education and Training of the Mentally Retarded, 19,* 114–124.

Spradlin, J. E., Cotter, V. W., & Baxley, N. (1973). Establishing a conditional discrimination without direct training: A study of transfer with retarded adolescents. *American Journal of Mental Deficiency, 77,* 556–566.

Spradlin, J. E., & Dixon, M. H. (1976). Establishing conditional discriminations without direct training: Stimulus classes and labels. *American Journal of Mental Deficiency, 80,* 555–561.

Spradlin, J. E., & Saunders, R. R. (1986). The development of stimulus classes using match-to-sample procedures: Sample classification versus comparison classification. *Analysis and Intervention in Developmental Disabilities, 6,* 41–58.

Squier, L. H. (1969). Auto-shaping key responses in fish. *Psychonomic Science, 17,* 177–178.

Squires, N., & Fantino, E. (1971). A model for choice in simple concurrent and concurrent-chains schedules. *Journal of the Experimental Analysis of Behavior, 15,* 27–38.

Staats, A. W., & Staats, C. K. (1969). Attitudes established by classical conditioning. *Journal of Abnormal and Social Psychology, 57,* 37–40.

Staddon, J. E. R. (1977), In W. K. Honig & J. E. R. Staddon (Eds.), *Handbook of Operant Behavior* (pp. 125–152). Englewood Cliffs, NJ: Prentice-Hall.

Staddon, J. E. R., & Ayres, S. L. (1975). Sequential and temporal properties of behavior induced by a schedule of periodic food delivery. *Behaviour, 54,* 26–49.

Staddon, J. E. R., & Innis, N. K. (1969). Reinforcement omission on fixed-interval schedules. *Journal of the Experimental Analysis of Behavior, 12,* 689–700.

Staddon, J. E. R., & Simmelhag, V. L. (1971). The "superstition" experiment: A reexamination of its implications for the principles of adaptive behavior. *Psychological Review, 78,* 3–16.

Stamps, J. (1995). Motor learning and the value of familiar space. *American Naturalist, 146,* 41–58.

Stamps, J., Kus, B., Clark, A., & Arrowood, P. (1990).

Social relationships of fledgling budgerigars, *Melopsitticus undulatus. Animal Behaviour, 40,* 688–700.

Stanley, W. C., & Rowe, M. I. (1954). Extinction by omission of food as a function of goal-box confinement. *Journal of Experimental Psychology, 48,* 271–274.

Steinhauer, G. D., Davol, G. H., & Lee, A. (1977). A procedure for autoshaping the pigeon's key peck to an auditory stimulus. *Journal of the Experimental Analysis of Behavior, 28,* 97–98.

Stevenson, J. G. (1967). Reinforcing effects of chaffinch song. *Animal Behaviour, 15,* 427–432.

Stevenson, M. F., & Poole, T. B. (1982). Playful interactions in family groups of the common marmoset (*Callithrix jacchus jacchus*). *Animal Beahviour, 30,* 886–900.

Stiers, M., & Silberberg, A. (1974). Autoshaping and automaintenance of lever-contact responses in rats. *Journal of the Experimental Analysis of Behavior, 22,* 4–506.

Stockhorst, U., Klosterhalfen, S., & Steingrüber, H.-J. (1998). Conditioned nausea and further side-effects in cancer chemotherapy: A review. *Journal of Psychophysiology, 12*(Suppl. 1), 14–33.

Stoddard, L. T., & Sidman, M. (1967). The effects of errors on children's performance of a circle-ellipse discrimination. *Journal of the Experimental Analysis of Behavior, 10,* 261–270.

Stoneking, M. (1993). DNA and recent human evolution. *Evolutionary Anthropology, 2,* 60–73.

Stoner, E. A. (1947). Anna hummingbird at play. *Condor, 49,* 36.

Strager, H. (1995). Pod-specific call repertoires and compound calls of killer whales, *Orcinus orca* Linnaeus, 1758, in the waters of northern Norway. *Canadian Journal of Zoology, 73,* 1037–1047.

Stringer, C., & McKie, R. (1996). *African exodus: The origins of modern humanity.* London: Cape.

Stromer, R., & Osborne, J. G. (1982). Control of adolescents arbitrary matching-to-sample by positive and negative stimulus relations. *Journal of the Experimental Analysis of Behavior, 37,* 329–348.

Struhsaker, T. T. (1967). Auditory communication among vervet monkeys (*Cercopithecus aethiops*). In S. A. Altman (Ed.), *Social communication among primates* (pp. 281–324). Chicago: University of Chicago Press.

Stuart, E. W., Shimp, T. A., & Engle, R. W. (1987). Classical conditioning of consumer attitudes: Four experiments in advertising context. *Journal of Consumer Research, 54,* 334–349.

Stubbings, V., & Martin, G. L. (1995). The ABLA test for predicting performance of developmentally disabled persons on prevocational training tasks. *International Journal of Practical Approaches to Disability, 19,* 12–17.

Stubbings, V., & Martin, G. L. (1998). Matching training tasks to the abilities of people with mental retardation: A learning test versus experienced staff. *American Journal on Mental Retardation, 102,* 473–484.

Sugiyama , Y., Fushimi, T., Sakura, O., & Matsuzawa, T. (1993). Hand preference and tool use in wild chimpanzees. *Primates, 34,* 151–159.

Sundberg, M. L., Michael, J., Partington, J. W., & Sundberg, C. A. (1995). The role of automatic reinforcement in early language acquisition. *Analysis of Verbal Behavior, 13,* 21–37.

Sussman, R. W. (1977). Socialization, social structure, and ecology of two sympatric species of *Lemur.* In S. Chevalier-Skolnikoff & F. E. Poirier (Eds.), *Primate bio-social development: Biological, social, and ecological determinants* (pp. 515–526). New York: Garland Publishing.

Swaddle, J. P., & Innis, C. C. (1994). Preference for symmetric males by female zebra finches. *Nature, 367,* 165–166.

Swartz, K. B., Chen, S., & Terrace, H. S. (1991). Serial learning by rhesus monkeys: I. Acquisition and retention of multiple four-item lists. *Journal of Experimental Psychology: Animal Behavior Processes, 17,* 396–410.

Swisher, C. C., Curtis, G. H., Jacob, T., Getty, A. G., & Widiasmoro, A. S. (1994). Age of the earliest known hominids in Java, Indonesia. *Science, 263,* 1118–1121.

Switzer, St. C. A. (1933). Disinhibition of the conditioned galvanic skin response. *Journal of General Psychology, 9,* 77–100.

Symons, D. A. (1973). *Aggressive play in a free-ranging group of rhesus monkeys* (Macaca mulatta). Unpublished doctoral. dissertation, University of California, Berkeley.

Tait, R. W. (1974). *Assessment of the bidirectional conditioning hypothesis through the UCS$_1$-UCS$_2$ conditioning paradigm.* Unpublished doctoral dissertation, University of Iowa.

Tait, R. W., Quesnel, L. J., & Ten Have, W. N. (1986). Classical-classical transfer: Excitatory associations between "competing" motivational stimuli during classical conditioning of the rabbit. *Animal Learning & Behavior, 14,* 138–143.

Tait, R. W., & Saladin, M. E. (1986). Concurrent development of excitatory and inhibitory associations during backward conditioning. *Animal Learning & Behavior, 14,* 133–137.

Takahashi, M., & Iwamoto, T. (1986). Human concurrent performances: The effects of experience, instruction, and schedule-correlated stimuli. *Journal of the Experimental Analysis of Behavior, 45,* 257–267.

Takahashi, R. N., & Singer, G. (1980). Effects of body weight levels on cannabis self-injection. *Pharmacology, Biochemistry, & Behavior, 13,* 877–881.

Talmy, L. (1985). Lexicalization patterns: Semantic structure in lexical forms. In T. Shopen (Ed.), *Language typology and syntactic description* (pp. 57–149). Boston: Cambridge University Press.

Talmy, L. (1988). The relation of grammar to cognition. In B. Rudzka-Ostyn (Ed.), *Topics in cognitive linguistics* (pp. 165–205). Philadelphia: Benjamins.

Tatham, T. A., Wanchisen, B. A., & Hineline, P. N. (1993). Effects of fixed and variable ratios on human behavioral variability. *Journal of the Experimental Analysis of Behavior, 59,* 349–359.

Talton, L. E., Higa, J. J., & Staddon, J. E. R. (1999). Interval schedule performance in the goldfish *Carassius auratus. Behavioural Processes, 45,* 193–206.

Taub, E., Crago, J. E., Burgio, L. D., Groomes, T. E., Cook, E. W. III, DeLuca, S. C., & Miller, N. E. (1994). An operant approach to rehabilitation medicine: Overcoming learned nonuse by shaping. *Journal of the Experimental Analysis of Behavior, 61,* 281–293.

Tayler, C. K., & Saayman, G. S. (1973). Imitative behavior by Indian Ocean bottlenose dolphins (*Tursiops aduncus*) in captivity. *Behaviour, 44,* 286-298.

Taylor, D. B., & Lestor, D. (1969). Schedule-induced nitrogen "drinking" in the rat. *Psychonomic Science, 15,* 17-18.

Taylor, R. J. (1974). Role of learning in insect parasitism. Ecological Monographs, 44, 89-104.

ten Cate, C. (1989). Behavior development: Toward understanding processes. In P. P. G. Bateson & Ph. H. Klopfer (Eds.), *Perspectives in ethology* (Vol. 8): *Wither ethology?* (pp. 243–269). New York: Plenum.

Terrace, H. S. (1963). Discrimination training with and without errors. *Journal of the Experimental Analysis of Behavior, 6,* 1–27.

Terrace, H. S. (1964). Wavelength generalization after discrimination learning with and without errors. *Science, 144,* 78–80.

Terrace, H. S. (1966a). Behavioral contrast and the peak shift: Effects of extended discrimination training. *Journal of the Experimental Analysis of Behavior, 9,* 613–617.

Terrace, H. S. (1966b). Stimulus control. In W. K. Honig (Ed.), *Operant behavior: Areas of research and application* (pp. 271–344). New York: Appleton-Century-Crofts.

Terrace, H. S. (1983). Simultaneous chaining: The problem it poses for traditional chaining theory. In M. L. Commons, R. J. Herrnstein, & A. R. Wagner (Eds.), *Quantitative analyses of behavior* (vol. 4): *Discrimination processes* (pp. 115–137). Cambridge, MA: Ballinger.

Tharinger, D., Schallert, D., & Kerr, N. (1977). Use of AVC tasks to predict classroom learning in mentally retarded children (Monograph). *Rehabilitation Psychology, 24,* 113–118.

Thomas, A. R. (1958). Some variables affecting latent extinction. *Journal of Experimental Psychology, 56,* 203–212.

Thomas, D. R., & Sherman, L. (1986). An assessment of the role of handling cues in "spontaneous recovery" after extinction. *Journal of the Experimental Analysis of Behavior, 46,* 305–314.

Thomas, D. R., & Switalski, R. W. (1966). Comparison of stimulus generalization following variable-ratio and variable-interval training. *Journal of Experimental Psychology, 71,* 236–240.

Thomas, J. R. (1964). Multiple baseline investigation of stimulus functions in an FR chained schedule. *Journal of the Experimental Analysis of Behavior, 7,* 241–245.

Thomas, J. R. (1965). Time-out avoidance from a behavior-independent contingency. *Psychonomic Science, 3,* 217–218.

Thomas, J. R. (1968). Fixed-ratio punishment by timeout of concurrent variable-interval behavior. *Journal of the Experimental Analysis of Behavior, 11,* 609–616.

Thomas, J. R. (1969). Maintenance of behavior by conditioned reinforcement in the signaled absence of primary reinforcement. In D. P. Hendry (Ed.), *Conditioned reinforcement* (pp. 77–90). Homewood, IL: Dorsey.

Thomas, R. K., & Boyd, M. G. (1973). A comparison of *Cebus albifrons* and *Saimiri sciureus* on oddity performance. *Animal Learning & Behavior, 1,* 151–153.

Thomas, R. K., Fowlkes, D., & Vickery, J. D. (1980). Conceptual numerousness judgments by squirrel monkeys. *American Journal of Psychology, 93,* 247–257.

Thomas, R. K., & Kerr, R. S. (1976). Conceptual conditional discrimination in Saimiri sciureus. *Animal Learning & Behavior, 4,* 333–336.

Thompson, A. L. (1964). *A new dictionary of birds.* London: Thomas Nelson and Sons.

Thompson, D. M. (1964). Escape from S^D associated with fixed-ratio reinforcement. *Journal of the Experimental Analysis of Behavior, 7,* 1–8.

Thompson, R. F., & Spencer, W. A. (1966). Habituation: A model phenomenon for the study of neuronal substrates of behavior. *Psychological Review, 73,* 16–43.

Thompson, R. H., Iwata, B. A., Conners, J., & Roscoe, E. M. (1999). Effects of reinforcement for alternative behavior during punishment of self-injury. *Journal of Applied Behavior Analysis, 32,* 317–328.

Thompson, R. K. R., Foltin, R. W., Boylan, R. J., Sweet, A., Graves, C. A., & Lowitz, C. E. (1981). Tonic immobility in Japanese quail can reduce the probability of sustained attack by cats. *Animal Learning & Behavior, 9,* 145–149.

Thompson, R. K. R., Oden, D. L., & Boysen, S. T. (1997). Language-naive chimpanzees (*Pan troglodytes*) judge relations between relations in a conceptual matching-to-sample task. *Journal of Experimental Psychology: Animal Behavior Processes, 23,* 31–43.

Thompson, T. I. (1964). Visual reinforcement in fighting cocks. *Journal of the Experimental Analysis of Behavior, 7,* 45–49.

Thompson, T., & Sturm, T. (1965). Classical conditioning of aggressive display in Siamese fighting fish. *Journal of the Experimental Analysis of Behavior, 8,* 397–404.

Thorndike, E. L. (1911). *Animal intelligence: Experimental studies.* New York: Macmillan.

Thornhill, R. (1992). Fluctuating asymmetry and the mating system of the Japanese scorpianfly, *Panorpa japonica. Animal Behaviour, 44,* 867–879.

Thornhill, R., & Gangestad, S. W. (1993). Human facial beauty: Averageness, symmetry, and parasite resistance. *Human Nature, 4,* 237–269.

Thornhill, R., & Gangestad, S. W. (1999). The scent of symmetry: A human sex pheromone that signals fitness? *Evolution and human behavior, 20,* 175–201.

Thorpe, W. H. (1963). *Learning and instinct in animals* (Second edition). London: Methuen.

Thorpe, W. H. (1966). Ritualization in ontogeny. I. Animal play. *Philosophical Transactions of the Royal Society of London. Series B: Biological Sciences, 251,* 311–319, 351–358.

Thorpe, W., & Jones, F. (1937). Olfactory conditioning in a parasitic insect and its relation to the problem of host selection. *Proceedings of the Royal Society of London, 124,* 56–81.

Thorpe, W. H., & North, M. E. W. (1965). Origin and significance of the power of vocal imitation: With special reference to the antiphonal singing of birds. *Nature, 208,* 219–222.

Timberlake, W. (1977). The application of the matching law to simple ratio schedules. *Journal of the Experimental Analysis of Behavior, 25,* 215–217.

Timberlake, W. (1982 a). Controls and schedule-induced behavior. *Animal Learning & Behavior, 10,* 535–536.

Timberlake, W. (1982 b). The emperor's clothes: Assumptions of the matching theory. In M. L. Commons, R. J. Herrnstein, & H. Rachlin (Eds.), *Quantitative analyses of behavior* (vol. 2): *Matching and maximizing accounts* (pp. 549–568). Cambridge, MA: Ballinger.

Timberlake, W. (1983). The functional organization of appetitive behavior: Behavior systems and learning. In M. D. Zeiler & P. Harzem (Eds.), *Advances in the analysis of behavior* (vol. 3). *biological factors in learning* (pp. 177–221). Chichester, UK: Wiley.

Timberlake, W. (1994). Behavior systems, associationism, and Pavlovian conditioning. *Psychonomic Bulletin & Review, 1,* 405–420.

Timberlake, W., & Allison, J. (1974). Response deprivation: An empirical approach to instrumental performance. *Psychological Review, 81,* 146–164.

Timberlake, W., & Fanselow, M. S. (1994). Symposium on behavior systems: Learning, neurophysiology, and development. *Psychonomic Bulletin & Review, 1,* 403–404.

Timberlake, W., & Grant, D. L. (1975). Auto-shaping in rats to the presentation of another rat predicting food. *Science, 190,* 690–692.

Timberlake, W., & Lucas, G. A. (1989). Behavior systems and learning: From misbehavior to general principles In S. B. Klein & R. R. Mowrer (Eds.), *Contemporary learning theories: Instrumental conditioning theory and the impact of biological con-*

straints on learning (pp. 237–275). Hillsdale, NJ: Erlbaum.

Timberlake, W., & Lucas, G. A. (1991). Periodic water, interwater interval, and adjunctive behavior in a 24-hour multiresponse environment. *Animal Learning & Behavior, 19,* 369–380.

Timberlake, W., & Peden, B. F. (1987). On the distinction between open and closed economies. *Journal of the Experimental Analysis of Behavior, 48,* 35–60.

Timberlake, W., & Silva, K. M. (1995). Appetitive behavior in ethology, psychology, and behavior systems. In N Thompson (Ed.), *Perspectives in ethology* (pp. 211–253). New York: Plenum.

Timberlake, W., Wahl, G., & King, D. (1982). Stimulus and responses contingencies in the misbehavior of rats. *Journal of Experimental Psychology: Animal Behavior Processes, 8,* 62–85.

Timberlake, W., & White, W. (1990). Winning isn't everything: Rats need only food deprivation and not food reward to efficiently traverse a radial arm maze. *Learning and Motivation, 21,* 153–163.

Timberlake, W., & Wozny, M. (1979). Reversibility of reinforcement between eating and running by schedule changes: A comparison of modules. *Animal Learning & Behavior, 7,* 461–469.

Tinklepaugh, O. (1928). An experimental study of representative factors in monkeys. *Journal of Comparative Psychology, 8,* 197–236.

Todorov, J. C. (1971). Concurrent performances: Effect of punishment on the switching response. *Journal of the Experimental Analysis of Behavior, 16,* 51–62.

Todorov, J. C. (1973). Interaction of frequency and magnitude of reinforcement on concurrent performances. *Journal of the Experimental Analysis of Behavior, 19,* 451–458.

Todorov, J. C., Ferrari, E. A. M., & de Souza, D. G. (1974). Key pecking as a function of response-shock and shock- shock intervals in unsignalled avoidance. *Journal of the Experimental Analysis of Behavior, 22,* 215–218.

Tomasello, M. Do apes ape? In C. M. Heyes & B. G. Galef, Jr. (Eds.), *Social learning in animals: The roots of culture* (pp. 319–346). San Diego: Academic Press.

Tomasello, M. (2000). Do young children have adult syntactic competence? *Cognition, 74,* 209–253.

Tordoff, M. G., & Friedman, M. I. (1986). Hepatic portal glucose infusions decrease food intake and increase food preference. *American Journal of Physiology, 251,* R192–R196.

Torgesen, J. K. (1996). A model of memory from an information processing perspective: The special case of phonological memory. In G. R. Lyon & N. A. Krasnegor (Eds.), *Attention, memory, and executive function* (pp. 157–184). Baltimore: Paul H. Brookes.

Torgrud, L., & Holborn, S. W. (1990). The effects of verbal performance descriptions on nonverbal operant responding. *Journal of the Experimental Analysis of Behavior, 54,* 274–291.

Tranberg, D. K., & Rilling, M. (1980). Delay-interval illumination changes interfere with pigeon short-term memory. *Journal of the Experimental Analysis of Behavior, 33,* 39–49.

Traupmann, K. L. (1972). Drive, reward, and training parameters, and the overlearning-extinction effect (OEE). *Learning and Motivation, 3,* 359–368.

Trevett, A. J., Davison, M. C., & Williams, R. J. (1972). Performance on concurrent interval schedules. *Journal of the Experimental Analysis of Behavior, 17,* 369–374.

Tulving, E. (1972). Episodic and semantic memory. In E. Tulving & W. Donaldson (Eds.), *Organization of memory* (pp. 381–403). New York: Academic Press.

Tulving, E. (1983). *Elements of episodic memory.* Oxford: Oxford University Press.

Tustin, R. D. (1994). Preference for reinforcers under varying schedule arrangements: A behavioral economic analysis. *Journal of Applied Behavior Analysis, 27,* 597–606.

Twyman, J. S. (1995). The functional independence of impure mands and tacts of abstract stimulus properties. *Analysis of Verbal Behavior, 13,* 1–19.

Ulrich, R. E., & Azrin, N. H. (1962). Reflexive fighting in response to aversive stimulation. *Journal of the Experimental Analysis of Behavior, 5,* 511–520.

Ulrich, R. E., Hutchinson, R. R., & Azrin, N. H. (1965). Pain-elicited aggression. *The Psychological Record, 15,* 111–126.

Ulrich, R. E., Wolff, P. C., & Azrin, N. H. (1964). Shock as an elicitor of intra- and inter-species fighting behavior. *Animal Behaviour, 12,* 14–15.

Underwood, B. J. (1945). The effect of successive interpolations on retroactive and proactive inhibition. *Psychological Monographs, 33*(59, Serial No. 3).

Underwood, B. J. (1957). Interference and forgetting. *Psychological Review, 64,* 49–60.

Underwood, B. J. (1966). *Experimental Psychology* (2nd ed.). New York: Appleton-Century-Crofts.

Urbain, C., Poling, A., & Thompson, T. (1979). Differing effects of intermittent food delivery on interim behavior in guinea pigs and rats. *Physiology & Behavior, 22,* 621–625.

Urcuioli, P. J., & Honig, W. K. (1980). Control of choice in conditional discriminations by sample-specific behaviors. *Journal of Experimental Psychology: Animal Behavior Processes, 6,* 251–277.

Valsecchi, P., & Galef, B. G., Jr. (1989). Social influences on the food preferences of house mice (*Mus musculus*). *International Journal of Comparative Psychology, 2,* 245–256.

van Haaren, F. (1992). Response acquisition with fixed and variable resetting delays of reinforcement in male and female Wistar rats. *Physiology & Behavior, 52,* 767–772.

van Hest, A., van Haaren, F., Kop, P., & van der Schoot, F. (1986). Stimulus- and feeder-directed behavior in a long-box: Effect of fixed versus variable time schedules of food presentation. *Animal Learning & Behavior, 14,* 168–172.

Vaughan, W., Jr. (1981). Melioration, matching, and maximization. *Journal of the Experimental Analysis of Behavior, 36,* 141–149.

Vaughan, W., Jr. (1982). Choice and the Rescorla-Wagner model. In M. L. Commons, R. J. Herrnstein, & H. Rachlin (Eds.), *Quantitative analyses of behavior* (vol. 2): *Matching and maximizing accounts* (pp. 263–279). Cambridge, MA: Ballinger.

Vaughan, W., Jr. (1997). Melioration and contiguity. *Journal of the Experimental Analysis of Behavior, 67,* 253–255.

Vaughan, W., Jr., & Herrnstein, R. J. (1987). Choosing among natural stimuli. *Journal of the Experimental Analysis of Behavior, 47,* 5–16.

Verhave, T. (1966). An introduction to the experimental analysis of behavior. In T. Verhave (Ed.), *The experimental analysis of behavior: Selected readings* (pp. 1–47). New York: Meredith.

Vernon, W. M., & Ulrich, R. E. (1966). Classical conditioning of pain-elicited aggression. *Science, 152,* 668–669.

Videl, J. M. (1980). The relations between filial and sexual imprinting in the domestic fowl: Effects of age and social experience. *Animal Behaviour, 28,* 880–891.

Vila, C. J. (1989). Death by pentobarbital overdose mediated by Pavlovian conditioning. *Pharmacology, Biochemistry & Behavior, 32,* 365–366.

Villarreal, J. (1967). *Schedule-induced pica.* Paper presented at the Eastern Psychological Association, Boston, April.

Vincent, L. E., & Bekoff, M. (1978). Quantitative analyses of the ontogeny of predatory behaviour in coyotes, *Canis latrans. Animal Behaviour, 26,* 225–231.

Vogel, R., & Annau, Z. (1973). An operant discrimination task allowing variability of reinforced response patterning. *Journal of the Experimental Analysis of Behavior, 20,* 1–6.

vom Saal, W., & Jenkins, H. M. (1970). Blocking the development of stimulus control. *Learning and Motivation, 1,* 52–64.

von Fersen, L., Wynne, C. D. L., Delius, J. D., & Staddon, J. E. (1991). Transitive inference formation in pigeons. *Journal of Experimental Psychology: Animal Behavior Processes, 17,* 334–341.

von Frisch, K. (1938). Zur psychologie des Fisch-Schwarmes. *Naturwissenschaften, 26,* 601–606.

von Frisch, K. (1967). *The dance language and orientation of bees.* Cambridge, MA: Harvard University Press.

Wacker, D. P., Kerr, N. J., & Carroll, J. L. (1983). Discrimination skill as a predictor of prevocational performance of institutionalized mentally retarded clients. *Rehabilitation Psychology, 28,* 45–59.

Wacker, D. P., Steil, D. A., & Greenbaum, F. T. (1983). Assessment of discrimination skills of multiply handi-

capped preschoolers and prediction of classroom task performance. *Journal of the Association for the Severely Handicapped, 8,* 65–78.

Wade, M. J., & Pruett-Jones, S. G. (1990). Female copying increases the variance in male mating success. *Proceedings of the National Academy of Sciences of the United States of America, 87,* 5749–5753.

Wagner, A. R. (1959). The role of reinforcement and nonreinforcement in an "apparent frustration effect." *Journal of Experimental Psychology, 57,* 130–136.

Wagner, A. R. (1981). SOP: A model of autonomic memory processing in animal behavior. In N. E. Spear & R. R. Miller (Eds.), *Information processing in animals: Memory mechanisms* (pp. 5–47). Hillsdale, NJ: Erlbaum.

Walker, D. J., & Branch, M. N. (1998). Effects of variable-interval value and amount of training on stimulus generalization. *Journal of the Experimental Analysis of Behavior, 70,* 139–163.

Walker, M. M., Baird, D. L., & Bitterman, M. E. (1989). Failure of stationary but not of flying honeybees (*Apis mellifera*) to respond to magnetic field stimuli. *Journal of Comparative Psychology, 103,* 62–69.

Wallace, M., & Oei, T. P. S. (1981). Differences in schedule induced behavior as a function of reinforcer in humans. *Physiology & Behavior, 27,* 1027–1030.

Wallace, M., & Singer, G. (1976). Adjunctive behavior and smoking induced by a maze-solving schedule in humans. *Physiology & Behavior, 17,* 849–852.

Wallace, M., Singer, G., Wayner, M. J., & Cook, P. (1975). Adjunctive behavior in humans during game playing. *Physiology & Behavior, 14,* 651–654.

Waller, M. B., & Waller, P. F. (1963). The effects of unavoidable shocks on a multiple schedule having an avoidance component. *Journal of the Experimental Analysis of Behavior, 6,* 29–37.

Wang, G. H. (1923). Relation between "spontaneous" activity and oestrus cycle in the white rat. *Comparative Psychological Monograph, 2,* (6, Serial No. 27).

Wasserman, E. A. (1973). Pavlovian conditioning with heat reinforcement produces stimulus-directed pecking in chicks. *Science, 181,* 875–877.

Wasserman, E. A., Hugart, J. A., & Kirkpatrick-Steger, K. (1995). Pigeons show same-different conceptualization after training with complex visual stimuli. *Journal of Experimental Psychology: Animal Behavior Processes, 21,* 248–252.

Watkins, M. J. (1979). Engrams as cuegrams and forgetting as cue-overload: A cueing approach to the structure of memory. In C. R. Puff (Ed.), *The structure of memory* (pp. 347–372). New York: Academic Press.

Watkins, M. J. (1990). Mediationism and the obfuscation of memory. *American Psychologist, 45,* 328–335.

Weatherly, J. N., McSweeney, F. K., & Swindell, S. (1995). On the contributions of responding and reinforcement to within-session patterns of responding. *Learning and Motivation, 26,* 421–432.

Weaver, C. A., III. (1993). Do you need a "flash" to form

a flashbulb memory? *Journal of Experimental Psychology: General, 122,* 39–46.

Weiner, H. (1962). Some effects of response cost upon human operant behavior. *Journal of the Experimental Analysis of Behavior, 5,* 201–208.

Weiner, H. (1969). Controlling human fixed-interval performance. *Journal of the Experimental Analysis of Behavior, 12,* 349–373.

Weiner, H. (1982). Histories of response omission and human operant behavior under a fixed-ratio schedule of reinforcement. *The Psychological Record, 32,* 409–434.

Weiner, H. (1983). Some thoughts on discrepant human-animal performances under schedules of reinforcement. *The Psychological Record, 33,* 521–532.

Weiss, B., & Laties, V. G. (1959). Titration behavior on various fractional escape programs. *Journal of the Experimental Analysis of Behavior, 2,* 227–248.

Weiss, B., & Laties, V. G. (1963). Characteristics of aversive thresholds measured by a titration schedule. *Journal of the Experimental Analysis of Behavior, 6,* 563–572.

Weiss, K. M. (1978). A comparison of forward and backward procedures for the acquisition of response chains in humans. *Journal of the Experimental Analysis of Behavior, 29,* 255–259.

Weiss, S. J. (1967). Free-operant compounding of variable-interval and low-rate discriminative stimuli. *Journal of the Experimental Analysis of Behavior, 10,* 535–540.

Weiss, S. J., & Dacanay, R. J. (1982). Incentive processes and the peak shift. *Journal of the Experimental Analysis of Behavior, 37,* 441–453.

Weiss, S. J., & Panlilio, L. V., (1999). Blocking a selective association in pigeons. *Journal of the Experimental Analysis of Behavior, 71,* 13–24.

Weiss, S. J., & Schindler, C. W. (1981). Generalization peak shift in rats under conditions of positive reinforcement and avoidance. *Journal of the Experimental Analysis of Behavior, 35,* 175–185.

Welker, W. I. (1961). An analysis of exploratory and play behavior in animals. In D. W. Fiske & S. R. Maddi (Eds.), *Functions of varied experience* (pp. 175–226). Homewood, IL: Dorsey.

Welker, W. I. (1971). Ontogeny of play and exploratory behaviors: A definition of problems and a search for new conceptual solutions. In H. Moltz (Ed.), *The ontogeny of vertebrate behavior* (pp. 171–228). New York: Academic Press.

Wells, G. L., Malpass, R. S., Lindsay, R. C. L., Fisher, R. P., Turtle, J. W., & Fulero, S. M. (2000). From the lab to the police station: A successful application of eyewitness research. *American Psychologist, 55,* 581–598.

Wells, M. (1964). Detour experiments with octopus. *Journal of Experimental Biology, 41,* 621–642.

Wells, M. (1967). Short-term learning and interocular transfer in detour experiments with octopuses. *Journal of Experimental Biology, 47,* 383-408.

Wells, M. (1978). *Octopus: Physiology and behaviour of an advanced invertebrate.* London: Chapman and Hall.

Wells, M., & Young, J. Z. (1970 a). Single session learning by octopuses. *Journal of Experimental Biology, 53,* 779–788.

Wells, M. J., & Young, J. Z. (1970 b). Stimulus generalization in the tactile system of Octopus. *Journal of Neurobiology, 2,* 31–46.

Wells, P. H. (1967). Training flat worms in a van Oye maze. In W. C. Corning & S. C. Ratner (Eds.), *Chemistry of learning: Invertebrate research* (pp. 251–254). New York: Plenum.

Wenner, A. M., & Johnson, D. L. (1967). Honeybees: Do they use direction and distance information provided by the dance? *Science, 158,* 1076–1077.

Wenner, A. M., Wells, P. H., & Johnson, D. (1969). Honey bee recruitment to food sources: Olfaction or language? *Science, 164,* 84–86.

Werner, E. E., Gilliam, J. F., Hall, D. J., & Mittelbach, G. G. (1983). An experimental test of the effects of predation risk on habitat use in fish. *Ecology, 64,* 1540–1548.

West, M. J., & King, A. P. (1988). Female visual displays affect the development of male song in the cowbird. *Nature, 334,* 244–246.

West, M. J., King, A. P., & Eastzer, D. H. (1981). The cowbird: Reflections on development from an unlikely source. *American Scientist, 69,* 56–66.

West, M. J., King, A. P., & Freeberg (1994). The nature and nurture of neophenotypes. In L. A. Real (Ed.), *Behavioral mechanisms in evolutionary ecology* (pp. 238–257). Chicago: University of Chicago Press.

Westbrook, R. F. (1973). Failure to obtain positive contrast when pigeons press a bar. *Journal of the Experimental Analysis of Behavior, 20,* 499–510.

Westerman, R. A. (1963). A study of the habituation responses to light in the planarian *Dugesia dorotocephala. Worm Runner's Digest, 5,* 6–11.

Wetherby, B., Karlan, G. R., & Spradlin, J. E. (1983). The development of derived stimulus relations through training in arbitrary-matching sequences. *Journal of the Experimental Analysis of Behavior, 40,* 69–78.

Wetherington, C. L. (1979). Schedule-induced drinking: Rate of food delivery and Herrnstein's equation. *Journal of the Experimental Analysis of Behavior, 32,* 323–333.

Wetherington, C. L., & Brownstein, A. J. (1979). Schedule control of eating by fixed-time schedules of water presentation. *Animal Learning & Behavior, 7,* 38–40.

Wetherington, C. L., & Brownstein, A. J. (1982). Comment on Roper's discussion of the language and generality of schedule-induced behavior. *Animal Learning & Behavior, 10,* 537–539.

Wetherington, C. L., & Riley, A. L. (1985). Differences in food consumption under intermittent and continuous reinforcement schedules of water delivery: Some implications for schedule-induced behavior. *Animal Learning & Behavior, 13,* 331–337.

Wexley, K. N., Yukl, G. A., Kovacks, S. Z., & Sanders, R. (1972). Importance of contrast effects. *Journal of Applied Psychology, 56,* 45–58.

Whalen, T. E., & Wilkie, D. M. (1977). Failure to find schedule-induced polydipsia in the pigeon. *Bulletin of the Psychonomic Society, 10,* 200–202.

White, A. J., & Davison, M. C. (1973). Performance in concurrent fixed-interval schedules. *Journal of the Experimental Analysis of Behavior, 19,* 147–153.

White, K. G. (1995). Action at a temporal distance: Component transition as the relational basis for successive discrimination. *Journal of the Experimental Analysis of Behavior, 64,* 185–213.

White, L. A. (1979). Erotica and aggression: The influence of sexual arousal, positive affect, and negative affect on aggressive behavior. *Journal of Personality and Social Psychology, 37,* 591–601.

Whitlow, J. W., Jr., & Wagner, A. R. (1972). Negative patterning in classical conditioning: Summation of response tendencies to isolable and configural components. *Psychonomic Science, 27,* 299–301.

Wilcoxon, H. C., Dragoin, W. B., & Kral, P. A. (1971). Illness-induced aversions in rat and quail: Relative salience of visual and gustatory cues. *Science, 171,* 826–828.

Wilkenfield, J., Nickel, M., Blakely, E., & Poling, A. (1992). Acquisition of lever-press responding in rats with delayed reinforcement: A comparison of three procedures. *Journal of the Experimental Analysis of Behavior, 58,* 431–443.

Wilkie, D. M. (1973). Signalled reinforcement in multiple and concurrent schedules. *Journal of the Experimental Analysis of Behavior, 20,* 29–36.

Wilkie, D. M. (1974). Stimulus control of responding during a fixed interval reinforcement schedule. *Journal of the Experimental Analysis of Behavior, 21,* 425–432.

Wilkie, D. M. (1977). Behavioral contrast produced by a signaled decrease in local rate of reinforcement. *Learning and Motivation, 8,* 182–193.

Wilkie, D. M. (1978). Delayed symbolic matching to sample in the pigeon. *The Psychological Record, 28,* 463–469.

Wilkie, D. M. (1983). Pigeons' spatial memory: II. Acquisition of delayed matching of key location and transfer to new locations. *Journal of the Experimental Analysis of Behavior, 39,* 69–76.

Wilkie, D. M., Carr, J. A. R., Siegenthaler, A., Lenger, B., Liu, M., & Kwok, M. (1996). Field observations of time-place behaviour in scavenging birds. *Behavioural Processes, 38,* 77–88.

Wilkie, D. M., Mak, T., & Saksida, L. M. (1994). Pigeons' landmark use as revealed in a 'feature-positive,' digitized landscape, touchscreen paradigm. *Behavioural Processes, 32,* 87–100.

Wilkie, D. M., & Masson, M. E. (1976). Attention in the pigeon: A reevaluation. *Journal of the Experimental Analysis of Behavior, 26,* 207-212.

Wilkie, D. M., Mumby, D. G., Needham, G., & Smeele, M. (1992). Sustained arm visiting by nondeprived, nonrewarded rats in a radial maze. *Bulletin of the Psychonomic Society, 30,* 314–316.

Wilkie, D. M., Saksida, L. M., Samson, P., & Lee, A. (1994). Properties of time-place learning by pigeons, Columba livia. *Behavioural Processes, 31,* 39–56.

Wilkie, D. M., & Spetch, M. L. (1978). The effect of sample and comparison ratio schedules on delayed matching to sample in the pigeon. *Animal Learning & Behavior, 6,* 273–278.

Wilkie, D. M., & Summers, R. J. (1982). Pigeons' spatial memory: Factors affecting delayed matching of key location. *Journal of the Experimental Analysis of Behavior, 37,* 45–56.

Wilkie, D. M., Wilson, R. J., & Kardal, S. (1989). Pigeons discriminate pictures of a geographical location. *Animal Learning & Behavior, 17,* 163–171.

Williams, B. A. (1976). The effects of unsignalled delayed reinforcement. *Journal of the Experimental Analysis of Behavior, 26,* 441–449.

Williams, B. A. (1979). Contrast, component duration, and the following schedule of reinforcement. *Journal of Experimental Psychology: Animal Behavior Processes, 5,* 379–396.

Williams, B. A. (1981). The following schedule of reinforcement as a fundamental determinant of steady state contrast in multiple schedules. *Journal of the Experimental Analysis of Behavior, 35,* 293–310.

Williams, B. A. (1983). Another look at contrast in multiple schedules. *Journal of the Experimental Analysis of Behavior, 39,* 345–384.

Williams, B. A. (1988). Reinforcement, choice, and response strength. In R. C. Atkinson, R. J. Herrnstein, G. Lindzey, & R. D. Luce (Eds.). *Stevens' handbook of experimental psychology* (2nd ed., pp. 167–244). New York: Wiley.

Williams, B. A. (1994). Conditioned reinforcement: Neglected or outmoded explanatory construct? *Psychonomic Bulletin & Review, 1,* 457–475.

Williams, D. A., Dyck, D. G., & Tait, R. W. (1986). Excitatory backward conditioning in conditioned punishment and conditioned suppression in rats. *American Journal of Psychology, 99,* 367–384.

Williams, D. R., & Williams, H. (1969). Auto-maintenance in the pigeon: Sustained pecking despite contingent non- reinforcement. *Journal of the Experimental Analysis of Behavior, 12,* 511–520.

Wilson, J. F. (1982). *Nonregulatory eating in rats.* Unpublished doctoral dissertation, Columbia University.

Wilson, J. F., & Cantor, M. B. (1987). An animal model of excessive eating: Schedule-induced hyperphagia in food- satiated rats. *Journal of the Experimental Analysis of Behavior, 47,* 335–346.

Wilson, S. C., & Kleiman, D. G. (1974). Eliciting play: A comparative study. *American Zoologist, 14,* 341–370.

Wilson, W. J., & Butcher, L. L. (1980). A potential shock-reducing contingency in the backshock technique: Implications for learned helplessness. *Animal Learning & Behavior, 8,* 435–440.

Windsor, A. L. (1930). Experimental extinction and negative adaptation. *Psychological Review, 37,* 174–178.

Winkelspecht, S. M., & Mowrer, R. R. (1999). Memory distortion: Can accurate memory be preserved? *The Psychological Record, 49,* 137–144.

Winter, J., & Perkins, C. C. (1982). Immediate reinforcement in delayed reward learning in pigeons. *Journal of the Experimental Analysis of Behavior, 38,* 169–179.

Witt, J. C., & Wacker, D. P. (1981). Teaching children to respond to auditory directives: An evaluation of two procedures. *Behavior Research of Severe Developmental Disabilities, 2,* 175–189.

Wittgenstein, L. (1953). *Philosophical investigations* (Third edition; trans: G. E. M. Anscombe). New York: Macmillan.

Wolf, M. M. (1963). Some effects of combined S^{D}s. *Journal of the Experimental Analysis of Behavior, 6,* 343–347.

Wolfe, J. B. (1936). Effectiveness of token-rewards for chimpanzees. *Comparative Psychology Monographs, 12*(60), 1–72.

Wolpe, J. (1958). *Psychotherapy by reciprocal inhibition.* Stanford, CA: Stanford University Press.

Wolpe, J. (1968). *Behavior therapy.* Stanford, CA: Stanford University Press.

Wolpe, J. (1990). *The practice of behavior therapy* (Fourth edition). New York: Pergamon.

Wolpe, J. (1995). Reciprocal inhibition: Major agent of behavior change. In W. O'Donohue & L. Krasner (Eds.), *Theories of behavior therapy: Exploring behavior change.* Washington, DC: American Psychological Association.

Wong, P. T. P. (1979). A behavioral field approach to general activity: Sex differences and food deprivation in the rat. *Animal Learning & Behavior, 7,* 111–118.

Wood, D. C. (1973). Stimulus specific habituation in a protozoan. *Physiology & Behavior, 11,* 349–354.

Wood, K. A., Martinez, E. S., & Willis, R. D. (1975). Ratio requirement and reinforcer effects in concurrent fixed-interval fixed-ratio schedules. *Journal of the Experimental Analysis of Behavior, 23,* 87–94.

Wood, K. A., & Willis, R. D. (1974). Reinforcer and ratio requirement effects on concurrent fixed-interval fixed- ratio schedules. *Bulletin of the Psychonomic Society, 4,* 541–543.

Woolverton, W. L., & Johanson, C. E. (1984). Preference in rhesus monkeys given a choice between cocaine and d,l-cathinone. *Journal of the Experimental Analysis of Behavior, 41,* 35–43.

Wright, A. A. (1999). Visual list memory in capuchin monkeys (*Cebus apella*). *Journal of Comparative Psychology, 113,* 74–80.

Wright, A. A., & Rivera, J. J. (1997). Memory of auditory lists by rhesus monkeys (*Macaca mulatta*). *Journal of Experimental Psychology: Animal Behavior Processes, 23,* 441–449.

Wright, A. A., Santiago, H. C., Sands, S. F., Kendrick, D. F., & Cook, R. G. (1985). Memory processing of serial lists by pigeons, monkeys, and people. *Science, 229,* 287–289.

Wright, W. G., McCance, E. F., Lu, T., & Carew, T. J. (1992). Delayed-onset sensitization emerges after dishabituation in developing Aplysia. *Behavioral and Neural Biology, 57,* 170–174.

Wyckoff, L. B., Jr. (1952). The role of observing responses in discrimination learning. Part 1. *Psychological Review, 59,* 431–442.

Wyckoff, L. B., Jr. (1969). The role of observing responses in discrimination learning. In D. P. Hendry (Ed.), *Conditioned reinforcement* (pp. 237–260). Homewood, IL: Dorsey.

Wynne, C. D. L., von Fersen, L., & Staddon, J. E. R. (1992). Pigeons' inferences are transitive and the outcome of elementary conditioning principles: A response. *Journal of Experimental Psychology: Animal Behavior Processes, 18,* 313–315.

Wyrwicka, W. (1978) Imitation of mother's inappropriate food preference in weaning kittens. *Pavlovian Journal of Biological Science, 13,* 55–72.

Yeomans, M. R. (1993). The appetiser effect: Sensory enhancement of feeding as a measure of reward. *Appetite, 21,* 219.

Yerkes, R. M., & Morgulis, S. (1909). The method of Pavlov in animal psychology. *Psychological Bulletin, 6,* 257–273.

Yerkes, R. M., & Tomilin, M. L. (1935). Mother-infant relations in chimpanzees. *Journal of Comparative Psychology, 20,* 321–359.

Yoburn, B. C., & Cohen, P. S. (1979). Assessment of attack and drinking in White King pigeons on response-independent food schedules. *Journal of the Experimental Analysis of Behavior, 31,* 91–101.

Yoburn, B. C., Cohen, P. S., & Campagnoni, F. R. (1981). The role of intermittent food in the induction of attack in pigeons. *Journal of the Experimental Analysis of Behavior, 36,* 101–117.

Yoburn, B. C., & Flory, R. K. (1977). Schedule-induced polydipsia and reinforcement magnitude. *Physiology & Behavior, 18,* 787–791.

Young, J. M., Krantz, P. J., McClannahan, L. E., & Poulson, C. L. (1994). Generalized imitation and response-class formation in children with autism. *Journal of Applied Behavior Analysis, 27,* 685–697.

Young, M. E., Wasserman, E. A., & Garner, K. L. (1997). Effects of number of items on the pigeon's discrimination of same from different visual displays. *Journal of Experimental Psychology: Animal Behavior Processes, 23,* 491–501.

Zahavi, A. (1975). Mate selection—a selection for handicap. *Journal of Theoretical Biology, 53,* 205–214.

Zahavi, A. (1977). The cost of honesty (further remarks on the handicap principle). *Journal of Theoretical Biology, 67,* 603–605.

Zaragoza, M. S., & Lane, S. M. (1994). Source misattributions and the suggestibility of eyewitness memory. *Journal of Experimental Psychology: Learning, Memory, and Cognition, 20,* 934–945.

Zaragoza, M. S., & Mitchell, K. J. (1996). Repeated exposure to suggestion and the creation of false memories. *Psychological Science, 7,* 294–300.

Zeaman, D. (1949). Response latency as a function of the amount of reinforcement. *Journal of Experimental Psychology, 39,* 466–483.

Zeiler, M. D. (1968). Stimulus control with fixed-ratio reinforcement. *Journal of the Experimental Analysis of Behavior, 11,* 107–115.

Zeiler, M. D. (1999). Reversed schedule effects in closed and open economies. *Journal of the Experimental Analysis of Behavior, 71,* 171–186.

Zeiler, M. D., & Blakely, T. F. (1983). Choice between response units: The rate constancy model. *Journal of the Experimental Analysis of Behavior, 39,* 275–291.

Zellner, D. A., Rozin, P., Aron, M., & Kulish, C. (1983). Conditioned enhancement of human's liking for flavor by pairing with sweetness. *Learning and Motivation, 14,* 338–350.

Zentall, T. R. (1973). Memory in the pigeon: Retroactive inhibition in a delayed matching task. *Bulletin of the Psychonomic Society, 1,* 126–128.

Zentall, T. R., Hogan, D. E., & Edwards, C. A. (1984). Cognitive factors in conditional learning by pigeons. In H. L. Roitblat, T. G. Bever, & H. S. Terrace (Eds.), *Animal cognition: Proceedings of the Harry Frank Guggenheim Conference, June 2–4, 1982* (pp. 389–405). Hillsdale, NJ: Erlbaum.

Zentall, T. R., Hogan, D. E., Edwards, C. A., & Hearst, E. (1980). Oddity learning in the pigeon as a function of the number of incorrect alternatives. *Journal of Experimental Psychology: Animal Behavior Processes, 6,* 278–299.

Zentall, T. R., Hogan, D. E., & Holder, J. (1974). Comparison of two oddity tasks with pigeons. *Learning and Motivation, 5,* 106–117.

Zentall, T. R., Hogan, D. E., Howard, M. M., & Moore, B. S. (1978). Delayed matching in the pigeon: Effect on performance of sample-specific observing responses and differential delay behavior. *Learning and Motivation, 9,* 202–218.

Zentall, T. R., Roper, K. L., & Sherburne, L. M. (1995). Most directed forgetting in pigeons can be attributed to the absence of reinforcement on forget trials during training or to other procedural artifacts. *Journal of the Experimental Analysis of Behavior, 63,* 127–137.

Zettle, R. D., & Hayes, S. C. (1982). Rule-governed behavior: A potential theoretical framework for cognitive-behavioral therapy. In P. C. Kendall (Ed.), *Advances in cognitive-behavioral research and therapy* (vol. 1, pp. 73–118). New York: Academic Press.

Zillmann, D., Bryant, J., Comisky, P. W., & Medoff, N. J. (1981). Excitation and hedonic valence in the effect of erotica on motivated intermale aggression. *European Journal of Social Psychology, 11,* 233–252.

Zimmerman, J. (1963). Technique for sustaining behavior with conditioned reinforcement. *Science, 142,* 682–684.

Zimmerman, J., & Baydan, N. T. (1963). Punishment of S[delta] responding of humans in conditional matching-to-sample by time-out. *Journal of the Experimental Analysis of Behavior, 6,* 589–597.

Zimmerman, J., & Ferster, C. B. (1963). Intermittent punishment of SD responding in matching-to-sample. *Journal of the Experimental Analysis of Behavior, 6,* 349–356.

Zimmerman, J., & Ferster, C. B. (1964). Some notes on time-out from positive reinforcement. *Journal of the Experimental Analysis of Behavior, 7,* 13–19.

Zimmerman, J., & Hanford, P. V. (1967). Differential effects of extinction on behaviors maintained by concurrent schedules of primary and conditioned reinforcement. *Psychonomic Science, 8,* 103–104.

Zimmerman, J., Hanford, P. V., & Brown, W. (1967). Effects of conditioned reinforcement frequency in an intermittent free-feeding situation. *Journal of the Experimental Analysis of Behavior, 10,* 331–340.

Ziriax, J. M., & Silberberg, A. (1984). Concurrent variable-interval variable-ratio schedules can provide only weak evidence for matching. *Journal of the Experimental Analysis of Behavior, 41,* 83–100.

Author Index

Subject Index

FIGURE ACKNOWLEDGMENTS

The Authors and Publishers are grateful to the following for permission to reproduce the figures in this book. Please see Reference section for full citation. Every effort has been made to contact the respective copyright owners for permission clearance. If we have overlooked any copyright owner, please contact us.

Figure 1.1: Bradshaw & Rogers (1993). Reprinted with the permission of Academic Press.

Figure 1.2: Art by Lynda D'Amico; first appeared in "The Quest for Adam" by Jean-Jacques Hublin. Reprinted with the permission of Archaeology Magazine, Vol. 52 No. 4 (Copyright the Archaeological Institute of America, 1999).

Figure 2.1: Dielenberg & McGregor (1999). Copyright 1999 by the American Psychological Association. Reprinted with permission.

Figure 2.2: Reprinted with permission from Hess, E.H. (1959). Imprinting. Science, 130, 133-141. Copyright 1959 American Association for the Advancement of Science.

Figure 2.3: Kandel (1979). Art by Patricia J. Wynne. Reprinted with permission.

Figure 3.1: Adapted from Yerkes & Morgulus (1909).

Figure 3.2: Adapted from Verhave (1966); Routenberg (1978); Rohles (1961), Copyright 1961 by the Society for the Experimental Analysis of Behavior, Inc.; Talton et al. (1999), Reprinted with permission from Elsevier Science.

Figure 3.3: Hoffman (1996). Reprinted with the permission of Authors Cooperative, Inc.

Figure 3.4: Hoffman (1996). Reprinted with the permission of Authors Cooperative, Inc.

Figure 4.1: Saltzman (1950). Copyright 1950 by the American Psychological Association. Reprinted with permission.

Figure 4.3: Skinner (1938). Courtesy of the B. F. Skinner Foundation.

Figure 4.4: Skinner (1938). Courtesy of the B. F. Skinner Foundation.

Figure 4.5: Skinner (1938). Courtesy of the B. F. Skinner Foundation.

Figure 4.6: Fester & Skinner (1957). Courtesy of the B. F. Skinner Foundation.

Figure 4.7: Fester & Skinner (1957). Courtesy of the B. F. Skinner Foundation.

Figure 4.8: Fester & Skinner (1957). Courtesy of the B. F. Skinner Foundation.

Figure 4.9: Fester & Skinner (1957). Courtesy of the B. F. Skinner Foundation.

Figure 4.10: Fester & Skinner (1957). Courtesy of the B. F. Skinner Foundation.

Figure 4.11: Fester & Skinner (1957). Courtesy of the B. F. Skinner Foundation.

Figure 4.12: Fester & Skinner (1957). Courtesy of the B. F. Skinner Foundation.

Figure 4.13: Fester & Skinner (1957). Courtesy of the B. F. Skinner Foundation.

Figure 4.14: Blough (1961). Copyright 1961 by the Society for the Experimental Analysis of Behavior, Inc. Reprinted with permission.

Figure 4.15: Terrace (1966a). Copyright 1996 by the Society for the Experimental Analysis of Behavior, Inc. Reprinted with permission.

Figure 5.1: Adapted from Solomon & Wynne (1953).

Figure 5.2: Heyes & Dawson (1990). Reprinted with permission.

Figure 6.1: Garcia, et al. (1973). Reprinted with permission of Kluwer Academic/ Plenum Publishers.

Figure 6.2: Adapted from Sidman (1960).

Figure 7.1: Eckerman et al. (1980). Copyright 1980 by the Society for the Experimental Analysis of Behavior, Inc. Reprinted with permission.

Figure 7.2: Pear & Eldridge (1984). Copyright 1984 by the Society for the Experimental Analysis of Behavior, Inc. Reprinted with permission.

Figure 7.4: Catania & Reynolds (1968). Copyright 1968 by the Society for the Experimental Analysis of Behavior, Inc. Reprinted with permission.

Figure 7.5: Pear (1985). Copyright 1985 by the Society for the Experimental Analysis of Behavior, Inc. Reprinted with permission.

Figure 8.1: Hearst et al. (1964). Copyright 1964 by the Society for the Experimental Analysis of Behavior, Inc. Reprinted with permission.

Figure 8.2: Honig et al. (1963). Copyright 1963 by the permission of the American Psychological Association. Reprinted with permission.

Figure 8.3: Guttman (1965). Reprinted with the permission of Stanford University Press.

Figure 8.4: Sidman & Stoddard (1967). Copyright 1967 by the Society for the Experimental Analysis of Behavior, Inc. Reprinted with permission.

Figure 9.1: Carter & Werner (1978). Copyright 1978 by the Society for the Experimental Analysis of Behavior, Inc. Reprinted with permission.

Figure 9.2: Schusterman & Kastak (1993). Reprinted with the permission of The Psychological Record.

Figure 9.3: Lanza, Starr & Skinner (1982). Copyright 1982 by the Society for the Experimental Analysis of Gehavior, Inc. Reprinted with permission.

Figure 9.4: Savage-Rumbaugh & Lewis (1994). Reprinted with the permission of John Wiley & Sons, Inc.

Figure 10.1: Torgesen (1996). Reprinted with the permission of Paul H. Brookes Publishing Co., Inc.

Figure 10.2: Author original.

Figure 10.3: Roper et al. (1995). Reprinted with the permission of the Psychonomic Society.

Figure 10.4: Olton (1977). Artwork by Alan D. Iselin.

Figure 10.5: Reprinted from Behavioral Processes, Vol. 31, Wilkie et al., Properties of time-place learning by pigeons, Columbia livia, pp. 39-56, 1994, with permission of Elsevier Science.

Figure 10.6: Wright & Rivers (1997). Copyright 1997 by the American Psychological Association. Reprinted with permission.

Figure 10.7: Wright & Rivers (1997). Copyright 1997 by the American Psychological Association. Reprinted with permission.

Figure 10.8: Anderson & Spellman (1995). Copyright 1995 by the American Psychological Association. Reprinted with permission.

Figure 12.1: Skinner (1957b). Reprinted with permission.

Figure 12.2: Tustin (1994). Copyright 1994 by the Journal of Applied Behavior Analysis.

Figure 12.3: Fantino (1969). Copyright 1969 by the Society for the Experimental Analysis of Behavior, Inc. Reprinted with permission.

Figure 13.1: Hineline (1978). Copyright 1978 by the Society for the Experimental Analysis of Behavior, Inc. Reprinted with permission.

Figure 15.1: Adapted from Azrin et al. (1966).

Figure 15.2: Adapted from Staddon (1977).

Figure 15.3: Hineline (1986). Reprinted with the permission of Lawrence Erlbaum Associates, Inc.

Figure 15.4: Kelly & Hake (1970). Copyright 1970 by the Society for the Experimental Analysis of Behavior, Inc. Reprinted with permission.

Figure 16.1: Roots (1988). Tropical birds of the world. Winnipeg: Hyperion Press.

Figure 16.2: Adapted from Schenkel (1967), published by the Society for Integrative and Comparative Biology.

Figure 16.3: Krebs & Davies (1993). Reprinted with the permission of Blackwell Science Publications.

Figure 17.1: Adapted from Schultz (1968).

Figure 17.2: Bradshaw & Rogers (1993). Reprinted with the permission of Academic Press.

Figure 17.3: Eccles (1989). Reprinted with the permission of Routledge.